OF THE FARM
by John Updike
GOLD MEDAL s1191
CANARY IN A CAT HOUSE & THE SIRENS OF
VONNEGU
An American traitor's astonishing confessi
mournful, macabre, diabolically funny—writt
natural candor in a foreign death ce
NIGHT
KOV'S
OZEN
LOLITA
The EXECUTIONER'S Song
The EXECUTIONER'S Song
A TRUE LIFE NOVEL BY
ORMAN MAILER

DICTIONARY OF LITERARY BIOGRAPHY

DOCUMENTARY SERIES

AN ILLUSTRATED CHRONICLE

VOLUME THREE

Depicting The Lives And Work Of Authors—Including Photographs, Manuscript Facsimiles, Letters, Notebooks, Interviews, And Contemporary Assessments

DICTIONARY OF LITERARY BIOGRAPHY

DOCUMENTARY SERIES

AN ILLUSTRATED CHRONICLE

VOLUME THREE

SAUL BELLOW
JACK KEROUAC
NORMAN MAILER
VLADIMIR NABOKOV
JOHN UPDIKE
KURT VONNEGUT

EDITED BY MARY BRUCCOLI

A BRUCCOLI CLARK BOOK

GALE RESEARCH COMPANY BOOK TOWER
DETROIT, MICHIGAN 48226

Matthew J. Bruccoli, *Editorial Director*
C. E. Frazer Clark, Jr., *Managing Editor*
Richard Layman, *Project Editor*

Manufactured by Braun-Brumfield, Inc.
Ann Arbor, Michigan
Printed in the United States of America

Library of Congress Cataloging in Publication Data
Main entry under title:

Dictionary of literary biography documentary series.

Vol. 3 edited by Mary Bruccoli.
"A Bruccoli Clark Book."
1. Authors, American—Biography—Sources. 2. American literature—History and criticism—Sources. I. Bruccoli, Mary. II. Title: Documentary series.
PS129.D48 1983 810'.9 [B] 82-1105
ISBN 0-8103-1115-1 (v. 3) AACR2

PERMISSIONS

SAUL BELLOW

TEXTS: p. 4, copyright © 1944, 1972, reprinted by permission of Farrar, Straus & Giroux, all rights reserved; p. 5, copyright 1948 by Kenyon College, reprinted by permission of the author and *The Kenyon Review*; p. 6, copyright © 1953 *Saturday Review*, reprinted by permission; p. 9, © 1953 *New York Times*, reprinted by permission; p. 12, © 1954 *New York Times*, reprinted by permission; p. 14, © 1956 *New York Times*, reprinted by permission; p. 15, © 1959 *New York Times*, reprinted by permission; p. 20, copyright © 1963 by Saul Bellow, reprinted by permission; p. 28, © 1964 *New York Times*, reprinted by permission; p. 30, copyright © 1964, all rights reserved, reprinted by permission of *The Nation*; p. 33, copyright © 1964, by The Atlantic Monthly Company, Boston, Mass., reprinted with permission; p. 37, copyright © 1965 *Saturday Review*, reprinted by permission; p. 38, copyright © 1970 by *Saturday Review*, reprinted by permission; p. 44, published by the R. R. Bowker Co., © 1973 Xerox Corporation; p. 49, © 1974 by Saul Bellow, reprinted by permission; p. 52, copyright © 1975 *Newsweek*, reprinted by permission, all rights reserved; p. 58, © 1976 *New York Times*, reprinted by permission; p. 62, copyright © 1977 The Nobel Foundation, reprinted by permission, all rights reserved; p. 69, copyright 1982 Time Inc., all rights reserved, reprinted by permission from *Time*.

ILLUSTRATIONS: pp. 7, 10, 11, 16, 18, 19, 57, reprinted by permission of the author, courtesy of the Regenstein Library, University of Chicago; pp. 8, 13, 63, 66, Wide World Photos; p. 14, courtesy of Humanities Research Center, University of Texas, Austin; pp. 25, 39, 54, courtesy of University of Chicago; p. 29, Joseph Abeles Studio; p. 46, courtesy *Publishers Weekly*; p. 61, Black Star; p. 68, © 1981, Thomas Victor.

JACK KEROUAC

TEXTS: p. 77, copyright © by *Saturday Review*, all rights reserved, reprinted by permission; p. 88, reprinted by permission of *The Village Voice*, copyright © News Group Publications, Inc., 1957; p. 91, by permission of The Sterling Lord Agency, Inc., copyright © 1958 by Jack Kerouac; p. 91, by permission of The Sterling Lord Agency, Inc., copyright © 1957 by Jack Kerouac; p. 93, reprinted by permission of *The Village Voice*, copyright © News Group Publications, Inc., 1958; p. 96, reprinted by permission; p. 98, copyright © by *Newsweek*, all rights reserved; p. 98, copyright © 1959 by Avon Books; p. 99, by permission of The Sterling Lord Agency, Inc., copyright © 1959 by Jack Kerouac; p. 105, reprinted by permission from *The Hudson Review*, XII, 4 (Winter 1959-60), copyright © 1960 by The Hudson Review, Inc.; p. 112, reprinted by permission of *The National Observer*, published by Dow Jones & Co., Inc., 5 February 1968; p. 114, reprinted by permission; p. 116, by Eric Ehrmann & Stephen Davis from *Rolling Stone*, 29 November 1969, #47, by Straight Arrow Publishers, Inc. © 1969, All Rights Reserved, Reprinted by Permission; p. 119, reprinted by permission of John Tytell, copyright © *Partisan Review*, XI, 2 (1973).

ILLUSTRATIONS: p. 73, photos by Marshall Clements; pp. 76, 77, 85, 86, courtesy of Allen Ginsberg; p. 81, photo © by Gerard Malanga; pp. 82, 83, 84, courtesy of Carolyn Cassady; p. 85, courtesy of John Clellon Holmes; pp. 110, 111, 118, by Ann Charters; p. 112, by James F. Coyne; p. 122, from *Moody Street Irregulars*, by Robert B. Perreault.

NORMAN MAILER

TEXTS: p. 130, copyright © 1948 by *Saturday Review*, all rights reserved, reprinted by permission; p. 131, reprinted by permission, © 1948, 1976, The New Yorker Magazine, Inc.; p. 132, copyright © 1951-R 1979, by The Atlantic Monthly Company, Boston, Mass. 02116, reprinted with permission; p. 133, reprinted by permission of Commonweal publishing Co., Inc.; p. 135, reprinted by permission of Alfred Kazin; p. 137, reprinted by permission of *The Nation*; p. 138, reprinted by permission of *The New Statesman*; p. 142, excerpted from "Letter Home" by James Jones, in *Esquire* (December 1963), copyright © 1963 by Esquire Publishing Inc.; p. 143, copyright © 1965 by R. R. Bowker Company; p. 143, © 1965 by National Review, Inc.; p. 149, © 1968 *New York Times*, reprinted by permission; p. 154, by permission of Norman Mailer, all rights reserved; p. 155, © 1971 *New York Times*, reprinted by permission; p. 157, © 1975 *New York Times*, reprinted by permission; p. 160, copyright Newsday, Inc., reprinted by permission; p. 167, copyright © 1979 by *Saturday Review*, all rights reserved, reprinted by permission; p. 171, copyright © 1981 by *Saturday Review*, all rights reserved, reprinted by permission.

ILLUSTRATIONS: pp. 124, 130, Culver Pictures; pp. 126, 127, 128, 129, 141, 146, 156, 157, 158, 159, 168, by permission of Norman Mailer, all rights reserved; pp. 140, 142, 144, 151, 154, 165, 175, Wide World Photos; p. 153, © Daniel Kramer, 1968; p. 161, photo by C. Brownie Harris from Black Star; p. 166, copyright © 1978 by Norman Mailer, published by Howard Fertig, Inc., New York, 1978; p. 170, by Molly Malone Cook.

VLADIMIR NABOKOV

TEXTS: p. 184, reprinted by permission of *The New Republic*, © 1944, The New Republic, Inc.; p. 186, copyright © 1979 by Véra Nabokov, Executrix of the Estate of Vladimir Nabokov, by permission of Harper & Row, Publishers, Inc.; p. 192, reprinted by permission of *The New Republic*, © 1958, The New Republic, Inc.; p. 196, reprinted by permission of *Encounter*, all rights reserved; p. 204, reprinted by permission from *The Progressive*, 409 East Main Street, Madison, Wisconsin 53703, copyright © 1958, The Progressive, Inc.; p. 208, copyright © 1959 by *Saturday Review*, all rights reserved, reprinted by permission; p. 209, © copyright 1962 by Mary McCarthy, all rights reserved; p. 217, reprinted with permission from *The New Leader*, copyright © 1963, The American Labor Conference on International Affairs, Inc.; p. 220, copyright © 1964 by John Updike. Reprinted from *Assorted Prose*, by John Updike, by permission of Alfred A. Knopf, Inc.; p. 224, reprinted by permission of *Encounter*, all rights reserved; p. 226, © 1966 *New York Times*, reprinted by permission; p. 227, © 1966 *New York Times*, reprinted by permission; p. 232, © 1967 *New York Times*, reprinted by permission; p. 233, copyright 1968 Time, Inc., all rights reserved, reprinted by permission from *Time*; p. 234, © 1970 *New York Times*, reprinted by permission; p. 236, © 1971 *New York Times*, reprinted by permission; p. 240, reprinted with permission from *The New York Review of Books*, copyright © 1972 Nyrev, Inc.; p. 242, copyright © 1973 by McGraw-Hill, reprinted by permission; p. 246, copyright © 1974 by John Updike. Reprinted from *Picked-Up Pieces*, by John Updike, by permission of Alfred A. Knopf, Inc. Originally appeared in *The New Yorker*; p. 249, copyright © 1977 by McGraw-Hill, used with the permission of McGraw-Hill Book Company.

ILLUSTRATIONS: pp. 178, 179, 180, 181, 183, 187, 188, 189, 200, 202, 206, 207, 210, 244, 249, by permission of Véra Nabokov, all rights reserved; pp. 190, 192, Library of Congress, by permission of Véra Nabokov, all rights reserved; p. 210, photo by Horst Tappe, courtesy Véra Nabokov.

JOHN UPDIKE

TEXTS: p. 256, from Louise Bogan, *A Poet's Alphabet* (McGraw-Hill, 1970), originally published by *The New Yorker*, 18 April 1958, reprinted by permission of Ruth Limmer, literary executor, Estate of Louise Bogan; p. 256, copyright © Commonweal Publishing Co., Inc.; p. 259, © 1960 *New York Times*, reprinted by permission; p. 264, copyright © 1975, by John Updike. Reprinted from *Picked-Up Pieces*, by John Updike, by permission of Alfred A. Knopf, Inc.; p. 266, copyright © 1965 by *Saturday Review*, all rights reserved, reprinted by permission; p. 268, copyright © 1968 by *Saturday Review*, all rights reserved, reprinted by permission; p. 269, © 1968 *New York Times*, reprinted by permission; p. 272, copyright © 1975 by John Updike. Reprinted from *Picked-Up Pieces* by permission of Alfred A. Knopf, Inc.; p. 275, copyright © 1969 by John Updike. Reprinted from *Picked-Up Pieces* by permission of Alfred A. Knopf, Inc.; p. 278, reprinted by permission of *The Listener* and John Updike, all rights reserved; p. 284, copyright 1970 Time, Inc., all rights reserved, reprinted by permission from *Time*; p. 286, © 1971, *New York Times*, reprinted by permission; p. 291, © 1971 *New York Times*, reprinted by permission; p. 294, copyright © 1974, by The Atlantic Monthly Company, Boston, Mass., reprinted with permission of Arthur Schlesinger, Jr.; p. 299, *Writer's Choice*, copyright © 1974 by Rust Hills, reprinted by permission of Longman, Inc., New York; p. 299, reprinted by permission of Georges Borchardt, Inc., copyright © 1975 George Steiner; p. 302, © 1975 *New York Times*, reprinted by permission; p. 305, copyright 1976 by Newsweek, Inc., all rights reserved, reprinted by permission; p. 306, © 1977 *New York Times*, reprinted by permission; p. 309, reprinted by permission of *The New Republic*, © 1979 The New Republic, Inc.; p. 315, reprinted by permission of *The Village Voice*, copyright © News Group Publications, Inc., 1981.

ILLUSTRATIONS: pp. 255, 257, 258, 260, 261, 263, 265, 267, 270, 285, 287, 303, 310, 313, 316, 317, by permission of The Houghton Library, Harvard University, and John Updike, all rights reserved; p. 254, photo of John Updike and Elizabeth Updike by Nancy Updike; p. 256, photo by Irving Fish; p. 259, photo by Earl Snyder; p. 262, photo by Ivan Massar from Black Star; p. 264, Wide World Photos; p. 275, Photo by Richard J. Patrick, *Reading Times*; p. 281, photo by Peter Simon from Black Star; p. 297, Wide World Photos; p. 307, photo by Terry Bauer; p. 319, photo by Martha Updike.

KURT VONNEGUT

TEXTS: p. 325, reprinted by permission of *The New Republic*, © 1952 The New Republic, Inc.; p. 327, © 1973 *New York Times*, reprinted by permission; p. 328, © 1965 Time, Inc., all rights reserved; p. 330, reprinted by permission of *The New Republic*, © 1966, The New Republic, Inc.; p. 334, copyright 1969 by Newsweek, Inc., all rights reserved, reprinted by permission; p. 336, copyright © 1970 by Esquire Publishing Inc., used by permission; p. 345, © CBS Inc. 1970, all rights reserved; p. 349, copyright 1970 by Newsweek, Inc., all rights reserved, reprinted by permission; p. 350, with permission, *Media & Methods*, American Society of Educators; p. 353, copyright © 1971 by *Saturday Review*, all rights reserved, reprinted by permission; p. 359, © 1975 *New York Times*, reprinted by permission; p. 361, reprinted by permission of *The New Republic*, © 1979, The New Republic, Inc.

ILLUSTRATIONS: p. 324, Charles Scribner's Sons; p. 350, Wide World Photos; p. 355, Wide World Photos; p. 355, © 1973, by permission of Delacorte Press, all rights reserved; p. 360, reprinted by permission of Delacorte Press; p. 366, photo by Steve Hunt, *Columbia* (S.C.) *State-Record*; pp. 370, 371, 373, © Jill Krementz; pp. 374, 375, reprinted by permission of International Paper Company, from the company's "The Power of the Printed Word" series.

CONTENTS

For
my family

PREFACE

DLB: Documentary Series is a new reference source with a twofold purpose: 1) it makes significant literary documents accessible to students and to scholars, as well as to nonacademic readers; and 2) it supplements the *Dictionary of Literary Biography* (1978-). The *Documentary Series* has been conceived to provide access to a range of material that many students never have the opportunity to see. By itself it is a portable archive. Used with *DLB*, it expands the biographical and critical coverage of the essays by presenting key documents on which these essays are based. *DLB* places authors' lives and works in the perspective of literary history; the *Documentary Series* chronicles literary history in the making.

Each volume in the *Documentary Series* concentrates on the major figures of a particular literary period, movement, or genre. These figures have been selected for their influence on literary history and because their careers generated documents of enduring interest. For each entry the *Documentary Series* staff works with an advisory editor who has studied the author's career extensively. Although entries vary according to an author's writing habits and the availability of his papers, several types of documents are routinely included: letters, notebook and diary entries, interviews, and book reviews. Each document has been chosen to illuminate the writer's personal or professional life.

Literary documents often convey a message beyond the words they record. An author's notes about his work provide insights into the shaping of his literary ideas. Because facsimiles of manuscripts and revised galley proofs vividly reveal the evolution of a work and the author's process of self-evaluation, specimens are included in the *Documentary Series*.

Letters are often the most reliable biographical evidence, recording an author's personal responses to the events of his life. A writer's aspirations or his private observations about his work are frequently revealed in his correspondence.

Notebook and diary entries also present the observations, experiences, and ambitions that determined the writer's career. Such private documents provide crucial perceptions into the creative process and frequently into the writer's artistic maturation.

Interviews contribute to the formulation of an author's public image, as he speaks directly to readers, often attempting to define and secure his place in literature. Some authors took a formal stance on interviews, answering questions straightforwardly. Others were manipulative and developed a public personality which was often misleading.

Book reviews by influential critics, contemporaries of the author, evoke the literary atmosphere of the era. Reviews influence public opinion as they chart the course of an author's critical reception. They are invaluable for the understanding of a writer's reputation, providing the basis from which subsequent assessments of his work evolved.

Fiction, as F. Scott Fitzgerald observed, is transmuted autobiography. Pictures from the author's life may explicate his work. The *Documentary Series* provides photographs of the author, his family, friends, and associates. Dust jackets, title pages, and advertisements—a book's packaging for the public—represent publishers' attempts to define the author's audience and establish impressions of his works. These illustrations in the *Documentary Series* present in the most direct way the stages of an author's publishing history, suggesting the tastes of his era as well.

Each author entry in *DLB: Documentary Series* is therefore a concise illustrated biography as well as a sampling of the diverse materials that have heretofore been accessible to a limited group of researchers. Too often readers see only the results of an author's painstaking toil and hear only the conclusions of others about the merits of his work. Students of literature rarely have the opportunity to glimpse a writer's work in progress, to consider firsthand the judgments of his contemporaries, and to examine extracts from his personal papers. *DLB: Documentary Series* offers these opportunities, facilitating the study of an author's life and career from a variety of perspectives, each of which enriches the appreciation and understanding of his enduring achievements.

ACKNOWLEDGMENTS

This book was produced by BC Research.

The production staff included Mary Betts, Donna Brasington, Arlyn F. Bruccoli, Joseph Caldwell, Angela Dixon, Lynn Felder, Joyce Fowler, Sharon K. Kirkland, Cynthia D. Lybrand, Alice A. Parsons, Joycelyn R. Smith, Robin A. Sumner, Margaret A. Van Antwerp, Charles Wentworth, and Lynne C. Zeigler.

The editor gratefully acknowledges the assistance of the following people and organizations: Laurie Bloomfield; Ellen Dunlap, Humanities Research Center, University of Texas, Austin; Philip B. Eppard; Janis Freedman; Dean Keller, Kent State University Libraries; Norman Mailer; Mrs. Vladimir Nabokov; Maurice Neville; Sem C. Sutter, Regenstein Library, University of Chicago; Mara Anne Tapp, Office of News and Information, University of Chicago; John Updike; Keith Walters; Jeffrey H. Weinberg; Yale University Library.

Anne Dixon and Walter W. Ross performed the library research with the generous assistance of the following librarians at the Thomas Cooper Library, University of South Carolina: Michael Freeman, Dwight Gardner, Michael Havener, David Lincove, Roger Mortimer, Donna Nance, Harriet Oglesbee, Jean Rhyne, Paula Swope, Jane Thesing, Ellen Tillett, Gary Treadway, and Beth Woodard. Assistance with the photographic copy work for this volume was given by Pat Crawford of Imagery, Columbia, South Carolina.

EDITORIAL ADVISERS

Dictionary of Literary Biography

1: *The American Renaissance in New England*,
edited by Joel Myerson (1978)

2: *American Novelists Since World War II*,
edited by Jeffrey Helterman and Richard Layman (1978)

3: *Antebellum Writers in New York and the South*,
edited by Joel Myerson (1979)

4: *American Writers in Paris, 1920-1939*,
edited by Karen Lane Rood (1980)

5: *American Poets Since World War II*, 2 volumes,
edited by Donald J. Greiner (1980)

6: *American Novelists Since World War II*, Second Series,
edited by James E. Kibler, Jr. (1980)

7: *Twentieth-Century American Dramatists*, 2 volumes,
edited by John MacNicholas (1981)

8: *Twentieth-Century American Science-Fiction Writers*, 2 volumes,
edited by David Cowart and Thomas L. Wymer (1981)

9: *American Novelists, 1910-1945*, 3 volumes,
edited by James J. Martine (1981)

10: *Modern British Dramatists, 1900-1945*, 2 volumes,
edited by Stanley Weintraub (1982)

11: *American Humorists, 1800-1950*, 2 volumes,
edited by Stanley Trachtenberg (1982)

12: *American Realists and Naturalists*,
edited by Donald Pizer and Earl N. Harbert (1982)

13: *British Dramatists Since World War II*, 2 volumes,
edited by Stanley Weintraub (1982)

Yearbook: 1980,
edited by Karen L. Rood, Jean W. Ross, and Richard Ziegfeld (1981)

Yearbook: 1981,
edited by Karen L. Rood, Jean W. Ross, and Richard Ziegfeld (1982)

Documentary Series, volume 1,
edited by Margaret A. Van Antwerp (1982)

Documentary Series, volume 2,
edited by Margaret A. Van Antwerp (1982)

Documentary Series, volume 3,
edited by Mary Bruccoli (1983)

DICTIONARY OF LITERARY BIOGRAPHY

DOCUMENTARY SERIES

AN ILLUSTRATED CHRONICLE

VOLUME THREE

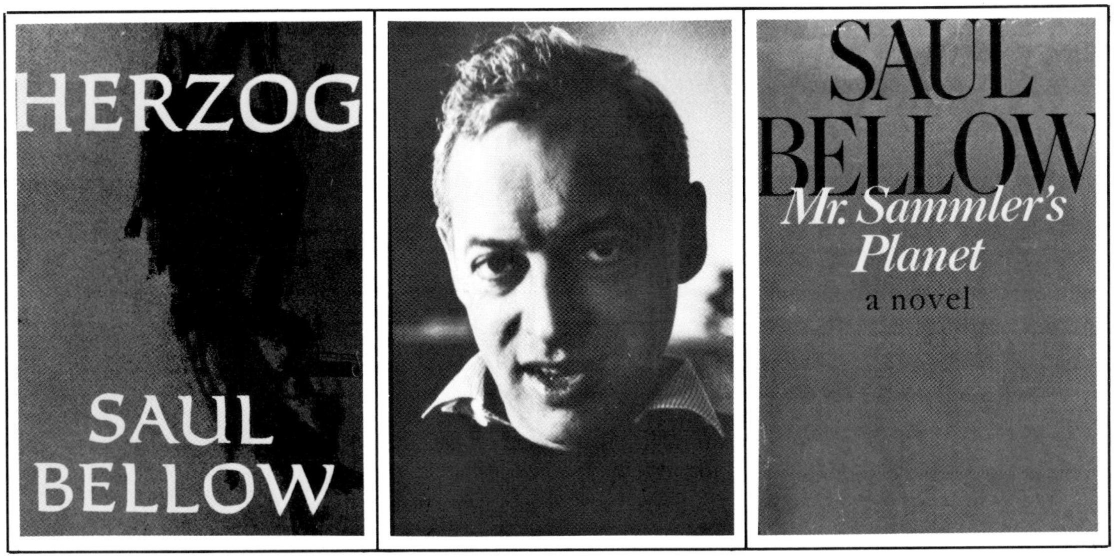

SAUL BELLOW

(10 June 1915-)

See the Saul Bellow entry in the Dictionary of Literary Biography, *volume 2,* American Novelists Since World War II.

MAJOR BOOKS:

Dangling Man (New York: Vanguard, 1944; London: Weidenfeld & Nicolson, 1960);

The Victim (New York: Vanguard, 1947; London: Weidenfeld & Nicolson, 1963);

The Adventures of Augie March (New York: Viking, 1953; London: Weidenfeld & Nicolson, 1954);

Seize the Day (New York: Viking, 1956; London: Weidenfeld & Nicolson, 1957);

Henderson the Rain King (New York: Viking, 1959; London: Weidenfeld & Nicolson, 1959);

Recent American Fiction (Washington, D.C.: The Library of Congress, 1963);

Herzog (New York: Viking, 1964; London: Weidenfeld & Nicolson, 1965);

The Last Analysis (New York: Viking, 1965; London: Weidenfeld & Nicolson, 1966);

Mosby's Memoirs and Other Stories (New York: Viking, 1968; London: Weidenfeld & Nicolson, 1969);

Mr. Sammler's Planet (New York: Viking, 1970; London: Weidenfeld & Nicolson, 1970);

The Portable Saul Bellow (New York: Viking, 1974);

Humboldt's Gift (New York: Viking, 1975; London: Secker & Warburg, 1975);

To Jerusalem and Back: A Personal Account (London: Alison Press/Secker & Warburg, 1976);

Nobel Lecture (New York: Targ Editions, 1979);

The Dean's December (New York: Harper & Row, 1982; London: Secker & Warburg, 1982).

BIBLIOGRAPHY:

B. A. Sokoloff and Mark Posner, *Saul Bellow: A Comprehensive Bibliography* (Folcroft, Penn.: Folcroft, 1972).

OTHER:

Great Jewish Short Stories, edited by Bellow (New York: Dell, 1963; London: Valentine, 1971).

LOCATION OF ARCHIVES:

The principal collection of Bellow's manuscripts and papers is at the Regenstein Library, University of Chicago.

Saul Bellow was born 10 June 1915 in Lachine, Quebec, Canada, the fourth child of Russian immigrant parents, Liza Gordon and Abraham Bellow. In the 1922 family portrait above, Bellow is at the far left. The family moved to Chicago in 1924, where Bellow attended Tuley High School and then entered the University of Chicago in 1933. He transferred to Northwestern University, graduating with honors in anthropology and sociology in 1937; he then entered the University of Wisconsin graduate school but left without a degree. In 1937 Bellow married Anita Goshkin, with whom he had a son, Gregory, born in 1944. He worked for the Works Progress Administration as a writer and then joined the faculty of the Pestalozzi-Froebel Teachers College in Chicago. From 1943 to 1946 he was on the Encyclopaedia Britannica *editorial staff, and in late 1944 he was in the Maritime Service training program.*

Book Review:

Edmund Wilson, "Doubts and Dreams," *New Yorker*, 20 (1 April 1944): 78, 81.

Bellow's first novel, Dangling Man, *was published in 1944. In a later interview he admitted that "when I wrote those early books I was timid. I still felt the incredible effrontery of announcing myself to the world (in part I mean the WASP world) as a writer and an artist. . . . In short, I was afraid to let myself go."*

"Dangling Man," by Saul Bellow (Vanguard), is the story, told in the form of a diary, of a young Jewish boy in Chicago who throws up a job in a travel bureau expecting to be inducted into the Army, but, owing to various technicalities, is left for a year without being called. In the meantime, he cannot get his job back, and "there is nothing to do but wait, or dangle, and grow more and more dispirited." He lives on his wife's earnings, sits at home and reads the paper, and, though naturally of studious tastes, cannot bring himself to concentrate on anything. He has a love affair in a half-hearted way; then, when it begins to prove a strain, gives it up. He finds himself getting more and more ill-tempered: he quarrels with his old friends, with his brother, with his wife, and finally comes to blows with his landlord. He has long, brooding dialogues with himself that never come to any conclusion. At last, he cannot stand it any longer and applies to the draft board to be taken, with the result that he is called at once.

And now he is immensely relieved, and everybody feels better about him. Yet the moral situation is ambiguous. From the conventional point of view and from that of his natural instincts as a young man sitting idle during a war, he has of course done the right thing. But his action implies the defeat of other instincts which he had felt to be important. He had not wanted to have to admit that he did not "know how to use his freedom," that he "had no resources—in a word, no character." He had hoped in some way to vindicate the value of the individual even in a crisis where the fate of Western culture seemed to hang on collective enterprise; he had hoped to sustain an example of the independence of the human mind even at a moment when the body had to wait on the orders of the State. But the pressure of the times has compelled his surrender.

This is all there is to the story, but the book is an excellent document on the experience of the non-combatant in time of war. It is well written and never dull—in spite of the dismalness of the Chicago background and the undramatic character of the subject. It is also one of the most honest pieces of testimony on the psychology of a whole generation who have grown up during the depression and the war, and has its affinities with certain other recent books that seem in some cases superficially quite different: the "War Diary" of Jean Malaquais, which shows the same kind of mentality persisting in the conditions of the war itself; "The Journal of Albion Moonlight," by the poet Kenneth Patchen, in which a similar helplessness in face of the war, a similar desperation, is transposed into a delirium of rhetoric; and "So It Doesn't Whistle," by Robert Paul Smith, a novel of the kind of sub-bohemian life, rootless and almost ambitionless, led by young people in big American cities. Most of these writers and the characters in their books have, like the hero of "Dangling Man," passed earlier through a period of Communist thinking. Events have since appeared to prove false the political predictions of the Communists, and the young men have discarded the philosophy without altogether destroying the attitude. They do not much want to defend the status quo, which in the thirties they had learned to distrust, but they cannot refuse the challenge to stand up to the barbarism of the Fascists. In the meantime, their impulses toward artistic creation or intellectual expression are frustrated, bewildered, and soured. The war world and the world at home both seem to present pretty black pictures.

A typical passage in "Dangling Man" shows the hero looking out the window at the winter streets and chimneys of Chicago. It is strikingly similar to Malaquais's thoughts on his companions and his duties in the army:

> It was my painful obligation to look and to submit to myself the invariable question: Where was there a particle of what, elsewhere, or in the past, had spoken in man's favor? There could be no doubt that these billboards, streets, tracks, houses, ugly and blind, were related to interior life. And yet, I told myself, there had to be a doubt. There were human lives organized around these ways and houses, and that they, the houses, say, were the analogue, that what men created they also were, through some transcendent means, I could not bring myself to concede. There must be a difference, a quality that eluded me, somehow, a difference between things and persons and even between acts and persons. Otherwise the people who lived here were actually a reflection of the things they lived among. I had always striven to avoid blaming them. Was that not in effect behind my daily reading of the paper? In their businesses and politics, their taverns, movies, assaults, divorces, murders, I tried continually to find clear signs of their common humanity.

BOOK REVIEW:

Leslie A. Fiedler, "The Fate of the Novel," *Kenyon Review*, 10 (Summer 1948): 519-527.

Bellow labored over his second novel, The Victim, *trying "to make it letter-perfect. . . . I accepted a Flaubertian standard. Not a bad standard, to be sure, but one which, in the end, I found repressive—repressive because of the circumstances of my life and because of my upbringing in Chicago. . . . I could not . . . express a variety of things I knew intimately."*

In Saul Bellow's book, it seems to me, the passion and the idea are unified, because they have never been separated. *The Victim* attempts the same mediation between the polarities of complete freedom and complete responsibility as Trilling's book, and in their abstract response the novels are extraordinarily alike. Bellow

The back of the dust jacket for a reprint of The Victim

chooses as his fable, however, the situation of a Jew, Asa Leventhal, accused fantastically of complicity in the downfall of an anti-semitic scoundrel who continues to abuse him even as he sponges upon him. The book might have stopped with a portrayal of the plight of the Jew, unnerved in advance before the charges of his enemy (who is entirely without guilt? who can feel a *right* to security before another's failure?), learning through the acceptance of his guilt and the assertion of his innocence to be free; but Leventhal is realized with such passionate patience and skill, achieved with such scrupulous regard for detail rising from a sense that the meanings of each trivial fact are inexhaustible and mysterious—that he becomes, deeply as he is a Jew, human, and, infinitely as he is particularized, universal. We think of Leopold Bloom, the urban man, the sojourner, the bastard artist, infinite in feeling, limited in expression; the style is at once low-keyed and violent with that baffled urge toward articulateness. Every aspect of that hot, lonely midsummer is felt at once as real and obsessive—Leventhal is what we are, and what, in terror, we dream we are. Secure for a moment, established in routines of decency and sufficiency in the blind institutionalized process of modern life—as we say, "lucky," and assailed suddenly by the accusation that is monstrously unfair and cannot be denied. To have rejected utterly his guilt and responsibility would have been for Leventhal a lie, and yet accepting them brings him in the end to a sullied house, to insolence and the point of death. It is difficult, after all, to be human—and nothing less is at stake.

The Victim is a fruitful and satisfying achievement, surely one of the most complexly moving books of the past ten years. The tension between its realistic surfaces and its symbolic implications is admirably sustained; the quality of its *achieved* ideas, their passionate implication in the fable, and their coherence with the tone and structure make a book whose unity, amazingly these days, is one of inclusion, not exclusion, a book whose pleasures are neither irrelevant nor unwitting, a novel that establishes in a single gesture its structure and its meaning. In each novel, the fate of the form is at stake, and we must be grateful to the young writer adequate to his responsibilities.

BOOK REVIEW:

Harvey Curtis Webster, "Quest Through the Modern World," *Saturday Review*, 36 (19 September 1953): 13-14.

When he published The Adventures of Augie March, *Bellow noted that "Augie was my favorite fantasy." The novel was warmly received; it won the National Book Award and brought Bellow a second Guggenheim Fellowship. At this time he was teaching at Bard College, having previously taught at the University of Minnesota, New York University, and Princeton.*

Reading "The Adventures of Augie March" in 1953 must be a good deal like reading "Ulysses" in 1920. Like Joyce before he wrote his first masterpiece, Saul Bellow is mainly known as the writer of two excellent, tightly organized works of fiction, neither of them too easy or too difficult to fit into the pattern of what one is accustomed to read. Not unnaturally, the reader used to the way most good writers follow or develop a pattern they or others have established is unprepared for an apparently complete break with both past technique and past subject matter. Anything deeply original is at first perplexing and

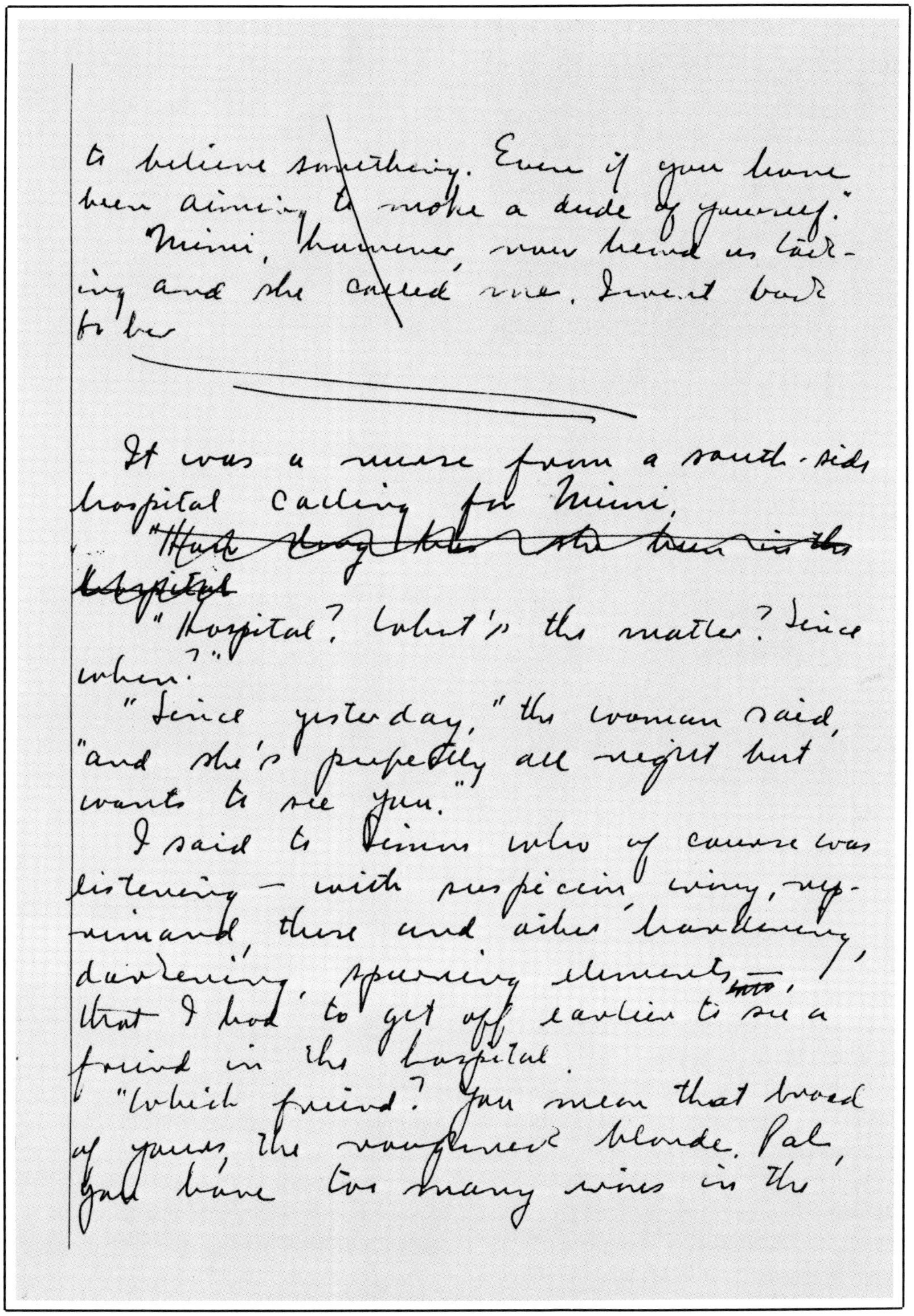
to believe something. Even if you have been aiming to make a dude of yourself."

Mimi, however, must have heard us talking and she called me. I went back to be

It was a nurse from a south-side hospital calling for Mimi.

"~~How long has she been in the hospital~~

"Hospital? What's the matter? Since when?"

"Since yesterday," the woman said, "and she's perfectly all right but wants to see you."

I said to Simon who of course was listening—with suspicion, irony, reprimand, these and other hardening, darkening, spurring elements, too—that I had to get off earlier to see a friend in the hospital.

"Which friend? You mean that broad of yours, the roughneck blonde. Pal, you have too many wires in the

Bellow felt that he had paid "my respects to formal requirements" in Dangling Man *and* The Victim; *but in writing about Augie March he "took off many of these restraints." He later commented, "I think I took off too many, and went too far, but I was feeling the excitement of discovery. I had just increased my freedom, and like any emancipated plebeian I abused it at once." Shown here is a page of an early manuscript for* The Adventures of Augie March *(Regenstein Library, University of Chicago).*

therefore likely to make the reader take refuge in either the dogmatics of damnation or of sanctification.

This does not mean that there is any marked similarity between Joyce's "Ulysses" and "The Adventures of Augie March." Both books are long, both ambitious; both can be read esoterically or as exercises in pornography. But Mr. Bellow's exercise in form and substance is, on the surface, readily intelligible; it is not so much concerned with the way its author sees the world as with the way someone quite unlike him does. While it is impossible for the "common" reader to go more than ten pages into "Ulysses" without deep perplexity, it is possible for the same reader to finish "The Adventures of Augie March" before his perplexity begins. Like Rabelais and Cervantes, Mr. Bellow makes easy sense from page to page, yet his total meaning is elusive.

This elusiveness is partially the consequence of the apparent simplicity and actual complexity of Augie March, the novel's protagonist. He has a "very weak sense of consequences" and a will to comply, but he also has a will to resist. He is "a sort of Columbus of those near-at-hand," a "laughing creature, forever rising up," one of those "people other people are always trying to fit with their schemes." He is "ambitious in general," not "concrete enough," a perpetual searcher for a "good enough fate," who always seems to be standing still. Though he is born in Chicago and most of his quest takes place in this city whose roughness does not encourage illusions, he believes that "we all catch up with legends," and that "there may gods turn up anywhere." In his life in Chicago, Mexico, and abroad he encounters almost all kinds of men and ideas and experiences more than any one man could (like Gulliver and Pantagruel). What he sees, thinks. and does is told in a style that mixes erudition and bawdiness. At first the style seems unconvincing and delightful; finally it becomes convincing and delightful. Whether one considers Augie a "man of hope or foolishness," whether one believes his lingo and experiences plausible or implausible, he should know after reading his adventures that the modern multiverse is his province and could be made so by no other method of presentation.

Augie's quest leads him to become a thief, a dog washer in a dog club, the trainer of an eagle, a merchant marine, a businessman, a down-and-outer in flop houses, a respectable gigolo, a questionable dealer in surplus goods abroad, a lover of more and more unusual women than any character in modern fiction. Augie almost succumbs to the ideas of Grandma Lausch, the Jewish empress of a Chicago boardinghouse, and to those of

Bellow at the time he was writing The Adventures of Augie March

Einhorn, a crippled Caesar who thinks one should know everything. He nearly follows his brother, Simon, who "had no peace or rest if he ever lacked dough," into the bondage of being a rich woman's husband. He is a CIO organizer, a great lover like Antony (but Augie survives), a man who nearly accepts a multiplicity of one-sided paths to salvation—but doesn't.

It is inevitable that one emphasize Augie in a novel about his adventures, but the book's interest and value inhere quite as much in the other characters as in him. Starting with Grandma Lausch, Five Properties, Jimmie Klein, Einhorn, and Sylvester—matriarch, milkman, thief-detective, Caesar, revolutionary—continuing to millionaire Robey, who worries about the effects of inevitable prosperity for everyone on everyone, to Thea, "the theoretician of love," and to Mintouchian, the man of secrets who thinks "only system taps the will of the universe," nearly all the secondary characters are as vivid as Augie himself. Even the very minor characters, met on a page or two—like Bluegren, the florist who trades with gangsters, and Lieutenant Nuzzo, the policeman with whom even his wife acted as though she were on probation—are memorable.

Looking back over what I have said I realize how much I have not. There is no mention of Mimi, of her abortion or of the inhumanity of hospitals to her; of Hooker Frazer, of Trotsky, of Mrs. Renling's "pale-fire concentration," of Mr. Renling, the "obstacle-eater." I have said little about the many philosophies and psychologies that make varied the book's texture: Clem's Freudianism, Sylvester's Trotskyism, Commissioner Einhorn's capitalism, Arthur Einhorn's estheticism. I have not pointed out how constantly Mr. Bellow's references to the past make the present seem as contemporary as Heraclitus or Aristotle. I have not quoted Caesar Einhorn, who said, "There's law, and there's Nature. There's opinion, and there's Nature." I have not given my final, undefinitive evaluation of a novel I enjoyed reading as much or more than any I have read in years.

Tentatively: Saul Bellow is perhaps a great novelist, "The Adventures of Augie March" perhaps a great novel. If "The Adventures of Augie March" is great it is great because of its comprehensive, not-naturalistic survey of the modern world, its wisely inconclusive presentation of its problems; because its author dares to let go (as so many very good and very neat modern writers do not); because the style of its telling makes the sequence of events seem real even when one knows they couldn't be; because the novel is intelligently and ambitiously conceived as a whole that esthetically comprehends its parts; because it is an achievement in and a promise of the development of a novelist who deserves comparison only with the best, even at this early stage of his development.

INTERVIEW:

Harvey Breit, "Talk With Saul Bellow," *New York Times Book Review*, 20 September 1953, p. 22.

The success of The Adventures of Augie March *established Bellow as a prominent literary figure, and he became the subject of interviews and critical articles.*

It was of Dostoevsky that André Gide once said all factions could find something in him to support their claims but no one faction could claim him exclusively. Some of this holds true for Saul Bellow. He came up as a writer out of the tough, tight literary magazines, established his beachhead, as it were, and is now successfully fanning out into the broader and brighter domains; his talents, valued from the start by the severer literary critics, have gradually begun to be noticed by greater numbers of the ordinary, intelligent vintage. Mr. Bellow's work contains innumberably diverse elements, it has variousness and is against the grain. His readers, therefore, are to be found anywhere and everywhere and they can be anyone at all.

Mr. Bellow's face has variousness too: sharply etched, the structure conveys scientific coldness; but the texture is bold, lyric, poetic. And similarly with his manner: he will talk on the most abstruse or delicate or complex subjects in a matter-of-fact, even breezy, colloquial. What he renders unto Caesar is public, what he renders unto God is a strictly private mater.

His first leap into the swaddling banded world was in 1915, in Quebec. His father, living in Petrograd, had been importing Egyptian onions. He decided to migrate to Canada because his sister was living there. In telling it, Mr. Bellow said in an aside that his father was a fascinating character. Since "The Adventures of Augie March" was a big novel, one wondered whether his father was in it? "No," Mr. Bellow said laughlingly, "I've saved him."

From Canada to Chicago, at the age of 9, and there the youthful Bellow remained for quite a while. Two years at the U. of Chicago brought him around to the conclusion that the study of literature was not the best way to become a writer. He decided to become an anthropologist and he buried himself in the stacks of Northwestern U., working under the famed Professor Herskovits (who wanted to make a pianist out of him). He next got a scholarship at Wisconsin, where he plugged at his master's thesis in anthropology. There Dr. Goldenweiser assured him he wasn't cut out for science. His papers had too much style. "It was a nice way of easing me out of the field," Mr. Bellow said.

"Goldenweiser played Chopin and wept. He was very Chekhovian. The old boy's heart was really in literature. Every time I worked on my thesis, it turned out to be a story. I disappeared for the Christmas holidays and I never came back." Mr. Bellow laughed a little, and then said, "This is my way of making a change. Disappearing from something and never coming back."

And so at this juncture began "The Adventures of Saul Bellow" because at this point he started to write. Between then and "Augie March," Mr. Bellow had written two novels, "Dangling Man" and "The Victim." Mr. Bellow nodded, but contradicted. "This is the third published novel. I threw two novels away because they were too sad."

Mr. Bellow has written steadily all the while—short stories, essays, literary articles. He won a Guggenheim Fellowship and a National Institute of Arts and Letters Award. Along the way he taught at the University of Minnesota and at Princeton. He has taken a job on the English staff of Bard College—which brings our author up to the immediate present. Except for "Augie." Would Mr. Bellow tell us what he could?

He thought a bit and then said, "I started 'Augie' in Paris. I wrote it in trains and cafes. I got used to writing on the roll. I hunted for the right cafe in Rome, and, when I found it, I worked there all the time. After I was there about a month, the waiter told me it was where D'Annunzio used to come to write. But," Mr. Bellow added dryly, "I don't expect to get into politics."

Had he had any trouble getting so right a name as Augie March? Mr. Bellow shook his head negatively, almost sleepily. "It just came to me," he said. "The great pleasure of the book was that it came easily. All I had to do was be there with buckets to catch it. That's why the form is loose."

Then it had just flowed easily and loosely and there

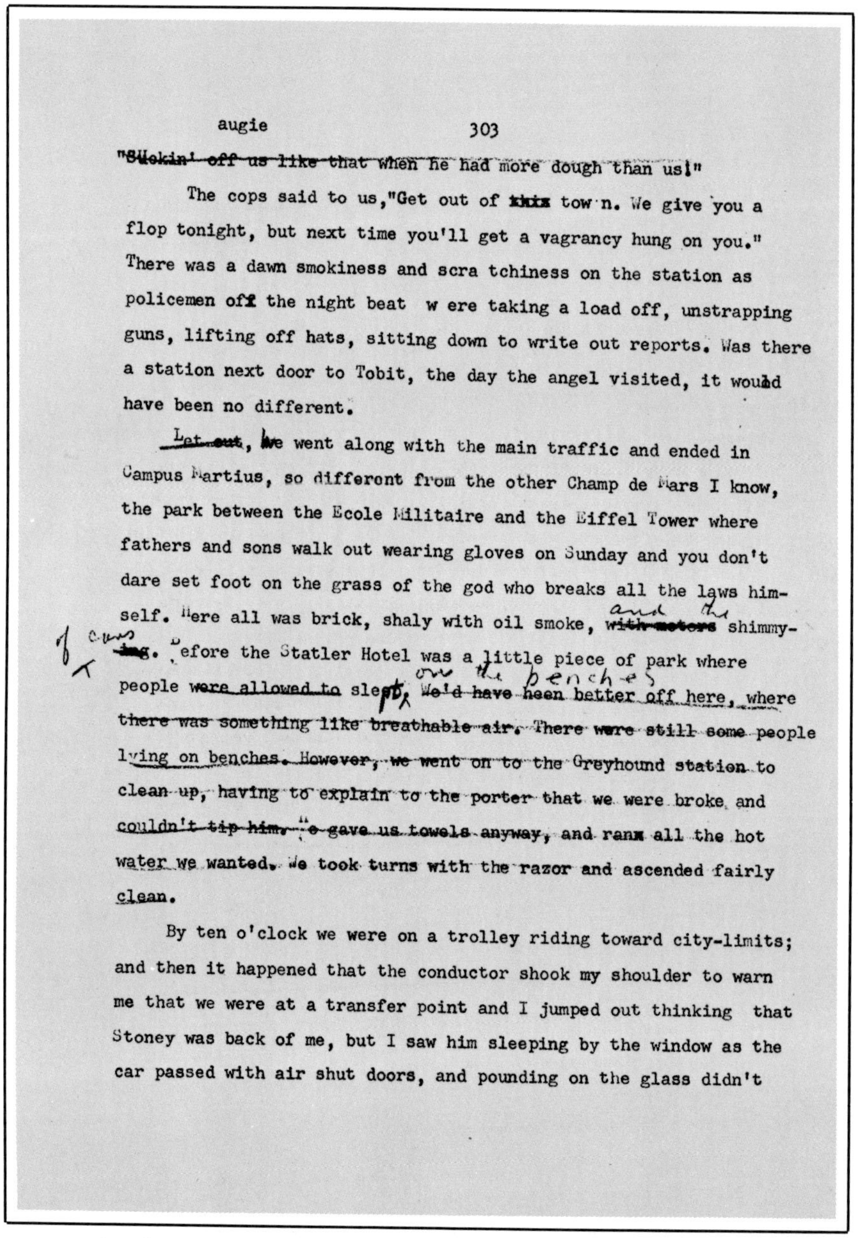
augie 303

~~"Suckin' off us like that when he had more dough than us!"~~

The cops said to us,"Get out of ~~this~~ tow n. We give you a flop tonight, but next time you'll get a vagrancy hung on you." There was a dawn smokiness and scra tchiness on the station as policemen off the night beat w ere taking a load off, unstrapping guns, lifting off hats, sitting down to write out reports. Was there a station next door to Tobit, the day the angel visited, it would have been no different.

~~Let out~~, we went along with the main traffic and ended in Campus Martius, so different from the other Champ de Mars I know, the park between the Ecole Militaire and the Eiffel Tower where fathers and sons walk out wearing gloves on Sunday and you don't dare set foot on the grass of the god who breaks all the laws himself. Here all was brick, shaly with oil smoke, ~~with motors~~ and the shimmy~~ing~~ of cars. Before the Statler Hotel was a little piece of park where people ~~were allowed to~~ slept on the benches. ~~We'd have been better off here, where there was something like breathable air. There were still some people lying on benches. However, we went on to the Greyhound station to clean up, having to explain to the porter that we were broke and couldn't tip him. He gave us towels anyway, and ran all the hot water we wanted. We took turns with the razor and ascended fairly clean.~~

By ten o'clock we were on a trolley riding toward city-limits; and then it happened that the conductor shook my shoulder to warn me that we were at a transfer point and I jumped out thinking that Stoney was back of me, but I saw him sleeping by the window as the car passed with air shut doors, and pounding on the glass didn't

Two pages of revised typescript for The Adventures of Augie March *(Regenstein Library, University of Chicago). Bellow has said of this novel that "one of my great pleasures was in*

was no literary principle back of the looseness? "Something like that," Mr. Bellow replied. "But I do think that the novel has imitated poetry far too much recently." How had it done that? "In its severity and style and devotion to exact form. In the great period of the novel, the novelist didn't care—there was a great mass of sand and gravel; there was diversity of scene, a large number of characters. One of the reasons the novel has diminished is that a great many people, writers, find it difficult to write dramatic scenes.

"After all, the novel grew out of daily events, out of newspapers. Today, the novelist thinks too much of immortality and he tries to create form. He tries to make his work durable through form. But you have to take your chances on mortality, on perishability. That's what I felt. I kicked over the traces, wrote catch-as-catch-can, picaresque. I took my chance."

Mr. Bellow shrugged, smiled and made his momentous novel seem casual. It was, we were convinced, what he wanted and needed to do. Obviously, Mr. Bellow was against the over-solemn, the too-pious manner, the inflated ego. Who could be against Mr. Bellow for that?

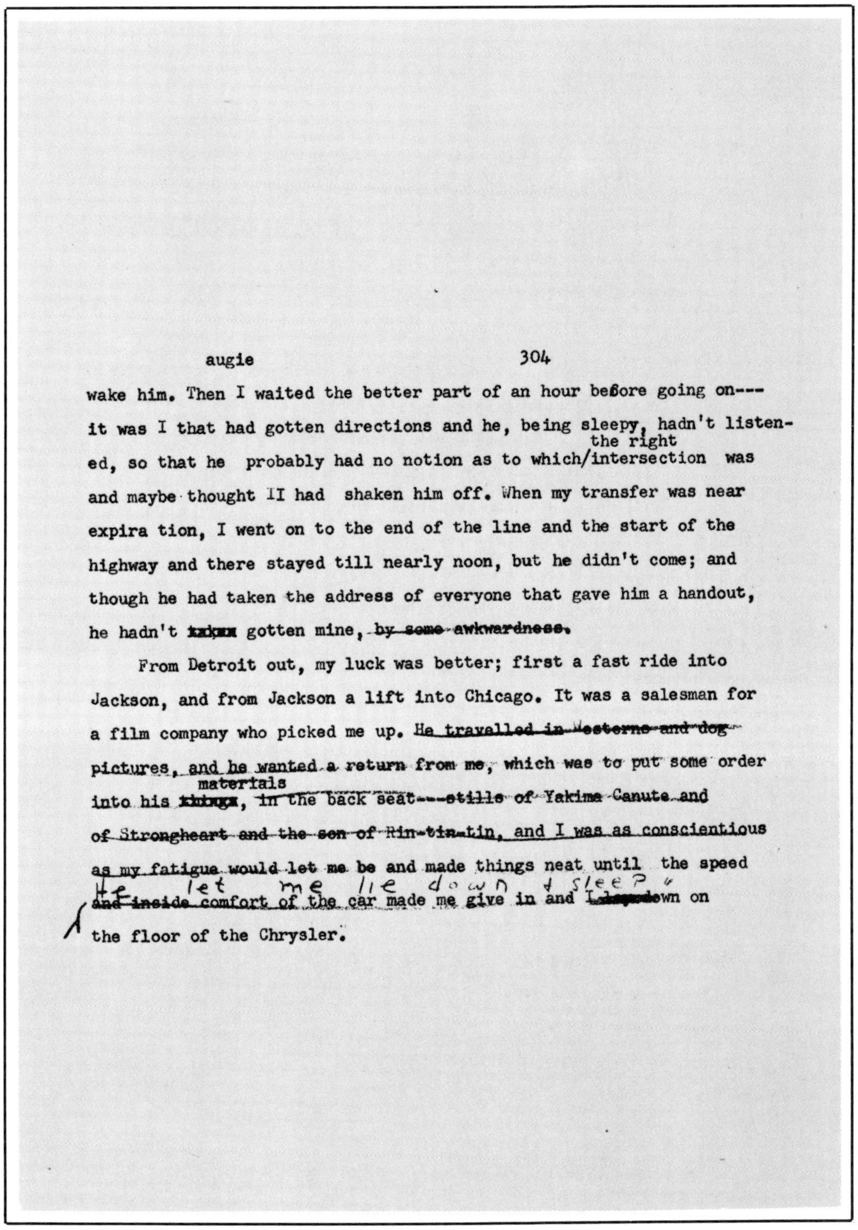

augie 304

wake him. Then I waited the better part of an hour beßore going on---
it was I that had gotten directions and he, being sleepy, hadn't listened, so that he probably had no notion as to which/the right intersection was
and maybe thought II had shaken him off. When my transfer was near
expira tion, I went on to the end of the line and the start of the
highway and there stayed till nearly noon, but he didn't come; and
though he had taken the address of everyone that gave him a handout,
he hadn't ~~[illegible]~~ gotten mine, ~~by some awkwardness.~~

From Detroit out, my luck was better; first a fast ride into
Jackson, and from Jackson a lift into Chicago. It was a salesman for
a film company who picked me up. ~~He travelled in Westerns and dog~~
~~pictures, and he wanted a return from me, which was to put some order~~
~~into his~~ ~~[illegible]~~ materials~~, in the back seat---stills of Yakima Canute and~~
~~of Strongheart and the son of Rin-tin-tin, and I was as conscientious~~
~~as my fatigue would let me be and made things neat until the speed~~
He let me lie down & sleep.
~~and inside comfort of the car made me give in and~~ ~~[illegible]~~own on
the floor of the Chrysler.

having the ideas taken away from me, as it were, by the characters. They demanded to have their own existence."

ARTICLE:

Saul Bellow, "How I Wrote Augie March's Story," *New York Times Book Review*, 31 January 1954, pp. 3, 17.

Bellow's Guggenheim Fellowship in 1948 enabled him to travel in Europe while he worked on his third novel, The Adventures of Augie March, *set in Chicago during the Depression.*

In a public statement Mr. Robert Penn Warren recently observed that he liked to write in a foreign country, "where the language is not your own, and you are forced into yourself in a special way." When I began to write "The Adventures of Augie March" I was living in Paris, where circumstances made me constantly aware that I was not a Frenchman. Americans at that time were forever being told what they were or were not. A friend of mine who blundered into his Parisian landlady's apartment was told before he could excuse himself, *"La France n'est pas un pays conquis, M'sieu."* He lacked the presence of mind to reply that he was not the American Army, either, but had merely been looking for the bathroom.

I was at that time writing in a tiny hotel room on Rue des Saints Pères. Across the street pneumatic drills were at work on the concrete of a hospital whose construction had been abandoned at the outbreak of the war. The noise did not disturb my thoughts; I lived in it like the salamander in the flames. The room below mine was occupied by an old Italian scholar, who was not much annoyed by it either. To protect his privacy I will call him M. Scaferlati. He had a large but frail body, an immense head of hair, feeble but severe-looking eyes, a small nervous laugh but a serious and learned mind. Most of the day he passed in bed drinking coffee and reading, favoring his left eye. M. Scaferlati was engaged in a study of heavy books at close range, the Merovingians.

While I was writing Chapter I, M. Scaferlati had an accident as he was washing his feet in the sink. He was soaping the left foot when the bowl of the washstand broke and a chunk of it fell on the instep of the supporting right foot, inflicting a deep gash. It was a painful wound. He wrapped a large bandage around it and did not leave his bed for an entire week, a week spent in conversation. Among his acquaintances there were some who said he had wounded himself on purpose, from resentment toward a friend who had tried to get him a job. A strange theory.

When one of his American visitors remarked that I did not seem to be getting what I should out of Paris, M. Scaferlati wisely replied, "But it is only natural that while he is here he should be thinking of America most of the time." Perhaps only a student of the Merovingians could be so discerning about the Chicagoans.

For it was Chicago before the Depression that moved my imagination as I went to my room in the morning, not misty Paris with its cold statues and its streams of water running along the curbstones.

After the theft of my typewriter from my room in the hotel I rented another place on Rue Vaneau, in the apartment of the French wife of a Swedish sea captain, a jolly woman who brought me coffee twice a day. She had once owned a bookshop, and hers was a literary house. For the fireplace she gave me, instead of ordinary wastepaper, copies of Le Rire for 1907 or thereabout.

Eventually Mme. L. rented half of her apartment to me, and since I had by this time gotten used to writing away from home I found another room in the vicinity of St. Sulpice, a gloomy region of shops specializing in ecclesiastical goods. The book was writing itself very rapidly; I was coming to be strangely independent of place. Chicago itself had grown exotic to me, and I began to realize that it is characteristic of any prolonged strangeness that it gradually begins to consider itself the invariable normalcy.

A descendant of Russian-Jewish immigrants; I was writing of Chicago in odd corners of Paris and, afterward, in Austria, Italy, Long Island and New Jersey. To speak of rootless or rooted persons is all very well. No man needs to bother his head about the matter whose emotions are alive. We are called upon to preserve our humanity in circumstances of rapid change and movement. I do not see what else we can do than refuse to be condemned with a time or a place. We are not born to be condemned but to live.

In the spring of 1950 I began to travel southward with my family. One chapter of "Augie"—I then had the notion of calling it "Life Among the Machiavellians"—was written at Schloss Leopoldskron, Salzburg, the late Max Reinhardt's baroque castle, while I was teaching in the American Seminar. Another was written in Florence

I have a longing, not for downright obscurity–I'm too egotistical for that–but for peace, and freedom from meddling.

From Writers at Work, Third Series *(New York: Viking Press, 1967)*

Saul Bellow at the National Book Awards ceremony, 26 August 1954, with Alistair Cooke, Cheryl Crawford, and Bruce Catton

in May, at various café tables. The late French novelist Bernanos once said that he preferred to do his writing in cafés and restaurants; he had a dislike for solitary labor. Of course one may argue that a novelist always has the company of his characters, or ought to have, but in my opinion there is nothing to be said in favor of a severe solitude.

In Rome I wrote every morning for six weeks at the Casino Valadier in the Borghese Gardens. In this marvelous place, overlooking the city from the Pincian Rock, I happily filled several student notebooks and smoked cigars and drank coffee, unaware of the close Roman heat as long as I did not move about. A waiter later told me that the poet D'Annunzio had enjoyed working in this same place. I didn't know whether or not he was saying this to please me but it did rather tickle me to hear it. Latterly, reading Goethe's "Conversations with Eckermann," I learned that the great poet had composed one of his tragedies in the Borghese Gardens. I am glad I was not aware of this historic fact at the time.

My old Mexican briefcase was growing fat with manuscript as we traveled. I wrote in all kinds of conditions, in hotels and eating places, on a rooftop in the town of Positano, south at Sorrento; at the Crystal Palace Hotel, London; in the apartment of my friend Lidov on West Ninety-fifth Street, in Forest Hills, in a cold-water flat on Hudson Street, in the Hotel Meany in Seattle, in a motel in Portland, Oregon; at Yaddo in Saratoga Springs, in the Pennsylvania Station, in a Broadway hotel, in an office at the Princeton Library. The last two paragraphs I completed on a Viking Press typewriter. Not a single word of the book was composed in Chicago.

From the point of view of a Chicagoan I suppose all these other places are foreign countries where, in Mr. Warren's words, "the language is not your own and you are forced into yourself in a special way."

BOOK REVIEW:

Alfred Kazin, "In Search of Light," *New York Times Book Review*, 18 November 1956, p. 5.

Three short stories, a play, and the short novel "Seize the Day"—which gave the volume its title—were collected by Bellow in 1956. This warm review was written by Bellow's friend Alfred Kazin.

The principal item in Mr. Bellow's new book is the long title story, virtually a novel in miniature, to which have been added three short stories and a one-act play. Although the different things in the book are by no means on the same level, the title story seems to me the most moving single piece of fiction that this young author has as yet written. It is all the more interesting because there is a plainness of feeling in it that contrasts sharply with the keyed-up virtuosity and the defiant humor of his long novel, "The Adventures of Augie March."

In all Mr. Bellow's fiction to date one has been aware of an unusual mind that has wryly put itself to situations for irony, burlesque, the macabre. In "Seize the Day" Mr. Bellow's very subject is the transparency of human weakness. It is the kind of weakness that is hard to conceal or to acknowledge. But if it is looked at as closely

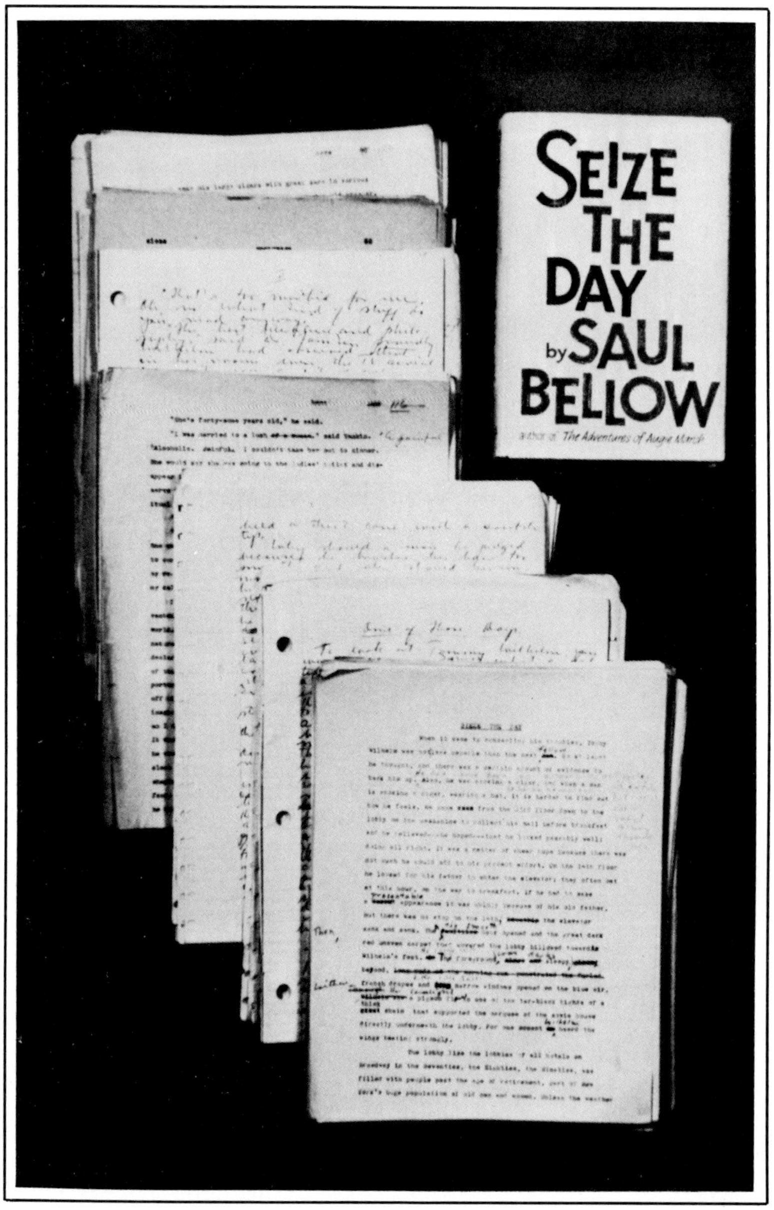

Seize the Day*: manuscript and four revised typescripts (Humanities Research Center)*

and compassionately as Mr. Bellow has done, it becomes a profoundly true image of human existence as it is lived through that single day, the human locus of time, which we try to make the most of as it dies on our hands.

Mr. Bellow describes Tommy Wilhelm (born Adler), a 42-odd-year old salesman who, despite a wife and two children, has not learned to think of himself as a grown and independent being. Separated from his wife, jobless because of his own impulsiveness, bedeviled by money worries, resentful of his father for withholding both cash and emotional protection, he has tied himself to a quack psychologist whom he profoundly distrusts—all the more because he cannot shake himself loose of the man's preposterous but haunting counsels.

Tommy finds himself prowling through a New York day searching for a place of support or rest. By the end of it, he has tossed away the last of his money on the market and is desperately frightened. Yet he gains an unexpected release when he is swept by the passing crowd into the funeral of a man he has never known—and, looking down at the dead man's face, at last finds himself able to feel, to accept his own suffering. Thus, at last, he is able to confront that larger suffering which (as we can see only at the end of the story) has been the dead weight of existence pressing on him without any release or passion in him of understanding.

It is the intense world of the ordinary, the mean daily detail, the outrage of being alive, the existential sense of one's self as human creature, which is bravely at the center of Mr. Bellow's fiction. Each detail is cruel, plain, irremediable, yet one feels that it is about to burst forth into the radiance of consciousness.

In the next-best story in the book, "A Father To Be," the hero, burdened by money worries, saddened by the careworn faces in the subway, reflects that "to think of money was to think as the world wanted you to think; then you'd never be your own master," and opposes to this world of necessity, which Mr. Bellow renders with so much honesty, the world of consciousness. "He went on to reflect how little people knew about this, how they slept through life, how small a light the light of consciousness was."

It is the special distinction of Mr. Bellow as a novelist that he is able to give us, step by step, the world we really live each day—and in the same movement to show us that the real suffering is always the suffering of not understanding, the deprivation of light. It is this double gift that explains the unusual contribution he is making to our fiction.

Book Review:

Carlos Baker, "To the Dark Continent," *New York Times Book Review*, 27 February 1959, pp. 4-5.

Henderson the Rain King, *a novel about a man who travels to Africa in an effort to understand his discontentment, was a popular and critical success. When told that it was inaccurate, Bellow replied, "I studied African ethnography with the late Professor Herskovits. Later he scolded me for writing a book like* Henderson. *He said the subject was much too serious for such fooling. I felt that my fooling was fairly serious. Literalism, factualism, will smother the imagination altogether."*

Genial Gene Henderson, successor to Augie March in Saul Bellow's roster of American heroes, is an enormous, rugged, bearlike creature with hair like Persian lambs' fur, three million dollars in the bank, and a Purple Heart medal in his basement trophy-room. At 52, he stands well over six feet, weighs well over two hundred, wears a size twenty-two collar, and raises pigs, gentleman-farmer-style, just outside Danbury, Conn.

But Henderson is afflicted with that disease of the soul whose classical name is Taedium Vitae and whose romantic name is Weltschmerz. All his life and deeds seem to him like a prison of fear and desire out of which he longs to break. Running through his head, with something like the insistent rhythmic swishing of the pendulum in Poe's pit, goes the perpetual refrain, "I want, I want, I want." Somewhere and soon he has to find the direct object of his transitive but baffled verb. Saul Bellow's original and important novel is not fifty pages old before Gene Henderson is literally winging his way to the Dark Continent in search of light. Readers who recall the philosophic dénouement of "Augie March" will not be surprised to learn that even Henderson, "a restless seeker, pitiful and rude, a stubborn old lush with broken bridgework," manages to find out certain answers before his returning plane sets him down once more on the concrete ribbon at Idlewild.

A great critic long ago observed that "every new genius produces some innovation which, when invented and approved, subverts the rules which the practice of foregoing authors had established." Mr. Bellow's "subversion" is in the direction of fantasy—a form of discourse to which the present reviewer is not strongly drawn. What may perhaps disappoint other readers who had expected or even hoped for a straight comic novel from Mr. Bellow is the degree to which the grotesque and the fantastic have now seized hold on his imagination. Although there was fantasy aplenty in "Augie March," the

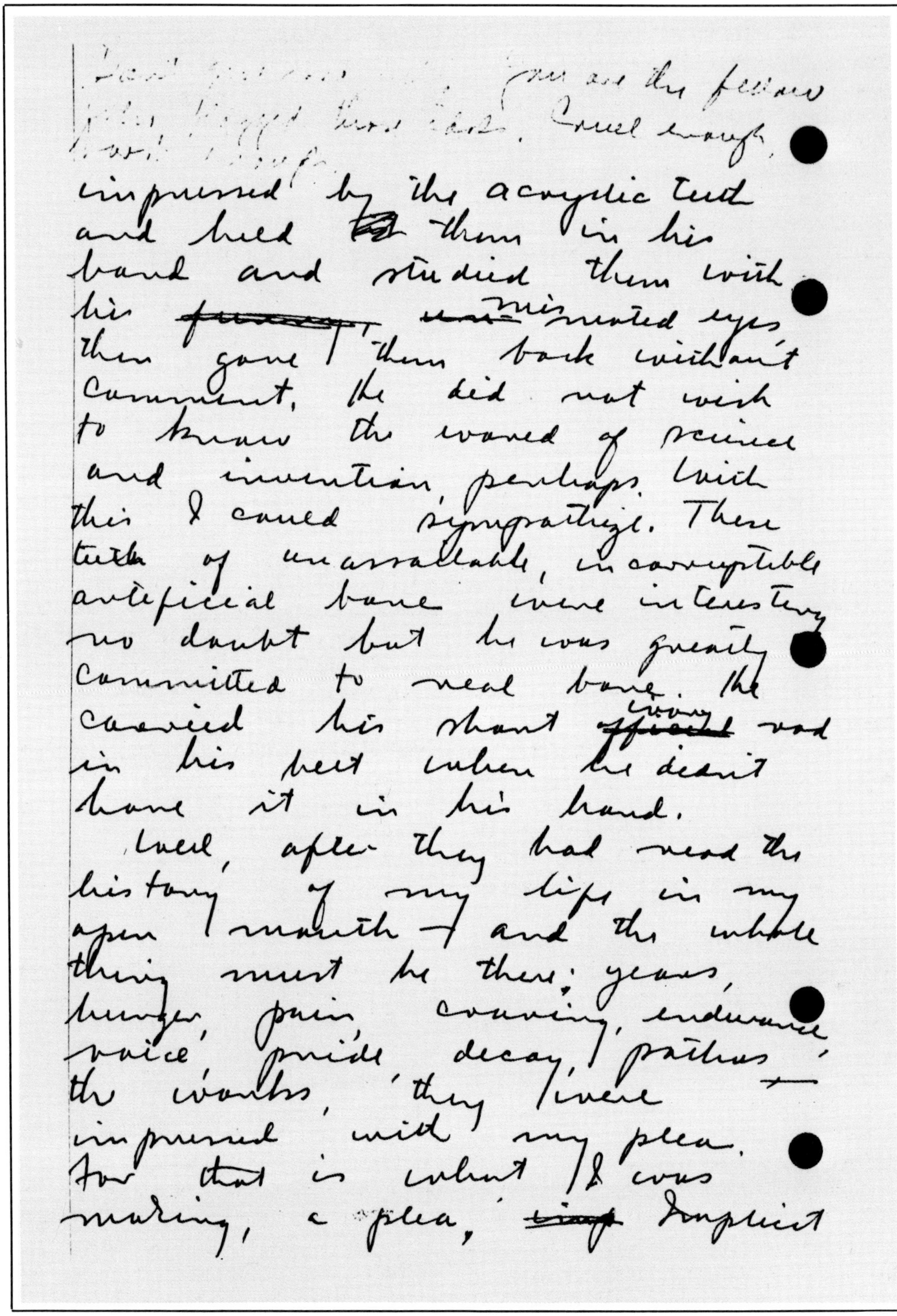

impressed by the acrylic teeth
and held ~~[illegible]~~ them in his
hand and studied them with
his ~~[illegible]~~ ~~un~~ mis-mated eyes
then gave them back without
comment. He did not wish
to know the wonders of science
and invention, perhaps. With
this I could sympathize. These
teeth of unassailable, incorruptible
artificial bone were interesting
no doubt but he was greatly
committed to real bone. He
carried his short ~~official~~ ivory rod
in his belt when he didn't
have it in his hand.
Well, after they had read the
history of my life in my
open mouth — and the whole
thing must be there; years,
hunger, pain, craving, endurance
voice, pride, decay, pathos,
the works, they were —
impressed with my plea.
For that is what I was
making, a plea, ~~[illegible]~~ Implicit

A page from the working draft of Henderson the Rain King *(Regenstein Library, University of Chicago)* balance has now shifted so far north-northwest that a former element has become a present dominant.

Even when we assert aggressively that every developing artist must follow the essential logic of his predispositions, it could be argued that Mr. Bellow, forcing his hand to invent, has here entered a corridor in wonderland none of whose doors open into new possibilities for serious fiction. Despite the fact, for example, that one of Henderson's heroes is Dr. Albert Schweitzer, the portrait of Africa in these pages is as far from the realities of Lambarene as "King Solomon's Mines" or "Tarzan of the Apes." Except for King Dahfu all the natives talk like a combination of Uncle Remus and the Emperor Jones. Most of the situations seem closer to Kipling's "Just So" stories than they do to any recognizable actuality. In certain respects, "Henderson the Rain King" looks more like anarchic romance than anything we have had in American fiction since Steinbeck's "Sweet Thursday." Still, in its zany manner, it is vastly amusing and often powerfully effective, particularly in passages like the lion hunt which ends King Dahfu's reign. Within its cocoon of craziness lurks the worm of wisdom, even though most readers will have trouble unwinding the filaments of the cocoon itself. "You are built," says one of the tribesmen to Henderson the Rain King, "like an old locomotif." What may be called the "loco-motif" has evidently been a strong influence in the building of this new novel.

For, like King Lear's Fool or Prince Hamlet's Hamlet, there is motive in Saul Bellow's method. Do we need to remind ourselves that just seventy years ago Mark Twain sent another Connecticut Yankee into the never-never land of Camelot? Or that Twain's picture of sixth-century England was approximately as far from the facts as Bellow's portrait of twentieth-century Africa? Or that the present novel could well have been called "A Connecticut Yankee in King Dahfu's Court"?

When Henderson succeeds in his crucial test of lifting and carrying Mummah, the monstrous wooden goddess of the Wariri tribe, rain falls on the drought-stricken land in fist-sized gobbets. The feat earns him the right to wear the title of Rain King and the official uniform of green silk drawers. It also serves to remind the wary reader of The Boss' success in confounding the Wizard Merlin and gaining favor with a beleaguered king whose cause he then vigorously adopts. The moral equivalent of Morgan Le Fay is a tall gilded girl whose face is tattooed with what might be a message in Braille; the Bunam of King Dahfu's court may be roughly equated with Sir Kay, King Arthur's Seneschal; and in place of the Knights of the

I think that art has something to do with an arrest of attention in the midst of distraction.

From Writers at Work, Third Series *(New York: Viking Press, 1967)*

Table Round, Henderson must reckon with a set of obese Amazons who toss him into a muddy cattle-pond to test his mettle.

For anyone interested in the shift of social attitudes during the past seventy years, however, the differences between Twain and Bellow are more instructive than the parallels. Where Twain's Connecticut mechanic gains temporary power by introducing modern technology to Camelot, Henderson's sole experiment with gunpowder is a miserable failure. The twentieth-century counterbalance to nineteenth-century faith in the machine is a renewal of belief in certain subliminal powers.

Twain's semi-skeptical mystique of Yankee know-how becomes in Bellow a semi-comical faith in the animalistic wisdom of the body. He who feels the "privation of noble conduct" on a New England pig-farm can doubtless profit by riding a Canadian roller-coaster with a beat-up bear named Smolak or by emulating the Biblical Daniel in an African lion's den. Perhaps, as Dahfu suggests, mankind is tired of itself and its technological triumphs, "and needs a shot in the arm from animal nature." The conversion of Nebuchadnezzar, as Henderson discovers, is an ancient case in point.

Wallace Stevens once remarked that "every poem is a poem within a poem: the poem of the idea within the poem of the words." The novel inside "Henderson" is a novel of an idea within a poetic novel of fantastically comic situations. The idea is definable in seven words: the needful rehabilitation of the cringing soul.

When Henderson wished to rearrange his values, he took to the green hills of Africa, as Thoreau to the green woods of Massachusetts. "My purpose," says he, "was to see essentials . . . and to guard against hallucinations." He learns the need of moving perpetually "from the states I make, I myself, into the states which are of themselves"—that is from what is hallucinatory to what is true and real. In the midst of our extravagant century, this roaring old boy makes, in his bizarre manner, a special kind of sense. The question is whether the fantastic vehicle in which he rides is the most sensible form of conveyance for Mr. Bellow's inside purpose.

My wife wept over the poor old woman. She said, "Poor thing. Why did you leave such a note?"

"Because nobody should touch her," I said, "except the coroner. I barely felt her. You know the law. Have a shot of whiskey with me." I opened the bottle but she declined, and I had several myself. The first only burned my heart. No fluid now could coat the terrible fact. I said, "Selma, maybe I ought to go with Charlie on this trip. Let's put the Buick in winter storage. You won't need two cars."

She didn't object.

I said, "I've got to do something. Life has got me down." I tried to explain to her that something was very wrong. Either I had shallow consciousness with deep experience, or deep consciousness with shallow experience andI could not bring the elements together. But there was no use trying to say such things, as she was shaken by Miss Lennox and frightened by me.

"Well," she said, "do whatever seems best to you."

So I did. I met Charlie and his bride and we flew to Cairo first, and then down into the Sohalis but after a couple of months, like Lot and Abraham Charlie and I parted company. I went my own way. Now that I had left the movie-making outfit I felt more free and mobile and I wandered south and east in search of unknown territory and I found places which if not utterly unknown were still far enough from the world to suit me. In a place called Baventai I left my jeep and most of my equipment and hired a guide named Romilayu recommended by a missionary

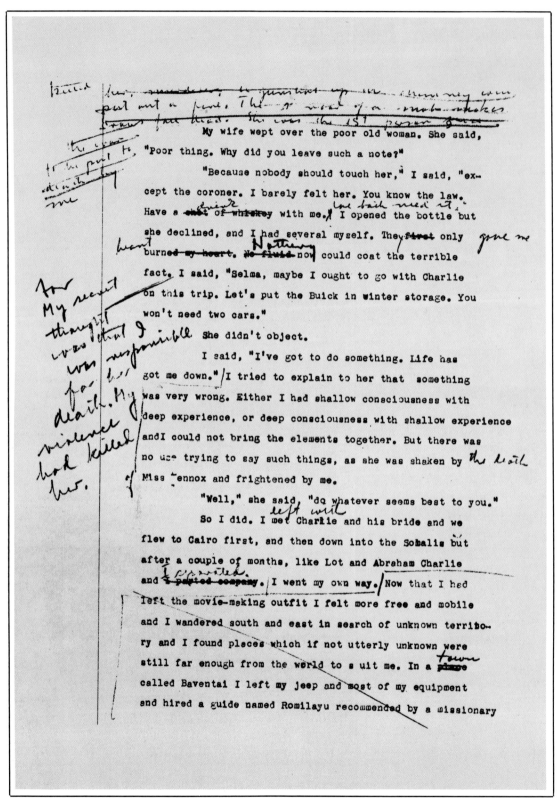

Two consecutive pages from the revised typescript for Henderson the Rain King *(Regenstein Library, University of Chicago). Bellow has explained, "I had to tame and restrain the style I developed in* Augie March *in order to write* Henderson *and* Herzog*."*

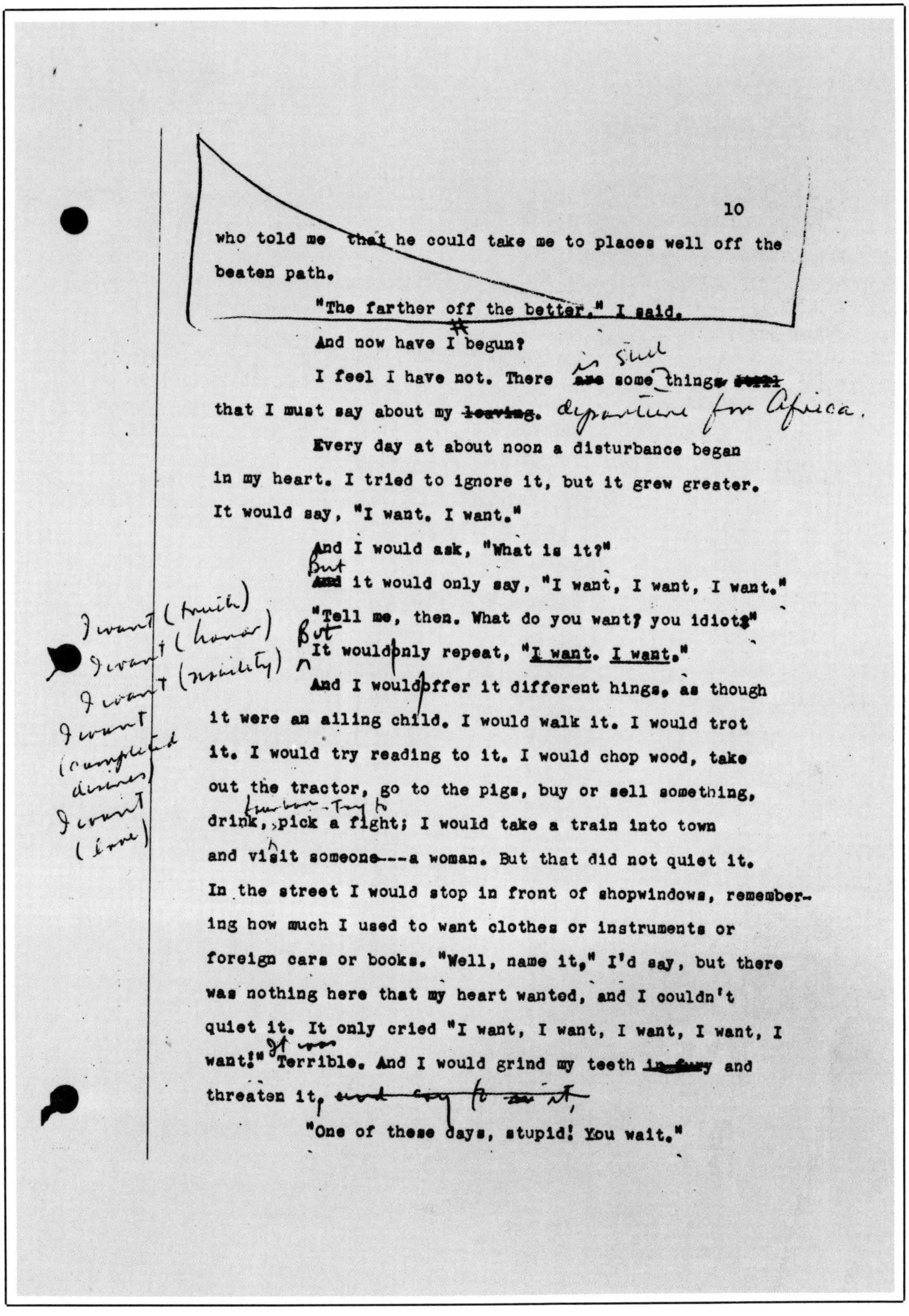

10

who told me that he could take me to places well off the beaten path.

"The farther off the better," I said.

And now have I begun?

I feel I have not. There ~~are~~ is still some things ~~still~~ that I must say about my ~~leaving.~~ departure for Africa.

Every day at about noon a disturbance began in my heart. I tried to ignore it, but it grew greater. It would say, "I want. I want."

And I would ask, "What is it?"

~~And~~ But it would only say, "I want, I want, I want."

"Tell me, then. What do you want? you idiot!"

But It would only repeat, "I want. I want."

And I would offer it different things, as though it were an ailing child. I would walk it. I would trot it. I would try reading to it. I would chop wood, take out the tractor, go to the pigs, buy or sell something, drink, pick a fight; I would take a train into town and visit someone---a woman. But that did not quiet it. In the street I would stop in front of shopwindows, remembering how much I used to want clothes or instruments or foreign cars or books. "Well, name it," I'd say, but there was nothing here that my heart wanted, and I couldn't quiet it. It only cried "I want, I want, I want, I want, I want!" It was Terrible. And I would grind my teeth ~~in fury~~ and threaten it, ~~and cry to it,~~

"One of these days, stupid! You wait."

I want (truth)
I want (honor)
I want (nobility)
I want (completed desires)
I want (love)

"Bigger, wilder and even better than The Adventures of Augie March (his 1954 National Book Award Winner). Henderson is a picaresque hero in the great tradition, full of a bizarre vitality with affinities both to Odysseus and Don Quixote."
Just published!
Henderson the Rain King
a novel by SAUL BELLOW
author of The Adventures of Augie March
SAUL BELLOW
Henderson the Rain King
$4.50
"The most brilliantly written novel to have come along in years....He has confirmed beyond any quibble his position as the great master of narrative prose in this period."
NORMAN PODHORETZ, N. Y. Herald Tribune
"As exciting a novel as has appeared in a long time....It is a book that should be read again and again."
GRANVILLE HICKS, Saturday Review
"A literary event. A remarkable novel."
PAUL PICKREL, Harper's
THE VIKING PRESS 625 Madison Ave., N. Y. 22

New York Times Book Review, *8 March 1959*

ARTICLE:

Saul Bellow, *Recent American Fiction* (Washington, D.C.: Library of Congress, 1963).

On 21 January 1961 Bellow delivered the Gertrude Clarke Whittall lecture at the Library of Congress.

Gertrude Stein is supposed to have explained to Hemingway that "remarks are not literature." Tonight I am offering some remarks, and I make no claim for them whatever. A writer's views on other writers may have a certain interest, but it should be clear that he reads what they write almost always with a special attitude. If he should be a novelist, his own books are also a comment on his contemporaries and reveal that he supports certain tendencies and rejects others. In his own books he upholds what he deems necessary, and usually by the method of omission he criticizes what he understands as the errors and excesses of others.

I intend tonight to examine the view taken by recent American novelists and short-story writers of the individual and his society, and I should like to begin by telling you the title of a new book by Wylie Sypher. It is *Loss of the Self in Modern Literature and Art*. I do not propose to discuss it; I simply want to cite the title of Mr. Sypher's book, for in itself it tells us much about the common acceptance of what the Spanish critic Ortega y Gasset described some years ago as "the dehumanization of the arts." One chapter of Mr. Sypher's book is devoted to the Beats, but, for the most part, he finds, as we might have expected, that the theme of annihilation of Self, and the description of an "inauthentic" life which can never make sense, is predominantly European and particularly French. The names he most often mentions are those of André Gide, Sartre, Beckett, Sarraute, and Robbe-Grillet. These are writers whose novels and plays are derived from definite theories which make a historical reckoning of the human condition and are peculiarly responsive to new physical, psychological, and philosophical theories. American writers, when they are moved by a similar spirit to reject and despise the Self, are seldom encumbered by such intellectual baggage, and this fact pleases their European contemporaries, who find in them a natural, that is, a brutal or violent acceptance of the new universal truth by minds free from intellectual preconceptions. In the early twenties D. H. Lawrence was delighted to discover a blunt, primitive virtue in the first stories of Ernest Hemingway, and 20 years later André Gide praised Dashiell Hammett as a good barbarian.

European writers take strength from German phenomenology and from the conception of entropy in modern physics in order to attack a romantic idea of the Self, triumphant in the 19th century but intolerable in the 20th. The feeling against this idea is well-nigh universal. The First World War with its millions of corpses gave an aspect of the horrible to romantic overvaluation of the Self. The leaders of the Russian Revolution were icy in their hatred of bourgeois individualism. In the communist countries millions were sacrificed in the building of socialism, and almost certainly the Lenins and the Stalins, the leaders who made these decisions, serving the majority and the future, believed they were rejecting a soft, nerveless humanism which attempted in the face of natural and historical evidence to oppose progress. A second great assault on the separate Self sprang from Germany in 1939. Just what the reduction of millions of human beings into heaps of bone and mounds of rag and hair or clouds of smoke betokened, there is no one who can plainly tell us, but it is at least plain that something was being done to put in question the meaning of survival, the meaning of pity, the meaning of justice and of the importance of being oneself, the individual's consciousness of his own existence.

It would be odd, indeed, if these historical events had made no impression on American writers, even if they are not on the whole given to taking the historical or theoretical view. They characteristically depend on their own observations and appear at times obstinately empirical. But the latest work of writers like James Jones, James Baldwin, Philip Roth, John O'Hara, J. F. Powers, Joseph Bennett, Wright Morris, and others shows the individual under a great strain. Laboring to maintain himself, or perhaps an idea of himself (not always a clear idea), he feels the pressure of a vast public life, which may dwarf him as an individual while permitting him to be a giant in hatred or fantasy. In these circumstances he grieves, he complains, rages, or laughs. All the while he is aware of his lack of power, his inadequacy as a moralist, the nauseous pressure of the mass media and the weight of money and organization, of cold war and racial brutalities. Adapting Gresham's theorem to the literary situation one might say that public life drives private life into hiding. People begin to hoard their spiritual valuables. Public turbulence is largely coercive, not positive. It puts us into a passive position. There is not much we can do about the crises of international politics, the revolutions in Asia and Africa, the rise and transformation of masses. Technical and political decisions, invisible powers, secrets which can be shared only by a small elite, render the private will helpless and lead the individual into curious forms of behavior in the private sphere. Public life, vivid and formless turbulence, news, slogans, mysterious crises, and unreal configurations dissolve coherence in all but the most resistant minds, and even to such minds it is not always a confident certainty that resistance can ever have a positive outcome. To take narcotics has become in some circles a mark of rebellious independence, and to scorch one's personal earth is sometimes felt to be the only honorable course. Rebels have no bourgeois certainties to return to when rebellions are done. The fixed points seem to be disappearing. Even the Self is losing its firm outline.

One recent American novel deals openly and consciously with these problems. It is *The Thin Red Line* by James Jones, a book which, describing the gross and murderous conditions of jungle combat, keeps a miraculously sensitive balance and does not weary us with a mere catalog of horrors. What Mr. Jones sees very precisely is the fluctuation in the value of the life of the individual soldier. Childhood in some cases ends for the fighting man as he accepts the lesson of realism. The attitude of Storm, one of the older soldiers, towards Fife, a younger man, is described as follows: "He [Fife] was a good enough kid. He just hadn't been away from home long enough. And Storm, who had started off bumming during the Depression when he was only fourteen, couldn't find kids like that very interesting." Storm, the mess sergeant, tolerates the inexperienced Fife, but

First Sergeant Welsh has no such tolerance. He cannot abide softness and the lack of realism, and he cruelly and punitively teaches the hard lesson to his undeveloped subordinates. Real knowledge as he sees it is brutal knowledge and it must be painfully and brutally learned. The heart of the lesson, as Welsh understands it, is that it matters little—it matters, therefore, not at all—whether any single man survives or falls. Welsh offers no indulgence to anyone and asks none for himself. When, under fire, a young soldier asks permission to dig his foxhole near him, Welsh curses him off savagely. When, under stress, unable to bear the groans of a dying man, Welsh leaves his shelter under fire to bring the soldier in, he wonders at himself. His heroism is useless and he returns. "Sobbing audibly for breath, he made himself a solemn unspoken promise never again to let his screwy wacked-up emotions get the better of his common sense." Sergeant Welsh has one word to which he refers all matters which press for explanation, and that magical word is Property. In Welsh's view the idea of Property alone makes the behavior of mankind intelligible. But Property is not an unassailable certainty. The word is used for purposes of incantation and has no real meaning to Welsh. His message to mankind is that you must cast the cold eye on life, on death.

Mr. Jones shrewdly understands that the philosophy of Welsh is not ultimately hard. Towards himself the sergeant is not fanatically severe, and his toughness betrays a large degree of self-pity. What Jones describes here is the casting off of a childish or feminine or false virtue, despised because it cannot meet the test of survival. In apprehending what is real, Jones' combat soldiers learn a bitter and levelling truth and in their realism revenge themselves on the slothful and easy civilian conception of the Self. The new idea cruelly assails the old, exposing its conventionality and emptiness. Young Fife, after he has gone the rugged course, kills like the rest, becomes quarrelsome, drinks and brawls, and casts off his hesitant, careful, and complaining childishness.

A very different sort of novel, in a peaceful sphere far removed from the explosions and disembowellings of Guadalcanal, is J. F. Power's *Morte d'Urban*, which does not so much study as brood over the lives of priests belonging to the Order of St. Clement. Father Urban, a well-known preacher and a man of some talent, is transferred for reasons not clearly understood from Chicago, where he has worked effectively, to a new Foundation of the Order in Duesterhaus, Minnesota. To Urban, a sociable and civilized priest, this transfer can only be seen as a mysterious banishment, and he is described by Mr. Powers looking from the train windows at the empty country beyond Minneapolis. ". . . flat and treeless, Illinois without people. It didn't attract, it didn't repel. He saw more streams than he'd see in Illinois, but they weren't working. November was winter here. Too many white frame farmhouses, not new and not old, not at all what Father Urban would care to come to for Thanksgiving or Christmas. Rusty implements. Brown dirt. Grey skies. Ice. No snow. A great deal of talk about this on the train. Father Urban dropped entirely out of it after an hour or so. The Voyageur arrived in Duesterhaus a few minutes before eleven that morning, and Father Urban was the only passenger to get off."

In more ways than one, Father Urban is viewed as the only passenger. At the new Foundation he is, without complaint, in a solitary situation. In charge of the Duesterhaus Foundation is Father Wilfred " . . . who, on account of his broad nose and padded cheeks, had been called Bunny in the Novitiate. Bunny Bestudik." Father Wilfred's concerns are all of a practical nature. His interests are the interests of any Midwestern American who has to run a place efficiently; he watches the fuel bills, thinks about the pickup truck and its rubber, the cost of paint, and is anxious to have good public relations. This religious Order is described as a community of cunsumers. It is the American and average character of activities whose ultimate aim is religious that Mr. Powers wants to describe. His tone is dry and factual as he tells of the discussions of the Fathers who have to heat, paint, and renovate their buildings, sand the floors, tear up old linoleum, lay new tile in the bathrooms, and this light and dry comedy cannot be maintained through such a long account of the effort to fill up a great emptiness with activity which is insufficiently purposeful. The religion of Father Urban is expressed in steadiness and patience, in endurance, not in fiery strength. His resistance to the prolonged barrenness and vacant busyness of this thoroughly American Order is made in a spirit of mild and decent martyrdom. Indeed the only violent and passionate person in the book is a certain Billy Cosgrove. Billy is rich and generous. He gives lavishly to the Order but he expects also to have his way. He and Father Urban eat shish kebab and drink champagne, play golf and go fishing. With Billy one talks of cars and sailing boats. Urban gets along rather well with spoiled and boisterous Billy until Billy tries to drown a deer in the water of Bloodsucker Lake. Billy has been fishing and is in an ugly mood because his luck has been bad. Seeing a swimming deer, he decides to seize it by the antlers and hold its head under water. As hungry for trophies as the soldiers in *The Thin Red Line*, Billy wants those antlers. Father Urban, who cannot bear his cruelty, starts up the motor of the boat, and Billy falls into the water. For this outrage Billy will never forgive him.

What Father Urban had been thinking just before the appearance of the deer was that in the Church there was perhaps too great an emphasis on dying for the faith and winning the martyr's crown. "How about living for the faith? Take Lanfranc and William the Conqueror—of whom it was written (in the Catholic Encyclopedia and Father Urban's notes on a book he might write someday): 'He was mild to good men of God and stark beyond all bounds to those who withsaid his will.' " Billy Cosgrove turns out to occupy the position of the Conqueror. He is stark beyond all bounds, and Urban is never again to see his face. Nor does Urban seem destined to write his book. He goes to the Novitiate of the Order as Father Provincial, there to deal with practical matters to the best of his ability. But he appears to be succumbing to a brain injury he received while playing golf. He had been struck in the head by a golf ball in Minnesota and is now subject to fits of dizziness. A martyr's crown seems to be awaiting Urban as the book ends.

Powers does not look at the issue of the single Self and the multitude as nakedly as Jones does, and it is a pity that he chose not to do so, for he might have been able to offer us a more subtle development of the subject. He would have been examining what Mr. Sypher calls "Loss of the Self" from the point of view of a Christian, that is, from the point of view of one who believes in the existence of something more profound than the romantic or secular idea of selfhood, namely, a soul. But there is curiously little talk of souls in this book about a priest. Spiritually, its quality is very thin. That perhaps is as Mr. Powers meant it to be. Even at play Father Urban is serving the Church, and, if he is hit in the head by a golf ball, we can perhaps draw our own conclusions from that about the present age viewed as a chapter in the spiritual history of mankind. Here great things will only be dimly apprehended even by the most willing servant of God. Still this seems to me unsatisfactory, and I am not sure that I can bring myself to admire such meekness. A man might well be meek in his own interests, but furious at such abuses of the soul and eager to show what is positive and powerful in his faith. The lack of such power makes faith itself shadowy, more like obscure tenacity than spiritual conviction. In this sense Mr. Powers' book is disappointing.

I am quite prepared to admit that being habitual liars and self-deluders, we have good cause to fear the truth, but I'm not at all ready to stop hoping. There may be some truths which are, after all, our friends in the universe.

From Writers at Work, Third Series *(New York: Viking Press, 1967)*

The individual in American fiction often comes through to us, especially among writers of "sensibility," as a colonist who has been sent to a remote place, some Alaska of the soul. What he has to bring under cultivation, however, is a barren emptiness within himself. This is, of course, what writers of sensibility have for a long time been doing and what they continue to do. The latest to demonstrate his virtuosity with exceptional success is John Updike, who begins the title story of his new collection, *Pigeon Feathers*, "When they moved to Firetown, things were upset, displaced, rearranged." The rearrangement of things in new and hostile solitude is a common theme with writers of sensibility. David, the only child of a family which has moved to the country, is assailed by terror when he reads in H. G. Wells' *The Outline of History* that Jesus was nothing more than a rather communistic Galilean, ". . . an obscure political agitator, a kind of hobo in a minor colony of the Roman Empire." The effect of this is to open the question of death and immortality. David is dissatisfied with answers given by the Reverend Dobson and by his parents. He cannot understand the pleasure his mother takes in her solitary walks along the edge of the woods. ". . . to him the brown sketches of slowly rising and falling land expressed only a huge exhaustion." " 'What do you want Heaven to be?' " asks David's mother. "He was becoming angry, sensing her surprise at him. She had assumed that Heaven had faded from his head long ago. She had imagined that he had already entered, in the secrecy of silence, the conspiracy that he now knew to be all around him." Young David in the end resolves the problem for himself aesthetically. Admiring the beauty of pigeon feathers he feels consoled by the sense of a providence. ". . . the God who had lavished such craft upon these worthless birds would not destroy His whole Creation by refusing to let David live forever." The story ends with a mild irony at the expense of the boy. Nevertheless, there is nothing to see here but the writer's reliance on beautiful work, on an aesthetic discipline and order. And sensibility, in such forms, incurs the dislike of many because it is perceptive inwardly, and otherwise blind. We suspect it of a stony heart because it functions so smoothly in its isolation. The writer of sensibility assumes that only private exploration and inner development are possible and accepts the opposition of public and private as fixed and indissoluble.

Perhaps it would be useful before I continue with my examination of recent American books of fiction to recapitulate. We are dealing with modern attitudes towards the ancient idea of the individual and the many, the single Self in the midst of the mass or species. In modern times the idea of the unique Self has become associated with the name of Rousseau. Nietzsche identified the Self with the God Apollo, the god of light, harmony, music, reason and proportion, and the many, the tribe, the species, the instincts and passions, with Dionysus. Between these two principles, the individual and the generic, men and civilizations supposedly work out their destinies. It is to Nietzsche, too, that we owe the concept of the "last man." His "last man" is an obituary on the unitary and sufficient Self produced by a proud bourgeois and industrial civilization. Dostoievsky's Underground Man is an analogous figure. Atheism, rationalism, utilitarianism and revolution are signs of a deadly sickness in the human soul, in his scheme of things. The lost Selves whose souls are destroyed he sees as legion. The living soul clearly discerns them. It owes this illumination to Christ the Redeemer. More optimistically, an American poet like Walt Whitman imagined that the single Self and the democratic mass might complement each other. But on this side of the Atlantic, also, Thoreau described men as leading lives of quiet desperation, accepting a deadly common life. The individual retires from the community to define or redefine his real needs in isolation beside Walden Pond.

Still later a French poet tells us "*Je* est an autre." Rimbaud and Jarry launch their bombs and grenades against the tight little bourgeois kingdom of the Self, that sensitive sovereign. Darwin and the early anthropologists unwittingly damage his sovereignty badly. Then come the psychologists, who explain that his Ego is a paltry shelter against the unendurable storms that rage in outer reality. After them come the logicians and physical scientists—people like Bertrand Russell and the late P. W. Bridgman—who tells us that "I" is a grammatical expression. Poets like Valery describe this Self as a poor figment, a thing of change, and tell us that consciousness is interested only in what is eternal. Novelists like Joyce turn away from the individualism of the romantics and the humanists to contemplate instead qualities found in dreams and belonging to the entire species—Earwicker is everybody. Writers like Sartre, Ionesco, and Beckett or like our own William Burroughs and Allen Ginsberg are only a few of the active campaigners on this shrinking front against the Self. One would like to ask these contemporaries, "After nakedness, what?" "After absurdity, what?" But, on the whole, American novels are filled with complaints over the misfortunes of the sovereign Self. Writers have inherited a tone of bitterness from the great poems and novels of this century, many of which lament the passing of a more stable and beautiful age demolished by the barbarous intrusion of an industrial and metropolitan society of masses or proles who will, after many upheavals, be tamed by bureaucracies and oligarchies in brave new worlds, human anthills.

These works of the first half of our century nourish the imagination of contemporary writers and supply a tonal background of disillusion or elegy. There are modern novelists who take all of this for granted as fully proven and implicit in the human condition and who complain as steadily as they write, viewing modern life with a bitterness to which they themselves have not established clear title, and it is this unearned bitterness that I speak of. What is truly curious about it is that often the writer automatically scorns contemporary life. He bottles its stinks artistically. But, seemingly, he does not need to study it. It is enough for him that it does not allow his sensibilities to thrive, that it starves his instincts for nobility or for spiritual qualities. But what the young American writer most often appears to feel is his *own* misfortune. The injustice is done to *his* talent if life is brutish and ignorant, if the world seems overcome by spam and beer, or covered with detergent lathers and poisonous monoxides. This apparently is the only injustice he feels. Neither for himself nor for his fellows does he attack power and injustice directly and hotly. He simply defends his sensibility. Perhaps the reason for this is the prosperity and relative security of the middle class from which most writers come. In educating its writers it makes available to them the radical doctrines of all the ages, but these in their superabundance only cancel one another out. The middle class community trains its writers also in passivity and resignation and in the double

Bellow in the fifties

enjoyment of selfishness and good will. They are taught that they can have it both ways. In fact they are taught to expect to enjoy everything that life can offer. They can live dangerously while managing somehow to remain safe. They can be both bureaucrats and bohemians, they can be executives but use pot, they can raise families but enjoy bohemian sexuality, they can observe the laws while in their hearts and in their social attitudes they may be as subversive as they please. They are both conservative and radical. They are everything that is conceivable. They are not taught to care genuinely for any man or any cause.

A recent novel like Philip Roth's *Letting Go* is a consummate example of this. Mr. Roth's hero, Gabriel, educated to succeed in this world and to lead a good life come hell or high water, is slightly uncomfortable in his selfishness. But nevertheless he wants his, as the saying goes, and he gets his. But he feels obscurely the humiliation of being a private bourgeois Self, the son of an unhappy but prosperous dentist, and he senses that a "personal life" with its problems of personal adjustment and personal responsibility and personal happiness, its ostensibly normal calculations of profit and loss, safety and danger, lust and prudence is a source of shame. But Gabriel's middle-class parents sent him into life to make the grade and that is precisely, with tough singlemindedness, what he does. His shame therefore becomes a province of his sensibility, and it is something he can be rather proud of as he does what he was going to do anyway. Roth's hero clings to the hope of self-knowledge and personal improvement, and he concludes that, with all his faults, he loves himself still. His inner life, if it may be called that, is a rather feeble thing of a few watts. Conceivably it may guide him to a more satisfactory adjustment, but it makes me think of the usher's flashlight in the dark theatre guiding the single ticket holder to his reserved seat. We are supposed to feel that Gabriel is unusually sensitive, but what we find is that he is a tough young man who cannot be taken in and who will survive the accidents of life that madden or kill genuinely sensitive young men.

I would like now to list the categories suggested by

my reading of current novels: the documentation of James Jones, the partially Christian approach of Powers, the sensibility of Updike, and the grievance of Philip Roth. I do not retract my earlier statement that in American novels—for I have decided rather arbitrarily to limit myself to examining these—the tone of complaint prevails. The public realm, as it encroaches on the private, steadily reduces the powers of the individual; but it cannot take away his power to despair, and sometimes he seems to be making the most of that. However, there are several other avenues commonly taken: stoicism, nihilistic anger, and comedy. Stoicism and comedy are sometimes mixed, as in the case of the late German dramatist Bert Brecht, but our own contemporary American stoicism comes from Hemingway, and its best American representative at present is Mr. John O'Hara.

Mr. O'Hara is properly impatient with people who suffer too intensely from themselves. The characters in his latest collection of stories, *The Cape Cod Lighter*, for whom he shows a decided preference, appear to be bluff, natural people, who know how to endure hurt and act with an elementary and realistic sense of honor. When Ernest Pangborn in the story "The Professors" learns that he has misjudged his colleague Jack Veech and understands at last that Veech's behavior has been decent and manly, he is moved to say something to him but does not know what to say. "A compliment would be rejected, and a word of pity would be unthinkable. Indeed the compliment was being paid to Pangborn; Veech honored him with his confidence and accorded him honor more subtly, more truly, by asking no further assurances of his silence." The emotion we feel here is made possible by long reticence, by the deep burial of self-proclamation or self-assertion. We recall the pure decencies of schooldays, and the old chivalrous or military origins of these. These, surely, are virtues of silence and passivity. We endure. We are rewarded by a vision of one another's complexities, but there is no possibility of a flourish, or of rhetoric, of anything that would make an undue personal claim. This is no longer the sovereign Self of the Romantics, but the decent Self of Kipling whose great satisfaction it is to recognize the existence of a great number of others. These numerous others reduce personal significance, and both realism and dignity require us to accept this reduction. Such stoicism of separateness is the opposite of sensibility with its large claims for the development of internal riches.

But the O'Haras are curiously like the Updikes in at least one respect. They are scrupulous craftsmen and extraordinarily strict about their writing. Nothing unrealistic, unnatural, or excessive (as they define these qualities) is suffered to appear. O'Hara insists upon a hard literalness in his language which reminds one of the simple crystalline code of his characters. There is a roughness in O'Hara which may make the writer of sensibility feel like a dude. O'Hara's self-identification is obviously with the workman, with the average, with plain people. Or perhaps he feels himself to be a part of the majority, which is to say, of the crowd. Certainly he does not merely react against what he judges an incorrect definition of the individual; he hates it violently. And conceivably he hates it in himself. His view of sensibility or of an intricate and conceivably self-indulgent privacy is, like Hemingway's (in *The Sun Also Rises*, for instance), entirely negative. He sees the romantic Self with the eyes of the crowd. And the crowd is a leveller. The average it seeks is anything but Whitman's divine average.

The absolute individualism of the Enlightenment has fallen. Contemporary writers like Brecht, or Beckett, or the Beats, and recently and most atrociously William Burroughs in his *Naked Lunch*, have repudiated it in a spirit of violence. Some have been violently comic at its expense, others ruthlessly nihilistic and vengeful. Among them there are some who gather unto themselves more and more and more power only to release it destructively on this already discredited and fallen individualism. In this they seem at times to imitate the great modern consolidations of power, to follow the example of parties and states and their scientific or military instruments. They act, in short, like those who hold the real power in society, the masters of the Leviathan. But this is only an imitation of the real power. Through this imitation they hope perhaps to show that they are not inferior to those who lead the modern world. Joint Chiefs or Pentagons have power to do as they will to huge populations. But there are writers who will not reckon themselves among these subordinate masses and who aim to demonstrate an independent power equal to the greatest. They therefore strike one sometimes as being extraordinarily eager to release their strength and violence against an enemy, and that enemy is the false conception of Self created by Christianity and by Christianity's successors in the Enlightenment. Modern Literature is not satisfied simply to dismiss a romantic, outmoded conception of the Self. In a spirit of deepest vengefulness it curses it. It hates it. It rends it, annihilates it. It would rather have the maddest chaos it can invoke than a conception of life it has found false. But after this destruction, what?

I have spoken of complaint, stoicism, sensibility, and nihilistic rage, and I would like to speak now of recent American writers who have turned to comedy. It is obvious that modern comedy has to do with the disintegrating outline of the worthy and humane Self, the bourgeois hero of an earlier age. That sober, prudent person, the bourgeois, although he did much for the development of modern civilization, built factories and railroads, dug canals, created sewage systems and went colonizing, was indicted for his shallowness and his ignoble and hypocritical ways. The Christian writer (see Dostoievsky's portrait of Mr. Luzhin in *Crime and Punishment*) and the revolutionary (see Mr. Mangan in Shaw's *Heartbreak House*) repudiated him and all his works. The First World War dealt a blow to his prestige from which it never recovered. Dada and surrealism raised a storm of laughter against him. In the movies René Clair and Charlie Chaplin found him out. He became the respectable little person, the gentlemanly tramp. Poets of the deepest subversive tendencies came on like bank clerks in ironic masquerade.

The trick is still good as James Donleavy has lately shown in his novel *The Ginger Man*. His hero, Sebastian Dangerfield, a free-wheeling rascal and chaser, presents himself with wickedly comic effect as an ultrarespectable citizen with an excellent credit rating, one who doesn't know what it is to hock other people's property for the price of a drink, the gentlemanly sack-artist.

The private and inner life which was the subject of serious books until very recently now begins to have an antique and funny look. The earnestness of a Proust towards himself would seem old-fashioned today. Indeed, Italo Svevo, a contemporary of Proust, in *The Confessions of Zeno*, made introspection, hypochondria, and self-knowledge the subjects of his comedy. *My* welfare, *my* development, *my* advancement, *my* earnestness, *my* adjustment, *my* marriage, *my* family—all that will make the modern reader laugh heartily. Writers may not wholly agree with Bertrand Russell that "I" is no more than a grammatical expression, but they do consider certain claims of the "I" to be definitely funny. Already in the 19th century Stendhal became bored with the persistent "I—I—I" and denounced it in characteristic terms.

Perhaps the change that has occurred can be clearly illustrated by a comparison of Thomas Mann's *Death in Venice* with Nabokov's *Lolita*. In both stories an older man is overcome by sexual desire for a younger person. With Mann, however, this sad occurrence involves Apollo and Dionysus. Gustave von Aschenbach, an overly civilized man, an individual estranged from his instincts which unexpectedly claim their revenge, has gone too far, has entered the realm of sickness and perversity and is carried away by the plague. This is a typically Nietzschean theme. But in *Lolita* the internal life of Humbert Humbert has become a joke. Far from being an Aschenbach, a great figure of European literature, he is a fourth- or fifth-rate man of the world and is unable to be entirely serious about his passion. As for Lolita's mother, the poor thing only makes him laugh when she falls in love with him—a banal woman. To a very considerable extent Humbert's judgment of her is based on the low level of her culture. Her banality makes her a proper victim. If her words about love and desire had not come out of a bin in which the great American public finds suitable expressions to describe its psychological and personal needs, she might have been taken more seriously. The earnestness of Mann about love and death might be centuries old. The same subject is sadly and maliciously comical in *Lolita*. Clare Quilty cannot be made to take even his own death seriously and while he is being murdered by Humbert, ridicules his own situation and Humbert's as well, losing at last a life that was not worth having anyway. The contemporary Aschenbach does not deny his desires, but then he is without the dignity of the old fellow and is always on the verge of absurdity. Wright Morris in his new novel *What a Way to Go* explicitly makes comedy of the *Death in Venice* theme. His American professors in Venice, discussing *Death in Venice* all the while, seem to feel that there is small hope for them. They decline to view themselves with full seriousness. They believe their day is over. They are unfit, and dismiss themselves with a joke.

We must carefully remind ourselves that, if so many people today exist to enjoy or deplore an individual life, it is because prodigious public organizations, scientific, industrial, and political, support huge populations of new individuals. These organizations both elicit and curtail private development. I myself am not convinced that there is less "selfhood" in the modern world. I am not sure anyone knows how to put the matter properly. I am simply recording the attitudes of modern writers, including contemporary Americans, who are convinced that the jig of the Self is up. What is the modern Self in T. S. Eliot's *Waste Land*? It is the many, crossing the bridge in the great modern city, who do not know that death has already undone them; it is the "clerk carbuncular" taking sexual liberties of brief duration with the "lovely lady" who, after she has stooped to folly, puts a record on the

Why should writers wish to be rated—seeded—like tennis players? Handicapped like racehorses? What an epitaph for a novelist: "He won all the polls"!

From Writers at Work, Third Series *(New York: Viking Press, 1967)*

gramophone. What is the Self for French novelists of the first postwar era like Louis Ferdinand Céline, or for writers like Curzio Malaparte or Albert Camus in the second postwar era? Man in a book like *The Stranger* is a creature neither fully primitive nor fully civilized, a Self devoid of depths. We have come a long way from Montaigne and his belief in a self-perfecting, self-knowing character.

Recent American comic novels like *Lolita*, or *The Ginger Man*, or Burt Blechman's *How Much?*, or Bruce Friedman's first novel *Stern* examine the private life. It is as if they were testing the saying of Socrates, that the unexamined life was not worth living. Apparently they find the examined life funny too. Some cannot find the life they are going to examine. The power of public life has become so vast and threatening that private life cannot maintain a pretence of its importance. Our condition of destructibility is ever-present in everyone's mind. Our submission seems required by public ugliness in our cities, by the public nonsense of television which threatens to turn our brains to farina within our heads, by even such trifling things as Muzak broadcasts in the elevators of public buildings. The Self is asked to prepare itself for sacrifice, and this is the situation reflected in contemporary American fiction.

As for the future, it cannot possibly shock us since we have already done everything possible to scandalize ourselves. We have so completely debunked the old idea of the Self that we can hardly continue in the same way. Perhaps some power within us will tell us what we are, now that old misconceptions have been laid low. Undeniably the human being is not what he commonly thought a century ago. The question nevertheless remains. He is something. What is he? And this question, it seems to me, modern writers have answered poorly. They have told us, indignantly or nihilistically or comically, how great our error is but for the rest they have offered us thin fare. The fact is that modern writers sin when they suppose that they *know*, as they conceive that physics *knows* or that history *knows*. The subject of the novelist is not knowable in any such way. The mystery increases, it does not grow less as types of literature wear out. It is, however, Symbolism or Realism or Sensibility wearing out, and not the mystery of mankind.

INTERVIEW:

Robert Gutwillig, "Talk With Saul Bellow," *New York Times Book Review*, 20 September 1964, pp. 40-41.

Bellow's play, The Last Analysis, *opened in New York on 29 September 1964 but ran only twenty-eight performances. During rehearsals he gave this interview about his new novel,* Herzog.

He came off the stage of the Belasco Theater, a cord jacket in one hand, an umbrella in the other, looking for all the world as wilted and dapper as that actor-philosopher Moses Herzog. We exchanged damp jokes about New York—a tropical paradise—he asked after my health (failing fast), and I asked after the Bellow family. Right on cue, he led me into a dressing room and introduced me to his young son.

I followed him into another dressing room that was bare of all amenities except for a hat tree from which dangled odd pieces of clothing (but no hats) and two chairs without backs. We dropped onto them. Shouted dialogue wafted over to us from the stage. A fellow came in and either took something from or put something on the hat rack. It seemed unaffected.

I had not seen Saul Bellow for four or five years, and meeting him again after all that time was a distinct shock, just as reading "Herzog" after not having read him since 1959 came as a real revelation. He is now 49 years old and he has grown almost alarmingly handsome. He has kept most of his hair and it has gone gray-white. His features—eyes, nose, mouth—are all large and full. This is an expressive face, and it expresses all the life he has seen and understood.

He roused me out of my glum study of his physiognomy (here's a guy who's got more talent than everyone else in the country, and now he's running for Robert Frost, too), and out of the room, the theater and into the street. I spotted the Blue Ribbon down the block and made for it, telling Bellow on the way that several writers had already called me after reading advance copies of the book and that he was making them feel pretty envious, pretty sick.

He laughed. "No, I'm doing them good. They do me good. Next time they'll make me feel sick."

Inside, it was cool and dark. There was no television. There was German beer on tap.

I said I thought "Herzog" was his best book, and Bellow said he thought so, too.

"Which makes it," I said, "better than everything else."

He smiled and ducked his head down.

A drunk at the end of the bar said, "That's the most confused [unprintable] in the whole damn country."

Wow," said Bellow. "That's pretty confused."

Saul Bellow takes a compliment better than any writer I know. And if you don't think that takes talent, just try complimenting a writer sometime. He submitted to a seemingly endless monologue about why "Herzog" was his best book, replete with copious references to "The Dangling Man," "The Victim," "The Adventures of Augie March," "Seize the Day" and "Henderson the Rain King," analyses of trends and developments, explication of recurrent themes, and said finally, "I think you're right about me." Any man who can and will lie so well after listening to that kind of thing can't be all bad.

New York is going to be a Bellow festival this fall. His first play, "The Last Analysis," starring Sam Levene, is opening Sept 29th, eight days after the publication of "Herzog." The play is a comedy about an aging comedian who is on his way down and out, partly because he feels he has a responsibility to tell people things. "I wanted to bring rhetoric back to the theater," Bellow said, "and I did. But I brought too much. About eight hours too much," he added, pretty much summarizing what rehearsals must have been like so far.

I said life must be pretty hectic between rehearsals and pre-publication duties, and Bellow said it was calm compared to last spring in Chicago when "I was trying to finish the book—again, and trying to finish the play—again, and teaching two courses and my wife was having a baby. I gave up sleeping." He said that starting with "Seize the Day" he has been re-writing heavily. "There must be fifteen drafts of "Herzog."

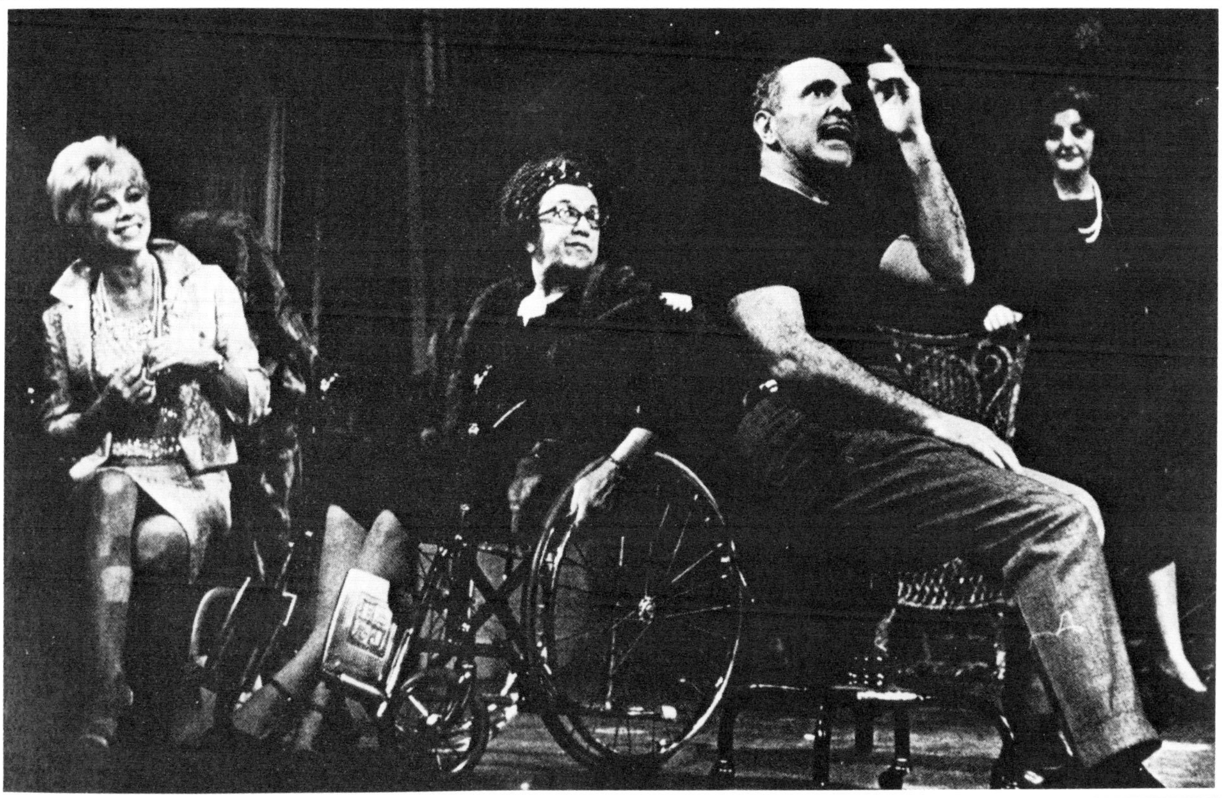

The Last Analysis: *Lucille Patton, Minerva Pious, Sam Levene, and Alix Elias.*

"In every generation there's a lunatic . . . " the drunk announced.

"We'd better not ask him who it is," Bellow said. "It might be me."

I said, "What do you want me to say about all the similarities between the life and hard times of Saul Bellow and Moses Herzog? Everyone's going to want to know about that. I mean, you're an artist. There aren't any accidents in your books. You don't find any surprises when you go back and look at them, do you?"

Bellow said he didn't go back to his old books, only to little pieces of "Henderson." "Say," he said, "when a writer runs out of other people to write about there's no reason why he can't use himself."

"Okay," I said.

After the opening here, Bellow is going back to Chicago to teach, and it looks as if he will continue to make Chicago his home base and go on teaching. We agreed that being attached to a university was not necessarily the fatal disease for writers that so many people seem to think. Bellow compared universities favorably to some of the other ways writers are making do these days, but said he had to teach in a large city. "At Princeton, it was the first time I was socially inferior to my students. But that was good too," he said, although he didn't say what was good about it.

Bellow told me about life in Chicago. Like Augie March and Moses Herzog, he is interested in all sorts of strange things (at one moment he was telling me something about the British Industrial Revolution, the next about an establishment called The Shamrock). He is certainly interested in other writers and their writing, and talked about the literary magazine, "The Noble Savage," he'd help run, and several young writers we both knew. I mentioned one who'd been having a hard time, and Bellow said, "That reminds me of what Samuel Butler once said. I've been having a lot of fun reading old Sam. Young people; I believe he said, should be careful about their aspirations. They might live to achieve them."

I thought about this and said at last that he was the only American writer I could think of who was getting better after 40. All the others in this century, anyway, seem to fall away. Bellow said it was something about American society, for in Europe writers were just beginning to hit their strides when they reached middle age. We talked a while about just what it was about American life that seemed so destructive. No conclusions.

Then it was time to go, back to rehearsals, back to his little boy. As we walked back to the Belasco, I was suddenly overcome by the emotion of this brief encounter and thought I probably wouldn't see him again for another four or five years. I remembered a sentence on Page 340 of the new book, after Moses Herzog had spent 339 pages suffering. "I am pretty well satisfied to be, to be just as it is willed, and for as long as I may remain in occupancy." It seemed to fit them both.

I said a friend of mine named Herzog was kind of upset and figured he was in for a few months of bad jokes.

Bellow stopped at the gate of the stage entrance and smiled his smile. "Tell him not to worry," he said. "Hey, what's he got to worry about? Suppose his name was Bellow!"

BOOK REVIEW:

George P. Elliott, "Hurtsog, Hairtsog, Heart's Hog?," *Nation*, 199 (19 October 1964): 252-254.

Herzog *is Bellow's most autobiographical novel. The protagonist shares with the author an immigrant bootlegger father, a Canadian past, a Chicago background, and two ex-wives. (Bellow married Alexandra Tschacbasov in 1956; they had a son, Adam.) Bellow has explained that while* Herzog *"ought to have been . . . obscure . . . with a total sale of 8,000," its success could be attributed to its appeal to "the unconscious sympathies of many people." The novel was on the* Publishers Weekly *best-seller list for forty-three weeks, occupying the number one position for twenty-five weeks.*

Herzog: what a title. On the realistic surface, the word is a name you can find in telephone books, free of English meaning or association. But there are cracks in the realistic façade. The name is German but is it also Jewish? And how is it pronounced, Hurtsog, Hurzog, Hairtsog? In the pidgin of the (American) unconscious, it puts "heart" and "hog" together in all sorts of silly ways, with "sog" in the offing. These, then, are juxtaposed to the literal German meaning "duke." Duke Heart's Hog. . . . No more silliness: Professor Moses Herzog, scholar. *Moses* Herzog! This middle-aged nut, this writer of unsent letters, this naive cuckold—a law-giver! Don't laugh. He suffered a lot. His second wife betrayed him with his best friend, he tried with all his mind to make sense of the crazy world, God knows he had his weaknesses, he was a little crazy himself there for a while. That's true, he suffered, he really did, even though he is a bit snobbish about his suffering like a good many Jews. . . . Herzog, a complicated man worth knowing.

Ceaseless mental play of words—the life of this

book is in the highwire play of mind. Without this verbal play, Herzog would not be worth knowing: neither the book nor the man.

When knowing the central character is the point of a book—biography, confession, novel—then the radical question is: "Why is this person worth knowing?" Usually he has some extraordinary qualities of his own (Dr. Johnson) or is part of a good tale (Cortez). It takes real nerve to build a whole book on an uneventful day in the life of a Leopold Bloom. Still, there are ways to write stories which can ruin the most interesting subject. Set a definitive biographer to work piling up facts, and even Gandhi's life would disappear shapeless under the cairn.

Herzog, like most characters, is neither a Gandhi, so interesting that it would take a perverted anti-writer to make him dull, nor a Bloom, so uninteresting that only a perverted super-writer would think of telling his nonstory. The book has no plot, but at least Herzog is in an intense situation, full of hate for the treacherous wife and friend; at least he does something, nowhere near enough to keep you reading for the story's sake, but something. He is a rather typical character in modern American fiction, alienated, baffled; but he has an intellect almost exactly as extraordinary as Saul Bellow's, one which raises him to a realm altogether brighter than the smog in which Chicago characters usually seem to live, Sister Carrie, Studs Lonigan, Bigger Thomas, Frankie Machine. But intellectual vigor is not in itself enough to make a character worth knowing. As a subject, Herzog is down toward the Bloom end of the scale: meager of story, somewhat colorless of person, his life is sustained in the reader's mind by his creator's prose. The play of Bellow's prose causes in the reader's mind a play analogous to the play of Herzog's mind. Of no live character, real or fictional, is it truer to say: "The style is the man."

Take those letters he is forever writing, seldom finishing, never sending:

> *Dear Mama, as to why I haven't visited your grave in so long . . .*
>
> *Dear Wanda, Dear Zinka, Dear Libbie, Dear Ramona, Dear Sono, I need help in the worst way. I am afraid of falling apart. Dear Edvig, the fact is that madness also has been denied me. I don't know why I should write to you at all. Dear Mr. President, Internal Revenue regulations will turn us into a nation of bookkeepers. The life of every citizen is becoming a business. This, it seems to me, is one of the worst interpretations of the meaning of human life history has ever seen. Man's life is not a business.*

Dust jacket for Bellow's fifth novel

Quirky, leaping, sometimes silly, sometimes piercing—such is Herzog's mind, such the prose of the letters and of the entire novel.

It is far from the self-effacing prose of most fiction, of realistic novels. It is much closer to the style of the "anatomy," Rabelais, Robert Burton. Among novelists, it has a good deal in common, functionally, with the prose of *Tristram Shandy* and *Ulysses*. That is, it is erudite, allusive, and full of tricks, and in itself it is the main source of the reader's pleasure. Because of the prose, Herzog is the first intellectual in American fiction whose mind is fully a part of him, who is all there in the reader's imagination. This is not the least of the reasons why the first round of literary-intellectual reviewers liked the book so much. To be sure, a style sets its own limits. How *Herzog* works on a willing reader who is nonliterary, nonintellectual and non-American, I cannot guess. Meanwhile let us revel in the book who can. Besides, as soon as Herzog gets to Chicago, everything picks up and the style expands to include all who will.

Of course Herzog isn't identical with the style. The book is not a confession, an arrangement of words projecting a self directly and immediately. The man personally is not as funny as the style. He is humorous, he sometimes does ludicrous things, he laughs at himself. But we readers laugh a lot more than he does. Our laughter may often be painful, since we do not cease to sympathize with him in his silliness and misfortune. Still, we do laugh.

Try telling someone what *Herzog* is about, all the time insisting that it's funny. Loneliness, betrayal, disillusionment, near murder, humiliation, half-madness, sorrow, severance, confusion, waste—comic, all comic! A strange combination. Why does Bellow insist on making the novel comic? In this book, the style is the man *plus* his author's looking at him. For example, Herzog goes to Chicago to visit his widowed stepmother, a strong, shrewd old woman. He gets her out of the room so that, on the pretext of taking some Czarist rubles from his dead father's desk he may filch his father's loaded pistol. (Neither he nor we are fully conscious of why he wants the pistol; it turns out he takes it with him when he goes to spy on his former wife and her lover, though he does not shoot.) Immediately after he pockets the gun, he goes to the old woman, Taube, and Bellow represents his thoughts as follows:

> *He knew it was not proper that he should think her expression sheeplike. This figurative habit of his mind crippled his judgment, and was likely to ruin him some day. Perhaps the day was near; perhaps this night his soul would be required of him. The gun weighed on his chest. But the protuberant lips, great eyes, and pleated mouth* were *sheeplike, and they warned him he was taking too many chances with destruction. Taube, a veteran survivor, to be heeded, had fought the grave to a standstill, balking death itself by her slowness.*

There is nothing comic about either the situation or his reflections. It is their juxtaposition which is comic, and this juxtaposing Bellow has caused so that he and we alike may keep our distance from Herzog.

Without the double distance of comedy, near and far simultaneously, all would have descended into a glop of free association and self-justification; no Herzog, no *Herzog*. As it is, the character and his self-justifyings remain *over there*; we see him, we laugh at him even as we feel for him, we can understand him. Usually. Nearly always, but not quite always. In one important respect, Bellow fails. Herzog's noncomic, anti-comic loathing of his false friend, Gersbach, almost totally obliterates that character for the reader. The faithless wife, Madeleine, we can see somewhat better, though nowhere near so well as his present mistress. But wife and friend we get only glimpses of, usually distorted, and we need to know them well if we are to size up Herzog fully. Here, and here only, Bellow allows Herzog's fantasy to supplant the reality almost entirely, rather than to play counterpoint to it. A serious flaw, fatal if the book had been realistically serious.

That is, according to realistic psychology, we know that Herzog, even in his middle age, was false-naive. Looking at a photograph of himself taken at the time he got his M.A., he thinks:

> *His younger face expressed the demands of ingenuous conceit. A man in years he then was, but in years only, and in his father's eyes stubbornly un-European, that is, innocent by deliberate choice. Moses refused to know evil. But he could not refuse to experience it. And therefore others were appointed to do it to him, and then to be accused (by him) of wickedness.*

This is the naïveté which made it possible for him to be so thoroughly duped, and his natural rage at his betrayers is magnified by rage at himself. As he knows: he puts himself into the position to shoot them, and then does not. He knows and Bellow knows, but we readers must know too. We must know more about Gersbach than externals, than that he was a poet-announcer with a wooden leg; we must know him in our hearts. *We* weren't victimized by him. After all, Herzog, an arrogant, intellectual, experienced man, had no business being so innocent at his age; he is guilty of innocence. The evil of Gersbach and Madeleine we cannot take on Herzog's word; Bellow must prove it, if we are to credit it fully enough to hate them on our own, and he does not. He seals us inside Herzog's mind too much, as he does not with the other secondary characters.

But, happily, the book is only partly about the rape of Herzog's naïveté. There is more to him than that, much more. According to another, older, moral psychology, Herzog is a man of sloth. He has his quota of the other sins, lust, pride, anger, but sloth dominates him. Not merely indolence, but busy-work too, furiously doing a thousand other things instead of what he ought to be doing. His soul wallows, and all the time his mind is thinking wildly, surrounding it with swarms of thoughts, attacking it, darting every which way, always coming back to it, prodding it till it shifts and grunts, jabbing at it. Sometimes the heaviness gets into the book. Late one afternoon his mistress phones and invites him over to dinner. He says he will be right there. It takes him thirty or forty minutes to get to the door of his apartment, during which time he does nothing but have twenty pages of thoughts. There is a lot of energy in these thoughts, but the inertia beneath them makes the passage drag.

Realistic or moral, whatever the psychology, there is the flaw in Herzog's character which we are grateful for and which the novel could not do without. He can't stop thinking: he is out of control of his thoughts a good deal of the time, he spills over, he darts all over the place. A lot of the thoughts he has are worth having, their energy is abundant, and they reek with vitality, even the silly ones. And the way Saul Bellow has put them together is a delight, a treat. On the next to last page occur the last words of Herzog's last imaginary letter: " 'But what do you want, Herzog?' 'But that's just it—not a solitary thing. I am pretty well satisfied to be, to be just as it is willed, and for as long as I may remain in occupancy.' " When you read this, you believe it. This is not just an easy upbeat ending. Herzog has earned the right to say this.

Still.

"For as long as I may remain in occupancy." Here he is, an English professor whose scholarly writing is good enough to put him in *Who's Who*, and he writes a sentence like that! The language of it may be more or less in character, but Bellow uses the locution to hold Herzog *over there* to the very end, so you won't take his sentiments too much to heart. You believe him, but you also believe Bellow's prose: Herzog has got through, all right, but only just, and there's plenty of trouble ahead. How long has Herzog, to our knowledge, ever been satisfied with anything, much less existence? "I am pretty well satisfied to be, to be just as it is willed." Come off it, Moses, we know you, Duke, you won't rest for long, you're about to get married again, your heart is gluttonous as a hog.

Novelists are wrong to put an interpretation of history at the base of artistic creation—to speak "the last word." It is better that the novelist should trust his own sense of life. Less ambitious. More likely to tell the truth.

From Writers at Work, Third Series *(New York: Viking Press, 1967)*

ARTICLE:

Alfred Kazin, "My Friend Saul Bellow," *Atlantic Monthly*, 215 (January 1965): 51-54.

This "informal profile" was written while Herzog *was on top of the best-seller lists.*

One day in 1942 I was walking near the Brooklyn Borough Hall with a young writer just in from Chicago who was looking New York over with great detachment. In the course of some startlingly apt observations on the life in the local streets, the course of the war, the pain of Nazism, and the neurotic effects of apartment-house living on his friends in New York, observations punctuated by some very funny jokes and double entendres at which he was the first to laugh with hearty pleasure for things so well said, he talked about D. H. Lawrence and James Joyce, Theodore Dreiser and Ernest Hemingway and Scott Fitzgerald, not as great names but as fellow artists. He said, as casually as if he were in a ball park faulting a pitcher, that Fitzgerald was "weak," but Dreiser strong in the right places. He examined Hemingway's style like a surgeon pondering another surgeon's stitches. And citing D. H. Lawrence with the intimacy of a brother-in-arms, he pointed to the bilious and smoke-dirty sky and said that like Lawrence he wanted no "umbrella" between him and the essential mystery.

The impression this conversation made on me was very curious. Bellow had not yet published a novel, and he was known for his stories and evident brilliance only to a small intellectual group drawn from the *Partisan Review* and the University of Chicago. Yet walking the unfamiliar Brooklyn streets, he seemed to be measuring the hidden strength of all things in the universe, from the grime of Brooklyn to the leading stars of the American novel, from the horror of Hitler to the mass tensions of New York. He was measuring the world's power of resistance, measuring himself as a contender. Although he was friendly, unpretentious, and funny, he was serious in a style that I had never before seen in an urban Jewish intellectual: he was going to succeed as an imaginative writer; he was pledged to grapple with unseen powers. He was going to take on more than the rest of us were.

As Bellow talked, I had an image of him as a wrestler in the old Greek style, an agonist contending in the games for the prize. Life was dramatically as well as emotionally a contest to him, and nothing of the agony or contest would be spared him. God would try him in his pride and trip him up, and he knew it; no one was spared; he had been brought up an orthodox Jew, and he had a proper respect for God as the ultimate power assumed by the creation. A poor immigrant's gifted son, he had an instinct that an overwhelming number of chances would come his way, that the old poverty and cultural bareness would soon be exchanged for a multitude of temptations. So he was wary—eager, sardonic, and wary; and unlike everybody else I knew, remarkably patient in expressing himself.

For a man with such a range of interests, capacities, and appetites, Bellow talked with great austerity. He addressed himself to the strength of life hidden in people, in political issues, in other writers, in mass behavior; an anthropologist by training, he liked to estimate other people's physical capacity, the thickness of their skins, the strength in their hands, the force in their chests. Describing people, he talked like a Darwinian, calculating the power of survival hidden in the species. But there was nothing idle or showy about his observations, and he did not talk for effect. His conceptions, definitions, epigrams, *apercus* were of a formal plainness that went right to the point and stopped. That was the victory he wanted. There was not the slightest verbal inflation in anything he said. Yet his observations were so direct and penetrating that they took on the elegance of achieved thought. When he considered something, his eyes slightly set as if studying its power to deceive him, one realized how formidable he was on topics generally exhausted by ideology or neglected by intellectuals too fine to consider them. Suddenly everything tiresomely grievous came alive in the focus of this man's unfamiliar imagination.

From New York Times Book Review, *27 September 1964*

Listening to Bellow, I became intellectually happy—an effect he was soon to have on a great many other writers of our generation. We were coming through. He was holding out for the highest place as a writer, and he would reach it. Even in 1942, two years before he published his first novel, *Dangling Man*, his sense of his destiny was dramatic because he was thinking in form, in the orbit of the natural storyteller, in the dimensions of natural existence. The exhilarating thing about him was that a man so penetrating and informed should be so sure of his talent for imaginative literature, for the novel, for the great modern form. We all knew brilliant intellectuals, academic conquistadores, geniuses at ideology, who demanded one's intellectual surrender. Every day I saw intellectuals clever enough to make the world over, who indeed had made the world over many times. Yet Bellow, who had been brought up in the same utopianism and was himself a scholar in the formidable University of Chicago style, full of the Great Books and jokes from the Greek plays, would obviously be first and last a novelist, a storyteller, creating new myths out of himself and everyone he had ever known, fought, loved, and hated. This loosened the bonds of ideology for the rest of us. It was refreshing to be with a man who so clearly believed himself headed for power in the novel: it disposed of many pedantic distinctions.

Saul Bellow was born in Montreal in 1915, but grew up in Chicago. Chicago from the 1890s until well past the First World War was a good town for novelists to grow up in, for it was a powerhouse of American life, it could give a writer the whole surrounding Midwest, and it promoted a fierce sense of rivalry with the East that made writers ambitious and cocky. Chicago, said Henry Blake Fuller in the nineties, was a great city built for the express purpose of making money; it was hard but bracing, brutal yet assimilable. A writer could understand it and feel equal to it. In no other great Northern city, up to our day, have Negroes and whites been so conscious of each other; no other great American city has been given so much of its character by the immigrant groups. New York, by contrast, has for a century been so big, complicated, and important that no novelist can be equal to all of it, as Dreiser and Anderson, Herrick and Fuller, Farrell and Algren have been representative of Chicago. New York has for so long been a center of culture and the literary business that what makes it a perpetual feast for the dilettantes makes it unreal even to writers who live in it. Chicago, for as much as half a century after the World's Fair of 1893, was a focus for all the rawness and power of American capitalism. Yet it was a human scene still open to a single novelist.

Much of the vividness of Bellow's novels, his powerful sense of place, comes out of Chicago. Two of his best books—*The Victim* (1947) and *Seize the Day* (1956)—are set in New York, and he manages to put into the city some quintessential urban quality which New York novelists themselves, usually absorbed in unrepresentative worlds like Madison Avenue and the Bronx, do not often see. "On some nights," *The Victim* opens, "New York is as hot as Bangkok. The whole continent seems to have moved from its place and slid nearer the equator, the bitter gray Atlantic to have become green and tropical, and the people, thronging the streets, barbaric fellahin among the stupendous monuments of their mystery. . . ." Bellow's senses have been tuned by the big city and the new situations always confronted by its immigrant masses. As Augie March says in the opening sentence of the book that established Bellow's reputation, "I am an American, Chicago-born—Chicago, that somber city—and go at things as I have taught myself, free-style, and will make the record in my own way. . . ."

And without the intellectual pugnacity that some Chicago novelists pick up because of their contempt for the old genteel culture, Bellow has the quicknesses that come from living on the firing line. He was brought up in a deeply Jewish spirit and with the Yiddish language, the life-thread of a cultural and religious tradition in Eastern Europe which the Nazis and Communists have destroyed along with three quarters of its speakers. To those who still possess this language, it is an incomparable assurance of identity. It is said of a new arrival in Israel who was berated for teaching her son Yiddish rather than Hebrew that she answered, "I want my son to be a Jew." This is Bellow's tradition, and of the many talented and interesting novelists of Jewish background in this country, there is probably no other who feels so lovingly connected with the religious and cultural tradition of his Eastern European grandfathers. And since he is at the same time the least ghettoized and least sentimental of "Jewish" novelists, one who makes the Jew a central figure because Bellow naturally thinks of the Jew as man at the end of his tether, which is where all dramas begin, his combination of many conflicting traditions and inclinations makes for remarkably vivid powers of mind, an unusual feeling for all the pressures and explosions inside the human community.

Bellow's most striking quality as a novelist is his ability to make the reader see dramatic new issues in situations that a great many people live with. The interest he arouses is very natural; he starts from the world we all know and share; many people recognize the stresses he writes about. Only one of his novels, *Henderson the Rain King* (1959), takes place in a wholly "arranged" setting, Africa, and is naturally preferred to his other books by those who like fiction allegorical and provoking to their subtlety. Yet even Henderson finds his marriages more real to him than he does Africa. Although Bellow's six novels, from *Dangling Man* (1944) to *Herzog* (1964), are frankly novels of development, *Bildungsromaner* without the cultural piety that the Germans attach to this form, they appeal to a very wide audience because, even more, they are novels of personal struggle, of life difficulties, domestic difficulties, common penalties and pains. Everyone can recognize the battle that Bellow puts his heroes through: it is made up of love and sex and marriage, of common apprehensions and natural catastrophes, of the struggles between parents and children, between victims and persecutors, between love and hatred, between life and death.

More than twenty years have passed since my first meeting with Bellow, twenty years in which he has become one of the most celebrated and influential of living novelists. Yet never in his life or work has he lost his prime sense of existence as one man's contest with terrible powers. As he nears fifty he looks considerably more benign than he used to. Yet the elegant aptness of his most informal observations, though more brilliant than ever, still yields easily to that tragicomic sense of buffoonery that urged some Yiddish genius to write: "If God lived on earth, His windows would always be broken." That wit is Bellow's habitat, and the terms of the joke are natural to him. The proud, moody, and handsome young writer who, like Joseph in the Bible, airily confided his dreams of greatness to his brothers has always been a man who suffers, as he would say, "in style"—with an air. In Bellow, anguish and wit have always been natural companions.

Characteristically, the hero of his new novel, *Herzog*, is a tortured scholar in his mid-forties, a specialist in intellectual history, author of *Romanticism and Christianity*, who has been abruptly turned out of his house and divorced by his formidable second wife, then discovers to his horror that he has been cuckolded all along by his best friend and former protégé. The nervous crisis into which this plunges him, one frantic midsummer in New York, compels a total exposure of his life and thinking to himself.

Herzog's fantastic mind is always the center of the book, so this is an operation on conscious flesh. Yet his thinking is wildly comic. At the mercy of the most primitive feelings, he writes letters that he will never mail, letters that he usually does not finish, burning scraps of thought addressed to Eisenhower, to Hegel, to Nietzsche, to his dead mother, to old girl friends. Herzog's suffering has become a lion in his path challenging him to overcome it. It is a sign from the unknown powers that surround us. Living entirely in his mind and on it, Herzog sends out his messages to the powerful and unseen, to the famous dead and to his own dead, in order to establish his suffering as a significant fact; he wants its seriousness to be acknowledged, its dignity to be respected. Herzog's pain is not something that other people have a right to pass over, to turn into another abstraction. Herzog is already suffering from too many abstractions. He is exasperated by "how quickly the visions of genius become the canned goods of the intellectuals. The canned sauerkraut of Spengler's 'Prussian Socialism,' the commonplaces of the Wasteland outlook, the cheap mental stimulants of Alienation, the cant and rant of pipsqueaks about Inauthenticity and Forlornness. I can't accept this foolish dreariness. We are talking about the whole life of mankind. The subject is too great, too deep for such weakness, cowardice—too deep, too great, Shapiro. It torments me to insanity that you should be so misled. A merely aesthetic critique of modern history! After the wars and mass killings! You are too intelligent for this. You inherited rich blood. Your father peddled apples."

When a brutal crippled lawyer tries to shout Herzog into submitting to his wife, the exhausted and much-tried scholar nevertheless resists him as one of those "reality instructors" who are always able to impose their coarse cynicism on sensitive minds. And when a delectable lady florist who has been consoling Herzog in his misery tries to persuade him that life can be perfect when sealed by her accomplished charms, Herzog remains obstinately convinced that his crisis is deeper, that it is attached to the age, and that by confronting it with all his intellectual and moral strength, he will attain some satisfying hold on the truth. Yet in the course of this struggle, Herzog naturally falls victim to people less perturbed than himself. Seeking some legal information, he spends a day in court, and there is so sickened by testimony on the murder of a child by its crippled mother and her lover that he runs off to Chicago, where his ex-wife and former friend are living. He digs up his father's old pistol and stalks his wife's house, but watching the lover bathe Herzog's child, he decides not to kill anyone. A day later, while driving with his daughter, his car is hit by a truck and he passes out; the police discover the loaded gun on him, and he lands briefly in jail. Yet in jail and out of it, he looks for a truth equal to the absoluteness of his suffering.

This search will never end; he is Herzog, a creature given to thought as a confrontation of the total human condition. Though he suffers to the root of his being every crisis in his affections, his intelligence is so powerful and obstinately independent that because of his intellectual adventure, *Herzog* becomes a vivifying experience. The reader finds himself drawn by Herzog's pace, thinking with Herzog's freedom, sending out manifestos of his own to the powers of this world. The bracing quality of the book stems from Herzog's mobility of spirit and the extremism of his emotions. As Blake said in *The Marriage of Heaven and Hell*, "Excess of sorrow laughs. Excess of joy weeps." Although Moses Elkanah Herzog is only a sometime professor having a nervous breakdown, his mind gives form to the novel and pace to its rhythms. Flashbacks, immediate experiences, and reflections move in and out of each other with ease; when Herzog is thinking, he can say "I" as easily as Bellow can say "Herzog," and the intricate sequences work because Bellow assumes they can.

Philosophers are authentic when they think as though their lives depended on it. This is already a dramatic subject, as Nietzsche knew about himself. But philosophers are hard to realize in fiction; thought is secret. How do you show thought in the contemporary novel, the unbreaking soliloquy of an obsessed and powerful mind, without giving up the common world that has come back for novelists despite the genius of James Joyce and Virginia Woolf? The interior world has grown stale, and the outer one is now actually more experimental. Herzog conveying the essence of Tolstoy and Hegel to Eisenhower in letters that the General will never see, mentally addressing a question to "Professor Nietzsche from the floor," or insisting on "moral realities" to another philosopher as he stands thinking in the subway expresses one way of moving between the private and public worlds.

It works in *Herzog* because of its inherent absurdity. Bellow's image of life is always a confrontation of opposites, a marriage of unlikely possibilities. A scholar betrayed and humiliated, so self-centered as to be unbearable to himself, finds life-enhancing powers of thought. Yet in the "post-quixotic, post-Copernican U.S.A., where a mind freely poised in space might discover relationships utterly unsuspected by a seventeenth-century man sealed in his smaller universe . . . in nine-tenths of his existence he was exactly what others were before him." Philosophers, even Nietzsche, once thought themselves the voice of reason, but reason now has to prove that it will not kill. In the glut of sex and culture, food and limitless self-expression, all things assume each other's identities. A couple lie naked in bed with heavy tomes of Russian spirituality all around them. Herzog's beautiful young mistress, a convert to Roman Catholicism, makes herself up to look older and more proper than she is, puts on a long old-fashioned skirt, and then catches her heel in it and falls down the subway steps. Herzog listening to testimony on the murder of a child by her mother and the mother's lover reflects that people get *up* to murder but *down* to make love. Herzog is cuckolded during the hours he is away getting psychoanalyzed. These harsh turns of thought, these absurd and brutal contingencies of existence, are capped by the most unlikely hope for the world as a whole. In the midst of death we are in life. "To realize that you are a survivor is a shock. At the realization of such election, you feel like bursting into tears. As the dead go their way, you want to call to them, but they depart in a black cloud of faces, souls. They flow out in smoke from the extermination chimneys, and leave you in the clear light of historical success—the technical success of the West. Then you know with a crash of the blood that mankind is making it—making it in glory though deafened by the explosions of blood. Unified by the horrible wars, instructed in our brutal stupidity by revolutions, by engineered famines directed by 'ideologists' (heirs of Marx and Hegel and trained in the cunning of reason), perhaps we, modern humankind (can it be!), have done the nearly impossible, namely, learned something."

ARTICLE:

Saul Bellow, "The Thinking Man's Waste Land," *Saturday Review*, 48 (3 April 1965): 20.

Herzog *won the International Literature Prize and Bellow's second National Book Award. This article was adapted from his speech accepting the NBA.*

The fact that there are so many weak, poor, and boring stories and novels written and published in America has been ascribed by our rebels to the horrible squareness of our institutions, the idiocy of power, the debasement of sexual instincts, and the failure of writers to be alienated enough. The poems and novels of these same rebellious spirits, and their theoretical statements, are grimy and gritty and very boring too, besides being nonsensical, and it is evident now that polymorphous sexuality and vehement declarations of alienation are not going to produce great works of art either.

There is nothing left for us novelists to do but think. For unless we think, unless we make a clearer estimate of our condition, we will continue to write kid stuff, to fail in our function; we will lack serious interests and become truly irrelevant. Here the critics must share the blame. They too have failed to describe the situation. Literature has for generations been its own source, its own province, has lived upon its own traditions, and accepted a romantic separation or estrangement from the common world. This estrangement, though it produced some masterpieces, has by now enfeebled literature.

The separatism of writers is accompanied by the more or less conscious acceptance of a theory of modern civilization. This theory says in effect that modern mass society is frightful, brutal, hostile to whatever is pure in the human spirit, a waste land and a horror. To its ugliness, its bureaucratic regiments, its thefts, its lies, its wars, and its cruelties, the artist can never be reconciled.

This is one of the traditions on which literature has lived uncritically. But it is the task of artists and critics in every generation to look with their own eyes. Perhaps they will see even worse evils, but they will at least be seeing for themselves. They will not, they cannot permit themselves, generation after generation, to hold views they have not examined for themselves. By such willful blindness we lose the right to call ourselves artists; we have accepted what we ourselves condemn—narrow specialization, professionalism, and snobbery, and the formation of a caste.

And, unfortunately, the postures of this caste, postures of liberation and independence and creativity, are attractive to poor souls dreaming everywhere of a fuller, freer life. The writer is admired, the writer is envied. But what has he to say for himself? Why, he says, just as writers have said for more than a century, that he is cut off from the life of his own society, despised by its overlords who are cynical and have nothing but contempt for the artist, without a true public, estranged. He dreams of ages when the poet or the painter expressed a perfect unity of time and place, had real acceptance, and enjoyed a vital harmony with his surroundings—he dreams of a golden age. In fact, without the golden age, there is no Waste Land.

Well, this is no age of gold. It is only what it is. Can we do no more than complain about it? We writers have better choices. We can either shut up because the times are too bad, or continue because we have an instinct to make books, a talent to enjoy, which even these disfigured times cannot obliterate. Isolated professionalism is death. Without the common world the novelist is nothing but a curiosity and will find himself in a glass case along some dull museum corridor of the future.

We live in a technological age which seems insurmountably hostile to the artist. He must fight for his life, for his freedom, along with everyone else—for justice and equality, threatened by mechanization and bureaucracy. This is not to advise the novelist to rush immediately into the political sphere. But in the first stage he must begin to exert his intelligence, long unused. If he is to reject politics, he must understand what he is rejecting. He must begin to think, and to think not merely of his own narrower interests and needs.

BOOK REVIEW:

Benjamin DeMott, "Saul Bellow and the Dogmas of Possibility," *Saturday Review*, 53 (7 February 1970): 25-28, 37.

Bellow won his third National Book Award for Mr. Sammler's Planet. *In this sad comedy, Artur Sammler, an old man who has outlasted the horrors of this century, speculates on the future of the Earth and other planets which man may reach.*

The lid is off, experience is in, Action is all: given this situation, have books a future? Can literary minds regain influence on the general culture? Will a voice of moral authority soon again sound—and be heeded—in a novel, poem, or play?

One current incitement to pessimism is the increasing polarization of literary opinion. (Conservatives are locked in the habit of fitting every observation of behavior or feeling into a grid of Cultural Decline; radicals are locked in the conviction that art can't be art unless it is revolutionary and anarchistic. The first view seals writers off from "unstructured" encounters with the age, the second abolishes literary form as a value.)

An incitement to optimism, on the other hand, is the ongoing productivity of the country's major literary talents—and among the latter none stands higher than Saul Bellow. This writer seldom slights his craft: no slovenly books or clownish cynicism or hints that art and

Bellow in the sixties

public relations are one. High spirits, humor, strong narrative rhythms, responsiveness to place as well as person, a swift idiomatic speaking voice, the power to nudge open a door upon common life without instantly banishing delight and wonder—these are but a few of his gifts. And equal to any of them, at least in the mind of people anxious about the survival of moral authority in letters, is Bellow's relish of talk and thought about the "conduct of life," and his custom of ventilating moral/cultural issues in his books. Usually the author of *Augie March* focuses on personal quandaries (the hero's unrestrainable appetite in *Henderson the Rain King*, Tommy Wilhelm's weakness and self-deception in *Seize the Day*). But even amidst absorption with the local and idiosyncratic, his eye glances off to items of larger implication—high-fashion enthusiasm for despair (*Herzog*), minority group self-pity (*The Victim*). And this tendency of mind, together with the gifts just mentioned, has fixed an estimate of Saul Bellow as a writer not only ambitious to speak general truth but exceptionally well-equipped to do so.

No book in Bellow's *oeuvre* addresses cultural agonies more directly than the one at hand; nowhere does representation of personal relations run on as regularly into impersonal counsel about how to live. From this it doesn't follow, of course, that narrative interest is neglected, or that a tractarian or essayistic posture is the book's norm, or that the hero—a Polish-born, English-educated septuagenarian—is to be identified with Mr. Bellow himself. (One surprising link between plus-seventy Sammler and plus-fifty Bellow—H. G. Wells—is worth a word. Sammler is presented as an intimate of Wells; Bellow corresponded with that author, an admirer of Bellow's first novel, in the 1940s.) *Mr. Sammler's Planet* is dense in character and anecdote, and if its narrative line is a shade less than gripping, it suffices for the display both of the central figure and of the novelist's comic inventiveness. It *is* true, though, that book and hero alike seek from the beginning a stance of detachment, and the search creates difficulties for both.

Artur Sammler, one-eyed man of mind, former London-based correspondent for Polish newspapers, icy, aristocratic, Bloomsbury habitue, escapee from a mass grave in a Nazi slaughter, lives on New York's West Side with his niece and his daughter as companions. A couple of his more extraordinary life adventures—hiding out in a Polish mausoleum after the escape from the mass grave, service as correspondent of sorts during an Arab-Israeli battle—are recounted in back-flashes. And the man does an occasional turn, center stage, most notably a lecture at Columbia on the British Scene in the Thirties, during which he's jumped by student radicals for approving intellectual freedom.

But Sammler is mainly an observer, not an actor. What he looks at is history in the large, the city roundabout (especially the habiliments of vanity and lunacy visible in strangers), and the appetites of relatives and acquaintances studied at close range. The human beings in question include an elegantly clad black pickpocket who works the bus between Columbus Circle and 72nd Street (the fellow at length detects Sammler's surveillance and chases him into an apartment lobby, trapping him in a corner and threatening him, wordlessly, by exposing himself). Others whom Sammler scrutinizes are Dr. Govinda Lal, an Indian astrophysicist guest-lecturing in America, author of a work called *The Future of the Moon*, the opening sentence of which reads, "How long will this earth remain the only home of Man?"; Dr. Elya Gruner, Sammler's benefactor, a Westchester surgeon

Dust jacket for Bellow's sixth novel

sick unto death in a Manhattan hospital, who stands forth by virtue of generosity and solidity of self as Sammler's model of human worth; and three members of the takeover generation—the surgeon's endlessly cosseted children, Angela and Wallace Gruner, and Sammler's own daughter, Shula-Slawa, lonely, lit'ry, loony.

The narrative net gathering these people is drawn by two actions—Shula-Slawa's theft of the astrophysicist's moon manuscript (the girl believes the document to be essential to a memoir of Wells that in her mind is the core of her father's life), and Wallace Gruner's attempted destruction of his father's house in pursuit of a cache of "dirty money" allegedly hidden in the pipes by the elder Gruner with the aid of a "Mafia plumber." The comic interludes that interrupt Sammler's reflections on this miscellaneous lot usually feature Wallace, a thoroughly original creation who shuttles from role to role and fantasy to fantasy, excusing himself with the remark that "I'm a different generation. I never had any dignity to start with."

> [Wallace] invented curious projects. Several years ago he flew out to Tangiers with the purpose of buying a horse and visiting Morocco and Tunisia on horseback. Not taking his Honda, he said, because backward people should be seen from a horse. He had borrowed Jacob Burckhardt's *Force and Freedom* from Sammler, and it affected him strongly. He wanted to examine peoples in various stages of development. In Spanish Morocco he was robbed in his hotel. By a man with a gun, hidden in his closet. He then flew on to Turkey and tried again. Somehow he managed to enter Russia on his horse. In Soviet Armenia he was detained by the police. After [his father] had gone five or six times to see Senator Javits, Wallace was released from prison. Then, once again in New York, Wallace, taking a young lady to see the film *The Birth of a Child*, fainted away at the actual moment of birth, struck his head on the back of a seat, and was knocked unconscious. Reviving, he was on the floor. He found that his date had moved away from him in embarrassment, changed her seat. He had a row with her for abandoning him. Wallace, borrowing his father's Rolls, let it somehow get away from him; carelessly parked, it ended up at the bottom of a reservoir somewhere near Croton. He drove a city crosstown bus to pay off debts. The Mafia was after him. His bookie gave him two months to pay. The handicapping hadn't worked. He flew with a friend to Peru to climb in the Andes. Said to be quite a good pilot . . . He volunteered for the domestic Peace Corps. He wanted to be of use to little black children, to be a basketball coach in playgrounds . . .

And the book's most hilarious moment occurs when Sammler delivers portentously to Dr. Lal the fruits of his meditation on the future of man just at the instant Wallace upstairs breaks the attic pipes, flooding the entire house. "Regularly, now, for generations," Sammler reflects minutes later, carrying plastic buckets up and down the stairs, "prosperous families brought forth their anarchistic sons—these boy Bakunins, geniuses of liberty, arsonists, demolishers of prisons, property, palaces. Bakunin had loved fire so. Wallace worked in water, a different medium."

As for the fruits of Sammler's meditation: their value lies in alertness to themes of Possibility, Experience, and Wholeness that are indeed central in contemporary thought and feeling, and that have never before in fiction been dealt with as explicitly as here. *Mr. Sammler's Planet* does, to be sure, offer up many commonplace ruminations about the odds against Western culture, and much fulmination against post-Enlightenment man. (". . . the struggles of three revolutionary centuries being won while the feudal bonds of Church and Family weakened and the privileges of aristocracy [without any duties] spread wide, democratized, especially the libidinous privileges, the right to be uninhibited, spontaneous, urinating, defecating, belching, coupling in all positions, tripling, quadrupling, polymorphous, noble in being natural, primitive, combining the leisure and luxurious inventiveness of Versailles with hibiscus-covered erotic ease of Samoa . . .") But the book's formulations concerning the nature of the new appetites are far less stale:

> . . . people want to visit all other states of being in a diffused state of consciousness, not wishing to be any given thing but instead to become comprehensive, entering and leaving at will . . .
>
> . . . Human beings, when they have room, when they have liberty and are supplied also with ideas, mythologize themselves . . . They legendize. They expand by imagination and try to rise above the limitations of the ordinary forms of common life . . . Separating themselves from the rest of their species, from the life of their species, hoping perhaps to get away . . . from the death of their species . . .
>
> Humankind had lost its old patience. It demanded accelerated exaltation, accepted no instant without pregnant meanings as in epic, tragedy, comedy, or films.

These formulations, furthermore, have an organic weight—nothing patched-on or abstract about them. Now they're validated by the observed life of the sidewalks:

> What one sees on Broadway while bound for the bus. All human types reproduced, the barbarian, Redskin or Fiji, the dandy, the buffalo hunter, the desperado, the queer, the sexual fantasist, the squaw, bluestocking princess, poet, painter, prospector, troubadour, guerrilla, Che Guevara, the new Thomas Becket . . .

Now they're validated by the sick non sequiturs of Wallace Gruner's funny-pathetic talk:

> ". . . They say that fellows that beef themselves up like that—'I was a ninety-pound weakling'—that such fellows are narcissistic pansies. I don't judge anybody. What if they are homosexuals? That's nothing any more. I don't think homosexuality is simply a different way of being human, I actually think it's a disease. I don't know why homosexuals fuss so much and proclaim themselves so normal. Such gentlemen. Of course they have *us* to point at—and we're not so great. I believe this boom in faggots was caused by modern warfare. One result of 1914, that slaughter in the trenches. The men were getting blasted. It was obviously healthier to be a woman than a man. It was better to be a child. Best of all is to be an artist, combining child, woman, or dervish—do I mean a dervish? A shaman? A necromancer is probably what I mean. Plus millionaire. Many a millionaire wants to be an artist, or a kid or woman and a necromancer. What was I talking about? . . ."

And before the tale is ended, the contrast between self-stability and its opposite is worked into the very texture of people's knowledge of each other. Sammler perceives his friend Gruner as a self-consistency embodying chosen dignity. And he himself in turn is placed by the restless money-maddened types who know him as pure stillness and fixity: "Feffer in the furious whirling of his spirit took him for a fixed point." (At length, true to his own ironic spirit, Sammler grins at the "still point" *schtick*. In "hyperenergetic revolutions," he reflects, men "fall in love with ideas of stability, and Sammler was an idea of stability.")

It's one thing to grant the pertinence of Bellow's account of the new sensibility, however, and another to accept *Mr. Sammler's Planet* as evidence of the trustworthiness of the literary mind now. For although there's much to praise in this work of fiction—spirited comedy, intermittent analytical brillance—it is nevertheless at bottom a troubled, uncertain book. The problems can be variously labeled. From one perspective they look to be consequences of an over-rigid, over-familiar (see above) "decline-of-culture" set of mind; from another they're traceable to esthetic confusion—a doomed effort to move freely, in a single work, between closed and open literary forms. But both perspectives are mere symptomatology: the strong impression is that the root of the book's trouble, both as argument and as art, is a defect of sympathy.

As might be assumed, Mr. Sammler the protagonist is wary of this defect, determined to guard against it. He understands that he is a man of the past. He knows that the appetite for multiple selves and for new ways of having experience has connections with past deprivation:

> . . . many have surged forward in modern history, after long epochs of namelessness and bitter obscurity, to claim and to enjoy (as people enjoy things now) a name, a dignity of person, a life such as belonged in the past only to gentry, nobility, the royalty or the gods of myth.

He tries to acknowledge that mere admonitions to "be human" can't instantly increase the attractions of humdrum humanness:

> Why should they be human? In most of the forms offered there is little scope for the great powers of nature in the individual, the abundant, generous powers. In business, in professions, in labor; as a member of the public; as an inhabitant of the cities, these strange pits; as experiencer of compulsions, manipulations; as endurer of strain; as father, husband obliging society by performing his quota of actions—the individual seems to feel these powers less, less and less.

And again and again he speaks of his struggle against certainty and the doctrinaire temper, his effort to preserve a measure of negative capability ("The best, I have found, is to be disinterested . . . by not judging").

But the struggle fails. Or, rather, it attains insufficient substance for the reader, seemingly belonging only to the surface structure of Sammler's mind and story. His "fairness," his qualifications, his hesitations, sound faint, as from the wings, whereas his scorn and vituperation come forth strongly as from the center:

> The mental masses, inheriting everything in a debased state, had formed an idea of the corrupting disease of being white and of the healing power of black . . .
>
> From the black side, strong currents were sweeping over everyone. Child, black, redskin—the unspoiled Seminole against the horrible Whiteman. Millions of civilized people wanted oceanic, boundless, primitive, neck-free nobility, experienced a strange release of galloping impulses, and acquired the peculiar aim of sexual niggerhood for everyone.
>
> Just look . . . at this imitative anarchy of the streets—these Chinese revolutionary tunics, these babes in unisex toyland, these surrealist warchiefs, Western stagecoach drivers—Ph.D.s in philosophy, some of them . . . They sought originality. They were obviously derivative. And of

From New York Times Book Review, *25 January 1970*

> what—of Paiutes, of Fidel Castro? No, of Hollywood extras. Acting mythic. Casting themselves into chaos . . .

Everywhere the limitations of his vision and sympathy have an invulnerable quality, as though the rigidity in his deep structure had been sanctified by his creator and was beyond the touch of any event, any sudden infusion of light, any breath of critical scrutiny.

And these limitations of vision bring in their train—a predictable sequel—novelistic flaws. As a "pure" gallery of fools, an enclosed world with a little of the flavor of a seventeenth-century "humours" comedy or Enlightenment dunciad, an instructive catalogue of the puerilities of "cultural revolution," *Mr. Sammler's Planet* would have edge and point. But the book aspires to a higher condition. Like the people it mocks—culture vultures, fops, dudes, academic entrepreneurs, SDSers, SAT wizards, indulgent parents, slobbish women, trust-fund swingers, "do-gooders"—it is haunted by a dream of wholeness. And the pressure of that dream forces it repeatedly out of "proper" key or genre: instead of accepting itself as satire, a distorting mirror, it undertakes to pass itself off as a genuine imaginative encounter with, and penetration of, forces and beings it despises.

To say that it doesn't succeed means, in terms of the book's felt argument, that too much that matters in present-day thought, feeling, and action is excluded. (*Mr. Sammler's Planet* is a world more or less without politics, without provocation to minority protest, without Merck or Mississippi, without entrenched economic power, without established, unshakable, ego-ridden plunderers and polluters, without the frustration and bitterness of "highminded" senseless war. In this world people's behavior is almost entirely a function of their "purely personal" braininess or stupidity.) In terms of the book's dimension as art—a work of fiction—it means that the moments of dramatic confrontation, as opposed to satiric revelation, are below Mr. Bellow's standard: blurred, hurried, implausible. Sammler's face-off with the pickpocket who exposes himself is filtered through a scrim of memory: it doesn't happen on the page in dramatic time. There is no spoken accent of black-white confrontation, no entrance into the relevant labyrinth of intensities—guilt, rationalization, oppression, revenge, and the rest. The confrontation between Sammler and radical studentdom is equally thin and hasty, lacking adequacy not only to the mind of the protester, but to the situation itself (no trace of the counter-forces and conflict that develop within audiences at any public shoutdown).

The effort to create a significant challenge to the Gruner children in the person of their father is even less telling. Sammler's claim is that his friend understood the human contract (life is only briefly lent to us), and was a kind man. But the presentation of the surgeon elsewhere hardly supports the attempt to elevate him before his children. Elya Gruner is good-hearted but timid, cynical, self-indulgent, trivial-minded, committed most fully to Respectability, Money, and a new Rolls next year.

In sum: the novelist attempts to use one character simultaneously as a voice of derision, a cataloguer of fools, and as a source of comprehensive moral and social wisdom. By thus inflating his enterprise, he obliges himself to overprotect his sage, weaken his own rejection of the dogmas of possibility, and bring forth news of the world that isn't merely partial (partiality could have been a strength, in other circumstances) but narrow, tight, even at moments mean.

What follows from this on the matter of moral authority in books? Not total depression, surely. If no sage, not even Sammler deserves exemption from a creator's critical examination, no cultural revolution, no human direction, deserves exemption either. Clear images of the perversion and sentimentalization of brains and hope—whether they're called Gruner or Feffer, Shadwell or Cibber—are valuable. But the question does arise whether, in what is left of high literary culture, hostile and suspicious responses to themes of possibility haven't lately become a kind of fixed obligation, expressive of a pinched acquiescence in is-ness, a fear of that openness on behalf of which great wars of poetry were once fought.

As Sammler would say, the subject doesn't lend itself to "short views." It's helpful, for instance, to know that Wallace Gruner is among the hazards on our course: thanks to the chart-maker for his alertness. But it's wrong, is it not, to imply that because the hazard exists, the course is ridiculous? Or again: it's likely that Saul Bellow may have been pushed into intolerance by the cliché-mongering protesters rumored to have told him at a White House party that "having made you, we can break you." But it must be remembered that the love of, and need for, negative words run deep in literary minds in all ages. (Most good prose, Ezra Pound wrote, *arises* "from an instinct of negation: in the detailed, convincing analysis of something detestable, of something which one wants to eliminate.")

After these and the other appropriate arguments, qualifications, rationalizations, etc., have been roughed out, no conclusion, only a reprise: the instinct for openness, for a "world of possibility," seemingly isn't standard equipment for the late-twentieth-century literary mind. Grasping that within the human effort to make men new there could be something more than a self-destructive urge, meeting with no trace of hatred or scorn our will to transcend an unsatisfactory humanity, our desire to feel forward toward a more habitable life—these acts would constitute on literary turf a breakthrough, a precedent, a New Record. Just at the moment the writer who is to set that record isn't, regrettably, in easy sight.

INTERVIEW:

Joyce Illig, "An Interview with Saul Bellow," *Publishers Weekly*, 210 (22 October 1973): 74-77.

Bellow discusses his position as a Midwestern—or, specifically, a Chicago—novelist and his early writing jobs.

Saul Bellow doesn't like to be interviewed. Even if you hadn't been told this by several people at his publishing house (Viking), you could figure it out from the company he keeps. Moses Herzog wouldn't like it. Neither would Artur Sammler. Bummidge might consent but then hide behind the curtains with his shoes showing, or lie down on a couch with his glasses on so he wouldn't have to face the questions but could see his answers better. It's painful enough to try to be private when you've gone public with seven novels, short stories and a play—all of which make you an important American writer and a spokesman for the Midwest. Augie March exhaled Chicago and Saul Bellow has lived there for most of his life.

Bellow agreed to talk and to meet me in New York on a visit to his publisher. (He's rewriting his next novel "Humboldt's Gift.") When he appeared in the doorway of Viking's conference room, he was already in a rush to leave.

His clothes were dandy—all in one brown or another. He wore a hat pulled down like a guy standing under a street lamp in the opening of an Alan Ladd movie. He could have been on his way to Belmont. Instead, he sat down and looked worried.

PW: Does a school of writers still exist in Chicago?

SB: There used to be, in the old days, something called a "Chicago school." It had a certain reality in the days of Dreiser or Anderson, Carl Sandburg, Floyd Dell and Ben Hecht. There really was such a group in Chicago. There is no such group today. The earlier group reflected the fact that Chicago had become a regional capital. Gifted people were coming from the surrounding region and states—Iowa, Indiana, Wisconsin, Michigan—and Chicago was then *the* big city, they say, which brought them together. It had the excitement of a city. It had art. It had new architecture. Sullivan architecture. Above all, it had newspaper jobs for them. For the most part they were employed by the newspapers. Newspapers in those days were something more than advertising throwaways with a margin of copy on each page allowed by the business department of the paper. Several things happened all at once to put that to an end. One was the mechanization of news gathering. The other was the professionalization of journalism. You no longer had literate people doing a job. You had old "leg men" or city room guys or people of that sort or graduates of journalism schools. It no longer attracted people of talent nor did it want to. Journalism didn't give them jobs and so Chicago began to lose its hold on these people. They were drawn away by two rival centers, California and New York. They headed either for Broadway or for Hollywood and so Chicago as a regional literary center was drained.

PW: When did the exodus take place?

SB: That began to take place in the late twenties. By the time the depression hit Chicago, there was nothing to make Chicago a literary center except the WPA [Works Progress Administration], which was Roosevelt's gift to the arts in America. I suppose the intention really was to keep the bums out of trouble and to prevent them from joining subversive organizations. When we got out of school and had no jobs and no income, we were all tickled to have a WPA Writers Project job.

PW: What was your Writers Project job?

SB: It was to sit in the Newberry Library mainly and to organize the statistics about newspaper publishing. For a time, it was that. Then, John D. Frederick, who was the head of the project in Chicago, a very decent and imaginative man, gave me a job of writing biographies of Middle Western authors. None of them, I'm sure, were ever meant to be used. I'm glad to say that they've all disappeared. I kept no copies and I'm certain that there are none in the files.

> *. . . I think that realistic literature from the first has been a victim literature. Pit any ordinary individual—and realistic literature concerns itself with ordinary individuals—against the external world, and the external world will conquer him, of course.*

From Writers at Work, Third Series *(New York: Viking Press, 1967)*

PW: Wouldn't you like to see them now?

SB: No, I'd hate to see them.

PW: Why?

SB: I'd be distressed. I was only 22 years old and I knew nothing.

PW: Aren't you curious about the comparisons you could make?

SB: No, thanks, I know all about that. [*There is a long pause.*] No, I don't think that Chicago is a regional literary center. I don't think there is any such thing as a Chicago school of writers any more. There are writers who have lived in Chicago, who live in Chicago, who've been struck, if not stung, by Chicago, who've been knocked down and run over by Chicago. Or who have, as Nelson Algren once said, "an unrequited love affair with Chicago." But Chicago is an American city. That is to say vigorous, charming in its own brutal way, philistine, lacking in culture fundamentally, except for a few islands like the universities and the art establishments of the city. But it is for the most part a philistine city.

PW: Yet, you have spent most of your life writing there, haven't you?

SB: Yes, it's true that I have been there most of my life.

PW: Then, how does someone like yourself survive?

SB: That is a curious question. Well, where is an American writer to go? I had the good luck to miss New York in the sixties. Perhaps it was foresight to leave New York in the sixties, as if I knew intuitively that it was going to go mad. It did go mad. This was no place for a writer. This was a place for performers, virtuosi exhibitionists, self advertisers and promoters, people in the publicity game who describe themselves also as writers. It was no place for a writer. In fact, it was quite depressing for a writer. The country had no center for literature and the arts. New York is not a center for literature and the arts. New York is a place where all the stuff gets packaged, and where auxiliary or associated careers are made in publishing, in editing, among agents, among literary journalists, and for hustlers. But as for literature, it doesn't thrive in promotional centers like New York. I don't see that there are any interesting writers in New York itself, apart from these salamanders of the Mailer type who know how to live in the fire, and I'm not that sort. So I'd gone away. Was I to go back to Paris? Paris is deader than a doornail for an American writer. London is not a center, either, it looks toward New York. Then what one has is a group of imaginary centers each reflected elsewhere. So there is no locus for it anywhere. And one has to live with the brute facts of one's society. Though America is a fascinating country, to which I am devoted—I'd better be devoted to it because it possesses me heart and soul—I don't imagine for a moment that it's what one might call a cultivated society. There's a lot of public excitement about culture. But there is no such thing in actuality as American culture.

PW: Did you want to return to your roots?

SB: Well, I don't know whether they're actually roots. Sometimes I think they are a lot of tangled old wires. [*He laughs.*]

PW: Fine ones, though. But it seems that no matter where you were, you would come back to Chicago. Did it lure you back? Or was it a safe feeling?

SB: No, I wouldn't say that Chicago is safe. I think I live in one of the most dangerous neighborhoods to be found in North America. [*Laughs again, pleased.*]

PW: You know I mean creatively—was it a safe feeling?

SB: Well, I don't know about that. I had a hunch that it might be feasible there since it was hopeless elsewhere, and hopeless in a way which filled me with rage and despair. I don't thrive on rage and despair. I'm not by nature a desperate person. I am, however, an irritable and aggressive one, and get my dander up.

PW: I bet you do.

SB: So I knew that in the early sixties on the Eastern seaboard I was living in a state of high irritation which was incapacitating. I read the papers and the new books. I met the writers, the painters, the critics, the art establishment, the jet set, the flossy women and I responded with very little other than rage to all this. I thought I'd better remove myself from the scene.

PW: What's the longest you were here in New York in one chunk of time?

SB: Well, like every ambitious provincial, I came to take the big town. I showed up at the end of World War II. The job was done by about 1963 or 1964. So I would say that I was in the East for about 18 years. Two of these years I spent in Paris. Some of the time I was in Nevada, and also in Minnesota, but I lived in the East for about 14 or 15 years straight through. Everything in my life is a matter of decades. After the war I came back to Chicago and packed up my wife, my one-year-old child, my worldly goods and we took the train to New York. We had no place to stay. We barged in on some friends in Brooklyn Heights, on Pineapple Street. Then we heard of a place near Quarry, New York, so we went up there. I supported myself then by writing brief notices. I got $5 for novels and $10 for nonfiction books. I could turn out five or six a week if I stayed up nights reading. So I was able to make 40 and 50 bucks a week.

PW: How did you get the jobs and where did your work appear?

SB: The man who founded Penguin Books in this town and is now a publisher, Victor Weybright, was very kind to me. He was then preparing his first Penguin list. He was considering a great, great number of books. He used me to screen books for him. I wrote these reports for Weybright. I also did this for the *New Republic* and for the New York *Times Book Review*. There was a very generous man at the *Times* who knew what my situation was and who, if he didn't have any work for me, used to take an armload of review copies off the shelf and give them to me. I would take them to 59th Street and sell them to a secondhand dealer. So that was the way I supported myself for some time.

PW: Are you teaching now?

SB: Yes, I teach at the University of Chicago. I teach literature there. I don't teach writing courses.

PW: I see it's important to you to make the distinction.

SB: Yes, because I don't like teaching writing.

PW: Is there a profound reason for that?

SB: It makes me too unhappy to read some of the inept things.

PW: You're sensitive about your talent. Do you have a great deal of respect for yourself as a writer?

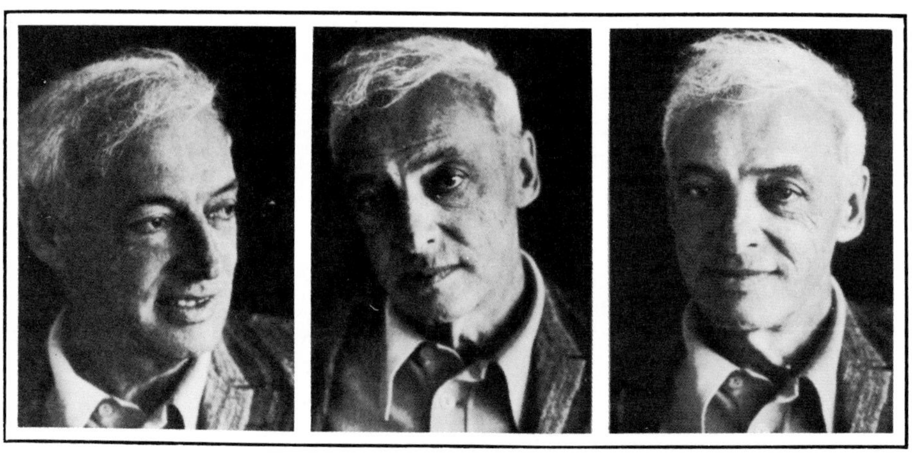

Bellow at the time he was interviewed for Publishers Weekly

SB: I think that people who write well are people who take a certain attitude toward themselves. Considerably more is involved than technique. One sees oneself as a certain kind of human being. I don't think that that peculiar act of initiation can be transmitted in a classroom. How am I going to describe to a young man or young woman the operation on one's soul which is necessary? You can't do that. So it's really misleading to say, well, I'll teach you to put together words on a page, or how to hook your reader or how to find a symbol or how to balance your narrative or anything of that sort.

PW: Who are you? What are you? [*After a long pause he doesn't answer.*] With the wealth of literature you've created, by now you could say, "I'm an amalgam of all the characters I've created." I don't want to put words in your mouth.

SB: No, don't. I'll take them right out. I don't know that that's really so, and I wouldn't like to describe myself because I would rather remain mysterious even for myself. We've all adopted from science the practice of telling ourselves what the critter is, in so many words, and I don't think that any act of positive cognition will really surface. We don't know who this is or what this is. [*pause*] But writing courses are very helpful to young people who leave home to go to the university, secretly craving to write and who are then able to tell their parents, the folks back home, that it's OK, I'm taking a course in it at the U. . . . This gives them a cover which they don't otherwise know how to create for themselves.

PW: The New York *Times* had an article about the physical and attitudinal changes in Chicago. Does this affect you?

SB: What abides in Chicago is the people of the city, many of whom I've known from childhood. These are intrinsically interesting to me. I don't care what happens to the Loop. It's of interest to me, but I don't live by that. I've seen too many neighborhoods in Chicago—familiar to me from childhood—destroyed, razed to the ground, rebuilt or left empty, to attach myself to the city in that way. That can only breed sadness in your heart. No, what I'm attached to in Chicago is a certain kind of person or to put it differently, a form of personality with which one becomes familiar in Chicago after many years.

PW: Is there a way of making me feel what that form of personality is?

SB: Only through what one writes.

PW: But don't you think that even in a small way, the environment makes a difference to you as a writer?

SB: I would adore a thriving and nourishing environment in which people of all sorts met in a common language, extraordinary interests, wonderfully developed personalities and all the rest of that rich, nutritious bed which we associate with culture of the great ages: Elizabethan England, Renaissance Italy, 19th century Paris, but that has never existed in the United States for anyone. It didn't exist for Poe or for Melville. Whitman insisted that it existed here. That he could discover it and prove that it was here. Mark Twain attached himself to a frontier society. Henry James and T. S. Eliot ran away from it altogether because they felt the poverty of it. But we who have grown up in this have no choice except to struggle with it. We know in the depths of our being how humanly significant it is, so we listen to what the schools have always described as culture. It's something else. It's a strange, new condition that's shared by the rest of mankind which is rapidly approaching it too. The British, the French and the Italians are speeding towards it in their own fashion. They, too, lack the vital food of culture which was so easily available in the past. They haven't got it anymore. All of civilized mankind is entering this peculiar condition in which we were pioneers. That's why Chicago is significant. We experienced it before the others did. We experienced the contemporary condition before the others were aware of it.

PW: In what way is that development unique to Chicago?

SB: Well, Chicago, I believe, is a symbol of it. In Chicago things were done for the first time, which the rest of the world later learned and imitated. Capitalist production was pioneered in the stockyards, in refrigerator cars, in the creation of the Pullman, in the creation of farm machinery, and with it also certain urban and political phenomena which are associated with the new condition of modern democracy. All that happened there. It happened early.

PW: I hear a lot of so-called image makers in New York trying to adopt Chicago. They talk about new buildings and fancy shops along Michigan Avenue, museums and theater. Isn't most of that just creating a new face, not a new pulse?

SB: That's right, but this country is great for that kind of thing. I go to the Art Institute and look at pictures. I also talk to intelligent people in Chicago. There are many there. They live in a sort of Fort Dearborn condition, behind palisades, so to speak, because the streets are not safe. The city empties at night, just as much as Dubuque, Iowa. You don't go down to the Loop any more because at night it's dangerous. Anyhow there's nothing to see in the Loop at night except a black movie where some super 007 with fancy pistols is shooting down whitey. I don't exaggerate when I say Fort Dearborn situation because one feels that one is surrounded by hostile savages. There's quite a lot of that in every city; it's all the more naked in Chicago because the city at night is so uninviting that one doesn't venture out except to go and see intelligent friends. I don't know what medieval Spain was like, but I imagine that there are certain similarities. You ride from one castle keep to another and you gallop over the drawbridge and the portcullis rises for you, and you spend an agreeable evening with your friends eating good food. What else is there to do? As you get older and flirtations dwindle or become less interesting, you spend . . . [*His laughter finishes the sentence*.] You can go out and admire the city as a tableau. You can admire it scenically. You can go downtown and visit the marvelous structures, look at the skyline, admire the color of the lake, show your visiting friends the wonders of the Miracle Mile and all the rest of that. But what is it really? It is really a sort of stirring and dramatic showpiece which at certain hours you can enjoy.

PW: Bill Styron gathers a literary and political crowd at his house in Martha's Vineyard. Are your intelligent friends a more diversified group?

SB: Styron is, if I may say this without offending him, on a Scott Fitzgerald system. Beautiful people and so on. I adore them when I meet them but I don't go out of my way to encounter them. I'm aware that I'm living through some sort of crisis in the history of civilization and I like to talk to people who know a great deal about various aspects of it. This entertains me much more than drinking with the boys and girls. Now I do divert myself in Chicago. I leave the university fortress to go to play squash twice a week downtown with businessmen, stockbrokers, lawyers, psychologists, builders, real estate people, and a sprinkling of underworld characters and old school friends who are not particularly aware of the fact that I am a writer. I make liberal use of the professional camouflage so they are a bit undecided in their mind as to which I am. Consequently, I am not continually identified by people as a writer. This I find a great blessing. I don't like to appear always under the single aspect: the writer. I like to be anonymous, diffuse, unnoticed. But of course, many Americans when they become writers, having performed enough and performed well the killing job of writing a book or two, want to unbend and enjoy the fruits of being a writer. Being a writer is extremely agreeable socially. Writing is damned hard.

PW: Will you appear on television to promote your books?

SB: I don't think I should appear on television to huckster my books because that's no part of my deal.

PW: With whom?

SB: With myself. With the gods, or with the public. I'm delighted when my books reach a large public. I want as many people as possible to read and understand my books. But I see no point whatever in hustling them on television because I am not a soup or a cleanser. And I feel polluted when I make a public pitch for it. I haven't done it since the days of Tex and Jinx and Mary Margaret McBride, when it brought my gorge up, and I quit then and there. I haven't done it since.

PW: Are you bringing your new novel out soon?

SB: In answer, may I quote E. M. Forster, in a favorite statement?

PW: You're compared to him a lot.

SB: Well, I don't like to be compared to him. We're sexually so different. But he said, and I appreciate this greatly, "How do I know what I think till I see what I say?" And I'm not done saying, so I don't know what I think.

"One of the pleasures of writing is being able to deal in certain primitive kinds of knowledge banished from ordinary discourse, like the knowledge brought by smells. I must be a great smell-classifier."

From Life, *3 April 1970, p. 59*

ESSAY:

Saul Bellow, "Starting Out in Chicago," *American Scholar*, 44 (Winter 1974/75): 71-77.

Bellow delivered the commencement address at Brandeis University in Spring 1974; he revised his speech into this essay on the benefits and disadvantages of growing up in Chicago during the Thirties.

What was it, in the thirties, that drew an adolescent in Chicago to the writing of books? How did a young American of the depression period decide that he was, of all things, a literary artist? I use the pretentious term literary artist simply to emphasize the contrast between such an amibition and the external facts. A colossal industrial and business center, knocked flat by unemployment, its factories and even its schools closing, decided to hold a World's Fair on the shore of Lake Michigan, with towers, high rides, exhibits, Chinese rickshaws, a midget village in which there was a midget wedding every day and other lively attractions, including whores and con men and fan dancers. There was a bit of gaiety, there was quite a lot of amoebic dysentery. Prosperity did not come back. Several millions of dollars were invested in vain by businessmen and politicians. If they could be quixotic, there was no reason why college students shouldn't be impractical too. And what was the most impractical of choices in somber, heavy, growling, low-brow Chicago? Why it was to be the representative of beauty, the interpreter of the human heart, the hero of ingenuity, playfulness, personal freedom, generosity, and love. I cannot even now say that this was a bad sort of crackpot to be.

The difference between that time and this is that in the thirties crackpots were not subsidized by their families. They had to go it alone for several years. Or at least until the New Deal (thanks largely to Harry Hopkins) recognized that a great government could *buy* the solution of any problem and opened WPA projects in many parts of the country. I think it possible that Hopkins and Roosevelt, seeing how much trouble unhappy intellectuals had made in Russia, Germany, and Italy between 1905 and 1935, thought it a bargain to pay people twenty-three dollars a week for painting post-office murals and editing guidebooks. This plan succeeded admirably. If I am not mistaken, America continued to follow the Hopkins hint in postwar Europe and perhaps in Vietnam.

I know, for instance, that John Cheever has been conducting creative writing courses at Sing Sing. Writers and criminals have often found that they had much in common. And correctional officials seem to understand, thanks to the psychology courses they take in the universities, that it is excellent therapy to write books and that it may soften the hearts of criminals to record their experiences. Politicians, too, when they fall from power or retire, become writers or university professors. Thus Hubert Humphrey and Dean Rusk became lecturers, Eugene McCarthy became a poet, and an altogether different sort of politican, Spiro Agnew, a novelist. Interviewed not long ago in the *New York Times*, Mr. Agnew said that, having suffered greatly, he felt the need to do something creative to recover his spirits, and was setting to work writing a novel because he was not yet strong enough to do serious mental work.

But I started out to recall what it was like to set oneself up to be a writer in the Midwest during the thirties. For I thought of myself as a midwesterner and not a Jew. I am often described as a Jewish writer; in much the same way one might be called a Samoan astronomer or an Eskimo cellist or a Zulu Gainsborough expert. There is some oddity about it. I am a Jew, and I have written some books. I have tried to fit my soul into the Jewish-writer category, but it does not feel comfortably accommodated there. I wonder, now and then, whether Philip Roth and Bernard Malamud and I have not become the Hart, Schaffner and Marx of our trade. We have made it in the field of culture as Bernard Baruch made it on a park bench, as Polly Adler made it in prostitution, as Two Gun Cohen, the personal bodyguard of Sun Yat-Sen, made it in China. My joke is not broad enough to cover the contempt I feel for the opportunists, wise guys, and career types who impose such labels and trade upon them. In a century so disastrous to Jews, one hesitates to criticize those who believe that they are making the world safer by publicizing Jewish achievements. I myself doubt that this publicity is effective.

I did not go to the public library to read the Talmud but the novels and poems of Sherwood Anderson, Theodore Dreiser, Edgar Lee Masters, and Vachel Lindsay. These were people who had resisted the material weight of American society and who proved—what was not immediately obvious—that the life lived in great manufacturing, shipping, and banking centers, with their slaughter stink, their great slums, prisons, hospitals, and schools, was also a human life. It appeared to me that this one thing, so intimately known that not only nerves, senses, mind, but also my very bones wanted to put it into words, might contain elements that not even Dreiser, whom I admired most, had yet reached. I felt that I was born to be a performing and interpretive creature, that I was meant to take part in a peculiar, exalted game. For there are good grounds to consider this, together with other forms of civilized behavior and ceremony, a game. At its noblest this game is played, under discipline, before God himself—so Plato said, and others as well. The game can be an offering, a celebration, an act of praise, an acknowledgment also of one's weaknesses and limitations. I couldn't have put it in this manner then. All that appeared then was a blind, obstinate impulse expressing itself in bursts of foolishness. I loved great things. I thought I had a right to think of that exalted game. I was also extremely proud, ornery, and stupid.

I was, in 1937, a very young, married man who had quickly lost his first job and who lived with his in-laws. His affectionate, loyal, and pretty wife insisted that he must be given a chance to write something. Having anyone pay attention to my writing wasn't a real possibility. I am as often bemused as amused at the attention my books have since received. Neglect would have been frightful, but attention has its disadvantages. The career of a critic, when I am feeling mean about it, I sometimes compare to that of a deaf man who tunes pianos. In a more benevolent mood I agree with my late father that people must be encouraged to make as honest a living as they can. For this reason I don't object to becoming a topic. When I visited Japan, I saw that there were prayer-and-fortune-telling papers sold for a penny at each temple. The buyers rolled up these long strips of paper and tied them by threads to bushes and low trees. From the twigs there dangled hundreds of tightly furled papers. I sometimes compare myself to one of these temple trees.

So I sat at a bridge table in a back bedroom of the apartment while all rational, serious, dutiful people were at their jobs or trying to find jobs, writing something. My table faced three cement steps that rose from the cellar into the brick gloom of a passageway. Only my mother-in-law was at home. A widow, then in her seventies, she wore a heavy white braid down her back. She had been a modern woman and a socialist and suffragette in the old country. She was attractive in a fragile, steely way. You felt Sophie's strength of will in all things. She kept a neat house. The very plants, the ashtrays, the pedestals, the doilies, the chairs, revealed her mastery. Each object had its military place. Her apartment could easily have been transferred to West Point.

Lunch occurred at half past twelve. The cooking was good. We ate together in the kitchen. The meal was followed by an interval of stone. My mother-in-law took a nap. I went into the street. Ravenswood was utterly empty. I walked about with something like a large stone in my belly. I often turned into Lawrence Avenue and stood on the bridge looking into the drainage canal. If I had been a dog I would have howled. Even a soft howl would have helped. But I was not here to howl. I was here to interpret the world (its American version) as brilliantly as possible. Still I would have been far happier selling newspapers at Union Station or practicing my shots in a poolroom. But I had a discipline to learn at the bridge table in the bedroom.

No wonder a writer of great talent and fine intelligence like John Cheever volunteers to help the convicts with their stories. He knows how it feels to be locked in. Maybe he thinks the prisoners, being already locked in, may as well learn the discipline. It is the most intolerable of privations for people whose social instincts are so highly developed that they want to write novels to be confined in rooms. Nuns fret not, perhaps, but writers do. Bernanos, the French religious novelist, said that his soul could not bear to be cut off from its kind, and that was why he did his work in cafés. Cafés indeed! I would have kissed the floor of a café. There were no cafés in Chicago. There were greasy-spoon cafeterias, one-arm joints, taverns. I never yet heard of a writer who brought his manuscripts into a tavern. I have always taken an interest in the fact that Schiller liked to smell apples when he was writing, that someone else kept his feet in a tub of water. The only person whose arrangements seemed to me worth imitating was the mystic and guru Gurdjieff. Gurdjieff, when he had work to do, set forth from headquarters in Fontainebleau with his disciples in several limousines. They carried hampers with caviar, cold fowl, champagne, cheese, and fruit. At a signal from the master the cars would stop. They would picnic in a meadow, and then, with all his followers around him, Gurdjieff did his writing. This, if it can be arranged, seems to me worth doing.

I am glad to say that I can't remember what I was writing in Ravenswood. It must have been terrible. The writing itself, however, was of no importance. The important thing was that American society and S. Bellow came face to face. I had to learn that by cutting myself off from American life in order to perform an alien task, I risked cutting myself off from everything that could nourish me. But this was the case only if you granted the monopoly of nutrients to this business-industrial, vital, brutal, proletarian, and middle-class city that was itself involved in a tremendous struggle. It was not even aggressively hostile, saying, "Lead my kind of life or die." Not at all. It simply had no interest in your sort of game.

Quite often, in the Hudson belonging to J. J., my brother-in-law, my mother-in-law and I drove to the cemetery. There we tended her husband's grave. Her trembling but somehow powerful, spotty hand pulled weeds. I made trips with a Mason jar to the faucet and made water splotches about the nasturtiums and sweet williams. Death, I thought, Chicago-style, might not be such a bad racket after all. At least you didn't have to drive down Harlem Avenue in rush hour back to the house with its West Point arrangements, with its pages of bad manuscript on the bridge table, and the silent dinner of soup and stew and strudel. After which you and your wife, washing dishes, enjoyed the first agreeable hours of the day.

J. J., my brother-in-law, born Jascha in the old country, practiced law in the Loop. He was a Republican, member of the American Legion, a golfer, a bowler; he drove his conservative car conservatively, took the *Saturday Evening Post*, he wore a Herbert Hoover starched collar, trousers short in the ankle, and a hard straw hat in summer. He spoke in a pure Hoosier twang, not like a Booth Tarkington gentleman but like a real Tippecanoe country dirt farmer. All this Americanism was imposed on an exquisitely oriental face, dark, with curved nose and Turkish cheekbones. Naturally a warm-hearted man, he frowned upon me. He thought I was doing something foreign.

There was an observable parallel between us. As I was making a writer of myself, this exotic man was transforming his dark oriental traits and becoming an American from Indiana. He spoke of Aaron Slick from Punkin' Crick, of Elmer Dub: "Ah kin read writin', but ah can't read readin'." He had served in the Army—my wife wore his 1917 overcoat (too small for me), and J. J. told old, really old, La Salle Street Republican sex jokes about Woodrow Wilson and Edith Bolling. It was common in that generation and the next to tailor one's appearance and style to what were, after all, journalistic, publicity creations, and products of caricature. The queer hunger of immigrants and their immediate descendants for true Americanism has yet to be described. It may be made to sound like fun, but I find it hard to think of anyone who underwent the process with joy. Those incompetents who lacked mimetic talent and were pure buffoons were better off—I remember a cousin, Arkady, from the old country who declared that his new name was now, and henceforth, Lake Erie. A most poetic name, he thought. In my own generation there were those immigrants who copied even the unhappiness of the Protestant majority, embracing its miseries, battling against Mom; reluctant, after work, to board the suburban train, drinking downtown, drinking on the club car, being handed down drunk to the wife and her waiting station-wagon like good Americans. These people martyred themselves in the enactment of roles that proved them genuine—just as madly wretched in marriage as Abe Lincoln and Mary Todd. Cousin Arkady, a clown who sold dehydrated applesauce on the road, giving dry applesauce demonstrations to housewives in small-town department stores, was spared the worst of it. He simply became "Archie," and made no further effort to prove himself a real American.

The point of this brief account, as I see it, is to evoke that mixture of imagination and stupidity with which people met the American Experience, that murky, heavy, burdensome, chaotic thing. I see that my own error, shared with many others, was to seek sanctuary in what corners of culture one could find in this country, there to enjoy my high thoughts and to perfect myself in the symbolic discipline of an art. I can't help feeling that I overdid it. One didn't need as much sanctuary as all that.

If I had to name the one force in America that opposes the symbolic discipline of poetry today as much as brutal philistinisms did before World War II, I would say the Great Noise. The enemy is noise. By noise I mean not simply the noise of technology, the noise of money or advertising and promotion, the noise of the media, the noise of miseducation, but the terrible excitement and distraction generated by the crises of modern life. Mind, I don't say that philistinism is gone. It is not. It has found many disguises, some highly artistic and peculiarly insidious. But the noise of life is the great threat. Contributing to it are real and unreal issues, ideologies, rationalizations, errors, delusions, nonsituations that look real, nonquestions demanding consideration, opinions, analyses in the press, on the air, expertise, inside dope, factional disagreement, official rhetoric, information—in short, the sounds of the public sphere, the din of politics, the turbulence and agitation that set in about 1914 and have now reached an intolerable volume. Nadezhda Mandelstam, writing of poets in the Soviet

> *"I'm a very determined struggler. I've always sought exposure, and never really been any good at taking cover."*

From Life, *3 April 1970, p. 60*

Union, says of the Russian noise: "Nowhere else I believe were people so much deafened as they were here by the din of life—One after another poets fell silent because they could no longer hear their own voices." She adds: "The noise drowned out thought and, in the case of millions, conscience as well."

William Wordsworth, nearly two hundred years ago, expressed his concern over the effects of modern turbulence on poetry. He was right, too. But in the language of my youth—"He didn't know the half of it."

ARTICLE:

Walter Clemons and Jack Kroll, "America's Master Novelist," *Newsweek* (1 September 1975): 32-34, 39-40.

Bellow's eighth novel brought him a Newsweek *cover story and was awarded the Pulitzer Prize. It was on the* Publishers Weekly *best-seller list for twenty-two weeks and sold more than 100,000 copies in cloth.*

Saul Bellow watches the young man with a camera who circles him, crouches and moves in for a close shot. "What the hell are you and I doing?" he asks mildly. A handsome man, 60 this year, who dislikes being photographed, Bellow is submitting to a candid session in a London hotel room. "I'm getting paid and you're getting famous," says the photographer, snapping away in his cheerful, practiced way.

"I can't get any famouser. I'm already too famous," says Bellow. Then the notion of celebrity makes the foremost American novelist burst out laughing. "When I'm stopped in the street," he says, "I'm usually asked if I'm the guy who made 'Never On Sunday'—Jules Dassin, whom I'm said to resemble."

Bellow's career has been a striking refutation of Scott Fitzgerald's remark that there are no second acts in American lives. He has not succumbed to any of the classic fates America seems to reserve for most of its major writers. He did not crack up, like Fitzgerald; he was not consumed by his own myth, like Hemingway; he did not suffer from long-delayed recognition, like Faulkner. Nor is Bellow a specimen of that other American phenomenon, the writer as show-biz personality or sudden superstar. Unlike Norman Mailer, perhaps his chief rival in sheer significance as a contemporary American writer, he has never dramatized his own persona as a major component of his art. And, unlike E. L. Doctorow, whose recent "Ragtime" has made him an instant millionaire after several well-received but non-bonanza novels, Bellow has never felt the pressures of outlandish success.

He is indeed an enormous success, complete with best sellers, prizes and honorifics, but above all he is a major artist and steadfast craftsman who has, almost miraculously, steadily matured and deepened, in book after book. Now, with the publication this week of his eighth novel, "Humboldt's Gift," he consolidates the place assigned to him by Philip Roth, who identified "the great inventors of narrative detail and masters of narrative voice and perspective" as "James, Conrad, Dostoevski and Bellow."

"Humboldt's Gift" is an exuberant comedy of success and failure, in which Bellow deals directly for the first time with the writer's life in America, including, implicitly, his own. It is his funniest book and his most openly affectionate, even in its satiric side glances. It speaks most movingly of aging and the felt loss of the sorely missed dead. It even proposes—and this will make some readers restive—a supernatural dimension beyond the crowded comic stage on which its characters collide.

The story tracks the parallel careers of two American writers. Charlie Citrine is a Pulitzer Prize historian, successful Broadway playwright, "Chevrolet" (as a Chicago gangster malaprops) of the French Legion of Honor and, in his late fifties, "a goofy chaser" of a voluptuous younger woman named Renata, whom he will be unable to keep if his ex-wife succeeds in stripping him of his money in a fang-and-claw divorce action.

The book also deals with one of the keenest American anxieties—the fear of death. Charlie keeps trim playing paddle ball at his Chicago club. But he isn't entirely reassured by his doctor's comments about "my amazingly youthful prostate and my supernormal EKG. Strengthened in illusion and idiocy by these proud medical reports, I embraced a busty Renata on [a] Posturepedic mattress."

Above all, Charlie is haunted by the death of a friend of his youth, the brilliant poet Von Humboldt Fleisher. Charlie read Humboldt's first poems in the '30s and came out of the Midwest to look him up in Greenwich Village. In Humboldt's company Charlie met the best talkers in New York. "Under their eloquence," he remembers, "I sat like a cat in a recital hall." As Humboldt's fame began to sink in the late '40s, Charlie's began to rise. Humboldt dropped dead in a seedy Times Square hotel in the '60s. Charlie now dreams of him and wakes crying with happi-

"*Humboldt's Gift* recalls the
Saul Bellow who wrote *Herzog*
(though plainly a lot has happened
to him since then).
He's once again a writer who
is fervently amused, if not obsessed,
by worldly issues—status, success,
money, and sex, and self-regard
—as they are experienced on
the lovely, hypocritical island
known as the 'American
intellectual community.'"
—RICHARD TODD
The Atlantic Monthly
487 pages. $10.00
"If there is literature
(and this proves there is)
this... is where it's at."
—JOHN CHEEVER
SAUL
BELLOW
Humboldt's
Gift
a novel
THE
VIKING PRESS

From New York Times Book Review, *24 August 1975*

ness at his memory and with regret that he dodged Humboldt the last time he saw him, wasted and stumbling down a New York street.

It's no secret that Humboldt is a loving portrait of Delmore Schwartz, whose precocious early poems prefigured the flowering of the powerful generation of poets who came to the fore in the '40s—Robert Lowell, Randall Jarrell, John Berryman. A woman who remembers Schwartz's electrifying youth says that Humboldt's talk in this novel brings him back with heartbreaking clarity. As Charlie Citrine remembers him, Humboldt was "a hectic nonstop monologist and improvisator, a champion detractor. To be loused up by Humboldt was really a kind of privilege. It was like being the subject of a two-nosed portrait by Picasso or an eviscerated chicken by Soutine."

For Citrine—and Bellow—Humboldt's rise and fall personifies the fate of the American artist who hunts glory in a hard-nosed society. Charlie reflects that "Humboldt did what poets in crass America are supposed to do. He chased ruin and death even harder than he had chased women. He blew his talent and his health and reached home, the grave, in a dusty slide . . ." America, thinks Charlie, ghoulishly enjoys this spectacle. Charlie sees the poet as the great American scapegoat, who is loved precisely because he can't make it. Poets exist, he says, to "justify the cynicism of those who say, 'If *I* were not such a corrupt, unfeeling bastard, creep, thief, and vulture, I couldn't get through this either. Look at the good and tender and soft men, the *best* of us. They succumbed, poor loonies.' "

Bellow says that "the history of literature in America is the history of certain demonic solitaries who somehow brought it off in a society that felt no need for them. In Chicago, where I grew up, we dreamed of the literary life—we were mad for it, but never got a smell of it. I went to Greenwich Village like everybody after college. It wasn't very glamorous, but I did get a feeling in New York that you weren't a bum or an outcast if you wanted to write."

Bellow is now in a position to look back on the

writer's life from the vantage point of a survivor who has never even suffered from writer's block. But he looks back without complacency. "I feel I've fallen short of my talents," he says. "Always—in this new book, too. And I've fought inertia in myself. Charlie in 'Humboldt's Gift' feels he's snoozed through his life, missing the significance of the great events of his time. I've fallen short of full wakefulness too. I've struggled with torpor."

Bellow himself is intolerant of the shortcomings he sees in his early work. "In 'The Victim' I was very much under the spell of Dostoevski's 'The Eternal Husband.' In 'Augie March' I got stuck in a Sherwood Anderson ingénue vein: here are all those people and isn't life wonderful! By the last third of the book I wasn't feeling that way any more. I've always thought that the germ of a novel is found in the first few pages. You start a certain way because it's liberating, and before you're through you find it inhibiting. I didn't know what to do with those inhibitions in the last third of 'Augie March,' and I can't bear to reread it. I can reread 'Henderson the Rain King' with pleasure. I reread 'Herzog' two or three times a year—looking, mind you, for goofs I made."

With the confidence born of a mastery that few American writers have achieved, Bellow sees very few goofs in "Humboldt's Gift." "The nice thing about this book," he explains, "which I was really struggling with in 'Herzog,' is that I've really come into a cold air of objectivity about all the people in the book, including Charlie. It really came easily for me to see him as America saw him, and thereby America itself became clearer." It seems clear that Bellow is talking about himself as well as Charlie. When he says, "Charlie is a very funny fellow, isn't he?" Bellow is ratifying the comic muse as the chief agent of his vision and mastery.

For Saul Bellow is a very funny fellow—like such other funny fellows as Gogol, Dickens and Mark Twain. Philip Roth put it nicely when he referred to Bellow as "closing the gap, as it were, between Damon Runyon and Thomas Mann." Bellow himself refers to his method offhandedly as "kidding my way to Jesus." Precisely because he is basically pessimistic about the drift of things, Bellow knows the liberating power of comedy. " 'Humboldt'," he says, "is very much a comic book about death." Then he adds: "I'm going to have my knuckles rapped for this book. There's this lady who says to Charlie Citrine, 'You're laughing and kidding and having a wonderful time, but life will come crush you like an empty beer can.' Well, that was actually said to me by a very tough, existential lady who's a critic. She's the type who, if she got some handsome young man to sleep with her, would rake his face with her fingernails, just to prove an existential point."

Bellow autographing copies of Humboldt's Gift *in 1975*

Born in Lachine, Canada, in 1915, the youngest of four children of Russian immigrants, Bellow moved with his family to Chicago when he was 9. A friend of those days, Dave Peltz, remembers Solomon Bellows, known as "Solly"—he dropped the "s" from his surname and took the name Saul when he began to publish—as the outstanding member of a group of Tuley High School friends who dreamed of someday becoming famous writers.

Every Friday night, these precocious Chicago kids went to the Mission House in the tattered multi-ethnic neighborhood around Humboldt Park—a name possibly reflected in the title of Bellow's new book. Dave Peltz remembers these sessions well. "Anyone could get up and speak, and we'd sit and listen while they argued politics and religion." Solly Bellows was the most precocious of the lot—a good runner on the track team, a fair swimmer, middling tennis player, but a remarkable writer even then. Sam Freifeld, now a Chicago attorney, recalls that Solly was fond of reading his work out loud among friends. In the back leaf of a copy of Oscar Wilde's poems, Bellows and his friends scribbled the titles of books they would someday write, copping their favorite lines from Wilde's verse. Solly was particularly fond of the phrase, "Black leaves whirling in the wind," which he thought would make a terrific book title.

Peltz, who now owns a home-improvement company in Gary, Ind., lunches with his boyhood friend once a week. "Last week he gave me Diderot's 'Rameau's Nephew' to read," says Peltz. "I don't have time to educate myself in literary matters. So he feeds me the proper material and when I finish it we discuss it. And I bring him something different. My work takes me into all kinds of neighborhoods. I tell Saul stories that help keep him connected."

Bellow still draws on the raffish Chicago scene for such "connections." In a poker game with novelist Nelson Algren, columnist Studs Terkel and two underworld characters, Peltz lost heavily, was advised by Terkel not to pay and promptly got two cement blocks through the windows of his home and a threat on his life. "I paid up," says Peltz. From this incident came Charlie Citrine's encounter in "Humboldt's Gift" with the exquisite mobster Ronald Cantabile, one of Bellow's great comic creations.

The father of three sons by his first three marriages, Bellow lives quietly in Chicago with his fourth wife, Alexandra, a beautiful Romanian-born mathematician who teaches at Northwestern University. He plays racquet ball at a local athletic club but shuns the Chicago literary community. "Saul is not a pop character," says Peltz. "He enjoys a couple of drinks before dinner, a quiet meal and a glass of brandy afterwards. He prefers to sit in civilized circumstances." Some think Bellow's withdrawn life is eccentric, and Freifeld, who had a falling-out with Bellow while representing him in one of his three divorces, avows that "Saul Bellow is a great artist but a lousy friend." The complex truth was probably best summed up by Bellow himself when he told the lawyer: "I know you think I'm a square, Freifeld, but there's no name for the shape I'm in."

Bellow has been on the faculty of the University of Chicago since 1962, as a member of the Committee on Social Thought. This is a flexibly organized department that accepts only 25 to 30 students a year. "It was designed to break the academic lockstep, to free students from required courses, to allow more independent-minded work," explains sociologist Edward Shils. As a member of the committee, and its chairman since 1970, Bellow is not a mere ornamental writer-in-residence. Last year he taught tutorials on the novel from Defoe to Joyce and this fall he will be teaching Tolstoy's shorter works.

Bellow, who got a B.S. in anthropology and sociology from Northwestern in 1937, has had what he calls "intellectual romances" with various ideologies—Marxism in his youth, Reichian psychology later. But he has been conspicuously apolitical in a period when many of his fellow artists have taken strong activist positions. The most celebrated occasion was President Johnson's 1965 White House arts festival, which the poet Robert Lowell declined to attend, citing his disagreement with the Administration's Vietnam policy. Twenty leading artists and writers signed a telegram supporting Lowell's position; Bellow and John Hersey wouldn't sign. "The President intends, in his own way, to encourage American artists," Bellow's statement read. "I consider this event to be an official function, not a political occasion . . . I accept in order to show my respect for [the President's] intentions and to honor his high office." The statement won him few friends; some of his colleagues harshly accused him of having lost touch with history.

But Bellow's position is more complex than that. "What man with his eyes open at this hour could not be interested in politics?" he says. "I only wish people talked about it at a deeper level than Chappaquiddick or Scoop Jackson or who's-gonna-get-the-nomination. I don't think we know where we are or where we're going. I see politics—ultimately—as a buzzing preoccupation that swallows up art and the life of the spirit."

The life of the spirit is very much on his mind these days. Some early readers of "Humboldt's Gift" have been startled by Charlie Citrine's espousement of anthroposophy, the creed of the early twentieth-century occultist thinker Rudolf Steiner, who believed in the transmigration of souls and opposed the dominant scientific view of the universe. How seriously are we meant to take these passages in the novel? Answer: very seriously indeed. Bellow discovered Steiner through a book called "Saving the Appearances" by Owen Barfield, a remarkable British writer who now lives in retirement in Kent after a long career as a lawyer. One of the main purposes of Bellow's trip to England this summer was to talk with Barfield.

The self-destructive genius Von Humboldt Fleisher was modeled on poet Delmore Schwartz.

For Bellow, Barfield's work represents a vigorous claim for the importance of poetic imagination. "Read 'Saving the Appearances,' " he says, "and then Rudolf Steiner's little book on theosophy—your hair will stand on end! I was impressed by the idea that there were forms of understanding, discredited now, which had long been the agreed basis of human knowledge. We think we can know the world scientifically, but actually our ignorance is terrifying."

When he discusses these matters, Bellow's face lights up with youthful enthusiasm. Like Charlie Citrine, who receives a message left behind by his deceased friend Humboldt: "Remember: we are not natural beings but supernatural beings," Bellow in this most openhearted of his novels embraces, at least as an imaginative possibility, the notion that "*this* could not be *it* . . . We had all been here before and I would presently be here again."

A surprising turn in the thinking of a worldly Chicagoan who has tasted his share of the satisfactions of the here-and-now. But the forms of "successful" life in the American here-and-now prove illusory in "Humboldt's Gift." Charlie Citrine, on the one hand, realizes late in the day that he has slept through most of his life: "I have always had an exceptional gift for passing out," says Charlie. "I look at snapshots taken in some of the most evil hours of mankind and I see that I have lots of hair and am appealingly youthful. I am wearing an ill-fitting double-breasted suit of the Thirties or Forties, smoking a pipe, standing under a tree, holding hands with a plump and pretty bimbo—and I am asleep on my feet, out cold. I have snoozed through many a crisis (while millions died)."

Still more insidious than Charlie's lethargy is Humboldt's reaching for the high-voltage wire of fame, of being *someone*. Bellow's voice softens with regret when he speaks not only of destroyed poets who were his friends, but of Marilyn Monroe, with whom he was acquainted when she was married to Arthur Miller: "I always felt she had picked up some high-tension cable and couldn't release it," he says. "She couldn't rest, she found no repose in anything. She was up in the night, taking pills and talking about her costumes, her next picture, contracts and money, gossip. In the case of a beautiful and sensitive creature like that, it was a guarantee of destruction."

There's been nothing remotely comparable to that in Bellow's own life. But he wryly describes a recent White House dinner he watched from the sidelines. "I was not there as a celebrity, only as a marginal retainer," he says. "But I watched the celebrities falling into each other's arms—Kissinger and Danny Kaye in a tight embrace. The only people who behaved decently were those like Margaret Truman who had recovered their humanity or never lost it. The others, their eyes wildly rolling at other celebrities, you couldn't hold their attention when you talked to them. What was I doing there? Neither Hubert Humphrey nor Nelson Rockefeller function as I function. The common ground I could find with them would be *their* common ground, if by some mighty, transcendent act of imagination I could project myself there, alongside them."

As the most honored American novelist of his age, Saul Bellow now enters a dangerous period, of which he is cannily aware: "Many American writers cross the bar in their 60s and 70s," he says, "and become Grand Old Men, gurus or bonzes of the Robert Frost variety. This is how society eases us out. Sees us off on the immortal train, with waving and cheering and nobody listening. Just as well, because there's nothing but bombast coming from the rear platform. If I last long enough, I assume this will happen to me too. And then there are two possibilities. Either you've run out of imagination, in which case you're ready to be puffed up, held down like a barrage balloon by the cables before you float off into eternity. Or your imagination keeps cooking, in which case you're lucky. You're among the blessed. No man knows which way he's gonna go. He can only hope."

At 60, Saul Bellow is not ready to be puffed up, held down, or floated off. Instead he makes us the gift of a masterly novel—wise, challenging and radiant.

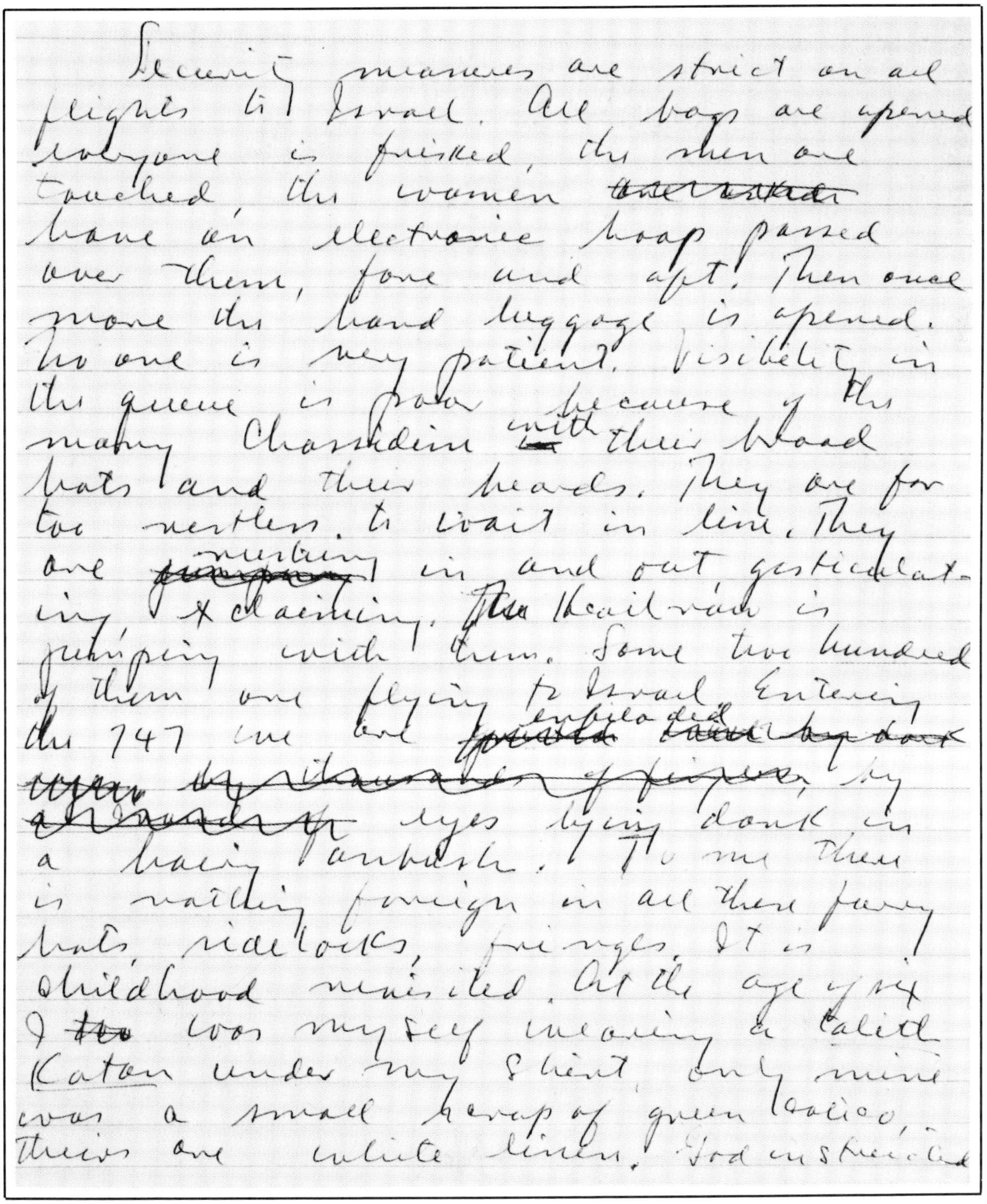

Security measures are strict on all flights to Israel. All bags are opened everyone is frisked, the men are touched the women have an electronic hoop passed over them, fore and aft! Then once more the hand luggage is opened. No one is very patient. Visibility in the queue is poor because of the many Chassidim with their broad hats and their beards. They are far too restless to wait in line. They are rushing in and out gesticulating & claiming. The [illegible] is jumping with them. Some two hundred of them are flying to Israel. Entering the 747 we are enfiladed by eyes lying dark in a hairy ambush. To me there is nothing foreign in all these furry hats, sidelocks, fringes. It is childhood revisited. At the age of six I ~~too~~ was myself wearing a talith katan under my shirt, only mine was a small scrap of green calico, theirs are white linen. God instructed

A manuscript page for Bellow's "book of conversations," To Jerusalem and Back *(1976)*

INTERVIEW:

Joseph Epstein, "A Talk with Saul Bellow," *New York Times Book Review*, 5 December 1976, pp. 3, 92, 93.

Bellow was the first American writer to win the Nobel Prize since John Steinbeck in 1962: "I knew Steinbeck quite well. And I remember how burdened he was by the Nobel Prize . . . I think it made him quite wretched. I hope it isn't going to make me wretched. But then I'm a more cynical character."

JOSEPH EPSTEIN: Noel, Nobel. The New York Times Book Review has asked me to interview you for its special Christmas Books issue. The mood is supposed to be celebratory, both of the season and, more important, of your having won the Nobel Prize for Literature. But I thought the occasion might be better used to ask you to formulate answers to some questions I have about your literary career and the Nobel Prize.

SAUL BELLOW: Well, you are not Eckermann, I am not Goethe, and this, our City of Chicago, is most distinctly not Weimar. But let's go ahead anyway. Shoot.

J. E.: What is the importance of praise to a writer? What, to you, is the best kind of praise?

S. B.: I think the answer is perhaps best put in an American context, for the question of praise is a trickier one here than in other countries, especially in countries where there is a literary establishment that is in a position to confer praise. In the United States, though, it is either feast or famine: one is either totally ignored, which is damaging, or becomes the center of attention, which is almost always unreal. Here it is the media which confer praise; and I think it is fair to say that the media aren't interested in literature but in publicity, in celebrity, in filling the space and killing the time allotted to them.

For myself, I have no reason to complain. I have had my share—and even more than my share—of recognition; and of all kinds and coming from all quarters. I think—I hope—I have received enough praise to have weaned myself away from the need for it. By now I think I have a clear enough eye to know both how good and how bad I am as a writer.

As for the second of your questions, the best praise I have had came from the young men with whom I started out in Chicago, most of whom are now dead. In particular I was much moved by the praise of my friend Isaac Rosenfeld, who was of course not only himself an estimable writer but who went out of his way to praise "Augie March," to tell me how significant he thought it was. His praise was, and shall always remain, very special to me.

J. E.: What, I wonder, would you have felt, especially after all the stories about your last year being a close runner-up to Montale, if you had been passed over for the Nobel Prize this year?

S. B.: Last year, after a momentary feeling of disappointment, I felt rather relieved that Montale won the prize. As I said, I have gotten a great deal of recognition, and I like to think I wouldn't have minded if I had been passed over. Perhaps this is the calm hindsight of a winner speaking, perhaps not.

One of the things one fails to realize till one has won it is that the Nobel Prize for Literature has many extra-literary aspects. Winning it makes you an eminent person; it gives you certain kinds of power. I have never had much taste for the power that goes with eminence.

As usual, there is the comic side. Journalists are fond of pointing out to me all the great writers who do not win a Nobel: Tolstoy, Proust, James, Joyce. They ask how it feels to be among the company of such distinguished literary figures as Sully-Prudhomme, Carl Spitteler, Wladyslaw S. Reymont, and Halldór K. Laxness. It causes me to scramble to remember that some pretty fair figures did win the Nobel Prize, among them Yeats, Mann, Eliot, Camus.

J. E.: As a writer who has shown himself fully alive to the world's status comedy, how do you think your own rise in status, as a Nobel Prize winner, will affect both your view of yourself and the day-to-day conduct of your life?

S. B.: One thing you may count on, and this is that I am not about to start thinking of myself as Saul Bellow who won the Nobel Prize for Literature for 1976. I am too old and canny for that. Moreover, I don't think that what recognition I have won thus far has turned my head; at least I hope it hasn't.

The worst fear I have as a writer is that of losing my feeling for the common life, which is, as every good writer knows, or should know, anything but common. To think of oneself as a Nobel Prize winner is finally to think of oneself as an enameled figurine in a China cabinet, and I don't intend to find myself in a China cabinet.

One of the things of interest about becoming a laureate is to note the attempt at exploitation of the Prize by institutions and the media. For a time the telephone here didn't stop ringing with offers: to accept honorary degrees, to go on talk shows, to make statements of one kind or another. A downtown club here in Chicago even offered me a free membership. We ought to go there one evening for dinner with our wives, order an enormous dinner, and not pay the bill.

One becomes aware of how many cultural promoters there are in this country: men and women whose job it is to drag you to the podium, to hold you tight while you are being photographed, propping you up like a corpse in a coffin. As a Nobel Prize winner one could become, if one is not careful, a cultural functionary, to be trundled out in honorific robes whenever the occasion requires. I wish I had the coldness, or strength of character, or whatever it takes, to turn my back on the publicity connected with the Nobel Prize, as Samuel Beckett has done. But I apparently do not. Instead when I am made an offer I usually just say thank you very much.

J. E.: Do you look forward to the award of the Nobel Prize increasing the size of the audience for your books? This might be a good place, too, to clear the air on the subject of your once supposedly calling yourself a "large-public" as opposed to a "small-public" writer.

S. B.: I truly do not know if the Nobel Prize brings a writer more readers. I do know that, as E. E. Cummings once put it, I would rather have "better than more readers." I am grateful to learn that someone has taken the time and trouble to read my books. Yet I am sometimes also a bit depressed when someone who has read something I have written comes up to me to ask "What does it mean?" As if a novel were a puzzle, or a code, to which only the author and certain highly erudite readers had the key. Such a response shows the rather demoralizing effect of the teaching of literature in our universities. But if the Prize should bring me more readers, and among those additional readers are better readers, then I should be most pleased, though, as I say, I am not at all sure that winning the Nobel Prize has such an effect.

On the question of "large-public" and "small-public" writers, the distinction, which is a useful one, was originally made by Wyndham Lewis, who noted that in the middle of the 19th century writers of great power—among them Dickens, Tolstoy, Dostoyevsky—wrote and seemed to be understood by a large public, whereas later in the 19th century and early in the 20th century a different kind of writer, no less of a genius but with something odd and difficult about him—Rilke, Joyce, Proust, Mallarmé are examples—appeared, though the difficulty of such writers made them perforce writers for a "small public." I grew up under the influence of these small-public writers. I revered them then, and in many respects continue to revere them now. But in an interview in The New York Times of some months ago, a reporter garbled the distinction badly, making me sound as if I thought myself a large-public writer and as if there was, in my view, something degrading about being a small-public writer. Of course, I neither think nor intended anything of the kind.

Which is not to say that I, along with every writer, do not want as large an audience as possible, but there are limits to such a desire. I want to be read on my own terms, which are small-public terms—to be, in my books, as odd, difficult, idiosyncratic as I need to be in order to get said what I feel needs to be said.

J. E.: Some time ago you remarked that you thought yourself a most fortunate man, because when you published a novel 50,000 people bought it in cloth covers, 5,000 people read it through, and 300 people reacted to it. Do those figures still apply? Or do they now need to be revised upwards?

S. B.: Perhaps this is a question better answered by an agent, or statistician, or literary accountant. But if pressed for an answer, I should say that the figures probably do need to be revised upward. I think I nowadays get more response from unknown readers than I used to get. Many of these letters are very penetrating; not all are completely approving, but then I am not completely approving of myself. In recent years, I would say that I have learned more from these letters than I have from formal criticism of my work. So many current critics—you can fill in the names for yourself—remind me of nothing so much as the figure of the man who steps to center stage with his thumbs looped in his suspenders, giving off an air of tremendous confidence, as if to say, "I've got the poop." Well, as I see it, he doesn't have the poop, just the suspenders.

> *"A radical stance is the ultimate luxury for those who already have everything else."*

From Life, *3 April 1970, p. 58*

But my view is that a writer should reach as many people as possible—not with a message but with a point of view arising from his freedom as a writer, the nonpartisanship of his heart, and the happy responsibilities of the imagination. When it is going well a novel affords the highest kind of truth; a good writer can lay claim to a disinterestedness that is as great as that of a pure scientist—when he is going well. In its complicated, possibly even mysterious, way, the novel is an instrument for delving into human truths.

J. E.: Do you imagine a perfect reader for your novels?

S. B.: Well, I do not start out assuming that I am *sui generis*. What I think I might have, apart from the techniques that I have learned about my craft over the years, is a certain clairvoyance about discovering issues, questions, problems before they are seen by most others—sometimes in a general, sometimes in a quite particular way. After publishing "Herzog," for example, I was interested to learn that all sorts of people wrote letters to the famous that they never sent, a la Moses Herzog. More generally, I find that the things that agitate, confuse and sometimes indeed frighten me about our time, agitate, confuse and frighten a great many others. As a novelist, it is a good part of my job to attempt to formulate, as dramatically and as precisely as I can, the pain and anguish that we all feel. Now more than ever, it seems to me, it becomes the writer's job to remind people of their common stock of emotion, of their common humanity—of the fact, if you will, that they have souls.

J. E.: One of the comforts of winning a Nobel Prize, I should think, is that you might now feel more free to compare your work with that of important writers of the past without seeming altogether vain in doing so. In this regard, will the winning of the prize in any way affect your work?

S. B.: To begin with, it is a cold comfort, if I may say so. The truth is, even though I have been at it for nearly four decades, I have always felt myself, as a writer, to be an apprentice or journeyman. Although I hope my books have given off greater reverberations than are perhaps to be found on their pages, I nonetheless feel that I have exercised my imagination on certain private kinds of people—with working out obsessions about people I loved who are now dead.

But now certain things have intervened to change my interests. In the book I recently did on Israel I discovered that it was as easy to write about great public matters as about private ones. All it required was more confidence and daring. Possibly the award of the Nobel Prize has, in an indirect way, bolstered that confidence further. Whatever the reasons, I feel it is time to write about people who make a more spirited resistance to the forces of our time. (True, they sometimes go under, such people, but that is another matter.) I am not saying that, as a novelist, I have suddenly become superambitious. Not at all. What I am saying is that I think that it is time for me to move on now.

J. E.: With a small handful of exceptions, I think it fair to say that the novel today does not generate the kind of excitement that it once did among intelligent readers. Is the writing of novels nowadays more difficult, or is it that our novelists are less good?

S. B.: I think it is hard to judge talent in a situation that is itself so difficult. It is harder for a novelist to cast his spell over a reality that is so convulsive as ours is at present. We're going through an interregnum at present, a terrible time of impatience. People are unquestionably more troubled, agonized, less certain of themselves. They are not only often without kindness but actively wickeder to one another. The cost of real virtue has gone up. Instead we have the false virtue of phony liberalism. In the midst of this one turns to the novelist and says: "Well, Bud, what have you got to say about this?" It's not to be wondered at if the novelistic imagination isn't often up to it. Besides, most novelists are little different than most people: they refuse to think things through anew but prefer instead to do the same old things in the same old way. But to answer your question: I am not sure if novelists today are less good than they once were—there has always been a great number of bad writers in the world—but I am sure that, the situation being what it is, they have to be very good indeed to make legitimate claims upon the attention of a public so deeply stirred and agitated.

J. E.: On more than one occasion, I have heard you refer to yourself as not a novelist but as a "historian of society." Could you elaborate a bit upon what that term means to you?

S. B.: I think of myself as a historian of society in that I cannot exceed what I see. I am bound, in other words, as the historian is bound by the period he writes about, by the situation I live in. I blame myself for not often enough seeing the extraordinary in the ordinary. Somewhere in his journals Dostoyevsky remarks that a writer can begin anywhere, at the most commonplace thing, scratch around in it long enough, pry and dig away long enough, and, lo!, soon he will hit upon the marvelous. I tend to believe that, at least most of the time.

Whether he is conscious of it or not, I think that every modern novelist has a theory of history. I think that I have, till recently, held for the most part to modernist assumptions about history. It is only recently that it has begun to occur to me that in fact we did not live with these assumptions, and that we were deeply moved by others. Therefore, I have begun to think of shucking these old assumptions off. At the moment that leaves me a historian of society without a theory of history.

J. E.: A great many of your readers were left confused about the emergence of interest in the work of Rudolf Steiner shown in your last novel. Many people who, I suspect, have never read Steiner, as I have not read Steiner, have been able to score rather easy points by remarking on the "vapidities of Rudolf Steiner" and taking other, similar cheap shots. But I wonder if your interest in such matters does not reflect an interest in the higher and wider questions: the design of the universe, the origin of evil, the origin (as mysterious, I should think) of goodness, and so forth. Do such questions occupy your thoughts more than they once did?

S. B.: I think people were confused by seeing Rudolf Steiner's work pop up in a novel a good part of which was comic in intent. I do admit to being intrigued with Steiner. I do not know enough to call myself a Steinerian. The college professor in me wants to administer a quick quiz to those who knock him to see whether they have done their homework. I think it enough for now to say that

In 1962 Bellow joined the University of Chicago Committee on Social Thought, which he chaired 1970-1976. He is the Raymond W. and Martha Hilpert Gruner Distinguished Service Professor and teaches tutorials in literature.

Rudolf Steiner had a great vision and was a powerful poet as well as philosopher and scientist.

When I was a child I read the Bible, when older I read Plato, St. Augustine and Dante. Should I, as an adult, erase all traces of this reading? Is it kid stuff compared with, say, R. D. Laing and The Village Voice? I am moved to take Plato, et al. seriously. I hope I will be forgiven if I choose not to see this as a sign that I am slipping.

J. E.: Shall we stop here?

S. B.: Let's. Before we weigh down too many Christmas stockings.

J. E.: Merry Christmas to all.

S. B.: And to all a good night.

SPEECH:

Saul Bellow, *Nobel Lecture* (New York: Targ Editions, 1979).

The Swedish Academy cited Bellow for portraying "a man who keeps on trying to find a foothold during his wanderings in a tottering world, one who can never relinquish his faith that the value of life depends on dignity, not its success, and that truth must triumph at last."

I was a very contrary undergraduate more than forty years ago. One semester I registered for a course in "Money and Banking" and then concentrated my reading in the novels of Joseph Conrad. I have never had reason to regret this. Perhaps Conrad appealed to me because he was like an American, speaking French and writing English with extraordinary power and beauty—he was an uprooted Pole sailing exotic seas. Nothing could seem more natural to me, the child of immigrants who grew up in one of Chicago's immigrant neighborhoods, than a Slav who was a British sea captain and knew his way around Marseilles. In England he was wonderfully exotic. H. G. Wells warned Ford Madox Ford, with whom Conrad collaborated in the writing of several novels, not to spoil Conrad's "Oriental style." He was valued for his oddity. But Conrad's *real* life had little oddity in it. His themes were straightforward—fidelity, the traditions of the sea, hierarchy, command, the fragile rules sailors follow when they are struck by a typhoon. He believed in the strength of these fragile-seeming rules. He also believed in his art. He stated in the preface to *The Nigger of the Narcissus* that art was an attempt to render the highest justice to the visible universe: it tried to find in that universe, in matter as well as in the facts of life, what was fundamental, enduring, essential. The writer's method of attaining the essential was different from that of the thinker or the scientist, who knew the world by systematic examination. To begin with, the artist had only himself; he descended within himself and in the lonely regions to which he descended he found "the terms of his appeal." He appealed, said Conrad, "to that part of our being which is a gift, not an acquisition, to the capacity for delight and wonder . . . our sense of pity and pain, to the latent feeling of fellowship with all creation—and to the subtle but invincible conviction of solidarity that knits together the loneliness of innumerable hearts . . . which binds together all humanity—the dead to the living and the living to the unborn."

This fervent statement was written some eighty years ago and we may want to take it with a few grains of contemporary salt. I belong to a generation of readers who knew the long list of noble or noble-sounding words, words such as "invincible conviction" or "humanity" rejected by writers like Ernest Hemingway. Hemingway spoke for the soldiers who fought in the First World War under the inspiration of Woodrow Wilson and other orotund statesmen whose big words had to be measured against the frozen corpses of young men paving the trenches. Hemingway's youthful readers were convinced that the horrors of the Twentieth Century with their deadly radiations had sickened and killed humanistic beliefs. I told myself therefore that Conrad's rhetoric must be resisted: resisted, not rejected, for I never thought him mistaken. He spoke directly to me. The feeling individual appeared weak—he felt only his own weakness. But if he accepted his weakness and his separateness and descended into himself intensifying his loneliness, he discovered his solidarity with other isolated creatures.

I feel no need now to sprinkle Conrad's sentences with skeptical salt. But there are writers for whom the Conradian novel—all novels of that sort—has become invalid. Finished. There is, for instance, M. Alain Robbe-Grillet, one of the leaders of French literature, a spokesman for "thingism"—*choseisme*. In an essay called "On Several Obsolete Notions" he writes that in great contemporary works, Sartre's *Nausea*, Camus' *The Stranger*, Kafka's *The Castle*, there are no characters; you find in such books not individuals, merely entities. "The novel of characters," he says, "belongs entirely in the past. It describes a period: that which marked the apogee of the individual." This is not necessarily an improvement; that Robbe-Grillet admits. But it is the truth. Individuals have been wiped out. "The present period is rather one of administrative numbers. The world's destiny has ceased, for us, to be identified with the rise and fall of certain men of certain families." He goes on to say that in the days of Balzac's bourgeoisie it was important to have a name and a character; character was a weapon in the struggle for survival and success. In that time, "It was something to have a face in a universe where personality represented both the means and the end of all exploration." Our world, he concludes, is more modest. It has renounced the omnipotence of the person. But it is more ambitious as well, "since it looks beyond. The exclusive cult of the 'human' has given way to a larger consciousness, one that is less anthropocentric." However, he offers in comfort a new course and the promise of new discoveries before us.

On an occasion like this I have no appetite for polemics. We all know what it is to be tired of "characters." Human types have become false and boring. D. H. Lawrence put it early in the century that we human beings, our instincts damaged by Puritanism, no longer care for—worse, had become physically repulsive to one another. "The sympathetic heart is broken," he said. "We stink in each other's nostrils." Besides, in Europe the power of the classics has for centuries been so great that every country has its "identifiable personalities" derived from Moliere, Racine, Dickens, or Balzac. An awful

Saul Bellow won the 1976 Nobel Prize in Literature. He is shown with other Nobel laureates; left to right: Burton Richter (physics), Carleton D. Gajdusek (medicine), William Lipscomb (chemistry), Bellow, Samuel C. Ting (physics), Milton Friedman (economics), and Baruch S. Blumberg (medicine).

phenomenon. Perhaps this is connnected with the wonderful French saying, *"S'il y a un caractère, il est mauvais."* It makes one think that the unoriginal human race tends to borrow what it needs from sources already at hand, much as new cities have often been made from the rubble of old ones. The viewpoint is perhaps confirmed by the psychoanalytic conception of character—that it is an ugly rigid formation, something to be resigned to, nothing to be embraced with joy. Totalitarian ideologies, too, have attacked individualism, sometimes identifying character with property. There is a hint of this in M. Robbe-Grillet's argument. Rejection of personality, bad masks, boring forms of being, have had political results.

But this is not my subject, what I am interested in here is the question of the artist's priorities. Is it necessary or even desirable that he begin with historical analyses, with ideas or systems? Proust speaks in *Time Regained* of a growing preference among young and intelligent readers for works of an elevated, analytical, moral or sociological tendency—for writers who seem to them more profound, "But," says Proust, "from the moment that works of art are judged by reasoning, nothing is stable or certain, one can prove anything one likes."

The message of Robbe-Grillet is not new. It tells us that we must purge ourselves of bourgeois anthropocentrism and do the classy things that our advanced culture requires. Character? "Fifty years of disease, the death notice signed many times over by the serious essayists," says Robbe-Grillet, "yet nothing has managed to knock it off the pedestal on which the Nineteenth Century had placed it. It is a mummy now, but one still enthroned with the same—phony—majesty, among the values revered by traditional criticism."

Like most of us, I share Robbe-Grillet's objection to the mummies of all kinds we carry about with us, but I never tire of reading the master novelists. Can anything as vivid as the characters in their books be dead? Can it be that human beings are at an end? Is individuality really so dependent on historical and cultural conditions? Is the account of those conditions we are so "authoritatively" given by writers and psychologists to be accepted? I suggest that it is not in the intrinsic interest of human beings but in these ideas and accounts that the problem lies. It is the staleness and inadequacy of the ideas that repels us. To find the source of trouble we must look into our own heads.

The fact that the death notice of charcter "has been signed by the most serious essayists" means only that another group of mummies—certain respectable leaders of the intellectual community—has laid down the law. It amuses me that these serious essayists should be empowered to sign the death notice of a literary form. Should art follow "culture"? Something has gone wrong.

A novelist should be free to drop "character" if such a strategy stimulates him. But it is nonsense to make such a decision on the theoretical ground that the period which marked the apogee of the individual, etc., is ended. We must not permit intellectuals to become our bosses. And we do them no good by letting them run the arts. Should they, when they read novels, find in them only the endorsement of their own opinions? Are we here to play such games?

Characters, Elizabeth Bowen once said, are not created by writers. They pre-exist and they have to be *found*. If we do not find them, if we fail to represent them, the fault is ours. It must be admitted, however, that finding them is not easy. The condition of human beings has perhaps never been more difficult to define. Those who tell us that we are in an early stage of universal history must be right. We are being lavishly poured together and seem to be experiencing the anguish of new states of consciousness. In America millions of people have in the last forty years received a "higher education"—often a dubious blessing. In the upheavals of the Sixties we felt for the first time the effects of up-to-date teachings, concepts, sensitivities, the pervasiveness of psychological, pedagogical, political ideas.

Every year we see scores of books and articles by writers who tell Americans what a state they are in. All reflect the current crises; all tell us what we must do about them—these analysts are produced by the very disorder and confusion they prescribe for. It is as a novelist that I am considering the extreme moral sensitivity of our contemporaries, their desire for perfection, their intolerance of the defects of society, the touching, the comical boundlessness of their demands, their anxiety, their irritability, their sensitivity, their tender-mindedness, their goodness, their convulsiveness, the recklessness with which they experiment with drugs and touch-therapies and bombs. The ex-Jesuit Malachi Martin in his book on the Church compares the modern American to Michelangelo's sculpture, *The Captive*. He sees "an unfinished struggle to emerge whole" from a block of matter. The American "captive" is beset in his struggle by "interpretations, admonitions, forewarnings and de-

"*. . . there are places, people, houses and women with whom I have a feeling of renewing very old antecedent relations. It's a sort of* déjà vu *when something about the light, the moisture, the plants or the color of stones gives me the sense of renewing an old and valuable connection—the Yiddish word is* angenehm. *The new not only recollects but* becomes *the old*."

From Life, *3 April 1970, p. 59*

scriptions of himself by the self-appointed prophets, priests, judges and prefabricators of his travail," says Martin.

If we take a little time to look more closely at this travail, what do we see? In private life, disorder or near-panic. In families—for husbands, wives, parents, children—confusion; in civic behavior, in personal loyalties, in sexual practices (I will not recite the whole list; we are tired of hearing it)—further confusion. It is with this private disorder and public bewilderment that we try to live. We stand open to all anxieties. The decline and fall of everything is our daily dread, we are agitated in private life and tormented by public questions.

And art and literature—what of them? Well, there is a violent uproar but we are not absolutely dominated by it. We are still able to think, to discriminate, and to feel. The purer, subtler, higher activities have not succumbed to fury or to nonsense. Not yet. Books continue to be written and read. It may be more difficult to cut through the whirling mind of a modern reader but it is still possible to reach the quiet zone. In the quiet zone we novelists may find that he is devoutly waiting for us. When complications increase, the desire for essentials increases too. The unending cycle of crises that began with the First World War has formed a kind of person, one who has lived through strange and terrible things, and in whom there is an observable shrinkage of prejudices, a casting off of disappointing ideologies, an ability to live with many kinds of madness, and an immense desire for certain durable human goods—truth, for instance; freedom, wisdom. I don't think I am exaggerating; there is plenty of evidence for this. Disintegration? Well, yes. Much is disintegrating but we are experiencing also an odd kind of refining process. And this has been going on for a long time. Looking into Proust's *Time Regained* I find that he was clearly aware of it. His novel, describing French society during the Great War, tests the strength of his art. Without an art that shirks no personal or collective horrors, he insists, we do not know ourselves or anyone else. Only art penetrates what pride, passion, intelligence and habit erect on all sides—the seeming realities of this world. There is another reality, the genuine one, which we lose sight of. This other reality is always sending us hints, which, without art, we can't receive. Proust calls these hints our "true impressions." The true impressions, our persistent intuitions, will, without art, be hidden from us and we will be left with nothing but a "terminology for practical ends which we falsely call life."

Proust was still able to keep a balance between art and destruction, insisting that art was a necessity of life, a great independent reality, a magical power. For a long time art has not been connected, as it was in the past, with the main human enterprise. Hegel long ago observed that art no longer engaged the central energies of man. These energies were now engaged by science—a "relentless spirit of rational inquiry." Art had moved to the margins. There it formed "a wide and splendidly varied horizon." In an age of science people still painted and wrote poetry but, said Hegel, however splendid the gods looked in modern works of art and whatever dignity and perfection we might find "in the images of God the Father and the Virgin Mary" it was of no use: we no longer bent our knees. It is a long time since the knees were bent in piety. Ingenuity, daring exploration, freshness of invention replaced the art of "direct relevance." The most significant achievement of this pure art, in Hegel's view, was that, freed from its former responsibilities, it was no longer "serious." Instead, it raised the soul through the "serenity of form above and painful involvement in the limitations of reality." I don't know who would make such a claim today for an art that raises the soul above painful involvements with reality. Nor am I sure that at this moment, it is the spirit of rational inquiry in pure science that engages the central energies of man. the center seems (even though temporarily) to be filled with the crises I have been describing.

There were European writers in the Nineteenth Century who would not give up the connection of literature with the main human enterprise. The very suggestion would have shocked Tolstoi and Dostoievski. But in the West a separation between great artists and the gen-

In 1974 he married Alexandra Ionescu Tulcea, a Romanian-born mathematician at Northwestern University. The Bellows are shown at the ball in honor of the Nobel Prize winners at Stockholm's City Hall, 1976.

eral public took place. Artists developed a marked contempt for the average reader and the bourgeois mass. The best of them saw clearly enough what sort of civilization Europe had produced, brilliant but unstable, vulnerable, fated to be overtaken by catastrophe.

Despite a show of radicalism and innovation our contemporaries are really very conservative. They follow their Nineteenth Century leaders and hold to the old standards, interpreting history and society much as they were interpreted in the last century. What would writers do today if it occurred to them that literature might once again engage those "central energies," if they were to recognize that an immense desire had arisen for a return from the periphery, for what is simple and true?

Of course we can't come back to the center simply because we wish to, though the realization that we are wanted might electrify us. The force of the crisis is so great that it might summon us back. But prescriptions are futile. One can't tell writers what to do. The imagination must find its own path. But one can fervently wish that they—that we—would come back from the periphery. We writers do not represent mankind adequately. What account do Americans give of themselves, what accounts of them are given by psychologists, sociologists, historians, journalists, and writers? In a kind of contractual daylight they see themselves in the ways with which we are desperately familiar. These images of contractual daylight, so boring to Robbe-Grillet and to me, originate in the contemporary world view: We put into our books the consumer, civil servant, football fan, lover, television viewer. And in the contractual daylight version their life is a kind of death. There is another life coming from an insistent sense of what we are which denies these daylight formulations and the false life—the death-in-life—they make for us. For it is false, and we know it, and our secret and incoherent resistance to it cannot stop—that resistance arises from persistent intuitions. Perhaps humankind cannot bear too much reality, but neither can it bear too much unreality, too much abuse of the truth.

We do not think well of ourselves; we do not think amply about what we are. Our collective achievements have so greatly "exceeded" us that we "justify" ourselves by pointing to them. It is the jet plane in which we commonplace human beings have crossed the Atlantic in four hours that embodies such value as we can claim. Then we hear that this is closing time in the gardens of the West, that the end of our capitalist civilization is at hand. This means that we are not yet sufficiently shrunken; we must prepare to be smaller still. I am not sure whether this should be called intellectual analysis or analysis by intellectuals. The disasters are disasters. It is worse than stupid to call them victories as some statesmen have done. But I am drawing attention to the fact that there is in the intellectual community a sizable inventory of atitudes that have become respectable—notions about society, human nature, class, politics, sex, about mind, about the physical universe, the evolution of life. Few writers, even among the best, have taken the trouble to re-examine these attitudes or orthodoxies. Such attitudes are everywhere and no one challenges them seriously. They only glow more powerfully in Joyce or D. H. Lawrence than in the books of lesser men. Since the Twenties, how many novelists have taken a second look at Lawrence, or argued a different view of sexual potency or the effects of industrial civilization on the instincts? Literature has for nearly a century used the same stock of ideas, myths, strategies. "The most serious essayists of the last fifty years," says Robbe-Grillet. Yes, indeed. Essay after essay, book after book, confirm the most serious thoughts—Baudelairean, Nietzchean, Marxian, Psychoanalytic, et cetera, et cetera—of these most serious essayists. What Robbe-Grillet says about character can be said also about these ideas, maintaining all the usual things about mass society, dehumanization and the rest. How poorly they represent us. The pictures they offer no more resemble us than we resemble the reconstructed reptiles and other monsters in a museum of paleontology. We are much more limber, versatile, better articulated, there is much more to us—we all feel it.

What is at the center now? At the moment, neither art nor science but mankind determining, in confusion and obscurity, whether it will endure or go under. The whole species—everybody—has gotten into the act. At such a time it is essential to lighten ourselves, to dump encumbrances, including the encumbrances of education and all organized platitudes, to make judgments of our own, to perform acts of our own. Conrad was right to appeal to that part of our being which is a gift. We must look for that gift under the wreckage of many systems. The collapse of those systems may bring a blessed and necessary release from formulations, from misleading conceptions of being and consciousness. With increasing frequency I dismiss as "merely respectable" opinions I have long held—or thought I held—and try to discern what I have really lived by, and what others really live by. As for Hegel's art freed from "seriousness" and glowing on the margins, raising the soul above painful involvement in the limitations of reality through the serenity of form, that can exist nowhere now, during this struggle for survival. However, it is not as though the people who engaged in this struggle had only a rudimentary humanity, without culture, and knew nothing of art. Our very vices, our mutilations, show how rich we are in thought and culture. How much we know. How much we can feel. The struggles that convulse us make us want to simplify, to reconsider, to eliminate the tragic weakness which prevented writers—and readers—from being at once simple and true.

Writers are greatly respected. The intelligent public is wonderfully patient with them, continues to read them and endures disappointment after disappointment, waiting to hear from art what it does not hear from theology, philosphy, social theory, and what it cannot hear from pure science. Out of the struggle at the center has come an immense, painful longing for a broader, more flexible, fuller, more coherent, more comprehensive account of what we human beings are, who we are, and what this life is for. At the center humankind struggles with collective powers for its freedom, the individual struggles with dehumanization for the possession of his soul. If writers do not come again into the center it will not be because the center is pre-empted. It is not. They are free to enter. If they so wish.

The essence of our real condition, the complexity, the confusion, the pain of it is shown to us in glimpses, in what Proust and Tolstoi thought of as "true impressions." This essence reveals, and then conceals itself. When it goes away it leaves us again in doubt. But our connection remains with the depths from which these glimpses come. The sense of our real powers, powers we seem to derive from the universe itself, also comes and goes. We are reluctant to talk about this because there is nothing we can prove, because our language is inadequate, and because few people are willing to risk the embarrassment. They would have to say, "There is a spirit" and that is taboo. So almost everyone keeps quiet about it, al-

Saul Bellow in 1981

though almost everyone is aware of it.

The value of literature lies in these intermittent "true impressions." A novel moves back and forth between the world of objects, of actions, of appearances, and that other world from which these "true impressions" come and which moves us to believe that the good we hang onto so tenaciously—in the face of evil, so obstinately—is no illusion.

No one who has spent years in the writing of novels can be unaware of this. The novel can't be compared to the epic, or to the monuments of poetic drama. But it is the best we can do just now. It is a sort of latter-day lean-to, a hovel in which the spirit takes shelter. A novel is balanced between a few true impressions and the multitude of false ones that make up most of what we call life. It tells us that for every human being there is a diversity of existences, that the single existence is itself an illusion in part, that these many existences signify something, tend to something, fulfill something; it promises us meaning, harmony and even justice. What Conrad said was true, art attempts to find in the universe, in matter as well as in the facts of life, what is fundamental, enduring, essential.

Book Review:

R. Z. Shepherd, "Truth and Consequences," *Time*, 199 (18 January 1982): 77-78.

Bellow's most recent novel, The Dean's December, *probes a double crisis in the life of Albert Corde; the settings are Chicago and Bucharest.*

At its richest, Saul Bellow's free-style prose reads as if a Division Street Dostoyevsky were writing a book called *Thus Spake the Nobel Savage*. In *Mr. Sammler's Planet* (1970), the author's tone took a Spenglerian edge as the novel's elderly New Yorker ruminated on the decline of the West Side and, inferentially, civilization as the author knows and reveres it. *Sammler* had political repercussions. Bellow was accused of being aloof, insensitive and a neoconservative. He has calmly and disdainfully rejected these labels as simplistic.

Any suggestion that the 1976 Nobel prizewinner was intimidated by his critics is dispelled in *The Dean's December*, a work that opens a second front in Bellow's war on cultural and intellectual nihilism. The scenes are set almost exclusively in Chicago and Bucharest, a disparity underscored by the line, "There was nothing too rum to be true." In fact, the book is largely based on a trip that the novelist and his wife made to Rumania a few years ago to visit her dying mother.

The literary result is Albert Corde, the latest and best of Bellow's old cogitators. Corde, a Chicago college dean, spends a great deal of time in an underheated Bucharest apartment waiting for his mother-in-law to die in a state hospital and mulling over the retreat of "personal humanity" before "the worldwide process of consolidation." The woman was an eminent psychiatrist and former Minister of Health whose humanism was incompatible with the Communist regime. Corde's wife Minna is an astrophysicist who defected to the U.S. and must now beg a vindictive bureaucracy for permission to see her failing mother.

The dean, a "hungry observer," describes the bleak utilitarianism and pinched daily life in the old Eastern European capital. Earthquake damage is crudely patched if repaired at all; the public crematorium is a factory where the dead are reduced unceremoniously to convenient size; his wife's childhood home, once a center of culture and comfort, is only a notch above a slum tenement: "Radiators turned cold after breakfast. The faucets went dry at 8 a.m. and did not run again until evening. The bathtub had no stopper. You flushed the toilet with buckets of water."

These are not cheap shots aimed to cripple Rumania's tourist industry or elicit smug agreement about Communist inefficiency. Corde has seen worse in Chicago. He has, in fact, written about it with appalling accuracy for *Harper's* magazine and caused a flap. The dean has also been criticized for his role in the arrest of two blacks accused of murder. Corde has been called a racist, a traitor to his home town and a fool. His boss is miffed at the publicity caused by his magazine piece, and his boyhood friend Dewey Spangler, now a famous columnist and "princely communicator," complains that Corde put too much poetry into Chicago.

Corde responds that Chicago put the poetry into him. He had to write the truth as he saw it on the streets. Pulling Corde's strings, Bellow leaves little doubt of his position: "What was the real explanation? Again, the *high* intention—to prevent the American idea from being pounded into dust altogether. And here is our American idea: liberty, equality, justice, democracy, abundance. And here is what things are like today in a city like Chicago. Have a look! How does the public apprehend events? It doesn't apprehend them. It has been deprived of the capacity to experience them."

Corde points to a prevailing materialism that deadens the senses with adgab, propaganda and information bits. He fingers professional explainers like his pal Spangler, whose theories and discourses usually distort rather than describe. "The first act of morality," Corde concludes, "was to disinter the reality . . . represent it anew as art would represent it."

The caul that separates mankind from nature and the power of art to restore perception and feeling are not new themes for Bellow. But never has he stated them with more force or political intent. This is not to say that the author has a future in politics. He lacks the facile answers that pull votes; he has only difficult questions, and he insists on talking up to his audience.

Where, then, does this leave *The Dean's December* as a novel to be read and enjoyed? Two generations of Bellow fans should not be disappointed. Although Corde is usually found shivering in one room in Rumania, he has total recall. There are flashbacks of Chicago as only Bellow can re-create it, boisterous, hard-nosed and advantageously backward: "By the time the latest ideas reach Chicago, they're worn thin and easy to see through."

There is no conventional plot other than the Cordes' efforts to see Valeria. But no writer turns an idea into a physical sensation as well as Bellow does. He has no contemporary equal in revealing the "mad clarity" of family relationships or in planting the seeds of metaphor in fertile situations. Corde's considerations of lead poisoning in the environment suggest an age of reverse alchemy in which the gold of Western civilization is turned into a crushing, toxic weight. The difference between an open society where the speculations grow spontaneously and a closed system with its sterile dogma is dramatized in a stunning juxtaposition. Corde and his wife ascend the telescope cage under the opening dome of the Mount Palomar observatory. He feels that he could go on forever. But he is also reminded of the rounded roof of the Bucharest crematorium, the dome "that never opened. You could pass through only as smoke."

Bellow's prose is unadorned, hard and penetrating. Yet even in such a serious work he cannot suppress his poetic impulses. Ignorant of astrophysics, Corde explains his wife's occupation as "bringing together a needle from one end of the universe with a thread from the opposite end." Elsewhere, he muses that if a film were made of one's life, every other frame would be death: "Destruction and resurrection in alternate beats of being, but speed makes it seem continuous." And there is Corde himself, whose name is French for string. A little obvious, but Bellow has never had much patience for furtive symbolism. Stretched tightly between Chicago and Bucharest, his fine fictional instrument is tuned perfectly to the dissonances of the times and the unheard but strangely felt music of a seductive eternity.

> *"Asking me what I might have been besides a writer is like asking an earthworm what else he considered becoming."*

From Life, *3 April 1970, p. 58*

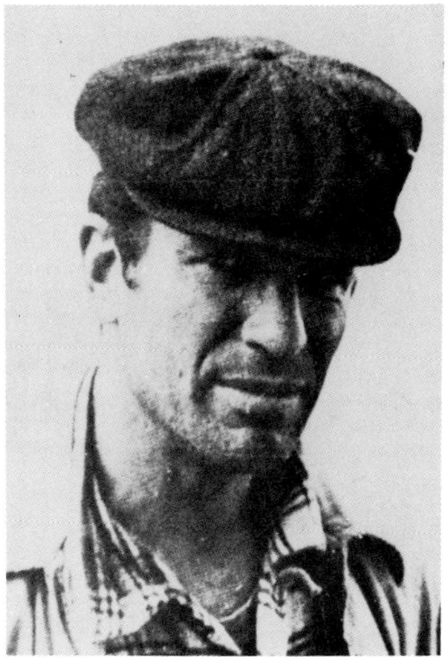

JACK KEROUAC

(12 March 1922-21 October 1969)

See the Jack Kerouac entry in the Dictionary of Literary Biography, *volume 2,* American Novelists Since World War II.

MAJOR BOOKS:

The Town and the City (New York: Harcourt, Brace, 1950; London: Eyre & Spottiswoode, 1951);

On the Road (New York: Viking, 1957; London: Deutsch, 1958);

The Subterraneans (New York: Grove, 1958; London: Deutsch, 1960);

The Dharma Bums (New York: Viking, 1958; London: Deutsch, 1959);

Doctor Sax: Faust Part Three (New York: Grove, 1959; London: Evergreen, 1961);

Maggie Cassidy (New York: Avon, 1959; London: Panther, 1960);

Mexico City Blues (New York: Grove, 1959);

Excerpts From Visions of Cody (New York: New Directions, 1960);

The Scripture of the Golden Eternity (New York: Totem Press in association with Corinth Books, 1960; London: Centaur, 1960);

Tristessa (New York: Avon, 1960; London: World, 1963);

Lonesome Traveler (New York: McGraw-Hill, 1960; London: Deutsch, 1962);

Rimbaud (San Francisco: City Lights Books, 1960);

Book of Dreams (San Francisco: City Lights Books, 1961);

Pull My Daisy (New York: Grove, 1961; London: Evergreen, 1961);

Big Sur (New York: Farrar, Straus & Cudahy, 1962; London: Deutsch, 1963);

Visions of Gerard (New York: Farrar, Straus, 1963); republished as *Visions of Gerard & Tristessa* (London: Deutsch, 1964);

Desolation Angels (New York: Coward-McCann, 1965; London: Deutsch, 1966);

Satori in Paris (New York: Grove, 1966; London: Deutsch, 1967);

Vanity of Duluoz: An Adventurous Education 1935-46 (New York: Coward-McCann, 1968; London: Deutsch, 1969);

Scattered Poems (San Francisco: City Lights Books, 1971);

Pic (New York: Grove, 1971);

Visions of Cody (New York: McGraw-Hill, 1972; London: Deutsch, 1973);

Trip Trap Haiku along the Road from San Francisco to New York 1959, with Albert Saijo and Lew Welch (Bolinas: Grey Fox Press, 1973).

BIOGRAPHIES:

Ann Charters, *Kerouac, A Biography* (San Francisco: Straight Arrow, 1973);

Charles E. Jarvis, *Visions of Kerouac* (Lowell: Ithaca Press, 1974);

Barry Gifford and Lawrence Lee, *Jack's Book: An Oral Biography of Jack Kerouac* (New York: St. Martin's Press, 1978);

Dennis McNally, *Desolate Angel: Jack Kerouac, the Beats and America* (New York: Random House, 1979);

Tim Hunt, *Kerouac's Crooked Road* (Hamden, Conn.: Archon Books, 1981).

BIBLIOGRAPHIES:

Ann Charters, *A Bibliography of Works by Jack Kerouac (Jean Louis Lebris De Kerouac), 1939-1975* (New York: Phoenix Bookshop, 1975);

Robert J. Milewski, *Jack Kerouac: An Annotated Bibliography of Secondary Sources, 1944-1979* (Metuchen, N.J.: Scarecrow Press, 1981).

LOCATION OF ARCHIVES:

There is no major collection of Kerouac's papers in any university library. One notebook is at the University of Texas, Austin; five notebooks and a typescript are in the Berg Collection of the New York Public Library; and collections of Kerouac letters are in the Allen Ginsberg archives at Butler Library, Columbia University, and in the Gary Snyder archives at the library of the University of California, Davis.

Jean Louis Lebris de Kerouac was born in the French-Canadian neighborhood of Lowell, Massachusetts, 12 March 1922, the third child of Gabrielle Ange L'Evensque (Mémère) and Leo Alcide Kerouac. His brother Gerard, five years older, died when Jack was four. His sister Caroline (called "Nin"), three years older, was close to her younger brother. "Ti Jean" (Little Jack), learned French at home, but was taught English by the nuns at his parochial school, St. Joseph's Brothers.

The Kerouac family regularly moved within Lowell, depending on the prosperity of Leo Kerouac's printing business. The fourth-floor apartment of this tenement at 736 Moody Street, where Jack had a room of his own, provided the source for Jacky Duluoz's home in Maggie Cassidy.

Kerouac carrying the ball for Lowell High School, fall 1938

Kerouac with his sister Caroline in Lowell, circa 1940. He was eighteen; she was twenty-one.

ARTICLE:

Jack Kerouac, "Count Basie's Band Best in Land; Group Famous for 'Solid' Swing," *Horace Mann Record*, 16 February 1940, p. 3.

Kerouac was offered football scholarships by Boston College and Columbia University. He chose Columbia, but first spent a year at Horace Mann prep school in the Bronx. During his year at Horace Mann, Kerouac wrote music articles, usually about swing bands, for the Horace Mann Record. *Jazz became a shaping influence on Kerouac's work, especially his poetry.*

"I want guts in my music!" Count Basie once said publicly. "No screaming brass for me," he had added, "but I do want plenty of guts in my music."

And so, without any screaming brass, the Count managed to weld his unit into a terrific gang of soloists and ensemble players. Much to the dismay of most of our present day "swing" bands, they cannot be terrific unless they tear off some deafening brass measures to send the jitterbugs out of the world. Count Basie's swing arrangements are not blaring, but they contain more drive, more power, and more thrill than the loudest gang of corn artists can acquire by blowing their horns apart.

Possibly excepting Duke Ellington, the Basie band is the most underrated and greatest band in the country today. Unlike the vacuous phraseology of pseudo-swing bands, Basie's stuff means something. As for solo work, there is no greater assortment of soloists to be found on any one band-stand.

Kerouac posing with his sister and their parents for a Times Square photographer, May 1944

Taking these stars apart, we can well realize why the Basie ensemble is the best in the land. Since the old days in Kansas City, these boys have been jamming together, causing a magnificent blend of musicians familiar with each other's peculiarities and ideas, and a subsequent precision of play.

To begin with, the Count has the greatest rhythm section in the history of jazz, and this has helped his other great musicians to improve. The Count himself is an outstanding soloist. He is a thrilling player with tremendous ideas. He ranks at least third among the best pianists of the swing world. The rest of his rhythm section is composed of Jo Jones, Walter Page, and Freddy Green.

Jones Finished Drummer

Jo Jones is the most finished drummer in existence. It is interesting to note how he keeps the beat going when he takes a solo on his hides, unlike the ordinary drummers who stop all activities when they set sail on their riflings. Freddy Green's steady guitar work has been unparalleled in jazz since the days of the old school guitarists. When Freddy Green starts his rhythm going, in unison with Walter Page's mighty bass-playing and Jo Jones chimes in on the drums, you have the rhythm section that every maestro dreams of.

But that is only half of it. The Count's soloists are all good, especially Lester Young, Dickie Wells, Harry Edison, and Buck Clayton.

Lester Young, who is now rated along with Coleman Hawkins on the hot tenor, is the Count's outstanding soloist. Lester uses a different riff on every chorus, and his enormous store of ideas enables him to take an unlimited number of solos. His phrasing on jump numbers is unequalled, while he is highly proficient when it comes to blues. It would be safe to say that Lester Young is actually popularizing the tenor sax, an instrument which the ordinary jitterbug cares little for, because he would prefer a screeching trumpet, a la Clyde Hurley. Young's playing may turn the trend of public interest to the tenor sax, because he is really a master-mind with that horn of his.

Besides Lester Young, Buddy Tate plays the tenor in the first chair. Tate is a stylist, and has an individual style definitely distinct from Young's, which adds a touch of variety to the Basie reeds. Earl Warren and Jack Washington are the other two saxists, each of whom are better than average. Lester Young is also a terrific clarinetist, but he rarely plays it except to mess around someone else's solo in the background. The same for Washington's alto yet to be heard.

Harry Edison, a powerhouse trumpeter, with a choice individuality of ideas, is featured in the brass section. His marvelous control, and the thrilling manner in which he delivers his trumpet solos makes him the equal of Buck Clayton, the other trumpet ace.

Clayton Ranks With Best

Clayton, who has improved a great deal in his long stay with Basie, has beautiful tone and some wonderful

Kerouac did well at Horace Mann. He remembered, "I scored all the winning touchdowns in the fall so they put me at the top of the literary magazine in the spring." The yearbook announced that "Brain and brawn found a happy combination in Jack, a newcomer to school this year. A brilliant back in football, he also won his spurs as a Record *reporter and a leading* Quarterly *contributor." He is shown above in his graduation suit in 1940 at the summer home of Edie Parker, who became Kerouac's wife on 14 August 1944.*

ideas. Clayton ranks, in fact, with the greatest trumpeters of all time. Al Killian, who recently joined the band at the Golden Gate Ballroom, has taken Shad Collins' place as lead trumpeter. Collins had been an amazing high note trumpeter. Ed Louis, a good hot player, occupies the other chair.

However, the thing which makes Basie's trumpet section what it is is the definite dash of style, provided by Edison and Clayton.

Dickie Wells, probably ranking alongside of Higginbotham, Keg Johnson and all the other great sliphorn men, is the man who provides those stirring trombone passages for the Count Basie orchestra. Dickie has a torrid accent on his phrasing, and is purely hot. It was unfortunate that Ben Morton had to leave the Basie band last month, but Wells will carry on. Vic Dickerson replaced Morton. The other trombonist is Dan Minor, the veteran first chair man. Morton had been Basie's straight player and hot man before leaving.

One could pick up a dictionary and cast all the superlatives in existence upon the Basie group, but it still wouldn't suffice. Words cannot explain the meaning of Basie's music, both to the listener, and to the good name of swing. A marvelous drive, borne by the assurance of over-talented musicians, makes this group what it is—the last word in hot music.

Supplied with an amazing group of soloists, Count Basie's orchestra has all the necessary harmonious technique and life conducive of REAL swing bands—and we do mean Basie.

Kerouac broke his leg in the second Columbia freshman football game of 1940 and missed the rest of the season. In his sophomore year he left Columbia after a disagreement with coach Lou Little; he returned in 1942, but quit again when Little refused to play him in the Army game. After repeated attempts to join the armed forces, he was inducted into the Navy in March 1943; six months later, he was given a psychiatric discharge. Edie Parker took this photograph of Kerouac and Lucien Carr at Columbia in 1944, before Carr went to prison for manslaughter. Jailed as a material witness, Kerouac married Edie in August 1944 in order to raise bail from her family; after two months he left her.

Hal Chase, Kerouac, Allen Ginsberg, and William Burroughs in New York, 1944. Kerouac and Ginsberg had met at Columbia, and Ginsberg acted as his literary agent. The next year Kerouac and Burroughs collaborated on an unpublished novel entitled "And the Hippos Were Boiled in their Tanks."

BOOK REVIEW:

Howard Mumford Jones, "Back to Merrimac," *Saturday Review of Literature*, 33 (11 March 1950): 18.

Kerouac began taking "bennies" in 1945, which caused him to develop thrombophlebitis in both legs. While in the hospital, Kerouac planned his first book, "a hugh novel explaining everything to everybody," in the manner of Thomas Wolfe. After Leo Kerouac died in the spring of 1946, Jack began to write in earnest to fulfill his promise to his father that he would take care of Mémère. The novel he had planned, The Town and the City, *was published in 1950. In this review Harvard professor Howard Mumford Jones called attention to the novel's lack of planning.*

In the present amorphous state of book reviewing this will likely be hailed as a novel displaying great life, energy, and realism. Life, energy, and realism of a kind it certainly has. It belongs to the category of the "big" novel—the lengthy book, in which a prodigious splashing about, general emotional appeals in the "lost, lost, lost" cadence of Thomas Wolfe, and a rather simple notion of what constitutes fictional characters are supposed to compensate for radical deficiencies in structure and style.

The fable concerns the ten members of the Martin family, originally domiciled on the Merrimac River in Massachusetts, and thence by time, circumstance, World War II, and the whim of the author dispersed. At the end the burial of the father in his native village formally concludes the story by bringing these lives momentarily back to the Merrimac. Some scenes, such as those of young Peter's first experiences as a football player, are memorable. But the novel starts a dozen themes without ever quite relating them to each other; it drowns itself in dull, repetitive dialogue intended as "life," and I, for one, am genuinely puzzled why the novelist spent the first seventy-five pages on the Merrimac phase of his story

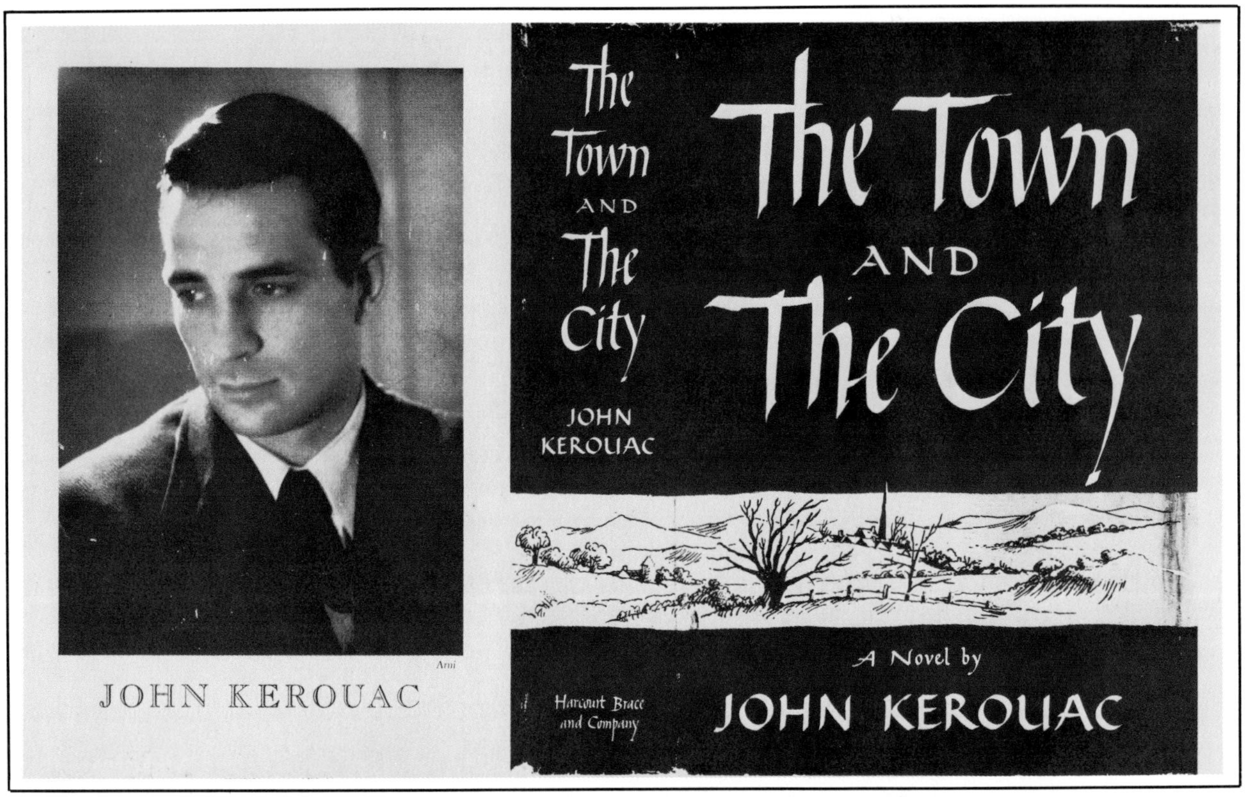

Kerouac later said he wrote his book "according to what they told me at Columbia University. Fiction. But . . . the novel's dead. Then I broke loose from all that and wrote picaresque narratives." Like almost everything Kerouac wrote, The Town and the City *is autobiographical. George and Marge Martin are based on Kerouac's parents. Kerouac can be seen in all five Martin sons, but most prominently in Peter, whose friends correspond to Kerouac's own Columbia buddies—Lucien Carr as Kenneth Wood; William Burroughs as Will Dennison; Allen Ginsberg as Leon Levinsky; and Dave Kammerer as Waldo Meister.*

only to abandon it for other material. A prodigious amount of liquor is drunk first and last, without affecting anybody's health or happiness, and we alternate between revelations of the "dark" emotions among the Martins and scenes of simple gaiety that, though they appeal, reduce the characters to the same level of emotion.

That classic stylist Willa Cather some years ago made a plea for the novel *demeuble*—the novel from which all the unnecessary furniture of realism, both words and things, had been removed, so that writer and reader might confront theme and character and so discover the graver issues of the tale. It is Mr. Kerouac's failure to throw the furniture out that leads to his confusion. A drive for "bigness" overcomes structure. There seems to be no special reason why the novel is as long as it is, none why it should not be half as long, none why it should not be the first of a series of novels quite as "big," following the Martins as far as Mr. Kerouac wants to go. But the pattern, the shape, the spire of meaning is here so overlaid one isn't sure whether even this would be his long-run intent.

One infers from the title that the conflict between town and city is to determine fate and perhaps character. The elements of the conflict are loose in the book, but the issue is never honorably joined. The Merrimac Valley opening is excellent writing but it remains merely excellent writing. There come whole rows of scenes elsewhere, including some queer ones laid in New York City and written with naive power, but these are so loosely integrated with the conflict (is there conflict?) one doesn't quite know how to take them. Time goes by in a series of jerks, but time as development (essential to the family novel, as in "Buddenbrooks") isn't there.

I suspect that if the unnecessary furniture of realism were removed, Mr. Kerouac would have seen what is wrong. But there are so many people, all motivated by a rather elementary notion of emotional drives, there are so many scenes presented in a kind of good-humored scramble, that the lives of the one are in many cases indistinguishable, and the purpose of the other never comes cleanly through this energetic prose. I think Mr. Kerouac has many of the essential attributes of the practising novelist—fecundity, invention, a kind of abundance (yet unchanneled)—but they do not here fuse into unity.

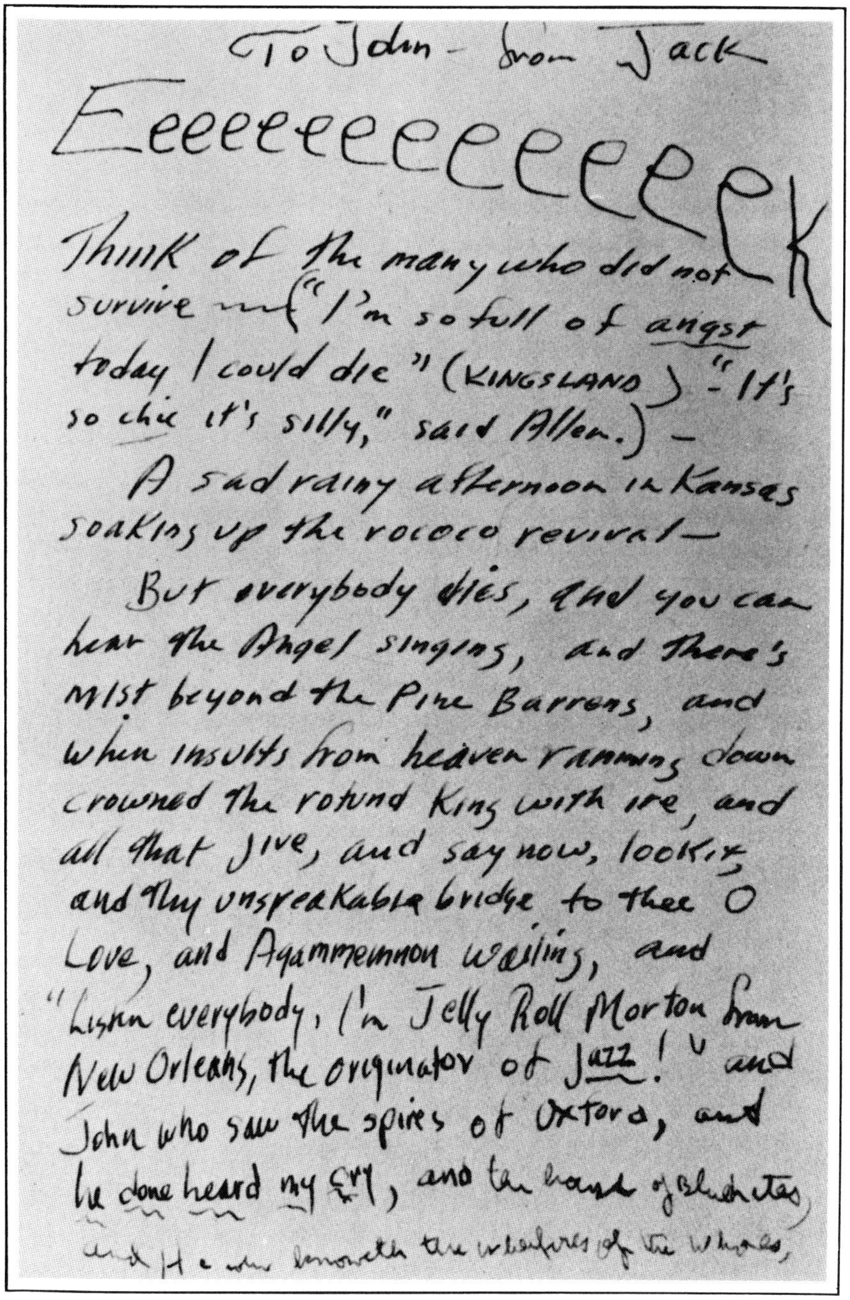
To John - from Jack
Eeeeeeeeeeeeek
Think of the many who did not survive me ("I'm so full of angst today I could die" (KINGSLAND) "It's so chic it's silly," said Allen.) —
A sad rainy afternoon in Kansas soaking up the rococo revival—
But everybody dies, and you can hear the Angel singing, and there's mist beyond the Pine Barrens, and when insults from heaven ranning down crowned the rotund King with ire, and all that jive, and say now, lookit, and thy unspeakable bridge to thee O Love, and Agammemnon waiting, and "Lissen everybody, I'm Jelly Roll Morton from New Orleans, the originator of Jazz!" and John who saw the spires of Oxford, and he done heard my cry, and the hand of [illegible], and He who knoweth the welfares of the Whales,

Inscription by Kerouac and Allen Ginsberg in The Town and the City *(Sotheby Parke Bernet sale 4109B). Addressed to their friend John Kingsland, the inscription covers three pages.*

Kerouac began to write On the Road *in November 1948 to tell Joan Haverty "what I'd been through." When it was published in 1957, the first printing sold out in fifteen days. Kerouac liked to remember the novel as something he had dashed off in just three weeks. The final version of* On the Road *was prepared from this paper roll typescript.*

This is a copy of the first edition of

ON THE ROAD

by

Jack Kerouac

It will be published in September 1957 by The Viking Press and is certain to cause violently conflicting reactions among readers and critics. We believe that readers will find truth in the book; to some this truth may be beautiful, to others it may be ugly, but no one can fail to be impressed by what this book says and the way it says it.

After World War I a certain group of restless, searching Americans came to be called "The Lost Generation." This group found its truest voice in the writings of the young Hemingway. For a good many of the same reasons after World War II another group, roaming America in a wild, desperate search for identity and purpose, became known as "The Beat Generation." Jack Kerouac is the voice of this group and this is his novel.

continued...

Advance review copy of On the Road. *When the novel was published, Kerouac commented: "It was my song for the beat children—And now if I become rich may God protect me from unkindness and vanity."*

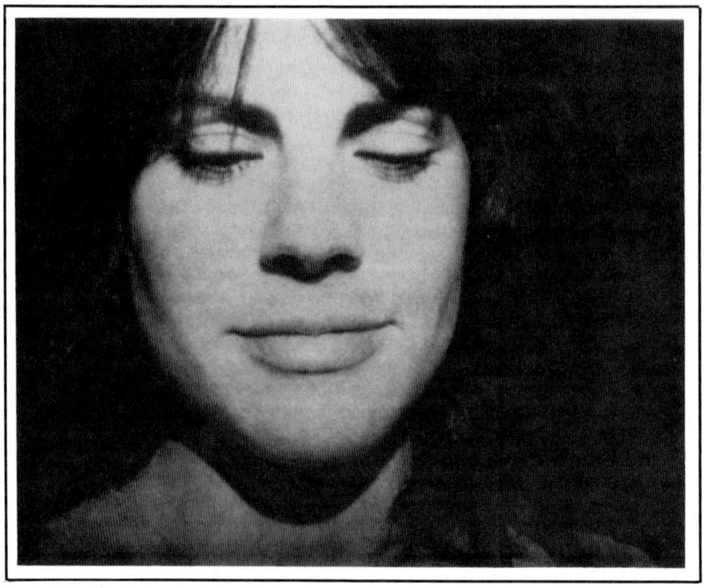

Kerouac married Joan Haverty in 1950. Their daughter Michelle (Jan) was born after they separated in 1951. Jan Kerouac's novel Baby Driver *was published in 1981.*

While writing The Town and the City, *Kerouac met Neal Cassady, who had a profound influence on him. Cassady was the model for Dean Moriarty, the hero of* On the Road, *and for Cody Pomeray, a main character in Kerouac's later books.*

In 1951, while writing On the Road, *Kerouac began another book in which the hero was modeled on Neal Cassady. Kerouac went to California, where he lived with the Cassadys from December 1951 until the following May. He recorded many conversations with Cassady which were later incorporated into* Visions of Cody. *Kerouac is shown above during his stay with Neal and Carolyn Cassady.*

Jack Kerouac drew this comic strip, "Doctor Sax and the Deception of the Sea Shroud," for the Cassady children about 1952 (Carolyn Cassady).

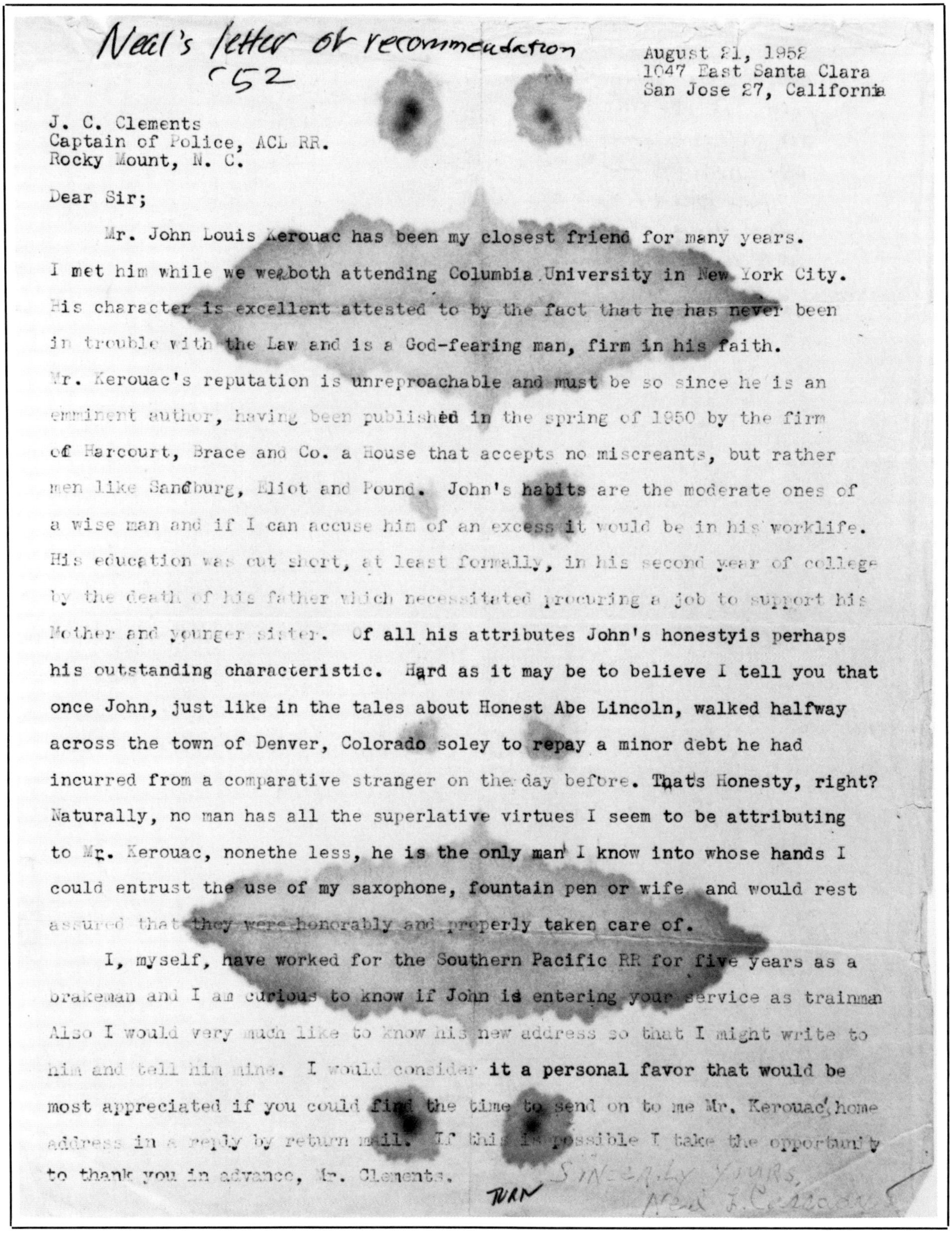

Neal's letter of recommendation
c52

August 21, 1952
1047 East Santa Clara
San Jose 27, California

J. C. Clements
Captain of Police, ACL RR.
Rocky Mount, N. C.

Dear Sir;

Mr. John Louis Kerouac has been my closest friend for many years. I met him while we were both attending Columbia University in New York City. His character is excellent attested to by the fact that he has never been in trouble with the Law and is a God-fearing man, firm in his faith. Mr. Kerouac's reputation is unreproachable and must be so since he is an emminent author, having been published in the spring of 1950 by the firm of Harcourt, Brace and Co. a House that accepts no miscreants, but rather men like Sandburg, Eliot and Pound. John's habits are the moderate ones of a wise man and if I can accuse him of an excess it would be in his worklife. His education was cut short, at least formally, in his second year of college by the death of his father which necessitated procuring a job to support his Mother and younger sister. Of all his attributes John's honestyis perhaps his outstanding characteristic. Hard as it may be to believe I tell you that once John, just like in the tales about Honest Abe Lincoln, walked halfway across the town of Denver, Colorado soley to repay a minor debt he had incurred from a comparative stranger on the day before. That's Honesty, right? Naturally, no man has all the superlative virtues I seem to be attributing to Mr. Kerouac, nonethe less, he is the only man I know into whose hands I could entrust the use of my saxophone, fountain pen or wife and would rest assured that they were honorably and properly taken care of.

I, myself, have worked for the Southern Pacific RR for five years as a brakeman and I am curious to know if John is entering your service as trainman Also I would very much like to know his new address so that I might write to him and tell him mine. I would consider it a personal favor that would be most appreciated if you could find the time to send on to me Mr. Kerouac's home address in a reply by return mail. If this is possible I take the opportunity to thank you in advance, Mr. Clements.

Sincerely Yours,
Neal L. Cassady

TURN

First page of Neal Cassady's character reference for Kerouac (Humanities Research Center). Kerouac's sister had moved to North Carolina, and he made long visits there.

John Clellon Holmes and Kerouac met in 1947. Five years later Holmes's novel Go *became the first to describe the lives of Kerouac, Ginsberg, and Cassady.*

After Kerouac left the Cassadys, he went to Mexico City, where he started a novel "of children and evil," called Doctor Sax. *Kerouac began working for the Southern Pacific in 1952 and from this experience wrote "October in the Railroad Earth" (1957). This 1953 photo shows Kerouac with the brakeman's handbook given to him by Cassady.*

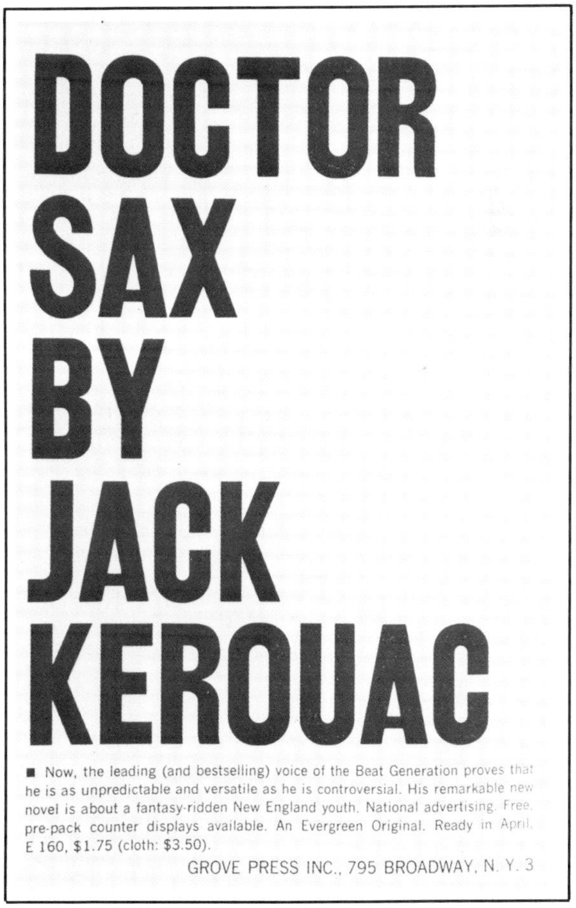

DOCTOR
SAX
BY
JACK
KEROUAC
■ Now, the leading (and bestselling) voice of the Beat Generation proves that he is as unpredictable and versatile as he is controversial. His remarkable new novel is about a fantasy-ridden New England youth. National advertising. Free pre-pack counter displays available. An Evergreen Original. Ready in April. E 160, $1.75 (cloth: $3.50).
GROVE PRESS INC., 795 BROADWAY, N. Y. 3

From Publishers Weekly, *23 February 1959*

Kerouac and Allen Ginsberg in 1953. Ginsberg's poem "Howl" (1959) was regarded as a major document of the Beat Generation.

Kerouac, Allen Ginsberg, Peter Orlovsky, Gregory Corso, and Lafcadio Orlovsky in Mexico City, 1956. During this stay in Mexico, Kerouac finished Tristessa*—a novel about a prostitute and morphine addict he had known in Mexico City.*

Bob Donlin, Neal Cassady, Allen Ginsberg, Bob LaVigne, and Lawrence Ferlinghetti in 1956 at the City Lights Bookstore. Ferlinghetti, a poet and proprietor of the bookshop, published many Beat works including Kerouac's Rimbaud, Book of Dreams, *and* Scattered Poems.

In February 1957 Kerouac went to visit William Burroughs in Tangier. There he occupied himself typing Burroughs's novel Naked Lunch. *While Kerouac was in Tangier,* On the Road *and* The Subterraneans *were being prepared for publication. This photo was taken by Burroughs at the Villa Mouneria.*

Saturday Review, *21 September 1957*

BOOK REVIEW:

Arthur Oesterreicher, *Village Voice*, 18 September 1957, p. 5.

Kerouac's most famous novel was widely praised; however, while Kerouac was lauded for his writing, he was also invariably labeled the spokesman for the Beat Generation—a position that made him increasingly uncomfortable.

As you have no doubt already gathered by now, the public emergence of Jack Kerouac from the hipsters' underground into American literature is upon us, and is going to be THE big thing for quite a while. (Another of his books is being published by Grove Press later this season.) The author of "On the Road" was on "Nightbeat" last week (looking and sounding remarkably like the late James Dean, incidentally), people are already leafing curiously through it in bookstores, toting it around the Village, hugging it under their arm as they ride the subway to work. I understand that, despite the complete and incomprehensible lack of publisher's advertising so far, the first printing sold out a week after publication.

A Voice

Some of us knew Kerouac's work before this—pieces of "On the Road" had appeared in New World Writing, New Directions, and the Paris Review, and another novel, "The Town and the City," was published in

1950. "On the Road" itself was written almost a decade ago; Malcolm Cowley was touting it as far back as 1951 or so, in his book "The Literary Situation." But now at last the news is out for good: Kerouac is not just a writer, not just a talent, but a *voice*, as Hemingway, Henry Miller, the early Gide were and are to those who are disposed to listen. Kerouac has taken the way he and his friends lived and felt about life in the years 1947-1950 and written a lusty, noisily lyrical, exuberantly overwritten book about it all. But more important than that, he offers a belief, a rallying point for the elusive spirit of the rebellion of these times, that silent scornful sit-down strike of the disaffiliated which has been the nearest thing to a real movement among the young since the end of World War II. "On the Road" is as crucial to the social history of the past 10 years in America as "The Lonely Crowd."

Misleading Phrase

The phrase "beat generation," coined by Kerouac, can be very misleading, though. John Wingate asked him on "Nightbeat" what it was all about, and Kerouac merely replied: "I feel beat, don't you?" But that's only part of it. The ugliness of American life appears on every page of "On the Road" but does not fill it. In telling the story of a bunch of young guys running like demented ants over the map of America, from New York to Denver, to San Francisco, to New Orleans, to Mexico, there are also adventures, kicks, discoveries—in a word, *joy*. In the midst of hung-upness there is ecstasy; in the midst of chaotic experience, a reverential order. Beneath the beatness of the surface of everything, Kerouac, like Henry Miller in "Tropic of Cancer," finds beatitude.

At least this is what Sal Paradise, the narrator of "On the Road," finds for himself. The most unforgettable character in the book, Dean Moriarty (its real hero), does not. In him the hunger for life, for *digging* everything, spells his destruction: the chaos of his marriages, of his adventures, of his perpetual appetite for motion, is too much to control. The arch-hipster of them all, he is at once saint and victim—and ultimately self-crucified.

Frenetic Trips

The story of Sal and Dean is spun out through a series of frenetic trips across the American continent, in which they see their friends and plan improbable, wonderful adventures, fall in and out of love and marriage with equal ease, get hung-up when friendships go wrong, drive through town after town and state after state, wherever the road goes. "I want to get on and on," Dean cries as they careen through Mexico. "This road drives *me*!!" The road is always there, the road along which you blast at 90 miles an hour into the future where "nobody knows what's going to happen to anybody besides the forlorn rags of growing old"; it is Whitman's road, Mark Twain's, and Thomas Wolfe's river which Kerouac has rediscovered.

But the road is too much for Dean. Each adventure leaves him madder, hungrier, a little more drained. In the end, when he has lost almost everything—including his very voice—he simply disappears, leaving Sal and his friends forever to wonder about him. Kerouac's somber moral, though unstated, is clear: the *total* rebels can either destroy themselves or be destroyed. There is no other choice.

Diary of Experience

But Kerouac does not concern himself very much with moralizing. His book is a diary of experience, pure and simple, too formless and plotless and wrapped up with action as an end in itself to be a tract such as Allen Ginsberg's "Howl" poem, which describes very similar people and experiences.

Inevitably "On the Road" suffers from the unevenness which is almost dictated by the scattered, episodic nature of the material. As an artist, Kerouac is all too frequently overcome by the sound of his own voice; there is a lot of mumbling mystical junk about "the wild American night" and the like. But the unforgettable scenes that stud the book (a tour of the San Francisco jazz joints stands out most vividly for this reader) more than make up for the hoarseness of Kerouac's cry. Sore throats are, after all, an occupational disease with rebels.

But what a lot of good things Kerouac has packed into this book! There are pages of hilarity, of despair, of tremendous excitement about merely being alive, of horror at being alive in today's America. It's an easy book to be cynical about because it is so thoroughly alive; academically literary fault-finders will have a holiday with it. (*Cf.* Carlos Baker's review in the Saturday Review.)

But man, like Kerouac's *got* it, really got it. And I'm very happy that he has and that his book is finally here.

> *"What's your road, man? holyboy road, madman road, rainbow road, guppy road, any road. It's an anywhere road for anybody anyhow."*

From On the Road

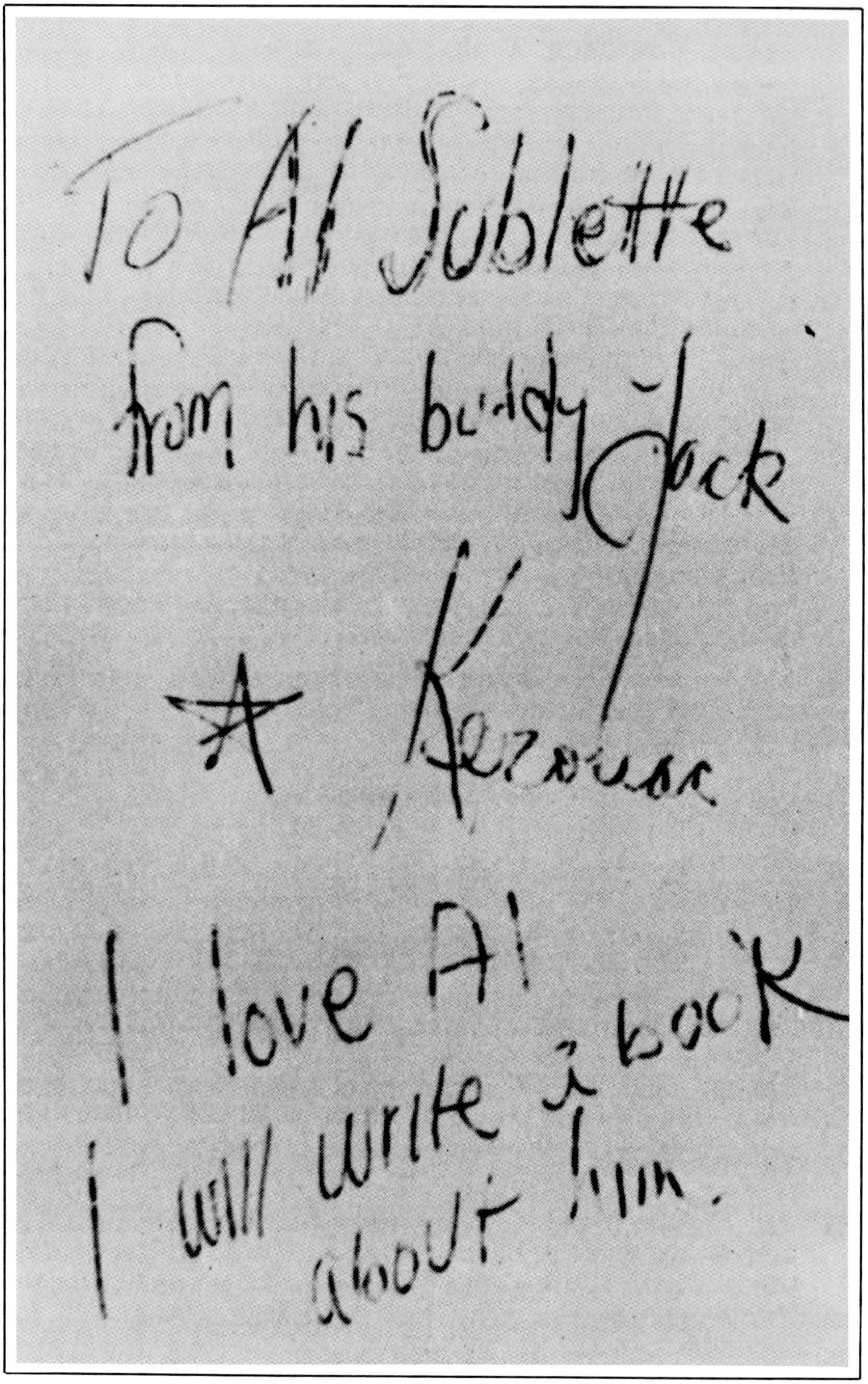

To Al Sublette
from his buddy Jack
Kerouac
I love Al
i will write a book
about him.

Kerouac's inscription in writer/jazz musician Al Sublette's copy of On the Road *(Bradford Morrow Catalogue 5). Sublette was a close friend while Kerouac was in San Francisco during the 1950s.*

ARTICLE:
Jack Kerouac, "Belief & Technique for Modern Prose," *Evergreen Review*, 2 (Spring 1959): 57.

Kerouac's protocols for spontaneous writing.

List of Essentials

1. Scribbled secret notebooks, and wild typewritten pages, for yr own joy
2. Submissive to everything, open, listening
3. Try never get drunk outside yr own house
4. Be in love with yr life
5. Something that you feel will find its own form
6. Be crazy dumbsaint of the mind
7. Blow as deep as you want to blow
8. Write what you want bottomless from bottom of the mind
9. The unspeakable visions of the individual
10. No time for poetry but exactly what is
11. Visionary tics shivering in the chest
12. In tranced fixation dreaming upon object before you
13. Remove literary, grammatical and syntactical inhibition
14. Like Proust be an old teahead of time
15. Telling the true story of the world in interior monolog
16. The jewel center of interest is the eye within the eye
17. Write in recollection and amazement for yourself
18. Work from pithy middle eye out, swimming in language sea
19. Accept loss forever
20. Believe in the holy contour of life
21. Struggle to sketch the flow that already exists intact in mind
22. Dont think of words when you stop but to see picture better
23. Keep track of every day the date emblazoned in yr morning
24. No fear or shame in the dignity of yr experience, language & knowledge
25. Write for the world to read and see yr exact pictures of it
26. Bookmovie is the movie in words, the visual American form
27. In praise of Character in the Bleak inhuman Loneliness
28. Composing wild, undisciplined, pure, coming in from under, crazier the better
29. You're a Genius all the time
30. Writer-Director of Earthly movies Sponsored & Angeled in Heaven

ARTICLE:
Jack Kerouac, "Essentials of Spontaneous Prose," *Black Mountain Review*, 8 (Spring 1959): 57.

With the publication of On the Road *Kerouac was recognized as a significant writer whose methods of producing poetry and fiction were influencing others. He explained the necessary elements for his writing in this article, published as* On the Road *was quickly gaining national attention.*

SET-UP. The object is set before the mind, either in reality, as in sketching (before a landscape or teacup or old face) or is set in the memory wherein it becomes the sketching from memory of a definite image-object.

PROCEDURE. Time being of the essence in the purity of speech, sketching language is undisturbed flow from the mind of personal secret idea-words, *blowing* (as per jazz musician) on subject of image.

METHOD. No periods separating sentence-structures already arbitrarily riddled by false colons and timid usually needless commas—but the vigorous space dash separating rhetorical breathing (as jazz musician drawing breath between outblown phrases)—"measured pauses which are the essentials of our speech"—"divisions of the *sounds* we hear"—"time and how to note it down."

SCOPING. Not "selectivity" of expression but following free deviation (association) of mind into limitless blow-on-subject seas of thought, swimming in sea of English with no discipline other than rhythms of rhetorical exhalation and expostulated statement, like a fist coming down on a table with each complete utterance, bang! (the space dash)—Blow as deep as you want—write as deeply, fish as far down as you want, satisfy yourself first, then reader cannot fail to receive telepathic shock and meaning-excitement by same laws operating in his own human mind.

LAG IN PROCEDURE. No pause to think of proper word but the infantile pileup of scatological buildup words till satisfaction is gained, which will turn out to be a great appending rhythm to a thought and be in accordance with Great Law of timing.

TIMING. Nothing is muddy that *runs in time* and to laws of *time*—Shakespearian stress of dramatic need to speak now in own unalterable way or forever hold tongue—*no revisions* (except obvious rational mistakes, such as names or *calculated* insertions in act of not writing but *inserting*).

CENTER OF INTEREST. Begin not from preconceived idea of what to say about image but from jewel center of interest in subject of image at *moment* of writing, and write outwards swimming in sea of language to peripheral release and exhaustion—Do not afterthink except for poetic or P. S. reasons. Never afterthink to "improve" or defray impressions, as the best writing is always the most painful personal wrung-out tossed from cradle warm protective mind—tap from yourself the song of yourself, *blow!—now!—your* way is your only way—"good"—or "bad"—always honest, "ludicrous" spontaneous, "confessional" interesting, because not "crafted." Craft *is* craft.

STRUCTURE OF WORK. Modern bizarre structures (science fiction, etc.) arise from language being dead, "different" themes give illusion of "new" life. Follow roughly outlines in outfanning movement over subject, as river rock, so mindflow over jewel-center need (run your mind over it, *once*) arriving at pivot, where what was dim formed "beginning" becomes sharp-necessitating "ending" and language shortens in race to wire of time-race of work, following laws of Deep Form, to conclusion, last words, last trickle—Night is The End.

MENTAL STATE. If possible write "without consciousness" in semi-trance (as Yeats' later "trance writing") allowing subconscious to admit in own uninhibited interesting necessary and so "modern" language what conscious art would censor, and write excitedly, swiftly, with writing-or-typing-cramps, in accordance (as from center to periphery) with laws of orgasm, Reich's "beclouding of consciousness." *Come* from within, out—to relaxed and said.

. . . the whole world's coming as the big engine booms and balls by with the madmen of the white cap california in there flossing and wow there's just no end to all this wine—

From "Conclusion of the Railroad Earth" (1960)

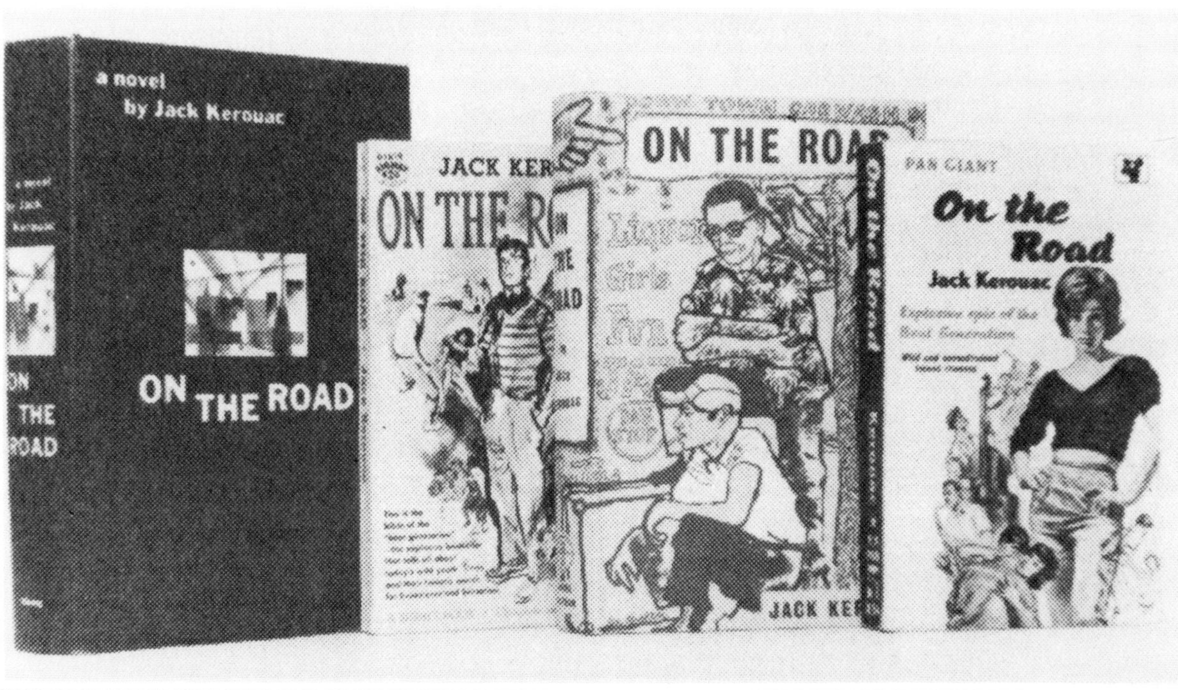

The first edition, first paperback, first English edition, and first English paperback of On the Road

ARTICLE:

Allen Ginsberg, "The Dharma Bums," *Village Voice*, 12 November 1958, pp. 3-5.

In 1953 Kerouac became interested in Buddhism, particularly identifying with the first of "the four truths"–Existence is Suffering. Kerouac wrote The Dharma Bums, *"my first and best miracle," in November of 1957. Allen Ginsberg had introduced both Kerouac and Cassady to Buddhist writings.*

A few facts to clear up a lot of bull. "On the Road" was written around 1950, in the space of several weeks, mostly on benny, an extraordinary project, sort of a flash of inspiration on a new approach to prose, an attempt to tell completely, all at once, everything on his mind in relation to the hero Dean Moriarty, spill it all out at once and follow the convolutions of the active mind for direction as to the "structure of the confession." And discover the rhythm of the mind at work at high speed in prose. An attempt to trap the prose of truth mind by means of a highly scientific attack on new prose method. The result was a magnificent single paragraph several blocks long, rolling, like the Road itself, the length of an entire onionskin teletype roll. The sadness that this was never published in its most exciting form—its original discovery—but hacked and punctuated and broken—the rhythms and swing of it broken—by presumptuous literary critics in publishing houses. The original mad version is greater than the published version, the manuscript still exists and someday when everybody's dead be published as it is. Its greatness (like the opening pages of Miller's "Cancer")—the great spirit of adventure into poetic composition. And great tender delicacy of language.

The long lines of "Howl" are piddling compared to the sustained imagic rhythms of that magnificent endless paragraph. Some of the original, a lot of it, can be seen in the published version though. The book took 7-8 years to appear in mutilated form. By then K had disappeared down that road and was invisible, magic art car soul.

The conception for such prose came from the hero of the Road himself, Moriarty's prototype, who sent K a long wild introspective 40-singlespace-page letter. It's been lost, by me, I think.

The next step (after the rejection of the original "Road") was to redo the subject, chronological account of the hero's life, in regular gothic-Melvillian prose.

That was started with one magic chapter about a Denver football field. But then K said, shove publishing and literary preconceptions, I want something I can *read*, some interesting prose, for my old age. "Visions of Neal" and "Dr. Sax" (1951-53) and another dozen subsequent books (prose, poetry, biography, meditation, translation, sketching, novels, nouvelles, fragments of brown wrapping paper, golden parchments scribbled at midnight, strange notebooks in Mexico and Desolation Peak and Ozone Park) follow.

Writing is like piano playing, the more you do it the more you know how to play a piano. And improvise, like Bach.

Not a mechanical process: the mechanical and artless practice would have been to go on writing regular novels with regular types form and dull prose. Well, I don't know why I'm arguing.

Too many critics (all incomplete because they themselves do not know how to write). Pound said not to take advice from someone who had not himself produced a masterpiece.

Am I writing for The Village Voice or the Hearing of God? In a monster mechanical mass-medium age full of horrible people with wires in their heads, the explanation is hard to make; after everybody's cash-conscious egotistical book-reviewing, trend-spotting brother has bespoke his own opinion.

It's all gibberish, everything that has been said. There's not many competent explainers. I'm speaking of the Beat Generation, which after all is quite an Angelic Idea. As to what non-writers, journalists, etc., have made of it, as usual—well, it's their bad poetry not Kerouac's.

Be that as it may, "The Subterraneans" (1953) and "The Dharma Bums" (1958) are sketchy evidence of the prose pilgrimage he's made.

The virtue of "The Subterraneans" was that it was, at last, published, completely his own prose, no changes.

An account of his method of prose (written 1953) about the time of the composition of "The Subterraneans" is reprinted in Evergreen Review, Vol. II, No. 8, from the No. 8 of the Black Mountain Review.

An excellent sample of the kind of sentence, the peculiar kind of rhythm, the appropriate alterations of square syntax, the juicy kind of imagery, the intimacy and juxtaposition of strange eternal detail, the very modernity of the thought, the very individuality (and therefore universality) of the specific sense perceptions, are to be found, for instance, in the long sentence that winds from the 6th line of p. 34 to the 13th line of p. 35 ("The Subterraneans").

(Please quote this if you have room.)

[*Not that kind of room*—Ed.]

Spontaneous Bop Prosody, a nickname one might

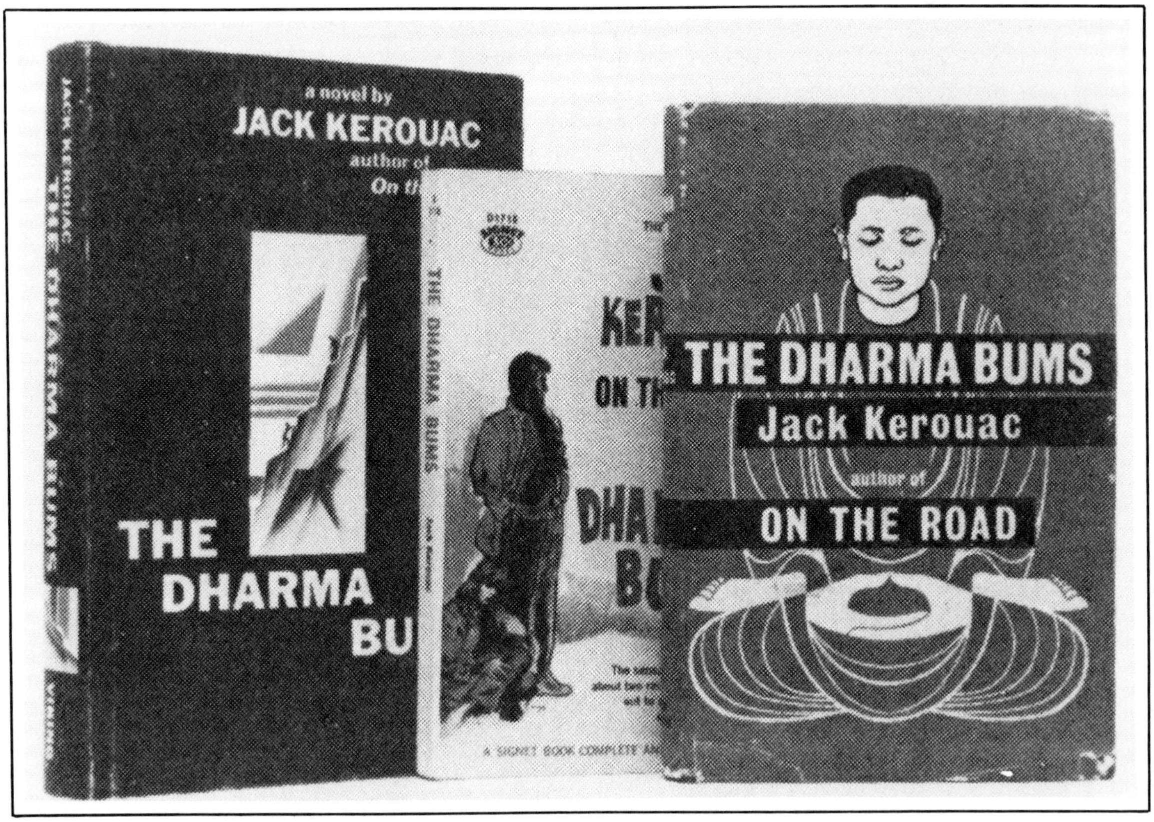

The first edition, first paperback, and first English edition of The Dharma Bums

give to this kind of writing—that is to say, read aloud and notice how the motion of the sentence corresponds to the motion of actual excited talk.

It takes enormous art (being a genius and writing a lot) to get to that point in prose. (And trusting God.)

Bop because, partly, in listening to the new improvisatory freedoms of progressive musicians, one develops an ear for one's own actual sounds. One does not force them into the old rhythm. Unless one wishes to protect one's old emotions by falsifying the new ones and making them fit the forms of the old.

Jack very concerned with the rhythm of his sentences, he enjoys that like he enjoys jazz, Bach, Buddhism, or the rhythm in Shakespeare, apropos of whom he oft remarks: "Genius is *funny*." The combinations of words and the rhythmic variations make masters laugh together (much as the two dopey sages giggling over a Chinese parchment—a picture in the Freer Gallery). All this ties in with the half-century-old struggle for the development of an American prosody to match our own speech and thinking rhythms. It's all quite traditional actually you see. Thus W. C. Williams has preached the tradition of "invention."

All this is quite obvious except to those who are not involved with the radical problems of artistic form.

"Dharma Bums" is a late and recent book, he's weary of the world and prose. Extraordinary mystic testament, however, and record of various inner signposts on the road to understanding of the Illusion of Being.

The sentences are shorter (shorter than the great flowing inventive sentences of *Dr. Sax*), almost as if he were writing a book of a thousand *haikus*—Buddhist Visionary at times. He's had an actual religious experience over a prolonged period of time. This book puts it, for convenience, in the form of a novel about another interesting friend. The passages of solitary meditation are the best I'd say. The wildest sentence, perhaps:

"Suddenly came the drenching fall rains, all-night rain, millions of acres of Bo-trees being washed and washed, and in my attic millenial rats wisely sleeping."

Now that's a very strange sentence, an oddly personal associative jump in the middle of it to the eternal rats. Not many prose writers alive (Céline, Genet, a few others) would have the freedom and intelligence to trust their own minds, remember they made that jump, not censor it but write it down and discover its beauty. That's what I look for in K's prose. He's gone very far out in discovering (or remembering, or transcribing) the perfect patterns that his own mind makes, and trusting them, and seeing their importance—to rhythm, to imagery, to the very structure of the "novel."

In this, in the present American scene in prose, he is the great master innovator. There are others (Robert Creeley, maybe I don't understand what he's doing in prose though his poetry is perfect I know). And our legendary unpublished Wm. S. Burroughs.

A few other notes. The meditation in the woods, published originally in Chicago Review, Zen issue, is an excellent sincere long passage. Reading it one wonders how anybody but a boor can vision Kerouac as anything but a gentle, intelligent, suffering prose saint. The abuse he's taken is disgusting, and the technical ignorance of most of his reviewers both pro and con is scandalous.

There has not been criticism that has examined his

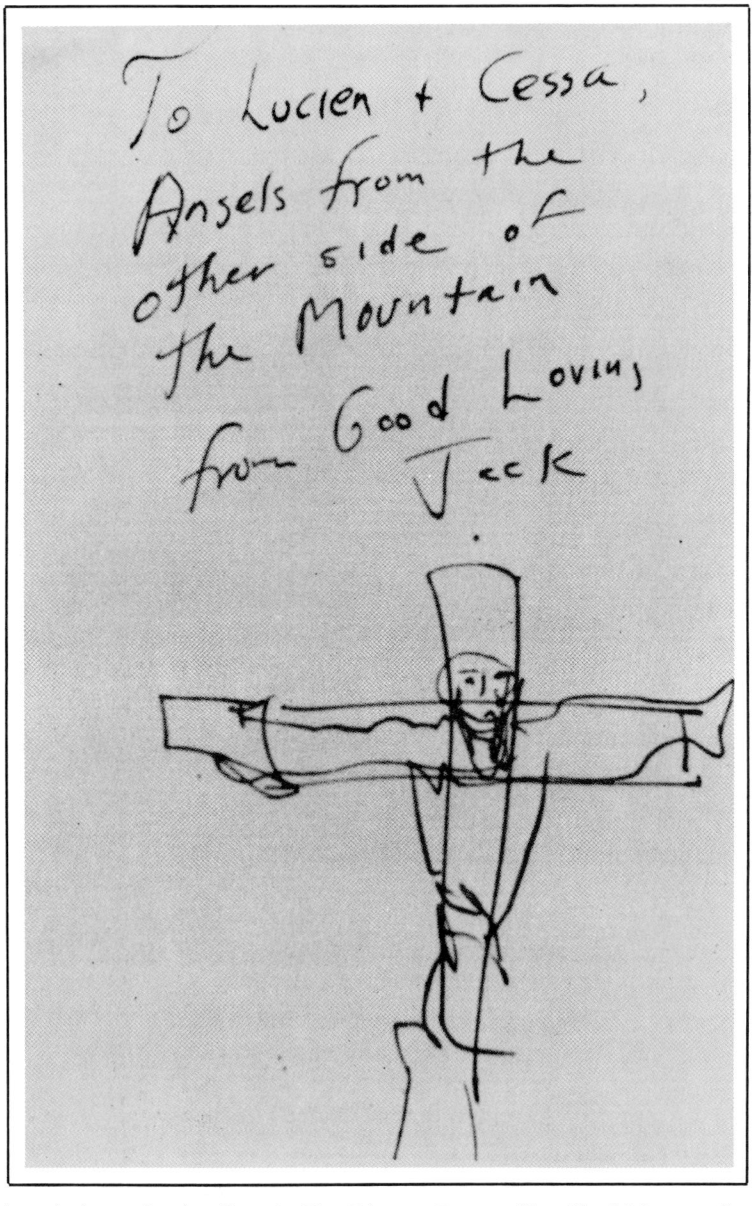

Kerouac's inscription to Lucien Carr in The Dharma Bums *(Bradford Morrow Catalogue 5)*

Advertisement in the New York Times Book Review, *12 October 1958*

prose purpose—nor his hip-beat insight and style—nor, finally, his holy content. It takes one to find one. Don't expect much understanding from academic journalists who, for all their pretense at civilization, have learned little but wicked opinion. (And you, Wicked Opinion—wrote Gregory Corso).

I'm only vomiting up some of the horror of Literature. Hacks in every direction. And a nation brainwashed by hacks. I begin to see why Pound went paranoiac, if he did. It's the same situation as 1910. There is a great revolution, innovation, in poetry and prose and going on now—continuing. That the academies have learned so little in the meantime—I feel betrayed. I'll stop before I go mad.

Chapter 34, "Dharma Bums," winds up with a great series of perfectly connected associations in visionary *haikus* (little jumps of the "freedom of eternity"). (Two images set side by side that make a flash in the mind.) Particularly pp. 241-2. Book ends with a great holy Blah! At last America has a new visionary poet. So let us talk of Angels.

ARTICLE:

Jack Kerouac, "The Last Word," *Escapade*, 3 (June 1959): 72.

Kerouac attempted to explain his own position—as well as the places of Allen Ginsberg, William Burroughs, Gregory Corso, and others—in American literature with this article in a "skin" magazine to which he contributed regularly during 1956-1961.

My position in the current American literary scene is simply that I got sick and tired of the conventional English sentence which seemed to me so ironbound in its rules, so inadmissable with reference to the actual format of my mind as I had learned to probe it in the modern spirit of Freud and Jung, that I couldn't express myself through that form any more. How many sentences do you see in current novels that say, "The snow was on the ground, and it was difficult for the car to climb the hill"? By the childish device of taking what was originally two short sentences, and sticking in a comma with an "and," these great contemporary prose "craftsmen" think they have labored out a sentence. As far as I can see it is two short sets of imagery belonging to a much longer sentence the total imagery of which would finally say something we never heard before if the writer dared to utter it out.

Shame seems to be the key to repression in writing as well as in psychological malady. If you don't stick to what you first thought, and to the words the thought brought, what's the sense of bothering with it anyway, what's the sense of foisting your little lies on others? What I find to be really "stupefying in its unreadability" is this laborious and dreary lying called craft and revision by writers, and certainly recognized by the sharpest psychologists as sheer blockage of the mental spontaneous process known 2,500 years ago as "The Seven Streams of Swiftness."

Those who will answer ESCAPADES's "The Beginning of Bop" letter contest (April issue) with disagreeing notes may be right, and I may be wrong, but it has been recorded in the *Surangama Sutra* that Gotama Buddha did

In 1959 three 33 1/3 recordings were made of Kerouac reading: Jack Kerouac Blues and Haikus, *with jazz accompaniment;* Jack Kerouac Steve Allen Poetry for the Beat Generation; *and* Readings by Jack Kerouac on the Beat Generation.

say "If you are now desirous of more perfectly understanding Supreme Enlightenment, you must learn to answer questions spontaneously with no recourse to discriminative thinking. For the Tathagatas (the Passers-Through) in the ten quarters of the universes, because of the straight-forwardness of their minds and the spontaneity of their mentations, have ever remained, from beginningless time to endless time, of one pure Suchness with the enlightening nature of pure Mind-Essence."

Which is pretty strange old news.

My opinion about current American literature is that the best of it has not been published yet. Only recently for instance have they begun to print some of William Seward Burroughs' huge *Naked Lunch*, a work that may prove repulsive to many, many people when they get to see it but in time will mellow in their minds with the changing of the times into a soft song of human love (*Lolita*'s nothing compared to it, *de Sade* pales). Some of it will mellow into a soft human song, that is, and the rest of it, the "reprehensible" part, will become known as high-grade American Humor in the great tradition, by the world's greatest living satirist. His language is Mid-American Missourian ("Motel Motel Motel loneliness moans across the continent like fog horns over still oily water tidal rivers").

A fabulous young American poet of the very first magnitude in the history of English is Gregory Corso, whose best long poems, *Bomb*, *Army*, *Marriage* and whole Mexicanas of notebooks of poetry he scribbled in Mexico have not been printed (and a lot of his best work he's personally rejected himself and hid under floorboards, and some he lost by the suitcaseful in buses!) ("O Atom Bomb, resound thy tanky knees!").

Allen Ginsberg's entire output since *Howl* and much of it before he hasn't even bothered to type up, let alone submit. His work is evenly Ginsbergian, I like best his wild little notebooks in which he thinks he's "making notes" for future poems and instead the poems are there, perfect ("Max who doesn't swing as much but paints asiatic mandalas is here, also great crowd of new people, african sculpting paranoiac spades and one short glitter-eyed egyptian who blows bop is a poltroon & works in bodybuilding school teaching").

My own best prose has yet to be published, my *Visions* and *Dreams* and *Dharmas*—when I want a friend to enjoy my style I hand him these unpublished things but the editors have been reluctant to go all out and print these. ("Madroad driving men ahead, lonely, leading around the bend into the openings of space towards the horizon Wasatch snows promised us in the vision of the West, spine heights at the World's end, coast of blue Pacific starry night—nobone halfbanana moons sloping in the tangled night sky, the torments of great formations in mist, the huddled invisible insect in the car racing onwards, illuminate.")

Poetry and prose rejects of people like Phil Whalen, Gary Snyder, Denise Levertov, Robert Creely, in fact e.e. cummings, Auden, James Jones, Algren, etc. are probably the most interesting things in American Lit today yet editors have been sifting through writers' manuscripts for the rocks of fool's gold and letting the real gold dust drop. Editors and writers have been engaged on a campaign of systematic rejection of everything except the most systematic manuscripts. In fact, the notebook should come back, printed, and like in France the cheap paperback editions of a writer's entire collected works, notes and outcries and doodle-drawings and all. This would institute a literature of the facts of life and writing, not of mere readability measurement—a rich *school* of writing, assisted by wise editors like Don Allen of *Evergreen Review* and Irving Rosenthal of *Chicago Review* and Leroi Jones, the emergence of something better than the novel (dead as the Victoria) and something better than fanciful versification, to be rejected as diarrhea of the mouth for fifty years by critics but accepted and enjoyed as unabashed language by *readers*.

ARTICLE:

Anonymous, "Downbeat," *Newsweek*, 19 December 1960.

Kerouac disliked being called a "Beatnik." When a columnist suggested that Kerouac had succeeded Norman Mailer as the Existentialist Party's candidate for Mayor, Kerouac said, "It is not my fault that certain so-called Bohemian elements have found in my writings something to hang their peculiar Beatnik theories on. . . . I hope before I die I'll be recognized for what I really am—someone who never was and never cared to be of the Beatnik clan."

Downbeat: In the Long Island pad that he shares with his mother, beatnik-branded author Jack Kerouac spends most of his time writing, he insisted. So how could there be any truth in the Broadway column note that he plans to run for mayor of New York City on an Existentialist Party ticket? "I don't even vote," Kerouac said. *"I never even leave the house except to go out and get drunk." Furthermore: "Existentialists are atheists. I believe in God; I have my rosary."* Most of all, Kerouac seemed to resent the column's reference to him as a beatnik: "I don't think I've ever said 'cool' in my life, and I've never had a beard. They itch."

INTRODUCTION:

Henry Miller, "Preface," *The Subterraneans* (New York: Avon, 1959).

Kerouac wrote The Subterraneans *in October of 1953. The book describes his two-month affair with a black woman he refers to as "Mardou." Keeping awake with benzedrine, Kerouac typed the manuscript in "three full moon nights." When* The Subterraneans *was reprinted in paperback, pre-beat figure Henry Miller provided this preface.*

Jack Kerouac has done something to our immaculate prose from which it may never recover. A passionate lover of language, he knows how to use it. Born virtuoso that he is, he takes pleasure in defying the laws and conventions of literary expression which cripple genuine, untrammeled communication between reader and writer. As he has so well said in "The Essentials of Spontaneous Prose"—"Satisfy yourself first, then reader cannot fail to receive telepathic shock and meaning-excitement by same laws operating in his own human mind." His integrity is such that he can give the semblance, at times, of running counter to his own principles. (*Cancer! Schmanser!* What's the difference, so long as you're healthy!) His learning, by no means superficial, he can bandy about as something of no consequence. Does it matter? Nothing matters. Everything is of equal importance or non-importance, from a truly creative standpoint.

Yet you can't say he's cool. He's hot, red hot. And if he's far out, he's also near and dear, a blood brother, an alter ego. He's there, everywhere, in the guise of Everyman. The observer and the observed. "A gentle, intelligent, suffering prose saint," Allen Ginsberg says of him.

We say that the poet, or genius, is always ahead of his time. True, but only because he's so thoroughly *of* his time. "Keep moving!" he urges. "We've had all this a thousand million times before." ("Advance always!" said Rimbaud.) But the stick-in-the-muds don't follow this kind of talk. (They haven't even caught up with Isidore Ducasse.) So what do they do? They pull him down off his perch, they starve him, they kick his teeth down his throat. Sometimes they are less merciful—they pretend he doesn't exist.

Everything Kerouac writes about—those weird, hauntingly ubiquitous characters whose names may be read backwards or upside down, those lovely, nostalgic, intimate-grandiose stereoptican views of America, those nightmarish, ventilated joy-rides in gondolas and hot rods—plus the language he uses (à la Gautier in reverse) to describe his "earthly-heavenly visions," surely even the readers of Time and Life, of the Digests and the Comics, cannot fail to discern the rapport between these hypergonic extravaganzas and such perennial blooms as the *Golden Ass*, the *Satyricon*, and *Pantagruel*.

The good poet, or in this case the "spontaneous Bop prosodist," is always alive to the idiomatic lingo of his time—the swing, the beat, the disjunctive metaphoric rhythm which comes so fast, so wild, so scrimmaged, so unbelievably albeit delectably mad, that when transmitted to paper no one recognizes it. None but the poets, that is. He "invented it," people will say. Insinuating that it was souped up. What they should say is: "He *got* it." He got it, he dug it, he put it down. ("You pick it up, Nazz!")

When someone asks, "Where does he get that stuff?" say: "From you!" Man, he lay awake all night listening with eyes and ears. A night of a thousand years.

The Subterraneans, *a book Kerouac warned his mother never to read, was made into a movie in 1960. Above is the Metro-Goldwyn-Mayer lobby poster.*

Heard it in the womb, heard it in the cradle, heard it in school, heard it on the floor of life's stock exchange where dreams are traded for gold. And *man*, he's sick of hearing it. He wants to move on. He wants to *blow*. But will you let him?

This is the age of miracles. The day of the killer-diller is over; the sex maniacs are out on a limb; the daring trapeze artists have broken their necks. Day of wonders, when our men of science, aided and abetted by the high priests of the Pentagon, give free instruction in the technique of mutual, but total, destruction. Progress, what! Make it into a readable novel, if you can. But don't beef about life-and-letters if you're a death-eater. Don't tell us about good "clean"—no fall outs!—literature. Let the poets speak. They may be "beat," but they're not riding the atom-powered Juggernaut. Believe me, there's nothing clean, nothing healthy, nothing promising about this age of wonders—except the telling. And the Kerouacs will probably have the last word.

ARTICLE:

Jack Kerouac, "The Origins of a Generation," *Playboy*, 6 (June 1959): 31-32, 42, 79.

In this article Kerouac attempted to explain his conception of the term beat *and his association with the "Beat Generation."*

This necessarily'll have to be about myself. I'm going all out.

That nutty picture of me on the cover of *On the Road* results from the fact that I had just gotten down from a high mountain where I'd been for two months completely alone and usually I was in the habit of combing my hair of course because you have to get rides on the highway and all that and you usually want girls to look at you as though you were a man and not a wild beast but my poet friend Gregory Corso opened his shirt and took out a silver crucifix that was hanging from a chain and said "Wear this and wear it outside your shirt and don't comb your hair!" so I spent several days around San Francisco going around with him and others like that, to parties, arties, parts, jam sessions, bars, poetry readings, churches, walking talking poetry in the streets, walking talking God in the streets (and at one point a strange gang of hoodlums got mad and said "What right does he got to wear that?" and my own gang of musicians and poets told them to cool it) and finally on the third day *Mademoiselle* magazine wanted to take pictures of us all so I posed just like that, wild hair, crucifix, and all, with Gregory Corso, Allen Ginsberg and Phil Whalen, and the only publication which later did not erase the crucifix from my breast (from that plaid sleeveless cotton shirt-front) was *The New York Times*, therefore *The New York Times* is as beat as I am, and I'm glad I've got a friend. I mean it sincerely, God bless *The New York Times* for not erasing the crucifix from my picture as though it was something distasteful. As a matter of fact, who's *really* beat around here, I mean if you wanta talk of Beat as "beat down" the people who erased the crucifix are really the "beat down" ones and not *The New York Times*, myself, and Gregory Corso the poet. I am not ashamed to wear the crucifix of my Lord. It is because I am Beat, that is, I believe in beatitude and that God so loved the world that he gave his only begotten son to it. I am sure no priest would've condemned me for wearing the crucifix outside my shirt everywhere and *no matter where* I went, even to have my picture taken by *Mademoiselle*. So you people don't believe in God. So you're all big smart know-it-all Marxists and Freudians, hey? Why don't you come back in a million years and tell me all about it, angels?

Recently Ben Hecht said to me on TV "Why are you afraid to speak out your mind, what's wrong with this country, what is everybody afraid of?" Was he talking to me? And all he wanted me to do was speak out my mind *against* people, he sneeringly brought up Dulles, Eisenhower, the Pope, all kinds of people like that habitually he would sneer at with Drew Pearson, *against* the world he wanted, this is his idea of freedom, he calls it freedom. Who knows, my God, but that the universe is not one vast sea of compassion actually, the veritable holy honey, beneath all this show of personality and cruelty. In fact who knows but that it isn't the solitude of the oneness of the essence of everything, the solitude of the actual oneness of the unbornness of the unborn essence of everything, nay the true pure foreverhood, that big blank potential that can ray forth anything it wants from its pure store, that blazing bliss, *Mattivajrakaruna* the Transcendental Diamond Compassion! No, I want to speak *for* things, for the crucifix I speak out, for the Star of Israel I speak out, for the divinest man who ever lived who was a German (Bach) I speak out, for sweet Mohammed I speak out, for Buddha I speak out, for Lao-tse and Chuang-tse I speak out, for D. T. Suzuki I speak out . . . why should I attack what I love out of life. This is Beat. Live your lives out? Naw, *love* your lives out. When they come and stone you at least you won't have a glass house, just your glassy flesh.

That wild eager picture of me on the cover of *On the Road* where I look so Beat goes back much further than 1948 when John Clellon Holmes (author of *Go* and *The Horn*) and I were sitting around trying to think up the meaning of the Lost Generation and the subsequent Existentialism and I said "You know, this is really a beat generation" and he leapt up and said "That's it, that's right!" It goes back to the 1880s when my grandfather Jean-Baptiste Kerouac used to go out on the porch in big thunderstorms and swing his kerosene lamp at the lightning and yell "Go ahead, go, if you're more powerful than I am strike me and put the light out!" while the mother and the children cowered in the kitchen. And the light never went out. Maybe since I'm supposed to be the spokesman of the Beat Generation (I *am* the originator of the term, and around it the term and the generation have taken shape) it should be pointed out that all this "Beat" guts therefore goes back to my ancestors who were Bretons who were the most independent group of nobles in all old Europe and kept fighting Latin France to the last wall (although a big blond bosun on a merchant ship snorted when I told him my ancestors were Bretons in Cornwall, Brittany, "Why, we Wikings used to swoop down and steal your nets!"). Breton, Wiking, Irishman, Indian, madboy, it doesn't make any difference, there is no doubt about the Beat Generation, at least the core of it, being a swinging group of new American men intent on joy. . . . Irresponsibility? Who wouldn't help a dying man on an empty road? No and the Beat Generation goes back to the wild parties my father used to have at home in the 1920s and 1930s in New England that were so fantastically loud nobody could sleep for blocks around and when the cops came they always had a drink. It goes back to the wild and raving childhood of playing the Shadow under windswept trees of New England's gleeful autumn, and the howl of the Moon Man on the sandbank until we caught him in a tree (he was an "older" guy of 15), the maniacal laugh of certain neighborhood madboys, the furious humor of whole gangs playing basketball till long after dark in the park, it goes back to those crazy days before World War II when teenagers drank beer on Friday nights at Lake ballrooms and worked off their hangovers playing baseball on Saturday afternoon followed by a dive in the brook—and our fathers wore straw hats like W. C. Fields. It goes back to the completely senseless babble of the Three Stooges, the ravings of the Marx Brothers (the tenderness of Angel Harpo at harp, too).

It goes back to the inky ditties of old cartoons (Krazy Kat with the irrational brick)—to Laurel and

Hardy in the Foreign Legion—to Count Dracula and his *smile* to Count Dracula shivering and hissing back before the Cross—to the Golem horrifying the persecutors of the Ghetto—to the quiet sage in a movie about India, unconcerned about the plot—to the giggling old Tao Chinaman trotting down the sidewalk of old Clark Gable Shanghai—to the holy old Arab warning the hotbloods that Ramadan is near. To the Werewolf of London a distinguished doctor in his velour smoking jacket smoking his pipe over a lamplit tome on botany and suddenly hairs grown on his hands, his cat hisses, and he slips out into the night with a cape and a slanty cap like the caps of people in breadlines—to Lamont Cranston so cool and sure suddenly becoming the frantic Shadow going mwee hee hee ha ha in the alleys of New York imagination. To Popeye the sailor and the Sea Hag and the meaty gunwales of boats, to Cap'n Easy and Wash Tubbs screaming with ecstasy over canned peaches on a cannibal isle, to Wimpy looking X-eyed for a juicy hamburger such as they make no more. To Jiggs ducking before a household of furniture flying through the air, to Jiggs and the boys at the bar and the corned beef and cabbage of old woodfence noons—to King Kong his eyes looking into the hotel window with tender huge love for Fay Wray—nay, to Bruce Cabot in mate's cap leaning over the rail of a fogbound ship saying "Come aboard." It goes back to when grapefruits were thrown at crooners and harvestworkers at bar-rails slapped burlesque queens on the rump. To when fathers took their sons to the Twi League game. To the days of Babe Callahan on the waterfront, Dick Barthelmess camping under a London streetlamp. To dear old Basil Rathbone looking for the Hound of the Baskervilles (a dog big as the Gray Wolf who will destroy Odin)—to dear old bleary Doctor Watson with a brandy in his hand. To Joan Crawford her raw shanks in the fog, in striped blouse smoking a cigarette at sticky lips in the door of the waterfront dive. To train whistles of steam engines out above the moony pines. To Maw and Paw in the Model A clanking on to get a job in California selling used cars making a whole lotta money. To the glee of America, the honesty of America, the honesty of oldtime grafters in straw hats as well as the honesty of oldtime waiters in line at the Brooklyn Bridge in *Winterset*, the funny spitelessness of old bigfisted America like Big Boy Williams saying "Hoo? Hee? Huh?" in a movie about Mack Trucks and slidingdoor lunchcarts. To Clark Gable, his certain smile, his confident leer. Like my grandfather this America was invested with wild selfbelieving individuality and this had begun to disappear around the end of World War II with so many great guys dead (I can think of half a dozen from my own boyhood groups) when suddenly it began to emerge again, the hipsters began to appear gliding around saying "Crazy, man."

When I first saw the hipsters creeping around Times Square in 1944 I didn't like them either. One of them, Huncke of Chicago, came up to me and said "Man, I'm beat." I knew right away what he meant somehow. At that time I still didn't like bop which was then being introduced by Bird Parker and Dizzy Gillespie and Bags Jackson (on vibes), the last of the great swing musicians was Don Byas who went to Spain right after, but then I began . . . but earlier I'd dug all my jazz in the old Minton Playhouse (Lester Young, Ben Webster, Joey Guy, Charlie Christian, others) and when I first heard Bird and Diz

First edition cover of Maggie Cassidy *(1959). Originally titled* "Springtime Mary," Maggie Cassidy *tells the story of Kerouac and his first love, Mary Carney.*

in the Three Deuces I knew they were serious musicians playing a goofy new sound and didn't care what I thought, or what my friend Seymour thought. In fact I was leaning against the bar with a beer when Dizzy came over for a glass of water from the bartender, put himself right against me and reached both arms around both sides of my head to get the glass and danced away, as though knowing I'd be singing about him someday, or that one of his arrangements would be named after me someday by some goofy circumstance. Charlie Parker was spoken of in Harlem as the greatest new musician since Chu Berry and Louis Armstrong.

Anyway, the hipsters, whose music was bop, they looked like criminals but they kept talking about the same things I liked, long outlines of personal experience and vision, nightlong confessions full of hope that had become illicit and repressed by War, stirrings, rumblings of a new soul (that same old human soul). And so Huncke appeared to us and said "I'm beat" with radiant light shining out of his despairing eyes . . . a word perhaps brought from some midwest carnival or junk cafeteria. It was a new language, actually spade (Negro) jargon but you soon learned it, like "hung up" couldn't be a more economical term to mean so many things. Some of these hipsters were raving mad and talked continually. It was jazzy. Symphony Sid's all-night modern jazz and bop show was always on. By 1948 it began to take shape. That was a wild vibrating year when a group of us would walk down the street and yell hello and even stop and talk to anybody that gave us a friendly look. The hipsters had eyes. That was the year I saw Montgomery Clift, unshaven, wearing a sloppy jacket, slouching down Madison Avenue with a companion. It was the year I saw Charley Bird Parker strolling down Eighth Avenue in a black turtleneck sweater with Babs Gonzales and a beautiful girl.

By 1948 the hipsters, or beatsters, were divided into cool and hot. Much of the misunderstanding about hipsters and the Beat Generation in general today derives from the fact that there are two distinct styles of hipsterism: the "cool" today is your bearded laconic sage, or schlerm, before a hardly touched beer in a beatnik dive, whose speech is low and unfriendly, whose girls say nothing and wear black: the "hot" today is the crazy talkative shining eyed (often innocent and openhearted) nut who runs from bar to bar, pad to pad looking for everybody, shouting, restless, lushy, trying to "make it" with the subterranean beatniks who ignore him. Most Beat Generation artists belong to the hot school, naturally since that hard gemlike flame needs a little heat. In many cases the mixture is 50-50. It was a hot hipster like myself who finally cooled it in Buddhist meditation, though when I go in a jazz joint I still feel like yelling "Blow baby blow!" to the musicians though nowadays I'd get 86d for this. In 1948 the "hot hipsters" were racing around in cars like in *On the Road* looking for wild bawling jazz like Willis Jackson or Lucky Thompson (the early) or Chubby Jackson's big band while the "cool hipsters" cooled it in dead silence before formal and excellent musical groups like Lennie Tristano or Miles Davis. It's still just about the same, except that it has begun to grow into a national generation and the name "Beat" has stuck (though all hipsters hate the word).

The word "beat" originally meant poor, down and out, deadbeat, on the bum, sad, sleeping in subways. Now that the word is belonging officially it is being made to stretch to include people who do not sleep in subways but have a certain new gesture, or attitude, which I can only describe as a new *more*. "Beat Generation" has simply become the slogan or label for a revolution in manners in America. Marlon Brando was not really first to portray it on the screen. Dane Clark with his pinched Dostoievskyan face and Brooklyn accent, and of course Garfield, were first. The private eyes were Beat, if you will recall. Bogart. Lorre was Beat. In *M*, Peter Lorre started a whole revival, I mean the slouchy street walk.

I wrote *On the Road* in three weeks in the beautiful month of May 1941 while living in the Chelsea district of lower West Side Manhattan, on a 100-foot roll and put the Beat Generation in words in there, saying at the point where I am taking part in a wild kind of collegiate party with a bunch of kids in an abandoned miner's shack "These kids are great but where are Dean Moriarty and Carlo Marx? Oh well I guess they wouldn't belong in this gang, they're too *dark*, too strange, too subterranean and I am slowly beginning to join a new kind of *beat* generation." The manuscript of *Road* was turned down on the grounds that it would displease the sales manager of my publisher at that time, though the editor, a very intelligent man, said "Jack this is just like Dostoievsky, but what can I do at this time?" It was too early. So for the next six years I was a bum, a brakeman, a seaman, a panhandler, a pseudo-Indian in Mexico, anything and everything, and went on writing because my hero was Goethe and I believed in art and hoped some day to write the third part of *Faust*, which I have done in *Doctor Sax*. Then in 1952 an article was published in *The New York Times* Sunday magazine saying, the headline, " 'This is a Beat Generation' " (in quotes like that) and in the article

> *Godamn it, FEELING is what I like in art, not CRAFTINESS and the hiding of feelings.*

From Writers at Work, Fourth Series *(New York: Viking Press, 1976)*

it said that I had come up with the term first "when the face was harder to recognize," the face of the generation. After that there was some talk of the Beat Generation but in 1955 I published an excerpt from *Road* (melling it with parts of *Visions of Neal*) under the pseudonym "Jean-Louis," it was entitled *Jazz of the Beat Generation* and was copyrighted as being an excerpt from a novel-in-progress entitled *Beat Generation* (which I later changed to *On the Road* at the insistence of my new editor) and so then the term moved a little faster. The term and the cats. Everywhere began to appear strange hepcats and even college kids went around hep and cool and using the terms I'd heard on Times Square in the early Forties, it was growing somehow. But when the publishers finally took a dare and published *On the Road* in 1957 it burst open, it mushroomed, everybody began yelling about a Beat Generation. I was being interviewed everywhere I went for "what I meant" by such a thing. People began to call themselves beatniks, beats, jazzniks, bopniks, bugniks and finally I was called the "avatar" of all this.

Yet it was as a Catholic, it was not at the insistence of any of these "niks" and certainly not with their approval either, that I went one afternoon to the church of my childhood (one of them), Ste. Jeanne d'Arc in Lowell, Mass., and suddenly with tears in my eyes and had a vision of what I must have really meant with "Beat" anyhow when I heard the holy silence in the church (I was the only one in there, it was five P.M., dogs were barking outside, children yelling, the fall leaves, the candles were flickering alone just for me), the vision of the word Beat as being to mean beatific. . . . There's the priest preaching on Sunday morning, all of a sudden through a side door of the church comes a group of Beat Generation characters in strapped raincoats like the I.R.A. coming in silently to "dig" the religion . . . I knew it then.

But this was 1954, so then what horror I felt in 1957 and later 1958 naturally to suddenly see "Beat" being taken up by everybody, press and TV and Hollywood borscht circuit to include the "juvenile delinquency" shot and the horrors of a mad teeming billyclub New York and L.A. and they began to call *that* Beat, *that* beatific . . . bunch of fools marching against the San Francisco Giants protesting baseball, as if (now) in my name and I, my childhood ambition to be a big league baseball star hitter like Ted Williams so that when Bobby Thomson hit that homerun in 1951 I trembled with joy and couldn't get over it for days and wrote poems about how it is possible for the human spirit to win after all! Or, when a murder, a routine murder took place in North Beach, they labeled it a Beat Generation slaying although in my childhood I'd been famous as an eccentric in my block for stopping the younger kids from throwing rocks at the squirrels, for stopping them from frying snakes in cans or trying to blow up frogs with straws. Because my brother had died at the age of nine, his name was Gerard Kerouac, and he'd told me "Ti Jean never hurt any living being, all living beings whether it's just a little cat or squirrel or whatever, all are going to heaven straight into God's snowy arms so never hurt anything and if you see anybody hurt anything stop them as best you can" and when he died a file of gloomy nuns in black from St. Louis de France parish had filed (1926) to his deathbed to hear his last words about Heaven. And my father too, Leo, had never lifted a hand to punish me, or to punish the little pets in our house, and this teaching was delivered to me by the men in my house and I have never had anything to do with violence, hatred, cruelty, and all that horrible nonsense which, nevertheless, because God is gracious beyond all human imagining, he will forgive in the long end . . . that million years I'm asking about you, America.

And so now they have beatnik routines on TV, starting with satires about girls in black and fellows in jeans with snapknives and sweatshirts and swastikas tattooed under their armpits, it will come to respectable m.c.s. of spectaculars coming out nattily attired in Brooks Brothers jean-type tailoring and sweater-type pull-ons, in other words, it's a simple change in fashion and manners, just a history crust—like from the Age of Reason, from old Voltaire in a chair to romantic Chatterton in the moonlight—from Teddy Roosevelt to Scott Fitzgerald . . . So there's nothing to get excited about. Beat comes out, actually, of old American whoopee and it will only change a few dresses and pants and make chairs useless in the livingroom and pretty soon we'll have Beat Secretaries of State and there will be instituted new tinsels, in fact new reasons for malice and new reasons for virtue and new reasons for forgiveness. . . .

But yet, but yet, woe, woe unto those who think that the Beat Generation means crime, delinquency, immorality, amorality . . . woe unto those who attack it on the grounds that they simply don't understand history and the yearnings of human souls . . . woe unto those who don't realize that America must, will, is, changing now, for the better I say. Woe unto those who believe in the atom bomb, who believe in hating mothers and fathers, who deny the most important of the Ten Commandments, woe unto those (though) who don't believe in the unbelievable sweetness of sex love, woe unto those who are the standard bearers of death, woe unto those who believe in conflict and horror and violence and fill our books and screens and livingrooms with all that crap, woe in fact unto those who make evil movies about the Beat Generation where innocent housewives are raped by beatniks! Woe unto those who are the real dreary sinners that even God finds room to forgive. . . .

Woe unto those who spit on the Beat Generation, the wind'll blow it back.

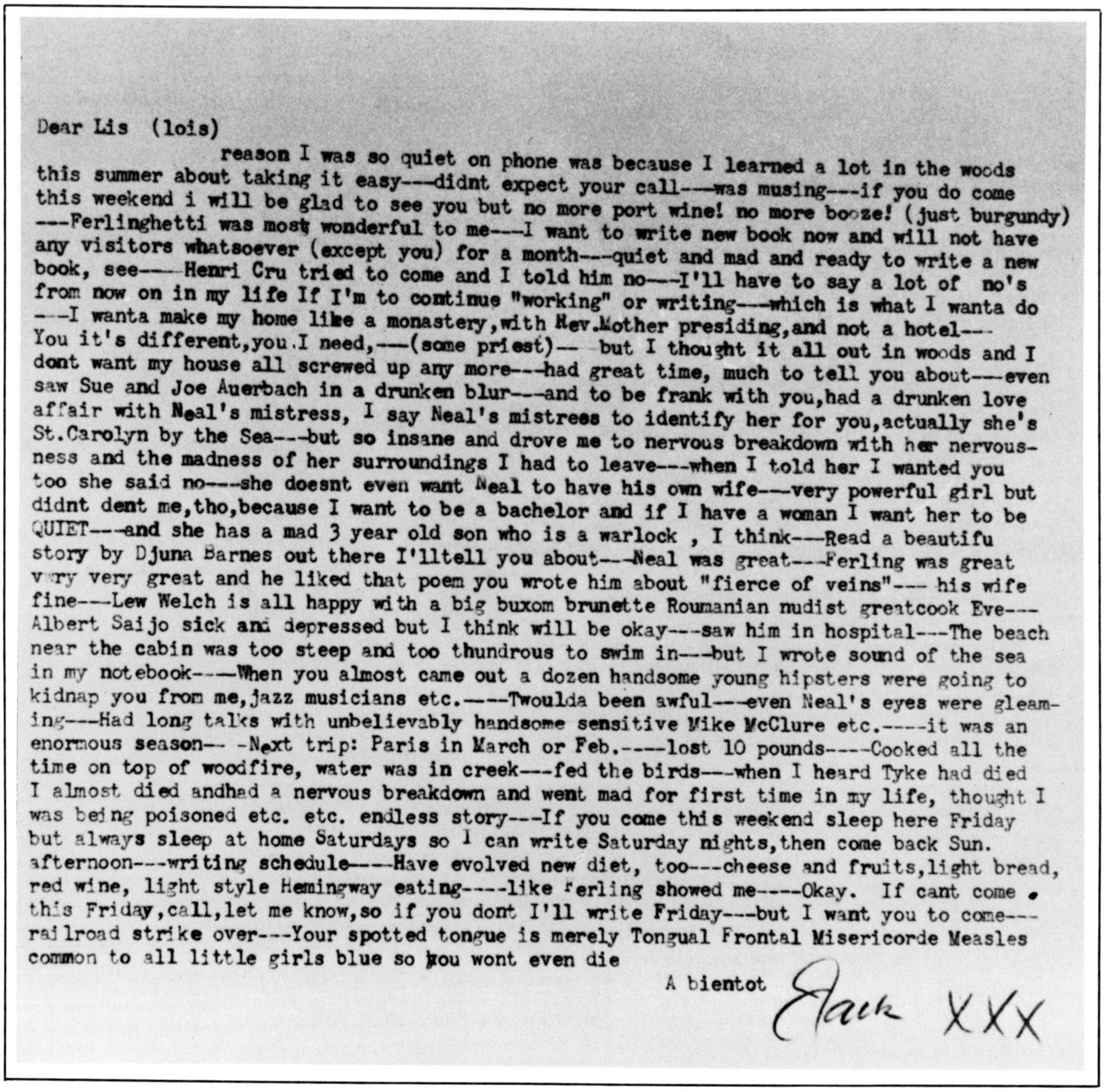

Dear Lis (lois)

reason I was so quiet on phone was because I learned a lot in the woods this summer about taking it easy---didnt expect your call---was musing---if you do come this weekend i will be glad to see you but no more port wine! no more booze! (just burgundy) ---Ferlinghetti was most wonderful to me---I want to write new book now and will not have any visitors whatsoever (except you) for a month---quiet and mad and ready to write a new book, see---Henri Cru tried to come and I told him no---I'll have to say a lot of no's from now on in my life If I'm to continue "working" or writing---which is what I wanta do ---I wanta make my home like a monastery,with Rev.Mother presiding,and not a hotel--- You it's different,you.I need,---(some priest)--- but I thought it all out in woods and I dont want my house all screwed up any more---had great time, much to tell you about---even saw Sue and Joe Auerbach in a drunken blur---and to be frank with you,had a drunken love affair with Neal's mistress, I say Neal's mistress to identify her for you,actually she's St.Carolyn by the Sea---but so insane and drove me to nervous breakdown with her nervousness and the madness of her surroundings I had to leave---when I told her I wanted you too she said no---she doesnt even want Neal to have his own wife---very powerful girl but didnt dent me,tho,because I want to be a bachelor and if I have a woman I want her to be QUIET---and she has a mad 3 year old son who is a warlock , I think---Read a beautifu story by Djuna Barnes out there I'lltell you about---Neal was great---Ferling was great very very great and he liked that poem you wrote him about "fierce of veins"--- his wife fine---Lew Welch is all happy with a big buxom brunette Roumanian nudist greatcook Eve--- Albert Saijo sick and depressed but I think will be okay---saw him in hospital---The beach near the cabin was too steep and too thundrous to swim in---but I wrote sound of the sea in my notebook---When you almost came out a dozen handsome young hipsters were going to kidnap you from me,jazz musicians etc.---Twoulda been awful---even Neal's eyes were gleaming---Had long talks with unbelievably handsome sensitive Mike McClure etc.---it was an enormous season--- -Next trip: Paris in March or Feb.---lost 10 pounds---Cooked all the time on top of woodfire, water was in creek---fed the birds---when I heard Tyke had died I almost died andhad a nervous breakdown and went mad for first time in my life, thought I was being poisoned etc. etc. endless story---If you come this weekend sleep here Friday but always sleep at home Saturdays so I can write Saturday nights,then come back Sun. afternoon---writing schedule---Have evolved new diet, too---cheese and fruits,light bread, red wine, light style Hemingway eating---like Ferling showed me---Okay. If cant come this Friday,call,let me know,so if you dont I'll write Friday---but I want you to come--- railroad strike over---Your spotted tongue is merely Tongual Frontal Misericorde Measles common to all little girls blue so you wont even die

A bientot Jack XXX

In this September 1960 letter to poet Lois Sorrells Beckwith Kerouac tells of his trip to San Francisco, where he stayed at Lawrence Ferlinghetti's Big Sur cabin and saw Neal Cassady, who had recently been released from prison (Sotheby Parke Bernet sale 4254). The Tyke mentioned was one of Kerouac's cats. This summer was later described in the novel Big Sur.

Book Review:

Anthony Hecht, *Hudson Review*, 12 (Winter 1959-1960): 601-603.

When Kerouac returned to Mexico City in 1955, he met Burroughs's friend William Maynard Garver—a sixty-year-old heroin addict after whom Kerouac modeled Old Bill Gaines of Tristessa *and* Desolation Angels. *Each day he smoked marijuana and composed the 242 "choruses" that make up* Mexico City Blues *while listening to Garver reminisce. Kerouac felt that of all his work, this was most closely related to jazz, especially bop.*

Mexico City Blues is composed of 242 poems, or "choruses," as Mr. Kerouac ingeniously calls them. They are all short, none longer than a page, and the proper way to read this book, taking a tip from Poe, is straight through at one sitting. What emerges is surprising in many ways, for Mr. Kerouac is not beyond offering some very misleading appearances. For example, there is his declaration: "I want to be considered a jazz poet blowing a long blues in an afternoon jam session on Sunday. . . . my ideas vary and sometimes roll from chorus to chorus or from halfway through a chorus to halfway into the next." His publishers have been delighted to amplify this note of American pastoralism, of the poet warbling his woodwind wild, spontaneous, simple, unbeguiled. They remark on his "improvised, nervous beat" and carry on in the heady vocabulary of *Metronome*. But this image of the seely swain is one of the poet's little impostures; his is a very "literary" book. It might have been called, "Kerouac's Cool Cantos, or, The Devaluated Pound." The structure of the whole volume is based on Pound's (as he called it) "fugal" method of interwoven themes, taking up one subject, dropping it, returning to it in altered words as a variation of the theme. (I like to wonder how many of Mr. Kerouac's admirers can comfortably imagine him writing fugues, or would be willing to trade Charley Parker for Johann Sebastian Bach.) And Pound is not the only derivative force at work: Dr. Williams is here, and so is Gertrude Stein, who has shown the poet how to make nonsense syllables out of words and words out of nonsense syllables. There is E. E. Cummings, who has shown him how to use nursery rhymes with wry and slapstick irony. There is a straightforward "Imagist" poem (chorus 151). There is even (bless his sophisticated literary soul) James Joyce: "Then all's wet underneath, to Eclipse / (Ivan the Heaven Sea-Ice King, Euclid, / Bloody Be Jupiter, Nucleus, / Nuclid, What's-His-Name—the sea / The sea-drang Scholar with mermaids, / Bloody blasted dadflap thorn it / —Neppy Tune—) / All's wet clear to Neptune's Seat."

If these writers give Mr. Kerouac a great many roles to play, they by no means exhaust his repertoire, for he also delights to adopt the garb of the Buddhist Sage. I know little about Buddhism, and am prepared to be instructed, but I do know that at the very least it is a taxing and difficult discipline to which serious and gifted men devote their entire lives; and I suspect that some of its more devout oriental practitioners would envy (if this were not contrary to the very spirit of their undertaking) the superb ease with which Mr. Kerouac attains his perfect exaltations. At least three or four times in this volume alone he "makes the scene," the seventh state of enlightenment, the first and last wisdom which is transcendent, ecstatic, coalescent. I think sadly of poor Plotinus, who in his small way, dedicated his life to just such a mode of apprehending ultimate truth, but who knew that in our present state of existence these visionary glimpses of totality were bound to be short and few, and who was forced to admit of himself and his most distinguished disciple, "I myself have realized it but three times as yet, and Porphyry hitherto not once."

And there is a related problem that can best be presented by quotation.

Got up and dressed up
and went out & got laid
Then died and got buried
in a coffin in the grave,
Man—
Yet everything is perfect,
Because it is empty
Because it is perfect
with emptiness,
Because it's not even happening.
(113th Chorus)

. . . . Death, the no-buzz,
no-voices, is, must be, the same,
as life. . . . .

I know that I'm dead.
I won't camp. I'm dead now.
. . . .
How do I know that I'm dead.
Because I'm alive
and I got work to do . . .
(235th Chorus)

What seems to me interesting here is the poet's obvious satisfaction with this complete identity of life and death. It is of course, as he realizes, an evasion of morality: in that timeless state nothing happens, so there are no consequences. I understand that Buddhists conceive of a state of being beyond morality, but I do not believe that their discipline directs them toward bliss by ignoring moral issues. Be that as it may, the interested reader is invited to compare passages like those above with another work on the same theme by T. S. Eliot, called "Sweeney Agonistes," with particular attention to the part that begins "I knew a man once did a girl in," and continuing through the line, "Death is life and life is death." Needless to say, in Eliot's little drama this conclusion is not arrived at with any composure or cheerfulness. As to which of these poets provides the most truthful and comprehensive vision of life, the reader must decide for himself.

But in spite of all the defences that have to be broken through, all the illusions Kerouac creates about himself as prophet of salvation, literary eclectic, Daphnis knocking off some hot licks on his oaten straw, there is something valuable and beguiling behind the poetry which is as curiously difficult to get at as if the book were translated from another tongue. The poet's gift for masquerade is first-class, and he is very hard to locate. But what seems to me to emerge at the end is a voice of remarkable kindness and gentleness, an engaging and modest good humor and a quite genuine spiritual simplicity that convinces as all the dogmatic assertions and affirmations did not. This is the voice of a man who has a lot of knick-knacks and hocus-pocus to get rid of, but it is the voice of a man.

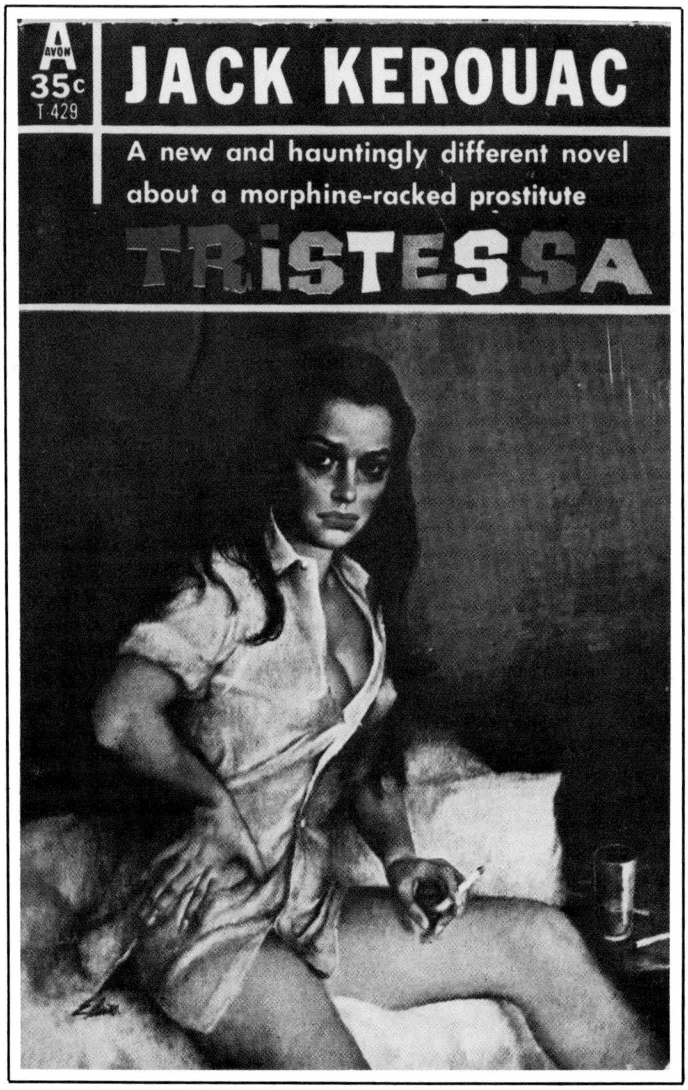

First edition cover of Tristessa *(1960), a book Kerouac regarded as sad and holy*

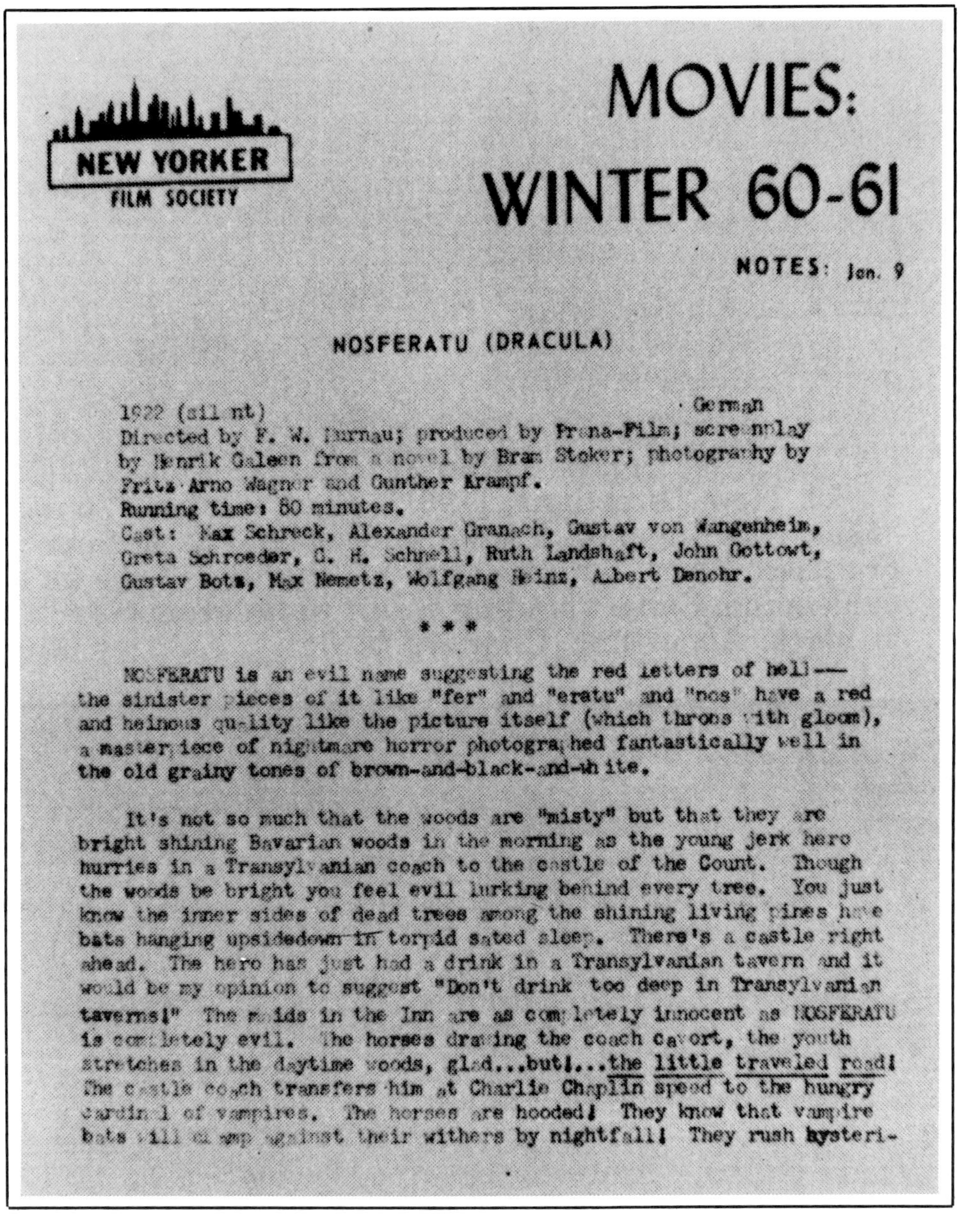

MOVIES: WINTER 60-61

NEW YORKER FILM SOCIETY

NOTES: Jan. 9

NOSFERATU (DRACULA)

1922 (silent) · German
Directed by F. W. Murnau; produced by Prana-Film; screenplay by Henrik Galeen from a novel by Bram Stoker; photography by Fritz Arno Wagner and Gunther Krampf.
Running time: 80 minutes.
Cast: Max Schreck, Alexander Granach, Gustav von Wangenheim, Greta Schroeder, G. H. Schnell, Ruth Landshaft, John Gottowt, Gustav Botz, Max Nemetz, Wolfgang Heinz, Albert Denohr.

* * *

NOSFERATU is an evil name suggesting the red letters of hell—the sinister pieces of it like "fer" and "eratu" and "nos" have a red and heinous quality like the picture itself (which throbs with gloom), a masterpiece of nightmare horror photographed fantastically well in the old grainy tones of brown-and-black-and-white.

It's not so much that the woods are "misty" but that they are bright shining Bavarian woods in the morning as the young jerk hero hurries in a Transylvanian coach to the castle of the Count. Though the woods be bright you feel evil lurking behind every tree. You just know the inner sides of dead trees among the shining living pines have bats hanging upsidedown in torpid sated sleep. There's a castle right ahead. The hero has just had a drink in a Transylvanian tavern and it would be my opinion to suggest "Don't drink too deep in Transylvanian taverns!" The maids in the Inn are as completely innocent as NOSFERATU is completely evil. The horses drawing the coach cavort, the youth stretches in the daytime woods, glad...but!...the little traveled road! The castle coach transfers him at Charlie Chaplin speed to the hungry cardinal of vampires. The horses are hooded! They know that vampire bats will clamp against their withers by nightfall! They rush hysteri-

Kerouac wrote the review of the film Nosferatu (Dracula) *for this January 1961 New Yorker Film Society flier.*

The heroes of On the Road, The Subterraneans, *etc. reappear here doing further strange things for no other particular reason than that the mind goes on, the brain ripples, the moon sinks, and everybody hides their heads under pillows with sleepingcaps.*

From "Foreword," Book of Dreams

Kerouac began keeping a spontaneous dream diary in 1952. Book of Dreams, *published in 1961, represents only a part of Kerouac's voluminous work as edited by his friend, poet Philip Whalen.*

INTERVIEW:
Farrar, Straus and Cudahy publicity release (1963).

During 1956 Kerouac wrote the first of the Duluoz Legends, which make up his fictional autobiography. Farrar, Straus & Cudahy released this interview upon publication of Visions of Gerard *in 1963.*

INTERVIEWER: At first glance, the Catholicism in your new novel, *Visions of Gerard* (Farrar, Straus September 6) seems to be something new for you. Is it?

KEROUAC: Catholicism in my books is not a new tack for me. Actually, there was some Catholicism in "The Dharma Bums" which the publishers saw fit to delete. There's a lot of Catholicism in "Big Sur," in "Lonesome Traveler," and even more in "Tristessa," and a running brief on the subject in "Maggie Cassidy." My first novel, "The Town and the City," was essentially a Catholic story. The "beat" theme in the hepcat books like "On the Road" and "The Subterraneans" is not opposed to Catholicism. I'm born a Catholic and it's nothing new with me.

At home or abroad, I always carry my rosary more or less for good luck. Most of the amateur painting I've done is of pietas, crucifixions, saints, and I have a nice collection of sacred music. I always give my stories and poems free to Jubilee Magazine as a contribution to the Church. I was baptized, received First Communion and feel quite calm about the whole thing.

INTERVIEWER: How was *Visions of Gerard* written?

KEROUAC: "Visions of Gerard" was written at the kitchen table of my sister's home in Big Easonburg Woods, North Carolina, over a ten-night stretch, midnight to dawn, ending with refreshing visits to the piney barrens out behind the cotton field at sunrise.

I did no rewriting or revising whatever, except for name changes and one important comma finally inserted somewhere, where I'd made a spontaneous mistake about it being needed, although I did reject a whole night's writing and started all over again on the section the next night.

It was all written by hand, in pencil, in little notebooks. Certain kinds of stories seem to deny the rackety typewriter.

INTERVIEWER: *Visions of Gerard* is part of the series you call the Duluoz Legend. What are your future plans for that?

KEROUAC: Future plans for the "Duluoz Legend" are to fill in the gaps left open in the chronological past. The sequel to "The Dharma Bums" is already written (called "Desolation Angels") and the sequel to that (already written) is called "Passing Through." The sequel to "Visions of Gerard" (not yet written) will be called "Vanity of Duluoz" and then come the post-"Big Sur" adventures of my future life, whatever it will be, if any.

The final scope of the Legend will be simply a completely written lifetime with all its hundreds of characters and events and levels interswirling and reappearing and becoming complete, somewhat a la Balzac and Proust. But each section, that is, each novel, has to stand by itself as an individual story with a flavor of its own and a pivot of its own. Nevertheless, they must all fit together on one shelf as a continuous tale.

INTERVIEWER: The setting for *Visions of Gerard* is your home town of Lowell. When were you last there?

KEROUAC: In October '62 and I got a big "celebrity" reception and had to run away back to New York. I'm sort of a hero there. Much fun. The people there, old football cronies, cousins, friends, new acquaintances, old newspaper confreres, the teaching fraternity, gossips, characters, all realize I just go there to bask and drink but we really have great rapports and I'm going back there soon because there are more books in that little Christian city than you could have packed in Carthage.

A golden Byzantine dome rises from the roofs along the canal; a Gothic copy of Chartres rises from the slums of Moody Street; little children speak French, Greek, Polish and even Portuguese on their way to school. And I have a recurrent dream of simply walking around the deserted twilight streets of Lowell, in the mist, eager to turn every known and fabled corner. A very eerie, recurrent dream, but it always makes me happy when I wake up.

INTERVIEWER: In a recent "Esquire" Alice Glaser says the Beats are no longer on the road, "that even Kerouac—their god—had settled down on Long Island with his mother?" Do you accept that?

KEROUAC: I've always been "settled with my mother" who supported me by working in shoe factories while I wrote most of my books years ago. She's my friend as well as my mother. When I go on the road I always have a quiet, clean home to come back to, and to work in, which probably accounts for the fact that I've published twelve books in the last six years.

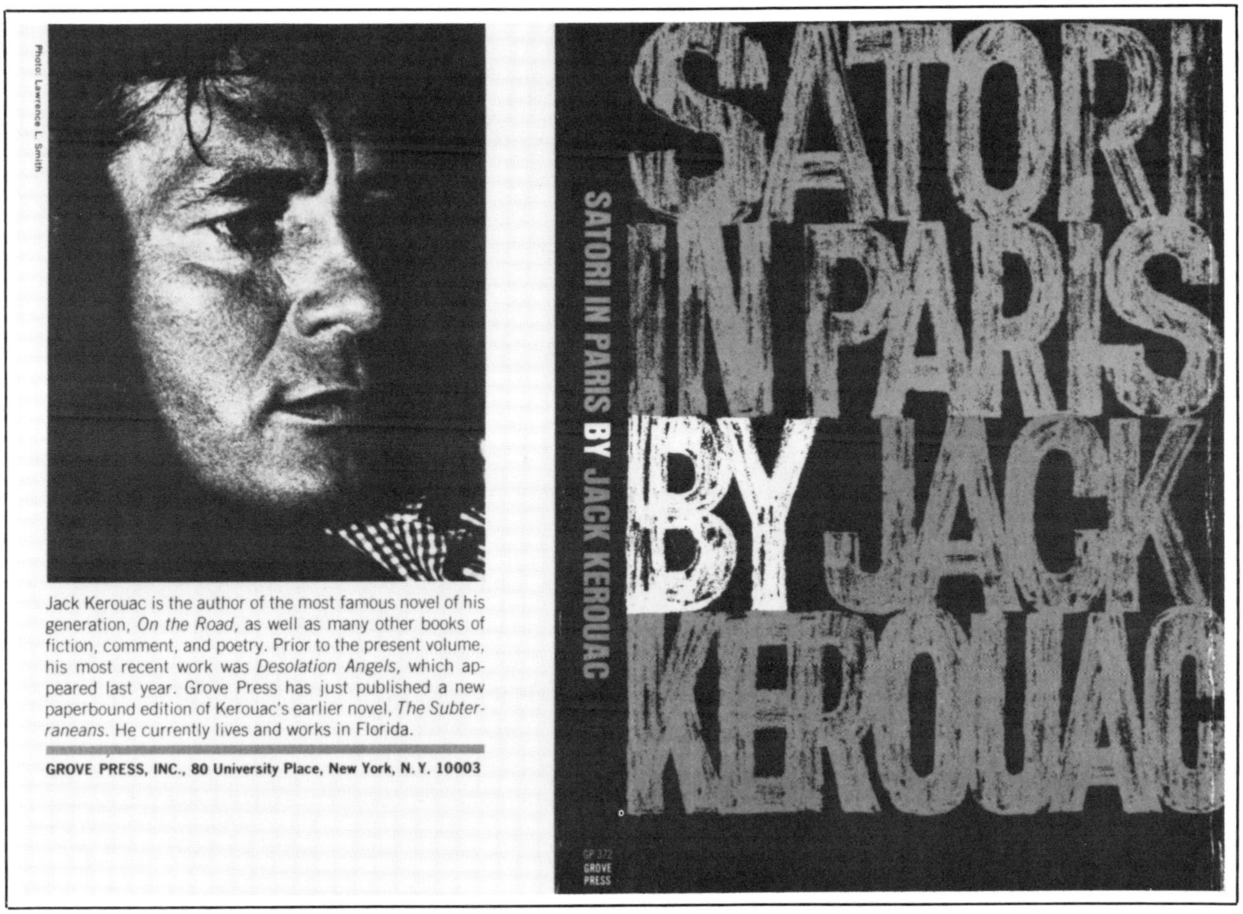
Photo: Lawrence L. Smith
Jack Kerouac is the author of the most famous novel of his generation, On the Road, as well as many other books of fiction, comment, and poetry. Prior to the present volume, his most recent work was Desolation Angels, which appeared last year. Grove Press has just published a new paperbound edition of Kerouac's earlier novel, The Subterraneans. He currently lives and works in Florida.
GROVE PRESS, INC., 80 University Place, New York, N.Y. 10003
SATORI IN PARIS BY JACK KEROUAC
SATORI IN PARIS BY JACK KEROUAC
GP 372
GROVE PRESS

In June 1965 Kerouac went to France in an effort to trace the de Kerouack family. He found little information and quickly returned home where he drank cognac and recorded his lonely trip in the novel Satori in Paris, *which was published in 1966.*

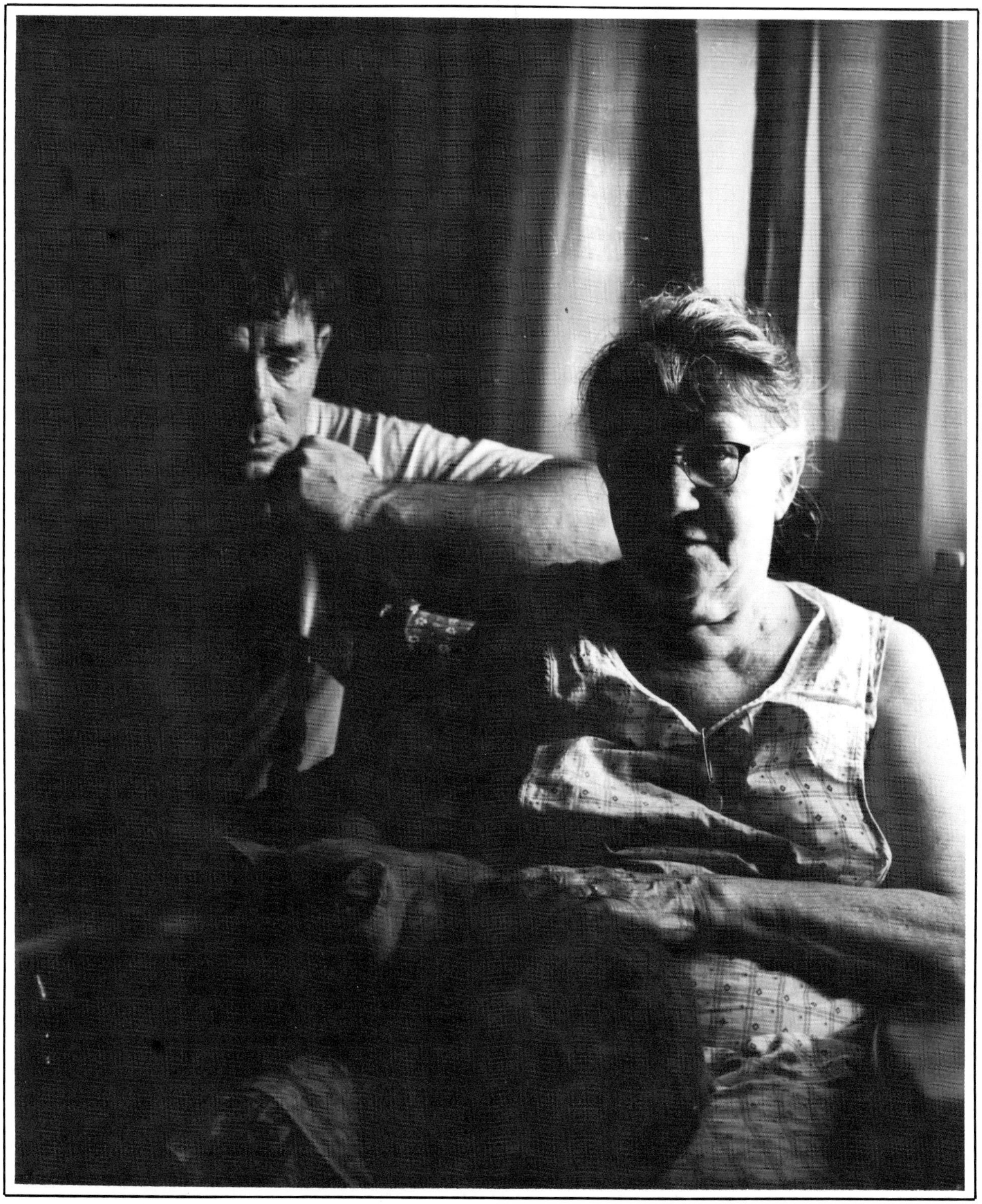

Kerouac and Memere at their home in St. Petersburg, Florida, 1966. Memere had supported her son by working in shoe factories until he was able to support them both with his writing.

Kerouac in 1966, Hyannis, Massachusetts

BOOK REVIEW:

John Clellon Holmes, "There's an Air of Finality to Kerouac's Latest," *National Observer*, 5 February 1968, p. 25.

In the fall of 1966 Mémère was invalided by a stroke. Shortly thereafter Kerouac married Stella Sampas of the Sampas family he had copied when writing The Town and the City. Vanity of Duluoz, *written in 1967 in Lowell, tells of his high school years and his life in New York as a young man. This book was the last he finished for his Legend of Duluoz cycle.*

Jack Kerouac's new book is a novel about uprootings. It is about how a gifted youth full of vaulting energies, ambitions, and ideals is uprooted into young manhood by success, war, and relativism. It is about how a traditional temperament, rooted in family warmth, religious belief, and innocent optimism, is "educated" by the dislocations of modern life. It is also about how the American provincial consciousness was wrenched into worldliness during World War II.

It is a bitter and an eloquent book, a Balzacian tale told in the accents of Ecclesiastes. It is about vanity—the vanity of youth that trusts the world because it trusts itself, the vanity of believing that outer achievements result in inner fulfilments, and that ultimate vanity of vanities: the notion that the race is to the swift and the battle to the strong, and that time and chance do not happen to us all alike.

It is the latest book in that sprawling, vivid, ruminative, slapdash series of books (11 so far) that Mr. Kerouac calls *The Duluoz Legend*, and there are good reasons for thinking that it may be the last. It has an unmistakable air of summation about it. It is the first book Mr. Kerouac has written since moving back to Lowell, Mass., where the *Legend* began. It is a book addressed to his new wife, who shares with him a Lowell growing-up, and it is thereby written in a new tone, a casual, almost domestic tone, an affectionate and impatient tone. The tone is occasionally arch when it becomes aware of the intrusive reader, but above all it is a sardonic, querulous, fatalistic, and *conclusive* tone.

Most importantly, this book fills the single remaining gap in the *Legend*: those years that Kerouac "fictionalized" in his very first book, *The Town and the City*. Those years changed Duluoz the boy—the reverent, imaginative, winning youngster of *Doctor Sax* who is the central figure in an evocation of small-city American youth during the '30s that has no peer in our literature—into Duluoz the man. The boy became the restless, saddened, boozy, Buddhistic, Beat Generation Duluoz, whose essential homelessness of soul made such books as *On the Road* so emblematic of postwar youth. In describing how that boy became this man, *Vanity of Duluoz* deals with the severing experience on which the entire *Legend* pivots.

Kerouac with his third wife, Stella

Scott Fitzgerald once wrote that the two keenest regrets of his youth were "not being big enough (or good enough) to play football in college, and not getting overseas during the war." *Vanity of Duluoz* is steeped in the keener knowledges of a writer who accomplished both these things, and it suggests that succeeding in such elementary endeavors prepares a young man for modern life no better than failing at them. Fitzgerald spent almost 10 years projecting his own image into imaginary Yale Bowls and Belleau Woods, prolonging his love affair with the Bitch Goddess of Success until well into his 30s. By contrast, Duluoz (Mr. Kerouac) is a brilliant high-school running back as well as a good student. He goes to Columbia on a football scholarship and shows promise of making All-American, only to discover that the dream of prowess on the playing field is really a kid's dream, which lacks substance in the world he is encountering—the world of challenging books, big-city amorality, and war.

He joins the Merchant Marine (and later the Navy), and serves on convoys in the North Atlantic only to discover that war, too, is a kind of grisly, inhuman game played by grown-up boys. "I realized either I was crazy or the world was crazy: and I picked on the world," making a *Catch-22* choice that lands him in the nuthouse for a time. By war's end he has drifted into the underground (of poets, junkies, and madmen) that flourished around Columbia and the Village in the New York of those days. There are love affairs, fledgling attempts to write, family upheavals, marginal involvement in a Gidean murder, and finally jail.

By the close of the book, the 22-year-old Duluoz has buried his father (and his youth) and has "settled down to write, in solitude, in pain . . . thinking 'When this book is finished, which is going to be the sum and substance . . . of everything I've been through, I shall be redeemed.' " To which the 45-year-old Mr. Kerouac, looking back with both irony and resignation, can only add: "Wifey, I did it all, I wrote the book, I stalked the streets . . . did everything you're supposed to do in life. But nothing ever came of it. . . . Go to sleep. Tomorrow's another day."

At its best, *Vanity of Duluoz* is a recapitulation of the themes that dominate the whole *Legend*, themes that most critics have failed to grasp, perhaps because the separate books were neither written nor published in any chronological sequence. From the beginning, Mr. Kerouac has been writing about the double evolution of a consciousness, a consciousness that *was* evolving in the Past the books describe, and *is* evolving in the Present of their composition.

As a result the *Legend* constitutes a prolonged search for a lost identity, for that singleness of vision, that sense of wholeness, that the uprootings of modern life

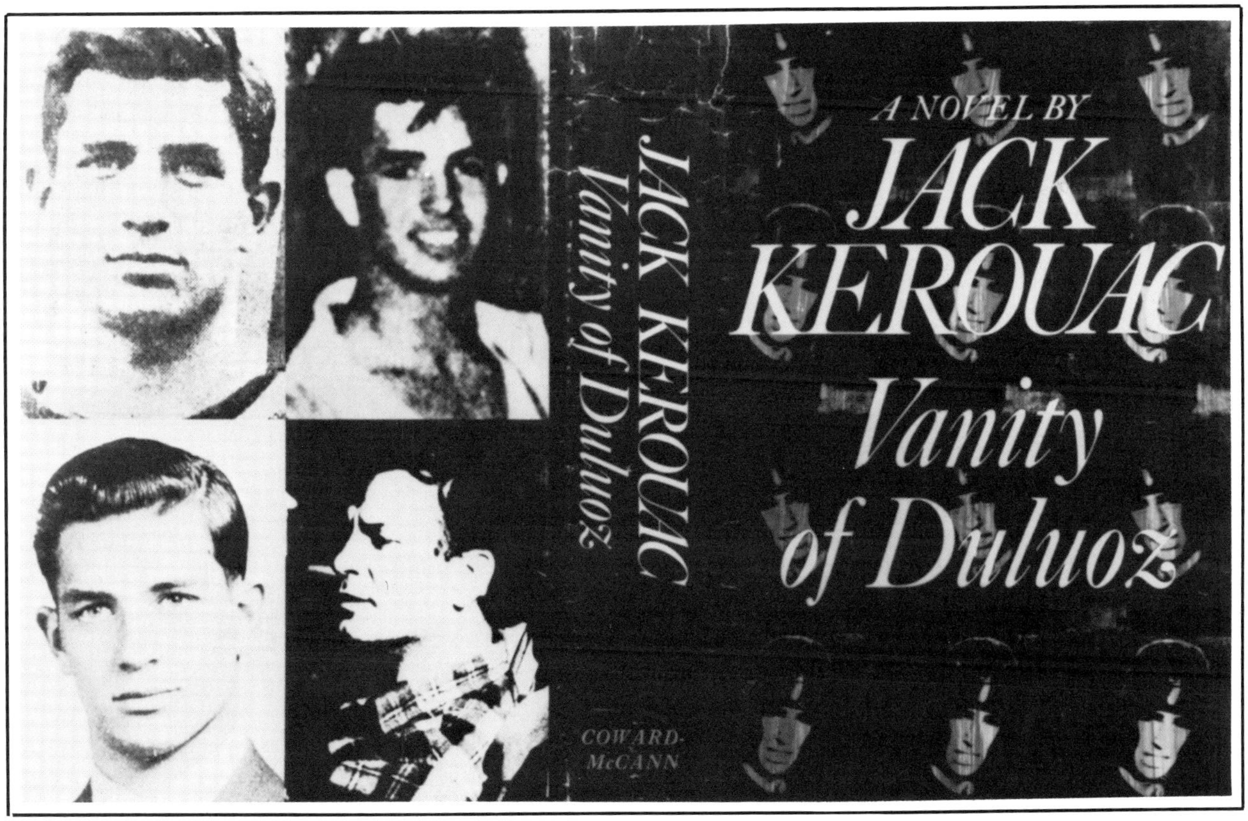

The year before he died Kerouac said of Vanity of Duluoz, *". . . earlier readers would come back and see what ten years had done to my life and thinking. . . . Which is after all the only thing I've got to offer, the true story of what I saw and how I saw it." The novel was subtitled "An Adventurous Education, 1935-46."*

have all but obliterated. If it celebrates innocence, it is because of a harrowing burden of experience.

A series of awful contrasts has wrenched Mr. Kerouac in his deepest nature—the way Tolstoi was wrenched, and Melville. His is a religious nature above all—mystical, poetic, cohesive, loving, and doomed to look for harmony in dissonance. Rarely has the religious temperament, in all its terrible contemporary forlornness and anguish, been more painfully expressed than in Mr. Kerouac's work. His is an orphaned voice, and *Vanity of Duluoz* is a record of that orphaning.

"I don't care who it is you love," he says. "You love the loyal, the helpless, the trusting. . . . What use the materialists [with] their clunkhead ignorance of their own broken hearts." If Kerouac is sometimes paranoid and sometimes sentimental, it is because this ignorance outrages him. But the trigger for that outrage is the suffering of his own broken heart.

Vanity of Duluoz is the capstone of one of the most extraordinary, influential, maddening, and ultimately prodigious achievements in recent literature. Its follies are our follies; its hopes are the hopes that we, too, have lost. And the broken heart that beats stubbornly within it is our own heart, to which (out of embarrassment of pseudohipness) we try so doggedly not to listen any more, thereby postponing any sort of mending.

As Kerouac might say: One last vanity.

ARTICLE:

Jack Kerouac, "Kerouac: The Last Word from the Father of the Beats," *Washington Post*, 22 October 1969, B1, B15.

Kerouac wrote this article to explain his politics in relation to those of the Beat Generation. It was first published as "Man, Am I the Granddaddy-O of the Hippies" and reprinted as "After Me, the Deluge."

What am I thinking about? I'm trying to figure out where I am between the established politicians and the radicals, between cops and hoods, tax collectors and vandals.

I'm not a Tax-Free, not a Hippie-Yippie—I must be a Bippie-in-the-Middle.

No, I'd better go around tell everybody, or let others convince me, that I'm the great white father and intellectual forebear who spawned a deluge of alienated radicals, war protesters, dropouts, hippies and even "beats" and thereby I can make some money maybe and a "new Now-image" for myself (and God forbid I dare call myself the intellectual forebear of modern spontaneous prose), but I've got to figure out first how I could possibly spawn Jerry Rubin, Mitchell Goodman, Abbie Hoffman, Allen Ginsberg and other warm human beings from the ghettos who say they suffered no less than the Puerto Ricans in their barrios and the blacks in their Big and Little Harlems, and all because I wrote a matter-of-fact account of a true adventure on the road (hardly an agitational propaganda account) featuring an ex-cowhand and an ex-footballer driving across the continent north, northwest, midwest and southland looking for lost fathers, odd jobs, good times, and girls and winding up on the railroad. Yup, I'd better convince myself that these thinkers were not on an entirely different road.

House Appropriations Chairman, assistants, Health Directors, Commission Chairman, assistants, Assistants to the Director of Regional Planning, Neighborhood Center Directors, Executive Presidents of Banks, Chairmen of Interior Subcommittees, Officials of the Department of Rehabilitative Services, Planners of the Preliminary Regional Plan, ethical Members of Rules Committees, House Insurance Committees, Utilities Commission entrepreneurs, Expressway Authority directors, county news hacks, spokesmen, pleaders, applauders, aides and wives in organdy, $2,500 worth of food and $5,000 worth of booze and the caterer's cut thrown in, for one "lunch," tax-exempt, televised for a 15-second spot on the evening news to show how well they can put on the dog. At your expense.

Here every handshake, every smile, every gibberous applause is shiny hypocrisy, is political lust and concupiscence, a ninny's bray of melody backed by a ghastly neurological drone of money-grub accompanied by the anvil chorus of garbage can covers being banged over half-eaten filet mignons which don't even get to the dogs, let alone hungry children of the absent "constituency."

I'll try to forget that the hippie flower children out in the park with their peanut butter sandwiches and their live-and-let-live philsophy nevertheless are not too proud of being robbed of their simplified attempt at primitive dignity, but the banquet guests are proud, proud.

The banquet guests, the politicos and their grinnish entourage in glistering suits and dresses, papershufflers all, plutocrats salient with hind paws and forepaws together, last night's nouveau riche, would be even prouder if they could get the "nonproductive parasite hippies" to get to work digging new roads and cooking and washing

> *Nobody'll ever know America completely because nobody ever knew Gatsby, I guess.*

From "He Went on the Road, as Jack Kerouac Says"

dishes at these fund raising galas so the dirty punks could at least make cash contributions, or, at best, pay taxes to enable the papershufflers to order more paper and copying machines with which they now rampant could form a further "planning" committee (of three-year duration, on pollution, sex, think of anything dirty) while sitting back and admiring the view of their back lawn where all the trees that only God can make have been cut down along with the bird's nests.

No, I think I'll go back to the alienated radicals who are quite understandably alienated nay disgusted by this scene, but I'll have to try to overlook the fact that the "alienated" radicals and activist yippies and SDS'ers who pretended holily inside the hippie flower movement of a few years ago till their colors withdrew into the basal portions of the chromotophores like the dwarf lizard's have no better plan to offer the griefstricken American citizenry but fund-raising dinners of their own, and if not for the same reasons, I'd better forget I'd be willing to bet for worse reasons.

Because so what if these brand new alienated radical chillun of Kropotkin and Bakunin don't believe in Western-style capitalism, private property, simple privacy even of individuals or families, for instance, or in Jesus or any cluster of reasons for honesty; or in education of course, that is, the bigotry of classic historical scholarship which enables one to know one, the better to see what other ambitious vandals and liars did before; or don't believe in government wrenched away by any others but themselves? Ah, so what if they don't believe in the written word which is the only way to keep the record straight?

Really, so what's new if they would like to see to it that under Timothy Leary's guiding proselytization no one in America could address a simple envelope or keep a household budget or a checkbook balanced or for that matter legible?

In fact, who cares, shucks, Toronto, that if Marshall McLuhan had wanted to be the biggest barbarianizing influence in the globe he couldn't have come up with a better idea (even if you can't go to the toilet nowadays without having an affidavit on it) than that linear reasonableness of the printed word is out, and the jiggling behinds in back of placards are in? (Electronic all-now mosaic dots on said behinds somewhat suspect.)

Of course the alienated radicals, the would-be fund-raisers of the Peking-oriented Castro-jacketed New Left who hate be-necktied plutocrats so much because clothes don't make the man, themselves won't take LSD or STP acid (which stupefy the mind and hand for weeks on end) but will keep perfect records of their own, even incorporate tax-exempt Libertarian Foundations for vocal poets who are really agitational propagandists, why, the alienated radicals, they'll be exuding transactions maybe with the help of a relative who's a lawyer.

Their anarchism extends just so far, after all. The relative wants to be a commissar too, hey. No sense starting trouble unless you get a "top job" straightening it out. Commissar of Chaos, say.

Addresses anyone? Red China's international propaganda and subversive apparatus is the Teh Wu (do-thus) section of Peking's overall Hai-Wai-Tiao-Cha-Pu espionage organization.

Russia: The Kremlin's KGB (State Security Committee) at 19 Stanislavskaya St. opposite the East German Embassy in Moscow.

Viet Cong: propaganda headquarters near the late Ho Chi Minh's French mansion in center of Hanoi. This leaves everybody "poor peasants" except the bastard Party cadres who figured it all out, even if they have to compromise a little with the "bourgeois" now, although I wish I could tell them that the only bourgeois I ever knew was Paul Bourgeois, a rough-and-tumble French-Canadian Indian high-steel worker on bridges who would tell them to go jump in the Lake of St. Louis de Ha Ha.

O New World!—Yay, if joy were proponent of coin, what grand economy. It's much like: what do you think a parasite is thinking when he's sucking on the belly of a whale or the back of a shark? "Where did this big stupid brute get all that blood, not being a parasite like me? How come he's so strong and free, not knowing how to live like I do?" So with human parasites feeding on their juicy national, personal, political, or racial host.

But now, I'll have to switch and become a "war protestor" and stick to my guns and try to insult the Military-Industrial Complex for safeguarding our offensive weapons inside of an electronic armory instead of leaving them out in the rain. I'll try to forget old armory raids. Maybe Jerome Weisner of M.I.T. already does.

At least I can always yell "ABM system too expensive!" but who'm I going to blame, Military Industrial Complex? or Industrial Military Complex? or Industrial Civilian Military Labor Academic complex? or . . . or maybe, yippee! no national right at all to be granted to the United States to defend itself against its own perimeter of enemies in its own bigger scale, that's best. Advised by the pacifists who faced Genghis Khan. By international pacifist demonstrators who now face further demonstrations by Chairman Mao's IBM warheads.

Or I can always try to see aggression by the U.S. in Vietnam as different from other armies' "defensive ripostes" and "counterfoils" and the good old brisk reply to "blind hatred": a "lesson" not an attack.

I'll try to see the difference between bombing of "civilians" in one town and bombing of "women and children" in another and "reprisals" instead of raids, and, elsewhere on our map, rocket "warnings" on the very ricepot rooftops of Saigon and Hue by the Viet Cong and brutal U.S. Imperialist bombings of Ho Chi Minh trail and rails round Hanoi.

Warm human beings everywhere. In Flanders Field they're piled 10 high.

The Mekong, it's just a long, soft river.

I'll do this, I'll do that—

You can't fight City Hall, it keeps changing its name—

Ah phooey on 'em—you pays your taxes and you passes to your grave, why study their "matters"? Let them present their problematical matters before the zoning board, or present complaint six on matters before the kidnapped Dean (problem planning committees for planning problem solutions) 'cause "I've got," as Neal Cassady said, "my own lil old bangtail mind."

I think I'll drop out—Great American tradition—Dan'l Boone, U. S. Grant, Mark Twain—I think I'll go to sleep and suddenly in my deepest inadequacy nightmares wake up haunted and see everyone in the world as unconsolable orphans yelling and screaming on every side to make arrangements for making a living yet all bespattered and gloomed-up in the nightsoil of poor body and soul all present and accounted for as some kind of sneakish, craft gift, and all so lonered.

Martin Heidegger says "Why are there existing essential things, instead of nothing?" Founder of Existentialism, never mind your Sartre, and also said: "And there is no philosophy without this doozie as a starter." Ever look closely at anybody and see that particularized patience all their own, eyes hid, waiting with lips sewn down for time to pass, for something to lift them up, for their yesterday's daily perseverance to succeed, for the long night of life to take them in its arms and say "Ah, Cherubim, this silly stupid business . . . What is it, existence."

A lifelong struggle to avoid disaster. Idiot PTA's and gurus call it Cre-a-tive? Politics, gambling, hard work, drinking, patriotism, protest, pooh-poohings, all therapeutic shifts against the black void. To make you forget it really isn't there, nor you anywhere.

It's like saying, if there are no elephants in the room, then you can safely say the room is empty of elephants. Ah, your immemorial golden ashes shall seem to be scattered anywhere in Paradise.

All caught in the middle.

Ah! I know what I'll do, I'll be like Andy Capp the British comic strip character and go to the rub-a-dub-dub for a bout-a-doubt (Cockney lingo for "pub" and "stout"). After all, doubt parades a lout. And I'll yell "WHAT I NEED IS LESS PEOPLE TELLIN' ME WHAT I NEED!" (Copyright 1969 by Smythe).

So I'll be "generous with the liberality of poets, which is conservative to the bone." (Copyright 1969 by Donald Phelps).

"*No cede malis*" (cede not to malfortune) (don't give in to bad times). Copyright 130 A.D. by Juvenal).

Some deluge.

ARTICLE:

Eric Ehrmann and Stephen Davis, "There Is Really Nothing Inside," *Rolling Stone*, 29 November 1969, p. 34.

Kerouac took his wife and his mother to St. Petersburg, Florida, in 1968. It was there that he died of massive abdominal hemorrhage resulting from alcoholism on 21 October 1969 at the age of forty-seven. Following is an account of his funeral, which took place in Lowell on 24 October 1969.

A small placard in the front hallway of the A. Archambault & Sons Funeral Parlor, one of a string of funeral homes along Pawtucket Avenue in this dreary mill town, directed mourners to the back room where the wake for Jack Kerouac was being held.

Jack Kerouac's people were all there in their Sunday best, sharp-featured French-Canadian people. Old ladies gushed and moaned in French *patois*, their heads bobbing up and down as they gossiped about what Father

Morrissette had told the young Kerouac many years before. They were cordial enough.

One led the way down a small hallway and around a corner to meet one of Jack's friends, Allen Ginsberg, who sat comforting Kerouac's wife, Stella. Peter Orlovsky, Ginsberg's constant companion and fellow poet, was taking a drink from the electric water cooler. A small toothless man in a gigantic blue overcoat paced nervously about, his thick black hair tousled, blue sunglasses peering anxiously about. It was Gregory Corso, the poet who had been right there, in New York and San Francisco and everywhere, with Kerouac and Ginsberg and the others, from the start.

Arms pressed tight to his body, head down, shoulders hunched, Corso stalked the room in perfect 1950s beat style, as if he still lives that crazed agony. He kept aiming those "What should I do now?" looks at Ginsberg.

Orlovsky and Ginsberg led the way to have a look at Kerouac. "You must see him," Ginsberg said. "He looks like a happy clay buddha."

Jack Kerouac, dead at 47, of a massive abdominal hemorrhage, on October 21. He symbolized an era. Whether or not his friend John Clellon Holmes was first to call it the Beat Generation in print, Holmes later attributed the term to Kerouac. "This," Kerouac told Holmes in 1948, "is really a beat generation." Nobody was in a better position to know.

They had laid out his body in a grey houndstooth sports jacket (at least one size too small), a yellow shirt and red bow tie with white pin dots. His face, heavily made-up, waxy and dull, had been molded into a cheery, vacant smile. The silver rosary clutched between his hands was faintly discolored by the heavy makeup caked upon his fingers.

"Touch him," said Ginsberg. "There's really nothing inside."

Not surprisingly, Kerouac's forehead was quite cold to the touch.

"This," Ginsberg continued, "is exactly the way he wanted it. Listen." He read aloud from Kerouac's *Mexico City Blues*. Ginsberg's manner was entirely reverent; this was his service over the body. Orlovsky fought back the tears.

Among the wreaths was a very special one that Ginsberg and Orlovsky had brought. A typical wreath, really, except for the senders, whose names—*Bill, Terry, Allen* and *Peter*—were spelled out in glittery sequins. (William Burroughs, Terry Southern, Ginsberg and Orlovsky.)

As Ginsberg departed the bier, Corso came over, ill at ease, that same wild Lower East Side-Brooklyn huckster rap from the coffee house poetry readings of the 50s, and asked: "What are the young people saying about Jack?"

He shuffled back and forth, talking more than he listened. The old Village style. For Corso, the young people are another group—a set of people he does not know. He does not know what they are saying about Jack. The *young people* have rock and roll as their common shared experience. Kerouac and Corso and Ginsberg broke on through to the other side, kicked out the jams, long before any of those ideas ever passed through the heads of Jim Morrison or the MC5 or the Rolling Stones. They were on the road and turning on a decade before the drop out/tune in/turn on litany was first sounded.

The following morning, Friday, was the day of the funeral, in the Paroisse St. Jean Baptiste Church. The weather was unseasonably cold for the New England October: in fact, it was the coldest day in months. The pallbearers (Kerouac's relatives, Ginsberg, and a man dressed as an Italian gangster who was uptight at the sight of so many cameras, from Gregory Corso's Bolex to about twenty Kodak Instamatics and Brownies that kept flitting about) all wore overcoats. Corso was filming the entire funeral, panning up and down the sub-Gothic facade of St. Jean and back to Ginsberg carrying the coffin. He said he was doing it for himself.

One missing figure at the funeral was Lawrence Ferlinghetti, whose City Lights bookstore was Kerouac's mailing address during the quintessential San Francisco years of Beat. "I don't like funerals," Ferlinghetti said later. "I've been asked by all sorts of big publications to write something about Jack. I can't do that. I don't write about dead men. They should have done something for him two years ago, when he needed it."

The gunmetal black casket was trundled toward the altar on a good-sized coffin dolly with the trademark *Eurak* embossed on its dies. A nice touch.

Father Armand Morrissette celebrated mass for Kerouac's soul in front of a congregation whose majority hadn't been inside a church in years, except to see an avant-garde play in the basement. During the offertory someone quietly speculated whether the body had been flown up from Florida, where Kerouac had died. A writer from a Cambridge weekly said that he had heard that the corpse had to be forcibly restrained from hitching up the coast by itself.

It might seem out of character for one of the Beat

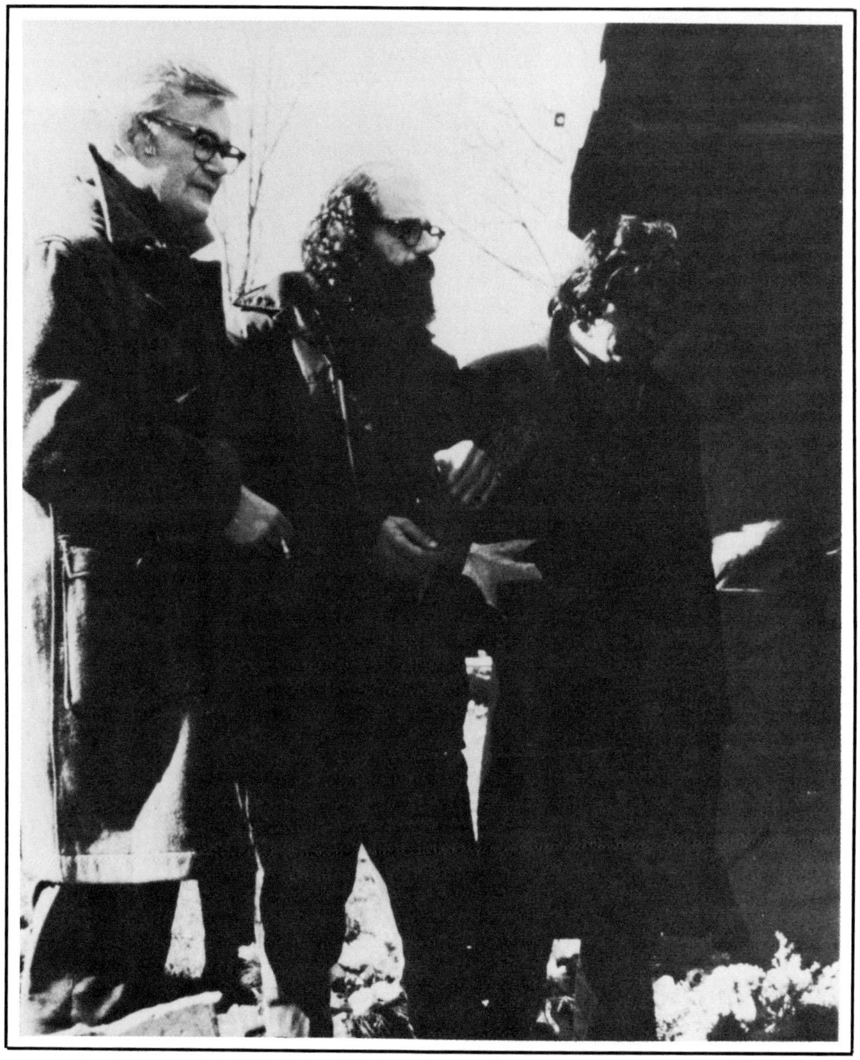

John Clellon Holmes, Allen Ginsberg, and Gregory Corso at Kerouac's grave, 24 October 1969

Generation's most renowned sons to be the object of the church's traditional religiosity. But Kerouac had always walked with Jesus, in his way. The Jesus of Sunday school atonement and redemption. "Horrors of the Jesus Christ of passion plays," wrote Kerouac in *Doctor Sax*, "in his shrouds and vestments of saddest doom mankind in the Cross Weep for Thieves and Poverty—he was at the foot of my bed pushing it one dark Saturday night (on Hildreth & Lilley second floor flat full of Eternity outside)—either He or the Virgin Mary stooped with phosphorescent profile and horror, pushing my bed."

In his address to the congregation, Fr. Morrissette said, in part, "Jack Kerouac embodied something of man's search for freedom: he refused always to be boxed in by the pettiness of the world. He had what Allen Ginsberg called 'the exquisite honesty,' the guts to express and live his ideas. Now he is on the road again, going on further, as he said, 'alone by the waters of life.' Our hope and prayer is that he has found complete liberation."

During his last days in Lowell, before he moved to St. Petersburg, Florida, to look after his invalid mother, he would walk into Mello's Bar, and bellow at the top of his lungs—"I'm Jack Kerouac!"—as if he had to prove it to himself. He had never played along with the beatnik hype that the media lavished upon some of his cronies.

Now, nearing his 50th year, Kerouac had become a lonely, embittered man, increasingly unsure of himself and upset with the world he saw around him. He was cut off. A dreadfully corny middle-aged gag-word—"bippie," from TV's *Rowan & Martin Laugh-In*—even figured in the title of his last published writing. It was called "I'm A Bippie in the Middle," it was published in the Washington Post, and it spoke his nightmare vision plainly if not clearly:

I think I'll drop out–Great American tradition–Dan'l Boone, U. S. Grant, Mark Twain–I think I'll go to sleep and suddenly in my deepest inadequacy nightmares wake up haunted and see everyone in the world as unconsolable orphans yelling and screaming on every side to make arrangements for making a living yet all bespattered and gloomed-up in the nightsoil of poor body and soul all present and accounted for as some kind of sneakish, craft gift, and all so lonered.

In his last years, his wife says, Jack Kerouac became a heavy drinker, a steady dope-smoker and tended to flip out often. There is a definite sense in his novels—in *On the Road, The Subterraneans, Dr. Sax*, certainly—that Kerouac was a free man. But he lost that freedom. Almost totally alienated from the free generation of the 1960s that he had, in a way, prophesied during the 1950s, the hippies and the dope freaks pissed him off. He grumbled in "I'm a Bippie in the Middle"—

Really, so what's new if they would like to see to it that under Timothy Leary's guiding proselytization no one in America could address a simple envelope or keep a household budget or a checkbook balanced or for that matter legible . . . Ah, so what if they don't believe in the written word which is the only way to keep the record straight.

As the mourners poured out of the church into the blinding reflection of the sun on the stone steps, Corso filming every move, a reporter sidled up to Jimmy Breslin and asked him what the reaction was to Kerouac's death in New York. Breslin said he didn't really know. But Breslin had some definite ideas about Kerouac the writer. "Yeah," he said, "you can say he opened a lot of doors for a lot of people. Tom Wolfe. Mailer a little bit. Nobody was publishing his kind of stuff in the fifties and then all of a sudden in '57, *On the Road* hit. He opened a lot of doors."

By now the cortege was pulling away for the cemetery. But the supposedly inviolate single file of cars, lights on, was quickly broken up by a huge oil truck making a quick turn to catch a light. The driver didn't seem to like the beatniks, so he stayed in line.

TV cameras caught the action at graveside: the cranes lowering the casket into the freshly dug earth. Corso filmed it, too, right on top of it, two feet from the grave. He tilted the big 16 MM camera right down into the hole, all the way, until Kerouac's casket settled into place.

Ginsberg lofted a handful of dirt onto the coffin as workmen shoveled away. A few other mourners followed suit with *their* handfuls, but most simply watched. The TV crews were packing up, the daily press men were departing, and it seemed like it had really ended a long time ago.

Allen Ginsberg, himself the model for various characters in Kerouac's works, had already said it at Yale a couple of days earlier. Speaking to an audience at Yale, Ginsberg said that Kerouac "broke open the fantastic solidity in America as solid as the Empire State Building—that turned out not to be solid at all. His vision was what the universe as we will experience it is—golden ash, blissful emptiness, a product of our own grasping speed."

BOOK REVIEW:

John Tytell, "Revisions of Kerouac," *Partisan Review*, 40 (Spring 1973): 301-305.

Kerouac's Visions of Cody, *originally published in 1960, was not published in full until 1972 after both Kerouac and Neal Cassady (Cody) were dead. Tytell subsequently wrote* Naked Angels: The Lives and Literature of the Beat Generation.

Recently, I interviewed Herbert Huncke who knew Burroughs, Kerouac, and Ginsberg in the time of their first friendship just after World War II. Huncke remarked that he never imagined that Kerouac was a writer then, believing that the ruggedly handsome and athletic figure was merely part of the scene around Columbia University in the forties. If Huncke, an incarnation of underground hip, didn't detect the writer's signals from Kerouac, I suppose the general public can't be blamed for taking him less than seriously, even after his nineteenth book. Of course the fashionable disparagement of Kerouac began long ago when the media circus, feeding on the apparent marketability of *On the Road*, created an awful vortex of publicity which somehow lessened Kerouac's credibility as spokesman for a generation in revolt.

In so many ways there is something essentially American about Kerouac's writing; his restless energies could never settle for a final form, and each of his novels demonstrates an eager variety in their differences from each other, and from conventional expectations of what the novel should be like. His voice, too, seemed representative of an endemic colloquialism in the American character: to listen to the recordings of Kerouac reading his poems is to attend to a purely natural inflection completely without literary affectation. Kerouac heard with raw ears (as Ginsberg said of William Carlos Williams) and fulfilled the romantic imperative of a language fashioned out of ordinary speech. But the demotic was only one of Kerouac's many voices. As John Clellon Holmes has asserted, Kerouac was gifted with an extraordinary range, almost responding stylistically to his own awe at the physical dimensions of his country, as his own exuberant bravado and gloomy sloughs were expressed in his great playfulness with words, his getting high with language as cascading rhythms resolved into Joycean sound games, or the baroque intricacies of *Dr. Sax*.

Visions of Cody was begun in 1951; intended as part of *On The Road*, it grew into a larger and perhaps more significant work. Part of it was issued by New Directions; most of it remained unprinted legend. The focus of the book was Neal Cassady, Dean Moriarty of *On The Road*, later busdriver for Ken Kesey's Merry Pranksters, now as authentic a part of American mythology as Paul Bunyan or Jesse James. Cassady's name in the book—Cody Pomeray—is an ironic testament to the writer's mythmaking powers. After all, wasn't Wild Bill Cody's reputation an invention of Ned Buntline, the original dime-novelist? Yet behind that legend was the fact that Bill Cody guided men like General Phil Sheridan, Lieutenant Colonel George Custer, and James Bennett (who published the *New York Herald*) to the buffalo hunt spectacle, just as later he would become cultural impresario of the forgotten West with his touring buffalo circus. Wild Bill died in Denver during World War I, and Denver was the hometown of Kerouac's cowboy without a range, destined to work out his frustrated quest for frontier freedom in countless journeys from coast to coast like some fugitive hounded by the classical Furies. Before dying near a railroad track in Mexico in 1968, Cassady guided Kerouac and Ginsberg along an excessively spectacular route of sex and drugs. In search of a vision of a lost America, "the immense indefinable charm of the wide open free sprawling America of railroads and distant mesas," they found Poe's charnel house of horrors, and *Visions of Cody* transcribes their attempted escape.

Kerouac presents Cassady in perpetual motion, like a man riding a wheel, impatiently intense, overspilling nervous anxiety, a torrent of words in a cage of restlessness. Virtually born on the road Steinbeck described in *Grapes of Wrath*, Cassady spent his early youth on the Denver bowery in the company of his father, a derelict wino. Hopping freights through the West, living with bums, Cassady became a Beat code figure, for the wandering hobo was to emerge as a foil for American materialism. Cassady's careening escapades became the wild accomplishments of legend: ten arrests, several years in jails, innumerable car-thefts; a supposedly irresistible attractiveness to both men and women, a Pan complete with the flute he loved to play; incongruously reading Proust, or wondering whether poets were more

Dust jacket for Kerouac's posthumously published novel

important than philosophers while recapping automobile tires!

Cassady wrote his story in lost letters to Kerouac, and in the posthumous *The First Third*, an autobiographical account of his early Denver years that seems flat and uninspired when compared to *Visions of Cody*. Kerouac's magic emerges as he evokes elegiac memories of popular culture as a backdrop by which to measure the Cassady legend: radio and The Shadow, comics and the Katzenjammer Kids, movies and the Three Stooges, burlesque shows and boxing matches. Cassady's untutored imagination responded to such forces; like Gatsby, he was the sort of primal force for whom a neon sign might represent hope and accomplishment instead of vulgarity. *The First Third* is straight narrative, brief, brutal, with the kind of antiliterary toughness so many American writers strain so hard to attain. *Visions of Cody* offers endless elaboration, is Kerouac's most literary composition, full of the formal play with fictional dimension that most of his work rather blatantly excludes. *Visions of Cody* is an exultation of Kerouac's best long-line sequences, passages combining the density of poetry with the compressed intensity of haiku, including at least two of his *Scattered Poems* run as prose. Digressively crowding impressions, anecdotes, tall-tales and cons, Kerouac's line approaches his own ideal of the jazz saxophonist, pursuing the ineluctable ultimate note, always furthering his sound with another association, always reaching and extending an oceanic continuum, secretly knowing that to cease is to die. A Shandyean profusion is compounded by a variety of means to enrich the texture: drawings and letters, imitations of Tom Sawyer and Bloom's trial in *Ulysses*, superbly rendered discontinuities and drug fantasies. The book becomes a realization of Kerouac's most apt mode—a kind of diary notation in which distinctions between fact and fancy, prose and poetry are deliberately blurred for the sake of imaginative recall.

In stark stylistic contrast, almost as relief from such complexities, stands the famous tape, a series of conversations between Kerouac and Cassady while inhaling benzedrine, smoking marijuana, and consuming quantities of alcohol. The tape—which is probably what prevented the book from appearing for so long—is valuable as the record of how the Beats sustained their friendships on an axis of drugs, sex, and jazz. The hipster scene is authentically detailed: the Times Square underground, the lower East Side Henry Street flat that Burroughs maintained and Huncke occupied as a place of sinister rendezvous and joyous release. Cassady describes Burroughs's life with Joan Adams and Huncke, in 1947 in New Waverly, Texas, where he and Ginsberg visited, and how he drove Burroughs and Huncke back to New York City in a jeep full of mason jars of marijuana that Burroughs had harvested. Cassady conjectures on how Burroughs, an expert marksman constantly shooting target practice in New Waverly, fatally shot his wife Joan through the head in Mexico the following year. These events are related in a manner that anticipated Pop realism with a graphic and relentlessly obsessive concentration on the ordinary; the catalyst is Rimbaud's aim of *derèglement des sens*, and when Kerouac passes out, Cassady's wife appears and the inexhaustible Cassady continues like an overflowing dam, a model of the blocked writer with a story to tell and the ability to recall it without the patience to set it down. His premise is that a story can only be told once to achieve its fullest impact, and this may well be the source of Kerouac's own publicized bias against revision, a reminder of how close the Beats are to the oral tradition and the improvisationary spirit of the blues. The real impunity of the tape follows from Cassady's premise of immediacy as it tries to violate the barriers between art and life. It doesn't succeed at all! Ironically, the tape almost becomes the justification of literary enterprise, revealing the inadequacies of natural speech when juxtaposed to the more poetic resources of the writer, suggesting also in the boring bareness of its antistyle that the genuinely "unspeakable visions of the individual" are the concern of art, and only the subject of life. Despite the stimulation of drugs, the talk is grounded in inhibition, never soaring or even searing, without the Zen zaniness of Kerouac's own more scintillating imitations of the tape where again craft courts the illusion of spontaneity with greater grace and deftness than the actual can provide. Curiously, despite their early fears of a bugged universe where no man could speak freely, Burroughs, Kerouac, and Ginsberg have all used tape recorders in their work, anticipating by light years the more recent innovations caused by the use of tapes in literary works by John Barth and others.

Jack Kerouac is right now our most misunderstood and underestimated writer. Like Henry Miller he was uninterested in the ideal of "literary" perfection or in the orderly fiction of his time, believing that even seemingly immutable tastes could change. His writing was always excessive, disorderly, and unbalanced because he responded to entirely different imaginative priorities than most writers of his time, not because he was unable to compose in the conventional mode of his first novel, *The Town and the City*. His attitudes were often raw and impulsive, as partial and erratic as his view of women was deplorable. Yet he seemed in touch with certain hidden vitalities of the future, verities beyond the ken of the middle class, like his warm response to black Americans that Eldridge Cleaver found so remarkable in *Soul on Ice*, or his involvement with the Buddhist notions that figure so significantly in his work. Like Neal Cassady in conversation, Kerouac had the gift of impromptu. Cassady's talent was in tirade, the tradition of the nightclub comic best exemplified by Lenny Bruce, the Jeremiah of the Dionysian outsider in ecstatic rout among the ashes of civilization. Kerouac, too, could write out of such abrupt and ungovernable impulses, but they were always tempered by the harmonies of his more meditative fancies, his essentially devotional sensibility. If the Cassady legend does become the lasting stuff of myth, it will be due largely to this generous and fiery book, published over a decade after the fact of writing, but all the more meaningful now that the bohemian releases once so privately explored have become so much more accepted and widespread.

Jack Kerouac's grave in Edson Cemetery, Lowell, on the tenth anniversary of his death

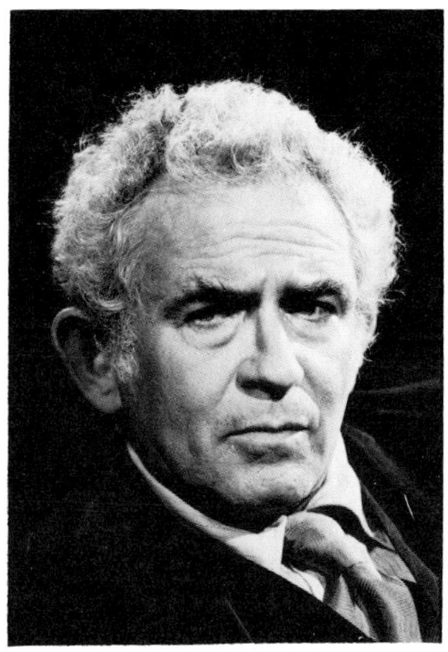

NORMAN MAILER

(31 January 1923-)

See the Norman Mailer entries in the Dictionary of Literary Biography, *volume 2,* American Novelists Since World War II, *and* Yearbook: 1980.

BOOKS:

The Naked and the Dead (New York: Rinehart, 1948; London: Wingate, 1949);

Barbary Shore (New York: Rinehart, 1951; London: Cape, 1952);

The Deer Park (New York: Putnam's, 1955; London: Wingate, 1957);

The White Negro (San Francisco: City Lights, 1957);

Advertisements for Myself (New York: Putnam's, 1959; London: Deutsch, 1961);

Deaths for the Ladies (New York: Putnam's, 1962; London: Deutsch, 1962);

The Presidential Papers (New York: Putnam's, 1963; London: Deutsch, 1964);

An American Dream (New York: Dial, 1965; London: Deutsch, 1965);

Cannibals and Christians (New York: Dial, 1966; London: Deutsch, 1967);

The Bullfight: A Photographic Narrative with Text by Norman Mailer (New York: Macmillan, 1967);

The Deer Park: A Play (New York: Dial, 1967);

Why Are We in Vietnam? (New York: Putnam's, 1967);

The Short Fiction of Norman Mailer (New York: Dell, 1967; London: Weidenfeld & Nicolson, 1969);

The Idol and the Octopus: Political Writings on the Kennedy and Johnson Administrations (New York: Dell, 1968);

The Armies of the Night (New York: New American Library, 1968; London: Weidenfeld & Nicolson, 1968);

Miami and the Siege of Chicago (New York: New American Library; London: Weidenfeld & Nicolson, 1969);

Of a Fire on the Moon (Boston: Little, Brown, 1970; London: Weidenfeld & Nicolson, 1970);

Maidstone (New York: New American Library, 1971);

The Prisoner of Sex (Boston: Little, Brown, 1971);

The Long Patrol (New York: World, 1971);

Existential Errands (Boston: Little, Brown, 1972);

St. George and the Godfather (New York: New American Library, 1972);

Marilyn (New York: Grosset & Dunlap, 1973; London:

Hodder & Stoughton, 1973);

The Faith of Graffiti (New York: Praeger, 1974); republished as *Watching My Name Go By* (London: Matthews, Miller, Dunbar, 1974);

The Fight (Boston: Little, Brown, 1975; London: Hart-Davis, 1976);

Genius and Lust: A Journey Through the Major Writings of Henry Miller (New York: Grove, 1976);

Some Honorable Men: Political Conventions 1960-1972 (Boston: Little, Brown, 1976);

The Executioner's Song (Boston: Little, Brown, 1979; London: Hutchinson, 1979);

Of Women and Their Elegance (New York: Simon & Schuster, 1980);

Pieces and Pontifications (Boston: Little, Brown, 1982).

BIOGRAPHY:

Philip H. Bufithis, *Norman Mailer* (New York: Ungar, 1978).

Hilary Mills, *Mailer: A Biography* (New York: Empire Books, 1982).

BIBLIOGRAPHY:

Laura Adams, *Norman Mailer: A Comprehensive Bibliography* (Metuchen, N.J.: Scarecrow Press, 1974).

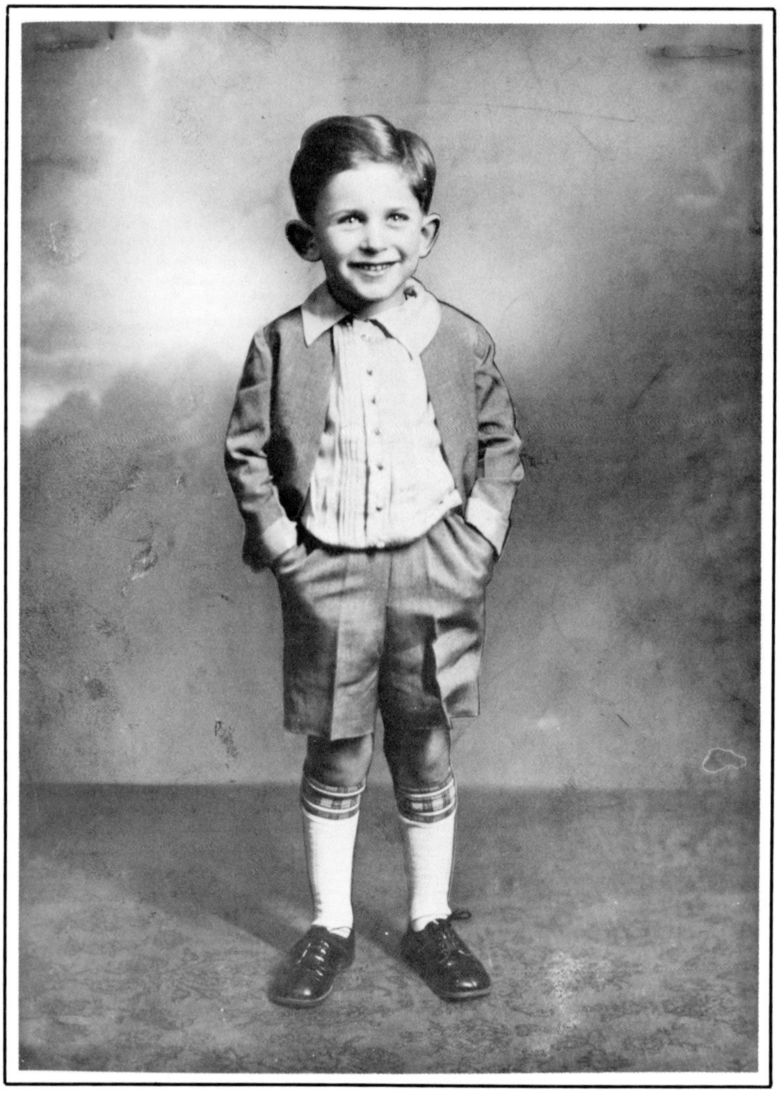

Norman Mailer was born 31 January 1923 in Long Branch, New Jersey, to Isaac Barnett and Fanny Schneider Mailer. When Norman was one, his family moved to the Eastern Parkway section of Brooklyn, "the most secure Jewish environment in America." He is five in this photo.

Mailer received his primary education in New York public schools. He is shown here at twelve, a member of the P.S. 161 class of 1935.

While at Boys' High School in Brooklyn, Mailer published his first article—a piece on building model airplanes. Upon graduation, Mailer wanted to go to the Massachusetts Institute of Technology and study aeronautical engineering, but, because he was only sixteen, the MIT admissions office recommended a year of college elsewhere first.

Norman Mailer
Dunster B-#1
Cambridge, Mass.

Manuscript submitted by a candidate in Harvard College appointed officially by a committee headed by Professor Robert Hillyer, Boylston Professor of Rhetoric + Oratory.

Three Fingers of Friendship

The subway car filled slowly; the three o'clock in the morning people sprawling tiredly on the dirty straw seats.

About two minutes before it was supposed to pull out of Maverick Station, a plump old gray-blond wavered in the doorway.

"I want to go to Scollay Square; is this the train to go to Scollay Square?" she asked the conductor. She was very drunk. At his nod, she tottered in, and sat down primly, smiling at him. Her streaked dyed hair was beginning to wander across her face, and she patted it into place with her fingers. "How do you go to Scollay Square?" she asked again. Taking out some rouge, she ran a streak from behind her ear to the edge of her mouth. She was smiling at something inside her.

The sailor sitting across from her straightened up. "Yaaaay, Scollay Square," he said, "what do you want with Scollay Square, momma? Only old folk's home there is the Crawford House." He laughed very loudly at this, showing a row of silver-capped teeth. For a sailor, he wasn't young at all; it must have been at least his

In his freshman year at Harvard, Mailer decided that he was going to become a major novelist. In his sophomore year, his Harvard Advocate *short story "The Greatest Thing in the World" won the* Story *magazine college fiction prize. Mailer wrote many short stories while at Harvard; above is the first page of a story, written in 1942 (Mailer papers). He graduated in 1943 with a B.S. in engineering.*

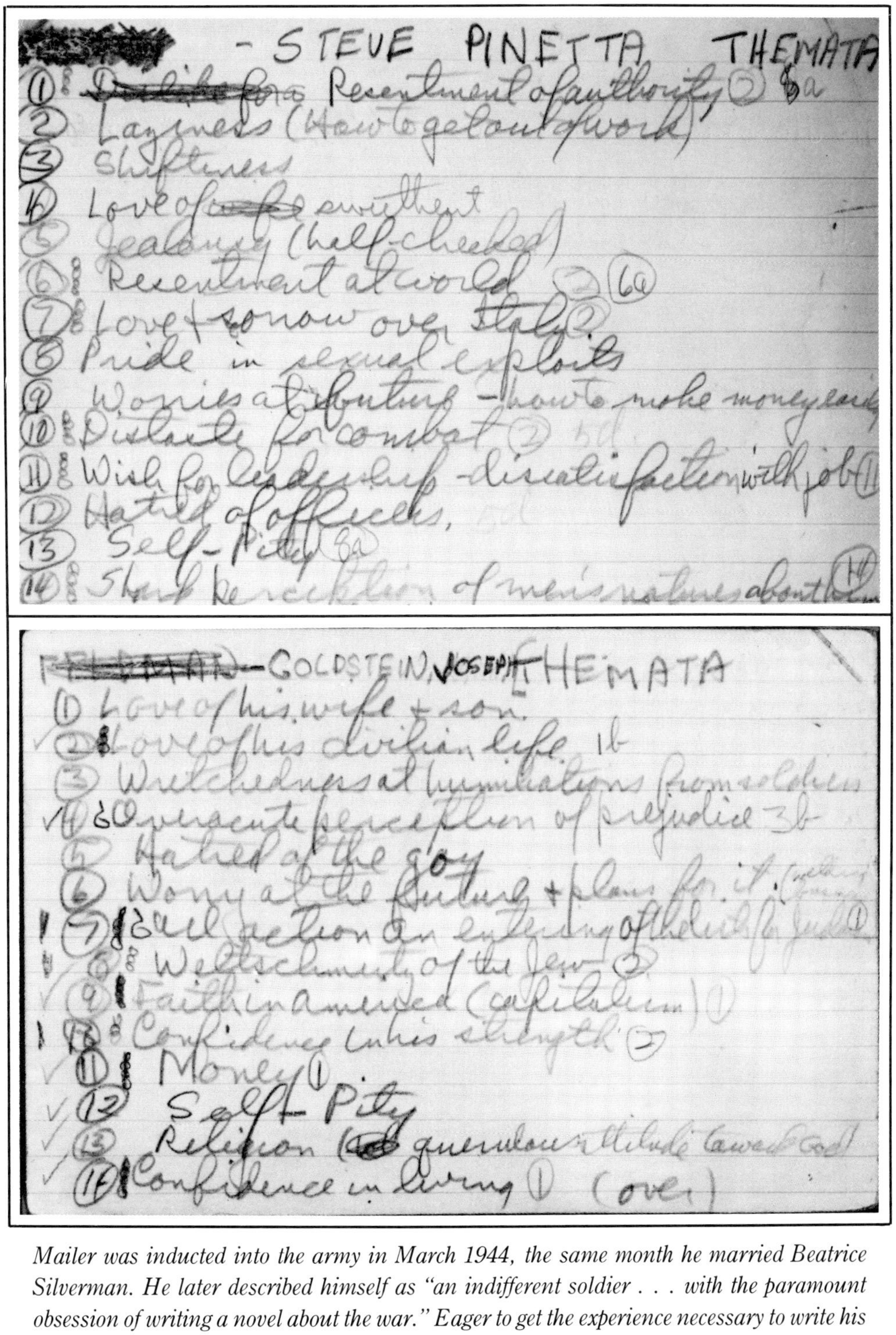

- STEVE PINETTA THEMATA
(1) Resentment of authority (2) 8a
(2) Laziness (How to get out of work)
(3) Shiftiness
(4) Love of sweetheart
(5) Jealousy (half-checked)
(6) Resentment at world (2) 6a
(7) Love + sorrow over Italy (2)
(8) Pride in sexual exploits
(9) Worries at future - how to make money easily
(10) Distaste for combat (2) 5d
(11) Wish for leadership - dissatisfaction with job (11)
(12) Hatred of officers,
(13) Self-Pity 8a
(14) Sharp perception of men's natures about him (14)

-GOLDSTEIN, JOSEPH THEMATA
(1) Love of his wife + son.
(2) Love of his civilian life. 1b
(3) Wretchedness at humiliations from soldiers
(4) Overacute perception of prejudice 3b
(5) Hatred of the goy
(6) Worry at the future + plans for it.
(7) Each action an extending of ... (1)
(8) Weltschmerz of the Jew (2)
(9) Faith in America (capitalism) (1)
(10) Confidence in his strength (2)
(11) Money (1)
(12) Self-Pity
(13) Religion (... querulous attitude toward God)
(14) Confidence in living (1) (over)

Mailer was inducted into the army in March 1944, the same month he married Beatrice Silverman. He later described himself as "an indifferent soldier . . . with the paramount obsession of writing a novel about the war." Eager to get the experience necessary to write his book, Mailer volunteered as a rifleman with a reconnaissance platoon in the Philippine mountains. Concerned that he might not survive to write his novel, he sent his wife long letters describing all he had seen. After his discharge in April 1946, Mailer spent fifteen months writing the novel. As he worked, he kept copious notes and a long dossier on each character. Above are notes for the characters Steve Pinetta and Joseph Goldstein (Mailer papers).

-1-

THE NAKED AND THE DEAD

1.

Nobody could sleep. When morning came, assault craft would be lowered and a first wave of troops would ride through the surf and charge ashore on the beach at Anopopei. All over the ship, all through the convoy, ~~theyknew~~ there was a knowledge that in a few hours some of them were going to be dead.

A soldier lies flat on his bunk, closes his eyes, and remains wide-awake. All about him,like the soughing of surf, he hears the murmurs of men dozing fitfully. "I won't do it, I won't do it," someone cries out of a dream, and the soldier opens his eyes and gazes slowly about the hold, his vision becoming lost in the intricate tangle of hammocks and ~~ankaxd~~ naked bodies and dangling equipment. He decided he wants to go to the head, and cursing a little, he wriggles up to a sitting position, his legs hanging over the bunk, the steel pipe of the hammock above cutting across his hunched back. He sighs, reaches for his shoes which he has tied ~~on~~ to a stanchion, and slowly puts them on. His bunk is the fourth in a tier of five, and he climbs down uncertainly in the half-darkness afraid of stepping on one of the men in the hammocks below him. On the floor he picks his way through a tangle of bags and packs, stumbles once over a rifle, and makes his way to the bulkhead door. He passes through another hold whose aisle is just as cluttered, and finally reaches the head.

Inside the air is ~~hvkvavd~~ steaming. Even now a man is using the sole fresh water shower which has been occupied ever since the troops have come on board. The soldier walks past the crap games in the unused salt water shower stalls, and squats down on the wet split boards of the latrine. He has forgotten his cigarettes and he bums one,

After Mailer's discharge, he and Beatrice lived in Brooklyn, where each worked on a novel. Mailer wrote furiously, averaging thirty pages a week. When he finished, the couple went to Paris to study at the Sorbonne. These are pages 1 and 25 from the revised typescript of

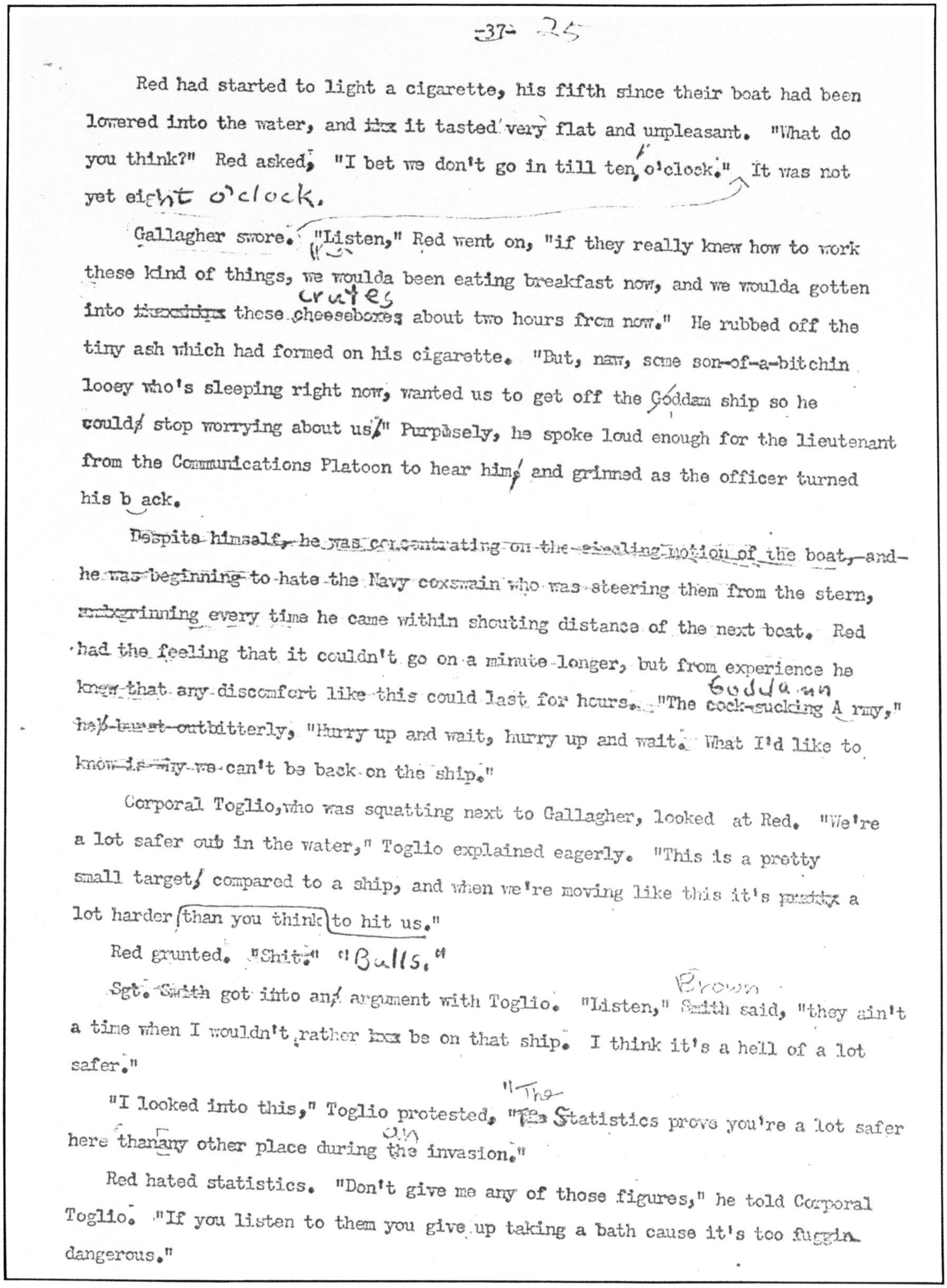

-37- 25

Red had started to light a cigarette, his fifth since their boat had been lowered into the water, and it tasted very flat and unpleasant. "What do you think?" Red asked. "I bet we don't go in till ten o'clock." It was not yet eight o'clock.

Gallagher swore. "Listen," Red went on, "if they really knew how to work these kind of things, we woulda been eating breakfast now, and we woulda gotten into these ~~cheeseboxes~~ crates about two hours from now." He rubbed off the tiny ash which had formed on his cigarette. "But, naw, some son-of-a-bitchin looey who's sleeping right now, wanted us to get off the Goddam ship so he could stop worrying about us." Purposely, he spoke loud enough for the lieutenant from the Communications Platoon to hear him, and grinned as the officer turned his back.

~~Despite himself, he was concentrating on the sickening motion of the boat, and he was beginning to hate the Navy coxswain who was steering them from the stern, grinning every time he came within shouting distance of the next boat. Red had the feeling that it couldn't go on a minute longer, but from experience he knew that any discomfort like this could last for hours.~~ "The ~~cock-sucking~~ Goddamn Army," ~~he burst out~~ bitterly, "Hurry up and wait, hurry up and wait. What I'd like to ~~know is why we can't be back on the ship.~~"

Corporal Toglio, who was squatting next to Gallagher, looked at Red. "We're a lot safer out in the water," Toglio explained eagerly. "This is a pretty small target compared to a ship, and when we're moving like this it's ~~pretty~~ a lot harder than you think to hit us."

Red grunted. ~~"Shit."~~ "Bulls."

Sgt. ~~Smith~~ Brown got into an argument with Toglio. "Listen," ~~Smith~~ Brown said, "they ain't a time when I wouldn't rather be on that ship. I think it's a hell of a lot safer."

"I looked into this," Toglio protested, "~~The~~ Statistics prove you're a lot safer here than any other place during ~~the~~ an invasion."

Red hated statistics. "Don't give me any of those figures," he told Corporal Toglio. "If you listen to them you give up taking a bath cause it's too fuggin dangerous."

Mailer's war novel The Naked and the Dead, *published 8 May 1948 (Beinecke Library, Yale University).*

Book Review:

Maxwell Geismar, "Nightmare on Anopopei," *Saturday Review*, 31 (8 May 1948): 10-11.

The Naked and the Dead, *the story of an infantry platoon's reconnaissance mission on a Pacific island, was an immediate success. It was at the top of the* New York Times *best-seller list for eleven weeks and sold 197,185 copies in its first year, bringing Mailer a reputation as one of America's most promising writers.*

Just when we have stopped talking about the new literary voices of the period, they seem to be appearing. Norman Mailer is a young American writer who grew up in Brooklyn, went to Harvard, and found himself, as a rifleman, in Leyte and Japan. His earlier work has appeared in *Story* magazine and *Cross Section*, but *The Naked and the Dead* is his first novel. It is a solid and interesting story of the capture of Anopopei, a typical Japanese island in the Pacific.

Mr. Mailer uses some of the technical devices which John Dos Passos initiated in the American novel, while there is also an influence of tone. But *Three Soldiers*, like most of the typical stories of World War I, was essentially a novel of individual protest. The military organization was something to escape from, not to understand. The virtue of *The Naked and the Dead*—and I think it will be the typical pattern of the new war novels—is that it sees the individual within the military organization. It attempts to evaluate the whole complex structure of the American Army in war and peace, as a manifestation of contemporary society, as well as a weapon of conquest and destruction. Or perhaps even, in the Tolstoian sense, as one-half of our "natural" existence.

That doesn't mean Mr. Mailer particularly approves of army life, or that the campaign on Anopopei was an idyl of human decency. The novel opens with an amphibious assault upon the island. The central group of characters are members of a reconnaissance squad. The slow, blundering, and tortured progress of the military action also marks their physical and moral disintegration as human beings. The plump and foul-mouthed Wilson, the superstitious and embittered Gallagher, the ambitious and servile Brown, the tough and rebellious Red Valsen, all are partially or completely destroyed by their ordeal. To live through it is not necessarily to have survived. Only the slow-thinking farm boy, Ridges, and the "intellectual" Brooklyn Jew, Goldstein, seem to have the necessary resources, whether of sheer animal vitality or of spiritual comprehension, to endure the impervious

Mailer at the time The Naked and the Dead *was published*

jungle, the sickening climate, the steady, demoralizing contact with filth, pain, and terror even more than the actual and paralyzing shock of combat.

Staff Sergeant Croft, an excellent soldier to begin with, becomes a rigid and implacable tyrant. If he has accepted the hatred of his men as part of his job, he soon begins to nourish it. As the novel moves up through the ranks of the military hierarchy, it is particularly good on the relationship of these men with the commissioned officers. There is an ironical episode in which Major Dalleson, a typical disciplinarian and drillmaster, goes into panic because the Japs have given him a chance for a breakthrough, and he is forced to use his troops. Lieutenant Hearn is a social rebel who has broken away from the conventions and prejudices of the ruling class, financial or military. General Cummings, who has given up human relationships completely, for the sake of organization and efficiency, who believes that the only value of a human soul is the use it can be put to, also believes that, after the war with Russia, the next century will belong to the reactionaries and the capitalists. And why not?

The antagonism between these last two figures, both human and theoretical, gives Mr. Mailer a chance to build up, often very eloquently, the historical and philosophical connotations of the war. In the end Hearn is broken and killed. Perhaps this represents Mr. Mailer's own conclusion about the future, yet Hearn is a curiously vapid character, and the ordinary soldiers in *The Naked and the Dead* lack the vitality and originality they should really have. Mr. Mailer leans rather heavily on the sexual experiences of his lower-class figures, too. These may be a solace for the common man, and even a source of strength, but they don't constitute his only achievement.

I think this is the main weakness of the novel, for there is no real balance of the dramatic forces in it, just as there is a final lack of emotional impact. The story ought to be more impressive than it is. Within these limits, however, *The Naked and the Dead* is a substantial work, and Mr. Mailer is a new novelist of consequence.

INTERVIEW:

"Rugged Times," *New Yorker*, 24 (23 October 1948): 25.

Mailer was in Europe when The Naked and the Dead *was published. He returned to the United States in July 1948 and actively compaigned for Progressive Party presidential candidate Henry Wallace. While engaged in the campaign, Mailer granted this interview discussing the reception of his first novel.*

We had a talk the other day with Norman Mailer, whose novel "The Naked and the Dead" has been at the top of the best-seller lists for several months now. We met him at Rinehart & Co., his publishers, in a conference room that had, along with other handy editorial equipment, a well-stocked bar. We'd heard rumors that Mailer was a rough-and-ready young man with a strong antipathy to literary gatherings and neckties, but on the occasion of our encounter he was neatly turned out in gray tweeds, with a striped red-and-white necktie and shined shoes, and he assured us that he doesn't really have any deep-seated prejudices concerning dress. "Actually," he said, "I've got all the average middle-class fears." He thinks the assumption that he hasn't got them grew out of his meeting some of the literati last summer when he was wearing sneakers and an old T shirt. He'd just come from a ball game, and it was a very hot day. "I figured anybody with brains would be trying to keep cool," he said.

Mailer is a good-looking fellow of twenty-five, with blue eyes, big ears, a soft voice, and a forthright manner. Locating a bottle of Scotch in the bar, he poured a couple of drinks. "If I'm ever going to be an alcoholic," he said, "I'll be one by November 2nd, thanks to the rigors of the political campaign. I've been making speeches for Wallace. I've made eighteen so far and have another dozen ahead of me. I'm not doing this because I like it. All last year, I kept saying that the intellectuals had to immerse themselves in political movements or else they were only shooting their mouths off. Now I am in the spot as a result of shooting my mouth off." In general, Mailer told us, the success of his novel has caused him to feel uncomfortably like a movie queen. "Whenever I make an appearance," he said, "I have thirty little girls crowding around asking for my autograph. I think it's much better when people who read your book don't know anything about you, even what you look like. I have refused to let *Life* photograph me. Getting your mug in the papers is one of the shameful ways of making a living, but there aren't many ways of making a living that aren't shameful. Everyone keeps asking me if I've ever been psychoanalyzed. The answer is no, but maybe I'll have to be by the end of another five years. These are rough times for little Normie."

Mailer's royalties will net him around thirty thousand this year, after taxes, and he plans to bank most of it. He finds apartments depressing and has a suspicion of possessions, so he and his wife live in a thirty-dollar-a-month furnished room in Brooklyn Heights. He figures that his thirty thousand will last at least five years, giving him plenty of time in which to write another book. He was born in Long Branch, New Jersey, but his family moved to Brooklyn when he was one, and that has since been his home. He attended P.S. 161 and Boys High, and entered Harvard at sixteen, intending to study aeronautical engineering. He took only one course in engineering, however, and spent most of his time reading or in bull sessions. In his sophomore year, he won first prize in *Story*'s college contest with a story entitled "The Greatest Thing in the World." "About a bum," he told us. "In the beginning, there's a whole *tzimes* about how he's very hungry and all he's eating is ketchup. It will probably make a wonderful movie someday." In the Army, Mailer served as a surveyor in the field artillery, an Intelligence clerk in the cavalry, a wireman in a communications platoon, a cook, and a baker, and volunteered, successfully, for action with a reconnaissance platoon on Luzon. He started writing "The Naked and the Dead" in the summer of 1946, in a cottage outside Provincetown, and took sixteen months to finish it. "I'm slowing down," he said. "When I was eighteen, I wrote a novel in two or three months. At twenty-one, I wrote another novel, in seven months. Neither of them ever got published." After turning in the manuscript of "The Naked and the Dead," he and his wife went off to Paris. "It was wonderful there," he said. "In Paris, you can just lay down your load and look out at the gray sky. Back here, the crowd is always yelling. It's like a Roman arena. You have a headache, and you scurry around like a rat, like a character in a Kafka nightmare, eating scallops with last year's grease on them."

Mailer has an uneasy feeling that Dostoevski and Tolstoy, between them, have written everything worth writing, but he nevertheless means to go on turning out novels. He thinks "The Naked and the Dead" must be a failure, because of the number of misinterpretations of it that he has read. "People say it is a novel without hope," he told us. "Actually, it offers a good deal of hope. I intended it to be a parable about the movement of man through history. I tried to explore the outrageous [proportions] of cause and effect, of effort and recompense, in a sick society. The book finds man corrupted, confused to the point of helplessness, but it also finds that there are limits beyond which he cannot be pushed, and it finds that even in his corruption and sickness there are yearnings for a better world."

BOOK REVIEW:

Charles Rolo, "A House in Brooklyn," *Atlantic*, 188 (June 1951): 82-83.

In 1949 Mailer went to Hollywood, where he wrote an original screenplay, which MGM rejected. After an unsuccessful attempt at producing the screenplay himself, Mailer returned East and finished Barbary Shore, *a novel he had started in Paris. The book, telling of people trapped by both American and Soviet authoritarianism, was strongly influenced by French left-wing intellectual Jean Malaquais, whom Mailer had known in Europe.* Barbary Shore *was not well received, getting, according to Mailer, "the worst reviews of any serious novel in recent years."*

In his second novel, *Barbary Shore*, Norman Mailer makes a sharp departure from the naturalism of *The Naked and the Dead*. The new book—also an ambitious story, with a fairly complex pattern of personal relationships and tensions—has a far stronger imaginative coloring, and it shows a remarkable advance in Mailer's writing: his style has become rounder, more flowing, and even tinged with poetry. But in *Barbary Shore* the parts are more impressive than the whole. In the final analysis, it is not, I feel, a successfully realized novel.

Mailer's narrator, Mikey Lovett, is a young man in his mid-twenties with "no past"—just a few hazy memories, such as that he was always poor. A scar behind his ear suggests that he was probably wounded in the war. Lovett takes a cheap room in a boarding house in Brook-

Dust jacket for Mailer's second novel

lyn Heights with the intention of writing a novel, but soon he finds himself increasingly absorbed in the lives of the other people under the same roof. His landlady, Mrs. Guinevere, is a blowzy, vulgarly genteel ex-burlesque queen, perennially in slippers and peignoir, and with a husband who remains invisible. The two lodgers are seemingly commonplace, but there is something indefinably puzzling about them. McLeod, a neat, solitary man of fifty, claims to be a window dresser in a department store. Hollingsworth is an oafish, nattily dressed young Babbitt, a mixture of Y.M.C.A. good fellowship and smug, small-time lechery. A third tenant moves in, a hysterical Bohemian girl, Lannie, who sometimes talks like a character out of Saroyan, and sometimes seems to have escaped from the world of Truman Capote.

In due course, it turns out that Hollingsworth is a government agent; Lannie is somehow associated with him; and McLeod was for fifteen years a leading figure in the Communist Party and is now a discredited "Old Bolshevik," anguished at the Party's betrayal of its early promise. Hollingsworth's assignment is to obtain an important "little object" which McLeod stole while working in a government office; but he decides to double-cross his organization and take over the "object" himself. After a curious series of interrogations, at which Lovett and Lannie are present, McLeod wearily agrees to Hollingsworth's terms, but insists on making an impassioned statement of his credo—that the two leading economic systems of today are both based on exploitation and both doomed; and that, after the Colossi are shattered by the coming war, men like Lovett, men unburdened by the guilt and failures of the past, will start the true Socialist Revolution.

The fuzzy political nihilism of the novel's underlying idea ("plague on both houses") has called for a story deliberately steeped in grotesquerie and in a kind of pointlessness. But in trying to create this tone, Mailer tends to produce an impression of outright make-believe. The characters seem to be playing a game of mystifying the reader; their motivation and their conduct are at times inexplicable. *Barbary Shore* never quite achieves—as it is clearly intended to achieve—the coherence of a political parable. It is a good illustration of what John Aldridge has to say about the new writers' failure to impose dramatic meaning on their material. It is also, I should add by way of corrective, an original and absorbing story of some very odd goings on in a house in Brooklyn Heights. Mailer has certainly furnished further evidence that he has one of the stronger talents of his generation. His work would gain considerably, I suspect, if he were to find a way out of the political purgatory in which he appears to be wandering.

BOOK REVIEW:

William Pfaff, "The Writer as Vengeful Moralist," *Commonweal*, 63 (2 December 1955): 230-231.

After the poor reception of Barbary Shore, *Mailer laboriously rewrote his next novel,* The Deer Park, *in which a Hollywood director is blacklisted and forced into retirement. Mailer's publisher, Rinehart, broke the contract when Mailer refused to delete a description of sex between an old producer and a call girl. The novel was rejected by six publishers before being accepted by Putnam's. Its critical reception was mixed, as indicated by this review in a Catholic journal. Mailer did not publish another novel until 1965.*

I wonder if the novelist is not dangerously overrated in this country. The key to national status as intellectual and spokesman for ideas is the writing of a novel. Critics have their journals, but a minute audience. Essayists and philosophers still exist, but we probably are seeing the last of them, and in another ten or twenty years they will be known to America only as reconstructed exhibits at the American Museum of Natural History. The journalists have come up fast but still have nothing of the peculiar status and influence of the novelist. And this development is highly dangerous to the novelist. He is no longer content to be only a novelist. He must provide us with whys, meanings and conclusions. Perhaps it would benefit the writer to be sent back to the time when he was entertainer or ghost kept on the string of a monarch to take over when the lutists and falconers tired.

Norman Mailer is a case in point. Mr. Mailer is an excellent writer with admirable and serious intentions, devotion and zeal. But he insists on explaining the meaning of life, and I, for one, would prefer to get that from someone other than the artist—explicitly, that is. If Mr. Mailer were content to show me art without explaining it, I would be happier with his work.

In this book he has taken a big and worthy subject: the people who make up the motion picture industry. His spokesman is a young military pilot who has been shaken up by his experiences in indiscriminately spewing napalm about and has come home with a large sum of money collected in a crap game and the desire to think things out. He goes to a desert resort in the southwest,where he falls in with the movie set: a first-rate director banished from Hollywood for having refused to name names at a Con-

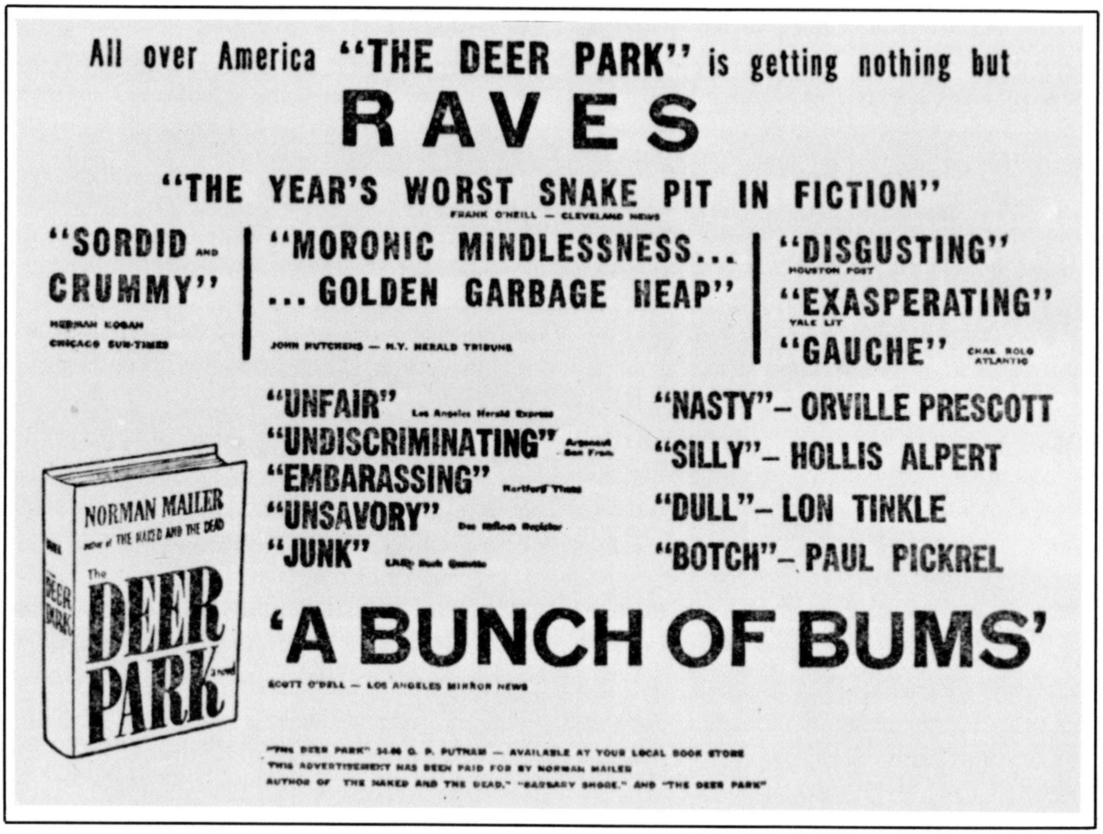

Mailer paid for this advertisement listing the worst critical judgments on The Deer Park.

gressional hearing on Communism; a star who falls in love, in her fashion, with the pilot; an Italian flamenco dancer who goes to live with the director; and an assortment of producers and pimps. Mr. Mailer then takes these people through their love and hate affairs with people and with Hollywood—that is, themselves. The director eventually decides to cooperate with the Congressional committee and reestablish himself in Hollywood with the flamenco dancer as his unhappy wife. The star decides that Hollywood is more important than the flier. The flier decides to go to Mexico and become a bullfighter. (And the man who popularizes a new dodge for writers to use as symbol of art-death-truth will have my thanks. What about jaguar hunting in Central America, or *jai-alai* or *Kendo*?)

All of this is done very well. Mr. Mailer tends to sacrifice form for getting it all in, but that is another national characteristic. (He also does not mind incongruity: in the middle comes a brittle, straight-faced farcical scene where the producer tries to marry off the stars. It could have been plucked out of *Black Mischief* and has nothing in common with anything else in this book.) The point is that these people do have real existence. Mailer has, I think, shown better than anyone else the position of the moviemaker, his fascination with his art, and the forces which affect him, from the uncomplicated desire for security to the exhilarating creation of a scenario to the bitter corner-blunting of professionalism. None of the motivations are cheap. Mr. Mailer makes the recantation of the director a comprehensible thing, and he makes the star an interesting—if less successful—figure of the ambitious young woman. The Italian girl is particularly successful because she is lifted out of what might have been terrible convention—the hot-blooded Latin half tramp half *hausfrau*. This one is a lot more than a convention.

So Mr. Mailer indignantly shows these people running, running, running. It is this which has caused the book to be compared with *The Last Tycoon*. But the difference between Mr. Mailer and Scott Fitzgerald is that Fitzgerald had as his spokesman a bond salesman, not a bullfighter seeking philosophy, and he had Dick Diver go back to the Fingerlakes where he probably is today, a rather old man now, and he did not have Diver sum it all up in the last chapter. Mr. Mailer sums it up by telepathic communication between Hollywood and Greenwich Village.

This book is being promoted as a sensational sex-book. But Mr. Mailer is not a panderer; he is a vengeful moralist. His story includes a good deal of sexual perversion, and the point of it all is to tell us how admirable true love is by contrast. (But true love remains as intangible as the meaning of life; I wonder if naïveté is not also part of the American novelists' baggage.) This is neither a cheap nor a simple book. There is a lot wrong with it, but more that is right. Mr. Mailer simply is not the kind of writer who produces books which can be judged successful or unsuccessful. He piles up enormously talented stuff, some of it incongruous, some of it boozy and pretentious, and it is both successful and unsuccessful, good and bad, but it is serious and worth the respect of the serious reader.

Book Review:

Alfred Kazin, "How Good is Norman Mailer?," *Reporter*, 21 (26 November 1959): 40-41.

After two unsuccessful novels, Mailer devoted himself to journalism. He helped found the Village Voice *in 1954 and wrote a weekly column from January to May of 1956. He also was a contributing editor for the leftist magazine* Dissent. Advertisements for Myself, *a collection of essays, fictions, and letters, on politics, sex, drugs, his own writing, and the works of others, appeared in 1959. It received unusual attention for a collection, mainly because of the autobiographical connecting pieces.*

Perhaps more than any other book since Scott Fitzgerald's *The Crack-up*, this book reveals how exciting, yet tragic, America can be for a gifted writer. It is a remarkably full book; all of Mailer up to now is in it, and that is exactly what is wrong with it. For at thirty-six, after following up *The Naked and the Dead* with an artistic failure, *Barbary Shore*, and one ambiguous *succès de scandale, The Deer Park*, Mailer (now embarked on a very long and extremely ambitious novel that may take many years) has obviously been hungry to make his mark again in one big smashing outrageous way. He has put together an anthology of all his works, from undergraduate short stories to two sections of the novel in progress, that includes his columns from a Greenwich Village weekly, social and political comment, his now famous essay on "The White Negro" and other socio-sexual themes, stories, spoofs, interviews, poems, and some shrewd but essentially subjective evaluations of his literary generation. In the "advertisements" to the different works he talks about himself and Hemingway, himself and marijuana, himself and sex, himself and Eisenhower's America. By the time you get through what is often a very brilliant if screamingly self-conscious book, you feel that Mailer has worked so hard to display everything he has done and everything he knows that it has all collected on the surface. Mailer's performance here reminds me of the brilliant talker who impresses the hell out of you at a cocktail party but who, when he turns his back to go home, seems vaguely lost.

Yet *Advertisements for Myself* is a remarkable performance, and it is clearer to me than ever that Mailer is a powerful, courageous talent admirably provoked by our culture. I admire him because he is naturally a radical, strong, and exuberant talent; this book is full of more penetrating comment on the America of Eisenhower, television, suburbia, and J. D. Salinger than anything I have seen in years. But as Mailer says, "I have been running for President these last ten years in the privacy of my mind," and he is probably the only Jew who has been. He wants to be not just a good novelist but the Hemingway of our period. Hemingway obsesses him (and ignores him); Faulkner once made fun of him for saying that whites are always jealous of Negro sexuality; the publisher who made so much out of *The Naked and the Dead* finally turned down *The Deer Park*; there are actually good writers in America who pay no attention to him.

In short, like many another American radical, desperado, Reichian stalwart of sexual frankness, Norman Mailer has been driven crazy by an affluent and greasily accommodating society which not only doesn't oppose him but which turns even his disgust and frankness into a form of literary capital. Just as the hipsters, whom Mailer admires, are not outlaws, not radicals, but the slobs and remittance men and spoiled brats of a society so wasteful

Very often after I've done the novel I realize that that beauty which I recognized in it is not going to be recognized by the reader. I didn't succeed in bringing it out. It's very odd—it's as though I had let the novel down, owed it a duty which I didn't fulfill.

From Writers at Work, Third Series *(New York: Viking Press, 1967)*

and indulgent and satiated with normal sex that it has to discover new thrills all the time, so the secret burn of Norman Mailer is that a book like this, which is meant to slap respectable America in the face, may not sell as much as it could. Like every American writer whose name is an instant password, who can support himself by his writing, who knows himself a celebrity because he moves largely in the company of celebrities, Mailer can no more stay off television or move back to Brooklyn than, being an honest and intransigent spirit, he can admire television or sentimentalize the Brooklyn which, as he says, is not the center of anything. Anyone who reads this book with as much attention and admiration as I have just done can, nevertheless, see that what obsesses Norman Mailer is not just the swarminess of our culture, the repressiveness of our official morals, the flabby gentility of our ruling intellectuals, but the fact that this same America is itself constantly coaxing Norman Mailer to share in the take and join the fun.

What makes this society so marvelous for the gifted rebel, and so awful, is that lacking all standards by which to counter or to question the new, it hungrily welcomes any talent that challenges it interestingly—but then holds this talent in the mold of its own shapelessness; the writer is never free enough of his neighbors and contemporaries to be not simply agin the government but detached from it. Mailer, who like all his generation has had to work against the overpowering example of Fitzgerald and Hemingway and Faulkner, now thinks that these older fellows had it easier, that our society did not drag them into its maw as compulsively as it does present writers. When I recall how desperately out of fashion Fitzgerald and Lewis and Anderson and Cather felt at the end of their careers, I doubt that the literary competition has ever been less punishing than Mailer obviously feels it to be. What has changed since the 1920's is first that there are more and more writers, as there are more and more people. Even "advanced" literature is beginning to get as crowded as the mass media, and Mailer cannot be sure, now that he has dismissed Bellow, ignored Malamud, and ruled out all women writers as unreadable, that there isn't someone in South Dakota who may yet outdistance him.

More important, Hemingway (of whom Mailer seems constantly to dream and to curse in his dreams) was still based enough on the old "inner-directed" Protestant culture to measure his need of courage against the moral abstractions of courage, duty, grace, etc. Mailer measures himself against others. Symbolically, Hemingway got his great experience in the first world madness by volunteering for the Italian Army long before Americans were in the war. Mailer in 1943 had to keep from becoming a clerk, for only as a rifleman could he collect the experience for the great Hemingwayish novel about the war that he was already prepared to write. And only in the Pacific, as he brilliantly estimated again, would he be able to gather experience for a really provocative novel, since there the growing reactionary tendencies in American life would be manifest.

Without his egotism, no writer is likely to carry much weight. But granted that he must fight for himself and push himself, what reserves of thought and imagination are left? A writer is not only what he knows himself to be, what he consciously fights for and hates and loves—he is the book he makes, the book that must surprise him in the making, the book that somewhere within itself is always greater than he is. Scott Fitzgerald's *The Crack-up*, moving as it may be, has less of Fitzgerald than *The Great Gatsby*. The question all over this book is: How good is Norman Mailer?—and the trouble is that Mailer thinks that he can answer it in terms of available competition. Only a highly self-conscious and rather stormily competitive fellow would have tried so hard to win the prize by dismissing so many writers whose books he hasn't read. This performance calls up the comment on the famous French writer who boasted in his journal that sexually he was more gifted than other men: "How does he know?"

Still, *we* have a right to ask, How good is Norman Mailer? How good are his books? Quite apart from the deleterious influence of our government, our publishers, our official morals—and apart from all the obscene words about television and the cowardice of the "squares" and the marvelous sexuality of Negroes and the necessity of Hip—how good are Norman Mailer's novels? My answer would be that *The Naked and the Dead* is a good novel, though too literary, with worked-up army detail that is thin compared with James Jones's *From Here to Eternity*, and with only one real character in it, the General, who is too obvious a villain; that *Barbary Shore* is hysterical politically and a bad novel by a writer of obvious talent and guts, so that everything in it makes its mark, but not as a work of art; that *The Deer Park* is an extraordinarily uneven and somehow sick book with something peculiarly closed and airless about it. I felt this painfully when I read the novel, and Mailer says in *Advertisements* that he rewrote the novel under marijuana. I am neither shocked by this nor moved to admire Mailer because of it; I do

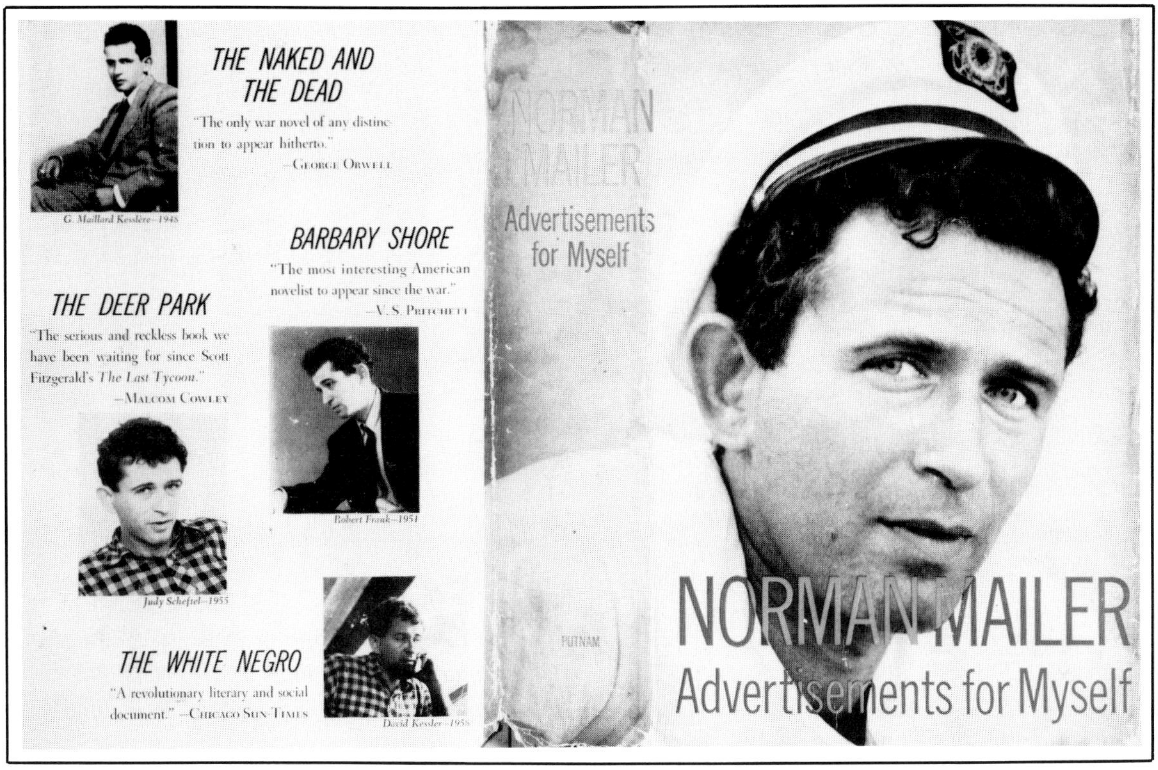

Dust jacket for Mailer's fourth book

think that *The Deer Park* is not what Mailer thinks it is. It seems to me ridiculous for Mailer to push his novel so hard in this book, since the question is not what Rinehart or the critics did to the book but what Mailer did.

How good is Norman Mailer? The answer varies from work to work, sometimes from page to page. Some of his new work, particularly a torrid story wholly about sexual intercourse, "The Time of Her Time," seems to me remarkable; the opening of his new book, "Advertisements for Myself on the Way Out," a lot of wind. Not only can Mailer not know how good he is; he is himself one of the most variable, unstable, and on the whole unpredictable writers I have ever read. He has a remarkable intelligence, and this book shows it; a marvelously forceful and inventive style; great objective gifts as a novelist. On the other hand, his intelligence, though muscular, has no real ease or quietly reflective power; he is as fond of his style as an Italian tenor of his vocal chords, and he sometimes tends to overpower when the more manly thing—if I may touch on a major concern in this book—would be to convince; his sense of reality, though boldly critical, is often obsessive in its self-consciousness. On the whole, Norman Mailer is very, very good indeed—not better than ten million other fellows, as he thinks one has to be, but good.

But what will become of him God only knows, for no one can calculate what so overintense a need to dominate, to succeed, to grasp, to win, may do to that side of talent which has its own rule of being and can never be forced.

LETTER:

Norman Mailer, "The Shiny Enemies," *Nation*, 190 (30 January 1960): inside front cover.

"Evaluations: Quick and Expensive Comments on the Talent in the Room," the section of Advertisements for Myself *containing Mailer's appraisals of seventeen contemporaries, angered many. Gore Vidal, whom Mailer called "imprisoned in the recessive nuances of narcissistic explorations," wrote an article for the 2 January 1960 issue of* Nation *denouncing* The Naked and the Dead *as a "clever, talented, admirably executed fake" and calling Mailer "a demagogue who should not be a novelist at all, or even a writer, despite formidable gifts." Mailer, relishing the controversy, wrote this response.*

Dear Sirs: I read Gore Vidal's review of *Advertisements for Myself* with attention. While I would and do disagree with parts of his piece, I must say Vidal did some good writing.

But in two places, I thought he was out of line. To quote him:

> . . . writers who are unduly eager for fame and acceptance will write novels which they hope might interest religious-minded critics. The results range from the sub-literary bleating of the Beats to Mailer's portentous: "I am the way and the life ever after, crucify me, you hackers, for mine is a ritual death! Oh, Scott, oh, Herman, oh, ancestral voices murmuring, take my flesh and my blood, partake of me and know mysteries!"

The quotation marks are unhappy. I never wrote such a sentence and I never spoke such a sentence. May this be put on the record before the sentence is quoted by others as the stricken heart of my credo.

Point Two is sly. I quote again from Vidal: "I noted with some amusement that, despite the air of candor, he makes no new enemies in this book. He scores off those who are lost to him anyway, thus proving that essentially the work is politic." Only a fool brags of making new enemies, but I was bruised to the bone by this quick assertion, and when Vidal called a few days later to discover my reactions to his piece, I gave documents to the man, page and paragraph, about the new enemies I had made, and by God yes I think even Gore V. would admit this day he was hasty. . . .

Norman Mailer

Mailer's essay "The White Negro: Superficial Reflections on the Hipster" was first published in the Summer 1957 issue of Dissent, *a magazine which describes itself as "a journal devoted to radical ideas and the values of socialism and democracy." The essay was included in* Advertisements for Myself *and separately published by City Lights in 1957.*

INTERVIEW:

Richard Wollheim, "Living Like Heroes," *New Statesman*, 52 (29 September 1961): 443-445.

The thesis of "The White Negro" is that the hipster "had absorbed the existentialist synapses of the Negro and for practical purposes could be considered a white Negro." Mailer continued his discussion of the hipster in this interview, which appeared in the British journal New Statesman *on the day* Advertisements for Myself *was published in England.*

NORMAN MAILER: What is a free act? It's an act for which there are no guides, when one has to make a moral judgment and there's no preparation for it because the life of the day has become more complex than the morality that covers it. The assumption here is that life always advances far ahead of morality. Morality is a quartermaster corps bringing up supplies to starving soldiers. Right. So the hipster acts and after he acts, he feels that it was either good or not good. He has a sensation which tells him which it was. This sensation is what Hemingway was writing about all the time. Now if the hipster always obeys this sensation, then he follows his unconscious, he acts on the basis of his id. He becomes the creature of the id.

RICHARD WOLLHEIM: But how do you get from the idea of the free act to that of a way of life flowing directly from the unconscious? Why shouldn't we identify the free act with the act that results from arbitrary choice?

MAILER: That's the Sartrean idea, isn't it? Well, I reject Sartre. I don't reject him entirely, because I've not read him entirely. But I think that a Sartrean logic can work psychologically for very few people. There *are* people who can do it. It works for Sartre, but Sartre is so much a man of will that he can literally recreate himself by acts. But most people can't: for most people there must also be expressions of nature which go counter to their will.

WOLLHEIM: Now this release of unconscious forces is obviously going to result in violence; and certainly in *The White Negro* you don't shrink from the consequences, though I'd say that certain critics make too much of this because they understand violence in too narrow a sense—violence as crime.

MAILER: But the violence must be violence for which full responsibility is accepted, and that's rare today. Today we have the violence of the man who won't look his victim in the face. Take Eichmann. If he had killed 500,000 people with his bare hands, he would have been a monster, but a heroic monster. He'd have gained some of our unconscious respect. He'd have worn the scar of his own moral wound.

WOLLHEIM: I agree that the denial of the existence of aggression is a bad thing in our society. But an ethic of violence, or one that tolerates violence, surely won't reduce anxiety?

MAILER: I think there are two anxieties. The first comes because one contains more hatred than one can express, and one's afraid that it will come out; and there's another that comes precisely when you release it, because when you do, there are consequences.

WOLLHEIM: But isn't there also anxiety that is more directly connected with the release of aggression, that isn't just fear of consequences, but an inherent fear we have of our own destructive forces. That's why hip morality will only increase anxiety.

MAILER: I know it's not easy to release the id. Incidentally I don't like the word 'id.' In America we have a better word: 'it.' You know, 'get with it.' But I don't see the real choice as one between violence and nonviolence. It's rather between the violence of the individual and collective violence.

WOLLHEIM: By 'collective violence' you mean the way in which certain aspects of society combine to destroy or deaden personality.

MAILER: Yes, and I mean a literal deadening. I believe there is a way in which a man's personality can die before his time, and that is worse than being killed in a concentration camp because—and this is where I am optimistic—if a man is killed in some most unjust way, then this will be taken account of in eternity; but if one's death isn't dramatic, if one is extinguished day by day by the society in which one lives, then one loses one's chance of eternity.

WOLLHEIM: This deadening of the personality is a great historical theme. But do you think that the method of destruction changes with the different historical phases, so that today we have it in the form of capitalist exploitation?

MAILER: I wouldn't like to say that I'm no longer a Marxist—I don't like the connotations of saying it. And since I happen to have got more from Marx than from anyone else I've ever read, I wouldn't want to jettison Grandfather. But I'm not orthodox. I don't believe that capitalist exploitation can be explained entirely in terms like surplus value. I think that Marxism revisited would have to take into account something else that goes much deeper than that. Deeper than the love of property is the fear of the past, the fear of the vitality of the lower classes, the fear that if all men were to walk the earth equal, the upper classes would not long survive. I have the impression that the upper classes of England are superior to the upper classes of America. For one thing, if they're hypocrites, they're hypocrites with a certain amount of style; if they're humbugs, they're humbugs with particularly interesting voices. Just as people there's something absolutely godawful about the upper classes of America—they really are horrible people.

WOLLHEIM: But however we think of this exploitation—and I agree that we ought to see it in part as a kind of emotional parasitism, as Lawrence did—it exists. Yet hip seems to me to raise what can't ever be more than a private or at best a minority protest. It demands a certain sophisitication, a special sense of style; in a way it's a variant of old-fashioned aestheticism.

MAILER: What separates hip from aestheticism is that it's not a man living in a country house, surrounding himself with the most beautiful works of art, receiving only those people with manners sufficiently attuned to his, and savouring every moment of it. Hip is living a little like a

After his 1951 divorce from Beatrice Silverman, mother of his daughter Susan, born in 1948, Norman Mailer married Spanish-Peruvian painter Adele Morales in 1954. They had two daughters–Danielle, born in 1957, and Elizabeth Anne, born in 1959. Mailer was charged with stabbing Adele on 20 November 1960 after a party at their Manhattan apartment. They are shown above in court, where she refused to press charges. Nonetheless, Mailer was required to undergo seventeen days of psychiatric observation at Bellevue Hospital, which he feared would be worse for his literary career than serving a jail sentence. They were divorced in 1962.

hero in a Hollywood Western. If you like, it's aestheticism with danger added.

WOLLHEIM: The danger thing seems to show that hip is essentially an ethic of protest, of rejection. But is it really beyond us to conceive of, or even bring about, a society in which, though dissent will still be necessary, protest won't, at least in this total form?

MAILER: Well, this depends on whether one thinks a society can solve its problems rationally. If one thinks it can, then hip will go nowhere. But if one thinks it can't, and that barbarism is closer, and that violence is in the seed, then at least hip introduces the notion of art into barbary.

WOLLHEIM: And you no longer think that Socialism provides a rational solution?

MAILER: If anything is to come of Socialism, the existential content will have to be changed altogether. I've never really been a Socialist, but I've always thought, 'Better Socialism than anything else—and what else is there?' The trouble with Socialists, I don't know about English Socialists, but the trouble with American Socialists—and some of my best friends are Socialists—is that they're prigs. They have very often failed to lead interesting lives, and they say, 'My God, I've had a lousy life, and I'm damned if it's my fault. Let's change the world and have a good time.' No, Socialism isn't terribly interesting if it means looking after the happiness of other people for them. And it doesn't solve the real problem. Socialism has never really considered that part of the establishment which puts emphasis on courage, on manners, on physical graces, on wit. I'd be much more excited about Socialism if it contained within itself the notion of the artist-warrior—and I don't mean myself by that.

WOLLHEIM: But why the warrior? It seems to me a historical accident that through centuries of oppression we've come to identify the free exercise of man's powers with conflict.

MAILER: There's a big problem here, one that Socialists won't face. And that is whether the nature of the universe is war. Because, if it is, it's important to have a good war. England had a war that wasn't nearly as good as it should have been, and it paid for it with a terrible greyness afterwards.

WOLLHEIM: You think psycho-analysis has nothing to say on the subject?

MAILER: I see it as an instrument of conformity. Psychoanalysts are sedentary middle-class people, and I see no reason to give nature and the universe over to sedentary middle-class people. In America now there's a new establishment, what I call the establishment of the centre: people who are right-wing Socialists and left-wing—no, that's inaccurate, moderate—Conservatives, who all work together. And their great handmaid is psychoanalysis. It's almost impossible for anyone now to do anything individual without being crucified in those very mediocre and dreary salons which pop up like mushrooms all over New York. I've seen the city dying over the last ten years. There's a psychic poverty in the city today, perhaps in the whole country. The thing that distresses me about America is that for all that country's done, I don't think it's done one quarter of what it should. I believe it was destined, by history if you will, to be the greatest country that ever existed. I don't think it's come near it.

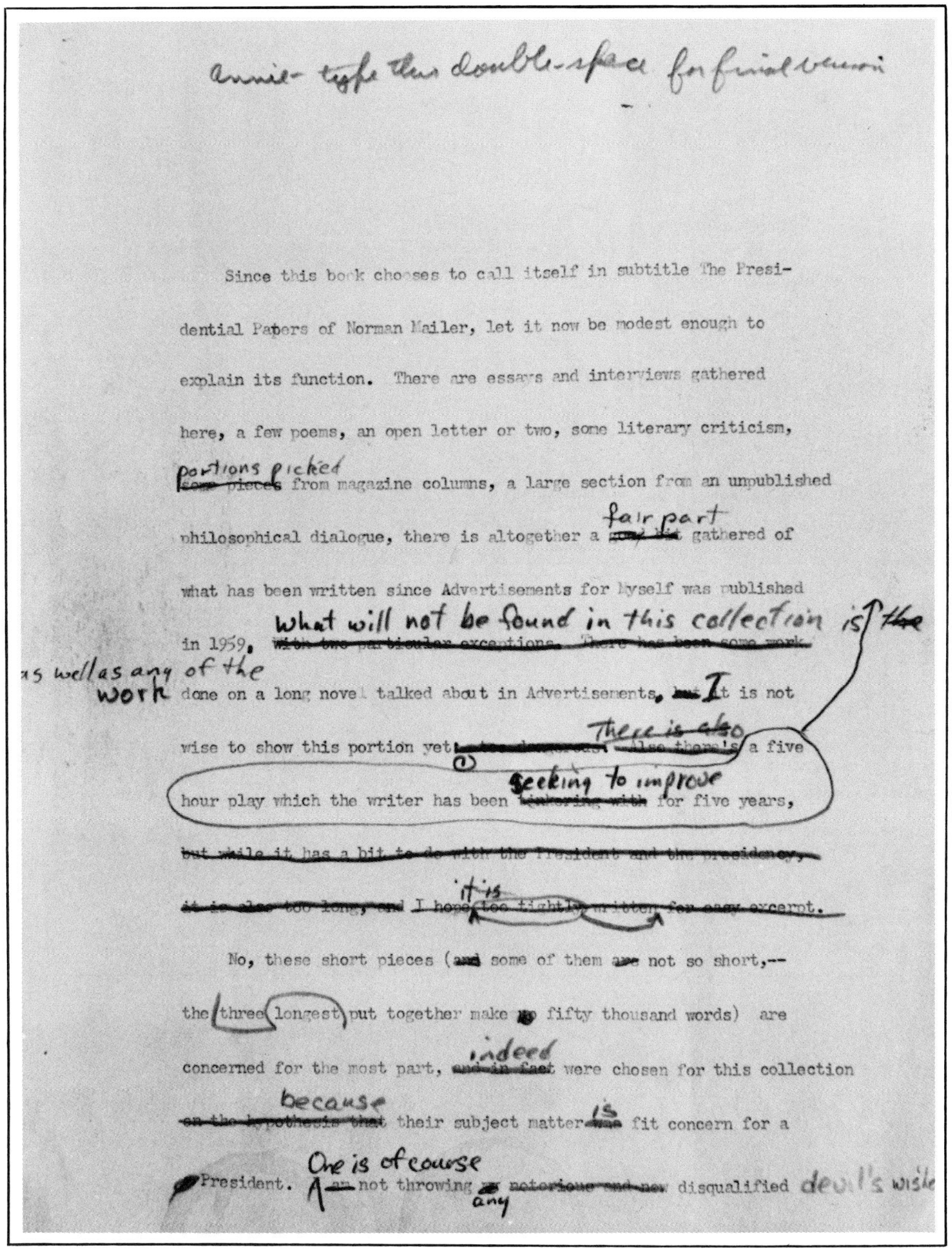

Since this book chooses to call itself in subtitle The Presidential Papers of Norman Mailer, let it now be modest enough to explain its function. There are essays and interviews gathered here, a few poems, an open letter or two, some literary criticism, portions picked from magazine columns, a large section from an unpublished philosophical dialogue, there is altogether a fair part gathered of what has been written since Advertisements for Myself was published in 1959. what will not be found in this collection is the work done on a long novel talked about in Advertisements, as well as any of the work. It is not wise to show this portion yet. There is also a five hour play which the writer has been seeking to improve for five years, but while it has a bit to do with the President and the presidency, it is also too long, and I hope too tightly written for easy excerpt.

No, these short pieces (some of them not so short,-- the three longest put together make fifty thousand words) are concerned for the most part, indeed were chosen for this collection because their subject matter is fit concern for a President. One is of course not throwing any notorious and new disqualified devil's wish

Working typescript for the first page of Mailer's "Prefatory Paper" to The Presidential Papers*—a collection of political commentaries published in 1963 (Mailer papers).*

Mailer married Beverly Bentley in 1963. They had two sons–Michael Burks, born in 1964, and Stephen McLeod, born in 1966. The family is shown above at their Brooklyn apartment in 1969, a year before Mailer and Bentley separated.

ARTICLE:

James Jones, "Small Comment from a Penitent Novelist," *Esquire*, 60 (December 1963): 40-44.

During 1962-1963 Mailer wrote a monthly column called "The Big Bite" for Esquire *magazine. Although novelist James Jones had not reacted to Mailer's "evaluation" of him in* Advertisements for Myself, *criticism of Jones in two* Esquire *articles prompted this reply.*

This is my first attempt at this type of magazine-column writing, and it may be my last. My fear is that the large ego gains reaped by this kind of writing, incommensurate with the relatively low value of the writing, may tend to relax a novelist's drive to write novels. And Esquire may have second thoughts about the idea, too.

One drunken evening, while I was railing against the work and personality of a contemporary writer, an old hood (retired) friend of mine who made up at least eighty percent of my audience of two, rasped: "Kid, don't never knock your own racket."

I think it's a good precept. And since then I've followed it closely, except for certain conversational lapses when drunk. But so far I have never given my railings the dignity and authority print gives.

However, after reading Norman Mailer's June and July columns in Esquire on the novel and contemporary novelists, I am hoping my old hood (retired) friend will let me off if I lapse One Time.

I read Norman's pieces with great seriousness. I was awed by his deep insights into all of our personalities, his profound grasp of what a novel ought to be. I hadn't really believed Norman was all that smart. I know I was helped immensely by his criticism of my writing, my courage, and my integrity; and whether they admit it or not I am sure that all of the others he took to pieces must be as grateful to him deep down as I am. What he did was

> *A really good style comes only when a man has become as good as he can be. Style is character.*

From Writers at Work, Third Series *(New York: Viking Press, 1967)*

so good, so much better than, say, Jack Aldridge's analysis of us, that I now wonder whether after all Norman, with his particular background, personality and gifts, was not cut out to be perhaps the greatest critic of our generation and not a novelist at all.

I was particularly struck by his use of the image of the novel as the Great Bitch. The Enemy, which each man has to fight and subdue, dominate. Or else he's no man at all. The Enemy: the Insatiable Great Gash. From which each man must walk away, "Peep, peep, peep." It's an apt description of the dark shadow so many American males fight and swing at, but can never hit in frantic efforts to save their masculinity through external objects.

I found this image particularly interesting because my own private image for the novel has always been that of the Sleeping Beauty: the one who—if I could only awaken her—not only would be the best hump in the world, but would also bring me, along with renown, the kingdom and those twenty-seven palaces to administer. And each time I toiled up that same old mountain by a different route, smarting from brambles and sweating profusely, fighting the fear-beasts who lay in wait to feed off cocky knights-errant, hanging by my cracking fingernails over precipices of self-destruction, each time I planted my confident kiss on that lovely cheek and she did not awaken, it was not so much that I had failed to *dominate*, as that I had failed to *awaken*. Maybe because I'd been eating garlic. My experience with women—Bitches, Princesses, and others—has been that no woman can ever be dominated by any male she does not choose to be dominated by. Garlic or no garlic.

Well, it's an old and romantic image, mine, nineteenth century, and earlier. And I know the broads have used it against us. And I'm sorry I've failed Norman, and that's my apology to him. I suffered as I read about Norman's fruitless search through the literature of his contemporaries to find a book good enough to give him the sense of competition he needs to get to work. I can only hope that my next novel—though I cannot speak for the rest of my contemporaries—will be good enough to be the stimulus he keeps asking for to get Norman off his ass. After all, that's my main reason for writing them.

And old hood friend, forgive me.

ARTICLE:

Publishers Weekly, 187 (22 March 1965): 44-45.

An American Dream, *Mailer's first novel since* The Deer Park, *was a radical departure from his earlier, more realistic, fiction. Shortly before publication of* An American Dream *Mailer made these remarks about his work at a Periodical Publishers Association press conference.*

Norman Mailer, whose first novel in nine years, "An American Dream," was published by Dial Press, on March 15, opened the final portion of the March 10 press conference for authors by saying, candidly, "Four years ago my life went out of control for a time. Once you become notorious your personality takes on a legendary quality. I am more and more surprised by what I am supposed to have done in the last two years."

Yes, said Mr. Mailer, it was quite true that in the past he had hurled obscenities at a lecture audience—"I thought I had God's message at the time"—but, looking back, "I regret it," he said.

Mr. Mailer was asked to comment on the National Book Awards acceptance speech of novelist Saul Bellow in which Mr. Bellow said, among other things, that "polymorphous sexuality and vehement declarations of alienation are not going to produce great works of art." He had only heard about the Bellow speech second hand, Mr. Mailer said, but he thought he would probably disagree with it entirely. The "moral nihilists' wing," to which he supposed Bellow would assign him, Mr. Mailer said, would probably also include William Burroughs, Allen Ginsberg, Terry Southern, among others, and "we are the ones who are doing something new, more creative and adventurous." Whether or not the surface actions of moral nihilists are negative is "irrelevant," Mr. Mailer said. What is important is that "they are concerned with the forefront of experience."

Mr. Mailer was not loath to give his opinion of the NBA-winner, "Herzog," as a novel or Saul Bellow as a writer, however. And what he had to say demonstrated neatly the Mailer dictum that "novelists left to themselves almost always become vicious gossip-mongers, so the only alternative is to air your differences publicly and ventilate the air."

Asked to define what he meant by "moral nihilism," Mr. Mailer said that the secret belief of all moral nihilists is that they can save the world. The moral nihilist believes that the moral attitudes with which most people regard existence are not so much false as that they do not fit reality. There are occasions, Mr. Mailer said, when in the view of the moral nihilist, obscenity can be brutal, shattering, cruel. There are also occasions when it can be warm, humorous, life-giving, boisterous. It can never be codified. For the moral nihilist, who wishes never to take anything for granted, the nature of reality is constantly shifting.

"I believe there is a God and a devil," Mr. Mailer said. "Morality is the battlefield. But the criminal in the act of committing a crime may be becoming a better man. The alternative to a sudden wild outburst of violence might be that he would have been running around poisoning the lives of all around him for 20 or 30 years. For the moral nihilist there is something worse than death."

In his own writing, Norman Mailer said, he tries never to introduce an abstract idea unless it is necessary. "Any intellectual discussions you can take out, should be taken out." He suggested as a working principle that a novelist should never put into his work what any other novelist would write.

Mr. Mailer, talking about "An American Dream," said that while it was substantially complete as originally written for *Esquire* in a series of monthly installments, adding up to eight chapters, he had worked on it extensively for style "and toning" before its publication in book form and "I really think it is a better book now."

Asked the central, driving influence that kept him working on such a tight schedule that he had to finish the novel in a year or less, Mr. Mailer said, "professionalism." He said he had wanted to try his hand at producing a novel under such pressure, "but if I had to follow such a schedule for five years it would kill me."

"An American Dream," Mr. Mailer said, seemed to write itself extremely naturally. "A book is prepared in one's unconscious. The words (call them the troops) start marching through your body. If you go out and get drunk one night the troops get bombed and you run into a writer's block. When you're working steadily this will not happen."

What effect has success had on him?, Mr. Mailer was asked. "A big hit changes your life altogether. You become a different person," he answered. " 'The Naked and the Dead' changed all my reflexes. Before that I had the value judgments of an infantryman. Once you have a lot of success you spend an awful lot of time with the officers. As James Jones once said to me, 'God damn it, Norman, I'm becoming an officer.' "

Mailer and Muhammed Ali in Puerto Rico in 1965, when Mailer was backing light-heavyweight champion José Torres

BOOK REVIEW:

Joan Didion, "A Social Eye," *National Review*, 17 (20 April 1965): 329-330.

An American Dream *appeared serially in* Esquire *magazine from January through August 1964 and was published in book form the following year. Mailer conceived this novel as a sequel to Theodore Dreiser's* An American Tragedy *(1925). Stephen Rojack, an intellectual whom Mailer describes as "in an incandescent state of huge paranoia and enormous awareness. . . . more heroic and more filled with dread than at any point in his life," murders his wife and then victimizes others to achieve his own rebirth.*

Norman Mailer, Living Legend. Known to gangsters, known to Presidents, known to readers of the *Daily News*. Wielder of the knife in the New York night. Actor in some national sexual fantasy. Candidate for Mayor, citizen-on-the-spot for civic improvement. Subject of the city's morning chorus, offered up with careful nonchalance by people he does not recall: "*Nor*man dropped up, late, drunk of course." "*Nor*man was there, and be*hav*ed *bad*ly." Norman Mailer, *Tout-New York*.

Let us try, for a moment, Norman Mailer, Novelist, a *persona* which many people who know *Nor*man prefer to patronize. Mailer is challenged to "writing contests" by advertising copywriters, condescended to by the kind of people who refer to Joseph Heller as "an authentic voice," deprecated by failed fashion models whose attention span for printed matter stops with the plane schedule to Montego Bay. He writes "a lot of voodoo about *cancer*," reports the *Herald Tribune*'s Writer of the Year. And if it had always been easy to laugh at Mailer, it was never easier than when he announced, clearly in trouble, running scared, that he had dared himself to write a novel in installments for *Esquire*. ("Only a second-rater would take a stupid dare like that," as Lulu says in *The Deer Park*.) Nonetheless, that novel, *An American Dream*, is one more instance in which Mailer is going to laugh last, for it is a remarkable book, a novel in many ways as good as *The Deer Park*, and *The Deer Park* is in many ways a perfect novel.

An American Dream is about a New York celebrity. War hero, congressman, husband to an heiress, professor of existential philosophy, television personality, *celebrity*. That is Stephen Rojack, whom we meet on the edge of something. "I was approaching my forty-fourth year," he explains, "but for the first time I knew why some of my friends, and so many of the women I had thought I understood, could not bear to be alone at night." In the thirty-some hours which follow he feels the pull of suicide, murders his wife, meets and falls in love with a singer named Cherry, witnesses Cherry's violent death, stands off the police, faces his father-in-law in the Waldorf Towers, discovers facts too dark to remember, and in the last few pages heads west, to Las Vegas, where "the sky was dark, the streets were light, the heat was a phenomenon." In the 110° night he walks out alone onto the desert and makes a deranged call to the dead from a roadside telephone with a rusty dial. (A roadside telephone booth, the night, the heat. Imagine it: a glass booth, with a light that goes on when the door closes, the only light on that desert road. Did Rojack close the door? He does not say. Just that he dialed, and asked for Cherry. That telephone booth alone is worth the whole of a couple of dozen of Mailer's contemporaries; it is distinctly the real thing.) He thinks he might make the call again, "but in the morning, I was something like sane again, and packed the car, and started on the long trip to Guatemala and Yucatán."

There it is. Detectives, columnists, the Waldorf Towers, gangsters, charity balls, The Big Guy, Harvard, the CIA, the Kennedys, Mrs. Roosevelt, the Cardinal, Harlem, East River duplexes with flocked wallpaper, women with names like Deborah Caughlin Mangaravidi Kelly. Sirens in the night, high places where the fix is in. Violence, the public memory of which fades with the next edition. New York. *An American Dream* is a "New York" novel, perhaps the only serious New York novel since *The Great Gatsby*. Other novels are set in New York, other novels are about Central Park West dentists who happen to live in New York; *An American Dream* is *about* New York, and Mailer is the first real novelist in a long time to perceive the obvious, to understand what legions of cheap writers and Walter Winchell have always known: that the essence of New York is celebrity, and that its true genius is tabloid melodrama.

In fact it is Fitzgerald whom Mailer most resembles. They share that instinct for the essence of things, that great social eye. It is not the eye for the brand name, not at all the eye of a Mary McCarthy or a Philip Roth; it is rather some fascination with the heart of the structure, some deep feeling for the mysteries of power. For both Mailer and Fitzgerald, as for the tellers of fairy tales, there remains something sexual about money, some sense in which the princess and the gold are inextricably one. In Deborah Caughlin Mangaravidi Kelly, Rojack sees "a vision of treasure, far-off blood, and fear." Sergius, in *The Deer Park*, thinks to linger awhile in Palm Springs,

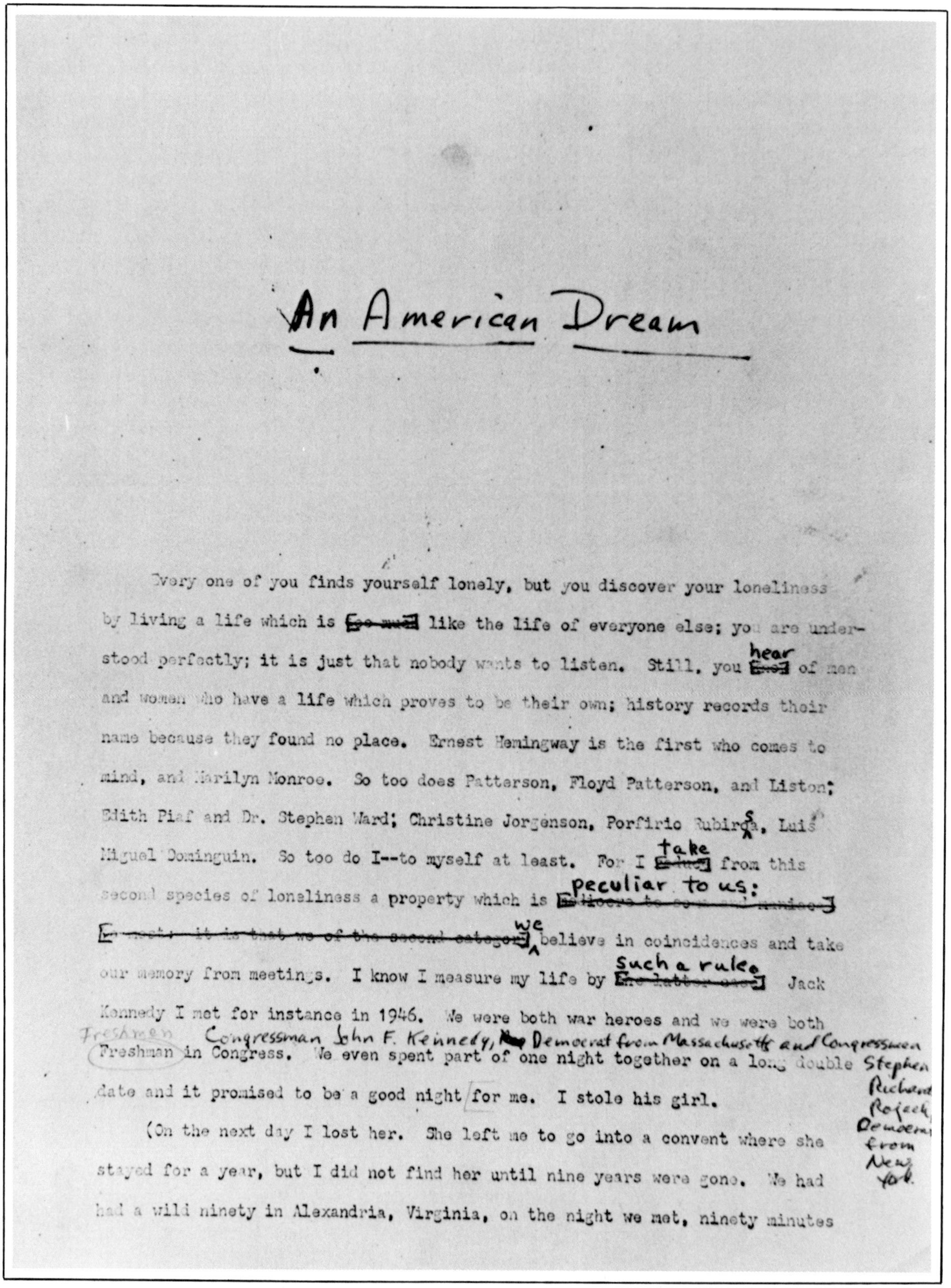

An American Dream

Every one of you finds yourself lonely, but you discover your loneliness by living a life which is [illegible] like the life of everyone else; you are understood perfectly; it is just that nobody wants to listen. Still, you hear [illegible] of men and women who have a life which proves to be their own; history records their name because they found no place. Ernest Hemingway is the first who comes to mind, and Marilyn Monroe. So too does Patterson, Floyd Patterson, and Liston; Edith Piaf and Dr. Stephen Ward; Christine Jorgenson, Porfirio Rubirosa, Luis Miguel Dominguin. So too do I--to myself at least. For I take [illegible] from this second species of loneliness a property which is peculiar to us: [illegible] we believe in coincidences and take our memory from meetings. I know I measure my life by such a rule. [illegible] Jack Kennedy I met for instance in 1946. We were both war heroes and we were both Congressman John F. Kennedy, Democrat from Massachusetts and Congressman Stephen Richard Rojack, Democrat from New York. Freshman in Congress. We even spent part of one night together on a long double date and it promised to be a good night for me. I stole his girl.

(On the next day I lost her. She left me to go into a convent where she stayed for a year, but I did not find her until nine years were gone. We had had a wild ninety in Alexandria, Virginia, on the night we met, ninety minutes

First page of the revised typescript for Mailer's fourth novel, whose protagonist expresses a condition of creative insanity that Mailer calls "psychopathy" (Mailer papers)

amid "the bright green foliage of its love and its money." One thinks of Daisy, whose voice was full of money. And Deborah herself: is she not, like Nicole Diver, a woman for whose sake "trains began their run at Chicago and traversed the round belly of the continent to California"?

Again, both Mailer and Fitzgerald have the kind of imagination that makes legend of experience. In *An American Dream* we meet an old woman who "had the reputation of being the most evil woman ever to live on the Riviera." In *The Deer Park* there was Don Beda, "married at different times to an actress, a colored singer, a Texas oil heiress with a European title—that had been a particular scandal—and to the madam of what was reported to be the most expensive brothel in South America." The most expensive brothel in South America, the most evil woman ever to live on the Riviera. What is the echo, the rhythm there? "The man who fixed the World's Series back in 1919."

They share a couple of other things, Mailer and Fitzgerald. The notoriety, the devastating celebrity which is probably in the end at least as nourishing as it is destructive. The immense technical skill, the passion for realizing the gift. The deep romanticism. And perhaps above all the unfashionableness, the final refusal to sail with the prevailing winds. Fitzgerald was "frivolous," and Mailer is "superstitious." Philip Rahv has spoken for the rationalist establishment: *An American Dream* lacks "verisimilitude." Rojack "hears voices." His suicidal thoughts seem induced by the moon, and "appear to have nothing to do with guilt-feelings or remorse." Mailer is entangled with "the hocus-pocus of power." Had Mailer not been so "entangled" he might have sent Stephen Rojack not to that telephone booth on the desert (not a "credible experience," Rahv chides) but to a good Morningside Heights analyst. Had Fitzgerald not been so "frivolous" he might have gone not to Hollywood but to Spain, and written *For Whom the Bell Tolls*. If only. Mailer thought to preface *The Deer Park* with this line from Gide: *Please do not understand me too quickly*. There seems little danger of that, and the loss is entirely ours.

Dust jacket for Mailer's 1966 collection of political essays.

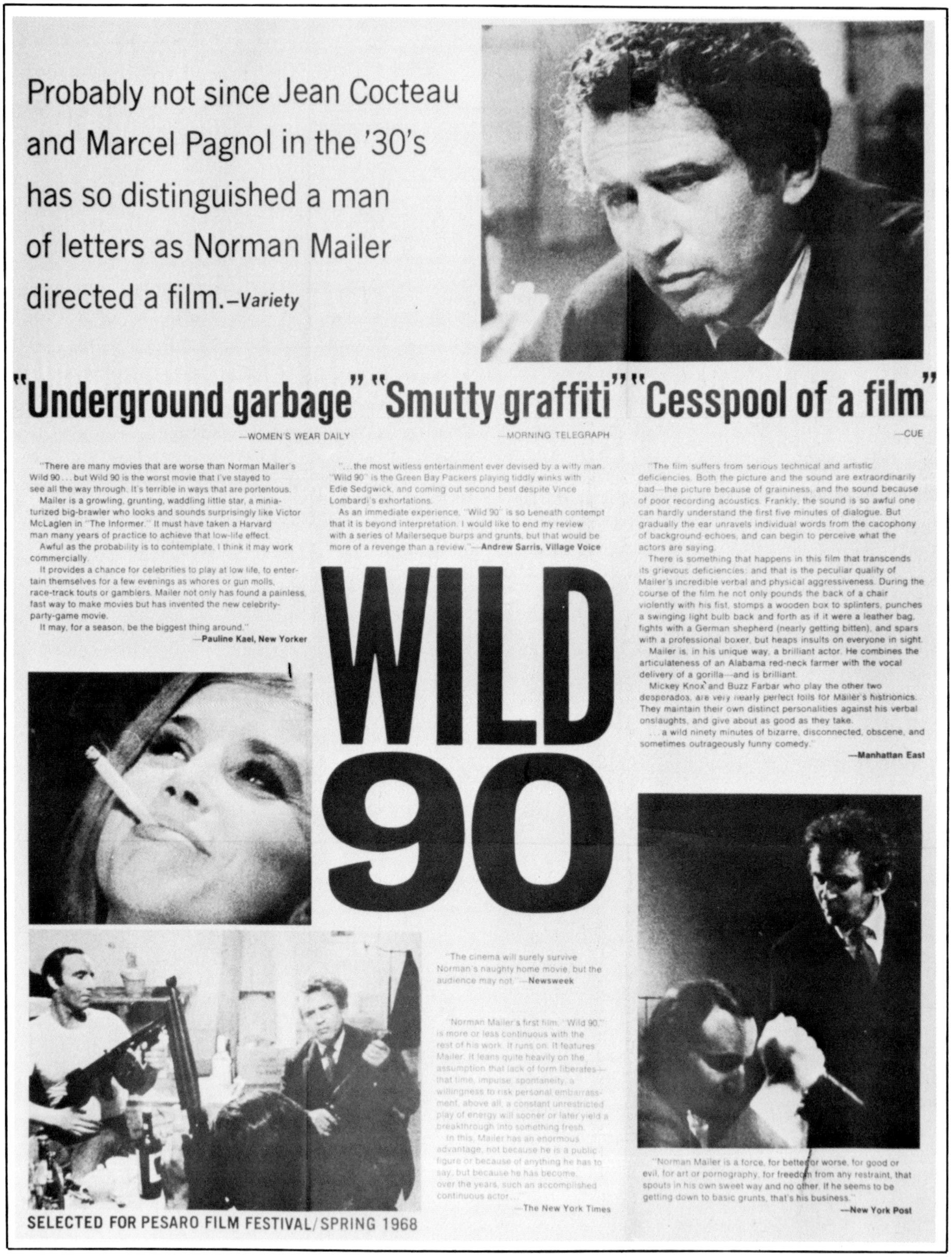

Probably not since Jean Cocteau and Marcel Pagnol in the '30's has so distinguished a man of letters as Norman Mailer directed a film.—Variety
"Underground garbage"
—WOMEN'S WEAR DAILY
"Smutty graffiti"
—MORNING TELEGRAPH
"Cesspool of a film"
—CUE
"There are many movies that are worse than Norman Mailer's Wild 90 . . . but Wild 90 is the worst movie that I've stayed to see all the way through. It's terrible in ways that are portentous.
Mailer is a growling, grunting, waddling little star, a miniaturized big-brawler who looks and sounds surprisingly like Victor McLaglen in "The Informer." It must have taken a Harvard man many years of practice to achieve that low-life effect.
Awful as the probability is to contemplate, I think it may work commercially.
It provides a chance for celebrities to play at low life, to entertain themselves for a few evenings as whores or gun molls, race-track touts or gamblers. Mailer not only has found a painless, fast way to make movies but has invented the new celebrity-party-game movie.
It may, for a season, be the biggest thing around."
—Pauline Kael, New Yorker
". . . the most witless entertainment ever devised by a witty man. "Wild 90" is the Green Bay Packers playing tiddly winks with Edie Sedgwick, and coming out second best despite Vince Lombardi's exhortations.
As an immediate experience, "Wild 90" is so beneath contempt that it is beyond interpretation. I would like to end my review with a series of Mailerseque burps and grunts, but that would be more of a revenge than a review."—Andrew Sarris, Village Voice
"The film suffers from serious technical and artistic deficiencies. Both the picture and the sound are extraordinarily bad—the picture because of graininess, and the sound because of poor recording acoustics. Frankly, the sound is so awful one can hardly understand the first five minutes of dialogue. But gradually the ear unravels individual words from the cacophony of background echoes, and can begin to perceive what the actors are saying.
There is something that happens in this film that transcends its grievous deficiencies: and that is the peculiar quality of Mailer's incredible verbal and physical aggressiveness. During the course of the film he not only pounds the back of a chair violently with his fist, stomps a wooden box to splinters, punches a swinging light bulb back and forth as if it were a leather bag, fights with a German shepherd (nearly getting bitten), and spars with a professional boxer, but heaps insults on everyone in sight.
Mailer is, in his unique way, a brilliant actor. He combines the articulateness of an Alabama red-neck farmer with the vocal delivery of a gorilla—and is brilliant.
Mickey Knox and Buzz Farbar who play the other two desperados, are very nearly perfect foils for Mailer's histrionics. They maintain their own distinct personalities against his verbal onslaughts, and give about as good as they take.
. . . a wild ninety minutes of bizarre, disconnected, obscene, and sometimes outrageously funny comedy."
—Manhattan East
WILD 90
"The cinema will surely survive Norman's naughty home movie, but the audience may not."—Newsweek
"Norman Mailer's first film, "Wild 90," is more or less continuous with the rest of his work. It runs on. It features Mailer. It leans quite heavily on the assumption that lack of form liberates—that time, impulse, spontaneity, a willingness to risk personal embarrassment, above all, a constant unrestricted play of energy will sooner or later yield a breakthrough into something fresh.
In this, Mailer has an enormous advantage, not because he is a public figure or because of anything he has to say, but because he has become, over the years, such an accomplished continuous actor . . ."
—The New York Times
"Norman Mailer is a force, for better or worse, for good or evil, for art or pornography, for freedom from any restraint, that spouts in his own sweet way and no other. If he seems to be getting down to basic grunts, that's his business."
—New York Post
SELECTED FOR PESARO FILM FESTIVAL/SPRING 1968

Mailer produced, directed, and appeared in his first movie, Wild 90, *in 1967. An adaptation of* The Deer Park, *it premiered 21 January and, despite terrible reviews, ran four months at New York's Theatre de Lys.*

Dust jacket for Mailer's fifth novel, published in 1967. The principal action is an Alaskan hunt narrated in a variety of styles by D. J., an eighteen-year-old Texan. The message about international matters is implicit until the final sentence: "Vietnam, hot damn."

Noam Chomsky, Mailer, and Robert Lowell at the Pentagon Building, 21 October 1967

BOOK REVIEW:

Alfred Kazin, "The Trouble He's Seen," *New York Times Book Review*, 5 May 1968, pp. 1, 2, 26.

On 21 October 1965 Mailer was arrested in an antiwar demonstration at the Pentagon Building in Washington, D.C. His account of the march appeared a year later in Armies of the Night: History as a Novel The Novel as History. *The book brought Mailer both popular and critical acclaim, winning the 1969 National Book Award and the Pulitzer Prize.*

Twenty years ago this week, when Norman Mailer published "The Naked and the Dead," became famous and rich and pleased everybody, even old novelists on their way out, it looked as if a safe type were off to a traditional career. The novel was "the best of the American World War II novels"; it was on the side of Lieutenant Hearn, the young American progressive, and made a villain of epicene, Fascist-minded General Cummings; its characters made a comprehensible "cross-section of American society," from Goldstein to Gallagher; the text was clearly indebted to many models—Dos Passos for narrative rhythm, Farrell for tough city background, Hemingway for nuance.

"The Naked and the Dead" is as intensely readable as it was in 1948, and still the only one of Mailer's novels that continually reads like a novel that is stable in conception, that doesn't become an exhibition or a Quest. There is a particular visual concentration behind its best scenes that was to reappear in everything he wrote later, a force of mind that had enabled this literary draftee out of Brooklyn and Harvard, in the Army often a clerk, to absorb other people's hardships and battles into himself. But what is most striking about it now is its intellectual discipleship. It could have been called "Main Currents in American Thought—A Novel." "The best of American World War II novels" is no great praise, for that war didn't produce any new forms. The novelists were competing with the reporters on their own ground, and amidst the mountains of gritty documentaries, Mailer's novel in fact pleased because it was more intelligent and better written, and so was more recognizable.

"Barbary Shore" (1951) was not just a "disappointment"; it showed that Mailer was not interested in being an "acceptable" novelist, that in his moody indignation with the moral failure of Socialism in Russia and the growth of authoritarian state power in the U.S.A., he was willing to throw a novel away in order to express political agony. He portrayed a struggle to the death between an ex-Bolshevik not yet ready to betray his dream of Socialism and an F.B.I. agent ready to betray anything. This dark, sad testament of a book, only distractedly a novel, was riddled with the intimations of a tie-up between the ex-Left and the Government's intelligence service. This (then) fantasy, one of many in Mailer's busy mind, nevertheless frightened him, demanded a solution, a reaffirmation of Socialism in Trotsky's terms. The author was stridently a moralist, disturbed by the lack of expected sequences. Faith seemed more important than fiction.

The author of "Barbary Shore" was still the nice Jewish boy from Harvard and very much a disciple—this time of the French radical, Jean Malaquais. But around the time Mailer had such trouble completing "The Deer Park" (1955) to his satisfaction, there appeared the toughie who hated the nice Jewish boy—and began talking about himself in public, with a bravado plainly designed to throw off anything that might soften him up in his opposition to America's cancer-breeding repressions. There was a new wife, a new Mailer and a new ideology—sexual courage, truth to the buried instincts. It looked as if Sade had displaced Marx, Wilhelm Reich had displaced Jean Malaquais. But the immediate crisis in this search for the politics and religion of sex, for solutions that would connect sex back to revelation, sex with the hidden message circuits of the mind that lead to God, was that Mailer never did like what he had finally made of "The Deer Park." Several publishers turned it down, he became obsessed with the book, and has been writing about it or dramatizing it ever since.

Mailer was now living "the crisis of the novel." He thought constantly about writing novels, saw everyone as a possible character, made grandiose announcements of a whole series of novels. But he was so sensitive to politics, power and society in America, so engrossed in the search for solutions and revelations, that the moralist and the "celebrity" left little time to the novelist. He now made a feat of writing books quickly, as if hurling "An American Dream" month by month into Esquire and turning all his powers of mimicry into the "Why Are We in Vietnam?" would finally earn him self-approval as a novelist. Both are certainly brilliant *performances*; but in the first you are always aware of Mailer's favorite fantasies, in the second of his pride in a linguistic tour de force.

Still, a significant reason for Mailer's impatience has also been his acute sense of the national crisis, his particular gift for detecting political deterioration—and his professional feeling that the American scene at this time may be too thorny a subject to be left to journalists. It is the coalescence of American disorder (always an obsession of Mailer's) with all the self-confidence he feels as a novelist doing reportage that has produced "Armies of the Night," his extraordinary personal tract on the unprecedented demonstration of Oct. 21-22, 1967, when thousands of the New Left attempted to "march on the Pentagon," fell into some brief but bloody skirmishes with armed guards, and a thousand people were arrested—among them, Norman Mailer.

Of course Mailer presents this book as *his* nonfiction novel—he simply cannot stop dreaming about himself as a novelist. But it is a fact that only a born novelist *could* have written a piece of history so intelligent, mischievous, penetrating and alive, so vivid with crowds, the great stage that is American democracy, the Washington streets and bridges, the Lincoln Memorial, the women, students, hippies, Negroes and assorted intellectuals for peace, the M.P.'s and United States marshals, the American Nazis chanting "We want dead Reds."

The book cracks open the hard nut of American authority at the center, the uncertainty of our power—and, above all, the bad conscience that now afflicts so many Americans. "Armies of the Night" is a peculiarly appropriate and timely contribution to this moment of the national drama and, among other things, it shows Mailer relieved of his vexing dualities, able to bring all his interests, concerns and actually quite traditional loyalties to equal focus. The form of this diary-essay-tract-sermon grew out of the many simultaneous happenings in Washington that weekend, out of the self-confidence which for writers is *style*, out of his fascination with power in America and his fear of it, out of his American self-dramatizing and his honest fear for his country.

"Armies of the Night" is a poorer title than the one Mailer gave to the portion of the book that appeared in the March issue of Harper's—"The Steps of the Pentagon"; but it does light up his main subject—the intellectuals, the students, the Negroes, the academic liberals and the marching women who personify the American opposition. From first to last, this book is about that opposition, its political and human awkwardness; that is why the book that seems too full of Mailer himself is really about Mailer's deepest political anxieties. Things are coming to a crisis, but the forces of protest symbolically assembled before the Pentagon seem to him limited in everything except courage. (It was the women particularly who, as the weekend drew to a close, were beaten by the guards.)

Mailer's second film, Beyond the Law *(1968), received praise from reviewers but failed to draw audiences. Mailer is shown above in July 1968 with some of the cast from his third movie,* Maidstone *(1971). Based on* Armies of the Night, *the movie received mixed reviews.*

What makes the tract exciting is the interpretation by Mailer's favorite persona, the novelist-in-charge-of-practically-everything, of the Left as well as of the Authority it would like to challenge. Mailer's gnawing sense of possibility makes the book, and it plainly grows out of his frustrations as a novelist, his wild imaginative resources, his constant brooding over all *he* might do with what he sees. So the American opposition has been frustrated by the way in which the Vietnam war particularly, but also Negro-white relations and even the old primacy of business in this country, have shown every day how little the forces of protest and "resistance" have to do with American *institutions*.

A century ago the Transcendentalists—the purest of Puritans—were already maddened by the power exercised by bankers, politicians, slaveholders. The feeling of the American opposition today, publicly if not actually led by such pillars of the Protestant establishment as the Rev. William Sloane Coffin Jr. and Dr. Benjamin Spock, is not merely that the American war in Vietnam is hideously brutal and wrong, that we have no right to be devastating this far-off country in the name of our theological anti-Communism, but that the political and moral sages who founded our culture have been succeeded by generals, politicians, executives, hucksters and "experts."

Nothing is more likely to drive a brilliant scholar at M.I.T. into a rage than the picture of ex-professor Walt Whitman Rostow of M.I.T. conferring with his boss on just where to bomb the North Vietnamese. "They" have all the power, and "we" have just imagination! This has been Mailer's grievance for many years. Given a novelist's belief that a novelist is the smartest of men anyway ("The novel is the one bright book of life," said D. H. Lawrence. "Only in the novel are *all* things given full play.") and *this* novelist's impatience to get into everything all the time and right away, one can see why

Some years ago I was asked by a magazine what were the ten most important books in my development. The book I listed first was Captain Blood. *Then came* Das Kapital. *Then* The Amateur Gentleman.

From Writers at Work, Third Series *(New York: Viking Press, 1967)*

Mailer in this book shows so much *brio*, so much wrath at the powerful, so much despair at those on the American Left who have been losing all their lives and perhaps like to lose.

For all his self-dramatization, Mailer is the right chronicler of the March on the Pentagon. For there is no other writer of his ability who, feeling so deeply about this "obscene war . . . the worst war the nation has ever been in," can yet be so aware of everything else around him—not least the intellectual staleness of his own side.

See him, for example, on the Friday night before the Saturday afternoon march, sipping bourbon from a coffee cup as he staggers up and down the stage of a Washington movie house, heckling his own audience and not forgetting to patronize Dwight Macdonald and Paul Goodman. All this was terrible, terrible, as that moral journal Time has told us. Mailer likes to be terrible, to clean all timidity, subservience and false respect out of his system. He is afraid of losers; they may be contagious.

But because these "Armies of the Night" are in reality his army, if not exactly an army after his own kind, it is a fact that Mailer does not trust his troops, or even his fellow writers on the Left, to be outrageous, strong and imaginative enough—to have *style* enough with the Kennedy panache. Can the American opposition really take on the corporations, the police, the mass media? America Mailer variously calls "corporation land," "technology land." Just as the stones of Egypt were formed from the "excremental" ooze of the Nile, so the walls of the Pentagon seem to him primeval, ancient, blind.

But that Saturday afternoon, as the incongruous crowd made its *symbolic* challenge, Mailer felt "as if he stepped through some crossing in the reaches between this moment, the French Revolution, and the Civil War, as if the ghosts of the Union Dead accompanied them now to the Bastille." Not drinking or eating a thing all day, he knew ". . . they were going to face the symbol, the embodiment, no, call it the true and high church of the military-industrial complex, the Pentagon, blind five-sided eye of a subtle oppression which had come to America out of the very air of the century . . . yes, Mailer felt a confrontation of the contests of his own life on this March to the eye of the oppressor, greedy stingy dumb valve of the worst of the Wasp heart . . . smug, enclosed, morally blind Pentagon, destroying the future of its own nation with each day it augmented its strength."

Overwritten? Overwrought? It doesn't read so in the context. And think of how many nice young students from the best families at the best colleges are mentally confronting the Pentagon today, how many of America's best young men in the graduate schools are in fact preparing *their* contest with authority—how many of America's children, if only in the privacy of their minds, now find themselves in one form of opposition or another. Yet Mailer is by no means happy about the young opposition. "These mad middle class children with their lobotomies from sin" are too facile in their thinking, spoiled by American affluence, indifferent to waste, too quick to obliterate the complexities of our situation by drugs and pills. Mailer calls himself a "Left Conservative" and at a marvelous moment, watching the young men turning in their draft cards, confesses that this mass ceremony shocks him.

Mailer's put-down of other writers (among the demonstrators only Robert Lowell is recognized as a "peer," but Lowell doesn't write fiction) is, of course, funny, because Mailer is always in character. If Ralph Ellison or Saul Bellow had passed by (hardly likely) Mailer would have been looking for Susan Sontag. But while he is careful to describe writers he can put down—or brilliant scholars like Noam Chomsky whose specialties he of course has ideas about—his judgments are infernally shrewd.

His portraits of the leaders are both impressive and funny—of Mailer's four wives, three used Dr. Spock's baby book, so Dr. Spock reminds him of all the trouble he has seen. For the first time one sees a leading American peacenik and resister addressing urgent questions to his "army"—Are *we* good enough? How can we overcome the "mediocrity of the middle-class middle-aged masses of the Left?" The general shoddiness of American standards just now? The marked tendency of authorities to lie? The general greediness of the middle classes? "The over-psychologized loins of the liberal academic intelligensia" and the general tendency of "liberal academics to become servants of the social machine of the future?"

Salinger once counseled us to recognize Jesus Christ in the fat old lady. But Mailer asks—what about "grandma with orange hair," madly playing the slot machines in Las Vegas and ignoring the burned children in Vietnam? The conformism, inertia, gluttony and moral indifference—to say nothing of the power now stored in piled banks of coded knowledge—may in fact be too much for the rhetoricians of the New Left. Mailer feels that there is a dead nerveless area in the American Left, "comprised of the old sense of paralysis before the horrors of the gas chambers." And since he grew up with the failure and failures on the Old Left, he is tired of the lack of style, wit and intellectual grace. J.F.K. is his model, and he is proud that he finally got himself arrested—by trying to run a line of U.S. marshals like a football player. Then, having got himself arrested, he found himself in the paddy wagon with an arrested American Nazi shrieking hate at him. Waiting in the detention center to pay his $25 and so get back to New York in time for a party, he unexpectedly spent the weekend in jail because the United States Commissioner in charge thought that a man with *his* literary reputation and all should not get off as easily as the others."

"I am the man," said Walt Whitman. "I suffer'd, I was there." When a writer gets old enough, like Whitman, one forgets that he was just as outrageous an egotist and actor as Norman Mailer is. Yet Whitman staked his work on finding the personal connection between salvation as an artist and the salvation of his country. The best American writers in the 19th century talked about themselves all the time—but, in the romantic American line, saw the self as the prime condition of democracy. I believe that "Armies of the Night" is just as brilliant a personal testimony as Whitman's diary of the Civil War, "Specimen Days," and Whitman's great essay on the crisis of the Republic during the Gilded Age, "Democratic Vistas." I believe that it is a work of personal and political reportage that brings to the inner and developing crisis of the United States at this moment admirable sensibilities, candid intelligence, the most moving concern for America itself. Mailer's intuition in this book is that the times demand a new form. He has found it.

Three of Mailer's wives on the set of Maidstone: *from left, Beverly Bentley; the mother of Mailer's fourth child, Kate, Lady Jeanne Campbell, who was married to him 1962-1963; and Adele Morales.*

In 1969 Mailer ran unsuccessfully for mayor of New York City. He and his running mate, Jimmy Breslin—standing next to him—proposed to make the city the fifty-first state.

INTRODUCTION:

Norman Mailer, "Deborah from *An American Dream*," in *This is My Best*, edited by Whit Burnett (Garden City: Doubleday, 1970), pp. 99-100.

When asked to choose a sample of his work for the anthology This is My Best, *Mailer picked his description of Deborah from* An American Dream. *Mailer's justification for his selection follows.*

Dear Whit:

Sometimes it seems to me useful to think of two kinds of novels—novels of manners, and modern explosive surrealistic novels in which the very notion of society, let alone manners, is bulldozed away in order to see which strange skeletons of fish and what buried treasure comes steaming up in the ore. Out of my own work I suppose *Why Are We In Vietnam?* would most satisfy the latter category, and *An American Dream* might prove for some to be my most substantial attack on the problem of writing a novel of manners. They are hard novels to do well. Now that we are approaching the end of the seventh decade of the twentieth century they are becoming novels which are almost impossible to do well. The old totemistic force of manners, the old totemistic belief that breaching a manner inspired a curse has been all but lost in the avalanche of social deterioration which characterizes our era. Yet what can appear more attractive and sinister to us than a tea ceremony at the edge of a cliff. So I often think *An American Dream* is my best book. I tried for more in this novel than anywhere else and hence was living for a while with themes not easily accessible to literary criticism, not even to examination. The passage I now choose is not obligatorily the best few thousand words in the work, but comes at least from the latter part of the first chapter and therefore offers few discomforts of orientation to the reader, and no demand on me for a synopsis of preceding events. Perhaps it may also serve to illumine the fine nerve of dread back of every good manner. Manner is the mandarin of mood, and in the shattering of every mood is an existential breath—does laughter or the murderous next ensue?

Yours,
Norman Mailer

Book Review:
Christopher Lehmann-Haupt, "Mailer's Dream of the Moon—II," *New York Times*, 8 January 1971, p. 29.

Mailer was able to apply his engineering training when he agreed to cover the 1969 Apollo 11 launch for Life. *To write* Of a Fire on the Moon *Mailer assumed the persona of "Aquarius, the truth seeker." After appearing in* Life, *the pieces were published as a book in 1970. Critic Christopher Lehmann-Haupt devoted two days' columns to this "magnificent book."*

In yesterday's column, on Norman Mailer's "Of a Fire on the Moon," . . . I registered complaints: dissatisfactions that arose from the installments of the book that appeared in Life magazine (which may have seemed unfair to bring up, but then many people I have spoken with are judging the book by the Life pieces, and the book is somehow a very different matter); and annoyances that persisted for a time in the book itself. But having catalogued these quibbles—the unresolved problem of Mailer's ego confronting cold interstellar space, his unjustifiable portentousness about the limits of technology, the tedium of scientific detail, the occasional theoretical murkiness, and the question of whether so much was needed so soon after the event—I described how nonetheless I read "Of a Fire on the Moon" with mounting interest and excitement, and how on reflection after finishing it, the book snapped into focus as an extraordinarily rich and complex work.

Actually, one's first real inkling of what Mailer is up to dawns about halfway through, when one is in the very throes of technological tedium, contemplating the phenomenon of earth orbit from this angle and by that analogy and every which way. Why, one wonders, must Mailer go to such pains to describe in such detail what we had all beheld in Sunday supplement diagrams such a short time ago?

One has at this point understood the rudimentary structure of the book. Mailer has traveled to the NASA Manned Spacecraft Center in Houston, sniffed out the terrain and found it odorless, tried to drill through the impenetrable casings of space personnel. It has been an unequal battle. He has grasped at straws. He has traveled to Cape Kennedy, wondered from across a lagoon at the magnificence of the Saturn V takeoff, drifted back into the plastic anonymity of the Houston Spacecraft Center, its press handouts, its bored reporters from everywhere without a story to catch by the jugular. (At one point, the reporters have even sought to interview him, Aquarius the water-bearer, as he refers to himself. He has refused.) Routinely, almost sketchily, with timeouts for philosophical probes, he has recounted the rest of the flight to and from the moon. And he has gone home to Provincetown, Mass.

And begun the story all over again, in loving, nearly solipsistic detail. One understands that he is making the moon flight his own, replaying it on the inside of his head with technical manuals and transcripts to guide him, *dreaming* it, in accordance with a theory he expounds that dreams are not wish-fulfillments at all, as Freud supposed, but projections of existential possibilities, psychic trial runs into the future based on new subliminal clues. The flight to the moon will be Mailer's dream. He will dream it to explore its possibilities for Aquarius.

But still, why the detail? And then it dawns on one that Mailer is not writing "Of a Fire on the Moon" for now, for us, but as a record of his dream for future generations—for generations that might also understand the effects of gravitational pull and the principles of orbital flight all too well, or conceivably might understand nothing at all. And once one has realized this—once one has projected oneself into the dream, into an innocence of the immediate present—one begins to experience an excitement that even the event of the flight itself, followed over television and through the newspapers and magazines and by word of mouth, did not arouse. One forgets that the mission was successful; one begins to consider the frightening possibilities, the yawning imminence of failure, the incredible risk of the venture not only for the astronauts but also for the philosophers. And removed from the category of a news report, recast in the imagination of the novelist, it is a far more thrilling story.

So that is what Mailer is up to: covering the best story of the century (if not quite the greatest story since the Creation, as some people have said) for 100, 200 years from now. And when one has finished the book, has reflected, has wondered at Mailer's reticence to attack those things one expected him to attack, when one has even registered surprise that Mailer comes to no final conclusions as to whether indeed this fantastic project was the work of God or the devil, one begins to understand what Mailer ultimately intended.

"Of a Fire on the Moon" is not Norman Mailer making final pronouncements on the space program, interpreting it for us, fitting it neatly into his view of things, giving hellfire and damnation to a plastic civilization, plastic technology, plastic politicians and technicians of plastic. (Although Lord knows he lands his share of punches.) No, this is the record—sad, angry, touching,

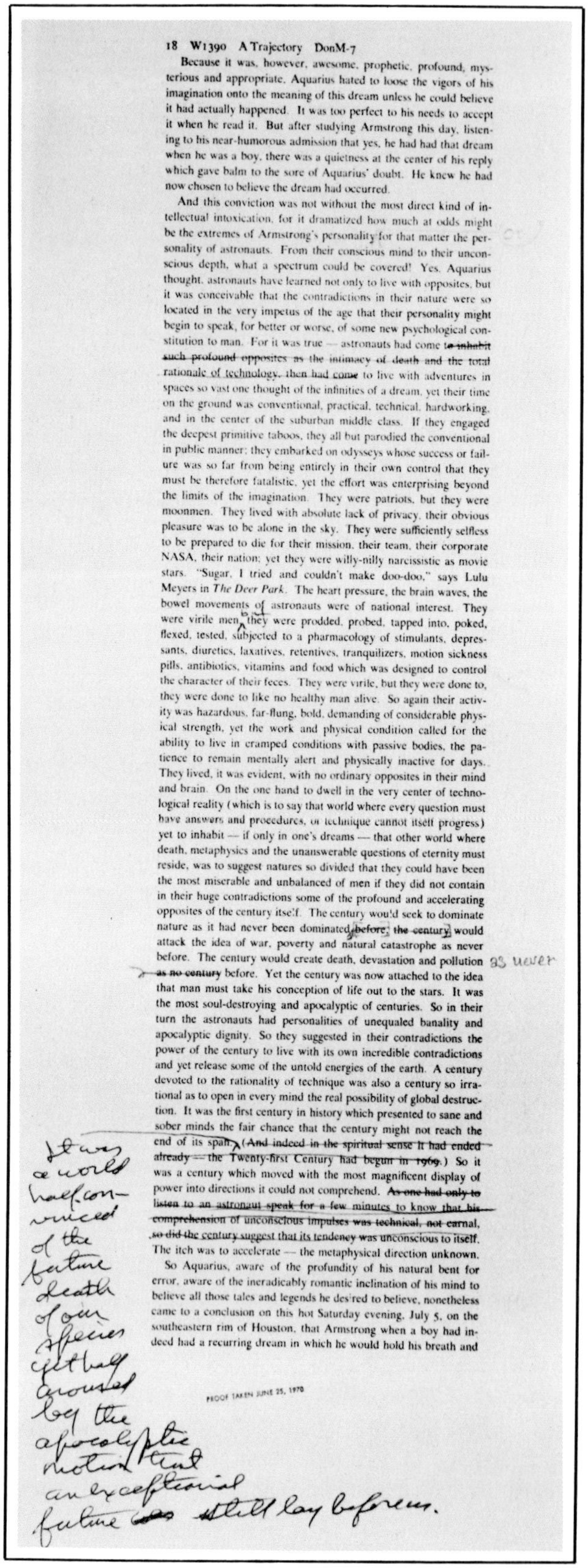

18 W1390 A Trajectory DonM-7

Because it was, however, awesome, prophetic, profound, mysterious and appropriate, Aquarius hated to loose the vigors of his imagination onto the meaning of this dream unless he could believe it had actually happened. It was too perfect to his needs to accept it when he read it. But after studying Armstrong this day, listening to his near-humorous admission that yes, he had had that dream when he was a boy, there was a quietness at the center of his reply which gave balm to the sore of Aquarius' doubt. He knew he had now chosen to believe the dream had occurred.

And this conviction was not without the most direct kind of intellectual intoxication, for it dramatized how much at odds might be the extremes of Armstrong's personality for that matter the personality of astronauts. From their conscious mind to their unconscious depth, what a spectrum could be covered! Yes, Aquarius thought, astronauts have learned not only to live with opposites, but it was conceivable that the contradictions in their nature were so located in the very impetus of the age that their personality might begin to speak, for better or worse, of some new psychological constitution to man. For it was true — astronauts had come ~~to inhabit such profound opposites as the intimacy of death and the total rationale of technology, then had come~~ to live with adventures in spaces so vast one thought of the infinities of a dream, yet their time on the ground was conventional, practical, technical, hardworking, and in the center of the suburban middle class. If they engaged the deepest primitive taboos, they all but parodied the conventional in public manner; they embarked on odysseys whose success or failure was so far from being entirely in their own control that they must be therefore fatalistic, yet the effort was enterprising beyond the limits of the imagination. They were patriots, but they were moonmen. They lived with absolute lack of privacy, their obvious pleasure was to be alone in the sky. They were sufficiently selfless to be prepared to die for their mission, their team, their corporate NASA, their nation; yet they were willy-nilly narcissistic as movie stars. "Sugar, I tried and couldn't make doo-doo," says Lulu Meyers in *The Deer Park*. The heart pressure, the brain waves, the bowel movements of astronauts were of national interest. They were virile men, they were prodded, probed, tapped into, poked, flexed, tested, subjected to a pharmacology of stimulants, depressants, diuretics, laxatives, retentives, tranquilizers, motion sickness pills, antibiotics, vitamins and food which was designed to control the character of their feces. They were virile, but they were done to, they were done to like no healthy man alive. So again their activity was hazardous, far-flung, bold, demanding of considerable physical strength, yet the work and physical condition called for the ability to live in cramped conditions with passive bodies, the patience to remain mentally alert and physically inactive for days. They lived, it was evident, with no ordinary opposites in their mind and brain. On the one hand to dwell in the very center of technological reality (which is to say that world where every question must have answers and procedures, or technique cannot itself progress) yet to inhabit — if only in one's dreams — that other world where death, metaphysics and the unanswerable questions of eternity must reside, was to suggest natures so divided that they could have been the most miserable and unbalanced of men if they did not contain in their huge contradictions some of the profound and accelerating opposites of the century itself. The century would seek to dominate nature as it had never been dominated ~~before; the century~~ would attack the idea of war, poverty and natural catastrophe as never before. The century would create death, devastation and pollution ~~as no century~~ before. as never Yet the century was now attached to the idea that man must take his conception of life out to the stars. It was the most soul-destroying and apocalyptic of centuries. So in their turn the astronauts had personalities of unequaled banality and apocalyptic dignity. So they suggested in their contradictions the power of the century to live with its own incredible contradictions and yet release some of the untold energies of the earth. A century devoted to the rationality of technique was also a century so irrational as to open in every mind the real possibility of global destruction. It was the first century in history which presented to sane and sober minds the fair chance that the century might not reach the end of its span. ~~(And indeed in the spiritual sense it had ended already — the Twenty-first Century had begun in 1969.)~~ So it was a century which moved with the most magnificent display of power into directions it could not comprehend. ~~As one had only to listen to an astronaut speak for a few minutes to know that his comprehension of unconscious impulses was technical, not carnal, so did the century suggest that its tendency was unconscious to itself.~~ The itch was to accelerate — the metaphysical direction unknown.

So Aquarius, aware of the profundity of his natural bent for error, aware of the ineradicably romantic inclination of his mind to believe all those tales and legends he desired to believe, nonetheless came to a conclusion on this hot Saturday evening, July 5, on the southeastern rim of Houston, that Armstrong when a boy had indeed had a recurring dream in which he would hold his breath and

PROOF TAKEN JUNE 25, 1970

It was a world half-convinced of the future death of our species yet half aroused by the apocalyptic notion that an exceptional future ~~was~~ still lay before us.

One of Mailer's corrected galley proofs for Of a Fire on the Moon *(Mailer Papers)*

humble, arrogant, sentimental, challenging, filled with wonder and despair—of a man, a sensitive and artistic man—his marriage breaking up, his friends in disarray, the things he loves gone aglimmering—trying to understand as best he can, trying to touch and smell and feel an event very nearly beyond the pale of human understanding.

It ends with a burial by the sea in Provincetown of an old junkheap of a car, with children slinging paint on the deceased and poets singing songs over it. The artists go thataway, the technicians have gone to the moon. Then Mailer, Aquarius, the dreamer and recorder of his dreams, goes to Houston and gazes upon a piece of moon rock. He sees it through layers of glass and thinks he can smell it. "Trust the authority of your senses" is his motto. Trusting the authority of his senses, he likes the moon. The reader, caught in the present still, glimpses in reflection a magnificent book.

In October 1973 Mailer gave twenty lectures at colleges and universities. During the tour he began to organize the Fifth Estate. This group proposed to investigate "the Invisible Government" of federal agencies such as the FBI and the CIA, and to prevent George Orwell's predictions in the novel 1984 *from becoming reality. This button was made for members of the organization.*

Mailer wrote two books about actress Marilyn Monroe, whom he never met, as well as the introduction to and captions for a calendar. His "biography in novel form," Marilyn, *was published in 1973, and his "false autobiography" or "imaginary memoir," originally entitled "Of Women and Their Elegance, by Marilyn Monroe as told to Norman Mailer," appeared in 1980 as* Of Women and Their Elegance.

BOOK REVIEW:

Michael Wood, "The Fight," *New York Times Book Review*, 27 July 1975, pp. 1-2.

To report the Ali-Foreman fight, Mailer stayed in Ali's training camp in Deer Lake, Pennsylvania, and traveled with the ex-champion's entourage to Zaire, Africa, where the match was held. After reading Mailer's account, Robert Lowell told him he was the world's greatest reporter.

The career of Muhammad Ali once looked like a sequence of magical, unrepeatable events. It was as if the fighters he defeated simply disappeared from the earth, and when he himself was beaten by Joe Frazier and then by Ken Norton it seemed impossible that he would ever come back. Yet here he is, heavyweight champion of the world, having straightened out the score with Frazier and Norton, having beaten George Foreman and held off a series of new contenders, including Joe Bugner a few weeks ago in Kuala Lumpur; here he is, promising to fight Frazier again in Manila in October, and after that to fight Norton and Foreman again. The unrepeatable has turned into a minuet, dancing bears revolving in the limelight to the rustle of millions of dollars. Still, losing some of his magic, Ali gains in stature, becomes a champion rather than a star, and one sees why he keeps calling off his proposed retirement. Being champion means proving you are the champion whenever proof seems required.

Norman Mailer's new book describes Ali's fight with Foreman last November to regain the title, and thus picks up Ali's story precisely at its turn, at the point where Ali's boasting was beginning to sound thin, where Ali really seemed to need all the psychic help that Mailer thought he might get from the heart of darkness. "If Ali can't win in Africa," Mailer had remarked when first hearing that Ali was to fight Foreman in Zaire, alias the Congo, "he can't win anywhere." During Ali's training Mailer hears "high-pitched hints of fear" in Ali's voice, and "large gouts of indignation." The hints of fear were probably lent to Ali by Mailer, but if Ali wasn't afraid of Foreman, everyone else was. In Mailer's account, even Ali's best jokes seem a promise of weakness, a buzzing,

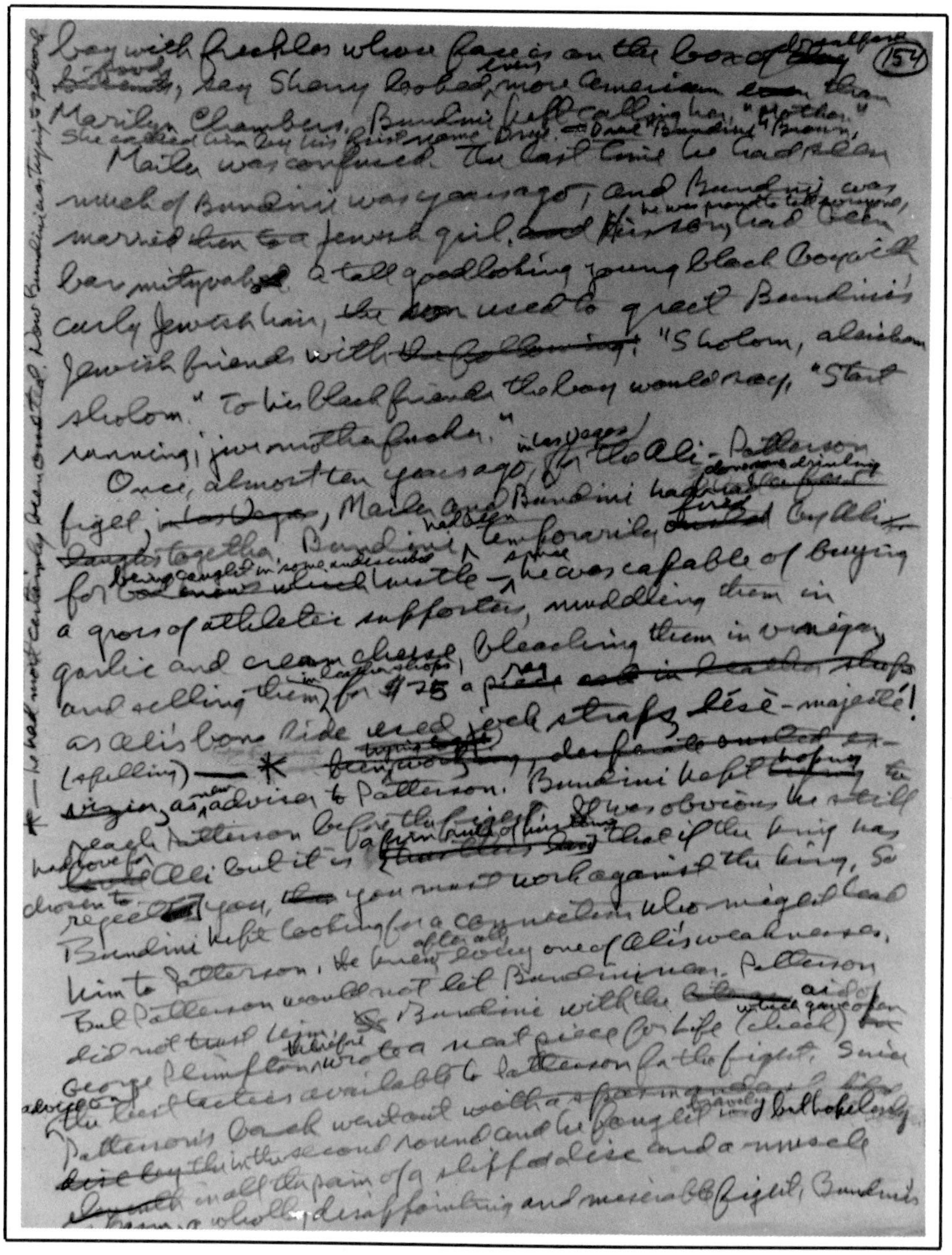

Two consecutive pages of manuscript for The Fight, *Mailer's account of the Ali-Foreman heavyweight championship boxing match (Mailer Papers)*

dispiriting counterpart to Foreman's strong silence. Ali, having said how impressed he is that blacks fly the planes in Africa ("Usually you feel safer if you see a white face flying a plane"), does this wonderful volte-face into vaudeville: "I never believe the bull—that the pilots is all Black. I keep looking for the secret closet where they hide the white man until the trouble starts." But Foreman offers the quiet, frightening logic of a giant who has been programmed by Harold Pinter. "Excuse me for not shaking hands with you," he says courteously to Mailer, "but you see I'm keeping my hands in my pockets."

Yet Ali won, because he was fit enough and fast enough and clearheaded enough to fight the way he wanted to. In the eighth round he knocked Foreman down (but not out, Foreman insisted afterwards), and Mailer, whose reporting in this book is quick and intelligent and sympathetic throughout, describes Foreman's descent from the championship in this way: "Foreman's arms flew out to the side like a man with a parachute jumping out of a plane, and in this doubled-over position he tried to wan-

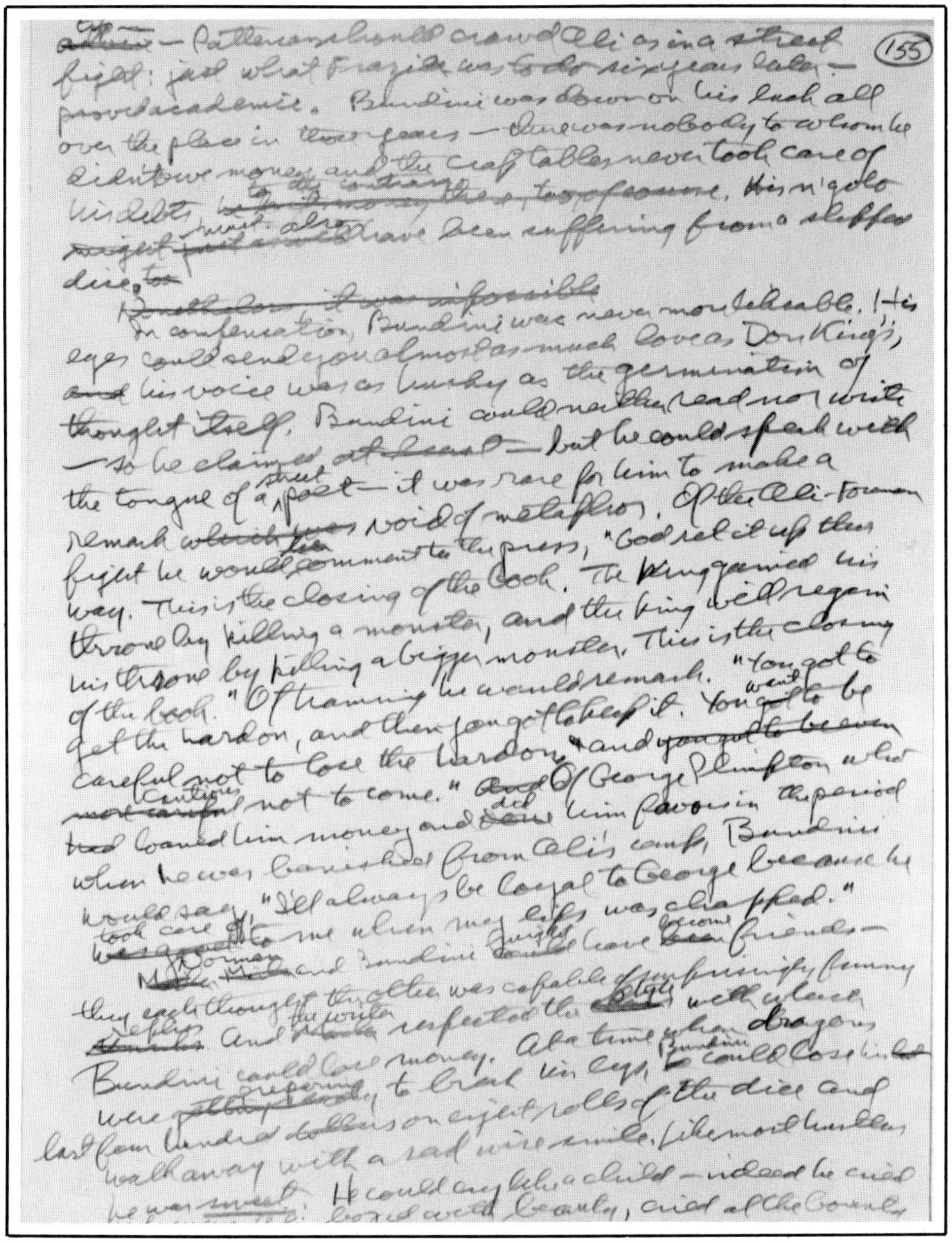
— Patterson should crowd Ali as in a street fight: just what Frazier was to do six years later — [illegible] academic. Bundini was down on his luck all over the place in those years — there was nobody to whom he didn't owe money and the crap tables never took care of his debts, [illegible]. His n'golo [illegible] have been suffering from a [illegible] disease.

In conversation, Bundini was never more likeable. His eyes could send you almost as much love as Don King's, his voice was as husky as the germination of thought itself. Bundini could neither read nor write — but he could speak with the tongue of a street poet — it was rare for him to make a remark void of metaphor. Of the Ali-Foreman fight he would comment to the press, "God set it up this way. This is the closing of the book. The king gained his throne by killing a monster, and the king will regain his throne by killing a bigger monster. This is the closing of the book." Of training he would remark, "You got to get the hardon, and then you got to keep it. You want to be careful not to lose the hardon, and [illegible] not to come." Of George Plimpton who had loaned him money and did him favors in the period when he was banished from Ali's camp, Bundini would say, "I'll always be loyal to George because he took care of me when my lips was chapped."

Norman and Bundini [illegible] become friends — they each thought the other was capable of surprisingly funny metaphors. And [illegible] respected the [illegible] with which Bundini could lose money. At a time when dragons [illegible] to break his legs, Bundini could lose [illegible] hundred dollars on eight rolls of the dice and walk away with a sad wise smile. Like most hustlers he was sweet. He could cry like a child — indeed he cried [illegible] with beauty, cried at the [illegible] der out to the center of the ring. All the while his eyes were on Ali and he looked up with no anger as if Ali, indeed, was the man he knew best in the world and would see him on his dying day. Vertigo took George Foreman and revolved him. Still bowing from the waist in this uncomprehending position, eyes on Muhammad Ali all the way, he started to tumble and topple and fall even as he did not wish to go down. . . . He went over like a six-foot sixty-year-old butler who has just heard tragic news. . . ."

There is an odd compassion in that last, comic image, and also, of course, a large element of stylistic risk. Mailer's writing is always on the edge of excess, much as Mailer himself is always walking parapets—he is trying to give it up, he says—and a cool look at almost any piece of his prose makes it look purple. It isn't purple, though, because Mailer is not after verbal effects, he is after his own shifting and elusive impressions, and the carelessness of Mailer's eloquence, the sense that it just came along as a means of saying what he had to say, is what makes it work: ". . . yes, impossible not to sense what everyone had been trying to say about Africa for a hundred years, big Papa first on line: the place was so [——] sensitive! No horror failed to stir its echo a thousand miles away, no sneeze was ever free of the leaf that fell on the other side of the hill."

It has become something of a commonplace to suggest that Mailer's vulnerability is his great charm: he is not afraid to appear ridiculous. This is true enough, but just appearing ridiculous, however bravely, won't take a writer all that far, and half a paragraph of Mailer on the Middle East, introduced because Ali is a Muslim, is already more than enough. Mailer hasn't been to Israel, but he's been to Cairo, and he knows where he stands: "Countries as gargantuan, fascinating, and godawful as Egypt did not deserve to dictate terms to one beleaguered Hebrew idea in the desert." Mailer's politics appear to be those of Moses, or indeed of God.

No, Mailer's great virtue is his ability to confess without apologizing. He is the most unrepentant of living writers, and it is very hard not to forgive a man who forgives himself so thoroughly. Every page in this book, for example, speaks implicitly of Mailer's dislike of blacks, converted into fascination and even affection by an act of sheer liberal will; but only Mailer, perhaps, would movingly and humorously admit to this dislike, "which had to be the dirtiest secret in his American life," and then go on blithely writing about blacks in the same spooked, mythologizing way, looking to boxing for "one more key to black emotion, black psychology, black love," and seeing a massage of Foreman as "Black fingers elucidating comforts for Black flesh." The Klan itself is hardly more prurient.

It is because he records his faults but scarcely ever corrects them that Mailer can be so marvelously funny without being ironic or even especially witty. When he describes himself as having seen a whale in Provincetown harbor, and having dreamed of a death that would link him with Melville forever; when he hears a lion in the African night and imagines another apposite literary demise ("who could fail to notice that it was Hemingway's own lion waiting down these years for the flesh of Ernest until an appropriate substitute had at last arrived?"), Mailer is not clowning or sending himself up. He is seeing the humor of his own perfect seriousness in such matters. A rare gift.

INTERVIEW:

Stan Isaacs, *Miami Herald*, 30 November 1975, pp. 3, 32-34, 36.

In 1974 Mailer signed a one-million-dollar contract with Little, Brown to write a multivolume novel. It has yet to appear, but Mailer has continued to publish other works. He granted this interview to discuss his latest book, The Fight, *and talk about the proposed Little, Brown work.*

INTERVIEWER: As a former fight reporter talking to a guy who has just written a fight book, I'll start with a standard sports question: What's been your greatest thrill in literature?

MAILER: In Literature? Oh boy, I don't know. Maybe *Anna Karenina*. Because when I got out of the Army and I was getting ready to write a war novel, all the time I was reading *Anna Karenina*. I read it on the boat coming back. And I was terrifically receptive to it and went through a huge experience reading it and every day I spent reading this book just to make my own novel better. I have a great love for that book.

INTERVIEWER: The question really refers to your greatest thrill, meaning yourself. What was your greatest thrill as a literary person, performer, etc.

MAILER: Listen, I never answer that question because I can't. You know, I have seven children, and if you ask me

Mailer in the seventies

which is my best child, or which is my favorite child, I couldn't give you the answer, you know, apart from the fact that I might have a few favorites among the seven. It's that it changes from day to day. You know, one day I see something reemerging in another kid, and so on. And with the books, it changes. On certain days I'd say *The Deer Park* and on other days I'd say *An American Dream*; I could say *The Armies of the Night*; I could say *Why We're in Vietnam* [*sic*]; I could say *The Naked and the Dead*. I could even say, on certain days when I get real mad, I could even say *Marilyn*.

INTERVIEWER: But you didn't say winning the Pulitzer Prize?

MAILER: No, that was during the (New York City 1969) mayoralty campaign and I was so geared to the mayoralty campaign that all I thought was, well, this'll probably get a few votes. You know, that's all I thought. You know, I've been bitter about the Pulitzer Prize for years because very often I felt it went to the wrong people as far as novelists went. So I wasn't altogether excited getting it.

INTERVIEWER: What do you think has been your best period as a writer?

MAILER: Ah, let's see, from about 1964 to about 1970. I wrote a lot of books in that period. You know, some of my best books are in that period. I started *An American Dream* in September of '63. So let's say from September of '63 through to about, well, I don't know, the middle of 1970 when I had finished *A Fire on the Moon*.

INTERVIEWER: What's been your worst period as a writer?

MAILER: The worst period was after *Naked and the Dead*. I really had about seven very slow years in which I wrote *Barbary Shore* and *The Deer Park*. All I wrote in seven years were those two novels. And each one I just pulled up out of my liver. I mean, I ended up with a bad liver writing *Deer Park*. It got that bad.

INTERVIEWER: In your new book, *The Fight*, you quote George Foreman calling you the champ among writers. Do you think you're the champion of writers?

MAILER: Well, if I am it would be only for two reasons. One is someone else thinks that way or cares that much. And the other thing is I wouldn't consider myself a great champ at all compared to the champs of the past. I'm like the equivalent of an Ezzard Charles, if you will.

INTERVIEWER: Ezzard Charles in relation to Jack Dempsey or Joe Louis?

MAILER: Yeah, as a Charles is to Dempsey or Louis or Muhammad Ali. I'm like a minor champ.

INTERVIEWER: With whom do you rank yourself from a literary standpoint?

MAILER: Well, like Charles in relation to Hemingway or Faulkner or Melville or Hawthorne. There are so many great American writers.

INTERVIEWER: At a Hofstra writing conference recently, Joseph Heller said, "I think more good novels are being written by Americans now than ever before in the history of the world. There are too many good writers now for anybody but literary critics to keep up with."

MAILER: Not a bad remark. I think there are a great number of novels being written at the next to the highest level. There are many more than at the time the *Great Gatsby* or *A Farewell to Arms* were being written. Then I think there were a few novels that really emerged, just stupendous novels. And below that category quite a way. You know, there weren't that many good books near that. Now you've got writers—I don't think there's a single writer around who's as great as Hemingway, Faulkner and probably even Fitzgerald. And maybe there's nobody around who's even as great as Thomas Wolfe and Dos Passos. But then below that rank you've got all those writers, Bellow, Updike, Heller, name 10 writers including myself, and more. And then under that 10 you've got 100 to 200 writers that any number of people will say are better than the first 10. But there's nobody around anyone will say is better than Hemingway; nobody around is better than Faulkner; we're not even near that line. We're just not doing what they were doing. I've been doing a lot of reading of Henry Miller because I'm going to do a small piece, a preface to an anthology of his stuff, and he's a great writer.

INTERVIEWER: John Updike wrote, "Mailer has abandoned fiction as a form of truth-seeking. He has become a 'pamphleteer.' " What's your reaction to that kind of thing?

MAILER: I think Updike said it in a weak moment of spleen. I've had a few of them myself. I don't take it too seriously. I haven't abandoned the novel. I've written 100,000 words of a new novel that's coming up—500,000 words. And I've never felt in my mind it's a matter of abandoning the novel. I thought I'd come to a point where I really needed years in which I wouldn't necessarily write novels because I find them very hard to write. And they get harder all the time. I mean I could sit down and tell a story easily enough that would run for 200 or 300 pages. But to tell a story that would really satisfy what I feel is necessary to a novel is something else altogether. I mean, I have a mystique about novels.

INTERVIEWER: I recall with some pain that in a conversation at a fight press room once I told you that your novels were not as significant as your journalism and that perhaps you should stick to journalism. You put me down with a good comment, which I don't remember.

MAILER: I don't remember the occasion.

INTERVIEWER: I didn't think you would. But, however, respectfully, I would still make that criticism.

MAILER: I think it's a legitimate criticism. You see, I don't take journalism as seriously as a novel, for one reason. Which is why I've always found it (journalism) easy. And I have terrible trouble with a novel's story. Characters come to me, situations, descriptions, but the story kills me. Because in a novel, you know, you've got to decide whether your character gets out of the bed and turns left when he gets up in the morning or turns right. And you have to keep making those decisions all through the book. And you make a wrong decision, you can ruin your novel. What I love about journalism, what makes it easy for me, is that I have the story. If I'd written this as a novel, *The Fight*, I'd have to decide does Foreman win or Ali. I'd lose six months deciding who wins. So, you know, there it is, Ali won, isn't that marvelous? But you know, it's a marvelous story told that way.

INTERVIEWER: You're talking in terms of heavyweight champ as a novelist—yet, you really haven't written that many novels.

MAILER: I've written as many novels as anyone else around. I've written five novels. And I think they're all good ones. I've written *The Naked and the Dead*, *Barbary Shore*, *Deer Park*, *The American Dream*, *Why Are We in Vietnam?*

INTERVIEWER: But it seems that lately the significant book is one like *Armies of the Night*, in which you're commenting so much better than the people in the newspapers on public issues.

MAILER: Now that book's a little different. That book's almost a novel, actually. It's almost when I'm kidding around I'll say that the *Armies of the Night* is the best 19th-Century novel that was written in the 20th Century. Because it's written in almost 19th-Century style, there's no sex in it, and it's a novel. I think of books like *Miami* and the *Siege of Chicago* as good, serious, responsible journalism.

INTERVIEWER: Somebody once said about you that your

failures are more exciting and exhilarating than the critical successes of less bold, dynamic contemporaries, but they're failures nevertheless.

MAILER: Well, every good novel's a failure. Not mine but everyone's. Dostoevski's career is a failure. He didn't write the book he had in mind. He died with a sense of frustration. He had this absolutely great book in which he was going to write about a saint. Yet, he'd written about people who had visions of being saints but lived in evil. That is, one saint up to that point, Alyosha in *The Brothers Karamazov*, is the least convincing of his characters. He died with a profound sense of failure in his novel and a profound sense of failure in his mission because he wanted to educate the Russian people to the nature of saintliness, which he felt was absolutely crucial to their survival as a nation. He might have been right. If you try hard enough at something, you're bound to create the failure by the very stretch of the imagination. But in the more limited technical sense, maybe, I don't know, maybe my novels are failures. I don't really—I don't think about them that way because I'm on the inside writing them. It's more a matter of, if that's the book I worked on that year, and you know, we're all professionals, we all do the best we can on a given day. So if it isn't as good as we wanted it to be, our feelings aren't so much that it's a failure as that we didn't really make the best run with the energies we had. You know, that's too bad, but there's today's work to do.

INTERVIEWER: In *The Fight*, at one point you say the news about your million-dollar contract for the new novel means it will have to be twice as good to overcome such financial news. Does that mean there is greater pressure on you in this book than you've ever felt before?

MAILER: Yeah, well I think there has to be. For one thing, I feel very responsible to the publisher because I feel they really acted the way I've always felt publishers should act, which is they're taking a big chance on one of their authors. And without their taking a big chance, I wouldn't have the chance of staying with this novel, because, you know, the amount of money I have to make a year is staggering, because of my personal situation, which I've brought on myself. You know, I've been married five times, seven children, and by the time I pay a full-time secretary, lawyer and all, I have to earn something like $100,000 a year before I can consider *myself*. Just alimony and the equivalent of business expenses is 100,000 bucks a year for me. I mean that's in terms of before I start paying on a mortgage on the house I own, and things like that. Well, the novel was for $1 million for 500,000 to 700,000 words. That's not an outrageous rate. It represents the rate that any number of good novelists would command. What's good about it though—different in the contract—is that the book may eventually be published as one novel or five novels or whatever. We'll all sit down and decide that when we're done. But what is good about it is I can really work on it and get my first draft done for the entire enormous project, possibly, before we have to decide what we'll do with it. So money can come in for five or six or seven years, however long it takes me, without my having to chop off a piece and say this is the book we'll put out. This is a very bad way to write long novels—to keep putting out pieces of it.

> *I think of craft as being like a Saint Bernard dog with that little bottle of brandy under his neck. Whenever you get into* real *trouble the thing that can save you as a novelist is to have enough craft to be able to keep warm long enough to be rescued.*

From Writers at Work, Third Series *(New York: Viking Press, 1967)*

INTERVIEWER: But my question is: Is the pressure much greater now than it's ever been?

MAILER: Well, that's one pressure—I feel responsible to the publisher. And I think everyone is going to be waiting for it, and that's a legitimate pressure. I don't mind the pressure altogether, I kind of half like it. Because my feeling is I kind of set it up that way. I wanted the pressure. I just was aghast when that news got out because it was a headline, in effect. Mailer gets a million dollars. And I know how I reacted when I heard about someone getting that kind of money. I don't like them. I don't have respect for them. And I feel an angry contempt toward them. And my feeling was—I know enough about how people read to know they hate your guts when they pick up that book of yours. They're not as likely to see what's in that book as someone who picks up a book sympathetically. So I just felt that's going to make it—the novel's really going to be better because it's really going to run into a lot of bad reviews. But actually, there's going to be so many years gone by before the book comes out that I think all of this will get digested, it'll be a different situation when the book comes out.

INTERVIEWER: Can you say anything about what the book's about?

MAILER: Well, a false story got out, that it was the story of a Jewish family from the time of the Pyramids to the future of the spaceship. And that's all wrong. What it is—a portion of the book starts in Egypt in the 20th Dynasty—about 1500 B.C. And there's also a portion of it that takes place in a spaceship. There's also a small portion of the book that has to do with a Jewish family about 40 years ago, 50 years ago—about the time of *Ragtime*—Ed Doctorow's book. I haven't been able to read *Ragtime* for just that reason. I'm going to cover the same period pretty much. Those are just three of the parts of it, but there's going to be a great deal of it that's contemporary. But I like to stick with something that has a lot to do with the structure of, oh, I don't know, the way time works. It's really going to be, to a certain extent, a full cyclical work if that isn't too pompous. Novelists are really very funny creatures. There's something really spooky about writing novels, because you're creating a world from just a half-life. The characters become real in your mind as you write. And you live with them and sleep with them, and even talk to them at a certain point, for they exist within you. And so they take on the same kind of funny life that movie stars take on for us when we think about them. I mean, there are a lot of people for whom Humphrey Bogart is the equivalent of an uncle, in terms of the psychic importance of their unconscious mind. And so a lot of that's going to go into this novel. One of the reasons I'm writing this novel is I want to try to show what an incredible vehicle, an incredible medium the novel is. How absolutely spooky it is because we don't really know where the beginning of it all is. More than that I don't want to say.

INTERVIEWER: In *The Fight* at one point you say, "He," meaning you, "was no longer so pleased with his presence. His daily reactions bored him." What do you think you would think of Norman Mailer, the writer, if you were Norman Mailer, the critic?

MAILER: I've often wondered if I would get as irritated with that—what's called that stylistic mannerism of mine. Of always placing myself in books in the third person—of always giving myself another name. And I really try to think and say would I get as irritated, because I feel I wouldn't. I can't do it any other way for a reason, which is I do not believe in objective truth. In my youth, there used to be these unsigned articles in *Time* magazine where they would tell you authoritatively that something was so, and of course it was always a matter that was moot. You know, that Marlene Dietrich could not play Swiss farm girls. Period. My argument is what you've always got to say is I, a spavined, semi-alcoholic writer at *Time* magazine, going out of my bird because I can't make Marlene Dietrich, now make this snide remark about Marlene Dietrich. Then you've got a reality. And so my feeling is it's important that I've always got to be in these things because I have a certain reality to Americans and they'd better know which reality is calling the tune for them. I mean, if I ever do write a book that's objective people are going to feel that there's something wrong with the book. You know, why aren't I in it.

INTERVIEWER: My question was: If you were Norman Mailer, the critic, what would you think of Norman Mailer, the writer? You've got a body of work to deal with. What would you say about him?

MAILER: I could deal severely with Mailer's limitations. But I don't want to answer it because I feel those critics out there are good enough without me helping them. I don't want to point out what I consider my flaws because they haven't quite hit them yet. I have what I consider a few flaws I haven't really gotten up to yet and I really don't want to accelerate that process. Let them discover my flaws on their own.

INTERVIEWER: The public sees you as a guy who's always out front, whether it's on a talk show or in his novels—always in the forefront, experiencing everything. People don't expect serious writers to behave the way you do.

MAILER: You know, it may seem like more than it is. I haven't been on television much. I've kind of decided it's kind of a dead end. I mean, you end up just being a character and a clown. I get on it now when a book is out and that's about it. From other people's point of view, when they hear about me they think I'm doing something. From my point of view, most of the time I'm not doing anything but being in a room and writing. Basically my life is boring most of the time.

INTERVIEWER: You refer to Hemingway four times in this new book. I had a feeling, almost, maybe to throw it at the critics.

MAILER: Oh, well if you're covering an athletic event and you've grown up in an American literary tradition as I did and you're reading all the American novelists in college, and I wanted to be an American writer. I never thought to myself, I want to be a writer, it was always I wanted to be an American writer, an American novelist. And how can you write about a fight without thinking of Hemingway all the time? I mean, his ghost hangs over the fight.

INTERVIEWER: If there had been no Hemingway, would Norman Mailer be different?

MAILER: Yes.

INTERVIEWER: In what way?

MAILER: I wouldn't be as good.

INTERVIEWER: Why not?

MAILER: Because he teaches you how to write, Hemingway. You know, if I were giving a writing course, he's one of the people I'd—well, let me put it this way. He's one of the people Nelson Algren used to assign to his students, and he'd get a lot of Hemingway stories written. And I asked him once why he did it, because I was sitting in on one of his classes many years ago. It was 20 years ago. And he said, you know, he said, well, you've got to let yourself be influenced by someone, so you may as well be influenced by someone who's pretty good. Let them write like Hemingway for a while. If they're really going to be any good, they'll get over that, and so on. And that's absolutely true. You know, you get over certain writers but, you know, you've picked up a lot of what they're doing.

In 1980 Mailer married Carol Stevens, with whom he had lived from 1969 to 1975, to legitimize their child, Maggie Alexander, born in 1971. Mailer and Stevens obtained a quick "civilized" Haitian divorce, and he then married his sixth wife, Norris Church, with whom he is shown above in 1976. They have one child, John Buffalo Mailer.

HOWARD FERTIG, INC., PUBLISHER
80 East 11th Street, New York, New York 10003

Announcing a Unique Literary Event:
Publication for the first time of an early
novel by Norman Mailer

A Transit to Narcissus
Norman Mailer

A Facsimile of the Original Typescript
with an introduction by the author

A Transit to Narcissus, now published for the first time, was written by Norman Mailer at the age of twenty while awaiting induction into the Army, and some three years before he began writing *The Naked and the Dead*.

He had spent a short time the summer before working in the violent ward of a mental hospital, and as he remarks

Promotional piece for the 1978 edition of Mailer's previously unpublished novel. He wrote in the introduction that his search for experience by working in a mental hospital provided "a first coming to grips with a theme that would not so much haunt me as stalk me for the rest of my writing life: what is the relation between courage and brutality?"

BOOK REVIEW:

Ted Morgan, "Last Rights," *Saturday Review*, 6 (10 November 1979): 57-58.

The Executioner's Song *follows the life of Gary Gilmore from his 1976 parole, through the murder of two Utah men, to his conviction and subsequent execution by firing squad in 1977. To write this long "true-life novel," Mailer studied transcripts of more than 1,000 hours of interviews with Gilmore, rented an apartment in Provo, slept in Gilmore's hotel room, interviewed Gilmore's friends, and corresponded with convict Jack Henry Abbott. Some critics thought the book too long, but the style and objective point of view were widely praised. It was awarded the 1980 Pulitzer Prize.*

No life is unworthy of a novel, Flaubert once said. Taking him at his word, Norman Mailer has devoted more than a thousand pages to nine months in the life of Gary Gilmore, from the time of his arrest in 1976 after killing two men to his execution in Utah by a firing squad.

Mailer calls this "a true-life novel." "Most nonfiction," he recently said to me, "is predigested. The writer ruminates on the material before he presents it to the reader." He went on to explain that fiction avoids that mistake by offering the reader the direct experience of the characters. It doesn't matter whether an incident is true or not, as long as it is convincing. The paradox of fiction is that an inventive narrative can seem more real than a verbatim report.

Mailer's "true-life novel"—which will remind many readers of Truman Capote's "nonfiction novel," *In Cold Blood*, since both books deal with senseless murder in heartland communities—tries to combine the immediacy of fiction with the strict accuracy of nonfiction.

In order to make the combination work, Mailer has done a disappearing act. The author of *Advertisements for Myself*, so aggressively present in most of his books, is absent from this one. Gone is the autobiographical narrator in his many guises, whether as Psychic Investigator, Prisoner of Wedlock, Aquarius, or just Norman.

The Executioner's Song is a "plain, unvarnished tale," stitched together from hundreds of hours of interviews, about half of them conducted by Mailer, with supporting characters and bit players in the Gary Gilmore saga. The story is told from several dozen points of view. Here, for instance, is Gilmore from his girl friend's point of view:

> Nicole made a pretense of ignoring the new fellow, but there was something about him. When their eyes met, he looked at her and said, "I know you." Nicole didn't say anything in reply. For a split second, something flashed in her mind but then she thought, No, I've never met him before, I know that. Maybe I know him from another time.

And here, by contrast, is Gilmore's cellmate Gibbs:

> Gilmore, tonight, would break off his arm if he could make a good joke. Cut off his head and hand it to you, if his mouth would spit nails. "What's your last best request when they're hanging you?" he asked, and answered, "Use a rubber rope." Pretended to be bouncing on the end, he put his face in a scowl, and said, "Guess I'll be hanging around for a while."

Mixing the different voices proved to be Mailer's highest hurdle. "I was brought up not to jump from one person's mind into another," he says. "I thought that was what poor writers did when they didn't have enough imagination to find a form. But then, I thought, the shifting point of view was a 19th-century form, it went back to a time when people believed in God and the novelist could play at being the All Knowing Supreme Deity."

In this case, the deity orchestrates the voices, but does not join in the song. The qualities (or flaws, depending on one's point of view) we look for in Mailer's work—the ripe style, the existential musings, the outrageous ideas, the overcharacterizing—are nowhere in sight.

What then, one might ask, is there of Mailer in the book, and why could it not have been written by any competent journalist who knows how to edit taped interviews? Mailer insists that "only someone who has been writing for 30 years would be willing to relinquish his ego. I couldn't have done it 15 years ago. It's hard for a writer who takes himself seriously to be nothing but a transmission belt."

But there is more to it than not getting in the way of his material. Mailer saw in Gilmore a character that he might have invented in a novel, for Gilmore personified the main theme of his entire *oeuvre*—namely, that the soul could conceivably have a separate existence from the body. Gilmore believed so fervently in an afterlife that he worried about bumping into his murder victims. Mailer wanted to show that Gilmore's wish to die was not a put-on or a publicity stunt; he wasn't just a proud con trapped in a role. He was doing it because he felt he deserved to die, could no longer tolerate life in prison, where he had spent half of his 35 years, and wanted to reach the Other Side. That was the kind of existential gamble Mailer could appreciate.

Mailer admittedly wrote *The Executioner's Song* "to

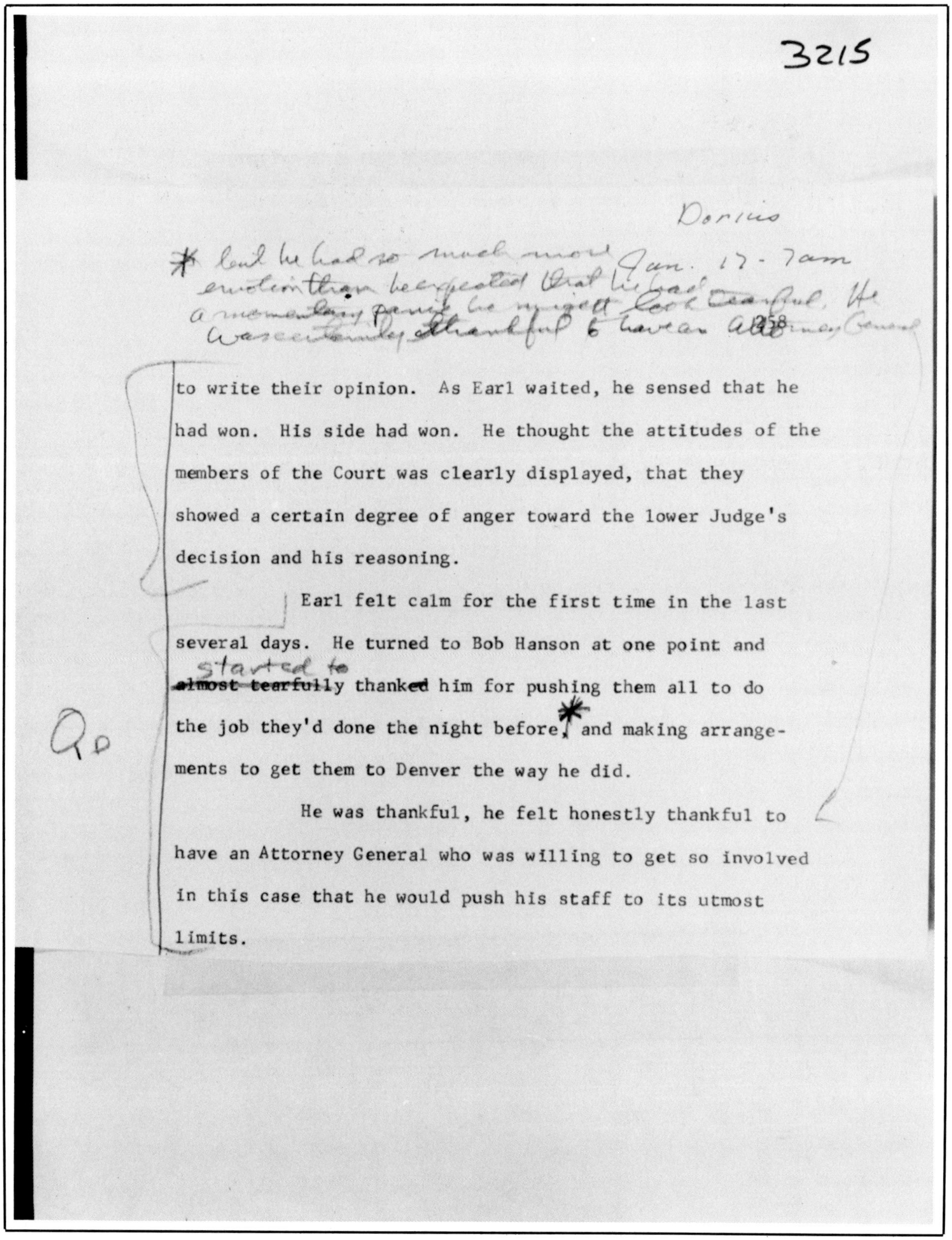

3215

Dorius

Jan. 17 - 7am

* but he had so much more emotion than he expected that he had a momentary panic he might look tearful. He was certainly thankful to have an Attorney General

258

to write their opinion. As Earl waited, he sensed that he had won. His side had won. He thought the attitudes of the members of the Court was clearly displayed, that they showed a certain degree of anger toward the lower Judge's decision and his reasoning.

Earl felt calm for the first time in the last several days. He turned to Bob Hanson at one point and ~~almost tearfully~~ started to thank him for pushing them all to do the job they'd done the night before,* and making arrangements to get them to Denver the way he did.

He was thankful, he felt honestly thankful to have an Attorney General who was willing to get so involved in this case that he would push his staff to its utmost limits.

Page of revised typescript from The Executioner's Song. *Mailer became involved in the project through Larry Schiller, a press agent who "packaged" the Gilmore material (Mailer Papers).*

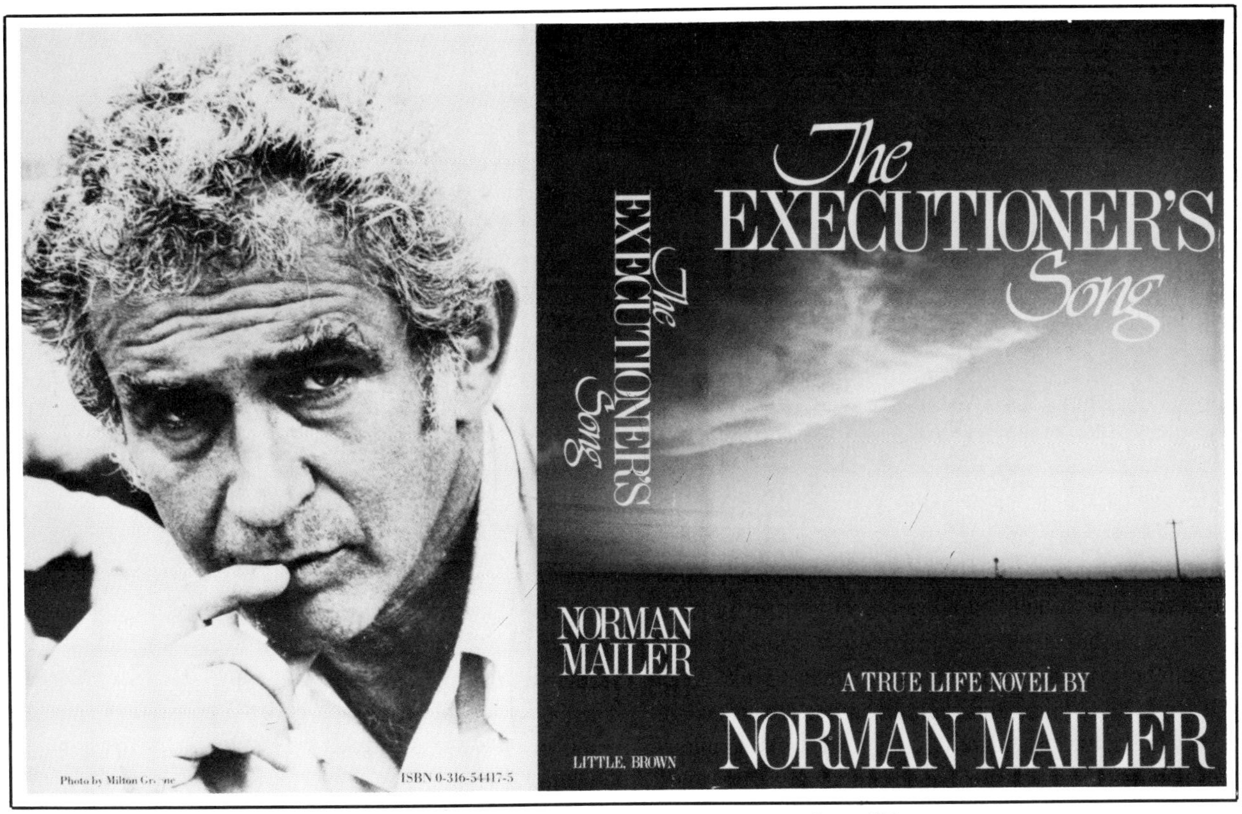

Dust jacket for Mailer's "true life novel" about Gary Gilmore

make a quick haul," interrupting the long novel he has been working on for years. Larry Schiller, the entrepreneur journalist who specializes in terminal cases, had tied up the rights to Gilmore's story and made Mailer an offer he couldn't refuse.

The result is Mailer's best book since *The Deer Park*, which may be a backhanded compliment in light of the author's unprecedented restraint. My first thought was, "How in the world can Gary Gilmore be worth a thousand pages?" But I found myself swept up and carried along by the narrative, and I began to see how artful the design is—how, by letting the characters speak in their own voices, and by having the events unfold as they appeared to witnesses, Mailer achieves an effect that is not unlike the homespun credibility of Thornton Wilder's *Our Town*. But this is the underside of *Our Town*, dealing as it does with misfits and murders. The overall tone made me think of Conrad's remark in *Lord Jim* concerning "that mysterious, almost miraculous, power of producing striking effects by means impossible of detection, which is the last word of the highest art."

This book is much more than the story of a man who wanted to die. It is a panorama of American life in the Seventies, of people at every level of society responding to an extreme situation. Gary Gilmore was the enemy of society. He had been in trouble since the age of 12, had gone to reform school and jail, and had finally killed two men, as though murder was the logical conclusion of his criminal destiny. Gilmore had killed a service-station attendant and a motel manager, men he did not know and had nothing against, in a completely impersonal manner, like an executioner. He asked in return to be killed by a firing squad in the same impersonal manner.

He became even more an enemy of society, which guarantees appeals procedures, by insisting on his right to die. Society rewards those who play the game, but Gilmore tilted the game, like a man playing chess on a slanted board.

With a convict's cunning, he seemed to sense the hypocrisy of keeping capital punishment on the books as a useful deterrent, even though it was no longer enforced—no one had been executed in Utah since 1963. Well, he seemed to be saying, let us test the system.

Everyone wanted to save him—his lawyers, who

filed an appeal against his wishes, the judges who granted stays, the ACLU, the Next-Friend petitioners, and assorted do-gooders. And everyone seemed to want a piece of him. The press wanted a story, Larry Schiller wanted rights, the prison psychologists wanted to understand him, and, after he had announced his intention of giving his body to science, people even wrote in asking for his eyes.

Mailer devotes one-third of his book to the transformation of a criminal case in Utah into a national media event, the shift from the saving of Gary Gilmore to the merchandising of Gary Gilmore. The man and his bizarre crusade were overshadowed by the deal—the movie and TV rights, the articles and interviews, and the foreign sales, which Larry Schiller kept hustling.

One end-product of this merchandising is Mailer's book, which redeems itself from the accusation of cheap (no, make that expensive) checkbook journalism by showing how the press distorts, makes over, and becomes a part of the event. Gilmore began to like the part and to play up to it, striking poses, chuckling over his mail, and enjoying the attention. Eventually, he got his way, and was shot by a firing squad early in 1977. The book is strewn with clues to explain his behavior, but it ends without a pat, predigested, conclusive answer.

Was Gary Gilmore, to paraphrase what was once said about Harry Truman, an example of mediocrity enlarged by history? Or was he a man of depth and artistic temperament, as his drawings and his rather eloquent letters to Nicole would indicate?

In tracing the causes of his violent behavior, a Freudian analyst might dwell on Gilmore's feeling that he was illegitimate because his father, a con artist, used different names, and the one on his birth certificate was not Gilmore. Even his mother, Bessie, "could never be certain that piece of paper had nothing to do with the armed robbery he did next and the terrible sentence of fifteen years at the age of twenty-two."

A behaviorist might prefer to stress his years in prison, where he spent long stretches in solitary and was given Prolixin, a drug used to calm the violent and psychotic. Surely it was in prison that hostility and violence became normal responses, and that he came to see himself as an outlaw and a failure.

A social biologist might argue that there was a missing component in Gary Gilmore. Most of us have shock absorbers to allow us to deal with frustration, with the gap between desire and fulfillment. Gilmore's response to frustration was an intolerable rage that he could relieve only by committing a crime. It was when the pressure built up, when Nicole left him and he had to find $400 as a down payment on a pick-up truck, that he became a killer.

The point Mailer makes is that even when we know everything about another human being we can never understand his ultimate moral nature. "I put in all I knew," he says, "and I have the answers we have in life, not hard concrete answers, but that Gilmore was a deck of cards, as many of us are. Perhaps he killed because he knew that what was best in him could never be expressed."

Mailer in the eighties

INTERVIEW:

Hilary Mills, "Norman Mailer," *Saturday Review*, 8 (January 1981): 46, 48-49, 52-53.

After twenty-two books, Mailer explains how he writes and describes his long Egyptian novel still in progress. The interviewer is the author of the first comprehensive biography of Mailer.

INTERVIEWER: You've used a lot of different literary forms over the past 32 years, yet it's always seemed as if you have the most respect for the form of the novel.

MAILER: Well, perhaps it's the professional respect I feel for the novel. I think it's the most difficult of all the forms I've tried. I've always been fond of journalism, but I don't respect it in the same way because I think it's easier. Artists always have a kind of regard for virtuosity, and although the fact that something is easier doesn't therefore mean it's a lesser form, deep down I think most artists feel that if it's hard you respect it more.

INTERVIEWER: Looking back on your career, it seems as if your novel *The Deer Park* was a kind of watershed. It was after that book came out in 1955 that you gradually moved away from the novel and into journalism. What happened at that point in your career?

MAILER: I really think the watershed book was *Advertisements for Myself* because that was the first book, oddly enough, that I'd say was written in what became my style. I never felt as if I had a style until that book, and once I developed that style—for better or for worse—a lot of other forms opened to it. It's an adaptable style, and of course when I finally discovered in *Armies of the Night* that I could put myself into a book and thereby paint all sorts of splendid effects, I began to enjoy going in many directions.

Between *Advertisements for Myself* which came out in 1959 and *Armies of the Night* which was written in 1967, I was going in a good many different directions but I wasn't enjoying it. I didn't know quite how to do it. I was having a terrible time with my journalistic pieces, but of course I was having a terrible time with everything I was writing. Writing was very difficult for me during that period and so much of it was tied up with my personal life.

INTERVIEWER: You've mentioned previously that you were smoking a lot of marijuana around this time; do you think this had anything to do with the difficulties you were encountering in your work?

MAILER: No. All it did was consume large tracts of my brain. I was doing to my brain what Barry Goldwater recommended we do to the foliage in Vietnam. I think parts of my head have been permanently sluggish ever since. But I don't think the damage to my head was what was giving me difficulty in writing. It was more timidity. I was a little aghast at what I was trying to do because no one had ever done it before. These days everybody is laying claim to having started the New Journalism. I mean Truman is screaming and Tom Wolfe has been writing manifestos for the last 10 years. But I think if I started any aspect of that New Journalism—and I did—it was an enormously personalized journalism where the character of the narrator was one of the elements not only in telling the story but in the way the reader would assess the experience.

I had some dim instinctive feeling that what was wrong with all journalism was that the reporter pretended to be objective and that was one of the great lies of all time. What this really was was an all-out assault on *New Yorker* writing, and at the same time I had—as all of us did—a vast respect for the *New Yorker*. So I was a little scared at what I was doing. I thought I was either all right or all wrong. The stakes were high, but by now it's more comfortable to write that way.

INTERVIEWER: You also pointed out in *Cannibals and Christians* that after the war American society was changing so rapidly that "the novel gave up any desire to be a creation equal to the phenomenon of the country." Did this have anything to do with your move away from the novel form and into journalism?

MAILER: Well, I wasn't taking journalism that seriously. I never felt that I was doing something more important than the novel. Wolfe feels it's more important, but I've never laid that claim since it's so much easier.

The thing that makes the novel so hellishly difficult is that you have to elucidate a story from the material. If you make a mistake then you may not discover it until the book is done and you're looking back on it 10 years later. It's very much like chess in a funny way. Good chess players always speak of the best line of continuation. They can analyze a game afterward and really replay the points of no return and see whether a knight should have been moved to another box. In the novel, you're left wondering.

INTERVIEWER: You've talked a lot about your economic

problems in the past. If economic necessity hadn't been a factor in your life, would you have written as much as you have?

MAILER: If I had no economic necessity I would have written about one and a half as many pages as Bill Styron and that's because I'm about one and a half times more energetic than old Bill.

INTERVIEWER: Would you have written the same kind of books as you have?

MAILER: No. I would have written books that are more like Styron's too, in the sense that they would have been more literary and more well-rubbed, and I would have spent more time on them and I would have polished them and I would have lived with them and would have sighed over them and I probably would have taken them more seriously than I take my books, although I do take them very seriously. But I mean I would have been truly solemn about them.

INTERVIEWER: Would all these books have been novels or would you have written journalism anyway?

MAILER: I probably would not have gotten into journalism. I'm speculating; I could have gotten into journalism anyway, particularly with the history we had in the Sixties. It was so much easier because there were all those wonderful stories. I'd never come up with a story of my own that was as good as the things that were happening all through the Sixties.

INTERVIEWER: So in a sense there has never been a conscious or premeditated orchestration of your own career; it just happened the way it did?

MAILER: Yes, I've always been reacting to the given.

INTERVIEWER: There seems to be a kind of tragic irony in American literary life: The youngest writers with the most brilliant first novels are the ones subjected to the most horrendous pressures. How would you say your early success affected you and your work?

MAILER: It changed my life. For a long time after the success of *The Naked and the Dead*, for seven or eight years, I kept walking around saying nobody treats me as if I'm real, nobody wants me for myself, for my five-feet eight-inches, everybody wants me for my celebrity. Therefore my experience wasn't real. All the habits I'd formed up to that point of being an observer on the sidelines were shattered. Suddenly, if I went into a room I was the center of the room, and so regardless of how I carried myself, everything I did was taken seriously and critically. I complained bitterly to myself about the unfairness of it until the day I realized that it was fair, that that was my experience. It's the simplest remark to make to yourself, but it took me 10 years to get to that point.

Then I began to realize the kind of writing I was going to do would be altogether different from the kind of writing I thought I would do. After *The Naked and the Dead* I thought I would write huge collective novels about American life, but I knew I had to go out and get experience and my celebrity made it impossible. I then began to realize that there was something else that I was going to get which hopefully would be equally valuable, and that was that I was having a form of 20th-century experience which would become more and more prevalent: I was utterly separated from my roots. I was successful and alienated and that was a 20th-century condition. This went into all my work after that in one way or another and will go on forever because by now I suppose I can say that kind of personality interests me more than someone who is rooted.

INTERVIEWER: Do you ever think of an audience when you write?

MAILER: No. I used to have a much clearer idea of who I was writing for—certain friends, certain intellectuals, certain critics, a certain sense of the kind of audience I wanted out there and who they might be. That was in the Sixties, but in the Seventies there was a stretch where I really didn't know who I was writing for. You go in and out of fashion as a writer, that's one of the periodicities in your life, and another is that your sense of who you're writing for goes in and out of phase or focus. I've gone through a period of about four or five years where I really didn't know who I was writing for anymore, and I must say with my Egyptian book I've gotten to the point where I don't care who I'm writing for. It's either going to be good or it isn't going to be good, but I wouldn't have a clue who's going to like it and who is not going to like it. You get old enough and realize there are gods in the cosmos but there are no literary gods left. That's not bad; there's something demeaning about being in awe of a critic.

INTERVIEWER: Is your concentration different when you work on a novel from when you work on journalism?

MAILER: The novel is much more demanding physically. I've found that I almost can't do serious writing without getting into a depression. The depression is almost a vital part of the process because, to begin with, it's dangerous beyond measure to fall in love with what you're doing while you're doing it. You lose your judgment and you lose it for the simplest reason—that the words, as you're reading them, are stirring you too much. The odds are, if they're stirring you too much, they are going to stir no one else.

You also get depressed for reasons that are impossible to explain. I think we sometimes get depressed when we're writing because we're destroying other possibilities. The deeper your theme, the more you're making it impossible for yourself to approach other themes that are collateral to it. So there's the gloom that certain things are probably not going to get written about.

INTERVIEWER: Once you commit yourself to a work do you write consistently every day?

MAILER: I've been working on the Egyptian novel on and off for 10 years so I hardly feel like desperate Ambrose when I get in in the morning. I'll work quietly on it, but the one invariable is if I tell myself the night before that I'm going to work, I go to work and it doesn't matter what kind of mood I'm in. When I was younger I used to shatter work all the time and could not finish things because I'd do some good writing then go out and celebrate and then unconsciously I'd be working on the continuation of what I'd been writing while I was celebrating. I was shattering my brain and I'd wake up the next morning and have to reconstruct it. Eventually the brain just rebels. I found I began to have blocks and the best way to get around a block is to tell yourself you're going to write. If you obey that promise you made to yourself—even if it takes 45 days—the unconscious will trust you again and begin to deliver the material.

INTERVIEWER: What time of day do you write?

MAILER: Usually in the morning, sometimes in the afternoon. I start around 10 and work till one, break for lunch, and then sometimes start again in the afternoon and sometimes not. I don't like to write twice in the day. It's somehow more nervous in the afternoon than it is in the morning.

INTERVIEWER: Where do you find the solitude you need to work?

MAILER: I had trouble for a while because I was working in a little room in the house in Brooklyn and it was hell because I was spoiled and used to a large studio room. But recently I found a small studio that's nice in Brooklyn Heights not too far from where I live.

INTERVIEWER: Do you type or write in longhand?

MAILER: Longhand.

INTERVIEWER: Are you one of those writers who build a book painstakingly from page one or do you like to get the material down and go back and revise?

MAILER: I'm not happy if I feel that what's behind me is wrong or needs work. The reason for that is I tend to build my books on the basis of what I have already. I never have a master plan for the entire book. Every time I have—and when I was younger I used to sit down and write out a complete plan for a book—I never wrote the book. Even with *The Executioner's Song* where, after all, I knew the story in great detail, I was very careful not to be versed in too many details of the story way ahead. In other words, I tended to do my research let's say 100 pages ahead of where I was because I wanted to keep the feeling that I didn't know how it was all going to turn out. I wanted to have the illusion that I was inventing each little detail as if I were writing a conventional novel.

INTERVIEWER: So you don't take many notes on plot or character development?

MAILER: A few notes. Usually if it's a powerful enough idea about the continuation of the book I don't need to take a note. If I can't remember that, then what kind of idea could it have been? Once in a great while I'll put together a note on something that should happen 200 pages ahead, just a thought the character might have, and I sort of know the place where it will come in; but I like the idea of a book not being too programmatic. I find some of the best ideas I get I receive because I haven't fixed other ideas in concrete and have to obey them. When you know your end, it's disastrous to get a good idea which takes you away from that end.

INTERVIEWER: Do you ever show your manuscript pages to someone while a work is in progress?

MAILER: Oh sure. I do it the way I box: I pick my sparring partners very carefully. Usually I'll box with people who are so good that I'm in no danger of being hurt because they consider it obscene to hurt me. Or I'll box with friends where we understand each other and are trying to bring out the best in each other as boxers. The same thing with an early stage of a manuscript. I'd no more dream of showing it to someone like John Simon than I would dream of carrying a kite to the Brooklyn Bridge and jumping off. But I'll show it to Norris or to Bob Lucid, who is a great friend of mine, or to Scott Meredith, my agent.

INTERVIEWER: You've worked on a number of other books while writing your big novel. Do you ever find it hard to get back in sync with the novel after doing these other projects?

MAILER: I've often said that this Egyptian novel is nicer to me than any of my wives. I leave it for two years and come back and it says, "Oh you look tired, you've been away, here let me wash your feet." I've been able to go back to it without trouble every time so far. But a novel is very much like that mythological creature: a good woman. You can't abuse her forever. So I think I've finally got to finish the Egyptian novel. The time has come.

INTERVIEWER: What is it about?

MAILER: It takes place in the reign of Ramses IX who was pharaoh in the 20th dynasty. The period is 1130 b.c. That's just the first novel. I'm two-thirds of the way through, and it's 1,000 pages long so far. The second novel will take place in the future and a third novel will be contemporary. I've got a very tricky way of tying them up, but I'm not going to talk about that because I've got to have something to keep me going.

INTERVIEWER: Is it written in first person or third?

MAILER: First person and the first person varies. But it's premature to start talking about it because it's a year or two from being done.

INTERVIEWER: Can you just say what the original inspiration for the book was?

MAILER: I thought I'd take a quick trip through Egypt. At one point I wanted the novel to be picaresque and have a chapter on Egypt of antiquity, a chapter on Greece, and a chapter on Rome just to show how marvelously talented I was to be able to do all these things. So I dipped into Egypt and I never got out. I'm kind of sluggish when you get right down to it.

INTERVIEWER: It's interesting that when you wrote *The Deer Park* back in 1955 it was originally supposed to be the first volume of an eight-novel project and now you've circled back to a novelistic scheme of almost equally monumental proportions. Do you feel more ready now?

MAILER: Well, I feel more ready but I don't feel ready. I mean I don't think you ever do. I suppose it's as much a question of me, that I'll really ever finish the three books and have them the way I want them. What I'm attempting in this book is a good reach or two beyond anything I've done before. I'm not at all confident that I'll be able to do it, but I'm hoping I will.

INTERVIEWER: Your work is totally unique, but do you see yourself as a direct descendent of any particular literary line?

MAILER: I must say that I have a fragmented soul when it comes to what I think are my traditions because my taste and my loyalties are all in separate places. My loyalties are to people like Dreiser and Farrell and maybe Steinbeck and Wolfe—all the people who were writing about working-class and lower middle-class people. They were the ones who first got me excited about writing. On the other hand, my taste quickly inclined toward Hemingway and Faulkner and Fitzgerald and I learned so many things from them that I didn't learn from the other bunch. Then, in a way, my actual roots and influences are so peculiar. Henry Adams, for instance, obviously had a vast influence on me but I never knew he did until I started to write *Armies of the Night*.

INTERVIEWER: Are you in the habit of socializing a lot with other writers?

MAILER: Not as much as some writers do. I have a distrust of the literary world which is not dissimilar to the kind of distrust a red-neck who starts to write has of the literary world—which is that they are all fancy double-talking phonies up in New York. My view is somewhat more sophisticated, but I think that the literary world is a very dangerous place to be in if you want to do an awful lot of writing because it's almost necessary to take on airs in order to protect yourself in that world. In a way you can't handle yourself skillfully unless your airs are finely tuned. Capote has a wonderful set of airs and he's also impregnable. He walks around like a little fortress—at least until lately. I think there are starting to be some cracks in the wall.

Hemingway committed suicide working on those airs. He took the literary world much too seriously and he's almost there as a lesson to the rest of us: Don't get involved in that world at too deep a level or it will kill you and kill you for the silliest reasons: for vanity and because feuds are beginning to etch your liver with the acids of frustration.

INTERVIEWER: On the other hand, you've put almost as much creative energy into your public performing self as you have into your work. Do you think that public self has helped or hurt your work?

MAILER: It's probably helped my mind and hurt my work. I think I've had the kind of experience that made me equipped to deal with certain kinds of problems that a writer who's more serious about keeping to his study and not venturing out too much—or certainly not venturing

Mailer leaving the courtroom during the 1982 murder trial of Jack Henry Abbott. Mailer had helped arrange Abbott's release from prison six weeks before he was charged with the killing.

out on quixotic ventures—would not have had. I think I have an understanding of the complexity of the world that I wouldn't have gotten if I stayed at home. I would have tended to have a much more paranoid vision of how sinister things are. Things are sinister but not in the way I used to think they were sinister.

INTERVIEWER: In your new book *Of Women and Their Elegance*, you assume the voice of Marilyn Monroe. Was this hard to do?

MAILER: No. That was the most enjoyable part of the book. I'd written the other book about Marilyn [*Marilyn*] in which I never entered her head once, because I just didn't feel ready to. But with *Marilyn*, something was obviously developing and got digested, and over the years, thinking about Marilyn, her voice just began to emerge. I always thought that if I had been a woman, then I probably would have been a little bit like Marilyn Monroe. I've always found her humor sympathetic to my own humor—such as it is.

INTERVIEWER: It's interesting that in your latest books, *The Executioner's Song* and *Of Women and Their Elegance*, Norman Mailer is conspicuously absent as narrator. Is this a conscious attempt on your part to get away from the autobiographical mode?

MAILER: I think I've just worn out my feeling that that was the style in which to keep writing. Because it was so difficult for me to arrive at my own style—after all I'd been a public writer for 10 to 12 years before I felt I'd come into my own style as such—I didn't start with an identity. I forged an identity through my experiences and through changing. Because of that, I think, in a funny way it was much easier to give up that style when the time came. I didn't feel as if I were giving myself away.

And I've always felt as if the way people react to me is not to me but they react to the latest photograph they've seen of me. So I can change the photograph and have the fun of observing the reactions. Also the devil in me loves the idea of being just that much of a changeling. You can never understand a writer until you find his private little vanity and my private little vanity has always been that I will frustrate expectations. People think they've found a way of dismissing me, like the mad butler—but I'll be back serving the meal.

Will we spoil the best secrets of life or will we help to free a new kind of man? It's intoxicating to think of that. There's something rich waiting if one of us is brave enough and good enough to get there.

From Writers at Work, Third Series *(New York: Viking Press, 1967)*

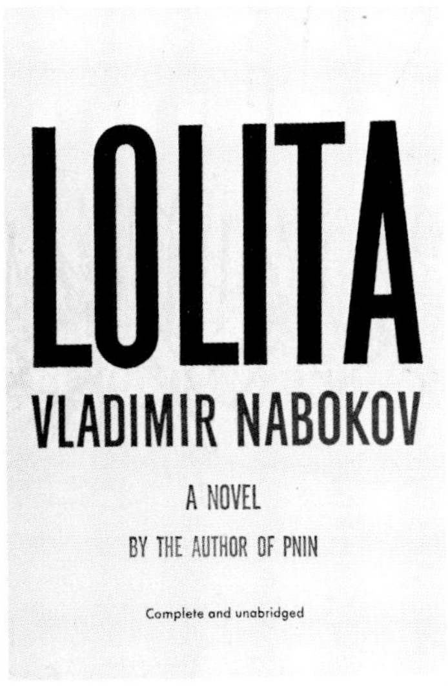

VLADIMIR NABOKOV

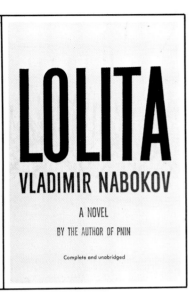

(23 April 1899-2 July 1977)

See the Vladimir Nabokov entries in the Dictionary of Literary Biography, *volume 2,* American Novelists Since World War II, *and* Yearbook: 1980.

MAJOR BOOKS:

Mashen'ka, as V. Sirin (Berlin: Slovo, 1926); translated as *Mary*, as Nabokov (New York: McGraw-Hill, 1970; London: Weidenfeld & Nicolson, 1971);

Korol', Dama, Valet, as Sirin (Berlin: Slovo, 1928); translated as *King, Queen, Knave*, as Nabokov (New York: McGraw-Hill, 1968; London: Weidenfeld & Nicolson, 1968);

Zashchita Luzhina, as Sirin (Berlin: Slovo, 1930); translated as *The Defense*, as Nabokov (New York: Putnam's, 1964; London: Weidenfeld & Nicolson, 1964);

Podvig, as Sirin (Paris: Sovremennye Zapiski, 1932); translated as *Glory*, as Nabokov (New York: McGraw-Hill, 1971; London: Weidenfeld & Nicolson, 1972);

Kamera Obskura, as Sirin (Paris: Sovremennye Zapiski, 1932); translated as *Camera Obscura*, as Vladimir Nabokoff-Sirin (London: John Long, 1935); translated again as *Laughter in the Dark*, as Nabokov (Indianapolis: Bobbs-Merrill, 1938; London: Weidenfeld & Nicolson, 1961);

Otchayanie, as Sirin (Berlin: Petropolis, 1936); translated as *Despair*, as Nabokov (London: John Long, 1937); translated again (New York: Putnam's, 1966; London: Weidenfeld & Nicolson, 1966);

Dar, as Sirin (Paris: Sovremennye Zapiski, Nos. 63-67, 1937-1938); translated as *The Gift*, as Nabokov (New York: Putnam's, 1963; London: Weidenfeld & Nicolson, 1963);

Soglyadataj, as Sirin (Paris: Russkie Zapiski, 1938)—includes novella and twelve stories;

Priglashenie na kazn', as Sirin (Paris: Dom Knigi, 1938); translated as *Invitation to a Beheading*, as Nabokov (New York: Putnam's, 1959; London: Weidenfeld & Nicolson, 1960);

The Real Life of Sebastian Knight (Norfolk, Conn.: New Directions, 1941; London: Editions Poetry, 1945);

Nikolai Gogol (Norfolk, Conn.: New Directions, 1944; London: Editions Poetry, 1947);

Bend Sinister (New York: Holt, 1947; London: Weidenfeld & Nicolson, 1960);

Nine Stories (Norfolk, Conn.: New Directions, 1947);

Conclusive Evidence (New York: Harper, 1951); republished as *Speak, Memory* (London: Gollancz, 1951; revised and enlarged edition, New York: Putnam's, 1967; London: Weidenfeld & Nicolson, 1967);

Lolita (Paris: Olympia Press, 1955; New York: Putnam's, 1958; London: Weidenfeld & Nicolson, 1959);

Pnin (Garden City: Doubleday, 1957; London: Heinemann, 1957);

Nabokov's Dozen (Garden City: Doubleday, 1958; London: Heinemann, 1959);

Poems (Garden City: Doubleday, 1959; London: Weidenfeld & Nicolson, 1961);

Pale Fire (New York: Putnam's, 1962; London: Weidenfeld & Nicolson, 1962);

Eugene Onegin, translated and annotated (Princeton, N.J.: Bollingen, 1964; London: Routledge & Kegan Paul, 1964; revised, Princeton, N.J.: Bollingen, 1975);

The Eye (New York: Phaedra, 1965; London: Weidenfeld & Nicolson, 1966);

The Waltz Invention (New York: Phaedra, 1966);

Nabokov's Quartet (New York: Phaedra, 1966; London: Weidenfeld & Nicolson, 1967);

Ada or Ardor (New York: McGraw-Hill, 1969; London: Weidenfeld & Nicolson, 1969);

Poems and Problems (New York: McGraw-Hill, 1971; London: Weidenfeld & Nicolson, 1972);

Transparent Things (New York: MacGraw-Hill, 1972; London: Weidenfeld & Nicolson, 1973);

A Russian Beauty and Other Stories (New York: McGraw-Hill, 1973; London: Weidenfeld & Nicolson, 1973);

Strong Opinions (New York: McGraw-Hill, 1973; London: Weidenfeld & Nicolson, 1974);

Look at the Harlequins! (New York: McGraw-Hill, 1974; London: Weidenfeld & Nicolson, 1975);

Tyrants Destroyed and Other Stories (New York: McGraw-Hill, 1975; London: Weidenfeld & Nicolson, 1975);

Details of a Sunset and Other Stories (New York: McGraw-Hill, 1976; London: Weidenfeld & Nicolson, 1976);

Lectures on Literature (New York & London: Harcourt Brace Jovanovich/Bruccoli Clark, 1980; London: Weidenfeld & Nicolson, 1980);

Lectures on Russian Literature (New York & London: Harcourt Brace Jovanovich/Bruccoli Clark, 1981; London: Weidenfeld & Nicolson, 1982);

Lectures on Don Quixote (San Diego, New York & London: Harcourt Brace Jovanovich/Bruccoli Clark, 1983).

BIOGRAPHY:

Andrew Field, *Nabokov: His Life in Part* (New York: Viking, 1977).

BIBLIOGRAPHIES:

Dieter Zimmer, *Vladimir Nabokov: Bibliographie des Gesamtwerks* (Hamburg: Rowohlt, 1963);

Andrew Field, *Nabokov: A Bibliography* (New York: McGraw-Hill, 1973);

Samuel Schuman, *Vladimir Nabokov: A Reference Guide* (Boston: G. K. Hall, 1979);

Stephen Jan Parker and others, "Nabokov Annual Bibliography," *The Vladimir Nabokov Research Newsletter* (Lawrence: The University of Kansas, 1979-).

LETTERS:

Simon Karlinsky, ed., *The Nabokov-Wilson Letters* (New York: Harper & Row, 1979).

LOCATION OF ARCHIVES:

The major collection of Nabokov's papers is at the Library of Congress, Washington, D.C.

Elema Ivanova Rukavishnikov and Vladimir Dimitrievich Nabokov before their marriage. Vladimir was the eldest of their five children.

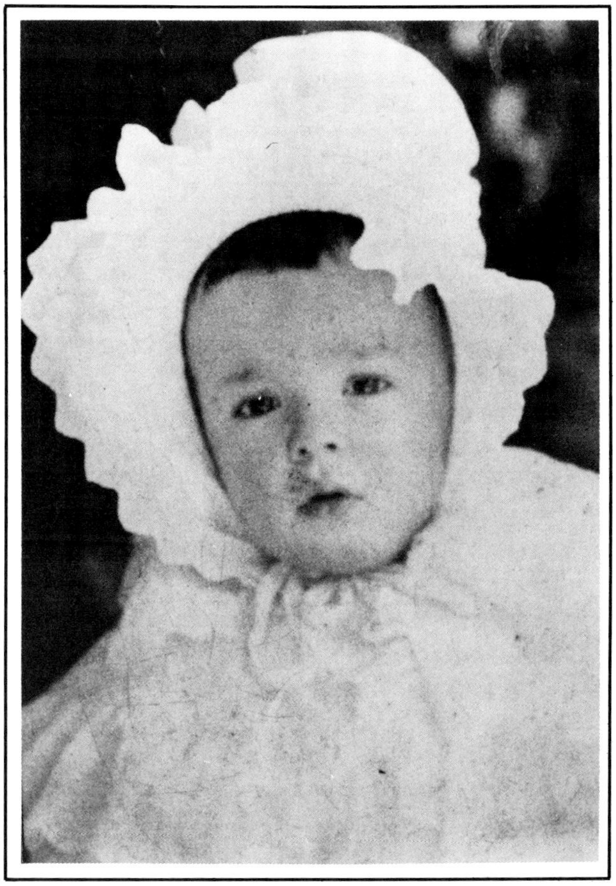

Vladimir Vladimirovich Nabokov was born 22 April 1899 in St. Petersburg (now Leningrad), Russia. He is shown above at five months old.

Nabokov learned to read English before Russian. He is shown at age seven with his brother Sergey, six. Sergey later became the model for Sebastian in The Real Life of Sebastian Knight.

Nabokov's family spent most summers at Vyra, their country estate located fifty miles south of their winter home in St. Petersburg.

Nabokov had published two books of poetry when the family left Russia in the spring of 1919, after the revolution. That fall he entered Trinity College, Cambridge, where he studied French and Russian literature. He is shown here during his Cambridge years.

On the evening of 22 March 1922 Nabokov's father, a founder of the Constitutionalist Democratic Party, which opposed Tsarist absolutism and advocated reform rather than revolution, was shot at a liberal political meeting in Berlin. The assassins had intended to kill another man. Young Nabokov published his Russian works under the name V. Sirin, feeling that his father, an editor of the Berlin Russian-language journal The Rudder, *had literary rights to the name Vladimir Nabokov.*

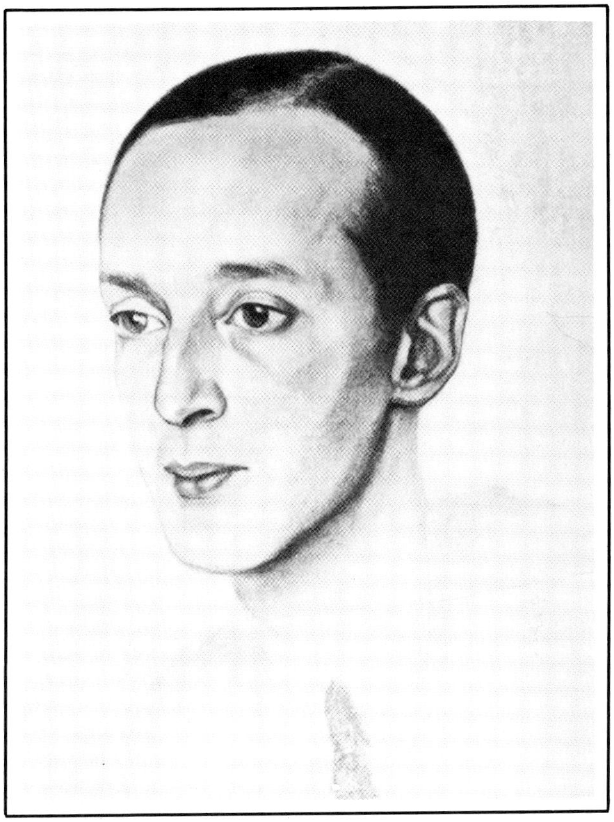

Portrait of Nabokov in 1933 by M. Nachman-Achazya

In 1923 Nabokov published two books of Russian poetry, A Cluster *and* The Empyrean Path. *At this time he was also contributing poems, reviews, chess problems, and short stories to* The Rudder. *He is shown above working on a farm at Solies-Pont, 1923.*

Nabokov married Vera Evaseevna Slonim in 1925. She took this 1929 photo of him at work on The Defense. *"Seldom does a casual snapshot compendiate a life so precisely," he later commented.*

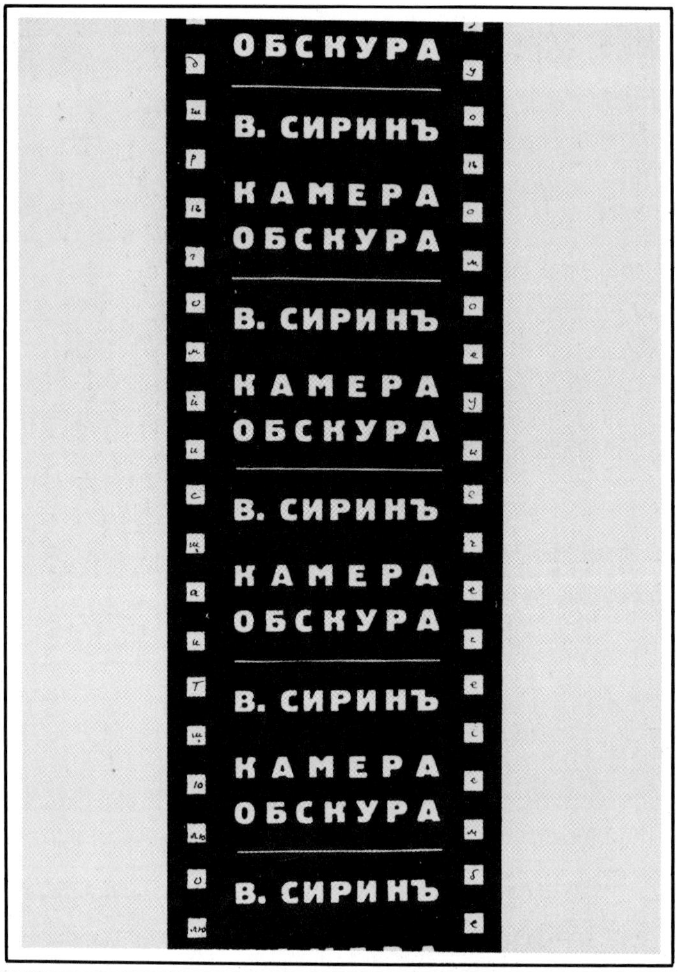

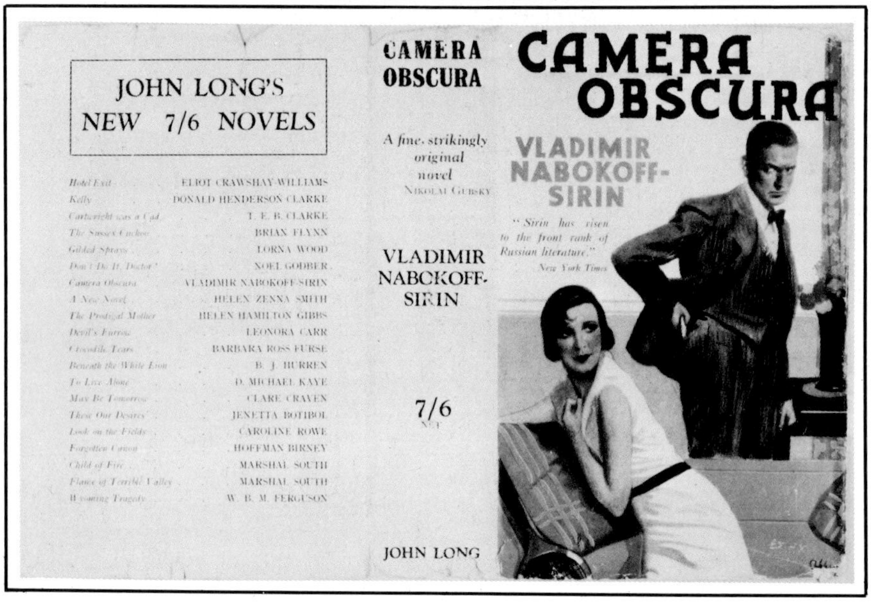

Kamera Obskura *was first published in Russian in 1932; the English translation was published in London as* Camera Obscura *in 1935.*

The Nabokovs' only child, Dmitri, was born in 1934. He is two years old in this photograph with his father.

In 1937 Nabokov left Berlin and moved to Paris, where he began to write in both French and English. Deciding that he would write in English exclusively, Nabokov came to America in 1940, leaving his Russian novel "Solus Rex" unfinished.

The Nabokovs in Salt Lake City, Utah, 1943

BOOK REVIEW:

Bernard Guilbert Guerney, "Great Grotesque," *New Republic*, 111 (25 September 1944): 376, 378.

In 1941 Nabokov began teaching at Wellesley College, where he was the Russian Department. Three years later he revised his classroom lectures on Dead Souls *and "The Overcoat" for publication in his short critical biography* Nikolai Gogol.

One fairly accurate cardiogram of just how violently the Anglo-American heart palpitates over one of Russia's supreme geniuses is furnished by the Britannica (fourteenth edition). GOGOL, NIKOLAI VASSILIEVICH, rates one column and a grudging third, a bibliography of four lines listing as many items (only one in English), and not even a cut of the man. GOLF, however, earns 18 columns (glossary, 3 columns; bibliography, one-third column; 10 line cuts and one plate of 9 halftones). And the never-to-be-praised-enough Slavonic Division of the New York Public Library lists, among hundreds of entries, in ever so many languages, under *Gogol, Works About*, five additional items written in English—all scholastic scrapiana. Gogol, in English criticism, has long since degenerated into a quintain for the professors and a whippingboy for ex-Russians who show themselves indubitably greater geniuses at engineering blood-ritual trials than at appraising literature and its creators.

It might therefore sound invidious to say that Nabokov's thoroughly mannered critical and biographical study of Gogol is the best in English—although it is precisely that.

Nabokov is a particularly rare orchid of the aerophyte Russian-literature-in-exile, and his fantasticism and exoticism received the cachet (something like fifteen years ago) from none other than the great and patriarchal Amphitheatrov. And since biography and even criticism are, for some reason, considered creative, Nabokov may be said to have created his own Gogol, adding one more to his phantasmal gallery of "strange creatures" where, in crepuscule, hang his Potato Elf, his chess-mad genius Luzhin. And one can't help feeling that he would have done as excellently with Hoffman, with Poe, with Baudelaire, with De Quincey, with St. John of the Apocalypse—save that, by choice, he would have made them all as realistic as bunion plasters.

The critic's main thesis (superbly defended) seems to be that Gogol was no realist, that he had an unreal, a looking-glass world of his own, that his catoptrics were not those of a mirror merely crooked but a mirror "of Gogol's own making and with a special refraction of its own," and that it wasn't necessarily nature he was holding it up to. If Chekhov could maintain (quite rightly) that his plays were really comedies, why shouldn't Nabokov describe "The Government Inspector" as a "dream play," "poetry-in-action," rather than a comedy? And in calling "Dead Souls" a "tremendous epic poem" he is simply adding an adjective to Gogol's own tag.

Of course, this approach will hardly create the uproar that Briussov's "He Who Has Burned Utterly into Ashes" ("Ispepelennyi") did three and a half decades ago. Rozanov also, even before Briussov, had shown that Gogol had created his own world and his own people, and to Merejkovsky Gogol was a phantast and a mystic—but then, Merejkovsky could make a Blakian tiger out of a tabbycat.

Gogol no realist? Perhaps. Yet the present writer believes (on the basis of experimentation) that "The Government Inspector," at least, would play Broadway to SRO merely by transposing the dialogue into American idiom, transferring the scene to any one of the hellholes in our own camellia-drenched, magnolia-stenchy South, and without changing the characters in any way save putting them in modern dress and trimming the *oviches* and *ovnas* into mintjulepy yet thoroughly Gogolian names. What was Huey Long save Skvoznik-Dmuhanovski, the amoral and immortal Mayor of the play?

Nabokov's brilliant causerie is concerned chiefly with "The Government Inspector," "Dead Souls" and "The Overcoat," with a kind word for only one comparatively insignificant fragment among Gogol's marvelous (in the Russian) Ukrainian stories (and a somewhat kinder nod for some of the "Arabesques"), since Gogol is to him a "false humorist." This attitude, it is very much to be feared, belongs to that dubious sophistication which in the United States expresses itself in a superior air toward the great arts of variety and the circus and poor old Longfellow, and which (at least in old Russia) was manifested in a let's-be-indulgent-about-the-humor-of-that-quaint-beggar-Chekhov. All Gogolators know of the Heresy of Kulish, who criticized the Ukrainian tales of Gogol, and there are pamphlets in Ukrainian plaintively entitled "Come, Was Gogol Really One of Us?" At any rate the reviewer, despite all the reasoned arguments, was caught utterly off his guard by certain passages given in Mr. Nabokov's own translation. And, after all, what other test of a humorist is there save his ability to make the reader (calloused or otherwise) laugh?

There are ever so many valiant gestures for which the author deserves a cluster of Distinguished Literary

Service Medals: his attempt to introduce *poshlust* (in the sense of vulgarity, philistinism) into English; his excoriation of Garnettian, Thousand-Pieces-Execution translations—so deep is his utterly correct feeling on this point that he spells Isabel Hapgood's name throughout as Hepgood; his refreshing attitude toward psychoanalysis: he doesn't exactly stick his tongue out at it, but, definitely and sensibly, keeps it in his cheek. He takes only a neat phrase or two to annihilate Gogol's very own Tsar, pulls no punches about Gogol's evil dæmon, an ignorant lout of a country priest, and shows quite objectively that when a good writer gets religion the result is inevitably bad writing.

It is therefore all the more regrettable to come upon a sour note or two. Nabokov creates every opportunity (coherent or otherwise) to flick out at the Soviets. Of course the author's anti-Sovietism (even if it be so very passé as not to be even sophisticated) has nothing to do with his book—which is precisely what makes it so very irritating. And such arbitrary pronunciamentos as that the written word has been dead in Russia for the last twenty-five years are (since Soviet literature is by no means a closed, even though a smudged, book in English) likely to prejudice the intelligent reader against better reasoned contentions where the author is fully able to maintain his ground. Then there is the overenthusiasm in implying (or seeming to imply) that his idol was somehow unique in creating what Nabokov calls peripheral, secondary, dream characters. Surely, there is a Mrs. Harris, and there are the Dream Children. And in playwriting the creative, evocative use of this exceedingly ancient device ranges from the Falstaff cycle ("And is Jane Nightwork

From 1942 until 1948 Nabokov, who had been introduced to lepidopterology by his father, was a fellow of the Museum of Comparative Zoology at Harvard, where he is shown above. Several butterflies and a moth have been named for him.

alive?"), through (good) French comedy, down to the "Toplitski Says" skits which died only with the music halls. And certain translations strike one irresistibly as an attempt to salvage exercises in that curious dead language, Anglo-English (wigging, waggish, bigwigs; little beggar, conjuror; old chap, old boy, old fellow). Everywhere else, where Mr. Nabokov has made something very like an anthology of next-to-impossible-to-English Gogolian passages, he has turned them into living Amer-English and acquitted himself nobly.

The work is, in the main, creative criticism, and as such quite often attains the caliber of "On the Knocking at the Gate in Macbeth." The author's perceptiveness is not only as keen but as bright and chill as a razor. Or (to use his own persistent figure of escamotage): Nabokov on Gogol is Dunninger eclaircissizing the *modae operandi* of Houdini. Biography is by no means scamped, but the critic handles it in his own way—fortunately. He is most fastidious in his use of anything smacking of the apocryphal or anecdotal, but there is no niggardliness as to fascinating and (occasionally) illuminating sidelights. (It is amusing to learn that Gogol was as great a facial contortionist as Morimoto.) He dismisses (quite correctly) Gogol's sex-life in a single sentence; but it is a pity that he has not devoted more than a sentence each to Gogol the actor (no one but a born actor could have written "The Inspector General"), to Gogol the draughtsman, and to that minor Ukrainian playwright but true theatromane, Gogol's father.

There is one English biography of Gogol, stoutly enough built but a slow-coach, available to the plodding student. But the creative reader (and student) who wishes to soar on Gogol's own wingéd-steed *troika* will choose Nabokov as his exhilarating courier.

LETTER:

Critic Edmund Wilson and Nabokov were close friends until they disagreed about Nabokov's four-volume translation of Pushkin's Eugene Onegin. *Their correspondence from 1940-1971 was published after Nabokov's death. Parts of this Nabokov letter appear in chapter thirteen of* Speak, Memory.

February 23, 1948

Dear Bunny,

You naively compare my (and the "old Liberals' ") attitude towards the Soviet regime (*sensu lato*) to that of a "ruined and humiliated" American Southerner towards the "wicked" North. You must know me and "Russian Liberals" very little if you fail to realize the amusement and contempt with which I regard Russian émigrés whose "hatred" of the Bolsheviks is based on a sense of financial loss or class *degringolade*. It is preposterous (though quite in line with Soviet writings on the subject) to postulate any material interest at the bottom of a Russian Liberal's (or Democrat's or Socialist's) rejection of the Soviet regime. I really must draw your attention to the fact that my position in regard to Lenin's or Stalin's regime is shared not only by Constitutional Democrats, but also by the Social[ist] Revolutionaries and various socialist groupings, and that Russian culture was built by liberal thinkers and writers which I think rather spoils your neat simile of "North and South." To spoil it completely I may add that the rather local and special difference between the North and South is much more comparable to that between first cousins, between, say, Hitlerism (Southern race prejudice) and the Soviet regime, than it is to the gap existing between fundamentally different systems of thought (totalitarianism and liberalism).

Incidental but very important: the term "intelligentsia" as used in America (for instance, by Rahv in *The Partisan* [*Review*]) is not used in the same sense as it was used in Russia. Intelligentsia is curiously restricted here to avant-garde writers and artists. In old Russia it also included doctors, lawyers, scientists, etc., as well as people belonging to any class or profession. In fact a typical Russian *intelligent* would look askance at an avant-garde poet. The main features of the Russian intelligentsia (from Belinsky to Bunakov) were: the spirit of self-sacrifice, intense participation in political causes or political thought, intense sympathy for the underdog of any nationality, fanatical integrity, tragic inability to sink to compromise, true spirit of international responsibility . . . But of course people who read Trotsky for information anent Russian culture cannot be expected to know all this. I have also a hunch that the general idea that avant-garde literature and art were having a wonderful time under Lenin and Trotsky is mainly due to Eisenstadt films—"montage"—things like that—and great big drops of sweat rolling down rough cheeks. The fact that pre-Revolution Futurists joined the party has also contributed to the kind of (quite false) avant-garde atmosphere which the American intellectual associates with the Bolshevik Revolution.

I do not want to be personal, but here is how I explain your attitude: in the ardent period of life you and other American intellectuals of the twenties regarded with enthusiasm and sympathy Lenin's regime which seemed to you from afar an exciting fulfillment of your progressive dreams. Quite possibly, had the position been reversed, Russian avant-garde young writers (living, say, in an Americoid Russia) would have regarded the burning of the White House with similar enthusiasm and sympathy. Your concept of pre-Soviet Russia, of her history and social development came to you through a pro-Soviet prism. When later on (i.e., at a time coinciding with Stalin's ascension) improved information, a more mature judgment and the pressure of inescapable facts dampened your enthusiasm and dried your sympathy, you somehow did not bother to check your preconceived notions in regard to old Russia while, on the other hand, the glamor of Lenin's reign retained for you the emotional iridescence which your optimism, idealism and youth had provided. What you now see as a change for the worse ("Stalinism") in the regime is really a change for the better in knowledge on your part. The thunderclap of administrative purges woke you up (something that the

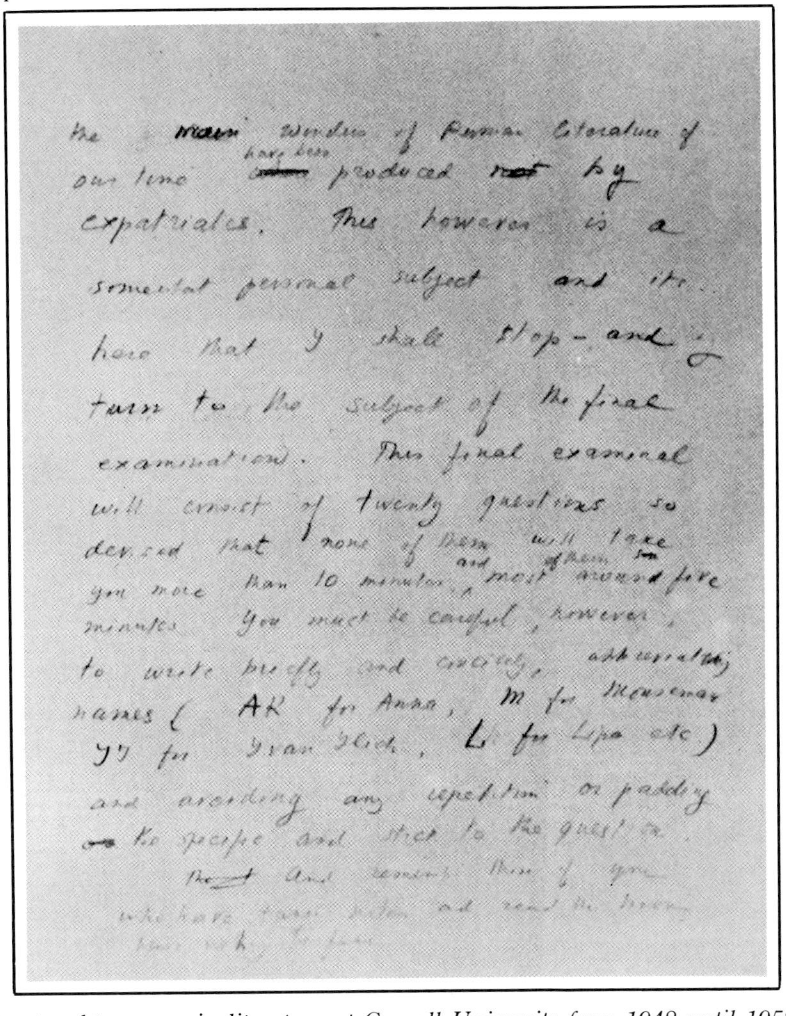
the main wonders of Russian literature of
our time have been produced ~~not~~ by
expatriates. This however is a
somewhat personal subject and it is
here that I shall stop — and
turn to the subject of the final
examination. This final examination
will consist of twenty questions so
devised that none of them will take
you more than 10 minutes, and most of them around five
minutes. You must be careful, however,
to write briefly and concisely, abbreviating
names (AK for Anna, M for Monsieur
II for Ivan Ilich, L for Lipa etc)
and avoiding any repetition or padding
Be specific and stick to the question.
And remember those of you

Nabokov taught courses in literature at Cornell University from 1948 until 1958. "My method of teaching precluded genuine contact with the students," he later said. "At best, they regurgitated a few bits of my brain during examinations. . . . Vainly I tried to replace my appearances at the lectern by taped records to be played over the college radio. On the other hand, I deeply enjoyed the chuckle of appreciation in this or that warm spot of the lecture hall at this or that point of my lecture. My best reward comes from those former students of mine who ten or fifteen years later write to me to say that they now understand what I wanted of them when I taught them to visualize Emma Bovary's mistranslated hairdo or the arrangement of rooms in the Samsa household. . . ." Above are his lecture notes explaining one of his final exams (Nabokov papers).

moans in Solovki or at the Lubianka had not been able to do) since they affected men on whose shoulders St. Lenin's hand had lain. You (or Dos Passos, or Rahv) will mention with horror the names of Ezhov and Yagoda—but what about Uritsky and Dzerzhinsky?

I am now going to state a few things which I think are true and which I don't think you can refute. Under the Tsars (despite the inept and barbarous character of their rule) a freedom-loving Russian had incomparably more possibility and means of expressing himself than at any time during Lenin's and Stalin's regime. He was protected by law. There were fearless and independent judges in Russia. The Russian *sud* after the Alexander reforms was a magnificent institution, not only on paper. Periodicals of various tendencies and political parties of all possible kinds, legally or illegally, flourished and all parties were represented in the Dumas. Public opinion was always liberal and progressive.

Under the Soviets, from the very start, the only protection a dissenter could hope for was dependent on governmental whims, not laws. No parties except the one in power could exist. Your Alymovs are specters bobbing in the wake of a foreign tourist. Bureaucracy, a direct descendant of party discipline, took over immediately. Public opinion disintegrated. The intelligentsia ceased to exist. Any changes that took place between November 1919 and now have been changes in the decor which more or less screens an unchanging black abyss of oppression and terror.

I think I shall eventually polish this letter and publish it somewhere.

Yours,
V

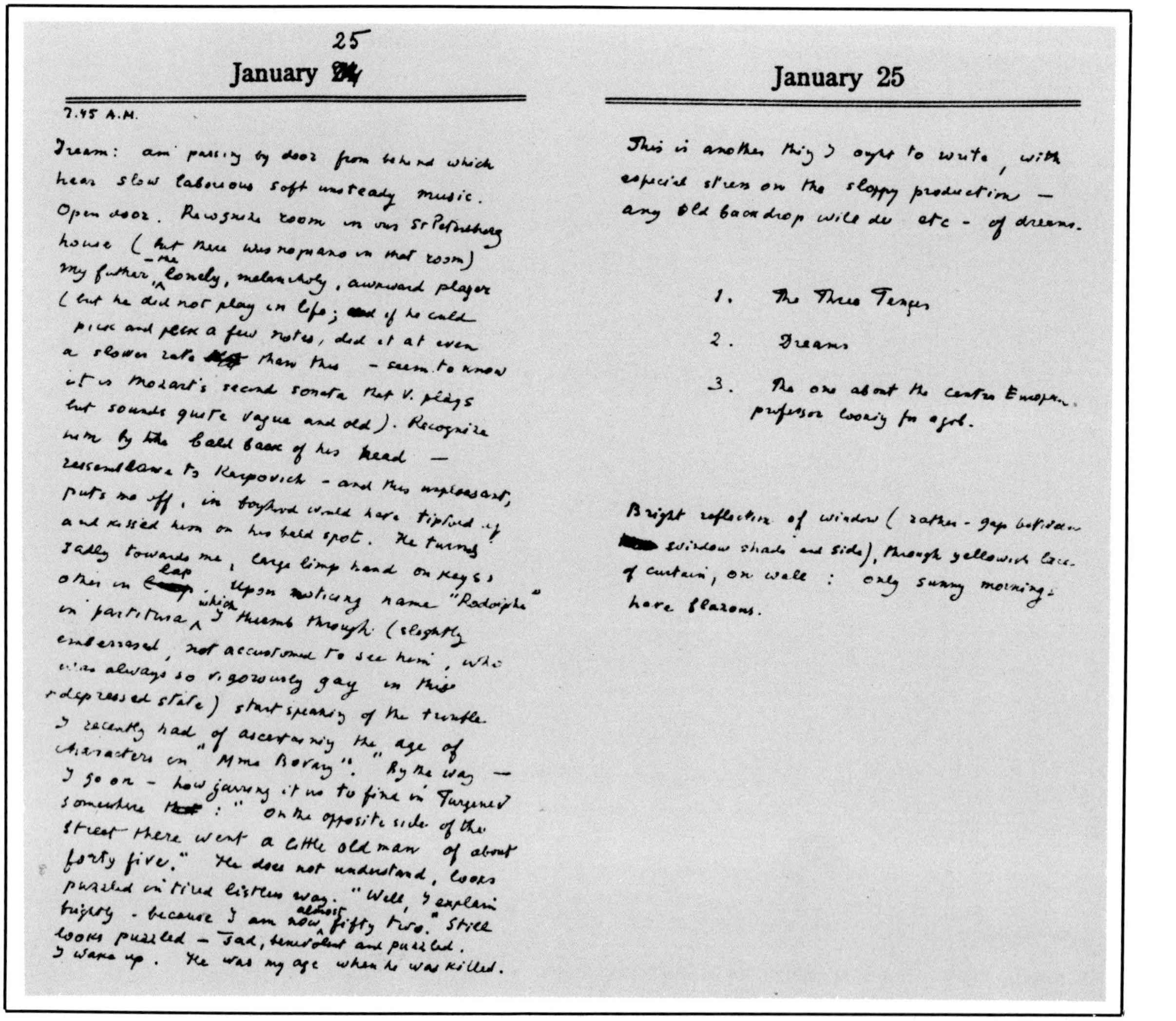

25
January ~~24~~

7.45 A.M.

Dream: am passing by door from behind which hear slow laborious soft unsteady music. Open door. Recognize room in our St Petersburg house (but there was no piano in that room) my father, the lonely, melancholy, awkward player (but he did not play in life; if he could pick and peck a few notes, did it at even a slower rate than this — seem to know it is Mozart's second sonata that V. plays but sounds quite vague and old). Recognize him by the bald back of his head — resemblance to Karpovich — and this unpleasant, puts me off, in boyhood would have tiptoed up and kissed him on his bald spot. He turns sadly towards me, large limp hand on keys, other in lap. Upon noticing name "Rodolphe" in partitura which I thumb through (slightly embarrassed, not accustomed to see him, who was always so vigorously gay in this depressed state) start speaking of the trouble I recently had of ascertaining the age of characters in "Mme Bovary". "By the way — I go on — how jarring it was to find in Turgenev somewhere: "On the opposite side of the street there went a little old man of about forty five." He does not understand, looks puzzled in tired listless way. "Well, I explain brightly - because I am now almost fifty two." Still looks puzzled — sad, benevolent and puzzled. I wake up. He was my age when he was killed.

January 25

This is another thing I ought to write, with especial stress on the sloppy production — any old backdrop will do etc — of dreams.

1. The Three Tenses
2. Dreams
3. The one about the Central European professor looking for a girl.

Bright reflection of window (rather - gap between window shade and side), through yellowish lace of curtain, on wall: only sunny mornings here blazons.

Nabokov's notes on dreams from a 1951 notebook (Nabokov papers)

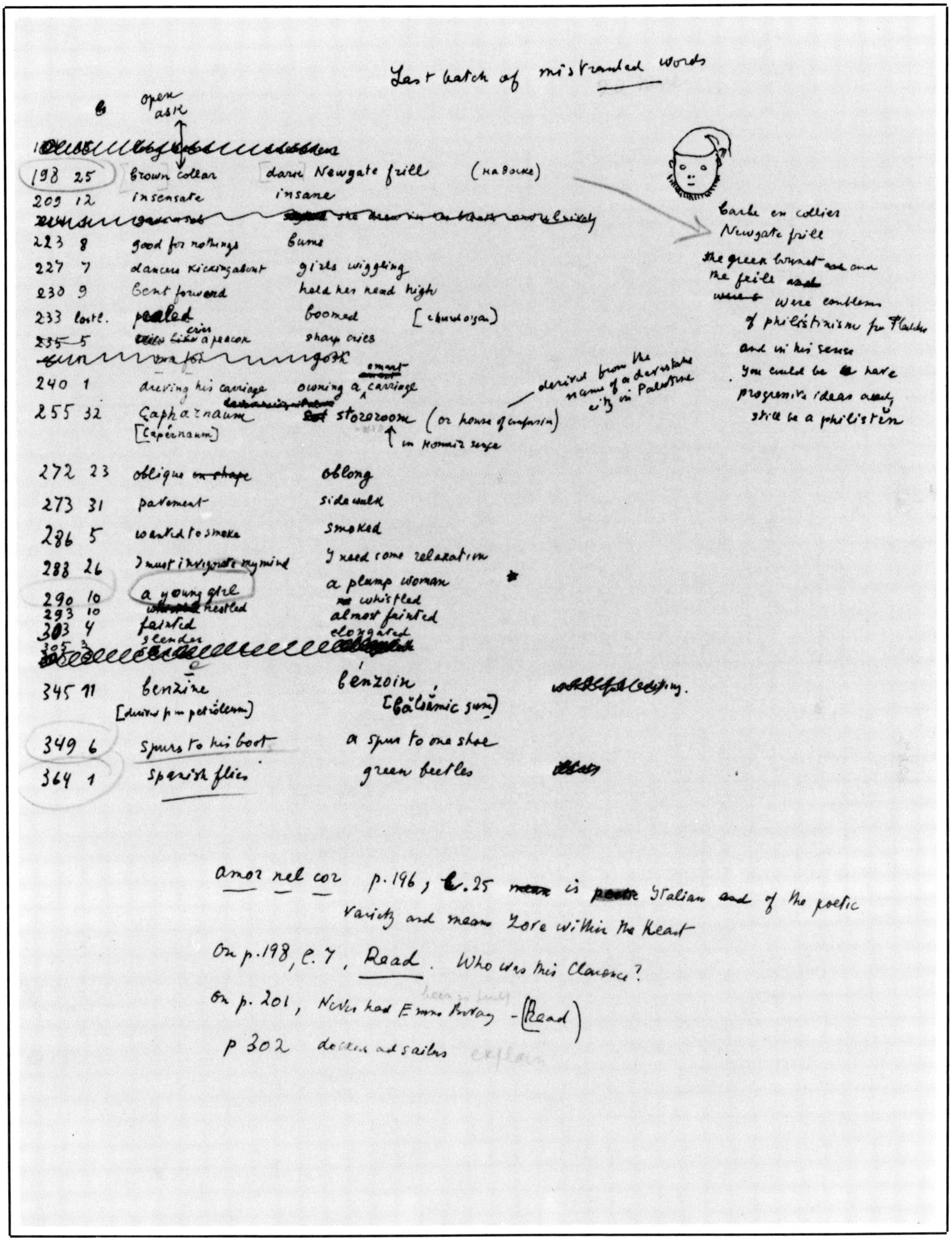

Last batch of mistranslated words

open
ask

198 25 brown collar — dark Newgate frill (набоике)
209 12 insensate — insane
223 8 good for nothings — bums
227 7 dancers kicking about — girls wiggling
230 9 bent forward — held her head high
233 last. pealed — boomed [chorus]
~~235 5~~ cries like a peacock — sharp cries
240 1 driving his carriage — owning a carriage
255 32 Capharnaum [Capernaum] — storeroom (or house of confusion) ↑ in Homais sense — derived from the name of a devastated city in Palestine
272 23 oblique ~~in shape~~ — oblong
273 31 pavement — sidewalk
286 5 wanted to smoke — smoked
288 26 I must invigorate my mind — I need some relaxation
290 10 a young girl — a plump woman
293 10 nestled — whistled
303 4 fainted — almost fainted
305 3 slender — elongated
345 11 benzine [derived from petroleum] — benzoin [balsamic gum]
349 6 spurs to his boot — a spur to one shoe
364 1 spanish flies — green beetles

barbe en collier
Newgate frill
the green bonnet and the frill were emblems of philistinism for Flaubert and in his sense you could be & have progressive ideas and still be a philistine

amor nel cor p. 196, l. 25 is Italian of the poetic variety and means Love within the Heart
On p. 198, l. 7, Read. Who was this Clarence?
On p. 201, Never had Emma Bovary [been so lovely] – (Read)
p 302 doctors and sailors explain

Above is a list of mistranslated words Nabokov discovered in the Eleanor Marx Aveling translation of Madame Bovary, *of which he disapproved. Nabokov taught Flaubert's novel in his survey course at Cornell University on English and continental literature.*

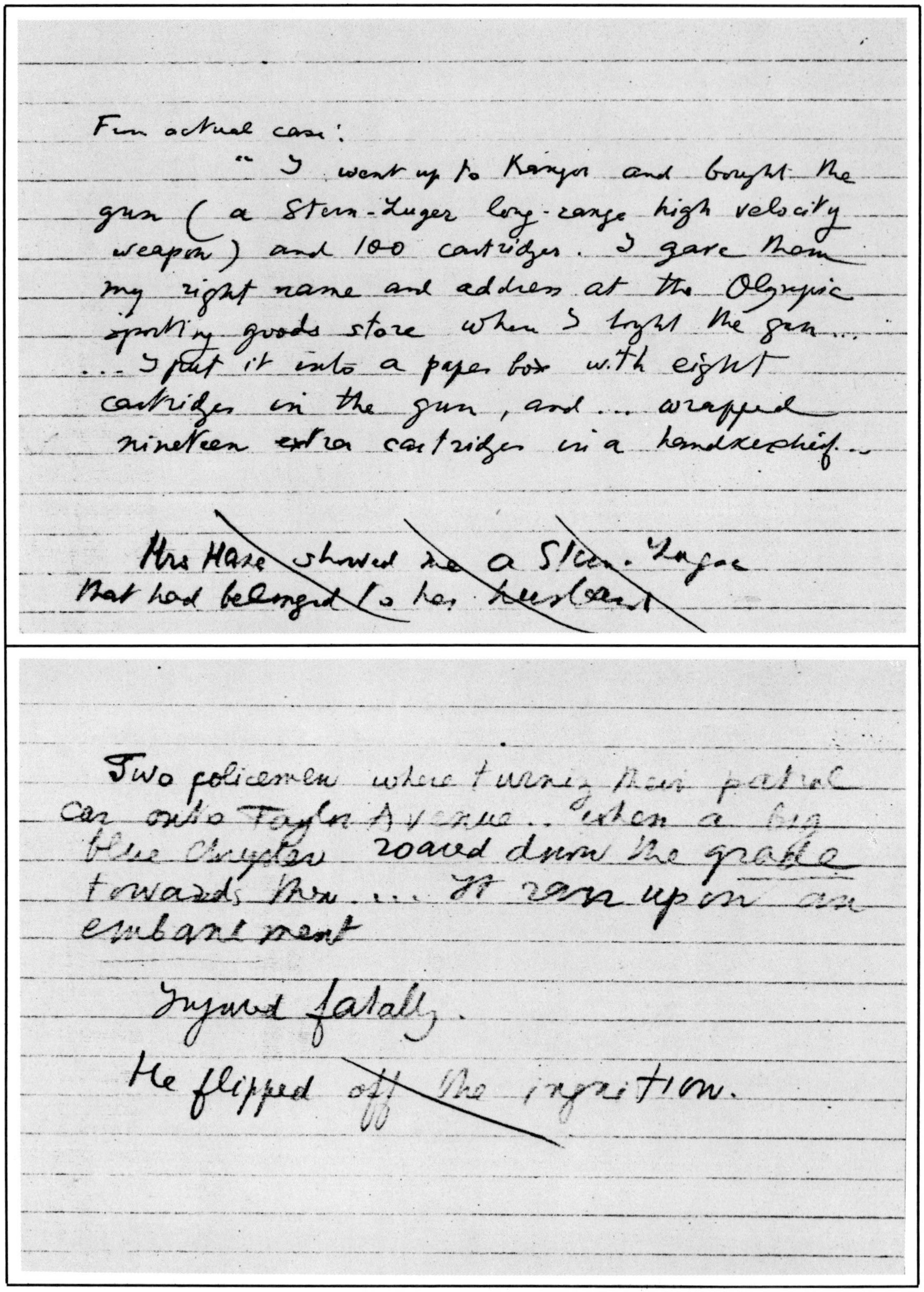

From actual case:
" I went up to Kenyon and bought the gun (a Stern-Luger long-range high velocity weapon) and 100 cartridges. I gave them my right name and address at the Olympic sporting goods store when I bought the gun...
... I put it into a paper box with eight cartridges in the gun, and ... wrapped nineteen extra cartridges in a handkerchief..

~~Mrs Haze showed me a Stern-Luger that had belonged to her husband~~

Two policemen where turning their patrol car onto Taylor Avenue.. when a big blue Chrysler roared down the grade towards them ... It ran upon an embankment

Injured fatally.

He flipped off ~~the ignition.~~

Nabokov wrote on index cards so that he could easily rearrange as he worked. These three cards are notes for Nabokov's 1955 novel, Lolita *(Library of Congress). Unable to find an American publisher, Nabokov had his book published in English by the Olympia Press of*

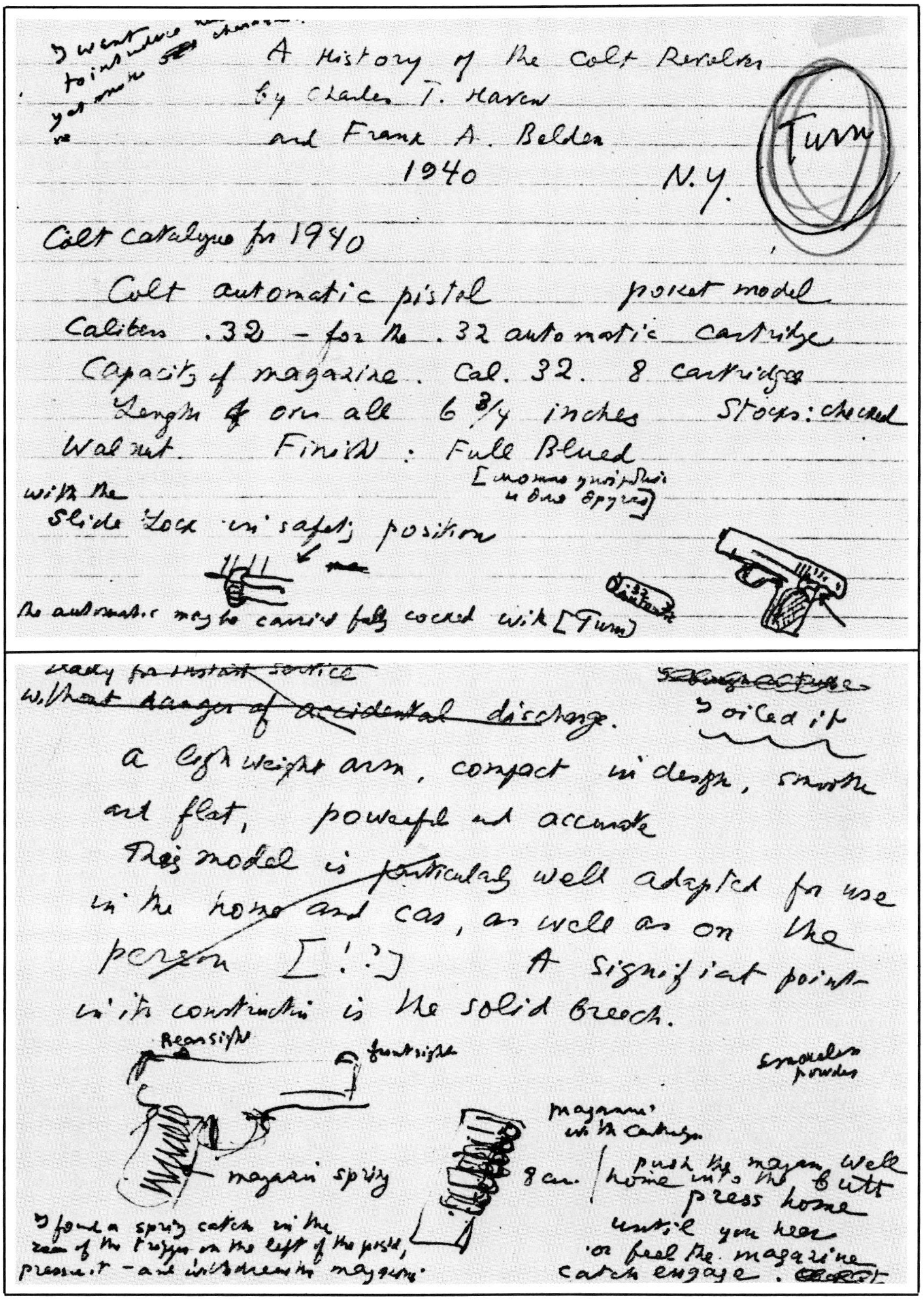

A History of the Colt Revolver
by Charles T. Haven
and Frank A. Belden
1940 N.Y.
Turn

Colt catalogue for 1940

Colt automatic pistol pocket model
Calibers .32 – for the .32 automatic cartridge
Capacity of magazine. Cal. 32. 8 cartridges
Length of over all 6 3/4 inches Stocks: checked
Walnut. Finish: Full Blued
with the
Slide Lock in safety position
The automatic may be carried fully cocked with [Turn]

ready for instant service
without danger of accidental discharge.
I oiled it

a light weight arm, compact in design, smooth and flat, powerful and accurate
This model is particularly well adapted for use in the home and car, as well as on the person [!?] A significant point in its construction is the solid breech.

Paris—known particularly for pornography. Lolita *quickly became an underground classic; but it was three years before it appeared in America, where it became a best-seller.*

BOOK REVIEW:

Conrad Brenner, "Nabokov: The Art of the Perverse," *New Republic*, 138 (23 June 1958): 18-21.

The impending publication of Lolita *in America generated interest in Nabokov's little-known earlier work and brought about attempts to define the nature of his genius.*

Vladimir Nabokov is best known, if he is known at all, as one of those ghostly heroes on the out-of-print register, fondly perpetuated by a mute coterie. It is quite in order, this soft pedal. Nabokov has at least two things going against him in this life which later on will make him the foremost retread of the day. He is wildly and liquidly sophisticated, and he writes as well as any man alive.

With the publication of *Lolita* (1955) by a wayward English press in Paris, some fresh irony was laid on the idyll of Nabokov's literary reputation. Irony of a high order, very much up to the level of its victim. Nabokov, who is now an American citizen, could not get his masterpiece printed here. *Lolita* was eventually brought out by the Olympia Press, tucked away in one of those *touriste* paper-bound series amid titles of dubious erotica.

Misunderstanding has come full circle as life imitates art. *Lolita* does not belong in trick luggage, but ideally, on every doorstep. If it is a "special" and "perverse" experience, if a taste for Nabokov is a special taste, there is nothing self-indulgent or peripheral about the book or its author. Nabokov is not special in the manner of a Henry James, a Virginia Woolf, or of any bad-boy writer of your acquaintance: his vision is neither parochial nor fragile, but entirely and transcendently private.

At his casual second-best, as in the recent *Pnin*, and indeed at all times, part of the impression Nabokov makes is that of the brilliant professional weaving his formula. For this reason, and his apparent feat of never laying an egg in-between creative waves, high praise should, I think, be rightly suspect. We live in an age which is largely content to assimilate the whole untidy house of its brackish avant-garde *and* its abundant professionalism (Scylla and Charybdis in the bookshops); loosely appraising, cataloging, leaving to posterity. Nabokov is both prodigiously off-beat and competent, but the more his art lends itself to one taxonomer or another, the more it transcends this quaint fury. The trouble is that the Nabokov formula (or the familiar props of a formula) keeps slipping away from the avid fingers; the conjuror has done it again. In pursuing this "formula," moreover, Nabokov is dedicated to the destruction of all other formulas meeting with his censure. Part of his mission consists in forcing the hand, not of the obviously fraudulent in literature, but of certain "serious" literary techniques and the attitudes which spawn them. To this end, he is a man of somewhat rigid but studied predispositions:

> The truth is that the play [*The Government Inspector*] is not a "comedy" at all, just as Shakespeare's dreamplays *Hamlet* or *Lear* cannot be called "tragedies." A bad play is more apt to be good comedy or good tragedy than the incredibly complicated creations of such men as Shakespeare or Gogol. . . . Gogol's play is poetry in action, and by poetry I mean the mysteries of the irrational as perceived through rational words. True poetry of that kind provokes—not laughter and not tears—but a radiant smile of perfect satisfaction, a purr of beatitude. . . . It [Gogol's style] gives one the sensation of something ludicrous and at the same time stellar, lurking constantly around the corner—and one likes to recall that the difference between the comic side of things, and their cosmic side, depends upon one sibilant. . . .

In describing Gogol's vision of St. Petersburg, Nabokov suggests his own circle of grotesquerie:

> . . . A reflection in a blurred mirror, an eerie medley of objects put to the wrong use, things going backwards the faster they moved forward, pale gray nights instead of ordinary black ones, and black days. . . . The door of a private house might open and a pig might come out—just like that. A man gets into a carriage, but he is not really a fat, sly, big-bottomed man—but your Nose. . . .

Nabokov fuses with Gogol for a while, like Dostoevsky, and then goes off, utterly himself in still a third way. There are no stray pigs or disembodied noses; what was in Gogol a poetic mural becomes a tight shadow-play. The satire, as of all great satirists, behaves in the same way—always lapped, negating its own utility, destroying itself, stepping beyond.

Nabokov's humor, though, is indescribably original:

> Uncle alone in the house with the children said he'd dress up to amuse them. After a long wait, as he did not appear, they went down and saw a masked man putting the table silver into a bag. "Oh uncle," they cried in delight. "Yes, isn't my make-up good?" said Uncle, taking his mask off. Thus goes the Hegelian syllogism of humor. Thesis: Uncle made himself up as a burglar (a laugh for the children);

> antithesis: it *was* a burglar (a laugh for the reader); synthesis: it still was Uncle (fooling the reader). . . .

None of the dazzling trickery is practiced for its own sake, but always as the key to individual scenes or the seminal conflict. Humor becomes a swathe blighting all those falsely heavy approaches to life and literature, disclosing by the way its own irresistible angles. The strength of Nabokov lies in the check (and balance) of the sinister obbligato.

Nabokov's figures teeter on the edge of the void, take one grotesque step, and blunder their way to the bottom. They are neither Stavrogins, men without qualities, men of action fighting death with destiny, nor simple victims of assorted "forces." In their own place, they aspire and fall on the strings of a vision profoundly matured rather than obsessed. Still, there is no lack of demons; they are there, convulsed, jerking those strings.

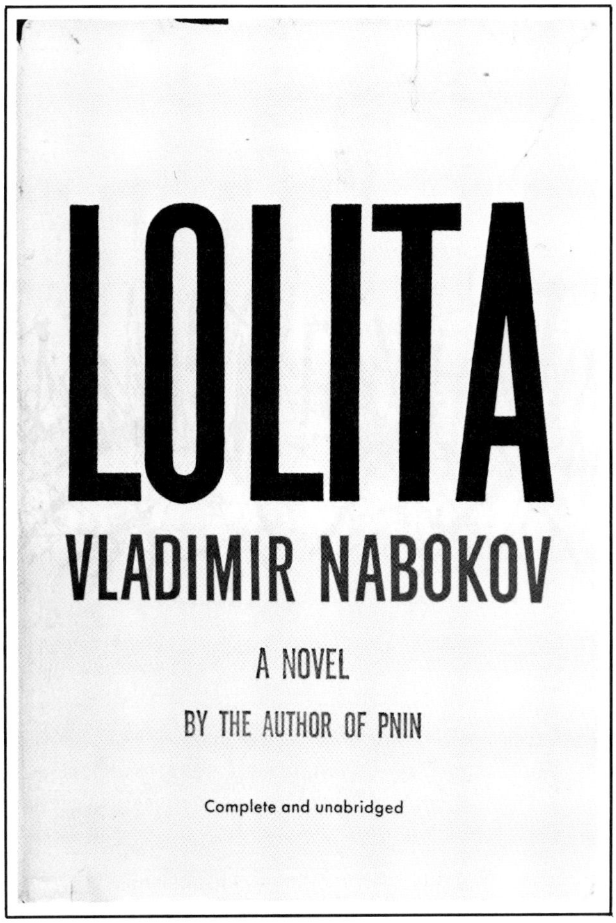

When Lolita *became a best-seller, Nabokov was able to give up teaching and devote all his energy to writing. He remarked, "I never imagined that I should be able to live by my writing, but now I am kept by a little girl named Lolita."*

Nabokov's pattern of limbo, search, disguise and discord is played in a variety of keys. The haunting short story, "That in Aleppo Once . . . ," puts his art to a very lyrical light. The narrator is a middle-aged Russian poet bolting France as the Germans come through. He marries hastily, and, it is hinted, a little desperately:

> It was love at first touch rather than at first sight, for I had met her several times before without experiencing any special emotions; but one night as I was seeing her home, something quaint she had said made me stoop with a laugh and lightly kiss her in the hair—and of course we all know of that blinding blast which is caused by merely picking up a small doll from the floor of a carefully abandoned house: the soldier involved hears nothing; for him it is but an ecstatic soundless and boundless expansion of what had been during his life a pinpoint of light in the dark center of his being.

The girl is young, and a little strange. In the south, on their way to Nice, they get separated, and a week later, after futile inquiries, he finds her there in a queue. She gives him first an innocent account of her movements, but later on amends it; she had lied to him, had stayed several nights in Montpellier with a man she met on the train. ("I did not want it at all. He sold hair lotions.") There follows a period of reciprocal torture as they fill out forms and wait for papers. One night she takes it all back: "You will think me crazy . . . but I didn't—I swear that I didn't. Perhaps I live several lives at once. Perhaps I wanted to test you. Perhaps this bench is a dream and we are in Saratov or on some star." He settles for the original story, morosely, and later they make it up.

On the day the visas and passage materialize, she disappears. He again makes inquiries, and discovers from one of the Russian families in Nice that she had been telling this story for weeks: she had fallen in love with a titled Frenchman, he had refused her a divorce and threatened to shoot both her and himself rather than sail to New York alone. It turns out that he has also hung in Paris a dog which they never had, and that she has gone to a chateau in Lozere with the mysterious young noble. The narrator gives it up and sails alone. On the fourth day out he is asked by a friend whether his wife might not be sick below, and he replies that he is alone. The man is taken aback: he had seen her in Marseilles, aimlessly walking along the embankment, two days before sailing. The narrator concludes:

> This is, I gather, the point of the whole story. . . . It was at that moment that I suddenly knew for certain that she had never existed at all. . . . Viewing the past graphically, I see our mangled romance engulfed in a deep valley of mist between the crags of two matter-of-fact mountains: life had been real before, life will be real from now on, I hope. Not tomorrow, though. Perhaps after tomorrow. . . . Yet the pity of it. . . . She keeps on walking to and fro where the brown nets are spread to dry on the hot stone slabs and the dappled light of the water plays on the side of a moored fishing boat. Somewhere, somehow, I have made a fatal mistake. . . .

That fatal mistake, these grotesque combinations of last-ditch defiance, these incredible errors and impossible results are Nabokov's stock-in-trade, and the very perverse angles of his relentless close-up. The narrator of this comedy of errors is more fortunate than most of Nabokov's questers; for him there is a visible crag in the future after all. Nonetheless, the story is quietly characteristic; the deep (and growing) unreality of human communion is sparely etched, and the only element of the novels tangibly missing is the presence of the exploiter, the smooth third party.

Perverse. Of all the words one should employ to tag Nabokov's art, this now seems to me by far the most accurate. *Lolita* has been called perverse because of the sacred ground it so blackly disrupts, and hence embargoed. But no one ought to be surprised. Nabokov has put in a working lifetime toward the cultivation of fruitful perversity, and it is probably this which gives him his great distinction as a conjuror and sets him apart from anyone. For the most "perverse" novel you are ever likely to encounter, there is nothing, not even *Lolita*, to equal *The Real Life of Sebastian Knight* (still, I think, in print). This book is quite openly a literary trick, astounding in the sleek deceitful contours, but you will be much mistaken to dismiss it as an exercise in ambiguity. Nabokov does not usually trade on this kind of straight ambiguity, so to speak, but in *Sebastian Knight*, it is an essential part of what he is trying to get across. At this point, I can only genuflect in the meek hope that he *has* come across, that I have got it "right" (and incidentally, that I do not take away too much from some tardy reader's delight).

The clue is the word *Real* in the title. An expatriate Russian novelist, writing in English, dies an early death in relative obscurity—of an incurable heart disease, we learn later. His life, a more or less continental one, with England for a base, his *story*, his *secret*, is shrouded in hermitic mist. His brother, who has not seen him more than twice since their divided college years, undertakes to seek out everyone who knew Sebastian, with the purpose of writing a conscientious biography (thus finally to come to know his brother)—and this book is, in fact, *The Real Life of Sebastian Knight*. The narrator is vaguely the business representative of a Paris firm, and he regards the small body of work published by his brother as the stuff of genius. These books are described in some detail through *Sebastian Knight*; they strike us—and this is an immense tribute to the fine line of Nabokov's craft—as both intriguing and somewhat precious. Ambiguity exhibit A. Another book has been published dealing with the dead author, a sort of bastard biography and critique by a literary opportunist who had been Knight's secretary. This book took the view that Knight was second-rate and what is known as a syptomatic product of his times, led astray. The narrator of *The Real Life* wishes to squash this fraud, and to that end visits (or does not visit), questions (or never gets to question) the false biographer himself, an Oxford friend of Sebastian's, his docile English mistress, and several others. Coincidences and chance meetings occur along the way (the "way" being the prelude to a biography, the brother's search), as they always and centrally do in Nabokov, until the book ends as the narrator, in still further retrospect, hurries to the deathbed of Sebastian himself with the hope of snatching something vital from his last words, and takes away instead the memory of one of those colossally edifying mix-ups which Nabokov so lovingly prepares. *Sebastian Knight* ends with the brother musing that perhaps he was Sebastian, or that Sebastian was he, or that both of them were somebody unknown to either of them.

These are the bones, but what of the points? They are viny. As the novel progresses, we become aware that Sebastian is less and less "known"; at the conclusion we are further than ever from even imagining him, his soul, his destiny. Both the man and the work are to remain an inaccessible proposition. We seem to learn more about the narrator, his brother's shadow—indeed the book appears to be really *his* book. But this notion is dispelled by the deliberate ambiguity of his (and Nabokov's) reflections in the final pages. The balance is so fine you could scream. We learn things about both men, and about each subsidiary character, yet we come away with less than nothing. A literary trick, yes, but it is impossible to show how convincingly this trick has been bolstered by Nabokov's visionary flare for the assorted mishaps which parody human soul-searching and soul-vamping. Discredited forever are the idea of the definitive biography; the revelatory Jamesian literature which little by little discloses the kernel or "essence" of a character; the secret-self view of life which that, and more notorious literatures, uphold; the attitude and literature of the Quest, in general.

Nabokov has been accused of writing masterpieces before, but *Lolita* is not that easy to brush off. For one thing, it is not bullet-proof like *Sebastian Knight*; it runs to excess and occasionally loses pitch (not necessarily a fault). Its prose is flamboyant, free, liberated; conceived in joy. It is a triangle—Nabokov's favorite scheme—to end all triangles, a work clearly foreshadowed in the body of his prose, and the high water mark of his career as *agent provocateur*. From the strategy of *Laughter in the Dark* (1938) to the inspiration of *Lolita* from minor to major key, the metamorphosis transpires.

Laughter in the Dark is a quietly brilliant novel. As to its themes, it does not really admit of this sort of approach; instead, what we get is almost purely a paradigm of one man's art, Nabokov's calling card. The first words announce his intention:

> Once upon a time there lived in Berlin, Germany, a man called Albinus. He was rich, respectable, happy; one day he abandoned his wife for the sake of a youthful mistress; he loved; was not loved; and his life ended in disaster. This is the whole of the story and we might have left it at that had there not been profit and pleasure in the telling; and although there is plenty of space on a gravestone to contain, bound to moss, the abridged version of a man's life, detail is always welcome.

In other words, a familiar and much-abused situation in literature will be taken up, and the author will show us how it ought to be done ("in the telling"), thereby pointing up for all time how it should not be done. (Before you can read Nabokov, you must put in a certain amount of spadework elsewhere). Of course, the situation itself seems to have been invented solely for Nabokov's patent; from right to left: the innocent bourgeois with his furtive dreams, the sleek trashy siren of sixteen summers, the unscrupulous rival. One against one, then one against two, and so on to infinity—the literature of downfall. The fatal flaw, nemesis, the rush of wings? Nabokov isn't buying any.

Laughter in the Dark applies the kiss of death to these: tragic pomp; abstract fatalism; mysterious forces; grave-faced determinism, and that provincial psychology which goes about meticulously evolving doom—a meager substitute for the true psychology which knows what doom is like and takes it from there. The protagonist of *Laughter in the Dark* is no grim victim, but a supreme fool and bungler. He is guilty of quitting his own demesne to trespass on another, leaving his pasture for a cesspool he cannot and dare not even begin to survey. Like all figures in the entire literature of decay, he is his own best goose. At his ruin, he is so far from being an object of pity or tragedy or human slime as to be raised to the highest perch of mockery. Both he and the melodramatic fixtures which always attend these sorry binges, are fried in hideous laughter. If he and his melodrama exist—and they do—Nabokov's version may be the only one to take seriously.

This brings up to *Lolita* and shapes of a more ominous order. The changeover is so complete that we are now in a world which positively defies the existence of types in its foreground.

In *Lolita*, Albinus has become Humbert, dilettante, rarefier, grotesquely aware of his bondage. He has vaulted so headlong from a season in limbo as to be the inventor and high priest of "nymphetry." A nymphet is no longer one at 16, like Margot in *Laughter in the Dark*. She must be something along the lines of Dolores Haze (Lolita is Humbert's drooling secret alias), vulgar, pubescent, first possessed at the age of twelve. And as though this coupling were not sufficiently perverse, the adored rival, still cruel, still worldly, still adored, now wears an impossible mask: aging, bloated, impotent—a veteran *fumiste* of vice. It is an old company gone sour, turned incontinently upside-down; inverting the process Dostoevsky thought of as taking things to their extremes, and then a step further. In *Lolita*, we get a vision of fragile little girls who are not really fragile, over-literary perverts who lack a final core of obsession, jaded dabbling exploiters who lurk about as resident parties of the third part.

Lolita brings us profoundly, rudely up-to-date: the surest sign that we have to hand a great novel. The conscience behind it is supremely public, supremely "topical," and the art of it supremely lonely, special. Revealed once more is the terrain proper to high fiction, that most totally distilled of forums. What has been renewed is nothing less than what Malraux would call the colloquy of the masters. (This is no idle phrase, in any case). Nabokov again takes the strands of an amazing number of traditions, gives them a new dimension or raps their importunate knuckles, by turns. That ultimate offense of Russian, and some European fiction—the horror of demon rape—is played out in a strange vacuum. So is the theme of revenge (murder will out). A new and chilling note is given to the literature of tragic waste. An advance is made on the old quest for reality, and the modern escape from reality. (What do you do with a world where every reality is rehearsed, abstracted, weirdly performed?) The need for glamor is refined endlessly, and ends in perversion. The vicious ring of the misfits, compulsively gravitating to and destroying one another, finds expression in a new bathos. Finally, life in America (*Lolita* is also an *American* novel) is drawn as some mad game, or daisy chain, and the poison is shown to be eating at the roots.

Among the ideas up for straight parody are the pursuit of happiness, the ultimate pill of the case-history, Freudian short-cuts in general, *and* the reverend literature of pornography. All these strands are gathered up in the one inspired conception, fused, and beamed obliquely, in Nabokov's demonic laughter, the better to fix that once-removed quality of life which seems to be our birthright. What *shall* we do with the drunken sailor, the recalcitrant byproduct, the uniquely masked, the violated who survive, the desperate clowns who go down in the search for a plausible *idée fixe*? What if we find, even in ourselves, the act dislodged from the passion, the act as some grotesque necessity, the mind as a neutral audience to the action, the action dissolving in a flow of analysis? For Lolita, the child, life is already the crazy game Humbert the pervert vainly seeks to out-maneuver.

Thus, the art of the perverse ultimately lashes everyone in its wake, and the highest farce tells the darkest tale. Yet who will publish it today, and who will put it on the syllabus tomorrow? alongside *Huckleberry Finn*, perhaps?

Vladimir Nabokov is an artist of the first rank, a writer in the great tradition. He will never win the Pulitzer Prize or the Nobel Prize, yet *Lolita* is probably the best fiction to come out of this country (so to speak) since Faulkner's burst in the thirties. He may be the most important writer now going in this country. He is already, God help him, a classic. He has written in Russian, French, German, and now wields an English that a native young writer would kill for. I am afraid that, in this respect, he puts Conrad in the shade. Where Conrad creaks, Nabokov dances. For the moment he writes for the happy few: not yet trussed up in the coils of idiot "discovery" by the breathless young, only mildly pooh-poohed by the doctoral old, left (as he would be in any circumstances) by the trenchermen to the unsure filters of posterity. So much the better. But it is one thing to be published, read by a handful, acclaimed posthumously, and something else to be virtually squelched.

COMMENT:

F. W. Dupee, " 'Lolita' in America: A Literary Letter from New York," *Encounter*, 12 (February 1959): 30-35.

Publication of Lolita *generated a cause celebre. The book was called the work of a genius, propaganda, and, often, pornography. Columbia University professor F. W. Dupee provided an overview of the critical reception in his article for the London* Encounter.

Seeing copies of *Lolita* in the bookstores here at the end of last summer, in a regular American edition with no conditions attached to its sale but the $5 price on its cover, was a curious experience for anyone with a prior knowledge of this magnificently outrageous novel and its earlier history. And what has happened to the book since—its conquest of the top place on the best-seller lists—as well as what has *not* happened to it so far—the failure of the expected opposition to materialise—makes another chapter of surprises.

But the surprises are getting to be an old story. Only three years of age, going on four, Vladimir Nabokov's little masterpiece has had a paradoxical history since its first appearance in print, in 1955, by way of an edition put out by the Olympia Press of Paris. What is in question is obviously not only a novel but a phenomenon, and a many-sided one. Like some flamboyant actress of the old school, *Lolita* has made her way by her personality as well as her art. Besides figuring as a work of literature which excites a variety of serious responses, *Lolita* represents a prodigy of the publishing business, a formidable addition to popular mythology, a major event in the career—already pretty fantastic—of its author.

Its publishing history goes back to the spring of 1954, when, Nabokov writes, "I finished copying the thing out in longhand . . . and at once began casting around for a publisher." He didn't find one among the four well-known American firms to which he submitted the manuscript by turns. Rejections tended to be decisive even though accompanied as a rule by rueful compliments on the book's undoubted merits. A book that described so vividly the mutual seduction of a middle-aged man and a twelve-year-old girl, as well as the disturbing events that precede and follow it, was likely to scandalise the press, mobilise the pressure groups, and finally bring about the sort of action in the federal courts which doomed Edmund Wilson's *Memoirs of Hecate County* a decade ago. Grotesque improvements were suggested by certain publishers, such as that Lolita be changed into a boy (an item I would include under "mythology" if the author had not vouched for its authenticity). So, refusing compromises, Nabokov turned to the Paris publishers.

It is not surprising that the American firms turned the book down in 1954. They would probably have done so even if the author had been as celebrated as William Faulkner. But Nabokov's literary reputation did not then,

New York Times Book Review, *24 August 1958*

one gathers, make him a particularly good risk, whatever the nature of the book he offered. Admirable but rather scattered, his work in English—as distinguished from his many earlier writings in Russian, French, and German, all virtually unknown here—consisted for the most part of *Bend Sinister* and *The Real Life of Sebastian Knight*, two novels which seemed to belong to the then obsolescent category of avant-garde writing; a critical book on Gogol which defied the prevailing modes of criticism; and *Speak Memory* (*Conclusive Evidence*, in the American edition), a volume of memoirs of the author's Russian childhood, which had always the reputation of being very beautiful and penetrating but was not exactly a public triumph.

So much for the fear of censorship and the comparative obscurity of Nabokov considered as probable reasons for the rejection of *Lolita* by publishers here. There was also a general literary situation which, although it may not have influenced them, ought to be taken into account, because it provided some of the background for the novel's subsequent success and because it probably affected to some extent the nature of the novel itself. Nabokov and his book were at odds with the general literary situation in at least two ways. In his personal and literary antecedents Nabokov was a hybrid, an unregenerate cosmopolitan, in a period which had gone native with a vengeance. By "gone native" I mean "become preoccupied with the national origins of literature, convinced of the sanctity of tribal traditions." The rediscovery of the ancestral Anglo-American pattern came first. Here was a neglected fireside which could be made to give out heat again; and the most prodigal of prodigal sons, all the old wanderers from Henry James to D. H. Lawrence, were hustled back there to be warmed. But any fireside would do for which a Great Tradition, a moral centre, could be claimed, with whatever disregard for the complexities of the particular case or of literary inspiration in general. And just as the "idea of the nation," in one critic's phrase, was thus rehabilitated, so the word "moral" became compulsory in criticism. Into this situation Nabokov failed to fit at all, not because of his actually mixed origins but because they show in his work, are proudly explicit in it, help to make it what it is. Where to place Nabokov, of whom someone has said that he is "Dostoevsky crossed with Voltaire," especially since this brilliant example of hybridisation resulted in *Lolita*, a book too shocking for any great tradition to want to own? Enter here the second negative consideration. *Lolita* was notoriously about sex and murder, subjects which modern American fiction had seemed to make compulsory on its side. Better a new William Dean Howells with his smiling horizons than another writer of the violent *Sanctuary* type. Indeed William Faulkner did not become the enormously respectable figure he now is until he had been naturalised, as it were, under the rubric of the "Southern Myth" and photographed at his ease in his hometown square between the Jail and the Courthouse. Nor did his violences become fully acceptable until they had been moralised, so to speak, as "melodrama." I would myself have predicted, at that time, that the next really new novel would not even be melodrama but would glorify those "common routines" which Mr. Lionel Trilling once tasked Mr. Eliot with having condemned; it would be a sort of sophisticated *Little Women*.

Not that *Lolita* is really without its complicated relations to the sentiments of those years, although the

> *There are three points of view from which a writer can be considered: he may be considered as a storyteller, as a teacher, and as an enchanter. A major writer combines these three—storyteller, teacher, enchanter—but it is the enchanter in him that predominates and makes him a major writer.*

From "Good Readers and Good Writers," in Nabokov's Lectures on Literature *(1980)*

opposite would seem to be true. If, as a reviewer has recently said, "the mind behind it is so original that it might have arrived here by flying saucer," that mind has nevertheless had us under observation from afar. Here, in *Lolita*, are the common routines in plenty: the American small town, the house with the Van Gogh prints, the humdrum poetry of cars, schools, neighbours, swimming lakes and country inns, the women big and little. Here also is melodrama, but of so bitter a kind that the label doesn't sweeten it. The melodrama turns this country of common routines into Lolitaland, a world of obscene innuendo, where the notices posted in motel bathrooms are cautionary come-ons, and the very highway signs are helpful-sinister. This raffish conjunction of the ordinary and the ghastly wasn't what influential people had in mind for the novel in 1954. No wonder the present victory of *Lolita* and its author could not be foreseen by American publishers when the manuscript was first submitted to them.

By itself, melodrama is only disappointed tragedy, inviting laughter. This, at least, is the way Nabokov seems to understand it, aided perhaps by the mating in him of Dostoevsky and Voltaire (or whatever pair of opposites). The American *pur sang* comes up with *The Bad Seed*. But Nabokov did not arrive by flying saucer, even figuratively. He came from nearer by, and *Lolita*, as I have suggested, was highly relevant in 1954, in the ironic way that original works are apt to be relevant to received opinion at any given time. A resident of the United States since 1940, a citizen for several years, the author has long made this country the centre of his life and observation, even submitting to the common routine of being an artist-in-residence (he teaches literature at Cornell University). Furthermore, the present book had been in his mind for many years.

"The first little throb of *Lolita* went through me in 1939," he says. He then lived in Paris, after having spent his youth in his native Russia, exiling himself in 1919 from the Revolution which had demolished the aristocracy he belonged to and undone his father, the famous Liberal statesman. For *Lolita*, "the initial shiver of inspiration was somehow prompted by a newspaper story about an ape in the Jardin des Plantes who, after months of coaxing by a scientist, produced the first drawing ever charcoaled by an animal: the sketch showed the bars of the poor creature's cage." This too Kafka-like inspiration led to a thirty-page story with an all-French setting, the prototype of Lolita being of that nationality while the original of Humbert Humbert, her *homme fatal*, was a Central European. In this form the story didn't satisfy the author. Some infusion of radically new experience seems to have been needed, and evidently his coming to America supplied it. "Around 1949, in Ithaca, upstate New York [seat of Cornell University], the throbbing, which had never quite ceased, began to plague me again." But now he wrote in English and what he began to bring forth "was new and had grown in secret the claws and wings of a novel." Much of it was written while he was on summer tours in the far West in his capacity as a part-time lepidopterist. While hunting rare butterflies in this cross-country fashion, he undoubtedly collected many specimens of common *vita Americana* for his novel.

Thus, from the point of view of Nabokov's development as a writer, *Lolita* probably sums up the progress, compounded of fear and fascination, disgust and laughter, by which he has become an American writer. He laughs off such interpretations, and sounds most like a know-nothing native writer when he does so. But as D. H. Lawrence said, "Never trust the artist. Trust the tale." Trusting the tale in this case means seeing that Nabokov's naturalisation has been on his own terms and is a triumph.

Meanwhile *Lolita* passed from his mind into literary and publishing history, and soon into myth, when it found a sponsor in the Olympia Press of Paris. Assorted works in English, some belonging to the category of frank erotica, a few to that of literature as well, are the specialty of this house. Out of *Lolita* it made an attractive pair of volumes, which some tourists began to bring home, while people at home began to order them by mail, often under the impression that another *Ulysses* or *Lady Chatterley's Lover* was being sneaked past the United States Customs. But one of *Lolita*'s many surprises was in store for them. In response to a query from the Olympia Press, the Collector of Customs in New York City replied that "certain copies of this book have been before this Office and that they have been released." Surprise turned into large-scale paradox when it became known that the book released by the traditionally strict American authorities was suddenly under a sort of ban in traditionally free-for-all Paris. Acting on an order signed by the French Minister of the Interior, as of December 10th, 1956, the Paris police had descended upon the Olympia Press, prohibiting the further sale and circulation on French territory of twenty-five titles, including *Lolita*, published by that firm. An appeal to the Ministry by a legal representative of the Press brought a belated reply, saying plainly, over an illegible signature, that "la mesure d'interdiction visant les dites publications" must stand. An appeal was also made to the *Syndicat National des Éditeurs*, but this powerful organisation of publishers stood by the Ministry just as the Ministry stood by the police. As sanction for their act, the authorities cited certain French statutes relating to the immunities and responsibilities of the press. But the Olympia Press was able to produce, and to reproduce in print, a letter headed "Home Office, Whitehall, Ministry of the Interior," dated September 3rd, 1953, and addressed to the *Section des Services de la Police Judiciare* of the French Ministry, calling attention to the International Convention for the Suppression of Obscene Publications and charging the Olympia Press with sending by post "des livres d'un caractére hautement obscéne."

The *gendarmes* were unwelcome enough in themselves; but the possibility that they had been set in motion by the British Home Office, after whatever lapse of time, made a literary scandal in France. The Olympia issued *L'Affaire Lolita*, a pamphlet containing the relevant

Sc.	Ft. Frs.	ACTION	SOUND 1/4
1	172 00	FADE IN:	
		EXT. FOG-SHROUDED COUNTRY ROAD - LS Humbert's car driving away - CAMERA TRACKING -	
2	188 12	DISSOLVE TO:	
		MLS - Humbert's car driving R-L - PAN with it to Ext. Pavor Manor.	
3 3	204 06	INT. PAVOR MANOR LS - HUMBERT coming in - PAN R. with him through room - he runs fingers over harp - TRACK BACK with him as he comes forward -	MUSIC STARTS
			HUMBERT: Quilty ! ... Quilty !
		Bottle falls in b.g. - QUILTY emerges from under dust sheet on chair.	
			QUILTY: Wha .. wha .. what's that ?
			HUMBERT: Are you Quilty ?
			QUILTY: No, I'm Spartacus. Have you come to free the slaves or something ?
			HUMBERT: Are you Quilty?
			QUILTY: Y-yeah .. I'm Quilty - yeah, sure.
		He gets up - knocks packing case over - Humbert puts gloves on as they move to either end of Table Tennis table.	Ah - ah - ah ... . Say, what you - er - what you putting your gloves ...
4	337 11	MS - HUMBERT putting gloves on	QUILTY: (o.s.) ... on for Captain - your hands cold or something ?
			HUMBERT: Shall we have a little chat before we start ?

In 1961 Stanley Kubrick directed a film version of Lolita *starring Peter Sellers, James Mason, and Shelley Winters. Above is the opening scene from Nabokov's screenplay.*

documents as well as various appeals to traditional French liberty. The response of writers everywhere was warmly sympathetic. And presently the Olympia Press was able to resume business, under a curious compromise evolved by the ministry. *Lolita* and the rest of her prohibited sisterhood could be sold, on the premises and by mail, but they could not be exhibited in the windows or otherwise advertised.

It was in the glare of these international ironies that *Lolita* came to the attention of the American press at large, most notably *Time* magazine, which made all the ironies plain in an article on the case (March 17th, 1957). Considering so much publicity, an American publisher could now probably take the chance of bringing the book out in the regular way in this country. Indeed the respectably sponsored *Anchor Review* not only got away with printing large sections of *Lolita*, together with my own detailed commentary, but also got enthusiastic reviews in many different quarters. What had formerly seemed a wonderful literary curiosity now began to be spoken of as an absolute masterpiece. It had its detractors too, and they sounded just angry or hurt enough to provide a further stimulus to interest.

With its publication here last August by the dignified firm of G. P. Putnam's Sons, *Lolita* therefore quickly became the best-seller it still is at this writing. Inevitably, yet surprisingly again (considering the grim subject), the movie rights were acquired—for the usual "sum in six figures"—by the independent producers, James B. Harris and Stanley Kubrick, Inc. These gentlemen are reported to be busy on the phone all day coping with Hollywood mothers who would like to see their youngest daughters in the leading role. Serio-comic speculations as to what the movie-makers will do to make *Lolita* palatable, stories of all kinds and all degrees of veracity, public controversies more or less earnest, witticisms delivered in print and in conversation, make up what I call the "mythology" of *Lolita*. But the mythology tends to be self-defeating, for reasons having to do with the nature of the book itself. *Lolita* is like Falstaff to the extent, at least, of being the cause that others *feel* witty. But what can others produce in this way that Humbert Humbert, the humbugging hero and purported author of the book, hasn't anticipated, hasn't said better? One's *double-entendres* have a way of being turned against one by that far more resounding frame of reference. He is as knowing, or more so, than the people who, inspired by a remark in the charming review of the book in the Sunday New York *Times*, have been filling the correspondence columns of that paper with news of the girl-child cult from Dante to Lewis Carroll. So, too, with Humbert's language. "Nymphet" and other new words, old words in shady new senses, are being fed into the vernacular by that eloquent source, without their ever meaning half as much mischief as they mean in the original. Even the innocently intended remarks one hears or reads on the subject often seem to have been invented by Nabokov's hero, in a lesser moment. A firm that specialises in advising libraries on purchases writes (I have its filing card on *Lolita* before me): "Thousands of library patrons conditioned to near-incest by *Peyton Place* may take this in their stride. However, better read before buying." This is minor Humbert. Nor does a woman pleasantly reviewing the book in the Cedar Rapids (Iowa) *Gazette* improve on his mastery of the dying fall when she says: "The writing is pure delight, the syntax admirable."

Pure or not, the delight given by the book appears to have exceeded any distress it has caused, thus immobilising the opposition. That there would be opposition and that it would try to take action seems to have been expected on all sides. A state of nerves braced by conscious courage may be felt in many of the early reviews, from New York to Texas. The courage seems to have had its effect, especially as represented in such a widely syndicated notice as that by W. G. Rogers, of the Associated Press, who wrote that *Lolita* is "concerned ostensibly with the flesh but [is] fascinating principally for the brilliant game of the mind." So far as action by censorship is concerned, therefore, *Lolita*'s story is a story without a plot. Two public libraries, those of Newark (New Jersey) and Cincinnati (Ohio), have refused to acquire the book, the director of the latter institution saying that "the theme of perversion seems to me obscene." *Lolita* is still sold in Boston despite some indignant notices in the local papers and despite the demand for a ban made by a Massachusetts state senator. The published advice of Dr. James Alexander Hamilton of the San Francisco Medical Society is probably typical of the more usual approach of disapproving authorities. He proposes that the book be given "the silent treatment" in San Francisco, which "is already a haven for wandering psychotics and goofballs of every description." So far as I can make out, the various religious groups are also applying the formula of silence. A brief, uninformative notice of *Lolita* in *The Catholic World* concludes that it is "a romp which does not amuse."

The Catholic World's refusal to be amused saves the dignity of institutions. It also spares *Lolita* the indignity of a whitewashing. This last has been the book's fate in many quarters where sincere admiration and unexceptionable literary judgment have otherwise prevailed. No doubt it was from a fear of scaring their readers and alerting the potential crusaders that many reviewers exercised restraint in reporting the starker aspects of *Lolita* considered as an imaginative experience. The tendency has been, as with W. G. Rogers, to leap athletically from the flesh to the word game. A review of the American edition in *Time* came to the consoling conclusion, missed by *The Catholic World*, that "Nabokov seems to be asserting that all of Creation is God." A Comic Masterpiece—again and again reviewers have arrived at something like this ultimate tribute without traversing the exquisitely painful ground between, the rank necessary purlieus of disgust and horror in *Lolita*. The book, they tend to say, is not pornographic, having no four-letter words in it. And again Humbert Humbert can be heard to laugh, this time at such saving formalities. In the person of his author he has been heard to say that pornography is only "the copulation of clichés"; there are worse things. He has also expressed amazement at the tendency of some of the best critics to get out on their favourite limbs—moral, metaphysical, or mythic—while trying to prune *Lolita* to shape. Trusting the tale means sticking to it. What he would say of Lionel Trilling's sober appraisal (*Encounter*, October 1958) can't be guessed. For this critic, the grimnesses of *Lolita*, to which he does full justice, are redeemed by its being about Love, a neglected subject in our merely sex-ridden literature, and he doesn't seem to allow the book a single laugh.

In his reserves concerning the book's stature, however, Mr. Trilling is more compelling than most of the outright enemies of *Lolita* have been. They have put on a poor show, lacking the theoretical equipment for a good attack, not to mention the rhetorical force, and falling back on the weakest strategies. These consist for the most part either in rude plain-speaking ("disgusting") or in attempts to sound superior and bored ("achingly tedious," "dull, dull, dull"). Both devices are so personal that they are likely to provoke only personal responses from the reader; and when the man who says "dull, dull, dull" happens to be the not famously brilliant daily reviewer of the New York *Times*, Orville Prescott, the reaction can be explosive.

The admirers of the book have certainly had the best of it, for several reasons. *Lolita* is a wonderful novel, however you take it. It acts with intricate force on anyone who lets himself be acted on. It has also had the luck to make its American appearance at just the right moment. The state of literary feeling—to speak only of that—has been undergoing something of a change here during the past year, from a kind of yearning conservatism to a kind of yearning dissidence. *Lolita* has both profited by the change and helped to crystallise it. There have been many similar manifestations; but no other novel, no periodical or work of criticism, no group of like-minded writers acting in concert, has done so much. *Lolita* works its magic in circles where the efforts of the Beat Generation, for example, pass for only further symptoms—there are so many already. Moreover, those approving circles are not exclusively made up of any of the familiar types into which literary Americans are commonly said to fall. All the brows—high, middle, and low—are to be found in them, celebrating together. It was someone writing in racy obscurity in the Louisville *Courier-Journal* who described *Lolita* as "undoubtedly one of the great comic novels of all time." It was a well-known younger critic

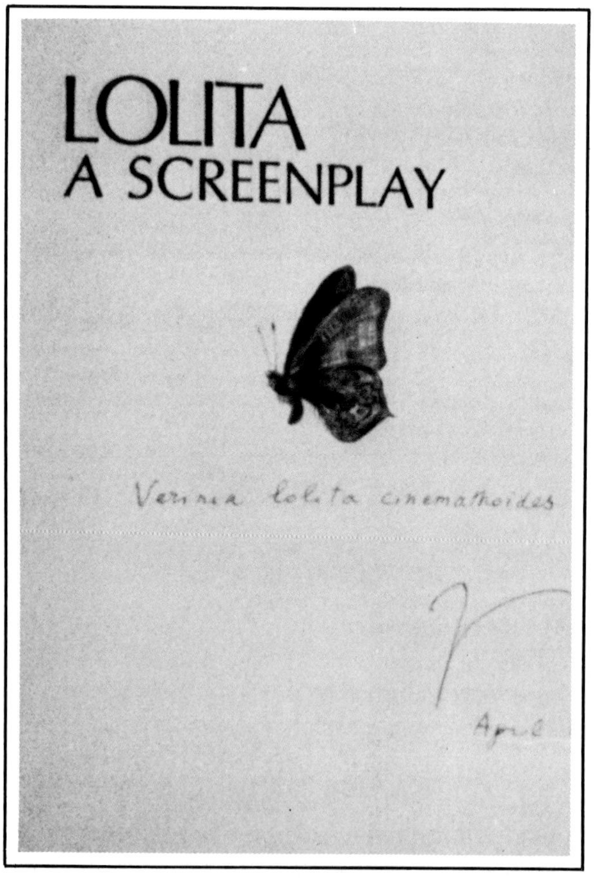

Nabokov's drawing of the imaginary Verina lolita cinemathoides butterfly on the title page of the 1961 Lolita *screenplay.*

writing with the conscious austerity of his kind (and in *The New Republic*) who called the book "a major literary event, worth all the attention we can spare." It was the book editor of the middling *Atlantic Monthly* who called it "an assertion of the comic spirit to wrest delight and truth from the most outlandish materials." It was a quite unclassifiable voice in the Milwaukee *Journal* that spoke out for Nabokov's style: "sparkling and volatile, a marvel beyond the reach of most of our own best writers." Nor are the detractors to be found only where one would expect to find them. They are in the fairly advanced *Nation* and, of all places, the Greenwich Village *Voice*, as well as in the newspapers of Dallas and Worcester. The old ranks will undoubtedly form again over other issues. Meanwhile, *Lolita* has contributed to a spectacle which many assorted individuals find irresistible. It has helped to make the fading smile of the Eisenhower Age give way to a terrible grin.

"Lolita" in London

Lolita *is about to be published in Britain. Remember* Lolita*? It is the pornographic novel recording in salacious detail the exploits of a middle-aged seducer of young girls, which on its publication in Paris Mr. Graham Greene recommended to unsuspecting readers of the sedate* Sunday Times *as good stuff.*

It has since been an immense moneymaking success in the U.S., where, of course, the pornography market is wide and profitable.

I hardly think the British publisher will find the market here so open and easy.

JOHN GORDON, SUNDAY EXPRESS

MR. R. JENKINS *(Lab., Stechford) referred to the difficulty of striking a balance between not allowing licence for pornography and giving reasonable security to literature of value. There was a more flourishing pornography trade here than in any other country—and a greater lack of security for genuine literature.*

He understood there was a proposal by a reputable firm to publish a book called "Lolita" *which had sold 240,000 copies in the United States.*

SIR GODFREY NICHOLSON *(C., Farnham): "It is thoroughly obscene."*

MR. JENKINS: *"I would not say that. It has been treated as a major work of art."*

SIR GODFREY *said he had only read an account in a newspaper. "It is uncontradicted that the book deals with a disgusting, revolting, and cruel vice and tends to encourage it."*

MR. JENKINS *said he was not trying to judge the matter. He was just saying that here was a book which many people considered of great value, which it was proposed to publish here. The debate would be valuable if it led to early legislation. . . .*

MR. BONHAM-CARTER *(Lib., Torrington) said that, as a publisher, he found in 1954 that it was difficult to know why one book was chosen for prosecution rather than another. One reason was that the English law appeared to work curiously. Anything to do with sex was automatically dangerous, while anything which described brutality, or violence, or pain was, for some reason, outside the scope of the law altogether.*

MR. N. NICOLSON *(C., Bournemouth E. and Christchurch), disclosing an interest as a partner in a firm of publishers, said the publishing profession shared the desire to eradicate pornography.*

His firm was given the opportunity to publish a novel, "Lolita" *written by a Russian exile who was professor of literature at Cornell University. The novel dealt with a perversion. It described the love of a middle-aged man for a girl of twelve. If this perversion had been described in such a way as to suggest that the practices were pleasant ones, and could lead to happiness, he would have advised against publishing the book. In point of fact,* "Lolita" *condemned what it described. He had come to the conclusion, therefore, that it was probably right to publish the book. . . .*

MANCHESTER GUARDIAN

"Well," I said, as I closed Lolita, *"if I were George Weidenfeld I would not publish that. . . ."*

KINGSLEY MARTIN, NEW STATESMAN

It is a remarkable book with a rancid taste. I do not believe it should be banned—because it is clearly a seriously-intended novel far removed from pornography. But I think it is regrettable that so much excited emotionalism should be building up around it—precisely the glare of publicity that may attract the eyes of people searching for twisted kicks.

The prevailing odds in the publishing trade are 60-40 chances of jail.

KENNETH ALLSOP, DAILY MAIL

Lolita *is not just another of the seamy sex-laden books that publishers sometimes label "controversial." It is one of the most extraordinary pieces of pornography ever written. However could a publisher think of issuing such a book? . . .*

It has been suggested that books, when you come to think of it, cannot really do harm to people who are intelligent enough to read them. What an extraordinary sentiment from the literary world that is. . . .

For Lolita, *as plainly as* Das Kapital *or* Mein Kampf, *is in effect a propagandist book. Every page pulsates with enthusiasm for the perversion which it describes. . . .*

Many of the most enlightened men in Britain's book-world have already denounced Lolita *in blunt terms. So, privately, have most of Britain's publishers, to whom the book was offered. One destroyed the copy which was sent him. Another threatened to resign from his firm if they issued the book.*

ROBERT PITMAN, SUNDAY EXPRESS

BOOK REVIEW:

Richard Schickel, "Nabokov's Artistry," *Progressive*, 22 (November 1958): 46, 48-49.

Nabokov published many short stories in Russian, French, and English. His first story collection published in America was Nine Stories *(1947), to which he added four more stories for* Nabokov's Dozen *(1958).*

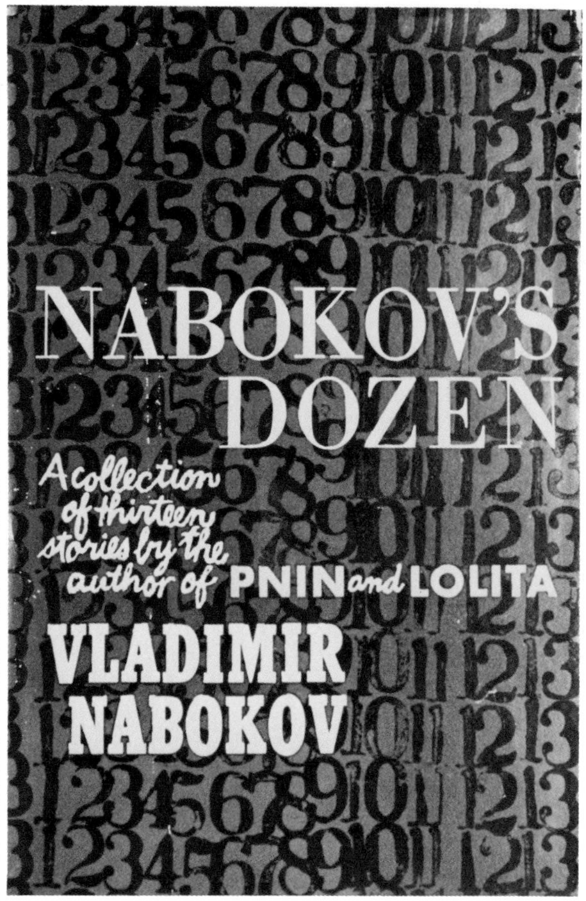
NABOKOV'S DOZEN
A collection of thirteen stories by the author of PNIN and LOLITA
VLADIMIR NABOKOV

Dust jacket for Nabokov's second volume of stories in English

Now that a couple hundred thousand Americans are feverishly thumbing through *Lolita* looking for the dirty parts (there aren't any), it might be well to take stock of the strange, brilliant talents of its author, Vladimir Nabokov.

He has been among us for years, his talents gaining increasing recognition from the small minority of literate readers—who will now, no doubt, summarily drop him for the sin of popularity. As those who picked up *Lolita* looking for a pornographic thrill have by now discovered, Nabokov's style is the very antithesis of that usually demanded in the cruel marts of best-sellerdom, as is his point of view.

For those who wish to test that point of view and that style, for those who are a little timid about the subject of *Lolita*, for those who shun literary controversy, there is, happily, an alternative. Doubleday has kindly provided us with *Nabokov's Dozen*, a collection of 13 short stories by the master. Here you may test him on your literary palate without the intervention of hot pepper seeds.

The first thing to note about the stories is that most of them are more plotless than anything of Chekov's. They go far beyond—most of them—the *New Yorker* school of plotlessness. But don't think for a moment that "plotless" means pointless. Take, for example, "Time and Ebb," a story which has absolutely no plot at all. It is merely the reminiscences of an old man written at the beginning of the Twenty-First Century. This device enables Nabokov to give an odd, brilliant insight into our own times: "They had their meals at large tables around which they grouped themselves in a stiff, sitting position on hard wooden chairs . . . Clothes consisted of a number of parts, each of which, moreover, contained the reduced and useless remnants of this or that older fashion . . . In their letters they addressed perfect strangers in what was—insofar as words have sense—the equivalent of 'beloved master' and prefaced a theoretically immortal signature with a mumble expressing idiotic devotion to a person whose very existence was to the writer a matter of complete unconcern."

The quotations indicate another of Nabokov's characteristics—his preoccupation with the significance of minutiae. He does not note detail with the dull, dogged persistence of the realist. But when a bit of it strikes his fancy he worries it about, digging the last morsel of meaning (in terms of his characters and in relation to the aesthetic niceties of his story). Typical is "Lance," in which he projects an as yet unborn descendant of the story's narrator into the position of being the first human to rocket to, and explore, another planet. But he is not concerned with the adventures of the explorer. No, his story is about the effect of the trip on the explorer's parents whose chief concern is, more or less, that their son remember to wear his rubbers. His adventure is, to them, simply too big to conceive in any other terms. Their reaction is a complex of simplicities, achingly human and sensitively rendered by Nabokov. He has a passionate desire for the right word, the right sound, the right rendering of color. Reading Nabokov is a marvelously creative experience, leading the receptive mind down dozens of delightful byways where, once the writer has pointed the way, it can find its own paths.

It is this quality in the work of Gogol which Nabokov admired so much in his fine little study of the Russian, published in 1944 by New Directions. It is obvious that Nabokov, in his own way, in a purely modern idiom, is following Gogol's lead. He too, as Turgenev once said of himself and his contemporaries, "crawled out from under Gogol's overcoat."

There is another, obvious quality in Nabokov's work which cannot go unremarked. That is its odd mingling of humor and sadness—something which is found in much Russian writing (Nabokov is a Russian emigre who now writes in English).

The other stories, all of them, deal with remembrances of things past. For example: "Mademoiselle O" is a sad, funny, oddly touching recollection of a grotesque governess Nabokov had in pre-revolutionary Russia. "First Love" is another autobiographical recollection of the sort the title describes. It is similar in mood to the section in *Lolita* dealing with the affair that first caused Humbert Humbert's passion for nymphets. "That in Alleppo Once" purports to be the letter of an emigre describing how his young wife went mad and was lost in the Nazi invasion (there is much mourning in Nabokov's work for people, places, things now lost forever). "Cloud, Castle, Lake" is the story of a sad, permanently displaced little Russian who wins a vacation hike with a group of Nazis and is made miserable by them for his inability to cope with the trip (so many of Nabokov's characters cannot cope with the people, places, things of the world) but who at last finds a scene of perfect beauty, a place he may recall from childhood, or, more likely, from the memories of childhood dreams. Of course, the Hitler youth forcibly drag him from his place of enchantment and it is lost.

Pnin, that delightful collection of short stories masquerading as a novel, is a quintessential Nabokovian piece. It is the story of an emigrant Russian professor teaching in America, funny in his ineffectual attempts to deal with the modern American world, sad in his wistfulness for times and places gone by. And *Lolita* is, in a sense, made up of the same ingredients. Humbert Humbert is obviously withdrawn from the world that threatens him. And his passion for little girls based on the aborted love of his childhood is obviously a bit of nostalgia carried to absurd lengths.

It is this recognition of nostalgia's absurdity which keeps Nabokov from falling into the bottomless pit of sentimentality. Behind every nostalgic reflection there is a sardonic laugh at the posturing involved in the recollection.

Above all, I believe, Nabokov is a poet of the absurd. He has written: "The absurd has as many shades and degrees as the tragic has. . . . You cannot place a man in an absurd situation if the whole world he lives in is absurd; you cannot do this if you mean by 'absurd' something provoking a chuckle or a shrug. But if you mean the pathetic, the human condition, if you mean all such things that in less weird worlds are linked up with the loftiest aspirations, the deepest sufferings, the strongest passions—then of course the necessary breach is there, and a pathetic human, lost in the midst of [a] nightmarish, irresponsible world would be 'absurd' by a kind of secondary contrast."

This is what Nabokov does to his lost, bewildered, but somehow indomitable people. You can see it in *Pnin*, in *Lolita*, in the stories in *Nabokov's Dozen*.

Perhaps only an emigre like Nabokov, who has at least twice had to flee the works of the madmen who inhabit our "nightmarish, irresponsible" world, can fully apprehend the full horror—and comedy—of the human condition's absurdity. Perhaps only he can know the full meaning of a nostalgia which is not merely, as I previously suggested, for times and places gone by, but for a world, and a place, which has never existed, and never can exist, in our world of men. Let me finally suggest that it is this vision of a higher reality which gives his work such importance, which transforms his memory-laden works into high art.

For, whatever the meaning of his work, his vision, we must always bear in mind the skill, the attention to meaning, the conscious skill with which he manipulates stubborn words. Many writers have had visions as sensitive as his. Many artists have had his word-skill without his vision. But high art is always a product of a combination of the two—vision and skill—in the mind of a genius. I risk that word with full consciousness of its dangers, with horrible examples of critics who have used it, and rued it, dancing before me. Vladimir Nabokov is a genius—one of the handful of major talents alive in our time.

> *Literature is invention. Fiction is fiction. To call a story a true story is an insult to both art and truth.*

From "Good Readers and Good Writers," in Nabokov's Lectures on Literature *(1980)*

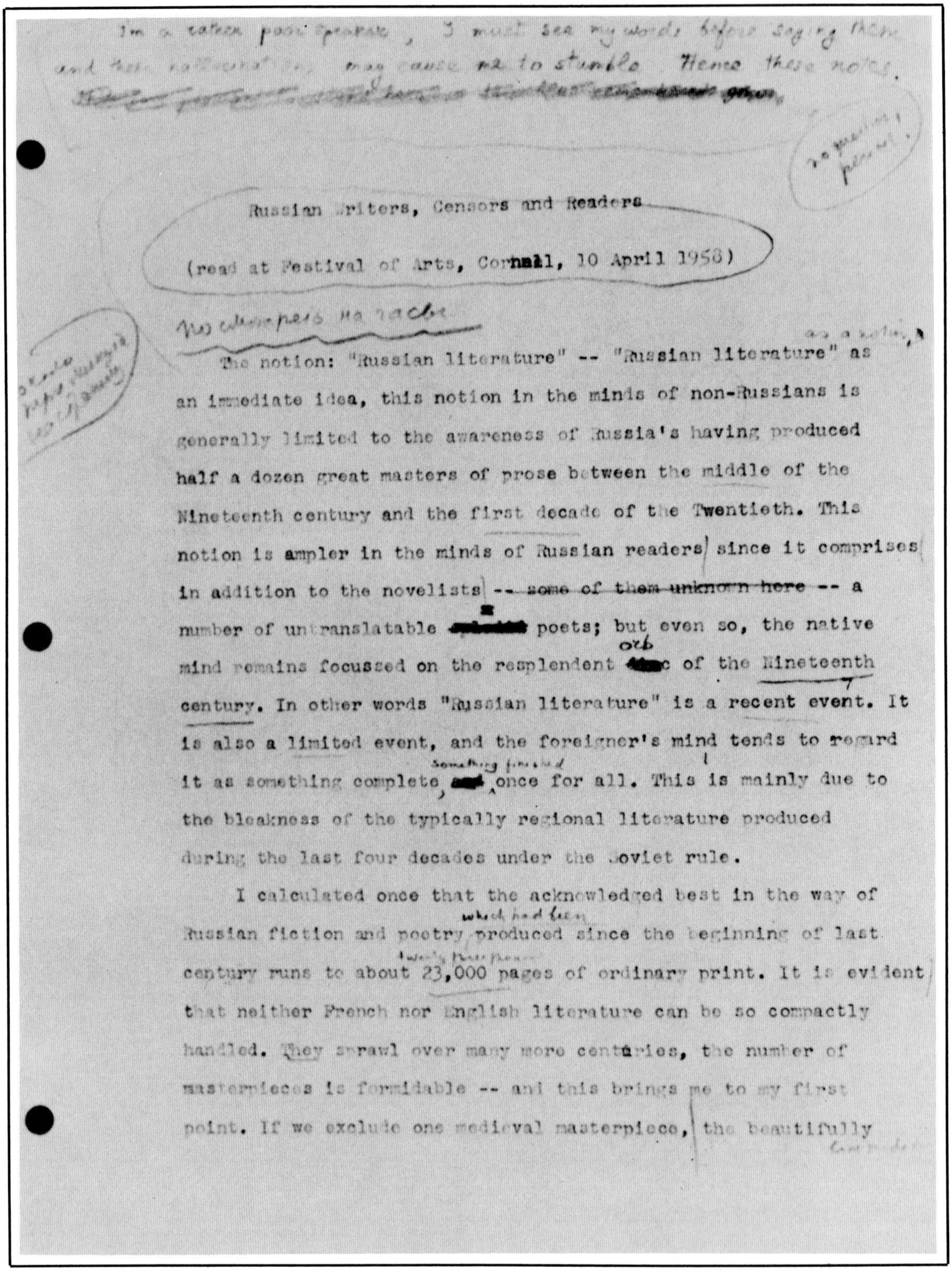

I'm a rather poor speaker, I must see my words before saying them and ... may cause me to stumble. Hence these notes.

Russian Writers, Censors and Readers

(read at Festival of Arts, Cornell, 10 April 1958)

The notion: "Russian literature" -- "Russian literature" as an immediate idea, this notion in the minds of non-Russians is generally limited to the awareness of Russia's having produced half a dozen great masters of prose between the middle of the Nineteenth century and the first decade of the Twentieth. This notion is ampler in the minds of Russian readers since it comprises in addition to the novelists ~~-- some of them unknown here --~~ a number of untranslatable [redacted] poets; but even so, the native mind remains focussed on the resplendent [redacted] orb of the Nineteenth century. In other words "Russian literature" is a recent event. It is also a limited event, and the foreigner's mind tends to regard it as something complete, something finished [redacted] once for all. This is mainly due to the bleakness of the typically regional literature produced during the last four decades under the Soviet rule.

I calculated once that the acknowledged best in the way of Russian fiction and poetry which had been produced since the beginning of last century runs to about 23,000 pages of ordinary print. It is evident that neither French nor English literature can be so compactly handled. They sprawl over many more centuries, the number of masterpieces is formidable -- and this brings me to my first point. If we exclude one medieval masterpiece, the beautifully

A page from the lecture "Russian Writers, Censors, and Readers" read at Cornell's Festival of Arts, 10 April 1958. In this account of the forces that have repressed Russian writers, Nabokov declared: "Let us not look for the soul of Russia in the Russian novel: let us look for the individual genius."

- 20 -

From Pushkin

I value little those much vaunted rights
that have for some the lure of dizzy heights;
I do not fret because the gods refuse
to let me wrangle over revenues,
or thwart the wars of kings; and 'tis to me
of no concern whether the press be free
to dupe poor oafs or whether censors cramp
the current fancies of some scribbling scamp.
These things are words, words, words. My spirit fights
for deeper Liberty, for better rights.
Whom shall we serve--the people or the State?
The poet does not care,--so let them wait.
To give account to none, to be one's own
vassal and lord, to please oneself alone,
to bend neither one's neck, nor inner schemes,
nor conscience to obtain some thing that seems
power but is a flunkey's coat; to stroll
in one's own wake, admiring the divine
beauties of Nature and to feel one's soul
melt in the glow of man's inspired design
--that is the blessing, those are rights!

(transl. by V.Nabokov)

Nabokov's translation of a Pushkin poem which he included in his 1958 speech at the Cornell Arts Festival

BOOK REVIEW:

Virgilia Peterson, "In Front of Reason He Waves a Red Cape," *Saturday Review*, 35 (24 October 1959): 35-36.

Nabokov's dream novel Priglashenie na kazn' (Invitation to a Beheading) *was published in 1938. It deals with Cincinnatus C., who is condemned to death for "gnostical turpitude"—a crime "so rare and so unutterable that it was necessary to use circumlocutions like 'impenetrability,' 'opacity,' 'occlusion'. . . ."*

With characteristic glee, Vladimir Nabokov complains, in his preface to "Invitation to a Beheading"—a tale first written in Russian in 1935 and now translated into English by Nabokov himself, together with his son—that he has been compared as a writer to "Gogol, Tolstoievski [sic], Joyce, Voltaire, de Sade, Stendhal, Balzac, Byron, Beerbohm, Proust, Kleist, Matar Marinski, Mary McCarthy, Meredith [!], Cervantes, Charlie Chaplin, Baroness Murasaki, Pushkin, Ruskin, and even Sebastian Knight" (the latter a writer whom Nabokov invented). In the light of his mockery, not of the august assemblage of suggested tutelary divinities but of the critics who claim to have discovered the influence of these deities on him, it behooves anyone henceforward attempting to impale the many-splendored wings of Nabokov's literary butterfly to compare him only to himself. Nor should this be too difficult, since in fact Nabokov is so entirely *sui generis* as to be incomparable.

If it were possible to lift from their various contexts and put together in one book all the seemingly parenthetical yet intensely relevant soundings of literary values that dot Nabokov's own pages, they would constitute a classic text for critics. In "Nicolai Gogol," the book in which he passionately defends Gogol as the foremost poet and fantast of Russian literature, he writes, "I have a lasting grudge against those who like their fiction to be educational, or uplifting or national, or as healthy as maple syrup and olive oil."

Nabokov need not be afraid, however, that these strictures are applicable in any conventional sense to him. He is "national" only in his evocation of a wildwood of firs or a floating island of water lilies recalled from the Russian landscape of his childhood; "educational," only in the scientific exactitude with which he describes the moths and butterflies he has been netting all his life, in the arrows of sarcasm with which he unfailingly bursts the balloon of human pretensions, and, of course, in his phenomenal (indeed, almost too phenomenal) range and use of the English language itself; he is "uplifting" only in the almost casual levitation by which, floating away from and above what we take for reality, he carries us up at his side. If he allows a certain sweetness, a certain sheen to appear in his literary texture, he manages so to imbed them in his jibes, his jokes, and his gall that they are no more than the deliberately precious jewel in the toad's head.

The time sequence in which Nabokov's books have appeared in English has little to do with his own private chronology. Long before "Lolita," there appeared the macabre and bitter "Laughter in the Dark," in whose sixteen-year-old heroine some have seen the foreshadowing of the unutterably besmirched Lolita herself. "Conclusive Evidence" was a tender evocation of his vanished home and family, while his stories collected under the title of "Pnin" told of a Russian refugee professor, Timofey Pnin, an unsentimental yet memorably vulnerable figure who puts to shame the two-dimensional Mr. Chippses and Miss Doves, and the stereotyped, absent-minded professors in contemporary fiction.

But since the appearance of "Lolita," and for this at least we must be grateful to it, there have reappeared several works which Nabokov wrote some time ago. There are the stories, peopled with faithless women, innocent poets, society rascals, nostalgic governesses, and mealy-mouthed bureaucrats, collected in the volume called "Nabokov's Dozen"; there is the little book of "Poems"; and now, this fall, there have appeared "The Real Life of Sebastian Knight," a reprint after twenty years of Nabokov's first book in English, which is at once a brilliant spoof of the art of biography and a beautifully tender example of that art, and "Invitation to a Beheading," originally written under the pen name of Sirin.

The man to whose beheading Nabokov invites us is a tiny, highly sentient figment of the author's imagination, with the stylized name of Cincinnatus. Not only at first sight but throughout the painful slice of his life that this book comprises, Cincinnatus seems to live in a picture-postcard, fortress-dominated town of a never-never land, in a never-never period of time when airplanes have become as obsolete as dinosaurs. He lives among people who, despite recognizable features and manners, are as improbable as only the people reflected in Nabokov's sometimes convex and sometimes concave mirrors can be. No one else in this seemingly unreal world is alive except Cincinnatus, and he is condemned to die for the crime of opacity, of being alone impenetrable when all the rest can be seen through by one another. Conceived and growing up, as it were, by accident, Cincinnatus, though

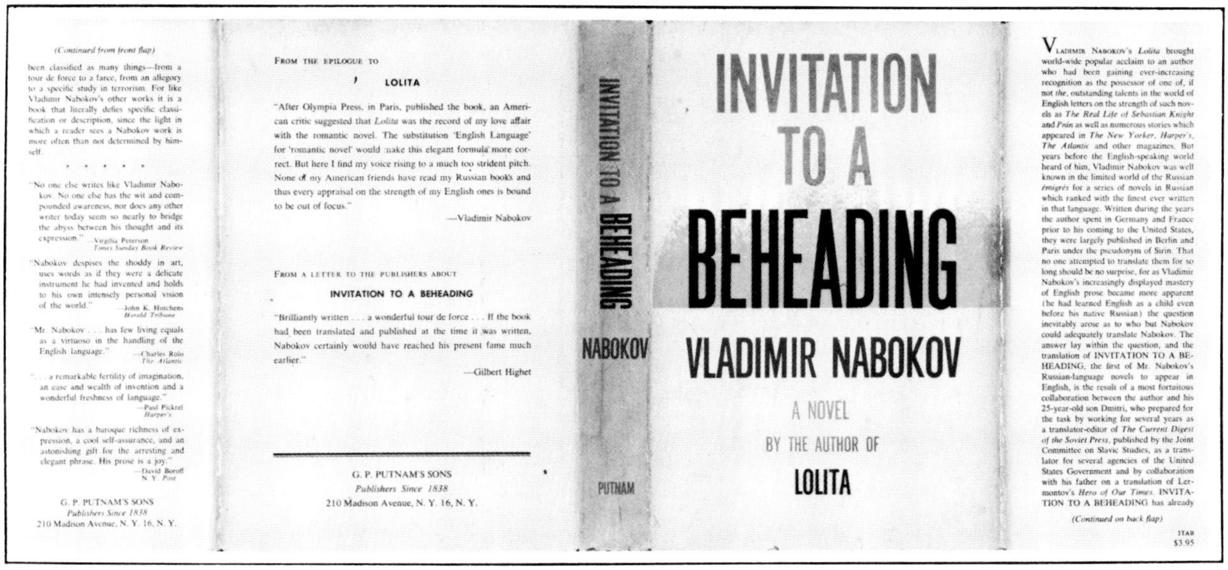

Dust jacket for the 1959 translation of Invitation to a Beheading

he has tried his best to feign translucence, has always somehow betrayed himself to his contemporaries. Shunned in school and later in the doll-factory where he works, he is favored only by a velvet-skinned, coarse-mouthed maiden named Marthe, who, once she has married him, deceives him with touching and candid regularity, and who, when the tide of opinion finally rises against him, helps to turn him in. Cincinnatus knows his crime, knows his sentence. What he does not know is which day, which hour, it will be carried out. From time to time his body trembles, but since, as he says, "a rider is not responsible for the shivering of his horse," he acknowledges his dread only to himself.

Today's shelves are stacked high with stories of trial, imprisonment, and sentence, but—on the face of it—these stories mention no such cuckoo court, no such monkey of a jailer, no such vainglorious prison director, no such coy executioner, no such cell, nor any such horrible little wife as Marthe. Yet this is the world, Nabokov hints, which we take for real, while the inner world of Cincinnatus, who can escape into real reality, we can neither see nor understand.

Nabokov's world is composed of reflections, whether in the mirror of another pair of eyes or in the multiple-faceted, constantly refracting complex imagination inside his head. No other writer reveals a greater contempt for sham, a more sophisticated insight into human foibles, a more convincing air of disillusion than Nabokov. At the same time, Nabokov reveals himself, whether consciously or unconsciously, as a wounded, but stubbornly persistent lover of life. "Great literature," he says in his study of Gogol, "skirts the irrational." By this definition, his constant waving of the red cape in the face of reason without ever allowing himself to be gored, makes him, if not an Olympian, at least a master of his trade.

BOOK REVIEW:

Mary McCarthy, "A Bolt from the Blue," *New Republic*, 146 (4 June 1962): 21-27.

Pale Fire *was the first novel Nabokov published in America after* Lolita. *It received mixed reviews but became a best-seller for a short time. Mary McCarthy had been married to Nabokov's friend Edmund Wilson.*

Pale Fire is a Jack-in-the-box, a Faberge gem, a clockwork toy, a chess problem, an infernal machine, a trap to catch reviewers, a cat-and-mouse game, a do-it-yourself novel. It consists of a 999-line poem of four cantos in heroic couplets together with an editor's preface, notes, index, and proof-corrections. When the separate parts are assembled, according to the manufacturer's directions, and fitted together with the help of clues and cross-references, which must be hunted down as in a paper-chase, a novel on several levels is revealed, and these "levels" are not the customary "levels of meaning"

Retaining his American citizenship, Nabokov moved to Montreux, Switzerland, in 1959 to be near his son, Dmitri, who was in Italy pursuing an opera career. He is shown above in his room at the Palace Hotel in Montreux.

Nabokov's sketch of the view from his balcony in Montreux

of modernist criticism but planes in a fictive space, rather like those houses of memory in medieval mnemonic science, where words, facts, and numbers were stored till wanted in various rooms and attics, or like the Houses of astrology into which the heavens are divided.

The poem has been written by a sixty-one-year-old American poet of the homely, deceptively homely, Robert Frost type who teaches at Wordsmith College in New Wye, Appalachia; his name is John Shade, his wife is called Sybil, nee Irondell or Swallow; his parents were ornithologists; he and his wife had a fat, plain daughter, Hazel, who killed herself young by drowning in a lake near the campus. Shade's academic "field" is Pope, and his poem, *Pale Fire*, is in Pope's heroic measure; in content, it is closer to Wordsworthian pastures—rambling, autobiographical, full of childhood memories, gleanings from Nature, interrogations of the universe: a kind of American *Prelude*. The commentator is Shade's colleague, a refugee professor from Zembla, a mythical country north of Russia. His name is Charles Kinbote; he lives next door to Shade in a house he has rented from Judge Goldsworth, of the law faculty, absent on sabbatical leave. (If, as the commentator points out, you recombine the syllables of "Wordsmith" and "Goldsworth," you get Goldsmith and Wordsworth, two masters of the heroic couplet.) At the moment of writing, Kinbote has fled Appalachia and is living in a log cabin in a motor court at Cedarn in the Southwest; Shade has been murdered, fortuitously, by a killer calling himself Jack Grey, and Kinbote, with the widow's permission, has taken his manuscript to edit in hiding, far from the machinations of two rival Shadians on the faculty. Kinbote, known on the campus as the Great Beaver, is a bearded vegetarian pederast, who has had bad luck with his youthful "ping-pong partners"; a lonely philologue and long-standing admirer of the poet (he has translated him into Zemblan), he has the unfortunate habit of "dropping in" on the Shades, spying on them (they don't draw theirs) with binoculars from a post at a window or in the shrubbery; jealous of Mrs. Shade, he is always available for a game of chess or a "good ramble" with the tolerant poet, whom he tirelessly entertains with his Zemblan reminiscences. "I don't see how John and Sybil can stand you," a faculty wife hisses at him in the grocery store. "What's more, you are insane."

That is the plot's ground floor. Then comes the *piano nobile*. Kinbote believes that he has inspired his friend with his tales of his native Zembla, of its exiled king, Charles the Beloved, and the Revolution that started in the Glass Works; indeed, he has convinced himself that the poem is *his* poem—the occupational mania of commentators—and cannot be properly understood without his gloss, which narrates Zemblan events paralleling the poet's composition. What at once irresistibly peeps out from Kinbote's notes is that he himself is none other than Charles the Beloved, disguised in a beaver as an academic; he escaped from Zembla in a motor boat and flew to America after a short stay on the Côte d'Azur; an American sympathizer, a trustee of Wordsmith, Mrs. Sylvia O'Donnell, has found him a post on the language faculty. His colleagues (read "mortal enemies") include—besides burly Professor Hurley, head of the department and an adherent of *"engazhay"* literature—Professor C., a literary Freudian and owner of an ultra-modern villa, a certain Professor Pnin, and an instructor, Mr. Gerald Emerald, a young man in a bow tie and green velvet jacket. Meanwhile the Shadows, the Secret Police of Zembla, have hired a gunman, Jakob Gradus, alias Jacques D'Argus, alias Jacques Degré, alias Jack Grey, to do away with the royal exile. Gradus' slow descent on Wordsmith synchronizes, move by move, with Shade's composition of *Pale Fire*; the thug, wearing a brown suit, a trilby, and carrying a Browning, alights on the campus the day the poem is finished. In the library he converges with Mr. Gerald Emerald, who obligingly gives him a lift to Professor Kinbote's house. There, firing at the king, he kills the poet; when the police take him, he masks his real purpose and identity by claiming to be a lunatic escaped from a local asylum.

This second story, the *piano nobile*, is the "real" story as it appears to Kinbote of the events leading to the poet's death. But the real, real story, the story underneath, has been transpiring gradually, by degrees, to the reader. Kinbote is mad. He is a harmless refugee pedant named Botkin who teaches in the Russian department and who fancies himself to be the exiled king of Zembla. This delusion, which he supposes to be his secret, is known to the poet, who pities him, and to the campus at large, which does not—the insensate woman in the grocery store was expressing the general opinion. The killer is just what he claims to be—Jack Grey, an escaped criminal lunatic, who has been sent to the State Asylum for the Insane by, precisely, Judge Goldsworth, Botkin's landlord. It is Judge Goldsworth that the madman intended to murder, not Botkin, alias Kinbote, alias Charles the Beloved; the slain poet was the victim of a case of double mistaken identity (his poem too is murdered by its editor, who mistakes it for something else). The clue to

Gradus-Grey, moreover, was in Botkin's hands when, early in the narrative, he leafed through a sentimental album kept by the judge containing photographs of the killers he had sent to prison or condemned to death: ". . . a strangler's quite ordinary-looking hands, a self-made widow, the close-set merciless eyes of a homicidal maniac (somewhat resembling, I admit, the late Jacques d'Argus), a bright little parricide aged seven. . . ." He got, as it were, a preview of the coming film—a frequent occurrence in this kind of case. Projected onto Zembla, in fact, are the daily events of the campus. Gradus' boss, Uzumrudov, one of the higher Shadows, met on the Riviera in a green velvet jacket, is slowly recognized to be "little Mr. Anon.," alias Gerald Emerald, alias Reginald Emerald, a teacher of freshman English, who has made advances to (read in reverse "had advances made to him by") Professor Botkin, and who is also the author of a rude anonymous note suggesting that Professor Botkin has halitosis. The paranoid political structure called Zembla in Botkin's exiled fantasy—with its Extremist government and secret agents—is a transliteration of a pederast's persecution complex, complicated by the "normal" conspiracy-mania of a faculty common room.

But there is in fact a "Zembla," behind the Iron Curtain. The real, real story, the plane of ordinary sanity and common sense, the reader's presumed plane, cannot be accepted as final. The explanation that Botkin is mad will totally satisfy only Professors H. and C. and their consorts, who can put aside *Pale Fire* as a detective story, with the reader racing the author to the solution. *Pale Fire* is not a detective story, though it includes one. Each plane or level in its shadow box proves to be a false bottom; there is an infinite perspective regression, for the book is a book of mirrors.

Shade's poem begins with a very beautiful image, of a bird that has flown against a window and smashed itself, mistaking the reflected sky in the glass for the true azure. "I was the shadow of the waxwing slain / By the false azure of the window pane." This image is followed by another, still more beautiful and poignant, a picture of that trick of optics whereby a room at night, when the shades have not been drawn, is reflected in the dark landscape outside.

> "Uncurtaining the night I'd let dark glass
> Hang all the furniture above the grass
> And how delightful when a fall of snow
> Covered my glimpse of lawn and reached up so
> As to make chair and bed exactly stand
> Upon that snow, out in that crystal land!"

"That crystal land," notes the commentator, loony Professor Botkin. "Perhaps an allusion to Zembla, my dear country." On the plane of everyday sanity, he errs. But on the plane of poetry and magic, he is speaking the simple truth, for Zembla is Semblance, Appearance, the mirror-realm, the Looking Glass of Alice. This is the first clue in the treasure-hunt, pointing the reader to the dual or punning nature of the whole work's composition. *Pale Fire*, a reflective poem, is also a prism of reflections. Zembla, the land of seeming, now governed by the Extremists, is the antipodes of Appalachia, in real homespun democratic America, but it is also the *semblable*, the twin, as seen in a distorting glass. Semblance becomes resemblance.

The word Zembla can be found in Pope's *Essay on Man* (Epistle 2, v); there it signifies the fabulous extreme north, the land of the polar star.

> "But where the Extreme of Vice was ne'er agreed.
> Ask where's the North? At York, 'tis on the Tweed;
> In Scotland, at the Oroades, and there,
> At Greenland, Zembla, or the Lord knows where;
> No creature owns it in the first degree,
> But thinks his neighbor farther gone than he."

Pope is saying that vice, when you start to look for it, is always somewhere else—a will-o'-the-wisp. This somewhere else is Zembla, but it is also next door, at your neighbor's. Now Botkin is Shade's neighbor and vice versa; moreover, people who live in glass houses. . . . Shade has a vice, the bottle, the festive glass, and Botkin's vice is that he is an *invest, i.e.*, turned upside down, as the antipodes are, relative to each other. Further, the reader will notice that the word Extreme, with a capital (Zemblan Extremists) and the word degree (Gradus is degree in Russian), both occur in these verses, in the neighborhood of Zembla, pre-mirroring *Pale Fire*, as though by second sight. Reading on, you find (lines 267-268), the following lines quoted by John Shade in a discarded variant:

> "See the blind beggar dance, the cripple sing,
> The sot a hero, lunatic a king . . ."

The second line is *Pale Fire* in a nutshell. Pope continues (lines 269-270):

> "The starving chemist in his golden views
> Supremely blest, the poet in his muse."

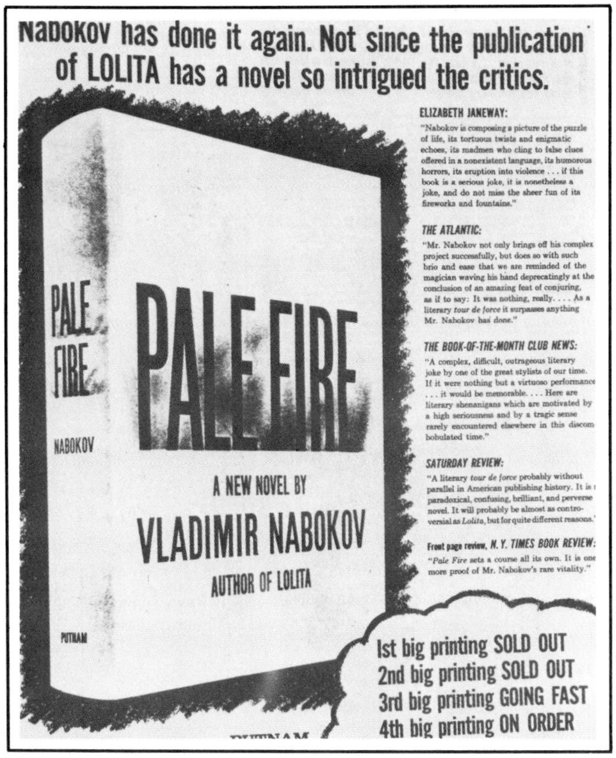

New York Times Book Review, *3 June 1962*

Supremely Blest is the title of John Shade's book on Pope. In this section of the poem, Pope is playing on the light and shade antithesis and on what an editor calls the "pattern of paradoxical attitudes" to which man's dual nature is subject. The lunatic Botkin incidentally, playing king, *inverts* his name.

To leave Pope momentarily and return to Zembla, there is an actual Nova Zembla, a group of islands in the Arctic Ocean, north of Archangel. The name is derived from the Russian Novaya Zemlya, which means "new land." Or *terre neuve*, Newfoundland, the New World. Therefore Appalachia Zembla. But since for Pope Zembla was roughly equal to Greenland, then Zembla must be a green land, an Arcadia. Arcady is a name often bestowed by Professor Botkin on New Wye, Appalachia, which also gets the epithet "green," and he quotes *"Et in Arcadia ego,"* for Death has come to Arcady in the shape of Gradus, ex-glazier and killer, the emissary of Zembla on the other side of the world. Green-jacketed Gerald Emerald gives Death a lift in his car.

The complementary color to green is red. Zembla has turned red after the revolution that began in the Glass Factory. Green and red flash on and off in the narrative like traffic signals and sometimes reverse their message. Green appears to be the color of death, and red the color of life; red is the king's color and green the color of his enemies. Green is pre-eminently the color of seeming (the theatrical greenroom), the color, too, of camouflage, for Nature, being green at least in summer, can hide a green-clad figure in her verdure. But red is a color that is dangerous to a wearer who is trying to melt into the surroundings. The king escapes from his royal prison wearing a red wool cap and sweater (donned in the dark) and he is only saved by the fact that forty loyal Karlists, his supporters, put on red wool caps and sweaters too (red wool yarn—yarn comes from Latin "soothsayer"—is protective Russian folk magic) and confuse the Shadows with a multitude of false kings. Yet when the king arrives in America he floats down with a green silk parachute (because he is in disguise?), and his gardener at New Wye, a Negro whom he calls Balthasar (the black king of the three Magi), has a green thumb, a red sweater, and is seen on a green ladder; it is the gardener who saves the king's life when Gradus, alias Grey, appears.

Now when Alice went through the looking-glass she entered a chess game as a white pawn. There is surely a chess game or chess problem in *Pale Fire*, played on a board of green and red squares. The poet describes his residence as "the frame house between / Goldsworth and Wordsmith on its square of green"; the Rose Court in the royal palace in Onhava (Far Away), the Zemblan capital, is a sectile mosaic with rose petals cut out of red stone and large thorns cut out of green marble. There is much stress, in place-descriptions, on framing, and reference is made to chess problems of "the solus rex type." The royal fugitive may be likened to a lone king running away on the board. But in problems of the solus rex type, the king, though outnumbered, is, curiously enough, not always at a disadvantage; for example, a king and two knights cannot checkmate a lone king—the game is stalemated or drawn. All the chess games played by characters in the story are draws. The plot of the novel ends in a kind of draw, if not a stalemate. The king's escape from the castle is doubtless castling.

Chess is the perfect mirror-game, with the pieces drawn up confronting each other as in a looking-glass; moreover, castles, knights, and bishops have their twins as well as their opposite numbers. The piece, by the way, called the bishop in English, in French is *"le fou"* or madman. In the book there are two opposed lunatics at large: Gradus and Kinbote. The moves made by Gradus from the Zemblan capital to Wordsmith in New Wye parallel spatially the moves made in time by the poet toward the completion of his poem; at the zero hour, there is a convergence of space and time. What is shadowed forth here may be a game of three-dimensional chess—three simultaneous games played by a pair of chess wizards on three transparent boards arranged vertically. A framed crystal land, the depth-echo of the bedroom projected onto the snow.

The moves of Gradus also hint some astrological progression. The magnum opus of old John Shade is begun July 1, 1959, at the dead center of the year. The poem is completed (except for the last line) the day of Gradus' arrival, July 21, on the cusp between Cancer and Leo. Botkin arrived at Judge Goldsworth's "chateau" on February 5, 1959; on Monday, February 16, he was introduced to the poet at lunch at the Faculty Club; on March 14, he dined at the Shades', etc. The fateful conjunction of three planets seems to be indicated, and the old astrological notion of events on earth mirroring the movements of the stars in the sky.

The twinning and doubling proliferate; the multiplication of levels refracts a prismatic, opaline light on Faculty Row. Zembla is not just land but earth—"Terra the Fair, an orbicle of jasp," as John Shade names the globe; a Zemblan feuilletonist had fancifully dubbed its capital Uranograd—"Sky City." The fate of Charles the Beloved is a rippling reflection of the fate of Charles II of England on his travels, of Bonnie Prince Charlie and of the deposed Shakespearean rulers for whom streets are named in Onhava—Coriolanus Lane, Timon Alley. Prospero of *The Tempest* pops in and out of the commentary, like a Fata Morgana, to mislead the reader into looking for "pale fire" in Shakespeare's swansong. It is not there, but *The Tempest* is in *Pale Fire*: Prospero's emerald isle, called the Ile of Divels, in the New World, Iris and Juno's peacock, sea caves, the chess game of Ferdinand and Miranda, Prospero's enchantments, his lost kingdom, and Caliban, whom he taught language, that supreme miracle of mirroring.

Nature's imitations of Nature are also evoked—echo, the mocking-bird perched on a television aerial ("TV's huge paperclip"), the iridescent eyes of the peacock's fan, the cicada's emerald case, a poplar tree's rabbit-foot—all the "natural shams" of so-called protective mimicry by which, as Shade says in his poem, "The reed becomes a bird, the knobby twig / An inchworm and the cobra head, a big / Wickedly folded moth." These disguises are not different from the exiled king's red cap and sweater (like the markings of a bird) or the impersonation of an actor. Not only Nature's shams but Nature's freaks dance in and out of the lines: rings around the moon, rainbows and sun dogs (bright spots of light, often colored, sometimes seen on the ring of the solar halo), the heliotrope or sunturner, which, by a trick of language, is also the bloodstone, Muscovy glass (mica), phosphorescence (named for Venus, the Morning Star), mirages, the roundlet of pale light called the *ignis fatuus*, fireflies, everything speckled, freckled, curiously patterned, dappled, quaint (as in Hopkins' poem, "Pied Beauty"). The arrowy tracks of the pheasant, the red heraldic barrings of the Vanessa butterfly, snow crystals. And the imitation of natural effects in manufactures: stained glass, paperweights containing snowstorms and mountain views, glass eyes. Not to mention other curios like the bull's eye lantern, glass giraffes, Cartesian devils. Botkin, the bearded urning, is himself a prime "freak of Nature," like Humbert. And the freakish puns of language ("Red Sox win 5/4 on Chapman's Homer"), "muscat" (a cat-and-mouse game), anagrams, mirror-writing, such words as versipel. The author loves the ampersand and dainty diminutives ending in "let" or "et" (nymphet). Rugged John Shade is addicted to "word-golf," which he induces Botkin to play with him. Botkin's best scores are hate-love in three (late-lave-love), lass-male in four (last-mast-malt-male), live-dead in five. If you play word-golf with the title words, you can get pale-hate in two and fire-love in three. Or pale-love in three and fire-hate in three.

The misunderstandings of scholarship, cases of mistaken word-identity, also enchant this dear author. *E.g.*, "alderwood" and "alderking" keep cropping up in the gloss with overtones of northern forest magic. What

> *If the mind were constructed on optional lines and if a book could be read in the same way as a painting is taken in by the eye, that is without the bother of working from left to right and without the absurdity of beginnings and ends, this would be the ideal way of appreciating a novel, for thus the author saw it at the moment of its conception.*

From "The Art of Literature and Commonsense," in Nabokov's Lectures on Literature *(1980)* can an alderking be, excluding chief or ruler, which would give king-king, a redundancy? "Erle" is the German word for alder, and the alder tree, which grows in wet places, has the curious property of not rotting under water. Hence it is a kind of magic tree, very useful for piles supporting bridges. And John Shade, writing of the loss of his daughter, echoes Goethe's "The Erl-King."

> "Who rides so late in the night and the wind?
> It is the writer's grief. It is the wild
> March wind. It is the father with his child."

Now the German scholar, Herder, in translating the elf-king story from the Danish, mistook the word for elf (*elle*) for the word for alder. So it is not really the alderking but the elf- or goblin-king, but the word alder touched by the enchanted word elf becomes enchanted itself and dangerous. Goethe's erl-king, notes Kinbote, fell in love with the traveler's little boy. Therefore alderking means an eerie, dangerous invert found in northern forest-countries.

Similar sorcerer's tricks are played with the word stone. The king in his red cap escaping through the Zemblan mountains is compared to a *Steinmann*, which, as Kinbote explains, is a pile of stones erected by alpinists to commemorate an ascent; these stonemen, apparently, like snowmen, were finished off with a red cap and scarf. The *Steinmann*, then, becomes a synonym for one of the king's disguised followers in red cap and sweater (*e.g.*, Julius Steinmann, Zemblan patriot). But the *Steinmann* has another meaning, not divulged by Kinbote; it is the *homme de pierre* or *homme de St. Pierre* of Pushkin's poem about Don Giovanni, in short the stone statue, the Commendatore of the opera. Anyone who sups with the stone man, St. Peter's deputy, will be carried off to hell. The mountain that the *Steinmann*-king has to cross is wooded by Mandevil Forest; toward the end of his journey he meets a disguised figure, Baron Mandevil, man of fashion, catamite, and Zemblan patriot. Read man-devil, but read also Sir John Mandeville, medieval impostor and author of a book of voyages who posed as an English knight (perhaps a chess move is indicated?). Finally the stone (glancing by glass houses) is simply the stone thrown into a pool or lake and starting the tremulous magic of widening ripples that distort the clear mirroring of the image—as the word stone itself, cast into the pool of this paragraph has sent out wavelets in a widening circle.

Lakes—the original mirrors of primeval man—play an important part in the story. There are three lakes near the campus, Omega, Ozero, and Zero (Indian names, notes Botkin, garbled by early settlers); the king sees his consort, Disa, Duchess of Payn (sadism; theirs was a "white" marriage) mirrored in an Italian lake. The poet's daughter was drowned herself in Lake Omega; her name (". . . in lone Glenartney's hazel shade") is taken from *The Lady of the Lake*. But a hazel wand is also a divining-rod, used to find water; in her girlhood, the poor child, witch Hazel, was a poltergeist.

Trees, lakes, butterflies, stones, peacocks—there is also the waxwing, the poet's alter ego, which appears in the first line of the poem (duplicated in the last, unwritten line). If you look up the waxwing in the OED, you will find that it is "a passerine bird of the genus Ampelis, esp. A. garrulus, the Bohemian waxwing. Detached from the chatterers by Monsieur Vieillot." The poet, a Bohemian, is detached from the chatterers of the world. The waxwing (belonging to the king's party) has red-tipped quills like sealing wax. Another kind of waxwing is the Cedar Waxwing. Botkin has fled to Cedarn. The anagram of Cedarn is nacred.

More suggestively (in the popular sense), the anal canal or "back door" or "*porte étroite*" is linked with a secret passage leading by green-carpeted stairs to a green door (which in turn leads to the greenroom of the Onhava National Theater), discovered by the king and a boyhood bedfellow. It is through this secret passage (made for Iris Acht, a leading actress) that the king makes his escape from the castle. Elsewhere a "throne," in the child's sense of "the toilet," is identified naughtily with the king. When gluttonous Gradus arrives in Appalachia, he is suffering from a severe case of diarrhea, induced by a conflict of "French" fries, consumed in a Broadway restaurant, with a genuine French ham sandwich, which he had saved from his Nice-Paris railway trip. The discharge of his bowels is horribly paralleled with the discharge of the automatic pistol he is carrying; he is the modern automatic man. In discharging the chamber of his pistol he is exercising what to him is a "natural" function; earlier the slight sensory pleasure he will derive from the act of murder is compared to the pleasure a man gets from squeezing a blackhead.

This is no giggling, high-pitched, literary camp. The repetitions, reflections, misprints, and quirks of Nature are taken as signs of the presence of a pattern, the stamp or watermark of a god or an intelligence. There is a web of sense in creation, old John Shade decides—not text but texture, the warp and woof of coincidence. He hopes to find "some kind of correlated pattern in the game,/

Plexed artistry, and something of the same/ Pleasure in it as they who played it found." The world is a sportive work of art, a mosaic, an iridescent tissue. Appearance and "reality" are interchangeable; all appearance, however deceptive, is real. Indeed it is just this faculty of deceptiveness (natural mimicry, trompe l'oeil, imposture), this power of imitation, that provides the key to Nature's cipher. Nature has "the artistic temperament"; the galaxies, if scanned, will be an iambic line.

Kinbote and Shade (and the author) agree in a detestation of symbols, except those of typography and, no doubt, natural science ("H^2O is a symbol for water"). They are believers in signs, pointers, blazes, notches, clues, all of which point into a forest of associations, a forest in which other woodmen have left half-obliterated traces. All genuine works contain pre-cognitions of other works or reminscences of them (and the two are the same), just as the flying lizard already possessed a parachute, a fold of skin enabling it to glide through the air.

Shade, as an American, is naturally an agnostic, and Kinbote, a European, is a vague sort of Christian who speaks of accepting "God's presence—a faint phosphorescence at first, a pale light in the dimness of bodily life, and a dazzling radiance after it." Or, more concessively, "Somehow Mind is involved as a main factor in the making of the universe." This Mind of Kinbote's seems to express itself most lucidly in dualities, pairs, twins, puns, couplets, like the plots of Shakespeare's early comedies. But this is only to be expected if one recalls that to make a cutout heart or lacy design for Valentine's Day all a child needs is a scissors and a folded piece of paper—the fold makes the pattern, which, unfolded, appears as a miracle. It is the quaint principle of the butterfly. Similarly, Renaissance artificers used to make wondrous "natural" patterns by bisecting a veined stone, an agate or a carnelian, as you would bisect an orange. Another kind of magic is the child's trick of putting a piece of paper on the cover of a school book and shading it with a pencil; wonderfully, the stamped title, *Caesar's Gallic Wars*, emerges, as though embossed, in white letters. This, upside down, is the principle of the pheasant's hieroglyph in the snow or the ripple marks on the sand, to which we cry "How beautiful!" There is no doubt that duplication, stamping, printing (children's transfers), is one of the chief forms of magic, a magic we also see in Jack Frost's writing on the window, in jet trails in the sky—an intelligent spirit seems to have signed them. But it is not only in symmetry and reproduction that the magic signature of Mind is discerned, but in the very imperfections of Nature's work, which appear as guarantees of authentic, hand-knit manufacture. That is, in those blemishes and freckles and streakings and moles already mentioned that are the sport of creation, and what is a vice but a mole?

Nabokov's tenderness for human eccentricity, for the freak, the "deviate," is partly the naturalist's taste for the curious. But his fond, wry compassion for the lone black piece on the board goes deeper than classificatory science or the collector's choplicking. Love is the burden of *Pale Fire*, love and loss. Love is felt as a kind of homesickness, that yearning for union described by Plato, the pining for the other half of a once-whole body, the straining of the soul's black horse to unite with the white. The sense of loss in love, of separation (the room *beyond*, projected onto the snow, the phantom moves of the chess knight, that deviate piece, *off* the board's edge onto ghostly squares), binds mortal men in a common pattern—the elderly couple watching TV in a lighted room, and the "queer" neighbor watching *them* from his window. But it is most poignant in the outsider: the homely daughter stood up by her date, the refugee, the "queen," the bird smashed on the window pane.

Pity is the password, says Shade, in a philosophical discussion with Kinbote; for the agnostic poet, there are only two sins, murder and the deliberate infliction of pain. In the exuberant high spirits, the wild laughter of the book, there is a cry of pure pain. The compassion of Nabokov stops violently short of Gradus, that grey, degraded being, the shadow of a Shade. The modern, mass-produced, jet-propelled, newspaper-digesting killer is described with a fury of intimate hatred; he is Death on the prowl. Unnatural Death is the natural enemy of the delicate, gauzy ephemerids who are Nabokov's special love. Kinbote makes an "anti-Darwinian" aphorism: "The killer is *always* his victim's inferior."

But except for the discussions between the poet and his neighbor and Kinbote's theological justification of suicide, the book is quite free of religion—a remarkable achievement for a work that plays on traditional associations. How was it possible to avoid the Holy Rood, the Trinity, the Harrowing of Hell, the Resurrection, etc.? Among the myriads of references, there seem to be only two to Christian legend: the oblique one to St. Peter as gatekeeper of Heaven and the chess-jesting one to the Black King of the Magi. The book is obstinately, adamantly secular. It flies this fact gallantly like a flag of difference. The author's attitude toward the mystery of the universe is closer to the old botanist's wonder than to the modern physicist's mysticism. His practical morality, like Kant's, seeks to reconcile the Enlightenment with universal maxims of conduct held as axioms. Nabokov's pantheism contains Platonic gleams: Kinbote's "phosphorescence" recalls the cave myth. Kinbote reverts to this notion when he concedes in his final remarks that Shade's poem, for all its deficiencies, has "echoes and wavelets of fire and pale phosphorescent hints" of the real Zemblan magic. This madman's estimate is also the author's apologia for his own work, in relation to the fiery Beyond of the pure imagination—Plato's Empyrean, the sphere of pure light or fire. But Plato's Empyrean is finished, a celestial storehouse or vault of models from which the forms of earthly life are copied. In Nabokov's view (see Shade's couplet, *"Man's life as commentary to abstruse / Unfinished poem.* Note for further use"), the celestial Poem itself is incomplete.

I have not been able to find, in Shakespeare or anywhere else, the source of "pale fire." In the commentary there is an account of the poet burning his rejected drafts in "the pale fire of the incinerator." An amusing sidelight on the question may be provided by the word ingle, used by Kinbote to mean a catamite or boy favorite, but which also means blaze, from the Gaelic word for fire. A Helena Rubinstein product is called Pale Fire. I think too of the pale fire of opals and of Wordsworth, one of the patron saints of the grotesquely named Wordsmith College: "Life like a dome of many-colored glass / Stains the pale radiance of eternity." Whether the visible world is a prismatic reflection of eternity or vice versa is perhaps immaterial, like the question of which came first, the chicken or the egg. In the game of signaling back and forth with mirrors, which may be man's relation with the cosmos, there is perhaps no before or after, only distance—separation—and, across it, the agitated flashing of the semaphore.

In any case, this centaur-work of Nabokov's, half poem, half prose, this merman of the deep, is a creation of perfect beauty, symmetry, strangeness, originality, and moral truth. Pretending to be a curio, it cannot disguise the fact that it is one of the very great works of art of this century, the modern novel that everyone thought dead and that was only playing possum.

I do love Chekhov dearly . . . it is his *works which I would take on a trip to another planet.*

From Nabokov's Strong Opinions *(1973)*

BOOK REVIEW:

Stanley Edgar Hyman, "Nabokov's Gift," *New Leader*, 46 (14 October 1963): 20-21.

Dar (The Gift), *Nabokov's last Russian novel, is generally considered his best in his native language. It appeared serially in* Sovremennye Zapiski *during 1937-1938, but without the controversial "political" fourth chapter which was not published with the novel until 1952. The English translation appeared in 1963. Nabokov said that "the last novel I wrote, or ever shall write in Russian" was difficult to translate because "its heroine is . . . Russian Literature."*

"I have no desire to twist and batter an unambiguous *apparatus criticus* into the monstrous semblance of a novel," says the mad critic Charles Kinbote in *Pale Fire*. He succeeded in producing the most ambiguous *apparatus criticus* imaginable, and his maniacal creator, Vladimir Nabokov, twisted and battered that into the finest comic novel since *Ulysses*. Now we have the first publication in English of Nabokov's last novel written in Russian, *The Gift* (translated by Michael Scammell with the collaboration of the author). Finished in 1937, it is as marvelous in its own way as *Pale Fire*, and it displays another variety of the same fantastic form: the novel as literary criticism and the spoof of literary criticism.

One would have to know a great deal more than I do about Russian literature to get all the references and parodies in *The Gift*. (This neatly reverses *Pale Fire*, where poor Kinbote didn't know enough about America to realize that Chapman's Homer was a home run by Sam Chapman.) The story itself, told alternately in the first and third person, is simple and delightful. Two young émigré Russians, Fyodor Godunov-Cherdyntsev and Zina Mertz, fall in love in Berlin about 1925. Fyodor is a poet and a *schlemiel*. When he goes swimming in the park, his clothes are inevitably stolen; when he spends his last coin to telephone Zina, of course he gets the wrong number. This figure of fun is nevertheless brilliant, talented, and good. Zina, the landlady's daughter, has "burning, melting, sorrowing lips," and is one of the two admirers of Fyodor's verse in the world. She is the principal "gift" of the title, and the tricks of fate that bring them together are the novel's plot.

We get glimpses of this chaste and tender love story, as though it were a lovely meadow, through periodic gaps in a fantastically elaborate topiary hedge, the literary criticism. Nabokov writes of the book, in his foreword: "Its heroine is not Zina, but Russian literature. The plot of Chapter One centers in Fyodor's poems. Chapter Two is a surge toward Pushkin in Fyodor's liter-

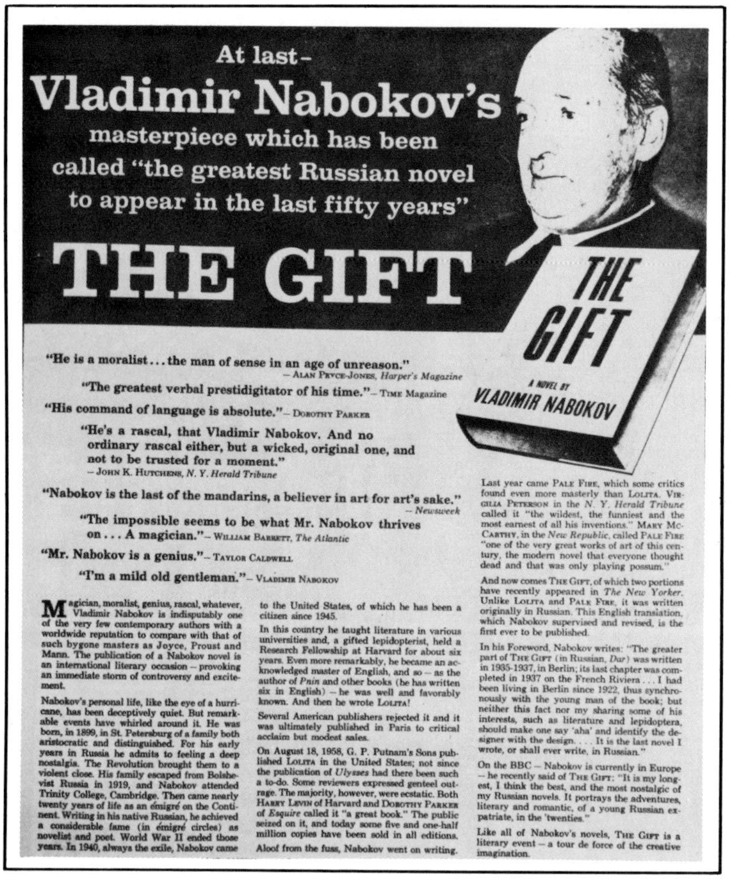

New York Times Book Review, *26 May 1963*

ary progress and contains his attempt to describe his father's zoological explorations. Chapter Three shifts to Gogol, but its real hub is the love poem dedicated to Zina. Fyodor's book on Chernyshevski, a spiral within a sonnet, takes care of Chapter Four. The last chapter combines all the preceding themes and adumbrates the book Fyodor dreams of writing some day: *The Gift*."

Nor is this the half of it. There are long literary discussions, of the greatest brilliance, that Fyodor has with another poet, Koncheyev, in his imagination. Fyodor endlessly meditates on earlier Russian writers, and his biography continually measures Chernyshevski against them. Fyodor quotes Marx in blank verse, "so it would be less boring." Chapter Four, the biography, is framed between the sestet and octave of a sonnet to Chernyshevski, making what Nabokov calls "a spiral within a sonnet." The last paragraph of the book conceals a parody Pushkin stanza.

As passionately as Fyodor loves Zina, Nabokov loves Words. The book's language dances and sparkles. An oil slick on the pavement is "asphalt's parakeet." After he has been writing poetry, Fyodor is unable to sleep because "discarded word-shells obstructed and chafed his brain and prickled his temples." A streetcar is "rare, almost legendary," and a lawyer is "repulsively small, almost portable." Of a symbiotic caterpillar-ant relationship, Nabokov writes: "It was as if cows gave us Chartreuse and we gave them our infants to eat." Sentences in *The Gift*, in the complexity of their syntax and the thrust of their images and metaphors, are poems. Here is a typical one:

"He was walking along streets that had already long since insinuated themselves into his acquaintance—and as if that were not enough, they expected affection; they had even purchased in advance, in his future memories, space next to St. Petersburg, an adjacent grave; he walked along these dark, glossy streets and the blind houses retreated, backing or sidling into the brown sky of the Berlin night, which, nevertheless, had its soft spots here and there, spots that would melt under one's gaze, allowing it to obtain a few stars."

Nabokov writes in the foreword: "I am not, and

never was, Fyodor Godunov-Cherdyntsev; my father is not the explorer of Central Asia that I still may become some day; I never wooed Zina Mertz, and never worried about the poet Koncheyev or any other writer. In fact, it is rather in Koncheyev, as well as in another incidental character, the novelist Vladimirov, that I distinguish odds and ends of myself as I was circa 1925." Reading this characteristic disclaimer, one is immediately reminded of the Freudian negative: The patient said the person in his dream was not his mother; so, then, it was his mother.

Of course Fyodor Godunov-Cherdyntsev is Vladimir Nabokov, and Zina Mertz is the wife Véra to whom he has dedicated a number of his books, including this one. Fyodor's childhood experiences repeat again and again those Nabokov recalls in his memoir, *Conclusive Evidence*; Fyodor's poems parody Nabokov's poems; in fact, in the 1920s Nabokov published his verse in émigré journals over the name "Godunov-Cherdyntsev." My consultant in Russian literature, to whom I am indebted for that last fact, also tells me that Koncheyev is the poet Vladislav Khodasevich, described with apparent irrelevance in *The Gift*'s foreword as "the greatest Russian poet that the twentieth century has yet produced."

The book, then, is Nabokov's mockery of himself, his writing, and his courtship of his wife, but it is a gentle and affectionate mockery. In similarly denying that the book is autobiographical in a recent BBC interview, Nabokov made the interesting statement: "I am very careful to keep my characters beyond the limits of my own identity." The truth behind this remark is that Nabokov inflates his self-portraits beyond the limits of his own identity. Fyodor is only one in a series of grotesque and wonderful self-caricatures—Humbert Humbert, Timofey Pnin, Charles Kinbote—and is the least grotesque and most engaging of them. In disguise in *The Gift*, Nabokov is able to parody and criticize his own work. A description of Fyodor's faults as a writer, given by Koncheyev in a dialogue Fyodor imagines, is, with Mary McCarthy's admirable review of *Pale Fire* in the *New Republic*, the best Nabokov criticism we have.

Along with Nabokov's passion for language, as great as that of Joyce, is a preoccupation with the past recalled by memory comparable to that of Proust. "Strange, strange are the mishaps of memory," Fyodor writes, dredging up an American dentist with a French mistress from his St. Petersburg childhood. Fyodor's poems are reminscences of childhood, his individual memories; his book on Chernyshevski is something like a national or collective memory. This 19th-century Russian revolutionary seems at first the least likely person for Nabokov to write about; he clearly, like Fyodor, detests him. But the detestation and mockery combine with a deep human sympathy and compassion, and the result is a biography that is frequently uproarious and ultimately heartbreaking.

But Chernyshevski too images—mirrors, really—Nabokov. His dreadful 20 years of Siberian exile are an ironic commentary on Nabokov's own exile from Russia, caused by men claiming to be Chernyshevski's heirs. The Minister of Justice who finally freed Chernyshevski was Nabokov's paternal grandfather, Dmitri, after whom Nabokov's son is named. And Chernyshevski as a rebel against the Little Father must obscurely speak for impulses deep in Nabokov, who loves and worships his wonderful father in *Conclusive Evidence*, as Fyodor loves and worships *his* wonderful father in *The Gift.*

Without pages of quotation it is hard to convey the brilliance and verbal corruscation of *The Gift*. Nabokov invents a painter and a whole series of loony paintings to go with him. When a foolish playwright stands up to read from his work, Nabokov writes a foolish play for him. Fyodor's father teaching him about butterflies and moths becomes a little lepidopteral treatise; Fyodor's father on an expedition to Central Asia becomes an article out of the *National Geographic*. To greet Fyodor's book on Chernyshevski, Nabokov writes a series of parody reviews, including one charging that Fyodor invented a biogapher (as I do not doubt that he did). A meeting of the Society of Russian Writers in Germany is the funniest scene I can recall since the Marx brothers split up.

The earliest of Nabokov's Russian novels available in English is *Camera Obscura* (published here as *Laughter in the Dark*), written in 1925, when he was 26. It is a sour and cruel comedy about the torments of a blind man. By the time of *The Gift*, 12 years later, Nabokov had become genial and benign. The mockery in *The Gift* is kindly, and if everyone gets sandpapered a little, no one gets flayed. (No Russians, anyway. Fyodor detests the Germans, and they are consistently portrayed in the book as fat, ugly, stupid, cruel, authoritarian, and swinish.)

One of the nicest inventions in *Pale Fire* is the Zemblan word *alfear*, defined as "uncontrollable fear caused by elves." We need a word (*nablaf?*) for uncontrollable laughter caused by Nabokov. He is wonderfully funny, while at the same time he is wonderfully serious. His books are intricate puzzles, Chinese ivories, Fabergé eggs; they represent the triumph of artifice. But his themes are profound: the interpenetration of illusion and reality in *Pale Fire*; the interpenetration of art and life in *The Gift*. Nabokov is a unique phenomenon in our literature (no one has yet had the temerity to imitate him except Thomas Pynchon in *V.*), as he was a unique phenomenon in Russian literature. *Pale Fire* and *The Gift*, which continually threaten to shatter the novel form, turn out finally to be enlargements of it, as *Ulysses* and *Finnegans Wake* are. It is about time we recognized that Vladimir Nabokov is a novelist of major importance.

BOOK REVIEW:

John Updike, "Grandmaster Nabokov," *New Republic*, 151 (26 September 1964): 15-18.

Nabokov says that of all his novels, Zashchita Luzhina *(*Luzhin's Defense, *published in 1964 as* The Defense*) has the most "warmth," and that it "has been found lovable even by those who understand nothing about chess and/or detest all my other books." Luzhin, the protagonist, sees life as a chess game he is losing to an unknown opponent. In an effort to find the unexpected move that will destroy his opponent's strategy, Luzhin commits suicide, "or rather sui-mate." John Updike is one of Nabokov's warmest admirers.*

One hesitates to call him an "American writer"; the phrase fetches to mind Norman Mailer and James Jones and other homegrown cabbages loyally mistaken for roses. Say, rather, that Vladimir Nabokov distinctly seems to be the best writer of English prose at present holding American citizenship, the only writer, with the possible exception of the long-silent Thornton Wilder, whose books, considered as a whole, give the happy impression of an *oeuvre*, of a continuous task carried forward variously, of a solid personality, of a plenitude of gifts exploited knowingly. His works are an edifice whose every corner rewards inspection. Each book, including the super-slim *Poems* and the uproariously pedantic and copious commentaries to his translation of *Eugene Onegin*, yields delight and presents to the aesthetic sense the peculiar hardness of a finished, fully meant thing. His sentences are beautiful out of context and doubly beautiful in it. He writes prose the only way it should be written—that is, ecstatically. In the intensity of its intelligence and reflective joy, his fiction is unique in this decade and scarcely precedented in American literature. Melville and James do not, oddly, offer themselves for comparison. Yet our literature, that scraggly association of hermits, cranks, and exiles, is strange enough to include this arrogant immigrant; as an expatriate Nabokov is squarely in the native tradition.

Very curiously, his *oeuvre* is growing at both ends. At one end, the end pointed toward the future, are the works composed in English, beginning with the gentlest of his novels, *The Real Life of Sebastian Knight*, and terminating, for the time being, in his—the word must be—monumental translation of *Onegin*, a physically gorgeous, sumptuously erudite gift from one language to another; it is pleasant to think of Nabokov laboring in the libraries of his adopted land, the libraries fondly described in *Pnin*, laboring with Janus-faced patriotism on the filigreed guy-wires and piled buttresses of this bridge whereby the genius of Pushkin is to cross after him into America. The translation itself, so laconic compared to the footnotes, with its breathtaking gaps, pages long, of omitted stanzas whose lines are eerily numbered as if they were there, ranks with Horace Gregory's Catullus and Richmond Lattimore's *Iliad* as superb, quirky, and definitive: a permanent contribution to the demi-art of "Englishing" and a final refutation, let's hope, of the fallacy of equivalent rhyme. In retrospect, Nabokov's more recent novels—obviously *Pale Fire* but there are also Humbert Humbert's mysterious "scholarly exertions" on a "manual of French literature for English-speaking students"—transparently reveal glimpses of the Pushkinian travail begun in 1950.

At the other end (an end, as in earthworms, not immediately distinguishable), Nabokov's *oeuvre* is growing backwards, into the past, as English versions appear of those novels he wrote in Russian, for a post-Revolutionary emigre audience concentrated in Paris and Berlin, during his twenty years of European residence (1919-1940), under the pen name of "V. Sirin." *The Defense*, originally *Zashchita Luzhina*, is the latest of these to be translated. In the chronology of his eight Russian novels, *The Luzhin Defense* (this literal title was used by *The New Yorker* and seems better, in clearly suggesting a chess ploy, though the ghosts of "illusion" and "losin' " fluttering around the proper name perhaps were worth exorcising) comes third, after two untranslated ones and just before *Laughter in the Dark*. It is thus the earliest Nabokov work now available in English. An author's foreword states that it was written in 1929—that is, when Nabokov was thirty, which is the age of Luzhin, an ex-chess prodigy and international grandmaster. Like his hero, the author seems older; few Americans so young could write a novel wherein the autobiographical elements are so cunningly rearranged and transmuted by a fictional design, and the emotional content so obedient to such cruelly ingenious commands, and the characterization so little colored by indignation or the shock of discovery. On this last point, it needs to be said—so much has been pointlessly said about Nabokov's "virtuosity," as if he is a verbal magician working with stuffed rabbits and hats nobody could wear—that Nabokov's characters live. They "read" as art students say; their frames are loaded with bright color and twisted to fit abstract schemes but remain anatomically credible. The humanity that has come within Nabokov's rather narrow field of vision has been illuminated by a guarded but genuine compassion. Two characters occur to me, randomly and vividly: Charlotte Haze of *Lolita*, with her blatant bourgeois Bohemianism, her cigarettes, her Mexican doodads, her touchingly clumsy sexuality, her utterly savage and believable war with her daughter; and Albinus Kretschmar of *Laughter in the Dark*, with his doll-like dignity, his bestial softness, his hobbies, his family feelings, his craven romanticism, his quaint competence. An American housewife and a German businessman, both observed, certainly, from well on the outside, yet animated from well within. How much more, then, can Nabokov do with characters who are Russian, and whose concerns circle close to his own aloof passions!

His foreword, shameless and disdainful in his usual first-person style, specifies, for "hack reviewers" and "persons who move their lips when reading," the forked appeal of "this attractive novel"—the intricate immanence in plot and imagery of chess as a prevailing metaphor, and the weird lovableness of the virtually inert hero. "Of all my Russian books, *The Defense* contains and diffuses the greatest 'warmth'—which may seem odd seeing how supremely abstract chess is supposed to be. In point of fact, Luzhin has been found lovable even by those who understand nothing about chess and/or detest all my other books. He is uncouth, unwashed, uncomely—but as my gentle young lady (a dear girl in her own right) so quickly notices, there is something in him that transcends . . . the coarseness of his gray flesh and the sterility of his recondite genius."

What makes characters endearing does not admit of such analysis: I would divide Luzhin's charm into (a) the delineation of his childhood (b) the evocation of his chess prowess. As to (a), Nabokov has always warmed to the subject of children, precocious children—David Krug, Victor Wind, the all-seeing "I" of *Conclusive Evidence*, and, most precocious and achingly childlike of all, Dolores Haze. The four chapters devoted to little Luzhin are pure gold, a fascinating extraction of the thread of genius from the tangle of a lonely boy's existence. The child's ominous lethargy: his father's brooding ambitiousness for him; the hints of talent in his heredity; the first gropings, through mathematical and jigsaw puzzles, of his peculiar aptitude toward the light; the bizarre introduction, at the hands of a nameless violinist who tinges the game forever with a somehow cursed musicality, to the bare pieces; his instruction in the rules, ironically counterpointed against an amorous intrigue of which he is oblivious; his rapid climb through a hierarchy of adult opponents—all this is witty, tender, delicate, resonant. By abruptly switching to Luzhin as a chess-sodden adult, Nabokov islands the childhood, frames its naive brightness so that, superimposed upon the grown figure, it operates as a kind of heart, as an abruptly doused light reddens the subsequent darkness.

As to (b), Nabokov has never shied from characters who excel. In *Pale Fire* he presumed to give us a long poem by an American poet second only to Frost; Adam Krug in *Bend Sinister* is the leading intellectual of his nation; no doubt is left that Fyodor Godunov-Cherdyntsev of *The Gift* is truly gifted. Luzhin's "recondite genius" is delineated as if by one who knows—though we know, from Chapter XIV of his autobiography, that Nabokov's *forte* was not tournament play but the "beautiful, complex and sterile art" of composing chess problems of a "poetico-mathematical type." On its level as a work-epic of chess (as *Moby Dick* is a work-epic of whaling) *The Defense* is splendidly shaped toward Luzhin's match with Turati, the dashing Italian grandmaster against whose unorthodox attack, "leaving the middle of the board unoccupied by Pawns but exercising a most dangerous influence on the center from the sides," Luzhin's defense is devised. Of Turati physically we are given the briefest glimpses, "rubbing his hands and deeply clearing his throat like a bass singer," but his chess presence is surpassingly vivid, and during the tournament in which Luzhin thinks himself into a nervous breakdown suspense mounts as to whether "the limpidity and lightness of Luzhin's thought would prevail over the Italian's tumultuous fantasy." Their game, a potential draw which is never completed, draws forth a display of metaphorical brilliance that turns pure thought heroic. Beneath the singing, quivering, trumpeting, humming battlefield of the chessboard, Turati and Luzhin become fabulous monsters groping through unthinkable tunnels:

> "Luzhin's thought roamed through entrancing and terrible labyrinths, meeting there now and then the

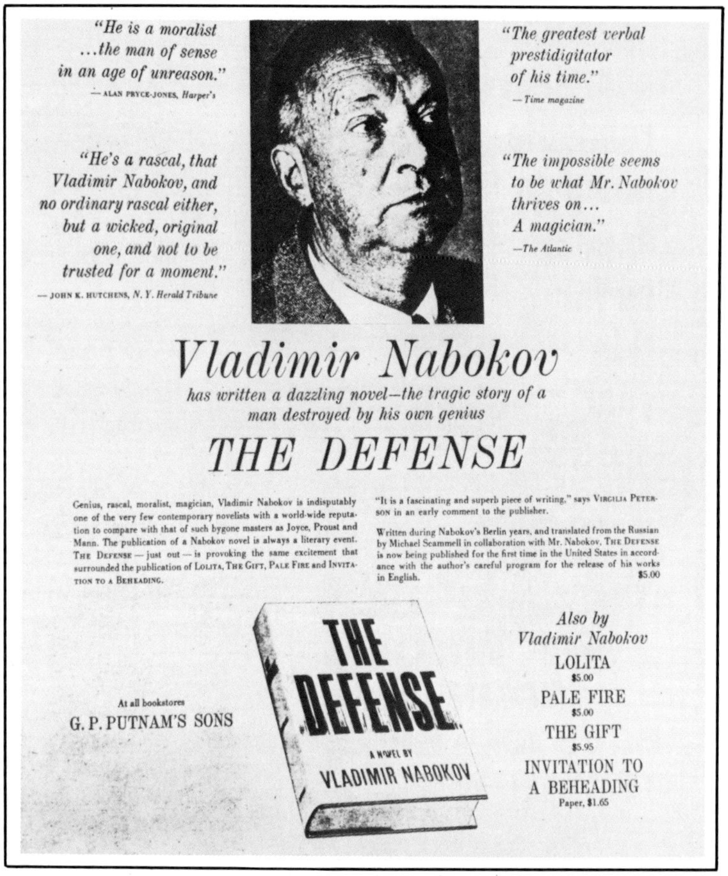

New York Times Book Review, *4 October 1964*

> anxious thought of Turati, who sought the same thing as he. . . . Luzhin, preparing an attack for which it was first necessary to explore a maze of variations, where his every step aroused a perilous echo, began a long meditation. . . . Suddenly, something occurred outside his being, a scorching pain—and he let out a loud cry, shaking his hand stung by the flame of a match, which he had lit and forgotten to apply to his cigarette. The pain immediately passed, but in the fiery gap he had seen something unbearably awesome, the full horror of the abysmal depths of chess."

The game is adjourned, and after such an evocation we have no difficulty in feeling with Luzhin how the chess-images that have haunted the fringes of his existence now move into the center and render the real world phantasmal. The metaphors have reversed the terms.

Chess imagery has infiltrated the book from all sides. Nabokov in his foreword preens perhaps unduly on the tiled and parqueted floors, the Knight-like leaps of the plot. His hero's monomania plays tricks with the objective world: "The urns that stood on stone pedestals at the four corners of the terrace threatened one another across their diagonals." "He sat thinking . . . that with a Knight's move of this lime tree standing on a sunlit slope one could take that telegraph pole over there . . ." ". . . Luzhin involuntarily put out a hand to remove shadow's King from the threat of light's Pawn." He warily watches the floor, "where a slight movement was taking place perceptible to him alone, an evil differentiation of shadows." Throughout the book, glimpses of black and white abound—tuxedoes, raspberries and milk, "the white boat on the lake, black with the reflected conifers." Many lamps are lit against the night; Luzhin's father thinks it "strange and awesome . . . to sit on this bright veranda amid the black summer night, across from this boy whose tensed forehead seemed to expand and swell as soon as he bent over the pieces," this boy for whom "the whole world suddenly went dark" when he learned chess and who is to glide, across the alternation of many nights and days, from the oblivion of breakdown into the whiteness of a hospital where the psychiatrist wears "a black Assyrian beard."

The squares on the board can also be construed as chess *vs.* sex. The child maneuvers his own initiation on the blind board of an illicit affair. His father, while he is poring over chess diagrams in the attic, fears that "his son might have been looking for pictures of naked women." Valentinov (!), his sinister "chess father," part manager and part pimp, "fearing lest Luzhin should squander his precious power in releasing by natural means the beneficial inner tension . . . kept him at a distance from women and rejoiced over his chaste moroseness." His marriage, then, is a kind of defensive castling undertaken too late, for the black forces that have put him in check press on irresistably, past his impotent Queen, toward certain mate. The Luzhin defense becomes abandonment of play—suicide. Such a design eminently satisfies Nabokov's exacting criteria of artistic performance, which, in a memorable section in *Conclusive Evidence* concerning butterflies, he relates to the "mysteries of mimicry": "I discovered in nature the non-utilitarian delights that I sought in art. Both were a form of magic, both were a game of intricate enchantment and deception."

However, I am not sure it perfectly works, this chess puzzle pieced out with human characters. In the last third of the book, the author's youth may begin to show; émigré parties, arranged by Mrs. Luzhin, are introduced for no apparent better reason than that Nabokov was going to such parties at this time. A "mercilessly stupid" Leningrad visitor pops up irrelevantly, as a naked index of editorial distaste for the Soviet regime. It is as if pawns were proliferating to plug a leaky problem. The reintroduction of Valentinov, though well-prepared, does not function smoothly; if the plot were scored like a game, this move would receive a (?). One becomes conscious of rather aimless intricacies: the chronic mention of a one-armed schoolmate (Nabokov's teasing of cripples, not the most sympathetic of his fads, deserves a monograph to itself), and the somewhat mannered withholding of the hero's first name and patronymic until the last sentences, which then link up with the first. In short, the novel loses inevitability as it needs it most. Suicide, being one experience no writer or reader has undergone, requires extra credentials to pass into belief. I can believe in the suicides of Anna Karenina and Emma Bovary as terrible but just—in the sense of fitting—events within the worlds the authors have evolved. I am even more willing to believe in Kirillov's suicide in *The Possessed* as the outcome of a philosophic-psychotic mental state explored with frightening empathy. But I am unable to feel Luzhin's descent into an eternity of "dark and pale squares" as anything but the foreordained outcome of a scheme that, however pretty, is less weighty than the human fictions it has conjured up.

Early in *The Defense* Nabokov describes an obtuse chess spectator who, exasperated by what seems to him a premature concession, itches to pick up the pieces and play the game out. So too, I cannot see why, now that Luzhin is equipped with a willing if not enthusiastic female caretaker and furthermore a wealthy father-in-law, the grandmaster is hopelessly blocked from pursuing, this side of madness, his vocation. He is lovable, this child within a monster, this "chess moron," and we *want* him to go on, to finish his classic game with Turati, and, win or lose, to play other games, to warm and dazzle the exquisite twilit world of his preoccupation with the "limpidity and lightness" of his thought. He seems blocked by something outside the novel, perhaps by the lepidopterist's habit of killing what it loves; how remarkably few, after all, of Nabokov's characters do evade the mounting pin. But in asking (irrationally, he has been dead for over thirty years) that Luzhin survive and be fruitful, we are asking no more than his creator, no pet of fate, has asked of himself and has, to his great honor, done.

Three grades of evil can be discerned in the queer world of verbal transmigration. The first, and lesser one, comprises obvious errors due to ignorance or misguided knowledge. This is mere human frailty and thus excusable. The next step to Hell is taken by the translator who intentionally skips words or passages that he does not bother to understand or that might seem obscure or obscene to vaguely imagined readers; he accepts the blank look that his dictionary gives him without any qualms; or subjects scholarship to primness: he is as ready to know less than the author as he is to think he knows better. The third, and worst, degree of turpitude is reached when a masterpiece is planished and patted into such a shape, vilely beautified in such a fashion as to conform to the notions and prejudices of a given public. This is a crime, to be punished by the stocks as plagiarists were in the shoebuckle days.

From "The Art of Translation," in Nabokov's Lectures on Russian Literature *(1981)*

BOOK REVIEW:

Anthony Burgess, "Pushkin & Kinbote," *Encounter*, 24 (24 May 1965): 74, 76, 78.

Nabokov translated and annotated Russian writer Alexander Pushkin's novel-in-verse Eugene Onegin. *He considered this four-volume work, published in 1964, one of his major achievements.*

> *Man's life as commentary to abstruse*
> *Unfinished poem.* NOTE FOR FURTHER USE.

That comes (lines 939-40) from John Shade's poem *Pale Fire*, and it is just the excuse that its commentator, Kinbote, needs for indulging in divagations disguised as an *apparatus criticus*. "The artistic correlation between the crown-crow-cow series and the Russian *korona-vorona-korova* series is something that would have, I am sure, enraptured my poet. I have seen nothing like it on lexical playfields and the odds against the double coincidence defy computation." This means that the memorable things in life won't submit to the stringencies of the literary forms that are supposed to be life's recorders—at least, not to the scholar or pedant who is also a literary artist. Nabokov, or Kinbote, is repelled by the economy that the novel demands—no room for *curiosa* like the above. He has made the *apparatus criticus* into a new artistic medium—first in *Pale Fire*, now in Volumes Two and Three of his edition of *Eugene Onegin*. If *Lolita* was a love affair with the English language, this new work is a massive act of copulation with scholarship.

Before considering it, I had better ask one question: how much do we think we know about Aleksandr Pushkin? I had better ask another question: how much do we think we know about foreign poetry in general? I don't refer to polyglots—Kuala Lumpur bar-boys or the sons of impresarios—nor to, rather a different thing, graduates in Modern Languages. I refer to *Englit* people, whether professional or not. The specification "foreign poetry" means, of course, poetry in the original tongue, not in "art" translations (like Pope's Homer or Roy Campbell's St. John of the Cross or FitzGerald's Omar Khayyam). We can rightly say that we "know" Proust and Dostoevsky and Mann if we only know them in English, since we have no sense of anyone but the original author (however modified or attentuated), the opacity of the translator's personality being minimal. But a translation of poetry is nearly all translator, and we recognise—however much we think it possible to separate content from style—that that won't really do. And so most of us read Mallarmé and Leopardi in the original, with a crib on the opposite page. We read Dante that way also, and *El Cid* and Lorca—Romance poetry being what our schools have best equipped us to read. We also read Goethe and Hölderlin, even though we had no formal lessons in German. After all, the Teutonic languages are more cognate with English than the Romance. It is when we start to move East that the trouble begins.

The trouble begins because of strange alphabets (they take only an hour to learn, but this is too long for many) and because of the apparent lack of familiar linguistic elements (few people are any good at piercing disguises). Here, it seems, arty translations are in order. Literary men who would scorn to read *L'Après-midi d'un Faune* in Aldous Huxley's translation drink up Arthur Waley, FitzGerald, and whoever has rendered (wasted labour) Evtushenko. One of my few endowments is an ability to read Persian, and I grow angry whenever I think of FitzGerald's falsification—a witty metaphysical tent-maker turned into a post-Darwinian romantic stoic. "Awake! for morning in the bowl of Night. . ." Omar has the muezzin cock-crowing *"Ishrabu!"* ("Drink!")—frightful blasphemy—and the *bam*, or dome, of the mosque is, in cosmic muscularity, inverted to become a *jam*, or cup, for the sun's wine to be poured into. And, later, Bahram, who was always catching wild asses (*gur*), has himself now been caught by the *gur* (grave).

If we want to read Omar, then, we must learn a little Persian and ask for a good, very literal, crib. And if we want to read Pushkin we must learn some Russian and thank God for Nabokov. If it were at all possible to render *Eugene Onegin* into English poetry, Nabokov would be the only man; but Nabokov himself starts off his Preface with this very impossibility. There are three kinds of translation, he says—the paraphrastic, the lexical, and the literal. The paraphrastic offers "a free version of the original, with omissions and additions prompted by the exigencies of the form, the conventions attributed to the consumer, and the translator's ignorance." In other words, the pretty stuff which makes the reviewer (a wretched hack who doesn't know the original) say: "It reads smoothly." The commercial poetiser, says Nabokov, traduces his author far more than the "schoolboy's boner." None of that, then. The lexical translation—rendering basic meanings and the original order—is a cybernetic job. Only the literal—"rendering, as closely as the associative and syntactical capacities of another language allow, the exact contextual meaning of the original"—is true translation. It is not a substitute for the original, though (as Keats thought Chapman a substitute for Homer); it is the original's complement.

Before reading Nabokov's translation, I thought it might be interesting to take a passage from the original and attempt my own literal rendering. Here is, first, a transliteration of a stanza from that section of the poem in which Tat'yana talks with her nurse. (I don't follow the 1837 text which makes up Nabokov's fourth volume but the Leningrad edition of 1954.)

"Nye spitsya, nyanya: zdyes' tak dushno!
Otkroiy okno, da syad' ko mnye."
–"Chto, Tanya, chto s toboiy?"–"Mnye skuchno,
Pogovorim o starinye."
–"O chom zhe, Tanya! Ya, buivalo,
Khranila v pamyati nye malo
Starinnuikh builyeiy, nyebuilits
Pro zluikh dukhov i pro dyevits;
A nuinche vsyo mnye tyomno, Tanya:
Chto znala, to zabuila. Da,
Prishla khudaya cheryeda!
Zashiblo . . ."–"Rasskazhi mnye, nyanya,
Pro vashi staruiye goda:
Buila tui vlyublyena togda?"

(The uninstructed reader will see from this how wise the Russians are to cling to their Cyrillic alphabet. Romanisation looks clumsy and is also uneconomical.) Here is my literal translation:

"I can't sleep, nanny: it's so stuffy in here! Open the window and sit by me."–"What is it, Tanya, what's the matter with you?"–"I'm depressed; let's talk about the old days."–"What about, Tanya? Once I kept in my memory no small number (nye malo—*not a little*) *of old stories and fables about wicked spirits and about young girls; but now everything is dark to me, Tanya: What I knew I've forgotten. Yes, the bad times are on us! My memory's gone. . ."–"Tell me, nanny, about your early days (old years): were you ever in love then?"*

Accurate enough, I think, but quite inelegant. Here comes Nabokov:

"I can't sleep, nurse: 'tis here so stuffy!
Open the window and sit down by me."
"Why, Tanya, what's the matter with you?" "I
am dull.
Let's talk about old days."

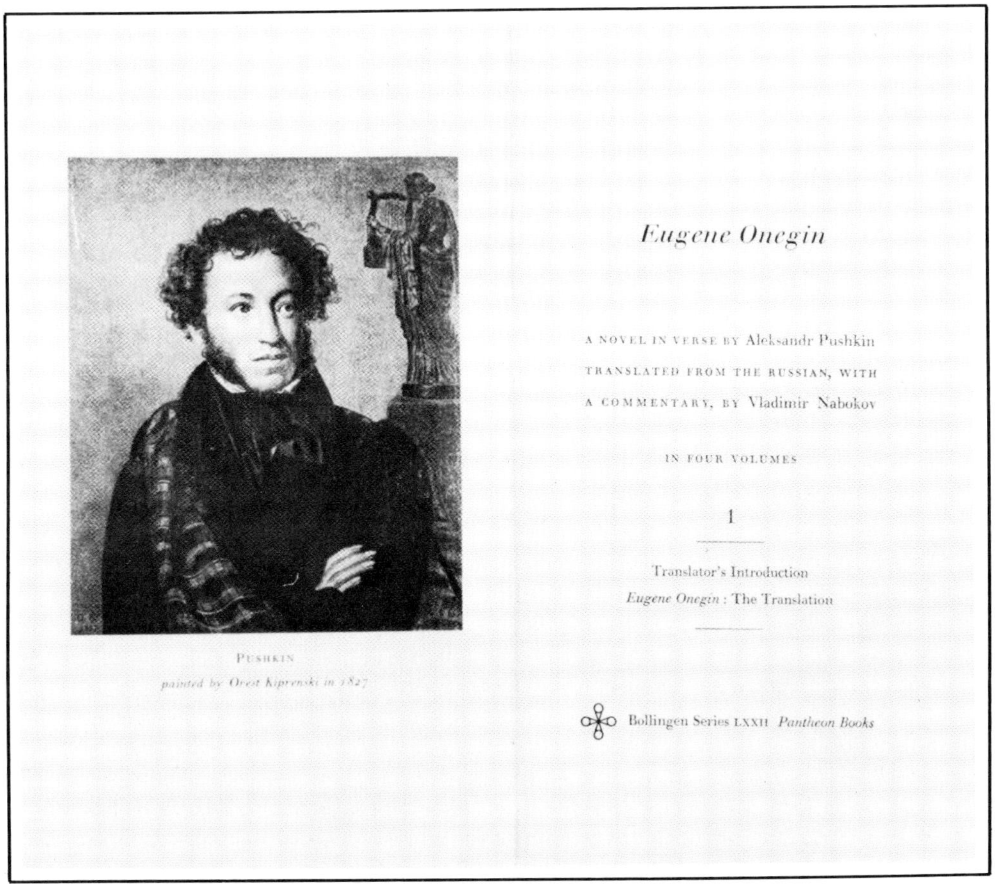
PUSHKIN
painted by Orest Kiprenski in 1827

Eugene Onegin

A NOVEL IN VERSE BY Aleksandr Pushkin
TRANSLATED FROM THE RUSSIAN, WITH
A COMMENTARY, BY Vladimir Nabokov

IN FOUR VOLUMES

1

Translator's Introduction
Eugene Onegin : The Translation

Bollingen Series LXXII *Pantheon Books*

Frontispiece and title page for Nabokov's translation of Eugene Onegin

"Well, what about them, Tanya? Time was, I
stored in my memory no dearth
Of ancient haps and never-haps
About dire sprites and about maidens;
but everything to me is dark now, Tanya:
I have forgotten what I knew. Yes, things
have come now to a sorry pass!
I'm all befuddled." "Nurse,
tell me about your old times. Were you then
in love?"

This is a fair example of Nabokov's technique. He cannot give us both the rhyme-scheme and a literal translation, but he can conjure a ghost of the stanza-form, remind us of the shape of Pushkin on the page and hint at his iambic rhythm. Some of his locutions have a period flavouring (" 'tis here so stuffy!"), but the quaint archaism of "ancient haps and never-haps" renders the Russian "*Starinnuikh builyeiy, nyebuilits*" better than my own more "sensible" translation. I don't much care for "I am dull," but "I'm all befuddled" is semantically exact as well as being in character. We have the feeling throughout of a literary experience, and sometimes the word-for-word technique evokes a new poetic *frisson*, as though Russian were fertilising English:

. . . the cork goes ceilingward,
the flow of comet wine spurts forth,
a bloody roast beef is before him,
and truffles, luxury of youthful years,
the best flower of French cookery,
and a decayless (nyetlyennuiy) *Strasbourg pie*
between a living Limburg cheese
and a golden ananas.

(Would "pineapple" be better there? Try it.)

I asked a question earlier but neglected to answer it, chiefly because the straight negative would have been embarrassing. But perhaps it would be going too far to say that Pushkin means nothing to us. We know *Eugene Onegin* as an opera, just as we know *Ruslan and Lyudmila* (or at least Glinka's Overture) and *Boris Godunov* and, to turn to the prose, *The Queen of Spades*. But we know only the paradigm behind the living richness, the generality of a plot, just as we know Pushkin himself only as a Byron by the Neva, killed untimely in a duel, an anonymous eroded statue of The Romantic Poet. We are neglecting our duty to literature (a hedonistic duty) if we prefer to remain satisfied with Tchaikovsky's Onegin (the bored dandy or *frant*), Lenski and Olga and Tat'yana. What appeals to Nabokov, or Kinbote, is the "variety of romantic, satirical, biographical, and bibliographical digressions that lend the poem wonderful depth and colour." In other words, it's the literature that counts:

> *Pushkin's composition is first of all and above all a phenomenon of style, and it is from this flowered rim that I have surveyed its sweep of Arcadian country, the serpentine gleam of its imported brooks, the miniature blizzards imprisoned in round crystal, and the many-hued levels of literary parody blending in the melting distance. It is not "a picture of Russian life"; it is at best the picture of a little group of Russians, in the second decade of the last century, crossed with all the more obvious characters of western European romance and placed in a stylised Russia, which would disintegrate at once if the French props were removed and if the French impersonators of English and German writers stopped prompting the Russian-speaking heroes and heroines.*

It is a kind of rococo which only *émigré* Russians are really qualified to appreciate, though westerners like ourselves will probably get more out of Pushkin than many of the comrades, even though they know more Russian than we do.

These four volumes (beautifully made, and each one with a bookmark) represent the very perfection of scholarship, though a scholarship that suggests no parallel talent to the one exhibited in the (now one comes to think of it) Pushkinesque novels. The Nabokov we know is very much here. I know of no other work which, ostensibly serving no higher purpose than to ease the way into an unknown piece of great art, itself approaches great art.

BOOK REVIEW:

Julian Moynahan, "Speaking of Books: Vladimir Nabokov," *New York Times Book Review*, 3 April 1966, pp. 2, 14.

The novella Soglyadataj (The Spy, *translated as* The Eye) *was originally published in 1930. The theme of a man seeking to recreate his life is introduced here, but appears more fully in Nabokov's next novel,* Podvig (Glory).

Vladimir Nabokov's short novel, "The Eye," appeared in Playboy last year and was published as a book during the New York newspaper strike last fall, with the result that it missed its normal quota of reviews. During the past few years, Nabokov has been bringing out in carefully supervised English translations most of his work written in Russian during the 1930's, when he belonged to Russian émigré circles in Berlin and elsewhere on the Continent. "The Eye" was composed in 1930 but is set further back, in the Berlin of 1924-25. It is a charming and funny book containing obliquities of narrative procedure which we have learned to call Nabokovian, and it should be read by anyone interested in what this singularly important modern writer is up to. Actually, "The Eye" strikes me as good Nabokov to practice on before exploring the non-Euclidean "plexed" spaces of "Pale Fire" (1962), or attempting to reach settled conclusions as to what, say, "The Real Life of Sebastian Knight" (1941) is "really" about.

"The Eye" is about a wincingly self-conscious young man named Smurov, who is presented to us by his own ghost in terms of images formed of him by various Russian expatriates frequenting a certain house in Berlin. Since the narrator purports to be dead and to survive only as a disembodied, registering eye—while Smurov is certainly "alive"—it becomes impossible to say who or what Smurov is, apart from people's imaginative construction of him. In fact, this mystery about "the true Smurov" is an entertaining and illuminating way of pointing to the problems of identity created by the stance of extreme self-consciousness. "The Eye" is, at once, a comic investigation of self-consciousness; the study of a shy, autistic and endearing young man who ought to take up writing; a fable about the vocation of the imagining and remarking artist, and the price he pays in isolation and self-effacement, for his special kind of awareness; and, finally, an early self-portrait of the great artist who wrote it.

"The Eye" is small-scaled and perhaps it is not quite major Nabokov. But Nabokov is major. He is, I believe, the most important novelist writing in English today. This claim rests on half a dozen books but preeminently on the two masterpieces, "Lolita" and "Pale Fire," of the period of his writing in English, which extends from about 1940 to the present. Furthermore, Nabokov is perhaps the last great Russian novelist in a succession stemming from the prose works of Pushkin and Lermontov, descending through Gogol, Turgenev and Chekhov, and avoiding God-tormented writers like Dostoevsky who, according to the epigram of one Nabokov hero, is "Bedlam turned back into Bethlehem."

Dust jacket for the English translation of The Eye *(1966)*

BOOK REVIEW:

Andrew Field, "Hermann and Felix," *New York Times Book Review*, 15 May 1966, pp. 5, 36, 37.

Otchayanie *(*Despair*) was written in Russian in 1932; it was serialized in* Sovremennye Zapiski *in Paris two years later and then published as a book in 1936. Nabokov translated the novel for English publication in 1937; but most of the copies were destroyed in the London blitz. The 1966 revised English translation is virtually a new novel.*

The common sea, or herring, gull is not a bird given to carefully ordered sky formations. Yet once I saw perhaps thirty to forty gulls in a swirling and loose but unmistakable figure-8 pattern—with, most likely, somewhere in its midst a gull or group of gulls directing the pattern's continuous unfolding. I hardly knew where to look, simultaneously seeking out a leader, attempting to determine the number of birds, and following those gulls that seemed about to roll out of the pattern, only to fall back into its very center.

Here, I thought, was a perfect aviary paradigm of Vladimir Nabokov's art: at once beautifully simple and mysteriously complex, ordered from memory and independence—and, above all, clearly apart from the linear angularity of most birds' flight patterns.

Nabokov, himself, has played with such a comparison in one of his English poems, in speaking of the Russian language and Russian poetry: "On mellow hills the Greek, as you remember/fashioned his alphabet from cranes in flight;/his arrows crossed the sunset, then the night./Our simple skyline and a taste for timber,/the influence of hives and conifers,/reshaped the arrows and the borrowed birds . . . all hangs together—shape and sound/. . . and all good worlds are round."

Such a description applies also to Nabokov's own prose, and thus, the reader of Nabokov's novels must attune himself not so much to their "Russianness" (which is and is not present; Nabokov's Russian critics have not fared better than his English ones) as to a certain unique conception of the novel.

Nabokov must be read differently—as with poetry, more attentively and slowly, to be sure, but also with greater abandon . . . to enjoyment as well as to the ever-present possibility of artistic duplicity. Because Nabokov uses litérature as readily as he does life, his reader could do with a solid background in almost all European literatures; but then such clues (often working against one another) would not disclose the sum of the author's intent. The most outstanding illustration of how easy it is to be seduced by detail in Nabokov's fiction is Mary McCarthy's well-known 1962 essay on "Pale Fire," in which, while pulling out veritable thickets of literary allusions, she somehow or other managed to miss the point of the whole thing.

Most often, in fact, the whole can best be perceived without undue preoccupation with the novel's minute particulars; I know of at least two reviews of "Pale Fire," both in provincial American newspapers (one by a poet), in which the reviewers' matter-of-fact exposition of the novel demonstrated that this simple comprehension can, in fact, be attained by the good reader even though he lacks knowledge of the Russian language and literature, of chess, lepidoptery, and several other refined subjects dear to Nabokov's heart. The close details may properly come later, for Nabokov's fiction demands rereading.

"Despair"—which was written in Russian in 1932, published serially in 1934 and as a book in 1936—is the "simplest" of Nabokov's major novels. But in spite of its narrative simplicity, it continually flits out of our grasp, a fact of which the author genially forewarns us in his Introduction: "Plain readers . . . will welcome its plain structure and pleasing plot—which, however, is not quite as familiar as [one character] assumes it to be."

There is a certain intrusive semblance of a retrospective echo in "Despair." It is present most of all perhaps in the rhetorical flourishes and sinister jollity of the novel's narrator-protagonist, Hermann, at times reproducing not only the psychic phase, but also the very verbal meter of "Lolita's" Humbert. Thus, in "Lolita": "All of a sudden I noticed that he had noticed that I did not seem to have noticed . . .": and, in "Despair": "He listened, that was certain. I listened to his listening. He listened to my listening to his listening." But Hermann and Humbert are only as alike as any two mad murderers, or, in Nabokov's own words: "Hermann and Humbert are alike only in the sense that two dragons painted by the same artist at different periods of his life resemble each other. Both are neurotic scoundrels, yet there is a green lane in Paradise where Humbert is permitted to wander at dusk once a year; but Hell shall never parole Hermann."

There is no direct correspondence between "Lolita" and "Despair." The two novels are comets moving in opposite directions, and we may do no more than appropriate a line from Byron ("The nympholepsy of some fond despair . . .") to mark their literary nexus. All the same, the reader who grasps the full, multifaceted

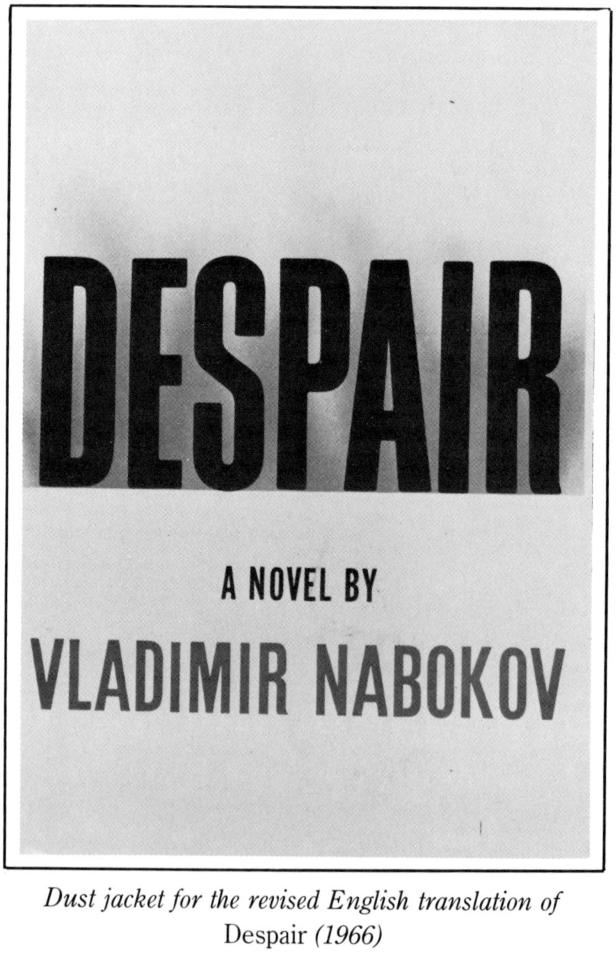

Dust jacket for the revised English translation of Despair *(1966)*

meaning of Hermann's carefully plotted assault on his double, Felix, in "Despair" will most likely find himself thinking back to Humbert and Quilty, wondering if he missed something in "Lolita."

A German chocolate manufacturer of Russian parentage is on the verge of bankruptcy. He goes on a business trip to Prague, where by chance he meets a tramp who is his perfect double, and—not too unpredictably—he proceeds to murder and change places with the tramp.

If the reader trustfully acquiesces in Hermann's train of exposition, "Despair" rolls steadily and evenly along its tracks. But when the shot has been fired and Hermann—now Felix, "the happy one"—has fled abroad, a switch is thrown in the tracks that turns the excursion into a mad, roller-coaster descent. The shock is one of re-cognition: for the densely bearded Felix learns from a newspaper story that the murdered Felix, although he was found wearing Hermann's clothes, in no way resembled him. At once, the entire narrative, in all its "simplicity," becomes something else again.

The theme of the double is in one sense eliminated as surely as poor Felix, but it is providentially replaced by many other doublings, both psychological and artistic.

The double motif is best known in Russian literature in Dostoevsky's short story "The Double" (a title that Hermann considers for his tale), but it figures prominently in the works of many other Russian writers, especially during the 1830's in the romantic prose of such minor figures as Antony Pogorelsky ("The Double, or My Evenings in Little Russia") and V. F. Odoevsky ("The Tale of the Body of Unclear Ownership"). Its most brilliant, albeit oblique expression in the 19th century was in the works of Nikolai Gogol ("The Nose," "The Inspector General"). The origin of the motif is the gothic fantasy of such German writers as Tieck and Hoffmann. To this genealogy may be added certain other writers—the German poet Heine (Nabokov printed an early fragment of "Despair" as a short story entitled "Still ist die Nacht," taken from Heine's "Die Heimkehr" in which the double motif figures) and, perhaps most important of all, Poe. Today the theme is generally regarded as one of literature's curious and interesting chestnuts.

Yet Nabokov is beyond any doubt the most subtle and imaginative manipulator of the *doppelganger* theme in the entire history of literatre. There are few Nabokov works in which the double motif does not at least poke its way into the narrative fabric, and there are many, such as "Despair," in which it constitutes the narrrative axis.

Nabokov makes of the double not so much a device as an artistic principle which may be used to examine and portray psychological, esthetic, and formal artistic problems, such as the relationship of the author to what he is writing. The doubles may stand in for author or character, and—fittingly enough—they are sometimes even double agents.

Nabokov uses and refers to them, now whimsically, now seriously, in a myriad of ways: "one of my representatives," "my disreputable namesake," "ever-present co-drinker," "my inner self," "I . . . the mimic and he the model" (that from "Despair"), "a bogus relative, a querulous imposter," "one of my literary impersonators" and "an elusive double, triple, self-reflecting magic, Proteus of a phantom." The doubles are reflections, refigurations and refractions, and their deployment in thoroughly palpable fiction constitutes a new and wonderfully malleable realism.

Hermann and Felix may be taken together, then, Felix playing the role not of Hermann's "secret self" but of the necessary and complementary mirror without which Hermann cannot be seen in proper focus. Significantly, after he has murdered Felix and assumed his place, Hermann cannot bear to look into a mirror and hides behind a luxuriant growth of beard. In a key sentence which has been added to the original text (one of those gifts which Nabokov grants the English readers of his Russian novels) the relationship is neatly stated as "Narcissus fooling Nemesis by helping his image out of the brook." In Greek mythology Nemesis is the personification of divine retribution for violation of sacred law. Hermann's murder of Felix, in other words, is not the primal violation.

On reading "Despair" first in the original Russian, my strong feeling was that Hermann's despair is (not exclusively by any means, but predominantly) sexual. Now there need be no doubt, for the 1966 "Despair" includes "an important passage which had been stupidly omitted in more timid times." This scene is Hermann's description of intercourse with his wife Lydia, whom he describes as "plump, short, rather formless, but then pudgy women alone arouse me." As he makes love to Lydia, Hermann suddenly finds that his place has been assumed by "that imp Split," and he himself sits off to the side in an armchair, naked, observing with delight the energetic exercises of Split and his wife. If we take the imp Split to be a double of Hermann's double, Felix, then Felix becomes an intimate, long-time acquaintance, and more of a threat than a victim.

New York Times Book Review, *15 May 1966*

The centripetal nature of Hermann's personality is clear enough, and yet Nabokov, especially when he plays the psychological novelist (Hermann has entrusted his diary to an emigre writer, "a well-known author of psychological novels . . . very artificial, though not badly constructed"), can always be counted on to leave the Freudians in despair. Hermann leers at the "rat-faced, sly little expert," who will discover a sure sign of psychic abnormality in his tale, and some of the embellishments are surely intended to be at the expense of his first reader and his secondary readers, ourselves.

The careful reader of "Despair" must always bear in mind two attributes which, by his own admission, govern Hermann's personality: his "gift of penetrating life's devices" and his "light-hearted, inspired lying." And anyway, Nabokov might remind us—in another novel, has, in fact—that, interesting as sexual matters are, "the breaking of a wave cannot explain the whole sea."

The "real" story of the novel can only be guessed at from the infrequent *lapses* in Hermann's commentary. Thus Lydia leaves a note for him one evening saying she has gone to the movies. Left alone at home, Hermann finds his own company "intolerable, since it excited me too much and to no purpose" and on impulse goes to visit the home of Lydia's cousin Ardalion ("a mountebank of a man, red-blooded and despicable") where he finds his wife lying half-dressed on Ardalion's bed.

Hermann, however, assures us many times that he has complete faith in his wife's fidelity and love, and it is only the taciturn and "stupid" Felix who can say (to Hermann): "I'd like to have a real friend. I'd serve with him as a gardener, and then afterwards his garden would become mine, and I'd always remember my dead comrade with grateful tears. We'd fiddle together, or, say, he'd play the flute and I the mandolin. But women . . . now, really, could you name a single one who did not deceive her husband?"

The possibility, indeed probability, that Lydia's affair with Ardalion is the "real" story of the novel leads to some most interesting further thoughts. For the meek

Lydia plays a key role in Hermann's crime, and, if she is not in fact the submissive and loyal wife Hermann portrays her as, it is quite likely that the crime and the entire story is a madman's fantasy. This view is corroborated by a technical detail at the end of the novel, for Hermann is writing a description of what he is doing *at the very moment* he is supposedly doing it.

To pay attention exclusively to such hints and details is to see Hermann only as a "case" (as is well known, Dr. Nabokov does not accept patients) and neglect the extraordinary story Hermann thinks he is telling. Hermann offers his own explanation of the tale's significance, and, surprisingly, it is a political one. For he is a convinced Communist, and it is his fondest hope that his story will be published in the U.S.S.R. "It even seems to me sometimes that my basic theme, the resemblance between two persons, has a profound allegorical meaning. . . . In fancy, I visualize a new world, where all men will resemble one another as Hermann and Felix; a world of Helixes and Fermanns; a world where the worker fallen dead at the feet of his machine will be at once replaced by his perfect double smiling the serene smile of perfect socialism." Hermann's ideal world, needless to say, is not a round but a square one.

This reading of "Despair" is perhaps only whimsical byplay on Nabokov's part—there is even less politics than sex in the novel. It is not nearly so intriguing as yet another interpretation, also courtesy of Hermann, which one émigré critic has taken to be the most important.

In his first paragraph Hermann compares himself to a poet. If one follows this curious analogy, the murder becomes the artist's assault upon his creation. "Any remorse on my part," Hermann says, "is absolutely out of the question: an artist feels no remorse, even when his work is not understood, not accepted." Hermann is striving to achieve not merely a perfect crime, but rather the "pride, deliverance, bliss" of artistic triumph. His inability to fashion himself out of his chosen image (in the manner he intends to, that is) is an allegory of the absurd pretension of realistic, "representational" art. There are but two truths in "Despair." One is stated by Hermann: "Every work of art is a deception," and Nabokov gives the other to Lydia's cousin Ardalion who, significantly, is an unsuccessful artist: "Every face is unique."

So, too, one might add, is every literary style, and Hermann's is a composite of "twenty-five different handwritings." The virtuosity with which he changes his narrative voice and the thrust and hilarity of his literary parodies (another rejected title for the book is "Crime and Pun") constitute almost a semiautonomous work of art within the novel. Most notably, there is a Pushkinian passage ("There is no bliss on earth: there's peace and freedom, though./An enviable lot I long have yearned to know")—Hermann's very name may hark back to Pushkin's "Queen of Spades"—and there are many uproarious passages at the expense of Dostoevsky. ("He kept covering my hands with kisses, and bidding me farewell. Even the waiters wept.")

The title word, despair, occurs (in the Russian text but, inexplicably, not the English) in a little snatch of Hermann's youthful poetry which, we are told (in the English text but not the Russian!), is a parody of Swinburne, and which has a certain playful, reverse-mirror affinity with the aforementioned Pushkin passage. For Swinburne, despair was "twinborn of devotion." Hermann may not receive Humbert's one day respite from Hell because his devotion has as its object that most dubious of beauties, oneself.

With each rereading the simplicity of "Despair" becomes more and more puzzling. (No review should betray the strange ending.) If he had written only this novel, Nabokov would deserve a significant place in world literature; no other author in half a century can claim a work of this magnitude as one of his "secondary" novels. A critic wrote some years ago that, although Vladimir Nabokov is the world's foremost living writer, he will never be awarded the Nobel prize. In the period immediately after "Lolita," it may have seemed so, but as Nabokov's Russian works and his newest English ones steadily come forth, his art can be seen in ever clearer perspective, and that prize seems all but inevitable.

One of the most florid tributes to Nabokov's art—"the very butterfly of poetry with the colored dust still left on its delicate wings"—has come from the pen of Dr. Anders Osterling, the head of the Nobel Committee. Nabokov himself has never ascribed any value to awards, of course, but one looks forward to the event anyway, if only for what will surely be the most eccentric and extaordinary acceptance speech in the history of that august body.

> *We shall do our best to avoid the fatal error of looking at so-called "real life" in novels. Let us not try and reconcile the fiction of facts with the facts of fiction.*

From Nabokov's "Introduction" to his Lectures on Don Quixote *(1983)*

BOOK REVIEW:

Eliot Fremont-Smith, "Evidence of the Hunt, Clues of a Past," *New York Times*, 9 January 1967, p. 37.

Nabokov's autobiography deals only with his life from childhood to his arrival in America. He originally wrote the book in English as Conclusive Evidence *(1952), translated it for Russian publication, and then reworked it back into English making changes and additions for the final version,* Speak, Memory: An Autobiography Revisited, *published in 1967.*

Vladimir Nabokov, the bilingual writer, has at one time or another been compared to Joseph Conrad. He objects to the comparison, noting (among other things) that Conrad never wrote in Polish. He himself, of course, has become something of an acrobat, supplely curling himself between his native language, Russian, and his first literate language, English. In a now-characteristic foreword (bibliography, 18th thoughts, rabbit punches for dunderheaded critics), he elucidates the genesis of this "present, final edition" of "Speak, Memory"—"a systematically correlated assemblage of personal recollections ranging geographically from St. Petersburg to St. Nazaire, and covering 37 years, from August, 1903 [when the author was 3 years old], to May, 1940 [when he migrated to America], with only a few sallies into later space-time."

As a matter of fact, the initial essay of the series was written in French and published in Paris in 1936; the rest were in English and written in America, in an order "established in 1936, at the placing of the cornerstone which had already held in its hidden hollow various maps, timetables, a collection of matchboxes, a chip of ruby glass, and even—as I now realize—the view from my balcony of Geneva lake, of its ripples and glades of light, black-dotted today, at teatime, with coots and tufted ducks."

The first assemblage of these recollections was published here in 1951 as "Conclusive Evidence" ("conclusive evidence of my having existed"). The English edition was retitled "Speak, Memory," which sounded less like a mystery story and was an acceptable modification of Nabokov's first choice of title, "Speak, Mnemosyne," which his publishers persuaded him was commercially debilitating.

"In the summer of 1953," he writes, "at a ranch near Portal, Arizona, at a rented house in Ashland, Oregon, and at various motels in the West and Midwest, I managed, between butterfly-hunting and writing 'Lolita' and 'Pnin,' to translate 'Speak, Memory,' with the help of my wife, into Russian. . . . For the present, final edition of 'Speak, Memory' I have not only introduced basic changes and copious additions [most identifiably, a much amplified biography of his adored father] into the initial English text, but have availed myself of the corrections I made while turning it into Russian. This re-Englishing of a Russian re-version of what had been an English re-telling of Russian memories in the first place, proved a diabolical task, but some consolation was given me by the thought that such multiple metamorphoses, familiar to butterflies, had not been tried by any human before." So much for Conrad.

These bibliographical data, seemingly so peripheral, are in fact central to much of Nabokov's work, and especially to this memoir. For he is concerned first of all, and to the point of obsession, with process. The book is "about" his extraordinary, cultured, aristocratic family and upbringing in imperial Russia—"the harmonious world of a perfect childhood," as he puts it—and the years of exile between 1919 and 1940 in Cambridge, England, Berlin and Paris.

But what primarily involves him, and makes the book a work of art, is the process of recollection, how the chip of ruby glass retrieves forgotten feelings and past events from dark corners of the prison of time in which both it and he are still and always entrapped; how what he calls the "spiral unwinding of things" can be stopped and penetrated at certain points by the senses, detectives and conjurers after clues; and how this evidence reasserts itself and can be reordered, re-energized and expressed, at once transformed and re-created into memory and art.

A Proustian exercise, also Joycean, also Nabokovian; and with Nabokov, the translation, reordering and extension of his own previous writing is not merely helpful to the estate but essential to his way of art, and has much to do with his early mathematical wizardry, his fascination with chess, his butterfly collecting, his (as Page Stegner notes in his recent study of Nabokov's English novels, "Escape Into Aesthetics") "deliberate strategy" of blending, as if for sanity's sake, appearance and reality in imitation of nature's intricate deceptions and endless metamorphoses.

It remains to be said here that "Speak, Memory" unmasks and evokes much that is factually fascinating. It is full of marvelous stories and fragments and portraits—especially of his liberal publisher-politician father, who was once jailed by the czar, took part in the uprising of March, 1917, and in the Lvov provisional government, fled the Bolsheviks (the author left behind a

Dust jacket for Nabokov's revised autobiography

$2-million inheritance) and was assassinated by monarchists in Berlin in 1922. The Nabokov residences—a town house in St. Petersburg, a country villa with "a permanent staff of about 50 servants and no questions asked" nearby—and the various wealthy watering-holes of Europe are all wonderfully described.

At the end, there is still the process, a source of art as well as of the meld of attitude it constantly, continuingly and cunningly takes on, a cross of farce and anguish. One is reminded throughout of a television interview done with Nabokov a year or so ago at his present home in Montreux, Switzerland. At the fadeout, the screen showed the view from Nabokov's terrace, while the author's voice could be heard in the background testing various pronunciations of his name, as if to see what each might now trick away from time, unmask, unlock, evoke. "Nabokov," you could hear—"NAbokov, NabOkov, Nabookov. . . ."

BOOK REVIEW:

"Great & Delightful Rarity," *Time*, 91 (17 May 1968): 102.

Nabokov "constructed" his second novel in the winter of 1927-1928. Although not as complex as his later work, Korol', Dama, Valet (King, Queen, Knave) *is the first of several plots based on cards or chess. Nabokov later said, "my first two novels are to my taste mediocre"; but publication of this second novel aroused critical interest. It was published in English in 1968.*

This is Vladimir Nabokov's second novel, written and published in Russian in 1928, when he was a 28-year-old émigré living in Berlin. It was recently roughed into English by Nabokov's son Dmitri, then tightened and buffed to a cold brilliance by the author. "Of all my novels," says Nabokov, "this bright brute is the gayest. Expatriation, destitution, nostalgia had no effect on its elaborate and rapturous composition."

Actually, his later novels, notably *Lolita* and *Pale Fire*, are far more elaborate. Even *Laughter in the Dark* (originally published in 1932 as *Camera Obscura*), which in setting, plot and theme strongly resembles *King, Queen, Knave*, is more intricately patterned. But *King, Queen, Knave* is tricky enough—the appearance-and-reality theme as applied to the eternal love triangle. In Nabokov's idiosyncratic geometry, all three angles are obtuse: Kurt Dreyer, fiftyish, owner of a prosperous department store, is suffused with a jocular egomania; Martha, his 34-year-old wife, beautiful and sybaritic, is dimmed by compulsively romantic restlessness and anticipation; Franz, Dreyer's youthful nephew and employee, is a myopic, precariously balanced bumpkin.

Dreyer and Franz occasionally attempt to squirm out of the two-dimensional plane in which Nabokov holds them captive. But most of the time, all three are as flat and glossy as the playing cards suggested by the novel's title. This enables Nabokov to give them the nimble shuffle that characterizes the mercurial plots of all his fiction.

Franz first encounters his uncle and aunt accidentally in a train compartment. They are unaware of his identity, as he is of theirs. Not a word is exchanged between him and them during the entire trip from his small home town to Berlin, where he will work in his uncle's department store. Dreyer idly casts a professional eye over the young spectacled passenger, sizing him up by the low quality of his haberdashery. In Martha's peephole of a mind, Franz registers as little more than a lifeless lump.

Nabokov lingers over the coincidence of the encounter, but his timing is nearly perfect. By drawing it out, he sharpens the anticipation of the impending adultery; before long, Martha, the frosty doll, and Franz, promoted from lifeless lump to "warm and pliant wax," can't get enough of each other.

The affair thrives, despite burlesqued escapes from detection, and Martha evolves a plan to drown Dreyer, inherit his millions and marry Franz. "My dining room, my earrings, my silver, my Franz," she muses. Martha, in fact, is so greedy that she aborts the murder plot at the last moment because her husband remarks that he is about to fatten his estate with $100,000 from the sale of a patent for mechanical mannequins. The appearance of these "automannequins" raises the question of who is real and who is not—one of those Nabokovian diversions that in later novels are more subtly conceived, often with the impish intention of trapping overanxious symbol hunters.

There are other such feints in the novel, including a jarring and inexplicable projection of Franz into a diseased old age, and a lunatic landlord who constantly threatens to break up the game but never does. But in the end, it is the author's stylized and intentionally visible hand that collects all bets. Martha succumbs meekly to pneumonia. Franz, relieved of his responsibilities as stud and killer, leaps into madness. Dreyer continues good-naturedly to misread all signs.

Here, as in Nabokov's more sophisticated novels, an important theme is the nature of fiction itself. By putting his comic trio through a series of abstract stances—a modification of the futurist and expressionist influences that swept the arts in the '20s—he never allows the reader to forget that fiction is essentially artifice. In *King, Queen, Knave*, the artifice may be a little too obvious, but intelligence and wit keep it working smoothly to the end. Nabokov himself could well have been thinking of this "bright brute" when he described a certain variety of butterfly he once discovered in the French Alps: "It may not rank high enough to deserve a name, but whatever it be—a new species in the making, a striking sport, or a chance cross—it remains a great and delightful rarity."

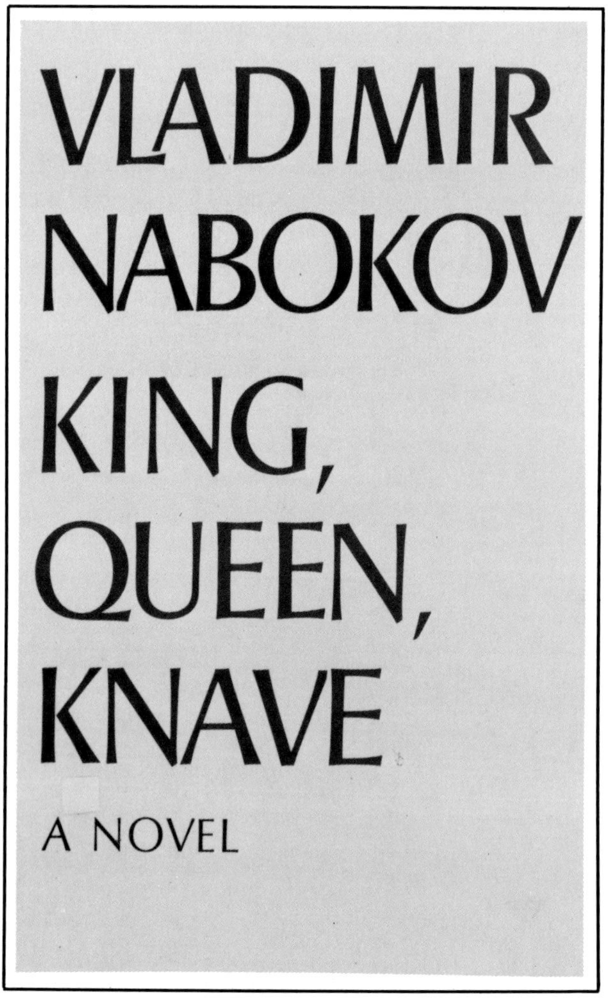

Dust jacket for the translation of Nabokov's second novel

BOOK REVIEW:

Marc Slonim, "An Early Act of Memory and Imagination," *New York Times Book Review*, 25 October 1970, pp. 4, 66.

After graduating with honors from Cambridge in 1923 Nabokov moved to Berlin. There he married Véra Evaseevna Slonim in 1925. His first novel, Mashen'ka (Mary), *was published in Russian the next year, and was generally unnoticed. Nabokov calls the character Mary "a twin sister" to his own first love, Tamara, whom he never saw after his family left Russia. Out of "attachment to* [his] *first book," Nabokov collaborated on its translation to produce a text in 1970 that follows the original very closely.*

I read "Mary" many years ago in the Russian original. It appeared in Berlin in 1926 as the first novel of Sirin—the pen name of young Vladimir Nabokov (born in 1899). At that time he was a beginner, an obscure poet and the author of a few short stories. Is it possible today to appraise "Mary" on its own merit, to overcome the almost irresistible temptation to examine it as a piece of literary history or biography, as a first step in a long and brilliant career, and abandon the search for elements brought to maturity and fulfillment in later creations of a famous writer?

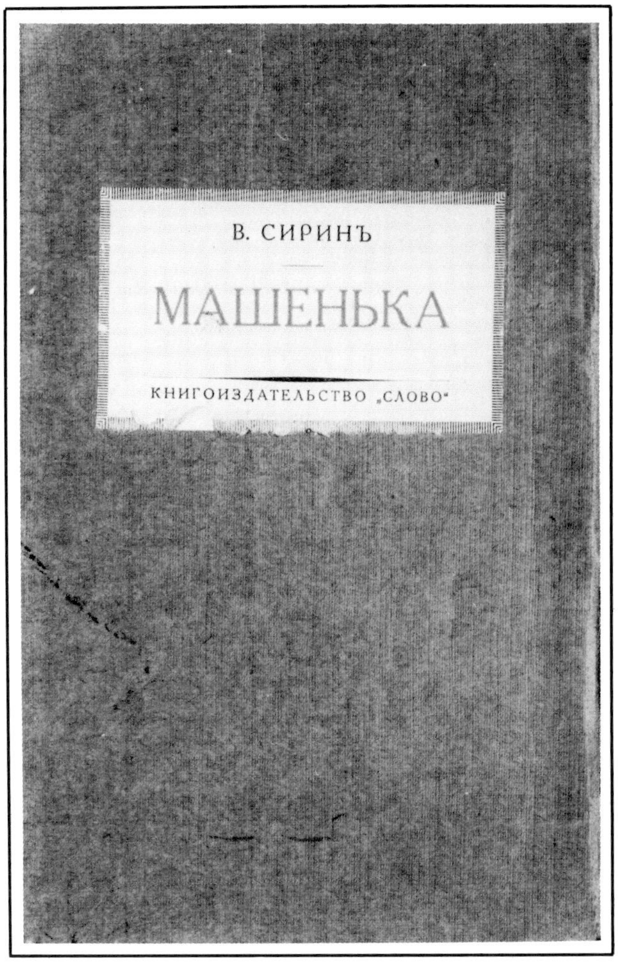

Cover of Nabokov's first Russian novel, Mashen'ka, *published under the pseudonym V. Sirin*

I liked "Mary" or "Mashenka"—this is how its title (an endearing diminutive) sounds in Russian—when I first read it, and I enjoyed rereading it in this very good English translation by Michael Glenny because of the spirit of youth and nostalgia its pages convey. Books, like people, can be lovely and charming—and I believe that this is the main attraction of "Mary." Otherwise, despite some questionable scenes and trite devices (such as the exchange of letters between two lovers) this minor work stands as a clever, compact story with a measured dosage of suspense resolved in an unexpected ending. Under the slight film of typical Nabokovian irony and verbal preciosity, one discovers the poetic and lyricism, let alone sentimentality, which the future master of parodies and sarcastic forays tried in the ensuing years to camouflage with his stylistic tours de force.

It would be a gross error to call "Mary" a realistic narrative describing the life of Russian émigrés in Berlin of the 1920's, but many readers and some critics did so in the past. In fact, Nabokov has as little to do with realism—whatever this arbitrary term means—as with symbolism and other "isms." He does describe visual, auditive and tactile sensations and brings out concrete significant details, but he uses them for his purely artistic purposes.

In "Mary" he presents sharp portraits of exiles huddled together in a shabby boarding house, always waiting for something to happen. The old poet Podtyagin, half-dead from heart disease, still hopes to leave for Paris; the flabby, ridiculous Alfyorov is counting the days before the arrival of his wife Mary from the Soviet Union; the two giggling young homosexuals look forward to dancing in a small theatrical company; the 26-year-old Klara, a brave, heavy, lonely girl and her vulgar silly friend Lyudmilla dream of great loves that will never come. These and other incidental characters are drawn with bold strokes and psychological incisiveness, free from any Freudian tricks.

But these characters only serve as background to Lev Ganin, the central figure of the novel. He is a typical expatriate, who went through all sorts of trials, worked as a movie extra, held odd jobs, and often felt himself a ghost among other shadows. Yet he is different because he possesses the gift of vivid remembrance. A whiff of carbide from a garage reminds him how the lamp of his bicycle smelled when years ago he was plunging into the autumn night hurrying to a tryst with his beloved. In the forced idleness of the unemployed, Ganin recreates his first love; and visions of the Russian countryside, of St. Petersburg, of Northern spring and snowy winter merge with the image of the young girl he adored.

Recollections bring him back to everything he has lost—youth, love, Russia—and this resurrected trinity has an intense immediacy. "It was not simply reminiscence," comments the author, "but life that was much more real, much more intense than life lived by his shadow in Berlin. It was a marvelous romance that developed with genuine, tender care." Thus the return to the native land—the dream of all exiles and the recurrent theme of Nabokov's early poems, stories and novels—is brought to fulfillment in Ganin's mind. And when the interplay of coincidences reveals the true identity of Alfyorov's wife Mary, Ganin understands that their love cannot be raised from the dead—as his Russia cannot. As the young woman arrives in Berlin, he leaves the city by another station.

"Mary" is a tale not only about love but primarily about the powers of memory and imagination. These two human aptitudes are both essential as the lifegiving source of all creative acts, and are the very foundations of art. Of course, Nabokov has traveled a long road and changed greatly since his twenties when he wrote "Mary," but throughout his work he has never failed to assert the basic truth that forms the core of his first novel.

BOOK REVIEW:

Simon Karlinsky, "Nabokov's Russian Games," *New York Times Book Review*, 18 April 1971, pp. 2, 10-14.

Nabokov combines his Russian and American influences in Ada or Ardor: A Family Chronicle. *An interior title, "Van's Book," is an anagram for "Nabokov's," suggesting that Nabokov and character Van Veen are closely related. Simon Karlinsky discussed both* Ada *and* The Gift *in the following review. Responding to this article Nabokov said that Karlinsky understood* The Gift *better than any other critic.*

After the Soviet cosmonaut Gherman Titov returned to earth from outer space not so many years ago, he vividly described his overwhelming experience of seeing the enlarged moon pass alarmingly close to his spacecraft. The sight reminded him of Gogol, Titov said. His impressions were front-page news and his remark was picked up by newspapers everywhere. One of the San Francisco papers that reported it felt obliged to explain to its readers that Nikolai Gogol was a Russian writer, gave his dates and, apparently exhausting its stock of information, ventured that Gogol was noted for his descriptions of the rising of the moon.

Titov was using a ploy that is fairly traditional among his countrymen: he was establishing his credentials as a man of culture and education by making an oblique and not fully stated literary allusion, paying his audience the compliment of assuming that they did not require a more explicit identification. He knew that he could trust his description of the huge moon and the mention of the author's name to lead all literate Russians to Gogol's tale "Christmas Eve," popular both in its own right and as the basis of two well-known operas: Rimsky-Korsakov's "Christmas Eve" and Tchaikovsky's "The Golden Slippers," sometimes called "Oksana's Caprices."

The hero of Gogol's tale, a Ukrainian village blacksmith, captures a devil and on his back flies to St. Petersburg to visit Catherine the Great. During his flight, the smith passes the moon at such close range that he has to stoop to avoid having his fur cap knocked off. Within the Russian cultural framework, Titov's allusion was both apt and accessible. It did not occur to him that he might also be stumping the copy desk of a California newspaper.

The situation in which Titov's offhand remark had put the unsuspecting American copyreaders is not unlike the position in which many American literary critics and scholars find themselves with the advent of Vladimir Nabokov as a major phenomenon on today's literary scene. A writer of wide-ranging, international culture Nabokov delights in projecting his literary likes and dislikes into his fiction, in interlarding his narratives with thinly disguised bits of literary criticism and in playing a variety of literary games involving allusion to and parody and citation of other men's writings.

In their turn, academic-minded American reviewers and exegetes, trained on Joyce and Eliot, love nothing better than unraveling this sort of literary puzzle for the edification of their readers and their less-informed colleagues. Thus, very soon after "Lolita" was published and acclaimed, several American commentators stepped forward to point out the numerous allusions to the work of Edgar Allan Poe in that novel; traces and paraphrases of Swift and Pope were quickly discovered in "Pale Fire"; and the better reviews of "Ada" emphasized the importance of its Byronic references and explained the several sets of variations on themes by Chateaubriand that the book contains.

But Nabokov was an accomplished, fully formed Russian writer before he ever wrote anything in English and it was in his Russian novels (which now, in translation, form an indispensable part of his total *oeuvre*) that he developed his art of incorporating literary allusion and reference as an inherent device of fictional narration. He drew mostly on Russian literature for this purpose in his early novels, and he continues to do so now that he writes in English. But competent critics, perfectly able to do the brilliance of Nabokov's verbal style and the elegance of his plotting full justice and to discern the subtlest and most veiled evocations of, say, Mérimée's "Carmen" or Poe's "Annabel Lee," have been known to stumble and fall on their faces the moment Nabokov mentions some work of Russian literature familiar to any child in the Soviet Union (or to any American college student who has taken a survey course on Russian literature in translation).

T. S. Eliot's absurdly uninformed dictum, enunciated in the 1920's, that Russian literature consists of half-a-dozen good novelists and possesses no poets or any other writers of note, may not necessarily be endorsed by most people who teach American literature or write about it today, but it does describe the extent of their factual grasp of it. This is why Matthew Hodgart, reviewing "Ada" for The New York Review of Books, was able to see significance in the similarity of the heroine's name to that of Lord Byron's daughter, but was thrown completely off the scent by the novel's subtitle, "A Family Chronicle."

Sergei Aksakov's "A Family Chronicle" is, of

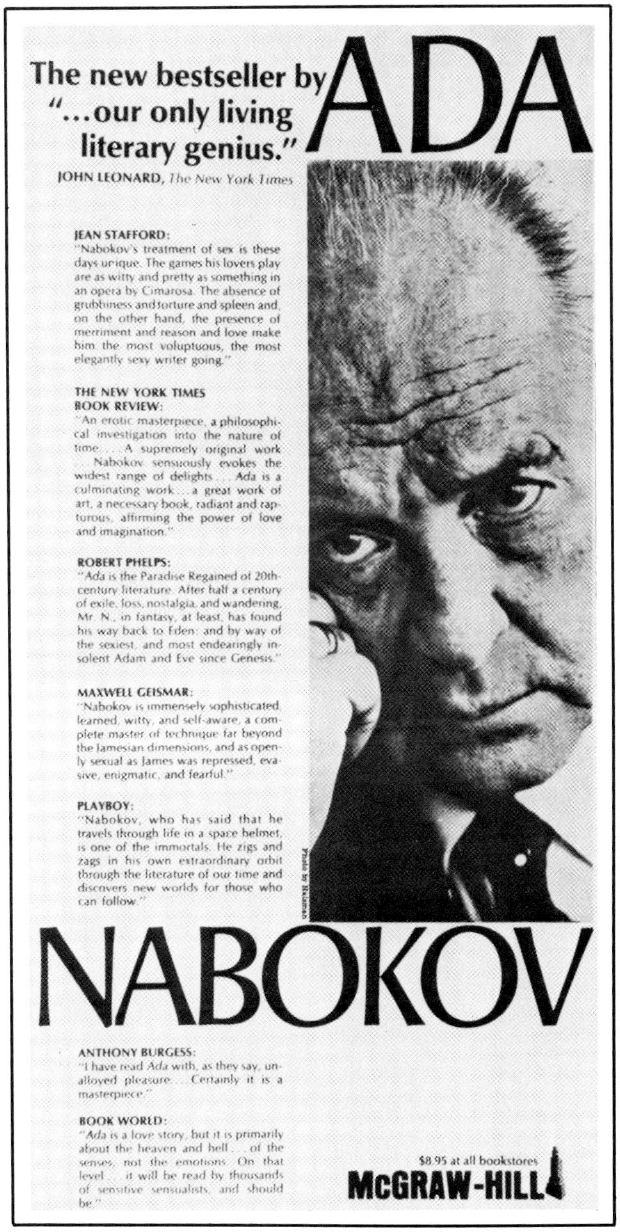

New York Times Book Review, *18 May 1969*

course, one of the most famous works of Russian 19th-century literature, long available in English translation and in no way minor or obscure. It is on that book's depiction of the leisurely and patriarchal life on a remote country estate in early 19th-century Russia that Nabokov draws for both the nostalgic and the parodistic aspects of "Ada's" quasi-Russian landed gentry setting. To drive the point home, he introduces into the novel minor characters named Aksakov and "Bagrov's grandson," the latter being the hero of Aksakov's sequel to "A Family Chronicle," "The Childhood Years of Bagrov-Grandson." Not aware of any of this, Mr. Hodgart decided that the subtitle "A Family Chronicle" indicated that "Ada" was a parody of the turn-of-the-century "family novel" of Galsworthy and Thomas Mann.

In a manner reminiscent of Alfred Hitchcock's celebrated walk-on scenes in every one of his films, Nabokov includes some Russian literary game in almost every one of his novels. Still, the unwary reader may miss the cryptic reference to a poem by Tiutchev in "Invitation to a Beheading" or fail to grasp the complex Franco-Russian puns in "Bend Sinister," which revolve around the Russian wording of Hamlet's soliloquy, and nevertheless have unimpeded access to the content of the novel. In three essential works, however, the quoted Russian literature serves as such a basic and central component, that to miss its significance is to miss much of the book's meaning. These works are "The Gift," the still-untranslated play "The Event" and the recent best-selling novel "Ada."

In the science-fiction-like narrative fabric of "Ada," the social and literary reality of 19th-century Russia is projected against the background of mid-20th century America, with results not unlike a double-exposed photograph. Russian language and literature (and to a lesser extent, French language and literature) permeate the verbal texture of the novel. Russian words and phrases are quoted, translated accurately, translated obliquely or deliberately mistranslated for punning or humorous effect. Quotations from Pushkin's "Eugene Onegin," from Griboedov's "The Misfortune of Being Clever," from Tolstoy, from several plays by Chekhov and from Russian poets too numerous to mention, are worked into the author's narration and into the characters' dialogue, with or without identification. Russian literary scholarship and scholars are twitted in ways that only they themselves could possibly perceive.

The lengths to which Nabokov can go in his verbal-literary games in "Ada" can be illustrated by his casting a girl named Dawn in the role of Natasha in a production of Chekhov's "Four Sisters" ("Three Sisters," plus Varya from the same author's "The Cherry Orchard") in which the heroine of the novel also appears. This enables Van to remark later: "Dawn *en robe rose et verte*, at the end of Act One," unexpectedly juxtaposing, for those who know about such things, the pink dress with its inappropriate green sash worn by Chekhov's vulgar Natasha with the rosy and green robe of Charles Baudelaire's shivering dawn (in his poem "Le Crépuscule du Matin") flying over the deserted Seine. The chapter wherein Van takes Ada and Lucette to a Russian-style New York nightclub gives Nabokov a chance to produce a series of virtuoso translations into English of the better-known torch songs of the Russian-Gypsy repertoire; however, the English of one of these translations, if read with a broad enough accent, will yield the Russian text of a popular song by Bulat Okudzhava, the current Soviet equivalent of Bob Dylan.

All this sort of thing did not prevent intelligent reviewers, such as Robert Alter and Alfred Appel Jr., from writing of "Ada" with distinction and perception, without delving too deeply into its Russian thickets; nor did this literary underbrush turn away thousands of satisfied readers, who found enough sustenance in the novel's other riches to ignore the cultural obstacles, which they for the most part did not even notice. But a very basic dimension of "Ada" was, however, almost universally overlooked by both critics and readers, despite Nabokov's numerous literary clues, and that was the demonic origin and nature of both the hero and the heroine.

The father of Ada and of Van is nicknamed Demon and the text of the novel constantly likens him to the hero of Mikhail Lermontov's *magnum opus* "The Demon," an iridescent-hued and somewhat tinseled narrative poem set in the Caucasus about the love of a Byronic demon for the ethereal Georgian girl Tamara, whom he kills with his kiss once she is able to reciprocate his love. The Russians also know this poem through Anton Rubinstein's bombastic opera, which they still inexplicably like, and through the series of beautiful, genuinely visionary oils and watercolors of the Demon by the turn-of-the-century painter Vrubel.

Although Nabokov draws heavily on both Lermontov and Vrubel ("I, Demon, rattling my crumpled wings" is a description of one of those paintings, and later on Ada herself refers to her father's portrait by Vrubel), his Demon Veen emerges both Victorianized and vulgarized when compared to his prototype in Lermontov. This is most clear in the passage (p. 180) where he is seen accompanied by a "temporary Tamara" (Lermontov's princess demoted to a harlot), and the pristine Caucasus landscape against which Lermontov's Demon is first glimpsed, the diamond-like facets (*gran' almaza*) of Mount Kasbek, is tellingly reduced to Demon Veen's ostentatious jewelry ("He wore a diamond ring blazing like a Caucasian ridge") and his companion's cheap cosmetics (her "kasbek rouge" and "Caucasian perfume, Granial Maza, seven dollars a bottle").

It is their descent from Demon that gives Van and Ada their superhuman stature, their immunity to scruples, and delivers their nondemonic half-sister Lucette into their power. The title "Ada or Ardor" may also refer to the heroine's infernal origin, but it may also be a rhyming device, designed to prevent the reader from pronouncing her name as Eh-dah. If the Lermontov references were more widely understood by the American reviewers of "Ada," the ridiculous comparisons of the diabolical sibling-lovers to the novelist himself and his wife in which some of these reviewers indulged would be instantly seen in all of their glaring absurdity.

While the Russian literary components in "Ada" are a part of an elaborate artistic game and a mechanism of plot structure, the similar component in the earlier novel, "The Gift," provides us with basic insights into Nabokov's views on the uses of literature and literary criticism and contains an explanatory key to many of Nabokov's controversial literary, political and social opinions. When the English translation of "The Gift" first appeared in 1963, it was greeted in the daily press with review headings such as "Early Nabokov Tale Wordy,

I confess I do not believe in time. I like to fold my magic carpet, after use, in such a way as to superimpose one part of the pattern upon another. Let visitors trip. And the highest enjoyment of timelessness—in a landscape selected at random—is when I stand among rare butterflies and their food plants. This is ecstasy, and behind the ecstasy is something else, which is hard to explain. It is like a momentary vacuum into which rushes all that I love. A sense of oneness with sun and stone. A thrill of gratitude to whom it may concern—to the contrapuntal genius of human fate or to tender ghosts humoring a lucky mortal.

From Nabokov's Speak, Memory *(1951)*

Confusing" and "Nabokov's Merry Pranks Hard to Follow in 'Gift'."

Even the remarkably eloquent and hugely favorable reviews of the novel by Granville Hicks and Stanley Edgar Hyman indicated that there was a dimension to the novel that they wished they had understood. Stephen Spender, writing in The Times Book Review, confessed that he had to read "The Gift" three times "in order to obtain an idea of the kind of novel it was." All reviewers read the book as an almost plotless record of a young émigré poet's solitary life in Berlin. None of them seemed to notice the exciting and eventful intellectual plot of the novel, dealing with the hero's literary researches, or that in fact, "The Gift" belonged to a totally new hybridized genre, combining as it does traditional fictional narration with lengthy sections of literary criticism and cultural history (a hybridization that was later continued in "Pale Fire").

What serves as the "internal" plot in "The Gift" is the hero's gradual discovery of some inescapable facts of Russian 19th- and 20th-century intellectual history and especially the oppressive character of the "men of the [eighteen-] sixties," the traditionally admired radical anti-government literary critics. As Fyodor plunges into his research on the life and writings of N. G. Chernyshevsky (1828-89), a figure almost unknown abroad, but venerated by Russians of every persuasion as a saint of human progress, the hero and the reader become convinced that it was Chernyshevsky (rather than his volatile, simple-minded predecessor Belinsky) who was the true originator of that grim anti-art, anti-beauty, anti-joy tradition in 19th-century Russian criticism which decreed any literature not aiding the cause of the oppressed Russian people in some universally perceptible and immediately relevant way to be harmful and in need of extermination.

The triumph of that tradition in the intellectual life of the country was what delayed the recognition of Dostoevsky's true stature for decades, caused generations of progressive university students to prefer a succession of now-forgotten Populist novelists to Tolstoy and to shun Chekhov as irrelevant and harmful. It was the great feat of Russian Symbolists at the turn of the century to break the stranglehold of Chernyshevskianism and to bring back complexity, mysticism, joy and literary craftsmanship as again respectable and desirable.

But the generation of Lenin (whose favorite novelist and critic Chernyshevsky was) was deeply imbued with the ideas of the sixties. The Soviet-Marxist aesthetics owes far more to the ideas of Chernyshevsky than to anything to be found in Marx and Engels. Where Chernyshevsky and his followers could only decry literary originality and independence as irrelevant and socially harmful in their editorials, their linear descendants of the 1930's, the decade when Nabokov wrote "The Gift," extended their methods of literary criticism to physical annihilation of excessively complex writers, such as Mandelstam and Babel.

Written when it was, "The Gift" is certainly the most engagé work Nabokov ever wrote. Its portrait of the morally righteous, aesthetically unimaginative Chernyshevsky fighting oppression and sowing the seeds of a later tyranny he could not have possibly imagined is all the more persuasive for the parodistic and burlesque terms in which Nabokov chose to couch it. Nabokov's daring challenge of some sacred traditions in "The Gift" caused a liberal émigré journal that first published it to delete an entire chapter from this novel.

It is a book that still makes elderly anti-Bolshevik Russian socialists, living in retirement in New York, to spit at the mention of Nabokov's name, and it has been known to move Soviet mathematicians visiting an American campus to break into an improvised dance of glee after perusing a few pages of the Chernyshevsky chapter. It is also, as Ellendea Proffer's recent article told us, Nabokov's most highly valued work among his underground fans in the Soviet Union. But until someone does "The Annotated Gift" (similar to Alfred Appel Jr.'s recent "The Annotated Lolita"), American critics and readers will continue closing this masterpiece of 20th-century Russian literature with a bored yawn.

Because of his paradoxical situation between Russian and American literatures, Nabokov will pose formidable problems to any American or British scholar who attempts to establish his literary genealogy and trace the influences that contributed to the formation of his art. The problem will have to be faced because of Nabokov's pervasive influence on literature written in English: from Stephen Schneck's gross "The Nightclerk" to John Fowles's elegant "The French Lieutenant's Woman," the Nabokov imprint is unmistakably there on any number of important novels of the last decade. But turning to Tolstoy and Turgenev for comparison, as some have tried, is fruitless: Nabokov was not directly influenced by them any more than James Joyce was by Dickens. Apart from his enormous debt to Pushkin, the roots of his innovative art are closer to us in time.

Although one would never know it from reading

Sholokhov, the Russian novel was as thoroughly reformed in the first decade of our century as the Western European novel was to be reformed a decade or two later by Proust, Joyce and Kafka. The three key writers of that Russian reformation have been so systematically downgraded or ignored by the neo-Chernyshevskians in their native country that the outside world is hardly aware of them, but those who care about Russian literature were never in doubt about their importance.

There was Fyodor Sologub, whose novel of transcendental evil, "The Petty Demon," written five decades before "Lolita," features a sexual affair between a 13-year-old boy and a sophisticated young woman of 25 and whose trilogy of novels, "The Created Legend," is situated partly in Russia during the revolution of 1905 and partly on a distant imaginary planet in a way that is reminiscent of "Ada." There was Andrei Belyi, who, had he written in any language other than Russian, would have long since received his due as one of the greatest novelists of the century and whose experimental novelistic techniques, tricky plot structures and shifting narrative viewpoints affected every Russian writer who wrote in the 1920's. And there was Alexei Remizov, a sort of Russian combination of Gertrude Stein and Raymond Queneau, whose writing career began in 1906 and ended with his death in Paris in 1957, and whose unique verbal art, based on the spoken rather than the written language, is so hypnotic that it can make one wonder whether anyone ever lived who knew Russian as well as this eccentric, half-blind man.

Nabokov has proclaimed his admiration for Belyi in a television interview, claiming for his novel "Saint Petersburg" a place on a par with Proust and Joyce; he mentions Remizov, whom he knew in Paris, in various memoirs, as one of the more important of Russian exiled writers; as to Sologub, chances are that his mysticism and fascination with absolute evil bore Nabokov. But whatever his current attitude may be, as a young beginning writer in 1916 he was sure to have been aware of the innovative novelists of the astounding Silver Age of Russian literature as he was certainly aware of its poets.

It is in the work of these predecessors, to whom he had to react either in imitation or rejection, that the origins of Nabokov's admired craftsmanship, verbal flair and thematic novelty are to be sought. By contributing to his formation, those Russian pioneers, banned or reviled in their own land, are now indirectly helping to turn the English and American novel to new and undreamed-of paths, enriching these two literatures with what the intolerant Soviet literary establishment forced Russian literature to reject. One handsome way that Nabokov's readers and critics could repay for all this largesse would be to learn a little more about the magnificent and much put-upon literature that so unexpectedly provided the English-speaking world with its currently reigning literary figure.

BOOK REVIEW:

V. S. Pritchett, "Genesis," *New York Review* (24 February 1972): 12-13.

The Russian term podvig is usually translated as exploit, *but Nabokov suggests* gallant feat, *or* high deed. *The working title for* Podvig, *his fourth novel, was "Romanticheskiy vek," " 'romantic times,' . . . because the purpose of my novel . . . lay in stressing the thrill and the glamour that my young expatriate finds in the most ordinary pleasures as well as in the seemingly meaningless adventures of a lonely life." Nabokov decided to change the title to* Glory *when the novel was translated into English by his son Dmitri to keep "the 'podvig,' the inutile deed of renown."*

The early Nabokov novels, written during the late Twenties and Thirties and published in the Russian *émigré* journals at the time, are now being carefully translated with the expected minute care by the master and his son. *Glory* has the prickly worded yet nonchalant detachment of the best young European writing of that period; one can think at once of half a dozen novels of that time, excellent in themselves, but vulgarly knocked out by fashion and history. Henry Green, for example, or the early Anthony Powell. It was a genre standoffish to outsiders, affectionately malicious to those within small, happy circles. For a decade or two the artist was to know himelf as an exile and not a journalistic joiner, and, to exiles, language and a few friends are the sacred country. The dictionary is the one holy book; as in another exile-creating period, there will be a turn to Stendhal's requirement of "exact chemistry" in the description of places, feeling, and people. This rejuvenates a stale world.

When the young man in Nabokov's fifth Russian novel takes one of the trying girls of the time to the piny and reedy outskirts of Berlin these are, they *must* be, "lacustrine." The sensations of being young lie between the rituals of being offhand and the hourly torment of pedantry. As for recording the general experience of growing a will and imposing it on the sensibility, the

Dust jacket for the English translation of Nabokov's 1932 Russian novel

sense of inner exile has been indispensable to decent writing and has nothing to do with being an aesthete. A youth like Nabokov's Martin is, in fact, a genuine Russian *emigre* and his only advantage is that he is a cosmopolitan—Swiss father, Russian mother, holidays at Biarritz before the revolution, flight, English education, and *Wanderjahre* afterward—but these accidental things do not explain why he knows in what way waves come in on any shore or why he grows, from day to day, by traveling back, forth, and crisscross in reverie. He may have had the luck to come from Yalta to London and Cambridge via Constantinople and Lausanne, in happy puberty, but his exotic journey will contain an inner one of greater interest.

In his Introduction to *Glory* Nabokov fires off a cheering shot or two at "the now discredited" Freudians and their "womby wonder" before Martin's final gesture in secretly getting back into Russia at the end of the novel. The author's difficulty in finding a title for the novel really contains the key. It was first to be called *Romanticheskiy vek* ("romantic times") but was changed to *Podvig*:

> . . . chosen partly because I had had enough of hearing Western journalists call our era "materialistic," "practical," "utilitarian," etc., but mainly because the purpose of my novel, my only one with a purpose, lay in stressing the thrill and glamour that my young expatriate finds in the most ordinary pleasures as well as in the seemingly meaningless adventure of a lonely life.

Podvig, it seems, literally means "gallant feat" or "exploit," but there was an overtone of usefulness here, and Nabokov was thinking of the "inutile deed of renown," something privately chivalrous. The now loaded word "fulfillment" was closer to the idea. Myself I find the finally chosen *"Glory"* too close to platform rhetoric, which is certainly not intended. There is no moralizing or exhorting in this gay book. Possibly Martin, who is to disappear across the policed Russian border into the forest, is crossing Conrad's shadow line, but in fact he is following the path of the secret imagination. His charming and impulsive career springs from a fantasy which has been born in his childhood, and the novel is an assertion of the excitement of that value against all others. One can, if one likes, read the story as an assertion of the kind of right an artist knows, but in a young man who is a doer "in training" and not an artist.

But the artist's coolness was required for the writing of a book so at ease with the everyday humors of people, so startlingly close to nature:

> Dinner proceeded in silence if one discounted the old-fashioned slurp with which Zilanov ate his soup.

Not entirely a comic sentence; it contains a historical judgment and even a tragic one in the placing of an old political plotter. It is an important part of the novel's intent to portray the Russian liberals whose existence has been crudely ignored in Europe and America.

The mixing of past and present and the sense of moving into a future is smoothly, sometimes strikingly, done. If Martin's mother daydreams of going back to her house in Russia, she will see herself and hear herself saying, "How tall the trees have grown," a heart-rending phrase that henceforth defines a life. Nostalgia, memory, and their tricks, so much a concern in Russian writing, are watched as they fizz away in the mind's retort. Back in Berlin after his visits there in his childhood, Martin cannot recover the city as he remembered it.

> It was as when you meet someone you have not seen for years; first you recognise his figure and his voice, then you look more closely, and there, before your eyes, the transformation imperceptibly wrought by time is run through in quick display. Features alter, likeness deteriorates, and you have before you a stranger, looking smug after having devoured his own youth and fragile double, whom it will henceforth be hard to picture, unless chance comes to the rescue.

But a novelist depends on his singular view of people as well as on the sensibility of his hero. I find Nabokov's Cambridge figures standardized but his Russian exiles admirable because they have two lives: what is open, what is concealed. All the love affairs, brief, long, or hopeless—it was a good time for the hopeless love affair with a disorganized girl—are done with a perfect lack of our contemporary exhibitionism. The episode of Martin's dangerous fancy play about the imaginary country called Zoorland, with Sonia, is brilliant.

The fantasy life of half-serious lovers is one of the central human subjects that is lost to later novelists who have forgotten that love is one thing and sexual messiness another. Sonia is a very real girl, bossy, rude, sweet, not always at her best, and certainly her allure is that she cannot be trusted from day to day. But her ugly rush of tears convinces us, more than anything else, of what Nabokov has told us in the fade-out of the last pages: that Martin has with quite awful and gallant finality gone irretrievably. The continuing gregarious good humor of the book sets off the "gallant feat," silently prepared from childhood, in all its singularity. Incidentally, prewar Berlin is very well done. Nabokov understands that objects have double lives too; they live in the mind. First lesson for the descriptive writer.

Let us not look for the soul of Russia in the Russian novel: let us look for the individual genius. Look at the masterpiece, not at the frame—and not at the faces of other people looking at the frame.

From "Russian Writers, Censors, and Readers," in Nabokov's Lectures on Russian Literature *(1981)*

INTERVIEW:

Vladimir Nabokov, *Strong Opinions* (New York: McGraw-Hill, 1973), pp. 185-193.

In October 1971 Kurt Hoffman interviewed Nabokov for German television's Bayerischer Rundfunk. *Nabokov selected these excerpts for publication in a collection of his interviews.*

ON TIME AND ITS TEXTURE

We can imagine all kinds of time, such as for example "applied time"—time applied to events, which we measure by means of clocks and calendars; but those types of time are inevitably tainted by our notion of space, spatial succession, stretches and sections of space. When we speak of the "passage of time," we visualize an abstract river flowing through a generalized landscape. Applied time, measurable illusions of time, are useful for the purposes of historians or physicists, they do not interest me, and they did not interest my creature Van Veen in Part Four of my *Ada*.

He and I in that book attempt to examine the *essence of Time*, not its lapse. Van mentions the possibility of being "an amateur of Time, an epicure of duration," of being able to delight sensually in the texture of time, "in its stuff and spread, in the fall of its folds, in the very impalpability of its grayish gauze, in the coolness of its continuum." He also is aware that "Time is a fluid medium for the culture of metaphors."

Time, though akin to rhythm, is not simply rhythm, which would imply motion—and Time does not move. Van's greatest discovery is his perception of Time as the dim hollow between two rhythmic beats, the narrow and bottomless silence *between* the beats, not the beats themselves, which only embar Time. In this sense human life is not a pulsating heart but the missed heartbeat.

PERSONAL PAST

Pure Time, Perceptual Time, Tangible Time, Time free of content and context, this, then, is the kind of Time described by my creature under my sympathetic direction. The Past is also part of the tissue, part of the present, but it looks somewhat out of focus. The Past is a constant accumulation of images, but our brain is not an ideal organ for constant retrospection and the best we can do is to pick out and try to retain those patches of rainbow light flitting through memory. The act of retention is the act of art, artistic selection, artistic blending, artistic re-combination of actual events. The bad memoirist retouches his past, and the result is a blue-tinted or pink-shaded photograph taken by a stranger to console sentimental bereavement. The good memoirist, on the other hand, does his best to preserve the utmost truth of the detail. One of the ways he achieves his intent is to find the right spot on his canvas for placing the right patch of remembered color.

ANCESTRAL PAST

It follows that the combination and juxtaposition of remembered details is a main factor in the artistic process of reconstructing one's past. And that means probing not only one's personal past but the past of one's family in search of affinities with oneself, previews of oneself, faint allusions to one's vivid and vigorous Now. This, of course, is a game for old people. Tracing an ancestor to his lair hardly differs from a boy's search for a bird's nest or for a ball lost in the grass. The Christmas tree of one's childhood is replaced by the Family Tree.

As the author of several papers on Lepidoptera, such as the "Nearctic Members of the Genus *Lycaeides*," I experience a certain thrill on finding that my mother's maternal grandfather Nikolay Kozlov, who was born two centuries ago and was the first president of the Russian Imperial Academy of Medicine, wrote a paper entitled "On the Coarctation of the Jugular Foramen in the Insane" to which my "Nearctic Members *et cetera*," furnishes a perfect response. And no less perfect is the connection between Nabokov's Pug, a little American moth named after me, and Nabokov's River in Nova Zembla of all places, so named after my great-grandfather, who participated at the beginning of the nineteenth century in an arctic expedition. I learned about these things quite late in life. Talks about one's ancestors were frowned upon in my family; the interdiction came from my father who had a particular loathing for the least speck or shadow of snobbishness. When imagining the information that I could now have used in my memoir, I rather regret that no such talks took place. But it simply was not done in our home, sixty years ago, twelve hundred miles away.

FAMILY TREE

My father Vladimir Nabokov was a liberal statesman, member of the first Russian parliament, champion of justice and law in a difficult empire. He was born in 1870, went into exile in 1919, and three years later, in Berlin, was assassinated by two Fascist thugs while he was trying to shield his friend Professor Milyukov.

The Nabokov family's estate was adjacent to that of the Rukavishnikovs in the Government of St. Petersburg. My mother Helen (1876-1939) was the daughter of Ivan Rukavishnikov, country gentleman and philanthropist.

My paternal grandfather Dmitri Nabokov (1827-1904) was State Minister of Justice for eight years (1878-1885) under two tsars.

My grandmother's paternal ancestors, the von Korffs, are traceable to the fourteenth century, while on their distaff side there is a long line of von Tiesenhausens, one of whose ancestors was Engelbrecht von Tiesenhausen of Livland who took part, around 1200, in the Third and Fourth Crusades. Another direct ancestor of mine was Can Grande della Scala, Prince of Verona, who sheltered the exiled Dante Alighieri, and whose blazon (two big dogs holding a ladder) adorns Boccaccio's *Decameron* (1353). Della Scala's granddaughter Beatrice married, in 1370, Wilhelm Count Oettingen, grandson of fat Bolko the Third, Duke of Silesia. Their daughter married a von Waldburg, and three Waldburgs, one Kittlitz, two Polenzes and ten Osten-Sackens later, Wilhelm Carl von Korff and Eleonor von der Osten-Sacken engendered my paternal grandmother's grandfather, Nicolaus, killed in battle on June 12, 1812. His wife, my grandmother's grandmother Antoinette Graun, was the granddaughter of the composer Carl Heinrich Graun (1701-1759).

BERLIN

My first Russian novel was written in Berlin in 1924—this was *Mary*, in Russian *Mashenka*, and the first translation of any of my books was *Mashenka* in German under the title *Sie kommt–kommt Sie?*, published by Ullstein in 1928. My next seven novels were also written in Berlin and all of them had, entirely or in part, a Berlin background. This is the German contribution to the atmosphere and production of all my eight Russian novels written in Berlin. When I moved there from England in 1921, I had only a smattering of German picked up in Berlin during an earlier stay in the winter of 1910 when my brother and I went there with a Russian tutor to have our teeth fixed by an American dentist. In the course of my Cambridge University years I kept my Russian alive by reading Russian literature, my main subject, and by composing an appalling quantity of poems in Russian.

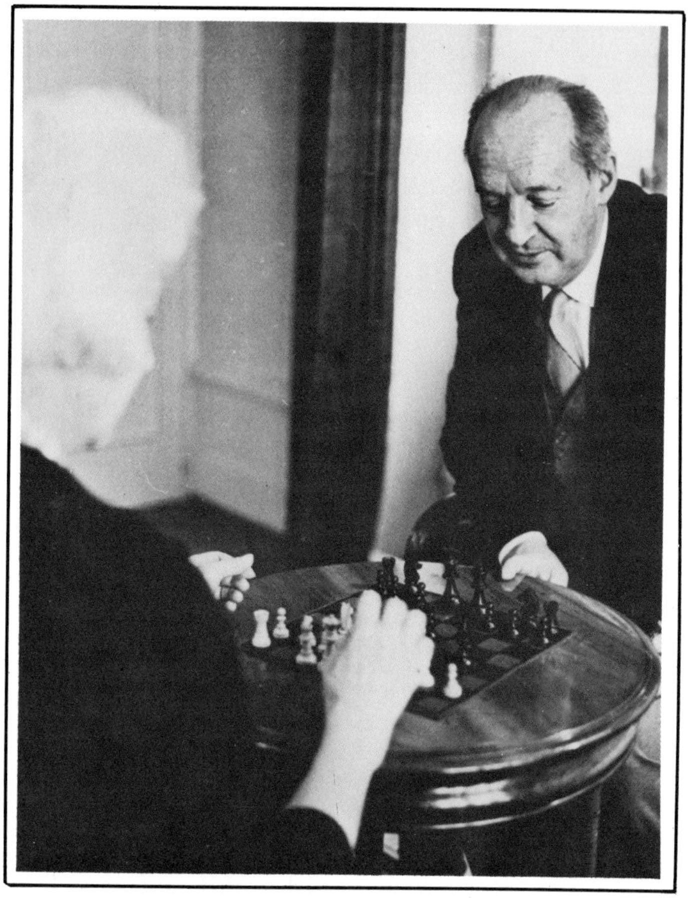

Vera and Vladimir Nabokov in Montreux

Upon moving to Berlin I was beset by a panicky fear of somehow flawing my precious layer of Russian by learning to speak German fluently. The task of linguistic occlusion was made easier by the fact that I lived in a closed émigré circle of Russian friends and read exclusively Russian newspapers, magazines, and books. My only forays into the local language were the civilities exchanged with my successive landlords or landladies and the routine necessities of shopping: *Ich möchte etwas Schinken*. I now regret that I did so poorly; I regret it from a cultural point of view. The little I ever did in that respect was to translate in my youth the Heine songs for a Russian contralto—who, incidentally, wanted the musically significant vowels to coincide in fullness of sound, and therefore I turned *Ich grolle nicht* into *Net, zloby net,* instead of the unsingable old version *Ya ne serzhus'*. Later I read Goethe and Kafka *en regard* as I also did Homer and Horace. And of course since my early boyhood I have been tackling a multitude of German butterfly books with the aid of a dictionary.

AMERICA

In America, where I wrote all my fiction in English, the situation was different. I had spoken English with the same ease as Russian, since my earliest infancy. I had already written one English novel in Europe besides translating in the thirties two of my Russian books. Linguistically, though perhaps not emotionally, the transition was endurable. And in reward of whatever wrench I experienced, I composed in America a few Russian poems which are incomparably better than those of my European period.

LEPIDOPTERA

My actual work on lepidoptera is comprised within the span of only seven or eight years in the nineteen forties, mainly at Harvard, where I was Research Fellow in Entomology at the Museum of Comparative Zoology. This entailed some amount of curatorship but most of my work was devoted to the classification of certain small blue butterflies on the basis of their male genitalic structure. These studies required the constant use of a microscope, and since I devoted up to six hours daily to this kind of research my eyesight was impaired for ever; but on the other hand, the years at the Harvard Museum remain the most delightful and thrilling in all my adult life. Summers were spent by my wife and me in hunting butterflies, mostly in the Rocky Mountains. In the last fifteen years I have collected here and there, in North America and Europe, but have not published any scientific papers on butterflies, because the writing of new novels and the translating of my old ones encroached too much on my life: the miniature hooks of a male butterfly are nothing in comparison to the eagle claws of literature which tear at me day and night. My entomological library in Montreux is smaller, in fact, than the heaps of butterfly books I had as a child.

I am the author or the reviser of a number of species and subspecies mainly in the New World. The author's name, in such cases, is appended in Roman letters to the italicized name he gives to the creature. Several butterflies and one moth have been named for me, and in such cases my name is incorporated in that of the described insect, becoming "*nabokovi*," followed by the describer's name. There is also a genus *Nabokovia* Hemming, in South America. All my American collections are in museums, in New York, Boston, and Ithaca. The butterflies I have been collecting during the last decade, mainly in Switzerland and Italy, are not yet spread. They are still papered, that is kept in little glazed envelopes which are stored in tin boxes. Eventually they will be relaxed in damp towels, then pinned, then spread, and dried again on setting boards, and finally, labeled and placed in the glassed drawers of a cabinet to be preserved, I hope, in the splendid entomological museum in Lausanne.

FAMILY

I have always been an omnivorous consumer of books, and now, as in my boyhood, a vision of the night's lamplight on a bedside tome is a promised treat and a guiding star throughout the day. Other keen pleasures are soccer matches on the TV, an occasional cup of wine or a triangular gulp of canned beer, sunbaths on the lawn, and composing chess problems. Less ordinary, perhaps, is the unruffled flow of a family life which during its long course—almost half a century—has made absolute fools of the bogeys of environment and the bores of circumstance at all stages of our expatriation. Most of my works have been dedicated to my wife and her picture has often been reproduced by some mysterious means of reflected color in the inner mirrors of my books.

It was in Berlin that we married, in April, 1925, in the midst of my writing my first Russian novel. We were ridiculously poor, her father was ruined, my widowed mother subsisted on an insufficient pension, my wife and I lived in gloomy rooms which we rented in Berlin West, in the lean bosoms of German military families; I taught tennis and English, and nine years later, in 1934, at the dawn of a new era, our only son was born. In the late thirties we migrated to France. My stuff was beginning to be translated, my readings in Paris and elsewhere were well attended; but then came the end of my European stage: in May, 1940, we moved to America.

FAME

Soviet politicans have a rather comic provincial way of applauding the audience that applauds them. I hope I won't be accused of facetious sufficiency if I say in response to your compliments that I have the greatest readers any author has ever had. I see myself as an American writer raised in Russia, educated in England, imbued with the culture of Western Europe; I am aware of the blend, but even the most lucid plum pudding cannot sort out its own ingredients, especially whilst the pale fire still flickers around it. Field, Appel, Proffer, and many others in the USA, Zimmer in Germany, Vivian Darkbloom (a shy violet in Cambridge), have all added their erudition to my inspiration, with brilliant results. I would like to say a lot about my heroic readers in Russia but am prevented from doing so—by many emotions besides a sense of responsibility with which I still cannot cope in any rational way.

SWITZERLAND

Exquisite postal service. No bothersome demonstrations, no spiteful strikes. Alpine butterflies. Fabulous sunsets—just west of my window, spangling the lake, splitting the crimson sun! Also, the pleasant surprise of a metaphorical sunset in charming surroundings.

All Is Vanity

The phrase is a sophism because, if true, it is itself mere "vanity," and if not then the "all" is wrong. You say that it seems to be my main motto. I wonder if there is really so much doom and "frustration" in my fiction? Humbert is frustrated, that's obvious; some of my other villains are frustrated; police states are horribly frustrated in my novels and stories; but my favorite creatures, my resplendent characters—in *The Gift*, in *Invitation to a Beheading*, in *Ada*, in *Glory*, et cetera—are victors in the long run. In fact I believe that one day a reappraiser will come and declare that, far from having been a frivolous firebird, I was a rigid moralist kicking sin, cuffing stupidity, ridiculing the vulgar and cruel—and assigning sovereign power to tenderness, talent, and pride.

BOOK REVIEW:

John Updike, "Motlier Than Ever," *New Yorker*, 50 (11 November 1974): 209-212.

Ada, Transparent Things, *and Nabokov's last novel,* Look at the Harlequins!, *are all highly autobiographical. John Updike, who has been strongly influenced by Nabokov's writing, reviewed this "trilogy of sorts."*

Vladimir Nabokov's last three novels form, in the squinting retrospect of at least this surveyor, a trilogy of sorts: "Ada," which is remarkably long; "Transparent Things," which is remarkably short; and the newly published (by McGraw-Hill) "Look at the Harlequins!," which is, like Mama Bear's chair, comfortably middle-sized. All three books feature on the jacket back (in three different tonalities, if you line them up) the same frontal, staring, intimidatingly cranial photograph of the author; and all three, composed in the sparkling and salubrious vacuum of Switzerland, are—in the nicest possible sense—narcissistic to a degree unprecedented in his other English-language fiction, where a distinct madness differentiates the narrator (Humbert Humbert, Charles Kinbote) from the author, or where at the end Nabokov himself breaks in, as if to establish that his unfortunate heroes (Krug, Pnin) are somebody else entirely. But no such disclaimer attaches to Van Veen of "Ada" or to R. of "Transparent Things"—creations that flagrantly flirt with our knowledge of their creator. And the main movement of "Look at the Harlequins!," the core of its "combinational delight" (to quote "Pale Fire"), is the reduction to zero of the difference between the author and the apparently contrasting Russian emigre author, Vadim, whose last name we never learn, though he is nicknamed MacNab and receives by mistake press clippings about a British politician called Nabarro.

Much of the fun of "Look at the Harlequins!" arises from Nabokov's apparent invention of a contemporary and peer who is nevertheless conspicuously unlike him—oft-married where Nabokov's monogamy is declared in every book's dedication to his wife, anti-athletic where Nabokov was a soccer player and a tennis instructor, dipsomaniacal where wholesome, outdoorsy Nabokov ("My own life is fresh bread with country butter and Alpine honey"—interview with James Mossman of the B.B.C.) is satisfied with "an occasional cup of wine or a triangular gulp of canned beer" (interview with Kurt Hoffman for the Bayerischer Rundfunk). Nabokov provides this alter ego with a list of works, but even at first glance the Master's oeuvre peeps through its mimotype: "Tamara" (1925) is surely "Mary" (1926); "Camera Lucida" ("Slaughter in the Sun") replicates "Laughter in the Dark" ("Camera Obscura"); "The Dare" mistranslates "The Gift" ("Dar"); "See Under Real" and "Dr. Olga Repnin" openly conceal "The Real Life of Sebastian Knight" and "Pnin;" "Ardis" (1970) is scarcely even a pseudonym for "Ada, or Ardor" (1969). The persona of Vadim, too, is thin to translucence, and rubs thinner as the book goes on. Though he advertises himself as "a complete non-athlete," he lapses into athletic imagery—"a crack player's brio and chalk-biting serve"—and likens his literary prowess in two languages to being World Champion of Lawn Tennis *and* Ski. Vadim's novels as he describes them are oneiric distortions of Nabokov's own; he signs himself Dumbert Dumbert in one nightmare episode of nymphetolatry, and his central psychological problem, an inability to imagine certain permutations of Space, transposes "Ada's" elaborate speculations on Time. Rightly, Vadim is haunted by "a dream feeling that my life was the non-identical twin, a parody, an inferior variant of another man's life, somewhere on this or another earth." When he comes to describe himself, his face is line for line the face on the back of the jacket. Even his three wives, so lovingly limned and so various—Iris, Annette, Louise—finally seem metamorphic phases of the nameless fourth mate, the "you" to whom this "autobiography" is addressed and who, when she enters Vadim's hospital room, is saluted as "Reality": "I emitted a bellow of joy, and Reality entered."

Nabokov's long joust and love feast with reality

New York Times Book Review, *6 October 1974*

seems notably good-humored in this novel—the best, in my view, of his last three. If "Transparent Things" is a splintered hand mirror, and "Ada" cotton candy spun to the size of sunset cumulus, "Look at the Harlequins!" is a brown briefcase, as full of compartments as a magician's sleeve and lovingly thumbed to a scuff-colored limpness. It holds, in sometimes crumpled form, all the Nabokovian themes, from ardor to Zembla, and shares with us more frankly than any book since "The Gift" his writer's bliss, "the endless re-creation of my fluid self":

> . . . I regarded Paris, with its gray-toned days and charcoal nights, merely as the chance setting for the most authentic and faithful joys of my life: the colored phrase in my mind under

the drizzle, the white page under the desk lamp awaiting me in my humble home.

Describing his three wives gives Vadim a quite contagious pleasure. First, there is Iris, a petite brunette, "a suntanned beauty with a black bob and eyes like clear honey":

> The moldings of her brown back, with a patch-size beauty spot below the left shoulder blade and a long spinal hollow, which redeemed all the errors of animal evolution, distracted me painfully. . . . A few aquamarines of water still glistened on the underside of her brown thighs and on her strong brown calves, and a few grains of wet gravel had stuck to her rose-brown ankles.

Then there is Annette, a Russian blonde, "with very attractive though not exceptionally pretty features":

> Her graceful neck seemed even longer and thinner. An expression of mild melancholy lent a new, unwelcome beauty to her Botticellian face: its hollowed outline below the zygoma was accentuated by her increasing habit of sucking in her cheeks when hesitant or pensive.

And, thirdly, Louise, an American, "porcelain-pretty and very fast":

> She . . . pulled off her wet sweater over her tumbled chestnut-brown, violet-brown curls and naked clavicles. Artistically, strictly artistically, I daresay she was the best-looking of my three major loves. She had upward-directed thin eyebrows, sapphire eyes registering (and that's the right word) constant amazement at earth's paradise (the only one she would ever know, I'm afraid), pink-flushed cheekbones, a rosebud mouth, and a lovely concave abdomen.

The manner in which these three wives (Nabokov's three languages?) travel in fictional space, enlarging from first glimpses into love objects and marriage partners and then diminishing through disenchantment into death or abandonment, is no mean feat of projection. And the hero describes other women as well—Lolita-like creatures, such as the whorish little Dolly and his elusive daughter Bel and the schoolmate of Bel's who turns out to be "you," and repulsive creatures, such as the adoring but subbrachially pungent Lyuba and the stocky, whiskery, pro-Soviet Ninella. But then Nabokov has always loved to describe women, and the landscapes of childhood, and the student chill of Cambridge, and twins, and butterflies, and insomnia, and all the gaudy mirages of "a happy expatriation that began practically on the day of my birth" (to quote a letter to the *Times*). But toward the end of "Look at the Harlequins!" Vadim does two things never, to our imperfect knowledge, experienced by Vladimir Nabokov: he travels to the Soviet Union, and he has a stroke.

Both these episodes show an exercising of the imaginative powers that one rather wishes had not had so strenuously to vie, over Nabokov's career, with his passion for trickery and annihilation. For a rabid Soviet-hater, the imagined return is surprisingly mild and calm in tone—and (to this onetime guest of the Soviet state) surprisingly accurate, from the smells on the Aeroflot turboprop to the insolence of the hotel lift operators and the slowness of the restaurant service to the "morose, drab, oddly old-fashioned aspect that Soviet kids have." The thrilleresque details of intrigue that get Vadim there are funny, and his conversation afterward, in a Paris airport, with a Soviet spy who has shadowed him all the way, is hilarious:

> "*Ekh!*" he exclaimed, "*Ekh*, Vadim Vadimovich *dorogoy* (dear), aren't you ashamed of deceiving our great warmhearted country, our benevolent, credulous government, our overworked Intourist staff, in this nasty infantile manner! A Russian writer! Snooping! Incognito!"

The agent (himself an old emigre turned Communist) confuses, as the conversation goes on in this bumptious style, Vadim with Nabokov, and when the elderly author (whoever he is) punches him, exclaims, with timeless Russian stoicism, "*Nu, dali v mordu. Nu, tak chtozh?*" ("Well, you've given me one in the mug. Well, what does it matter?") Somehow, absurd and sketchy as it is, this episode contains a warmth, humor, and suspense that only unguarded feeling bestows, and that are too much missing from the professedly ardent filigree of Nabokov's later fiction. The stroke, a moment of near-fatal paralysis that overtakes Vadim at the turning point of a preprandial walk, is amazing in its authentication, in the near-mystical swoops of its inner detail:

> Speed! If I could have given my definitions of death to . . . the black horses gaping at me like people with trick dentures all through my strange skimming progress, I would have cried one word: Speed! . . . Imagine me, an old gentleman, a distinguished author, gliding rapidly on my back, in the wake of my outstretched dead feet, first through that gap in the granite, then over a pinewood, then along misty water meadows, and then simply between marges of mist, on and on, imagine that sight!

The Master in his seventies

Or imagine any other writer since the beginning of time providing such a blend of sensation, metaphysics, and comedy.

Oh, yes, the title. Vadim's great-aunt, when he is an impressionable seven or eight, cries out to him, "Stop moping! . . . Look at the harlequins!"

> "What harlequins? Where?"
>
> "Oh, everywhere. All around you. Trees are harlequins, words are harlequins. So are situations and sums. Put two things together—jokes, images—and you get a triple harlequin. Come on! Play! Invent the world! Invent reality!"

Throughout the invented reality of this novel harlequins recur, as a butterfly glimpsed with Annette and as an Iranian circus troupe that boards a Soviet plane, as the "motley of madness" the hero wears and as a cunning multiplicity of lozenge shapes, some as small as a "sequence of suspension dots in diamond type." As the jacket design reminds us, a harlequin's traditional lozenge pattern is a chessboard made oblique. Beside him on the hospital table, as Vadim/Vladimir, "paralyzed in symmetrical patches," slowly reassembles the world, he notices "a pair of harlequin sunglasses, which for some reason suggested not protection from a harsh light but the masking of tear-swollen lids." Which hint of masked grief suggests, more strongly than is his wont, why our author has so insistently harlequinized the world and tweaked the chessboard of reality awry.

TRIBUTE:

Julian L. Moynahan, *In Memoriam: Vladimir Nabokov, 1899-1977* (New York: McGraw-Hill, 1977).

Vladimir Nabokov died in Montreux on 2 July 1977. Julian Moynahan delivered this tribute at the offices of Nabokov's publishers, McGraw-Hill.

I was first drawn to the work of Vladimir Nabokov just thirty years ago when parts of his study of Gogol, especially his illustration of the concept "poshlost" by the anecdote of the lovesick German who swam naked in the river beneath his mistress's window embracing two swans, made me laugh hard. It might seem questionable to bring up laughter on this occasion, but Nabokov was a great humorist and now that he has put down his pen there is no aspect of his many-sided work in humor, in criticism, in scholarship, in poetry, and above all in the bright inventions of his narrative art which we can afford to do without. He said of Pushkin that "he had a prismatic mind," but the phrase best characterizes Pushkin's most accurate translator and most stimulating commentator, that is, Vladimir Nabokov himself. He was a unique force, an original light in world literature, and there will be no one to replace him or carry on from where he leaves off. Of the supremely great writer, the poet Hopkins said that he was not a member of a class or genus but was an entire, an original species in and of himself. Few writers have ever lived up to this description. Nabokov is one of the few.

The most unrepentant of individualists, the most imperial of selves, Nabokov found in this Emersonian country and in the opulent American language the only dwelling place he was willing to call home after the utter disappearance into the past of the country and culture of his birth. We should feel gratitude even more than pride that he traveled "to the virgin woods of young America," as the exiled Russian poet Pushkin once dreamed of doing, and that his regard for America, his identification with the American scene held steady for all the recent years of residence abroad at Montreux. This country has always been fortunate in the exiles or refugees who found their way to our shores, but never more fortunate than in my lifetime when Mann, Broch, Stravinsky, Hoffmann, Auden, Gropius, Miës van der Rohe, Russell, to name a few, only a few, not only came here but also did some of their most creative work here. Yet I think it was Vladimir Nabokov among these great Europeans who made the deepest penetration into American life, who put his ripe creative powers most uninhibitedly at the service of American themes, subjects, possibilities, changing the map of contemporary writing more thoroughly and more usefully than anyone else.

There are spiritual depths in Nabokov's art, obviously present in the meditations on death and fate in *Pale Fire*, but no less substantial if more elusive in *Lolita*, *The Gift*, and in *Invitation to a Beheading*, that persuade me he understood death less as a termination than as an open question. His sense of the bizarre and enigmatic, the rich pleasure he took in descrying instances of deception, masking, mimicry, coincidence, and riddling throughout the life forms he studied, from "the little hushed worlds of luminous hues" under the microscope to the social and psychological dimensions of the European and American milieus depicted in his novels, imply a metaphysical or teleological cast of mind that settled neither for the solaces of conventional religion nor the mere reductions of the ordinary scientific outlook.

A sort of gnostic, he sensed that for all his keen love of the palpable world, it lay under a shadow and that there was a purer light elsewhere. Perhaps he now travels toward that light in a space and along pathways of his own imaginative devising.

Finally, there is great love in his work, centering, as I've written elsewhere, on a belief in marriage as an equal union where two people find their freedom in a bond of mutuality against "the loneliness of exile, the imprisoning world, the irredeemable nature of time, the voidness of eternity." Vladimir Nabokov lost Vyra Estate near St. Petersburg when young, and that loss persisted in memory as something like an expulsion from Eden. But he found Véra and they went on together, surviving extraordinary hardships and a cruelly long wait before world recognition of the writer's genius dawned. All sympathy to Véra Nabokov, who was Vladimir Nabokov's full and essential collaborator and who ought to be feeling a great pride along with her grief.

We are liable to miss the best of life if we do not know how to tingle, if we do not learn to hoist ourselves just a little higher than we generally are in order to sample the rarest and ripest fruit of art which human thought has to offer.

From "L'Envoi," in Nabokov's Lectures on Literature *(1980)*

JOHN UPDIKE

(18 March 1932-)

See the John Updike entries in the Dictionary of Literary Biography, *volume 2,* American Novelists Since World War II; *volume 5*, American Poets Since World War II; and Yearbook: 1980.

MAJOR BOOKS:

The Carpentered Hen and Other Tame Creatures (New York: Harper, 1958); republished as *Hoping for a Hoopoe* (London: Gollancz, 1959);

The Poorhouse Fair (New York: Knopf, 1959; London: Gollancz, 1964);

The Same Door (New York: Knopf, 1959; London: Deutsch, 1962);

Rabbit, Run (New York: Knopf, 1960; London: Deutsch, 1961);

The Magic Flute (New York: Knopf, 1962; London: Deutsch & Ward, 1964);

Pigeon Feathers (New York: Knopf, 1962; London: Deutsch, 1963);

The Centaur (New York: Knopf, 1963; London: Deutsch, 1963);

Telephone Poles and Other Poems (New York: Knopf, 1963; London: Deutsch, 1964);

Olinger Stories (New York: Vintage, 1964);

The Ring (New York: Knopf, 1964);

Assorted Prose (New York: Knopf, 1965; London: Deutsch, 1965);

A Child's Calendar (New York: Knopf, 1965);

Of the Farm (New York: Knopf, 1965; London: Deutsch, 1966);

Verse (Greenwich, Conn.: Fawcett, 1965);

The Music School (New York: Knopf, 1966; London: Deutsch, 1967);

Couples (New York: Knopf, 1968; London: Deutsch, 1968);

Midpoint and Other Poems (New York: Knopf, 1969; London: Deutsch, 1969);

Bottom's Dream (New York: Knopf, 1969);

Bech: A Book (New York: Knopf, 1970; London: Deutsch, 1970);

Rabbit Redux (New York: Knopf, 1971; London: Deutsch, 1972);

Seventy Poems (London: Penguin, 1972);

Museums and Women (New York: Knopf, 1972; London: Deutsch, 1973);

Buchanan Dying (New York: Knopf, 1974; London: Deutsch, 1974);

A Month of Sundays (New York: Knopf, 1975; London: Deutsch, 1975);

Picked-Up Pieces (New York: Knopf, 1975; London: Deutsch, 1976);
Marry Me (New York: Knopf, 1976);
Tossing and Turning (New York: Knopf, 1977; London: Deutsch, 1977);
The Coup (New York: Knopf, 1978; London: Deutsch, 1979);
Too Far to Go (New York: Fawcett Crest, 1979);
Problems (New York: Knopf, 1979);
Rabbit Is Rich (New York: Knopf, 1981);
Bech Is Back (New York: Knopf, 1982).

BIBLIOGRAPHIES:

C. Clarke Taylor, *John Updike: A Bibliography* (Kent, Ohio: Kent State University Press, 1968);

Michael A. Olivas, *An Annotated Bibliography of John Updike Criticism 1967-1973, and A Checklist of His Works* (New York: Garland, 1975);

Ray A. Roberts, "John Updike: A Bibliographical Checklist," *American Book Collector*, new series, 1 (January-February, March-April, 1980): 5-12, 40-44, 39-47;

Donald J. Greiner, "Selected Checklist of the Other John Updike," in his *The Other John Updike: Poems / Short Stories / Prose / Play* (Athens, Ohio: Ohio University Press, 1981), pp. 267-281.

LOCATION OF ARCHIVES:

Updike's papers are in the Houghton Library, Harvard University.

John Updike was born in Shillington, Pennsylvania, 18 March 1932, the only child of Wesley Russell and Linda Grace Hoyer Updike. He is shown here at about five years of age.

Updike and his father, who became the model for George Caldwell, the schoolteacher in The Centaur

The Updike family moved to a farm in Plowsville, Pennsylvania, in 1945. John attended high school in nearby Shillington, where his father taught science. Updike is shown here at fifteen with his mother, who encouraged her son to go to Harvard after she noticed that a large percentage of the writers in a Whit Burnett short story anthology were Harvard graduates. She has had some of her own stories published in the New Yorker *under her maiden name.*

Updike's first ambition was to be an animator for Walt Disney or a magazine cartoonist. At Harvard he joined the Lampoon *staff where his specialty was "Chinese jokes," such as this cartoon. He also "did a lot of light verse, and more and more prose" while in college.*

After graduating from Harvard in June 1954, Updike received a Knox Fellowship and attended the Ruskin School of Drawing and Fine Art at Oxford during the 1954-1955 academic year. He was in England when his first New Yorker *story, "Friends from Philadelphia," appeared in the 30 October 1954 issue. This photo was taken in Oxford by his wife Mary, whom he had married on 23 June 1953.*

The Updikes' first child, Elizabeth, was born in 1955. That year the family settled in Manhattan to be near the offices of the New Yorker, *where Updike had taken a position as a staff writer.*

Updike - Comment

John P. Marquand wrote many good books and ~~at least~~ one ~~xxxxx~~ for
which we ~~shall always~~ be permanently grateful.
cannot be grateful enough.
one. "The Late George Apley" is many things. It is a ~~somewhat~~
sentimental novel that fully satisfies the expectations aroused when
we approach a professional product. It is also the best and funniest
yet somewhat
extended parody composed by an American; the stately, cloying, ~~xxxxxx~~
and intermittently melodious
unmelodious ~~literary~~ ~~manner~~ of Mr. Willing, ~~xx~~ "Boston's Dean of
prose
Letters," ~~is~~ ~~xxxxxxxxxxxxxxxxxxxxxxxxxxxxxxxxxxxxxxxxxxxx~~
firmly
is so ~~firmly~~ wedded to its subject that ~~x~~ a ~~x~~ reader ~~forgets~~ is ~~xx~~
prodigy
inventi n
apt to ~~x~~ forget that this style is a continuous ~~invention~~ of ~~literary~~
prodigious
~~prodigious~~ literary wit. Also, "Apley" is a ~~xxxxxxxx~~ detailed
valentine to a city -- Boston -- such as no other American city has as
it is, finally, for us, fictional
yet received. And ~~xxx~~ ~~xxxxxxxx~~ ~~xxxxxx~~ the best-wrought monument
~~xxxxxxx~~ This class, at best
to the Protestant elite, whose grip on ~~this country~~ the country is like
nation's
the grip of a ~~small~~ small ~~x~~ but serious boy on an immense, wet, and
~~xxxx~~ frolicksome dog, ~~is so~~ apt to ~~xxxx~~ ~~xxxxx~~ raise, in reader and
tends
writer alike, ~~xxx~~ currents of prejudice and counter-prejudice that ~~all~~
such crowd
~~seem propaganda~~
~~xxxxxxxxxx~~ dramatizations ~~of it are apt to lose equilibrium and becom~~
~~propaganda of one distasteful sort of another. Marquand~~
of it lose equilibrium and tip into propaganda. Marquand, having made,
no less ferocios for being urbane,
with a satire ~~that approaches the ferocious~~ the point that the Apleys
are no better than other men, goes on, more remarkably, to suggest
that they are no worse. At the end of a life bounded on the south
by Providence and on the north by Portsmouth, a life ~~timorous and~~
smug and loving,
~~timid and narrow, mean and smug, timorous and mean~~ ~~timid,~~ mean,
laborious and timid,
timorous, and loving,
~~narrow, and smug~~, George Apley sits down to write a farewll letter
to his son in which snobbery and ~~xxx~~ ~~generosity~~ generosity, pomposity
and courage are ~~blended~~ ecstatically ~~blended.~~ confused. When he writes, ~~after~~
having
settl~~ing~~ the last detail of protocol at his funeral, "During the last

Draft for one of Updike's many "Notes & Comments" pieces in the New Yorker
(Harvard University)

Updike left New York and the New Yorker *in 1957 to concentrate on his own writing. This photo was taken a year later outside John and Mary Updike's first house in Ipswich, Massachusetts.*

lightest. The gift of wit, as unmistakable (and as inescapable) as a gift for chess or higher mathematics, has its limits and its dangers. It can be ephemeral to a degree when it shows up in verse, since part of its appeal is its timeliness. It needs stout underpinnings of neat thinking and sturdy observation, combined with a wide range of interest, to anchor it to reality. Updike's first collection, "The Carpentered Hen and Other Tame Creatures," possesses these fundamental requisites. In addition, it is wildly original and charmingly perceptive. Updike has an unmistakable voice, and it will be delightful to hear more of it as time goes on.

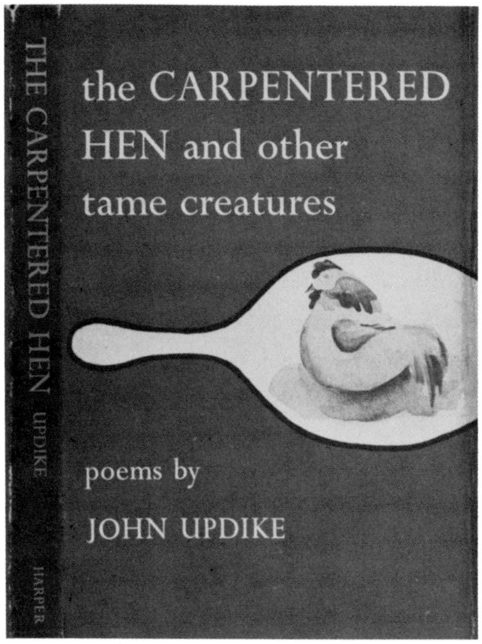

Dust jacket of Updike's first book, published in 1958; it was republished in Britain a year later as Hoping for a Hoopoe.

Book Review:

Louise Bogan, "Books: Verse," *New Yorker*, 35 (18 April 1958): 170.

The Carpentered Hen and Other Tame Creatures, *Updike's first book, was a collection of light verse first published in the* New Yorker *which, predictably, gave the volume its most favorable review. The enthusiastic remarks of Louise Bogan, highly respected poet and poetry critic, are typical of the few notices the book received.*

The poetry of a young American, John Updike, exhibits all the surface characteristics of verse at its

Book Review:

Richard Gilman, "A Last Assertion of Personal Being," *Commonweal*, 69 (6 February 1959): 499-500.

Updike rejected his earliest attempt at long fiction, titled "Home," because he felt it had too many of the problems characteristic of a first novel. The idea for his first published novel came to him on a visit to his old neighborhood in Shillington, when he saw the local poorhouse being torn down.

We have with us, to be sure, the uprising in San Francisco, but the present is plainly a period of literary retrenchment. For some time now we have been circumscribing our fields, consolidating our gains and being satisfied with mild discovering and advances that resemble the descents of small birds upon smaller worms.

John Updike is a small bird, of beautiful plumage and the sharpest beak imaginable. His first novel, *The Poorhouse Fair*, while betraying some of the deficiencies of our new mood of caution, has all its virtues too. It is bone-dry, with nothing excessive and nothing misplaced. It relies more directly on language than on thought, takes the closest insight as most useful and permits to metaphor a stabbing or flashing action but never an all-encompassing one. Turning a narrow plot of ground, it achieves the rarity of bounded, native truth, and comes forth as microcosm.

The Poorhouse Fair unfolds during a single day and upon a single scene. The poorhouse of the title, mythically situated in New Jersey, is occupied by elderly and ancient men and women who every year are allowed to stage a fête during which they set up stands and amid bunting and colored lights sell comforters, peach-stone carvings and penny candy to their visiting neighbors, while a uniformed band plays Sousa marches on the porch.

So it has always been. But on this particular fair-day everything converges toward a point of moral tension

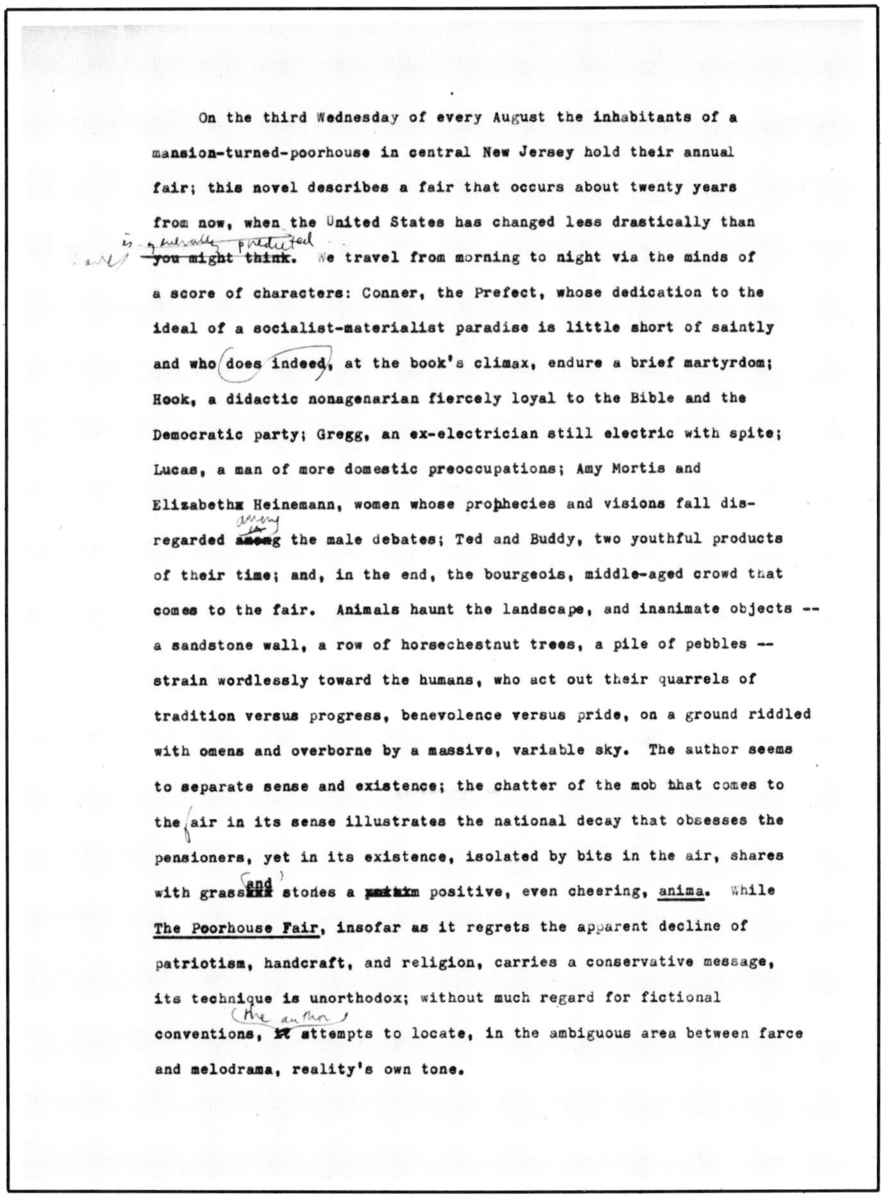

On the third Wednesday of every August the inhabitants of a mansion-turned-poorhouse in central New Jersey hold their annual fair; this novel describes a fair that occurs about twenty years from now, when the United States has changed less drastically than ~~you might think~~ is generally predicted. We travel from morning to night via the minds of a score of characters: Conner, the Prefect, whose dedication to the ideal of a socialist-materialist paradise is little short of saintly and who does indeed, at the book's climax, endure a brief martyrdom; Hook, a didactic nonagenarian fiercely loyal to the Bible and the Democratic party; Gregg, an ex-electrician still electric with spite; Lucas, a man of more domestic preoccupations; Amy Mortis and Elizabeth Heinemann, women whose prophecies and visions fall disregarded among the male debates; Ted and Buddy, two youthful products of their time; and, in the end, the bourgeois, middle-aged crowd that comes to the fair. Animals haunt the landscape, and inanimate objects -- a sandstone wall, a row of horsechestnut trees, a pile of pebbles -- strain wordlessly toward the humans, who act out their quarrels of tradition versus progress, benevolence versus pride, on a ground riddled with omens and overborne by a massive, variable sky. The author seems to separate sense and existence; the chatter of the mob that comes to the fair in its sense illustrates the national decay that obsesses the pensioners, yet in its existence, isolated by bits in the air, shares with grass and stones a positive, even cheering, anima. While The Poorhouse Fair, insofar as it regrets the apparent decline of patriotism, handcraft, and religion, carries a conservative message, its technique is unorthodox; without much regard for fictional conventions, ~~it~~ (the author) attempts to locate, in the ambiguous area between farce and melodrama, reality's own tone.

Updike's description of The Poorhouse Fair, *written as copy for the dust jacket (Harvard University)*

Oct 2 64

Foreword

The Poorhouse Fair was written in 1957 and was supposed to take place twenty years hence -- that is, in 1977. The future it portrays was intended less as a predictive blueprint than as a caricature of diffuse and decadant ~~present.~~ tendence I felt around me. Nevertheless, I did not expect that Hook's question on page 105, (ll. 14-15) "Isn't it significant, now, that of the three presidents assassinated, all were Re-publican?" would be rendered impossibly strange by unforseen events. I have left it stand as a vivid anachronism. I thought, in 1957, fondly composing this latter version of the stoning of St.Stephen, that the future did not radically differ from the past; and perhaps this curious notion was itself a product of those years of Eisenhower entropy.

Rabbit, Run was written in 1959 and was imagined by me to be so contemporaneous that the present tense seemed proper. The songs and news that Harry Angstrum hears on the car radio in his flight south, on night before Spring arrives, were what came over my own, more northerly radio (that very night,) ~~in those very hours.~~ I fell behind in this synchronization, but still worked with such haste that I found it necessary to rework all proofs heavily, and, after the book was published ~~printed,~~ to make further revisions for the Penguin paperback edition, published in England. ~~This present~~ The Modern Library, incorporates these last revisions, as well as some (trifling) ~~minor~~ emendations in the text of The Poorhouse Fair.

JOHN UPDIKE

Working typescript for Updike's foreword to the Modern Library edition of The Poorhouse Fair *(Harvard University)* unprecedented in the dim-flowing lives of the inhabitants. An opportunity for protest, for a last assertion of personal being, presents itself. Living stripped on the extreme edge of society's tolerance, the old people have let themselves be helped along to the grave. Now they turn on the young sociology-minded director of the home, whose vision of a clean ample future free of gods and suffering is the implicit denial of their present needful humanity. They shower him with an intellectual rain of stones, and thereby tip the balance toward something rich, unknown and saving.

This is the "action" of *The Poorhouse Fair*. But its true activity goes on beneath narration, like a humming around a core of vision or the breathing of language upon the coals of experience. Updike sees and hears before he judges or constructs: his prose aims at the immaculate immediacy of things perceived and at the freshest rhythms of intuited life. It modulates with absolute sureness from one sensory realm to another, from sight to sound, in order to establish oneness and simultaneity. And its unit of drama is the sentence.

This supple, most accurate prose is also capable of delights beyond itself—knowledge, insight, the restitution of truth displaced by sentiment. Updike has a marvelous understanding of old age (he is, remarkably, only twenty-six), but it is less philosophical than imaginative. He reveals it the way the aged experience it but cannot say: as the creaking of an inner bough, the attenuation of a wire, a dance of sorrow in the stillness of time.

". . . Hook felt the small condensed grief—that the past was so far, the end so near—secreted safe within his system well up and fill his head so exactly the thin arcs of his eyes smarted with what they contained."

Occasionally, Updike's hunger for precision leads him into a false approximation of it, into blueprints and a diction more proper to mathematics: ". . . a net of dark wrinkles had been thrown across his face, and his features seemed bright things pinned at the interstices of these diagonals."

Occasionally, too, his book suffers from what Pascal described as the wearying effect of continuous eloquence. He would profit from knowing that it is in the spaces between images that their resonance is nurtured and maintained.

Still, such overloading and being forced to maneuver at close quarters is one of the prices we pay for the loss of range and dimension in the novel. To people who write books about the path literature should take, this is no doubt alarming. Others will understand that one does the best one can, needlework where the big structures are impossible, small weights hefted and known in the hand where to wrap our arms around anything is denied us.

What Updike has held lovingly and explored in his hand is more worthy to be made known than all the paper towers and dragons of our hyperbolic age. And it is most worthy of being known in its own right.

Book Review:

David Boroff, "You Cannot Really Flee," *New York Times Book Review*, 6 November 1960, pp. 4, 43.

With his second novel Updike firmly established his literary reputation. Considered among his best books, Rabbit, Run *received high praise from most reviewers, although some critics felt Updike limited himself by choosing to write about a commonplace character.*

At the beginning of this moving and often brilliant novel, "Rabbit" Angstrom quietly watches a group of boys playing basketball. Then, shedding his coat, he joins them at play, demonstrating superbly the virtuosity that eight years earlier had made him the star of his high school team. This opening defines the mood of nostalgia and unquiet adulthood that characterizes John Updike's "Rabbit, Run."

Updike in 1960, the year Rabbit, Run *was published*

Rabbit is an older and less articulate Holden Caulfield. An urban cipher, he is trapped by wife, baby, an uncongenial job as demonstrator for a new kitchen utensil.

"You get the feeling," he says, "you're in your coffin before they've taken your blood out." Like his younger prototype, he is an uneasy, picaresque hero who discovers that you can run but cannot really flee. And in back of all the restlessness there is an unslaked thirst for spiritual truth.

Surfeited with his wife (who, highball in hand, sits glued to the television set), Rabbit gets in his car and drives into the night with a vision of falling asleep by the Gulf of Mexico and waking up "with the stars above perfectly spaced." However, after only one night on the road, he is drawn back to his home town and finds refuge and love of a kind with a local Lilith. A minister, a curious mixture of fallen saint and case worker, prevails upon him to return to his wife. They have their second child—but the old dissatisfactions rage and Rabbit runs again. Finally, disaster overtakes the hapless family.

This is the stuff of shabby domestic tragedy—and Mr. Updike spares the reader none of the spiritual poverty of the milieu. The old people are listless and defeated, the young noisily empty. The novel, nevertheless, is a notable triumph of intelligence and compassion; it has

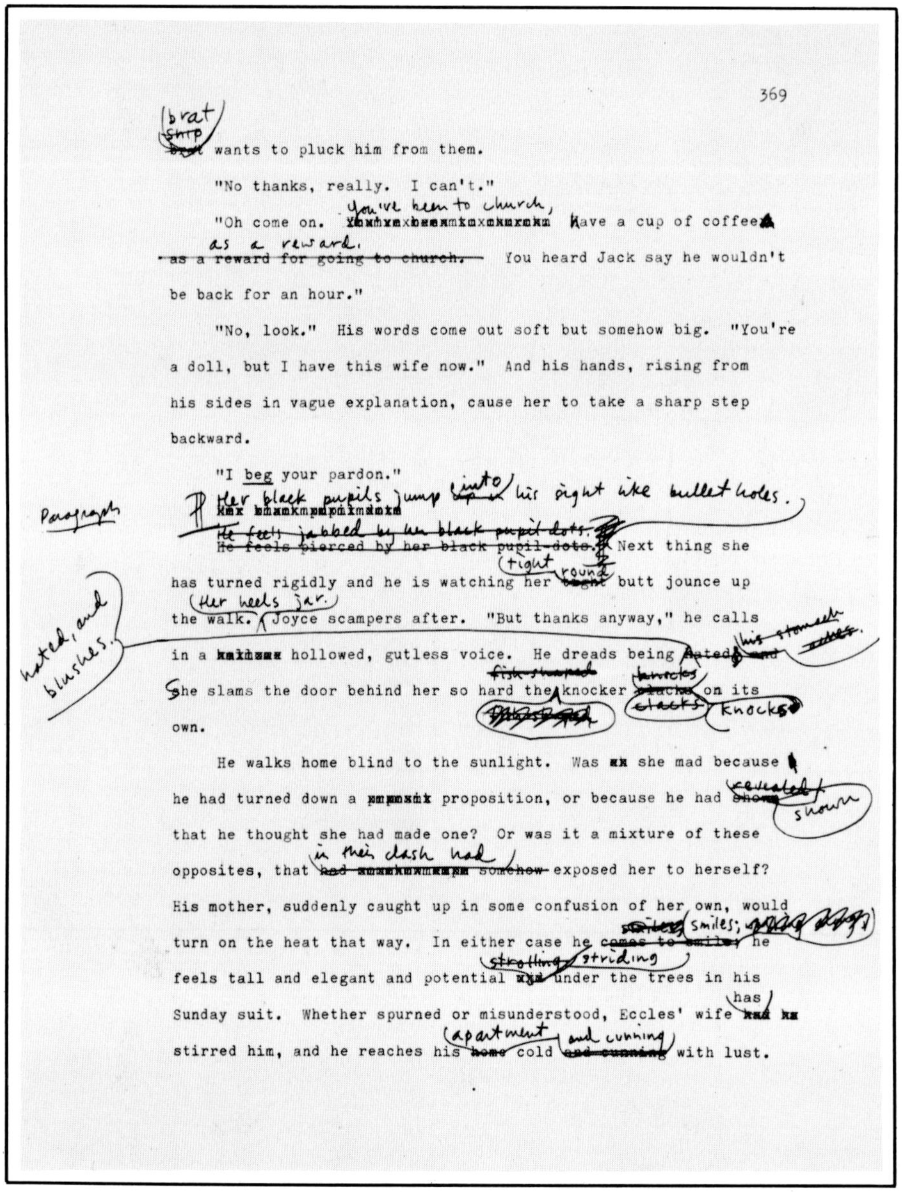

369

brat wants to pluck him from them.

"No thanks, really. I can't."

"Oh come on. You've been to church, Have a cup of coffee as a reward. You heard Jack say he wouldn't be back for an hour."

"No, look." His words come out soft but somehow big. "You're a doll, but I have this wife now." And his hands, rising from his sides in vague explanation, cause her to take a sharp step backward.

"I beg your pardon."

Paragraph

Her black pupils jump into his sight like bullet holes. Next thing she has turned rigidly and he is watching her tight round butt jounce up the walk. Her heels jar. Joyce scampers after. "But thanks anyway," he calls in a hollowed, gutless voice. He dreads being hated, and blushes. She slams the door behind her so hard the knocker knocks on its own.

He walks home blind to the sunlight. Was she mad because he had turned down a proposition, or because he had shown that he thought she had made one? Or was it a mixture of these opposites, that in their clash had exposed her to herself? His mother, suddenly caught up in some confusion of her own, would turn on the heat that way. In either case he smiles; he feels tall and elegant and potential striding under the trees in his Sunday suit. Whether spurned or misunderstood, Eccles' wife has stirred him, and he reaches his apartment cold and cunning with lust.

Revised typescript and corrected galley proof for Rabbit, Run *(Harvard University)* none of the glib condescension that spoils so many books of this type. The characters have an imposing complexity. The local Lilith is neither a golden-hearted harlot nor an item from a sociologist's work-book, but oddly lovable, stingingly real. Rabbit's wife is no self-indulgent slattern, but a woman with a rich and tortured consciousness—her interior monologues remind one of a less lascivious Molly Bloom. And Rabbit, neither an overaged delinquent nor a casual satyr, is a seeker and a sufferer—a man in impotent rebellion against all the people "advertising their belief that the world arches over a pit, that death is final, that the wandering thread of his feelings lead nowhere."

The author's style is particularly impressive; artful and supple, its brilliance is belied by its relaxed rhythms:

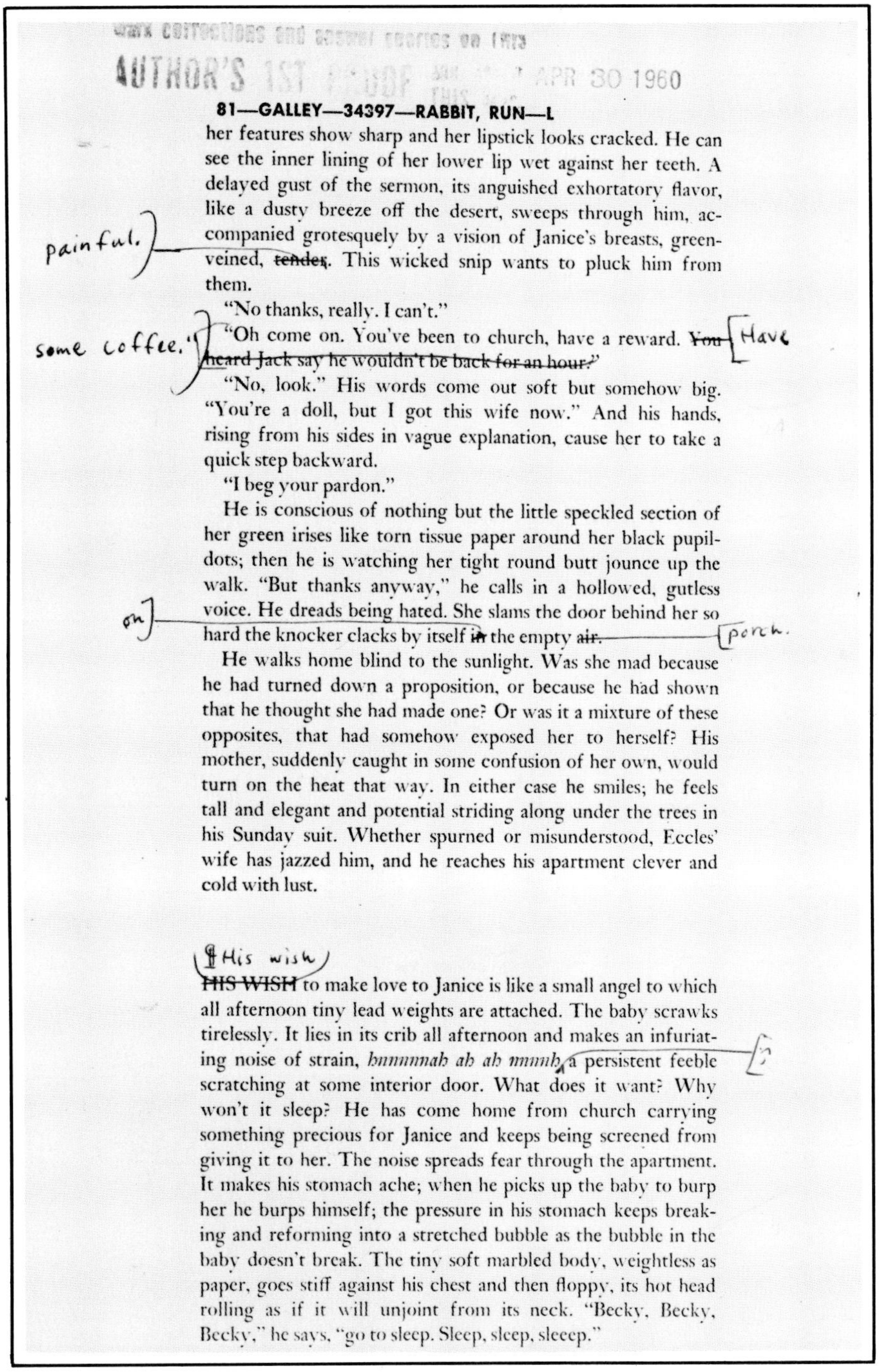

81—GALLEY—34397—RABBIT, RUN—L

her features show sharp and her lipstick looks cracked. He can see the inner lining of her lower lip wet against her teeth. A delayed gust of the sermon, its anguished exhortatory flavor, like a dusty breeze off the desert, sweeps through him, accompanied grotesquely by a vision of Janice's breasts, green-veined, ~~tender~~. This wicked snip wants to pluck him from them.

"No thanks, really. I can't."

"Oh come on. You've been to church, have a reward. ~~You heard Jack say he wouldn't be back for an hour?~~"

"No, look." His words come out soft but somehow big. "You're a doll, but I got this wife now." And his hands, rising from his sides in vague explanation, cause her to take a quick step backward.

"I beg your pardon."

He is conscious of nothing but the little speckled section of her green irises like torn tissue paper around her black pupil-dots; then he is watching her tight round butt jounce up the walk. "But thanks anyway," he calls in a hollowed, gutless voice. He dreads being hated. She slams the door behind her so hard the knocker clacks by itself ~~in~~ the empty ~~air~~.

He walks home blind to the sunlight. Was she mad because he had turned down a proposition, or because he had shown that he thought she had made one? Or was it a mixture of these opposites, that had somehow exposed her to herself? His mother, suddenly caught in some confusion of her own, would turn on the heat that way. In either case he smiles; he feels tall and elegant and potential striding along under the trees in his Sunday suit. Whether spurned or misunderstood, Eccles' wife has jazzed him, and he reaches his apartment clever and cold with lust.

~~HIS WISH~~ to make love to Janice is like a small angel to which all afternoon tiny lead weights are attached. The baby scrawks tirelessly. It lies in its crib all afternoon and makes an infuriating noise of strain, *hnnnnnah ah ah mmnh* a persistent feeble scratching at some interior door. What does it want? Why won't it sleep? He has come home from church carrying something precious for Janice and keeps being screened from giving it to her. The noise spreads fear through the apartment. It makes his stomach ache; when he picks up the baby to burp her he burps himself; the pressure in his stomach keeps breaking and reforming into a stretched bubble as the bubble in the baby doesn't break. The tiny soft marbled body, weightless as paper, goes stiff against his chest and then floppy, its hot head rolling as if it will unjoint from its neck. "Becky, Becky, Becky," he says, "go to sleep. Sleep, sleep, sleeep."

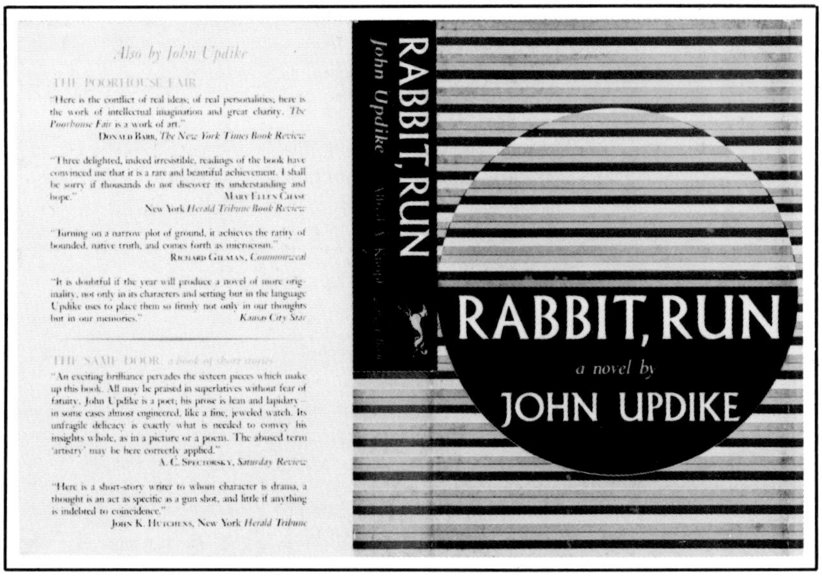

Dust jacket for Rabbit, Run, *the first of Updike's series of novels about Harry "Rabbit" Angstrom. He continued Angstrom's story in* Rabbit Redux *(1971) and* Rabbit Is Rich *(1981). A final "Rabbit" book has been promised for 1991.*

Mr. Updike has a knack of tilting his observations just a little, so that even a commonplace phrase catches the light. The prose is that rarest of achievements—a perfectly pitched voice for the subject.

The treatment of sex commands our attention. For Rabbit, its expression is the final measure of the quality of experience. The author is utterly explicit in his portrayal of Rabbit's divagations—but the description is as seemly as it is candid, for Mr. Updike is primarily interested in the psychic underside of sexuality. Nevertheless, there are some not-easily-ignored footnotes about the erotic sophistication of the post-war generation that will shock the prudish.

"Rabbit, Run" is a tender and discerning study of the desperate and the hungering in our midst. A modest work, it points to a talent of large dimensions—already proved in the author's New Yorker stories, and his first novel, "The Poorhouse Fair." John Updike, still only 28 years old, is a man to watch.

The contemporary attempts to shake off the heavy spell of realism, however seemingly formless and irresponsible, are a worthy phase of man's attempt to educate himself through literature.

From Updike's "Honest Horn," in his Assorted Prose

"A few places are specially conducive to inspiration—automobiles, church—private places."

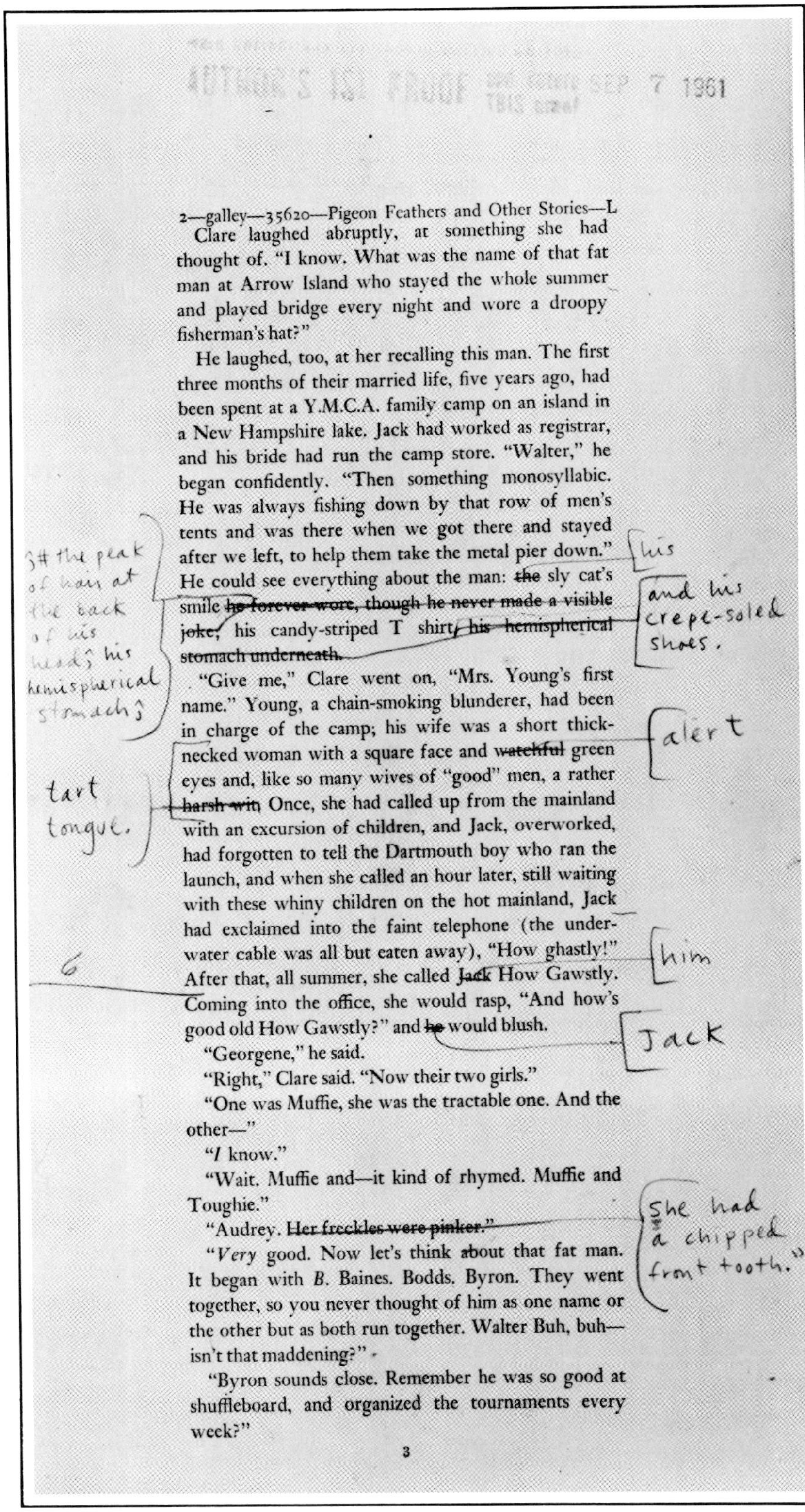

AUTHOR'S 1ST PROOF SEP 7 1961

2—galley—35620—Pigeon Feathers and Other Stories—L

Clare laughed abruptly, at something she had thought of. "I know. What was the name of that fat man at Arrow Island who stayed the whole summer and played bridge every night and wore a droopy fisherman's hat?"

He laughed, too, at her recalling this man. The first three months of their married life, five years ago, had been spent at a Y.M.C.A. family camp on an island in a New Hampshire lake. Jack had worked as registrar, and his bride had run the camp store. "Walter," he began confidently. "Then something monosyllabic. He was always fishing down by that row of men's tents and was there when we got there and stayed after we left, to help them take the metal pier down." He could see everything about the man: ~~the~~ sly cat's smile ~~he forever wore, though he never made a visible joke,~~ his candy-striped T shirt, ~~his hemispherical stomach underneath.~~

"Give me," Clare went on, "Mrs. Young's first name." Young, a chain-smoking blunderer, had been in charge of the camp; his wife was a short thick-necked woman with a square face and ~~watchful~~ green eyes and, like so many wives of "good" men, a rather ~~harsh wit~~. Once, she had called up from the mainland with an excursion of children, and Jack, overworked, had forgotten to tell the Dartmouth boy who ran the launch, and when she called an hour later, still waiting with these whiny children on the hot mainland, Jack had exclaimed into the faint telephone (the underwater cable was all but eaten away), "How ghastly!" After that, all summer, she called ~~Jack~~ How Gawstly. Coming into the office, she would rasp, "And how's good old How Gawstly?" and ~~he~~ would blush.

"Georgene," he said.

"Right," Clare said. "Now their two girls."

"One was Muffie, she was the tractable one. And the other—"

"*I* know."

"Wait. Muffie and—it kind of rhymed. Muffie and Toughie."

"Audrey. ~~Her freckles were pinker.~~"

"*Very* good. Now let's think ~~about~~ that fat man. It began with *B*. Baines. Bodds. Byron. They went together, so you never thought of him as one name or the other but as both run together. Walter Buh, buh—isn't that maddening?"

"Byron sounds close. Remember he was so good at shuffleboard, and organized the tournaments every week?"

3

his
and his crepe-soled shoes.
; the peak of hair at the back of his head; his hemispherical stomach;
alert
tart tongue.
6
him
Jack
She had a chipped front tooth."

Pigeon Feathers and Other Stories, *published in 1962, was Updike's second collection of* New Yorker *stories. This revised galley proof is from "Walter Briggs," one of three stories in the collection about a young married couple named Jack and Clare (Harvard University).*

SPEECH:

"Accuracy," in *Picked-Up Pieces* (New York: Knopf, 1975), pp. 16-17.

Updike's third novel, The Centaur, *is a modern version of the Greek myth of Chiron and Prometheus, written "to make a record of my father . . . a normal, good-doing Protestant man suffering in a kind of comic but real way." Although the book, complete with an index of mythological references, was considered pretentious by some critics, it was generally well received and won the 1963 National Book Awards fiction prize. Updike's March 1964 acceptance speech follows.*

I thank the donors of the prize and the judges of the award for this honor. Its receipt makes me both glad and uneasy—uneasy perhaps because the writing of fiction is so rewarding in itself, so intimately necessary, that public bonuses seem bestowed under some misapprehension, to somebody else, to that fantastical and totally remote person whose picture very occasionally appears in the Sunday book supplements and whose opinions of art, life, and technology are so hopefully solicited by the editors of undergraduate magazines. On his behalf, as it were, I gratefully accept; and since he has been asked to say a few words, I will mention, in the manner of writing fiction, a virtue seldom extolled these days, that of *accuracy*, or *lifelikeness*.

It may seem too daring of me to touch on this when my book appeared, to many, a bewildering, arbitrary, and forced mixture of uncongenial elements, of mythology and remembrance, of the drably natural and the bookishly supernatural. I can only plead that the shape of the book formally approximates, for me, the mixed and somewhat antic experience it was trying to convey. The book as well as the hero is a centaur. Anyone dignified with the name of "writer" should strive, surely, to discover or invent the verbal texture that most closely corresponds to the tone of life as it arrives on his nerves. This tone, whose imitation induces style, will vary from soul to soul.

Updike at the 1963 National Book Awards ceremony with Aileen Ward, winner of the Arts and Letters award, and John Crowe Ransom, winner of the poetry award

Glancing upward, one is struck by the dispersion of recent constellations, by how far apart the prose masters of the century—say, Proust and Joyce, Kafka and Hemingway—are from one another. It may be partly an optical illusion, but modern fiction does seem, more than its antecedents, the work of eccentrics. The writer now makes his marks on paper blanker than it has ever been. Our common store of assumptions has dwindled, and with it the stock of viable artistic conventions. Each generation—and readers and writers are brothers in this—inherits a vast attic of machinery that once worked and decorative dodads whose silhouettes no longer sing. We must each of us clear enough space in this attic so that we in turn can unpack. Does plot, for example, as commonly understood and expected, mirror Providential notions of retribution and ultimate balance that our hearts doubt? Is the syntactical sentence plastic enough to render the flux, the blurring, the endless innuendo of experience as we feel it? No aesthetic theory will cover the case; what is needed is a habit of honesty on the part of the writer. He must, rather athletically, instill his wrists with the refusal to write whatever is lazily assumed, or hastily perceived, or piously hoped. Fiction is a tissue of literal lies that refreshes and informs our sense of actuality. Reality is—chemically, atomically, biologically—a fabric of microscopic accuracies. Language approximates phenomena through a series of hesitations and qualifications; I miss, in much contemporary writing, this sense of self-qualification, the kind of timid reverence toward what exists that Cézanne shows when he grapples for the shape and shade of a fruit through a mist of delicate stabs. The intensity of the grapple is the surest pleasure a writer receives. Though our first and final impression of Creation is not that it was achieved by taking pains, perhaps we should proceed in the humble faith that, by taking pains, word by word, to be accurate, we put ourselves on the way toward making something useful and beautiful and, in a word, good.

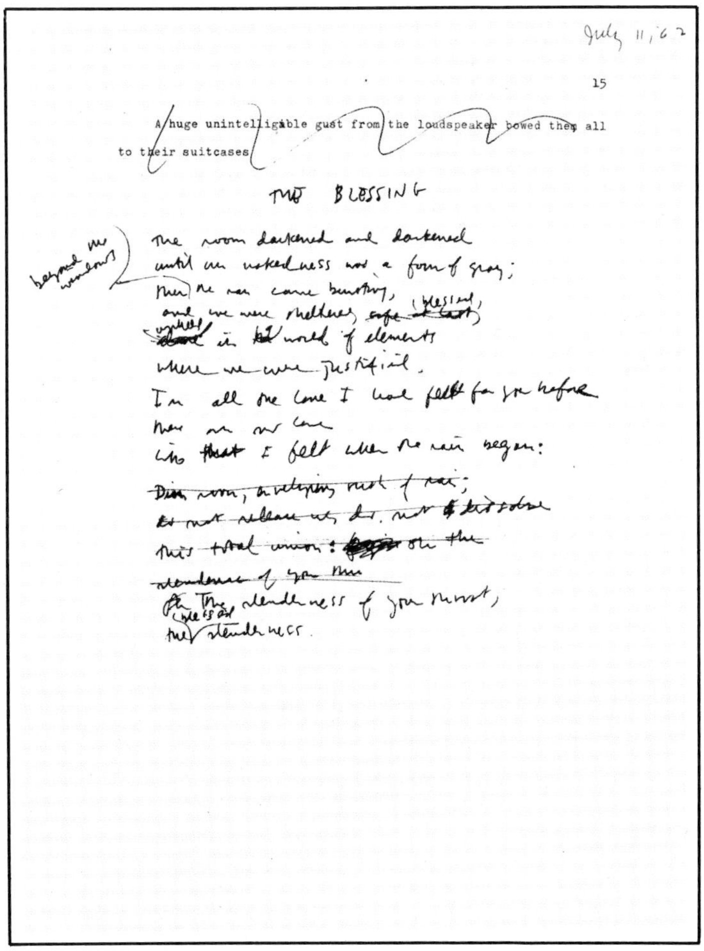
July 11, '62

15

A huge unintelligible gust from the loudspeaker bowed them all to their suitcases

THE BLESSING

The room darkened and darkened
until our nakedness was a form of gray;

Manuscript draft for "The Blessing," collected in Telephone Poles and Other Poems, *Updike's second volume of verse (Harvard University)*

BOOK REVIEW:

Granville Hicks, "They Also Serve Who Write Well," *Saturday Review*, 48 (15 May 1965): 25-26.

Although Updike is best known for his novels, he is an active literary journalist. Most of his nonfiction prose was written for the New Yorker. *His 1965 collection,* Assorted Prose, *included many pieces previously unrecognized as his. Granville Hicks was an unwavering supporter of Updike.*

Precocious and prolific, John Updike, born in 1932, has just published his eighth book, *Assorted Prose*. "In the ten years that I have written for a living," he states, "I have published a certain amount of nonfictional prose; this book collects all of it that I thought anyone might like to read."

At an early age Updike began writing for *The New Yorker*, and between August 1955 and March 1957 he was one of the bright young men in that magazine's office. During that period he contributed many pieces to "The Talk of the Town" and "Notes and Comment," and he has continued to write from time to time for these departments. Early in his career he managed to achieve the right tone, and in the pieces he has preserved we hear the true *New Yorker* voice. (He calls this section "First Person Plural.")

The variety of subjects is impressive: Russia's first moon shot, a dinosaur egg, style in sports writing, the quiz show scandal, the assassination of President Kennedy. There are also obituary notes on John P. Marquand, Grandma Moses, and T. S. Eliot. Two longer pieces, one on pigeons and one on Antarctica, show how well Updike could handle a *New Yorker* research job.

Among his other apprentice works were several parodies. "My first literary idols," he notes, "were Thurber and Benchley and Gibbs; these few *feuilletons* are what remains of my ambition to emulate them." In his review of Dwight Macdonald's anthology of parodies, Updike writes, "If great parodists are not great writers, great writers, conversely, are not great parodists." Whether or not Updike is, or someday may be, a great writer, he is not a great parodist. Although the parodies were pleasant enough to read as they appeared in the magazine, most of them—the principal exception is the parody of Harry Truman—scarcely seem worth republication.

Of greater interest are several longer pieces, especially "Hub Fans Bid Kid Adieu," an account of Ted Williams's final game in Boston. Updike, a true enthusiast, wrote about the great day *con amore*. Although I am sure that the article would delight any baseball fan, it is interesting to me as a piece of writing. It begins, "Fenway Park, in Boston, is a lyric little bandbox of a ballpark. Everything is painted green and seems in curiously sharp focus, like the inside of an old-fashioned peeping-type Easter egg." Updike proceeds by outlining Williams's career, and then describes the ceremonies that took place on this occasion and the game itself. Finally, in the eighth inning, came what everyone was waiting for—Ted Williams's last home run. "From my angle, behind third base, the ball seemed less an object in flight than the tip of a towering, motionless construct, like the Eiffel Tower or the Tappan Zee Bridge. It was in the books while it was still in the sky."

Of the more or less autobiographical pieces, the most interesting is "The Dogwood Tree," which was written for a volume called *Five Boyhoods*. Updike speaks of it disparagingly, but I find it fascinating, not merely as a vivid reminiscence but also as a commentary on his fiction. Here are the settings of *The Poorhouse Fair*, *Rabbit, Run*, *The Centaur*, and many of the short stories. The youthful John Updike, as he presents himself here, is readily identified with boys we have met in his fiction.

Then there are the book reviews. Updike is not, and does not pretend to be, a great critic, but he is a consistently interesting literary journalist. He has reviewed a variety of books for *The New Yorker* and other magazines, and he appears to have approached each of them with the liveliest kind of curiosity. He can write an incisive note on a novel by Richard Hughes, or he can write a long and considered discussion of a theological treatise by Karl Barth. (He says in the foreword that "Barth's theology, at one point in my life seemed alone to be supporting it.") He writes about Alan Sillitoe, J. D. Salinger, Muriel Spark, Vladimir Nabokov, and others, and he always has something to say.

The reviews are also interesting because they suggest some of Updike's values as a writer of fiction. Sillitoe's stories, he remarks, show "enviable assurance and abundance in the writer"—qualities that Updike surely possesses. He says that Sillitoe is "well-armed with intelligence, humor, and (my guess is) stamina." He describes Muriel Spark as "one of the few writers of the language on either side of the Atlantic with enough resources, daring, and stamina to be altering, as well as feeding, the fiction machine."

Updike's versatility is as obvious as his mastery of the language. But, some people ask, isn't he spreading himself too thin? Has he written anything that is worthy of

Self-portrait. In 1967 Updike said, "Of late I don't draw at all, don't even doodle beside the telephone. It's a loss, a sadness for me" (Harvard University).

his talents? Isn't it time he wrote a Great Book?

Updike himself has something to say on this general theme in his review of Salinger's *Franny and Zooey*: "When all reservations have been entered, in the correctly unctuous and apprehensive tone, about the direction he has taken, it remains to acknowledge that it *is* a direction and that the refusal to rest content, the willingness to risk excess on behalf of one's obsessions, is what distinguishes artists from entertainers, and what makes some artists adventurers on behalf of us all."

But, the opposition inquires, what risks has Updike taken; and is he driven by obsessions of any sort? So far as the use of language is concerned, he is extremely bold and extremely effective, but how often does one feel a sense of urgency in his fiction?

These are reasonable questions, but I should be sorry if Updike were to pay much attention to them. Certainly we want him to write a great book, but we don't want him to feel that he *must* do something great or be a failure. In a wise comment on James Agee, Updike says: "A fever of self-importance is upon American writing. Popular expectations of what literature should provide have risen so high that failure is the only possible success, and pained incapacity the only acceptable proof of sincerity." If, he goes on, Agee had justly estimated what he had done, instead of weeping over what he had wanted to do, he would not have taken so unhappy a view of his career. In the same way, it might be a good thing for critics to contemplate what Updike has accomplished in a decade—two excellent novels and many first-rate stories—and not to spend so much time worrying about the books he hasn't yet even attempted.

BOOK REVIEW:

Granville Hicks, "God Has Gone, Sex Is Left," *Saturday Review*, 51 (6 April 1968): 21-22.

Although Couples *did not receive overwhelming critical praise, it was a commercial success and made the* Publishers Weekly *best-seller list for thirty-six weeks. This novel brought Updike the first of his two* Time *cover appearances.*

Sex has been central in much of Updike's work, but never so strongly emphasized as in his latest novel, *Couples*. It is the story of a group of people in a Massachusetts town called Tarbox. (Tarbox is south of Boston and therefore not to be confused with Updike's hometown, Ipswich, which is north of Boston.) Ten couples figure in the novel, and, so far as the book is concerned, coupling is their most important activity. It is rather a mixed group, including two building contractors, three men concerned with science, two men concerned with finance, an airplane pilot, and one man so rich he only pretends to work. Their wives, at the beginning, have no jobs, but most of them do have children. The average age is probably in the neighborhood of thirty-five.

The couples see each other frequently, at weekend parties and, in varying combinations and at the proper seasons, in sports such as swimming, tennis, touch football, and skiing. At the parties there is much drinking, some dancing, some necking, occasionally a word game or something of the sort. They seldom talk about art, literature, philosophy, or even politics. Most of them seem rather unattractive at the outset and grow more so as the novel proceeds.

As has been indicated, Updike concentrates on the sexual relations, marital and extramarital, of these twenty people. There is at least one adulterer in nine of the families, and in several there are two. We are spared none of the details, nor any of the four-letter words, and I am not sure we ought to be. Since writers can be explicit these days, perhaps they ought to be if their theme is sex. At any rate Updike could not have done what he wanted to do if he had been more reticent, for it is only by being specific that he can show the variety in sexual behavior.

Although in the first part of the novel Updike moves freely from one character to another, he comes to concentrate more and more on Piet Hanema, one of the contractors, the other being his partner, Matt Gallagher. In the course of the novel Piet has intercourse with four of the wives in addition to his own. Involved with Georgene Thorne at the start, he soon turns to Foxy Whitman, and this is his grand affair although he has two other bed-partners before the book ends.

The relationship between Piet and his creator is puzzling. "Piet," we are told on the first page, "had red hair and a close-set body: no taller than Angela, he was denser." Updike, by his pictures, is tall and slender. Moreover, Piet didn't graduate from Harvard *summa cum laude*: he didn't go to college at all. He doesn't write

Dust jacket for Updike's most controversial book. "There's a lot of dry talk around about love and sex being somehow the new ground of our morality," Updike said of this novel. "I thought I should describe the ground and ask, is it entirely to be wished for."

books; he builds houses. But if the hands are the hands of a contractor, the voice is often the voice of John Updike. For example, after Piet has said goodbye to a friend who is dying of cancer, we are told that "the drug-dilated eyes, eyes that had verified the chaos of particles on the floor of matter, lifted, and dragged Piet down into omniscience; he saw, plunging, how plausible it was to die, how death, far from invading earth like a meteor, occurs on the same plane as birth and marriage and the arrival of the daily mail." Again: "The world was more Platonic than he had suspected. He found he missed friends less than friendship; what he felt, remembering Foxy, was a nostalgia for adultery itself—its adventure, the acrobatics its deceptions demand, the tensions of its hidden strings, the new landscapes it makes us master." Piet, it appears, has the mind of a poet, and we had hardly been prepared for that.

The book has two epigraphs, one of them from Paul Tillich's *The Future of Religions*: "There is a tendency in the average citizen, even if he has a high standing in his profession, to consider the decisions relating to the life of the society to which he belongs as a matter of fate on which he has no influence—like the Roman subjects all over the world in the period of the Roman empire, a mood favorable for the resurgence of religion but unfavorable for the preservation of a living democracy."

The members of the Tarbox group seem to give little thought to the affairs of the nation and the world. To underline their remoteness, Updike occasionally dates a scene by referring to some happening in the world at large that plays no part whatever in the action that follows. The conspicuous example of detachment is the fact that members of the group do not cancel plans for a party on the night after President Kennedy's assassination, and, though some of the people feel vaguely guilty, the party is pretty much like all their parties.

On the other hand, there are few signs of the resurgence of religion that Tillich predicted. Aside from the Gallaghers, who are practicing Catholics, Piet is the only member of the group who is seriously concerned with religious matters. He regularly attends the Congregational Church, and sometimes the service is important for him: "On command, Piet sat and prayed. Prayer was an unsteady state of mind for him. When it worked, he seemed, for intermittent moments, to be in the farthest corner of a deep burrow, a small endearing hairy animal curled up as if to hibernate. In this condition he felt close to a massive warm secret, like the heart of lava at the earth's core. His existence for a second seemed to evade decay." He says to Foxy: "I think America now is like an unloved child smothered in candy. Like a middle-aged wife whose husband brings home a present after every trip because he's been unfaithful to her." When Foxy asks him who the husband is, he answers, "God. Obviously. God doesn't love us any more. He loves Russia. He loves Uganda. We're fat and full of pimples and always whining for more candy. We've fallen from grace." In part because of his deep fear of death, Piet cares about God's grace.

Freddy Thorne, the ostentatiously cynical dentist, says, "People are the only things people have left since God packed up. By people I mean sex." But so far as the group is concerned—what one of its ex-members sardonically refers to as "the magic circle"—sex seems to be a poor substitute for religion. Perhaps it is Piet's strength that, important as sex is in his life, he enjoys sex as sex, not as a substitute for anything.

Couples is the longest book Updike has written, but it isn't the major novel many of us have been hoping for. For one thing, Piet, as I have suggested, is not quite real; the umbilical cord has not been severed. For another thing, the book is not different from what Updike has written before but simply more—more couples, more coupling, more trouble. However—and this is as much a cliché as saying it isn't the book we were hoping for—it is full of good things. I've written that or something like it about every book Updike has published, and it's always true. As almost everybody but Norman Podhoretz agrees, Updike writes like an angel. Although quantitatively, so to speak, *Couples* reminds me of the work of Updike's fellow-Pennsylvanian John O'Hara, there is no comparison in quality. Updike's style can carry the burden of details with which the book is filled. He uses even the four-letter words with distinction.

INTERVIEW:

Lewis Nichols, "Talk with John Updike," *New York Times Book Review*, 7 April 1968, pp. 37-38.

This interview appeared at the time Couples *was published. Updike was thirty-five and had written five novels.*

John Updike's office, a half mile from his 1680 salt box home, is one flight up over the Dolphin Restaurant—steaks, seafood—in the heart of town. It overlooks the Ipswich River, home of a New England delicacy, the

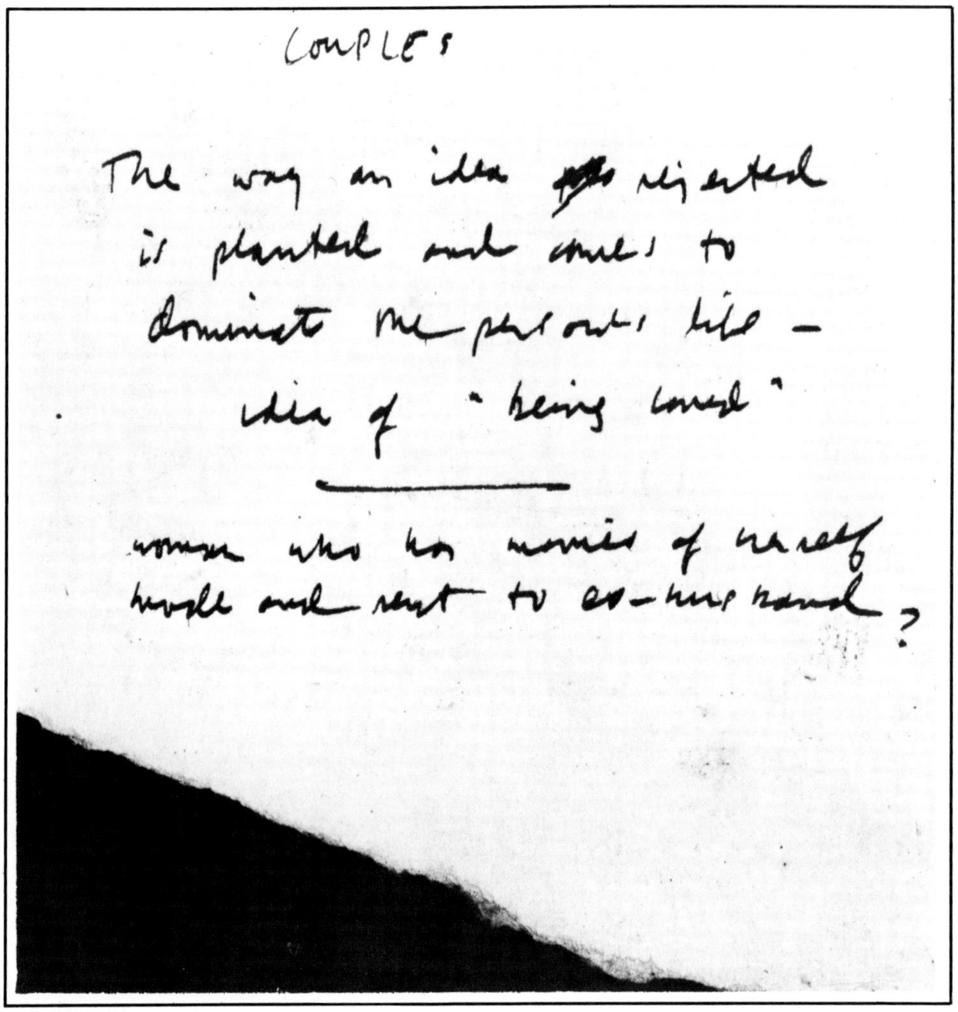

Updike has said he plotted Couples *almost entirely in church—"little shivers and urgencies I would note down on the program and carry down to the office Monday"* *(Harvard University)*

Ipswich clam. It has a leather sofa on one side, a littered bookcase across from it, a bureau along the wall facing the river. On top of the bureau are numerous paper containers which had held coffee from the Dolphin; under it a pile of empty packages from the small cigars he doesn't quite chain smoke. There, the other day, he answered questions about his writing and about "Couples."

He answered on the typewriter, saying that as an old Talk of the Town man for The New Yorker he knew interviews. The typewriter is a portable, standing on a table in the middle of the room. He typed rapidly, beating time with a half-off loafer clinging to his toes. A man of concentrations, he looked for the right word, didn't hesitate to X-out the wrong ones.

INTERVIEWER: In an interview some years ago, you said you hadn't lived in New England long enough to write about it. Now have you, since "Couples" is set on the Massachusetts shore?

UPDIKE: I've lived in New England now for 10 years, and still feel like a visitor, but a fascinated and fond visitor. Pennsylvania and Massachusetts—those two ancient Commonwealths—have become for me times of life rather than areas of geography. I do not intend, as a writer, to be a regionalist.

INTERVIEWER: Do you ever go back to Pennsylvania?

UPDIKE: About once or twice a year, to visit my parents. Returning, I feel the larger—dare I say coarser?—scale of the state, the intensity of the green, the something mythic—an intensity, perhaps, of ordinariness—that I have tried to express in the novels and Olinger stories. After "Of the Farm" I was determined to leave the state fictionally. I do still, however, want to write something—a play, a dreamy novel—about James Buchanan, the only President—a bachelor and a staller—to come from the Keystone State.

INTERVIEWER: Do you consider "Couples" a new departure for yourself? What was its conception?

UPDIKE: Every novel is a departure for me; I find I have no firm conception of what a "novel" is, and every one is in a sense an experiment. For every novel I have published, by the way, there exists one, or a fraction of one, that I have scrapped. "Couples" was first conceived as a short story, whose purpose was to show a group of couples as an organism, something like a volvox, making demands on and creating behavior in the individuals within it. The story was too cramped, and a novel, with enough space to work out a number of configurations, felt necessary. I didn't intend the book to be quite so long; but even so, there remain things—scenes, bits of gossip, further twists of fate—that happen, as it were, on the other side of the margins.

INTERVIEWER: There will be those who say that sex seems all too important in the book. Comment?

UPDIKE: Well, the book is about sex, in part. Sex, gossip and games are the ways in which the couples relate to each other. Alas, not all sex is the same; as the biochemist in the book says, there are different degrees and types of bond. I tried to show a variety of bonds, not only intra- but inter-couple. The hero, Piet Hanema, is an adventurer, and his conquests—the stages of his progress—deserved chronicling. As in "The Poorhouse Fair," in this novel I was asking the question, After Christianity, what? Sex, in its many permutations, is surely the glue, ambience, and motive force of the new humanism. Freddy Thorne is a prophet who brings, with his Grove Press books, the new gospel into the backwoods of Tarbox. On the general matter of sexual explicitness, I think it is to be preferred, as is explicitness in everything.

INTERVIEWER: Is Tarbox, Mass., of the book in effect Ipswich, Mass.?

UPDIKE: I confess to stealing a few bits of landscape from my surroundings, but even these are garbled. The people are altogether invented—indeed, I sometimes wondered, as I worked with my charts of hair-color, types of automobile, ages of children, etc., if they weren't too invented. At any rate, the couples were in my mind a microcosmic middle-class America who do breathe the same moral atmosphere we do, from Berkeley to Boston. They seem, and were meant to seem, somewhat fantastical, though ultimately plausible, residents of a fairy-tale New England. Plymouth County, in which Tarbox lies, is as vague to me cartographically as Purgatory.

INTERVIEWER: What about today's moral atmosphere? Do you think people act everywhere as they do in "Couples"?

UPDIKE: I think the search for love, for reassurance of sexual effectiveness, goes on, and that the American home-unit has given a rectangular shape to arrangements that in Europe took the form of a *ménage á trois*. But the ménages in the book are meant to be seen within the large ménage, of people who know each other, who are asked to know each other *really*, to accept and forgive each other in an almost psychoanalytical way. Friendship edges into group therapy. Group therapy hardens into institutions, miniature churches or cells. I don't think authors should try to spell out their schemes; in the end my descriptions, of landscapes or conversations, are called into being by nothing more complex than the sense that these things, these phenomena, are beautiful—glowing beautifully against a huge background of loss.

INTERVIEWER: I noticed, coming into Ipswich, a big, white Congregational Church on South Green, similar to the church which burned in Tarbox. Is there religious significance here?

UPDIKE: Yes, God does withdraw through the book, and the novel as a whole has the same ghostly relation to the Biblical story of Sodom and Gomorrah as "The Poorhouse Fair" did to the stoning of St. Stephen. What is new, and what I can't quite explain, is that the withdrawal and wrath of God are felt by the hero, Piet Hanema—he and Foxy are the only orthodox Protestants in the book—as a relief. When the rooster is brought down, and exposed to the children, Piet somehow dies—dwindles, moves to

Lexington, lives happily every after.

I *have* seen a church burn, by the way, not a Greek temple edifice, and very ably combatted by the local firemen—unlike the Tarbox firemen. The strange thing to report, as a member of that church, is how much healthier and happier the church body has been for the catastrophe. There *is* a sense I have of God having removed his blessing from America. Yet a kind of blessing remains. But—we seem to be tiptoeing into realms where I am inarticulate, or where the ambiguities of the book must speak for themselves.

INTERVIEWER: Some time ago Life magazine spoke of John Updike as a "nice guy." After "Couples," is he still the nice guy people are used to?

UPDIKE: It was Life, not me, who said I was a nice guy. I have, as a writer, never tried to be nice but to be accurate; writers have nothing to deliver but the truth, the truth in its details and shadings. In this book I was trying to describe a divorce, set in the context of marriages that did not end in divorce—a thin crack of fate, as it were, that slowly expanded.

Artistically, I don't feel that the book is any more a sloughing-off of old skin than the preceding novels were. I tried to subdue my antic disposition of style to the abundant furniture and circumstantiality of a broad social scene; my next novel, if any, would hopefully be shorter, more subjective, somehow less chunky and more hovering. Though I hope that "Couples" has its hovering moments, too.

INTERVIEWER: Granted that Ipswich is a pleasant place, there can't be too many writing colleagues here. Why live in Ipswich?

UPDIKE: We moved here, my wife and I, essentially to raise our children, in the faith that I could make a sufficient living writing what I pleased. Having been raised on the western rim of the Northeastern megalopolis, I have moved to the northern rim, and still consider myself a citizen of New York; the culture we live in, despite the fascinating nuances of difference, seems increasingly homogenized, and one need not feel, unless you love the Broadway theater, which I don't, deprived. As to writers, they weren't meant to be herd animals. They're like tigers, or maybe skunks—they need territory.

INTERVIEWER: Where, in a literary sense, do you go from here?

UPDIKE: Now 35, with half my allotted span expired, and this bulky book behind me, I feel the need to rethink the riddle of fiction, to simmer in the classics, to close some closet doors, and get a second wind. I would especially like to re-court the muse of poetry, who ran off with the mailman four years ago, and drops me only a scribbled postcard from time to time.

INTRODUCTION:

"To the Czech Edition of *Of the Farm*," in *Picked-Up Pieces* (New York: Knopf, 1975), pp. 82-83.

Three years after its American publication, Of the Farm *was translated by Igor Hajek for Czechoslovakian publication. Updike's special introduction, sympathizing with the Czechs after the August 1968 Russian invasion of Czechoslovakia, was not included.*

As I remember, I wrote *Of the Farm* (the title originally was simply *The Farm*, but this had a monumentality that seemed bogus to me, which the preposition "Of" suitably reduced; I intended to mean that the book was *about* the farm, and that the people in it belonged *to* the farm, were of the earth, earthy, mortal, fallen, and imperfect) in the late summer and early autumn of 1964, in pencilled longhand. Then I embarked on a trip through the Soviet Union and Eastern Europe that lasted six weeks; the last night of this tour, and perhaps the most pleasant and unconstrained, was spent in Prague, in the apartment of Mr. Igor Hájek, the brilliant and engaging young man then involved in translating my previous novel *The Centaur*. Upon returning to the United States, I rewrote and typed *Of the Farm*, and in due course it was published, enjoying the mild sale and mixed reviews that usually greet my productions. Now, when Eastern Europe presents an aspect more troubled yet more hopeful than four years ago, Mr. Hájek and I both find ourselves in London, and he is translating my novella. And it has amused him to point out to me that I, like Joey Robinson, now possess, if not a new wife, a Citroën station wagon. Of such circling strands are past and present, fact and fiction, woven.

Of the Farm was my first attempt at book-length fiction after the writing of *The Centaur*; it was undertaken after a long hesitant interval fruitful of short stories. Like a short story, it has a continuous action, a narrow setting, a small cast. I thought of it as chamber music, containing only four voices—the various ghosts in it do not speak,

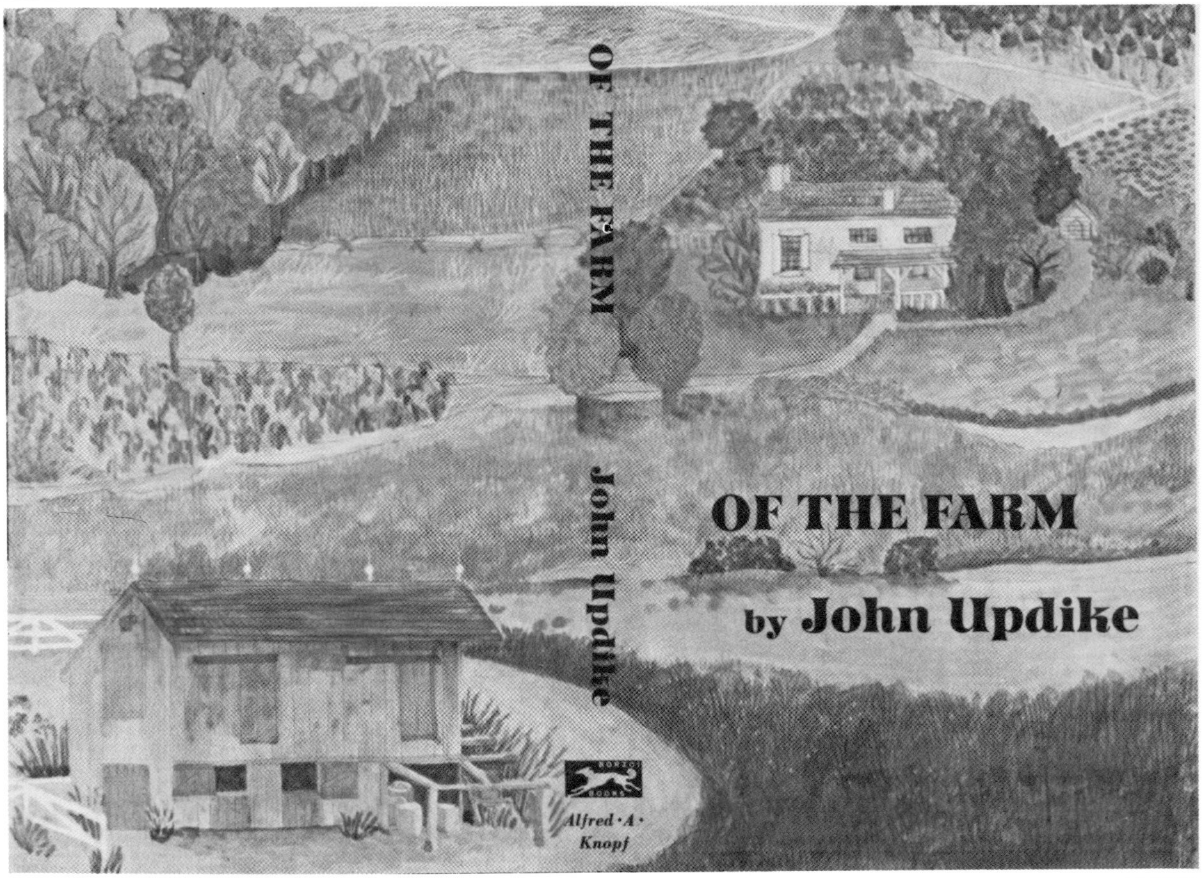

Although the characters' names are changed in Of the Farm *(1965), it is recognizable as the last of the Olinger cycle which began in* Pigeon Feathers *and continued in* The Centaur.

and the minister's sermon, you will notice, is delivered in close paraphrase, without the benefit of quotation marks. The voices, like musical instruments, echo each other's phrases and themes, take turns dominating, embark on brief narrative solos, and recombine in argument or harmony. The underlying thematic transaction, as I conceived it, was the mutual forgiveness of mother and son, the acceptance each of the other's guilt in taking what they had wanted, to the discomfort, respectively, of the dead father and the divorced wife.

Threads connect it to *The Centaur*: the farm is the same, and the father, even to his name, George, seems much the same in both books. Mr. Hájek has directed my attention to a strange phrase, "his humorous prancing whine," in which the prancing is purely a remnant, like a badly erased pencil line, of the half-horse half-man. In a sense this novella is *The Centaur* after the centaur has died; the mythical has fled the ethical, and a quartet of scattered survivors grope with their voices toward cohesion. And seek to give each other the stern blessing of freedom mentioned in the epigraph from Sartre.* Let us hope that all nations will in their varying languages seek to bestow this stern blessing upon one another. I am honored at this moment [that is, when the cultural liberalization under Dubček had just been crushed by Russian tanks] to be translated into Czech.

*"Consequently, when, in all honesty, I've recognized that man is a being in whom existence precedes essence, that he is a free being who, in various circumstances, can want only his freedom, I have at the same time recognized that I can want only the freedom of others." [*En conséquence, lorsque sur le plan d'authenticité totale, j'ai reconnu que l'homme est un être chez qui l'essence est précédée par l'existence, qu'il est un être libre qui ne peut, dans des circonstances diverses, que vouloir sa liberte, j'ai reconnu en même temps que je ne peux vouloir que la liberté des autres.*]

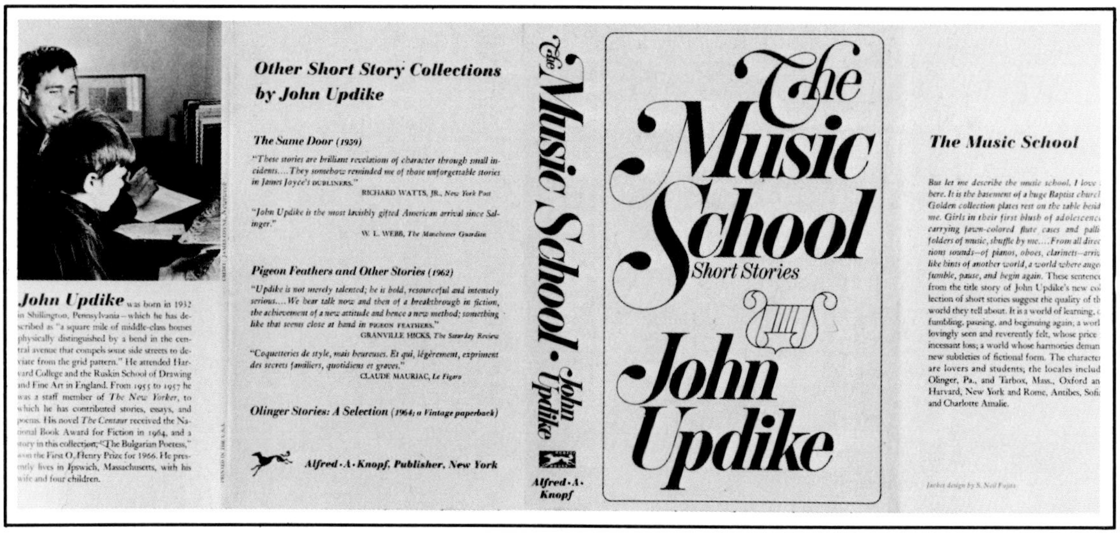

Dust jacket of The Music School, *Updike's third story collection, consisting of twenty stories published in the* New Yorker *between 1962 and 1966*

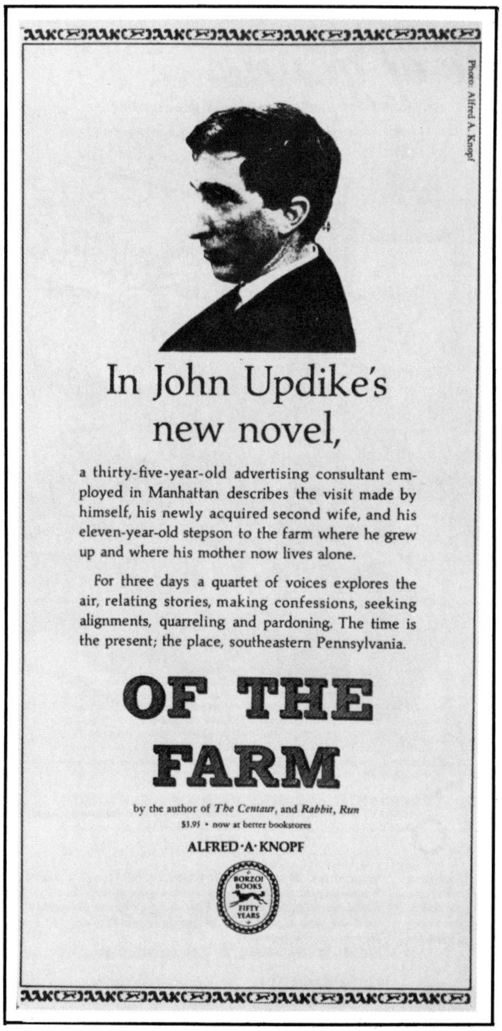

From New York Times Book Review, *21 November 1965*

Updike reading from Olinger Stories *at Governor Mifflin High School in Shillington, 23 June 1968*

SPEECH:

"The Future of the Novel," *Picked-Up Pieces* (New York: Knopf, 1975), pp. 17-23.

In February 1969, a year after publication of his fifth novel, Updike delivered this address to the Bristol Literary Society, Bristol, England.

First, let us ask, to what extent is The Future of the Novel a non-question, a non-issue repeatedly raised by literary journalists about a non-thing, the Novel? Do we worry ourselves with the future of the Poem? Surprisingly, not. Yet verse, compared to narrative prose, would seem to be the more fragile device, far more vulnerable to the clamorous counterclaims of television, the cinema, and traffic noise, far less likely to survive into an age of McLuhanism, Computerization, and whatever other polysyllables would dull our sensibilities and eclipse our humanistic heritage. In fact, poetry has survived. Great poets appear, do their work, and die. Waves of excitement and revolution occur, and are followed by lulls of consolidation and repose. An Ezra Pound or an Allen Ginsberg issues proclamations and generates apostles; relatively isolated and soft-spoken figures such as our Wallace Stevens and your Philip Larkin also meditate, and create. No doubt some decades are more fruitful of enduring verse than others; but each generation seems to supply its quota of poets and, odder still, of poetry readers. A certain slender ardent audience for poetry persists, and indeed in the United States seems to be widening; and if we include as "poets" (and why not?) the ubiquitous pop lyricists in the style of Bob Dylan and the Beatles, the audience is very wide indeed. The appetite for song—for things singingly said—would seem to be so fundamental to human nature that no foreseeable turn of technology or history could soon root it out.

Now, might we not assume the same of prose narrative? Perhaps; but the impression does linger that the Novel is not quite a category of human expression as eternal as Poetry, or the Dance, or the Joke, but is instead, like the Verse Epic, like the dramatic form called Tragedy, a genre with a life cycle and a death—a death, indeed, that may have already occurred.

Dr. Johnson, in his Dictionary, defined the word "novel" as "a small tale, generally of love." What he had in mind, of course, were the Italian *novelle*, written in great quantity from the 14th century to the 17th, of which Boccaccio's were the most famous, and from which Shakespeare derived the plots of, among other plays, *Romeo and Juliet* and *Othello*. The novel form in England was greatly enriched and broadened: Richardson brought to it the imitation of the epistle and Defoe the imitation of the journal; with Fielding and Jane Austen it becomes an inhabitable microcosm of society; and with Dickens the many-chambered Novel is expanded to include a courtroom for the indictment of social abuse. In the 19th century, length—physical bulk, the rendering of the sonorous music of passing time—becomes so intrinsic to the idea of the once-modest *novella* that Tennyson speaks of the ideal novel as one that will just "go on and on and never end." Throughout, however, and right down to the classics of modernism, love is a pervasive, perhaps obsessive, thread. The French say, "Without adultery, there is no novel," and while this may be more true of *their* novels than yours, it is indeed difficult to imagine a novel, even one by Lord Snow, without its—as the phrase goes—"romantic interest."

I would suggest that this is a *genre* trait of the Novel rather than an undistorted reflection of our lives. There *are* areas of concern in our lives apart from love; yet as a literary practitioner, and as a sometimes compulsory reader of unsuccessful novels, I have observed that it is difficult to make them interesting in a novel. Disease and pain, for instance, are of consuming concern to the person suffering from them, but while we will follow for eight hundred pages the course of a romance, and suffer with each love pang, the course of a physical disease, and the description of pain and discomfort, however sympathetic the character afflicted, weary us within a few paragraphs. Similarly, the amassment of sums of money, fascinating in reality, acquires interest in a novel only if the acquisition of wealth advances the hero or heroine toward that eventual copulation that seems to be every reader's insatiable and exclusive desire. Indeed, it is part of the peculiar democracy of fiction, and one way in which the air of its world is fresher than our own, that although in real life we *do* find wealthy and famous men more interesting than poor and obscure ones, in novels we do not. Even intelligence does not recommend a fictional character to us. No, in the strange egalitarian world of the Novel a man must earn our interest by virtue of his—how shall I say?—his *authentic sentiments*.

So we arrive at the not very spectacular inkling that the Novel is by nature sentimental. I use the word without pejorative intent, but merely as descriptive of the kind of coinage with which we transact our business in one literary realm. This coinage is not legal tender, I think, in the New Testament, or in *Beowulf*, or in *Prometheus Bound*, or to any predominant degree in the *Odyssey* or *Paradise Lost*. It is current, though not the only currency, in *The Divine Comedy*, and it would seem to have been introduced in Italy, with the breakup of the Middle Ages, and to be concurrent with the rise of capitalism. That is, when human worth began to be measured in terms of capital, and men became counters upon a board of productivity, the uneconomic emotions went underground, into literature. We can scarcely imagine it: but with the massive cosmic drama of Fall and Redemption always before him, and the momentous potentialities of sin and repentance always alive within him, medieval man may well have needed less reassurance than we that his emotions were substantial and significant, that his inner life and outward status were integrated. Even today, religious fundamentalists are not notable novel-readers.

This scale of generalization is uncomfortable for a novelist, concerned as he properly is with the strict small circumstance, the quizzical but verifiable fact. I wish to describe, merely, the Novel as a product of private enterprise, for which a market is created when the state, or tribe, or church, withdraws itself from the emotional sector of the individual's life. Erotic love then becomes a symbol, a kind of code for all the nebulous, perishable sensations which we persist in thinking of as *living*. Living and loving: the titles of two novels by the splendid Henry Green, and an equation, but for one transposed vowel, to which all novel readers consent—the housewife reading away the dull afternoon, the schoolboy concentrating amid the stupid family din, the banker sitting prim in the homeward commuting train. All are members of a

Updike and his wife Mary played tenor and alto recorders, respectively, in an Ipswich music group.

conspiracy to preserve the secret that people *feel*. Please do not suppose that I am describing only penny fiction, trash. The most elegant and respectable of modern novels, from *Remembrance of Things Past* to *Lolita*, enlist in this conspiracy with all the boldness of their virtuosity. Even as all-including and unyielding a masterwork as *Ulysses* is finally about lovers; Leopold and Molly Bloom are great lovers, great in compassion and fidelity, fidelity to each other and to their inner sensations, their authentic sentiments. Perhaps the reason Stephen Dedalus is slightly tedious in this novel is that he is not in love. Not to be in love, the capital N Novel whispers to capital W Western Man, is to be dying.

So much for the past; what of the future? The Novel's Victorian heydey has passed. If my impression is correct, that capitalism put sex in a treasure chest, the chest, after so many raids upon it, is battered to the point of collapse. The set of tensions and surprises we call *plot* to a great extent depends upon the assumption that bourgeois society discourages and obstructs free-ranging sex. In the 19th-century novels and the 20th-century movies, the punishment for adultery is death. Yet even in *Madame Bovary*, one feels, reading it, that the heroine in swallowing arsenic is being hysterical, that there is nothing in her situation a sudden inheritance of money wouldn't solve. In the novels, say, of Evelyn Waugh, adultery has become a dangerous pleasantry, and by now I think even the aura of danger is fading. As Denis de Rougemont has pointed out, the conventional obstructions to love no longer impress us; a somewhat extravagant situation, such as in *Lolita*, alone can bestow dignity upon a romantic passion. Freud, misunderstood or not, has given sex the right to be free, and the new methods of contraception have minimized the bail. Remove the genuine prohibitions and difficulty, and the three-dimensional interweave of the Novel collapses, becomes slack and linear. The novels of Henry Miller are not novels, they are acts of intercourse strung alternately with segments of personal harangue. They are closer to the *Arabian Nights* than to Tolstoy; they are not novels but *tales*.

Dr. Johnson defined "novel" as a type of tale; and, though the classic Novel, the sentimental underground of bourgeois Europe, may belong to a moment of history that is passing, the appetite for tales is probably not less fundamental to the human species than the appetite for songs. Books of prose about imaginary events will continue to appear, and they will be called, out of semantic inertia, novels.

What will be the shape of these books? Some will continue the direction of Miller, and be more or less angry personal accounts of coitus and conversation among bohemians. The tradition is not dishonorable—Dostoevsky's *Notes from the Underground* is such a book—and will veer very close to pornography, which itself has a tradition that is, at the least, venerable. The subversive burden will shift, I fear, from sex to violence, and the threat of society, and the problem for censorship, lies not, in my opinion, with the description of sexual acts but with fantasies of violence and torture. Books like *Last*

Exit to Brooklyn and *The Painted Bird*, with their unrelieved brutality, and the relish that seethes beneath their creditable surface pretensions, augur an unhappy direction. Cruel events do occur in reality, of course; but the obligation of the artist, when dealing with them, as with sex, is to be, not inexplicit, but accurately alive to their complicated human context. Today's bohemia, or hippiedom, seems to aspire toward a political effectiveness that precludes much compass of sympathy or subtlety of craft. Rather, a fanatic and dazed narrowing of comprehension seems to be in progress. The sour riots of the Sixties are not likely to call forth the ebullient rapture of a Kerouac, let alone the refined anguish of a Huysmans.

Other books of fiction will, I think, try to employ the inherited machinery of the romantic novel for drier purposes than the dramatization of erotic vicissitudes. The novels of Vladimir Nabokov already ingeniously toy with romantic triangles to produce more intricate patterns. His novels approach the condition of puzzles—*Pale Fire* was rigged on the scheme of an annotated poem and the introduction playfully invited us to buy two copies to read it properly. Novels by other men play hopscotch with us, or invite us to shuffle the pages and make our own plots. Robbe-Grillet gives us an overlapping sequence of repetitions of actions; all such inventions have a somewhat capricious air, but I think the two directions, of novel as philosophy, of novel as object, will be fruitfully pursued. Heightened intellectual demands should compress the conventional size of the novel; hundreds of thousands of words in Dickens' time, it may settle at around two hundred pages, the length of a mystery story, of *Candide*, or of a novel by Samuel Beckett.

The surface of the page, now a generally dead rectangle of gray, a transparent window into the action, could be a lively plane of typographic invention, as it was for Apollinaire—a surface that says "This is printing" much as Impressionism forsook the licked illusionistic surface and announced, "This is painting." The comic strip offers a blend of picture and word that, though it has not attained the status of high art, has, in strips like the old "Krazy Kat" and the contemporary "Peanuts," climbed rather high. I see no intrinsic reason why a doubly talented artist might not arise and create a comic-strip novel masterpiece. Artistically, this century has belonged to the eye; concrete poetry, medieval manuscripts, and Egyptian hieroglyphs all hint at paths of accommodation in an ecumenical movement among eye-oriented media.

If these suggestions sound frivolous, let me say that tale-telling *is* a kind of toying, and that something of primitive magic does linger about the manipulation of verbal dolls. When the speaker was an undergraduate student of "creative writing," a guest writer, John Hawkes, told our class—amazingly, I thought—"When I want a character to fly, I just say, 'He flew.' " We are, all of us novelists, like neoclassic playwrights captive to the three unities, prisoners of conventions we cannot imagine our way around; a wonderful freedom awaits us, and extraordinary opportunities. Let me admit to the hopeful fancy that some book such as I have imagined—a short novel, approaching the compact, riddling condition of an object—may serve as the vehicle of a philosophic revolution. That a new Rousseau or a new Marx or a new Kierkegaard may choose to speak to us through the Novel. That the Novel, relieved of some of its old duties as an emotional masseur, may prove to be a light and nimble messenger. That, though at the moment the Novel roosts a little heavily in the bookshops, to fly it only needs him to come along who will say, "It flies."

Fiction must recommend itself or remain unrecommended.

From Updike's foreword to his Olinger Stories

INTERVIEW:

Eric Rhode, "John Updike talks to Eric Rhode about the shapes and subjects of his fiction," *Listener*, 81 (19 June 1969): 862-864.

The following is a transcription of a BBC Third Programme radio broadcast.

UPDIKE: There is a concern, especially on the Continent, with formal problems of the art of fiction. I don't think you can really be very theoretical about it, especially if you're an American, but I do somehow look towards Europe for tools with which to say what I have to say.

INTERVIEWER: When you talk of formal problems you're thinking of French writers like Robbe-Grillet?

UPDIKE: Exactly. It's just a question of finding out what is dead in the novel and what really is alive. I don't think Robbe-Grillet has done anything very solid or helpful.

Nevertheless, he and Nathalie Sarraute are at least posing the problems in a way that anybody trying to earn his living at the art should be aware of. I'm not aware of the English being very interested in formal theory. On the other hand, it seems to me that you do have here a kind of tradition of—I hate to say it—craft, or of mastery, perhaps. Somebody like Iris Murdoch—whether or not you are totally persuaded by each book or whether or not her total philosophy seems, well, slightly hysterical—is somehow a master in that. She keeps inventing, keeps presenting new patterns, and keeps producing a book a year—which is a pretty hectic rate, but it's a healthy rate. As opposed to this, there is the awful sense in America of the writer being a kind of priest, and a constipated priest at that.

INTERVIEWER: I don't see any affiliation in your work to the French idea of experiment, or indeed to the kinds of experiment that go on in the States. It seems to me that you are much closer to the English novel: there is a very strong sense of the domestic in your work—of the world as it is.

UPDIKE: I'm just trying to think of the word 'domestic.' I suppose this is true. It may be less a matter of conscious choice than of the fact that I seem to be a domestic creature. My first novel, *The Poorhouse Fair*, was, at least in my mind, something of a *nouvelle vague* book, particularly in the ending: that is, I tried to create a pattern of tension and then, instead of resolving it, dissolved it. It ended with a kind of brainless fair: people come to a fair and you hear their voices and it all dissolves. In my mind it was a somewhat experimental book and my publishers then, Harper, seemed to think it was, because the ending puzzled them so much that I took it away from them and went to Knopf, where I've been happy ever since. In each of the books there has been, in my mind at least, a different experiment, an adventure: in *Rabbit, Run* the present tense may seem a mild adventure. It's more and more used now, but at that time it wasn't.

INTERVIEWER: Coming back to 'The Poorhouse Fair,' the most striking thing there, I think, is the fact that you have so clearly kept yourself out of the book, that you have created these very old men and women. This is an act entirely of the imagination, or so it feels. In fact Mary McCarthy said that she finds it a rather spooky accomplishment—like those boy actors who play old men—that you have created these characters so credibly. How far was it based on actuality?

UPDIKE: Not very. There was indeed a poorhouse a couple of blocks from where I grew up, but I very rarely went into it, and there was a fair that must have impressed me as a child. I had written prior to this, while living in New York City, a 600-page novel, called, I think, *Home*, and more or less about myself and my family up to the age of 16 or so. It had been a good exercise to write it and I later used some of the material in short stories, but it really felt like a very heavy bundle of yellow paper, and I realised that this was not going to be my first novel—it had too many of the traits of a first novel. I did not publish it, but I thought it was time for me to write a novel. I was—what?—25, 26. Getting to be an old man, as writers go in America. They were tearing the poorhouse down at Shillington and I went up and looked at the shell. My grandfather, who is somewhat like John Hook in that book, was recently dead, and so the idea of some kind of memorial gesture, embodying what seems to have been on my part a very strong sense of national decay, crystallised in this novel. I wrote it in three months and then rewrote it in three months. It was my first real venture into what you might call novelistic space and it was very exciting. I haven't read it since the last set of proofs, but I'd like to think that there was some love, and hence some life and blood, in these old people.

INTERVIEWER: I think it's a perfect, completely enclosed book and when I read it I thought: this is a masterpiece, how can he go on from here? I always have the feeling in your work that the short story, the novella, comes fairly easily to you. You've probably had enormous problems with the longer stretch. I would say this because I think your kind of writing, where you start from within the centre of a character, from the character's observations and impressions of the world, and then move on to a sense of the family, doesn't lead naturally to the discovery of a form. I feel, for instance, in your second novel, 'Rabbit, Run,' which is more ambitious, and where you have a strong plot, that the central situation is the man who is under strain, but then you do move into melodrama later in the book. This must have been difficult for you.

UPDIKE: I'm afraid melodrama comes quite easily to me. I'm in two minds about events in novels. One has this sense that the old-fashioned novel, and indeed films and television plays, are falsifying life terribly by making events happen, by creating tensions and then resolving them, by setting up trials and then handing down the verdicts—for in fact verdicts don't usually get handed down. All my books end on a kind of hesitant or ambiguous note. On the other hand, there is a delight in making things happen, in falling through or leaping through this fictional space. As for the accusation of being melodramatic which was levelled at the last book, or not melodramatic, perhaps, so much as Gothic or unreal or coarsely plotted: if there could be a defence it is my sensation that events, when they happen, do happen rather lurchingly and suddenly.

INTERVIEWER: Do you improvise or do you plot things out very carefully beforehand?

UPDIKE: I really begin with some kind of solid, coherent image, some notion of the shape of the book and even of its texture. *The Poorhouse Fair* was meant to have this sort of Y shape of the two things and then the disappearance, or the resolution. *Rabbit, Run* was a kind of a zig-zag. *The Centaur* was sort of a sandwich. I can't begin until I know the beginning and have some sense of what's going to happen between. There are some hinges, but really a novel, even quite a bulky one—you think of Henry James's 800 pages—has only a few hinges. I don't make an outline or anything. I figure that I can hold the events in my head and then hope that things will happen which will surprise me, that the characters will take on life and talk. I keep a kind of loose rein on the book. I would not begin a book, I would not advise people to begin a book, without knowing where it's going because one of the aesthetic delights one hopes for is a sense of resolution, of having heard that phrase before, an echo and a kind of click at the end.

INTERVIEWER: This image of the book that you have in mind is in fact a rather geometric image. It's not, say, a visual image, an image of events in the book which you're leading up to.

UPDIKE: It's sort of an abstract sensation, but of course you have to have a lot of other things to begin a book. You have to have at least some of the people and have to be in some ways stirred by the central people. The main motive force behind *The Centaur* would be some wish to make a record of my father. There was the whole sense of having for 15 years watched a normal, good-doing Protestant man suffering in a kind of comic but real way. What led me to write it and what keeps it going and what gives it its life now, at least in myself, is this thing of making a solid object and making a pattern. Also there is a certain element of having a message and wanting to get it across. My message has not been the kind that is especially congenial to my time. In a time concerned with urban and political issues, I've dealt with suburban, or rural, unpolitical man.

INTERVIEWER: Where I think you are unusual is that you're not a metaphysical writer in the sense that you might say Melville is a metaphysical writer: you deal with the actual world, with sensations and things. And yet religion, in an institutional sense, does appear in all your books. Often it's something you look at rather wryly, rather diffidently, as though it's a kind of electric force which your characters are a bit frightened of. I would think this is both part of the sense that you have of a tradition of the past, of the world existing as it is, and also of some anxiety, an inability to relate this to any sense of community.

UPDIKE: The ministers tend increasingly to become figures of fun, or rather, I'd say, more of a disappointment on the author's part. I seem to have some expectations of the ministry which it doesn't fulfil. The short story 'Pigeon Feathers,' which is about a boy's questions being answered, he thinks very badly, by his clergyman, is the central minister story. The church continues to exist in the modern world, and it seems to me to be something rather gallant.

INTERVIEWER: You are religious yourself?

UPDIKE: I'd say, yes, I try to be. I think I do tend to see the world as layered, and as there being something up there; certainly in *Couples* it would seem to be God, who in a certain sense destroys that inoffensive Congregationalist church. Moreover, and again it's worked out geometrically, I seem to see all my books in terms of children's drawings, they are all meant to be moral debates with the reader, and if they seem pointless—I'm speaking hopefully—it's because the reader has not been engaged in the debate. The question is usually, 'What is a good man?' or 'What is goodness?' and in all books an act is inspected. Take Harry Angstrom in *Rabbit, Run*: there is a case to be made for running away from your wife. In the late Fifties beatniks were preaching transcontinental travelling as the answer to man's disquiet. And I was just trying to say: 'Yes, there is certainly that, but then there

Updike observed in 1972: "On the golf course as nowhere else, the tyranny of causality is suspended, and men are free."

are all these other people who seem to get hurt.' That distinction is meant to be a moral dilemma.

INTERVIEWER: You see the institution of marriage, the institution of the Church, as something that carries you back to the past, which I think again is very important in your books. For instance, in 'The Poorhouse Fair' the one moment that I felt that you emerged as a person was close to the end when you say something about how we go backwards, how we become our father's opinions, and eventually our grandfather's.

UPDIKE: True enough, there is this interest in the past, but in a way the past is all we have. The present is very thin, it's less than a second wide, and the future doesn't exist. I think that *Of the Farm* is about moral readjustment, and the readjustment is somehow in terms of harsh deeds done in the past; the mother and boy need, in a way, to excuse each other, or somehow to give a blessing. It's a little hard for me to see my work from the outside, as it were, but I do notice a recurrence of the concept of a blessing, of approval, or forgiveness, or somehow even encouragement in order to go on. I wonder if 20th-century man's problem isn't one of encouragement, because of the failure of nerve, the lassitude and despair, the sense that we've gone to the end of the corridor and found it blank. So the characters beneath the surface are exhorting each other to action. In *Couples* Piet is quite a modern man in that he really can't act for himself because he's overwhelmed by the moral implications of any act—leaving his wife, staying with her . . . The women in that book are less sensitive perhaps to the oppressive quality of cosmic blackness, and it is the women who do almost all of the acting. I don't want to say that being passive, being inactive, being paralysed, is wrong in an era when so much action is crass and murderous. I do feel that in the generations that I've had a glimpse of—I can see my grandfather at one end, and I can see my boys coming up—there has been a perceptible loss of the sense of righteousness. But many evils are done in the name of righteousness, so perhaps one doesn't want it back. Nevertheless, I suspect that the vitality of women now, the way many of us lean on them, is not an eternal phenomenon but a historical one, and fairly recent.

INTERVIEWER: I wonder, in the case of 'The Centaur,' why you related the immediate experience of the schoolmaster to myth.

UPDIKE: It seemed to me that there was something mythical about the events. It's an experiment very unlike that of *Ulysses*, where the myth lurks beneath the surface of the natural events. In a way the natural events in my book are meant to be a kind of mask for the myth. The genesis of it was reading in an old book of my wife's this variant to the Hercules legend. It is part of the comedy of the man's plight that he is living in a town full of gods, and he's not quite a god himself, hence this failure of communication all the time. In fact, my father, who came from New Jersey, did have this feeling about Pennsylvania, that he wasn't quite clued in about what was going on. Secondly, there is a way in which to a child everything is myth-size: people are enormous and ominous and have great backlogs of mysterious information and of a life lived that you lack. I don't think that without the myth you'd have a book. It seemed to me to fit a kind of experience that I'd had: my father's immersion in the world of Christian morality, in trying to do the right thing and constantly sacrificing himself, always going off to church meetings, and yet complaining about it all the time. There was an ambivalence that seemed to make him very centaur-like. I think that initially art was tied in with theology and has to do with an ideal world: the artist is in some way a middleman between the ideal world and this, even though our sense of the ideal—and I'm speaking really of our gut sense, regardless of what we think we believe—is at present fairly dim. It may not always be so. And I find I cannot imagine being a writer without wanting somehow to play, to make these patterns, to insert these secrets into my books, and to spin out this music that has its formal side.

INTERVIEWER: Well, there are ideal worlds and ideal

Updike reading galleys on vacation in Martha's Vineyard

worlds. There's the ideal world of Plato, there's the world of the Music of the Spheres, and there's also the Titian world, the world of the sensuous. This other side to you has really found a fulfilment in 'Couples,' which, I now see with hindsight, was something you had to write. The whole interest in sensation, in the body, finds its fulfilment here. Were you conscious of this inevitability in writing 'Couples'?

UPDIKE: Well no, it's just my usual simple-minded attempt to portray something. Nothing annoys me more than books ostensibly about sex that don't really describe it.

INTERVIEWER: We're talking about 'Couples' as a book about sex. It's something quite different, isn't it? And I think it's certainly not sensationalist. What astonishes me is that these descriptions are written with extraordinary delicacy and tact. You must have found them very hard to write.

UPDIKE: They were no harder than landscapes and a little more interesting. It's wonderful the way people in bed talk, the sense of voices and the sense of warmth, so that as a writer you become kind of warm also. The book is, of course, not about sex really: it's about sex as the emergent religion, as the only thing left. I don't present the people in the book as a set of villains: I see them as people caught in a historical moment—a moment now past, by the way.

INTERVIEWER: That world no longer exists?

UPDIKE: It was pretty unthinkable in 1964 that there would be openly expressed this constant desire to tear everything down that you hear now from every Western city. It was basically still a world of acceptance where the abiding institutions were assumed to be substantial, though they received no real homage. The people in the book exist within a society, but have no wish to restructure it; rather, within its interstices they are seeking through each other's bodies, and really through each other's voices too—there's an awful lot of talk in that book—to console themselves.

INTERVIEWER: What's unusual about them is their particular promiscuity, isn't it?

UPDIKE: I don't think they are especially notable in that regard. These are the descendants of the Puritans, people who have inherited a work ethic and who find themselves really working no harder than they must. In part, the book is about affluence, which, in releasing at least this class of people from pressing financial anxiety, creates new anxieties.

INTERVIEWER: Not only is there much greater control of all these characters and a much larger canvas, but there is this kind of space in the book which I don't feel exists in the early work.

UPDIKE: At least you have a map of the town in your mind's eye and you sort of sail from one house to the other. I think a writer should perpetually be giving himself tough assignments in an attempt to see what he can do. It took courage initially to be able to write frankly about my own boyhood, which, funnily enough, was a very innocuous boyhood. Nevertheless it seemed to be a step forward to write some of the short stories that have been collected here and there. Then I thought: okay, enough of that, get out of this and write about adults making the usual sort of adult mess. In that sense the book was a change. But I see backwards through my books a certain continuity: in a way this book is describing a divorce and *Of the Farm* was about the consequences of a divorce. And certainly I've not, I don't think, been shy about erotic detail in the other books.

INTERVIEWER: It's only here that suddenly it has come right into the centre of the canvas. You probably won't want to write a book like this again.

UPDIKE: I wonder where I'm going to go now. I think it's very bad luck to talk about things you're doing.

INTERVIEWER: Well, talk in a rather magical and mysterious way about it.

UPDIKE: It's a rather magical or mysterious book. The proud State of Pennsylvania from which I come only produced one President, a man called James Buchanan who preceded Lincoln and who has always been dismissed as one of the weakest of a succession of weak Presidents between Jackson and Lincoln. I'm attached to him because he's a Pennsylvanian: he was a bachelor too, and he was very old, the oldest President till Eisenhower. I've read now maybe eight books about the 1850s, a period rather like the 1960s, a period of harsh debates, increasingly irrevocable rifts, a period of astounding invective. I was sort of shocked in my prim way by the kind of abuse that Johnson had to put up with, but that kind of abuse was American coin. I see Buchanan as a centre of some kind of investigation of what political power feels like. To what extent is it illusory? It certainly was very illusory in his case because he really didn't have much power, the country was paying no attention to him. And also I'm interested in taking a long, eventful life and shuffling it.

Book Review:

"The Lion That Squeaked," *Time*, 95 (22 June 1970): 82-84.

Bech: A Book *(1970) collects seven stories with the same protagonist–novelist Henry Bech. Five of the stories had originally appeared in the* New Yorker. *A sequel,* Bech Is Back, *was published in 1982.*

Now that John Updike's Bech stories from *The New Yorker* have been federated between hard covers, it is easier to see them for what they are: the funniest, most elegantly written and intelligently sympathetic renditions available about what happens when a writer stops being a writer and becomes a culture object.

Updike has ingeniously and elaborately invented Bech and his entire literary career. Verisimilitude is heightened by various Nabokovian cartouches, including an appendix containing Henry Bech's "Russian journal" and an introductory letter to Updike from Bech that shrewdly stops short of being a seal of approval: "I don't suppose your publishing this little *jeu* of a book will do either of us drastic harm."

It is the voice of a man who has already suffered the worst that his abundant society and his own easily seducible character have to offer. It is not the natural voice of John Updike, of course, though Bech experienced early fame like Updike and some of their travels have been the same. The basic Bech is a gently satiric caricature of a Jewish literary heavyweight. His qualities are drawn from the congregation of Eastern Liberal intellectuals whose ranks, incidentally, have sheltered some of Updike's more ferocious critics.

Updike's elfin revenge includes a six-page bibliography of Bech's works as well as criticism of them. *Travel Light*, Bech's highly praised first novel, seems to carry strains of Kerouac's *On the Road* and Bellow's *The Adventures of Augie March*. *Brother Pig*, a novella, hints ever so slightly of Mailer's stylishly oblique and politically muddled *Barbary Shore* ("Puzzling Porky" is Updike's title for the *Time* review). *When the Saints*, a collection of essays and sketches of the kind that often get published from the sheer momentum of a downsliding career, contains such elegies of West Side New York as "Sunsets over New Jersey" and such Commentariana as "Orthodoxy and Orthodontics." Bech has also succumbed to the siren song of journalism with such articles as "The Landscape of Orgasm" (*House and Garden*) and "My Favorite Christmas Carol" (*Playboy*).

Lately Bech's fiction has taken a 180-degree turn for the worse, but his life at least continues to be buoyed by his awareness of the irony of his situation: the quantity of his material rewards is inversely proportional to the quality of his production.

At 46, Bech looks like a "mob-controlled congressman from Queens hoping to be taken for a Southern Senator." Fat lecture invitations are as available as women anxious to add a famous notch to their bedposts. In the three funniest adventures, Bech is sent by the State Department on a cultural-exchange junket behind the Iron Curtain. The tableaux of culturecrats in opulent neo-czarist settings undoubtedly come from Updike's memories of his own U.S.-sponsored tour of Russia in 1964. For Bech, the trip proves to be a sort of thinking man's "Mission: Impossible," in which Bech must make his way through the claustrophobic air ducts of Communist literary life.

In Russia, where he endures the blatant irony of having a huge salad of royalty rubles thrust on him, Bech and the head of the Soviet Writers' Union joust with vodka glasses: "He toasts Jack London, I toast Pushkin. He does Hemingway, I do Turgenev. I do Nabokov, he counters with John Reed." Elsewhere, Bech vainly attempts to charm Yevtushenko by describing his own position in America not as a literary lion but as a "graying, furtively stylish rat indifferently permitted to gnaw and roam behind the wainscoting of a firetrap about to be demolished anyway."

In Rumania, where he comes to think of himself as "a sort of low-flying U-2," Bech attends an underground cabaret that features an endless number of variety acts, including an East German girl in a cowboy outfit singing *Dip in the Hot of Texas*. Humor at the expense of literal or imprecise translation is rampant. An admirer slathering to translate Bech into Bulgarian asks, "You are not a *wet* writer, no. You are a dry writer, yes?"

No and yes. As a dried-out writer, Bech loses some

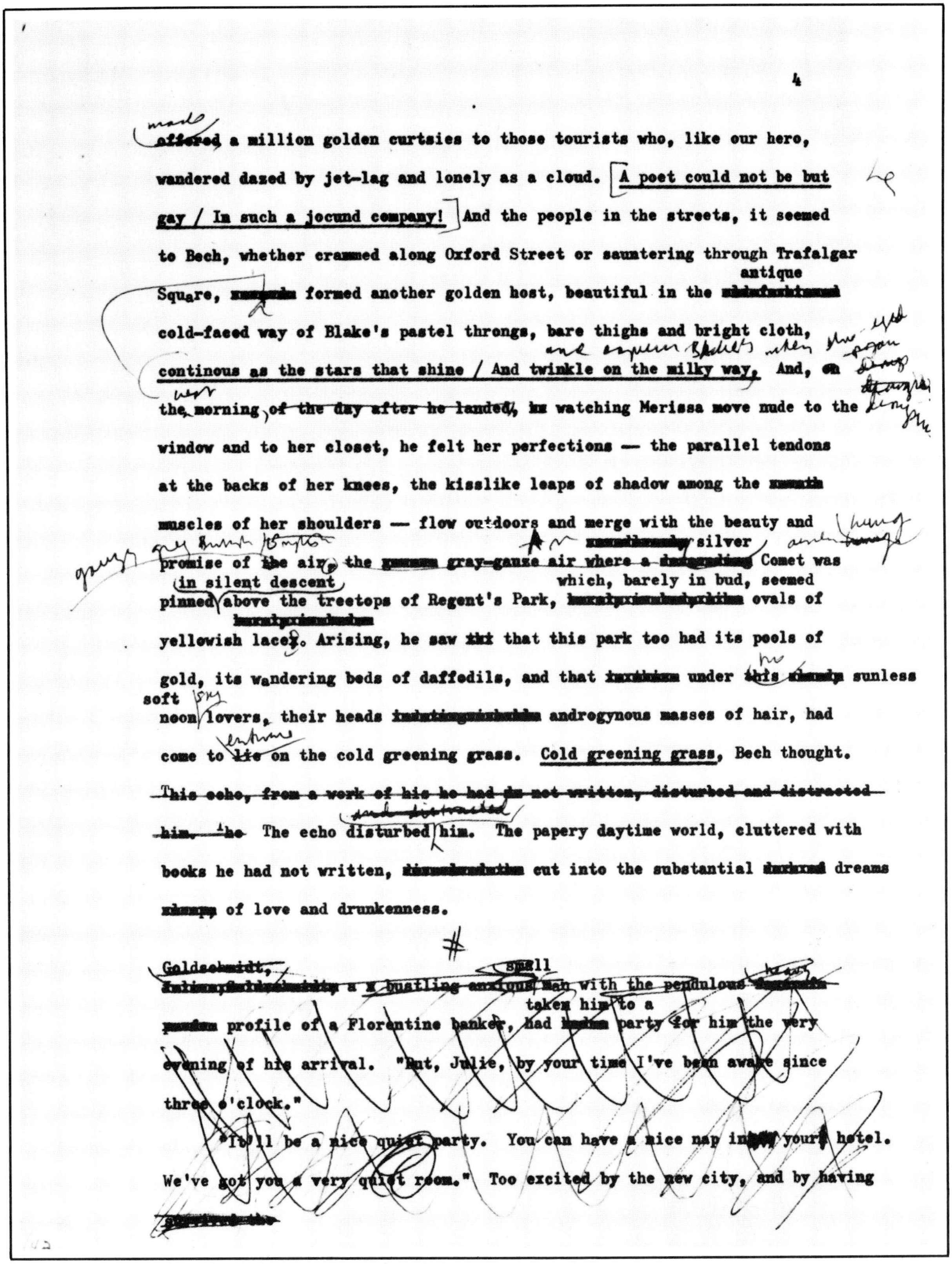

4

~~offered~~ made a million golden curtsies to those tourists who, like our hero, wandered dazed by jet-lag and lonely as a cloud. [A poet could not be but gay / In such a jocund company!] And the people in the streets, it seemed to Bech, whether crammed along Oxford Street or sauntering through Trafalgar Square, formed another golden host, beautiful in the antique cold-faced way of Blake's pastel throngs, bare thighs and bright cloth, continous as the stars that shine / And twinkle on the milky way. And, on the morning ~~of the day after he landed~~, watching Merissa move nude to the window and to her closet, he felt her perfections — the parallel tendons at the backs of her knees, the kisslike leaps of shadow among the muscles of her shoulders — flow outdoors and merge with the beauty and promise of the air, the gray-gauze air where a silver Comet was in silent descent which, barely in bud, seemed pinned above the treetops of Regent's Park, ovals of yellowish lace. Arising, he saw that this park too had its pools of gold, its wandering beds of daffodils, and that under this sunless soft noon lovers, their heads androgynous masses of hair, had come to ~~lie~~ on the cold greening grass. Cold greening grass, Bech thought. ~~This echo, from a work of his he had not written, disturbed and distracted him.~~ The echo disturbed him. The papery daytime world, cluttered with books he had not written, cut into the substantial dreams of love and drunkenness.

#

~~Goldschmidt,~~ ~~a bustling anxious small man with the pendulous heavy profile of a Florentine banker, had taken him to a party for him the very evening of his arrival. "But, Julie, by your time I've been awake since three o'clock."~~

~~"It'll be a nice quiet party. You can have a nice nap in your hotel. We've got you a very quiet room."~~ Too excited by the new city, and by having

Revised typescript for the story "Bech Swings?"–collected in Bech: A Book
(Harvard University)

Dust jacket for Bech: A Book, *a collection of stories about a writer ruined by success*

sustaining irony as he gets closer to home. In London, an aggressive young scholar browbeats Bech into explaining his work. A rich young cutie looks up from her pillow and smugly suggests that he "learn to replace ardor with art." Back home, a former student gives him pot and he vomits.

Yet Bech is never really pathetic. He never loses sight of his ludicrous position. Somewhere behind the Iron Curtain, Bech observes that "shallowness can be a kind of honesty." It is a remark worthy of Oscar Wilde. It is unlikely, however, that Wilde—who never lost the knack of drawing life from the surface of things—would have fudged with "kind of."

BOOK REVIEW:

Richard Locke, "Rabbit Redux," *New York Times Book Review*, 14 November 1971, pp. 1-2, 12, 14, 16, 20, 22, 24.

Rabbit Redux *deals with the life of Harry Angstrom from July to October 1969, ten years after the events of* Rabbit, Run.

In 1939 Thomas Mann sent his brother a fan letter. Heinrich's new novel, he wrote, "is great in love, in art, boldness, freedom, wisdom, kindness, exceedingly rich in intelligence, wit, imagination and feeling—a great and beautiful thing, synthesis and resumé of your life and your personality." Though fulsome and obviously written in the first flush of enthusiasm for Heinrich's now all but forgotten book, these are the hyperboles that come to mind after reading John Updike's new novel, "Rabbit Redux." "It must be said," Mann continues, "that such growth—such transformation of the static to the dynamic, such perseverance, and such a harvesting—is peculiarly European. Here in America the writers are short-lived; they write one good book, follow it with two poor ones, and then are finished."

There's truth as well as well-earned snobbery in this observation. American writers do tend to flash and then fizzle. The casualties in our postwar fiction are legion: writers as different as J. D. Salinger and Joseph Heller immediately spring to mind. John Updike knows this well: in an essay on Nabokov he argued that this Russian émigré was the only writer practicing in America "whose books, considered as a whole, give the happy impression of an *oeuvre*, of a continuous task carried forward variously, of a solid personality, of a plentitude of gifts explored knowingly. His works are an edifice whose every corner rewards inspection. Each book . . .yields delight and presents to the aesthetic sense the peculiar hardness of a finished, fully meant thing."

But, keeping this high professional standard in mind, are there any contemporary American writers who are steadily producing distinguished work, not one or two but say a minimum of four full-length books? Who are the novelists who have tried to keep a grip on our experience

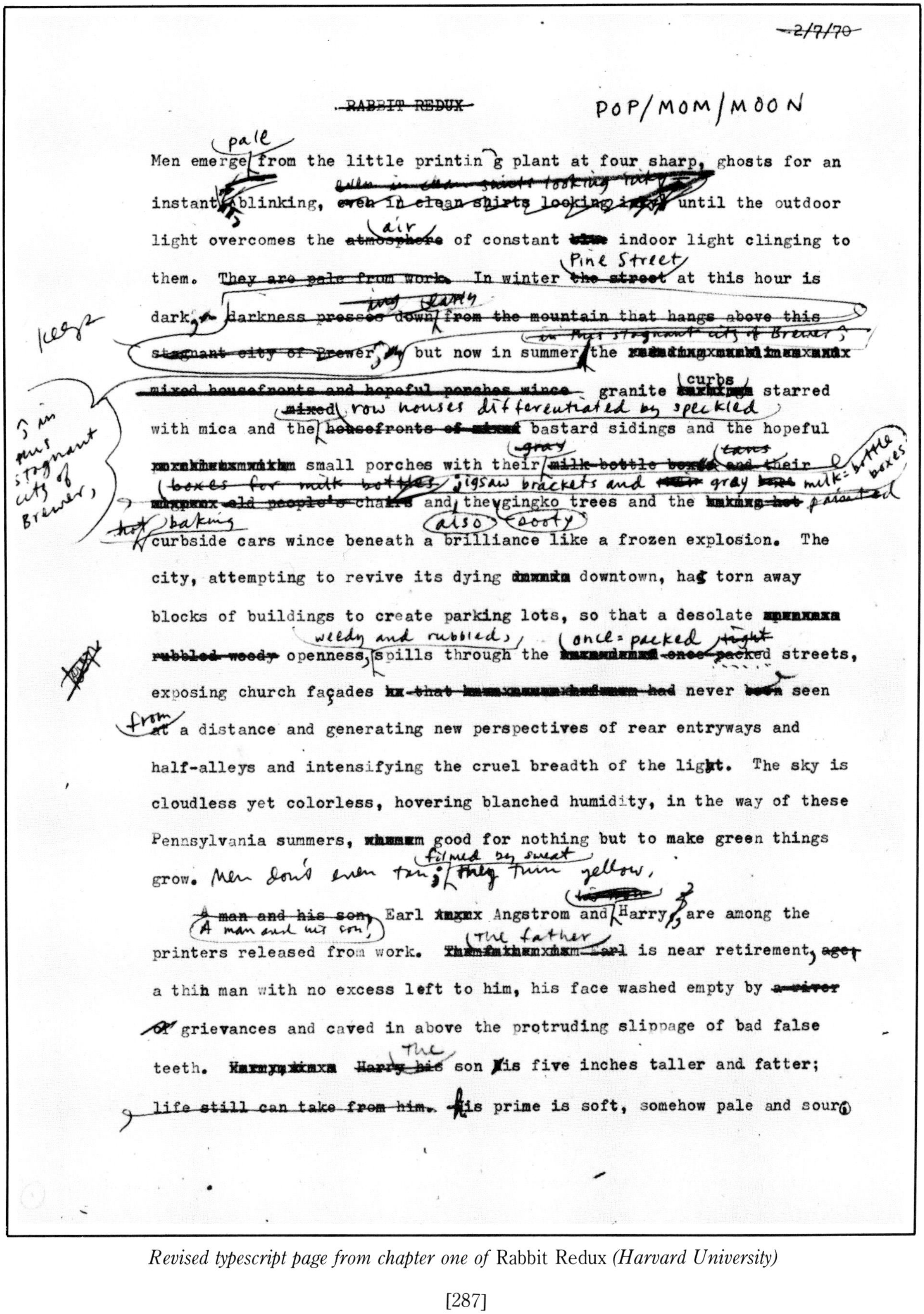
~~2/7/70~~

~~RABBIT REDUX~~ POP/MOM/MOON

Men emerge pale from the little printin g plant at four sharp, ghosts for an instant, blinking, ~~even in clean shirts looking inky~~ until the outdoor light overcomes the ~~atmosphere~~ air of constant indoor light clinging to them. ~~They are pale from work.~~ In winter ~~the street~~ Pine Street at this hour is dark, ~~darkness presses down from the mountain that hangs above this stagnant city of Brewer,~~ but now in summer the ~~mixed housefronts and hopeful porches wince~~ granite curbs starred with mica and the ~~mixed~~ row houses differentiated by speckled ~~housefronts of mixed~~ bastard sidings and the hopeful small porches with their ~~milk bottle boxes and their~~ jigsaw brackets and gray milk-bottle boxes ~~old people's chairs~~ and the also gingko trees and the sooty painted ~~baking hot~~ curbside cars wince beneath a brilliance like a frozen explosion. The city, attempting to revive its dying downtown, has torn away blocks of buildings to create parking lots, so that a desolate ~~rubbled weedy~~ weedy and rubbled, openness, spills through the once-packed ~~tight~~ streets, exposing church façades ~~that~~ never ~~been~~ seen ~~at~~ from a distance and generating new perspectives of rear entryways and half-alleys and intensifying the cruel breadth of the light. The sky is cloudless yet colorless, hovering blanched humidity, in the way of these Pennsylvania summers, good for nothing but to make green things grow. Men don't even tan; filmed by sweat they turn yellow.

~~A man and his son,~~ Earl Angstrom and Harry, (A man and his son!) are among the printers released from work. The father ~~Earl~~ is near retirement, ~~age~~ a thin man with no excess left to him, his face washed empty by ~~a river of~~ grievances and caved in above the protruding slippage of bad false teeth. ~~Harry his~~ The son is five inches taller and fatter; ~~life still can take from him.~~ His prime is soft, somehow pale and sour.

Revised typescript page from chapter one of Rabbit Redux *(Harvard University)* as we've wobbled along in the past decade or two, the writers to whom we turn to find out something of where we are and what we're feeling, the writers who give the secular news report? I'd suggest that there are five: Saul Bellow, Norman Mailer, Bernard Malamud, Philip Roth—and John Updike himself.

There are, to be sure, many other gifted authors at work, but these five (and possibly Joyce Carol Oates) are wrestling most fiercely with "the novel as history/ history as the novel." Barth, Vonnegut, Barthelme, Hawkes are up to something else. In the past two years, Bellow, Mailer, Malamud and Roth have written books that cluster like angry hornets around a few big news items, chiefly the moon shot and racial turmoil. Now, in a surprising return to the hero of his most unequivocally successful novel, "Rabbit, Run," John Updike plunges Harry "Rabbit" Angstrom, ten years older, into the late 1960's where he tries to cope with sex, fatherhood, marriage, drugs, Vietnam, blacks, the moon shot. And "Rabbit Redux" is the best book of the lot.

Of course to praise Updike on these terms, to place him in the company of the other four, is either an outrage or a truism, depending on who's listening. He began as the darling of The New Yorker in the mid 1950's and by the age of 30, in 1962, had published two novels, two collections of short stories, a children's book and a book of light verse. He seemed to have made it as nearly everybody's favorite best young American writer, from Granville Hicks in the Saturday Review, to Mary McCarthy in Paris, to Stanley Edgar Hyman in The New Leader. Yet even then there were qualms. Melvin Maddocks sounded a first graceful note in what became a symphony of critical opprobrium in a few years: "Infinite care is bestowed on infinitely small passions. When the time comes to touch the essential, the writer's grip slips, almost from embarrassment, into rhetoric, and feelings become esthetic sensations."

When Updike's third novel, "The Centaur," appeared in 1963, Commentary's editor, Norman Podhoretz, laced into him: Updike, he wrote, is callow, sentimental, cruel, adolescent and fashionably audacious in his treatment of sex, given to self-conscious efforts at verbal brilliance and fake profundity to cover up his lack of substance—"a writer who has very little to say and whose authentic emotional range is so narrow and thin that it may without too much exaggeration be characterized as limited to a rather timid nostalgia for the confusions of youth." When the novel won the 1964 National Book Award it was the kiss of death. Updike's books might be popular, but serious people didn't really have to read them.

In 1965 his short novel "Of the Farm" was almost universally misunderstood and dismissed as trivial. And then in 1968 came "Couples": a huge best seller, but a critical disaster. It was Alfred Kazin who sealed the coffin: "Among American novelists," he wrote, "John Updike is the college intellectual with genius. . . . I mean someone who can brilliantly describe the adult world without conveying its depths and risks, someone wholly literary, dazzlingly bright, the quickest of quick children, someone ready to understand everything and to describe anything, for nothing that can be put in words is alien to him. But when he describes situations that in life do bring terror to the human heart, his facility reminds one of many other college intellectuals brought up on Criticism, Psychoanalysis, the Death of God. Words become all, and what the words show most is the *will* to be as effective as one is gifted."

Nevertheless, when Updike brought out a collection of stories in 1970 about the imaginary Jewish writer Henry Bech, the critics loved it. Though many had reviled him for trivia, they lapped it up when the literary world they knew and loved became the focus of such elegant satirical attentions. "Bech" was proclaimed Updike's best book. But almost everybody knew the serious case against him was closed. He was precious, facile, pretentious. When he wrote about rural family life he was too small, they said, except when he dragged in all the highfaluting mythological nonsense in "The Centaur"—which was too big. When he wrote about suburban sexual behavior he was merely sociological and much too longwinded. Only in "Bech" did he keep his place as a country cousin with a charming eye. But he had nothing to say. Just a boyish cry of "Look ma, no hands" in the prose.

Or so they said. There remains at the very least one large, stubborn fact: in the 15 years since Updike began to write professionally he has published an astonishing range and volume of work that cannot be airily dismissed as the mindless gush of the steady best seller "pro" nor the dreary stream of a genteel "quality author." There are three collections of verse, a large anthology of parodies, essays and reviews, four children's books, four collections of short stories and six novels. This may not in Updike's mind or ours constitute a Nabokovian *oeuvre*, but when one sits down and begins to read through these books the variety and professional effort command respect and critical scrutiny. . . .

Updike's "Rabbit" novels—"Rabbit, Run" (1960) and its sequel "Rabbit Redux" (just published)—are his best books. The thesis novels failed because his will and intelligence took the place of emotional force. The autobiographical family novels were full of emotional force yet in the effort to keep it under esthetic control "The Centaur" sometimes became a shade too big and "Of the Farm" a shade too small. But in the Rabbit novels the use of the present tense and the choice of a character who stands at one remove from Updike's personal experience shield him from the overpowering rushes of feeling that result in ornate prose, willful intricacies or problems of scale in his other novels.

In "Rabbit, Run" a young man deserts his wife on an impulse, takes up with another woman, goes back to his wife and then runs off again. When the book first appeared, Richard Gilman described it well: "On one level, 'Rabbit, Run' is a grotesque allegory of American life, with its myth of happiness and success, its dangerous innocence and crippling antagonism between value and fact. But much more significantly, it is a minor epic of the spirit thirsting for room to discover and be itself, ducking, dodging, staying out of reach of everything that will pin it down and impale it on fixed, immutable laws that are not of its own making and do not consider its integrity."

Norman Mailer, writing in Esquire, greatly disliked Updike's prose but he did concede that "Updike has instincts for finding the heart of the conventional novel" and brilliantly expressed the emotional and ultimately religious intensity of the book: "the merit of the book is not in the simplicity of its problem, but in the dread Updike manages to convey, despite the literary commercials in the style, of a young man who is beginning to lose nothing less than his good American soul, and yet it is not quite his fault. The power of the novel comes from the sense, not absolutely unworthy of Thomas Hardy, that the universe hangs over our fates like a great sullen hopeless sky. There is real pain in the book, and a touch of awe."

What distinguishes "Rabbit, Run" from all of Updike's other work (until the appearance of its sequel) is its dynamic balance between description and narrative energy: as Rabbit escapes from one enclosing situation to another, the pace never flags and yet the physical and psychological details have never been more sharply in focus. The minutiae of the Eisenhower age—the paradigmatic Mickey Mouse TV show, the religious revival, the all-American glamor of high-school heroes, the cramped apartments of small town sweethearts who married too young, the hallowed authority of athletic coaches and parents—all are perfectly there.

But the verisimilitude is more than skin deep. Updike meticulously conveys the longings and frustrations of family life, the interplay of love, tenderness, aggression and lust with self-esteem, the differences of feeling and speech from class to class and generation to generation. The prose speeds along with grace and strength; the present tense has given it dramatic immediacy and yet permitted a rapid flow of psychological nuance. Rabbit's wife, his mistress, the disapproving parents, his old coach, an all too modern Episcopal priest and his wife, the two young children all are brilliantly drawn. Rabbit is caught in the center—a kind of anti-Job who won't aban-

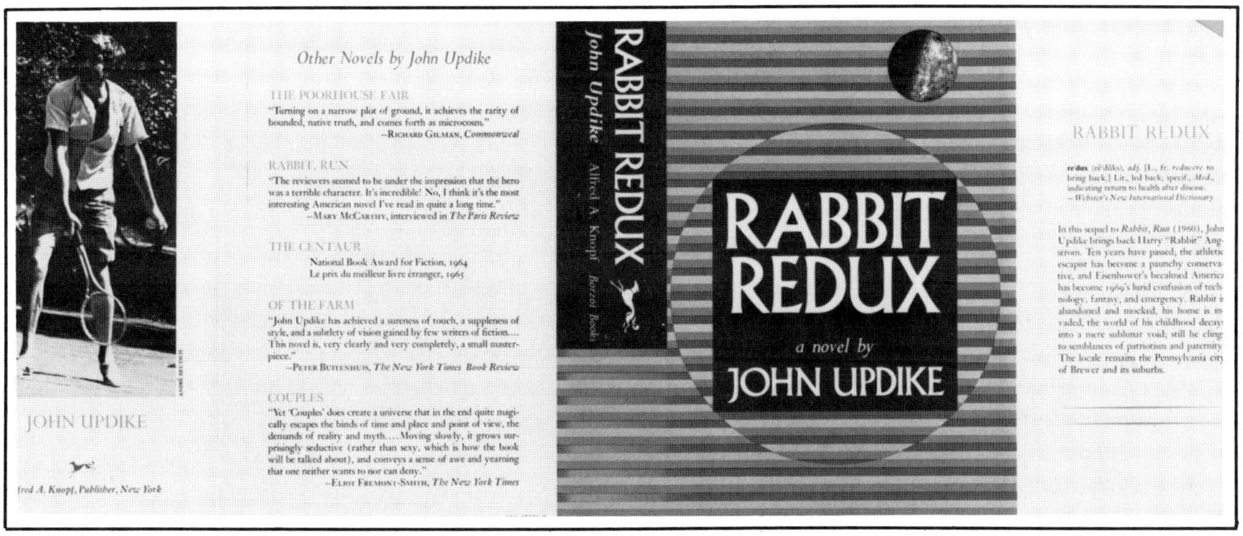

When Rabbit Redux *was published in 1971, it was hailed by Anatole Broyard in the* New York Times *as the work of "an awesomely accomplished writer." The title was explained on the front flap of the dust jacket.*

don the pleasure principle, or a male Madame Bovary who instead of killing himself simply runs away.

Thus, the essential theme of "Rabbit, Run" is civilization and its discontents: the opposing claims of self and society, the sacrifices of energy and individuality that civilization demands. In "Rabbit, Run" Updike pulled against the 1950's, defending the claims of the libidinous presocial self against the smothering complacencies of small town white America. Now in "Rabbit Redux" (that is, Rabbit "returns") he pulls against the 1960's and defends his hero's new commitment to civilization, his longing for social and personal continuity in an age where both are hard to come by.

In the new book Rabbit has greatly changed; it's been ten years since he last ran away. At 36 he's no longer a bounder, but plugs away, like his father, as a linotypist in a local print shop. He sticks to his responsibilities and lives by the old American rules which it cost him so much to learn: family loyalty, hard work, sexual compromise. But in the 1960's such rules no longer seem to apply. "Everybody's the way I used to be," he says.

Rabbit's wife, Janice, has also changed. She is restless, no longer the gloomy stay-at-home. Now she bustles out to work at her father's new Toyota agency, while Rabbit is stuck in his dwindling blue collar trade and is finally laid off as obsolete. Janice, not Rabbit, is the one who has an affair and runs away from home—for much the same reason as he once did. This time he is left behind, the town cuckold, caring for his teen-age son.

Lonely, adrift, Rabbit takes an 18-year-old runaway girl into his house; he becomes her lover and father. The family expands when she brings home another stray: a black Vietnam veteran on the run, who styles himself an agent of apocalypse—and indirectly brings down fire and brimstone on the house. Rabbit returns to his parents' home. Once again he sleeps in his old room, regresses into adolescent fantasies. But in the end his wife decides to let her lover go and comes back to her family. A more complex health and order is achieved.

The action takes place in the summer of 1969, and the Apollo moon shot is used as the organizing image of the book. As Rabbit and his father sit drinking in a bar and he first learns that his wife may be unfaithful, the astronauts are taking off. As Rabbit's life falls apart, Armstrong sets foot on the moon. Everything in the middle sections is in free fall as Rabbit spins around the dark side of the moon. In the end Rabbit and his wife home in like space capsules and, of course, like rabbits in a hutch. The lunar wasteland of contemporary America is everywhere. The tacky houses of the suburban development where Rabbit lives blister the landscape like craters on the moon. Downtown there are deserted lots and empty stores. Desolate shopping centers are lit by burger joints where the drinks all taste like chemical sludge and Luna specials (two cheeseburgers with an American flag on top) are sold. The endless electronic buzz of television fills the air with news reports of rocket launchings and racial turmoil. The young trip out on pot and heroin; their sexual license is bombed out, arid, frozen. All these elements are subtly brought together in the controlling image of space exploration, a journey out into a void and then back to earth.

In "Rabbit Redux," for the first time in his career, Updike deals in a large way with public subjects: violence, the Vietnam war, black revolution, drug addiction, middle American anger and frustration, hippie life-styles, the moon shot. With great narrative facility he has integrated these volatile elements within a realistic novel of suburban life in 1969. In outline, the book may seem populated with clichés, but on the page they are redeemed by Updike's accurate evocation of people's voices and feelings as well as his description of physical details. Updike has always written about the inner surface of banal experiences; in "Rabbit Redux" he shows highly familiar subjects in all their human particularity.

For example, Rabbit has a series of violent political arguments with his two sexual rivals: his wife's lover and the young black. In "Bech," Updike wrote "even in an age of science and unbelief our ideas are dreams, styles, superstitions, mere animal noises intended to repel or attract." In the give and take of these debates it is nearly impossible to detach the ideas and political opinions from their psychological, novelistic base. Rabbit gets wild about Vietnam when he feels personally and sexually threatened; he overcomes his fear and dislike of blacks when he himself is an outcast and a cuckold.

The wide range of tones and rhythms in black speech has never been so well reproduced in contemporary white writing. (The apposite comparison is Ralph Ellison's "Invisible Man.") Bernard Malamud's stereotyped black novelist in "The Tenants" and Saul Bellow's wordless menacing black pickpocket in "Mr. Sammler's Planet" come nowhere near the depth and accuracy of Updike's black characters: a printer, a lowlife singer, the young Vietnam veteran. Although symbolically Rabbit is clearly the "suffering servant" and father, and this young black is clearly the Antichrist—preaching sermons that mix Afro-American history and religious nihilism and administering the sacraments of drugs and sex—this black is portrayed with enormous sympathy and force and is anything but an allegorical cut-out.

In "Rabbit, Run" the hero confronted an essentially static social situation and dove into his inner spaces to avoid it. In "Rabbit Redux" he confronts an unnervingly dynamic social situation that plunges him into outer space—beyond his family, his class, his race and his normal earthbound feelings and behavior. "Rabbit, Run" was a major book about the fifties; "Rabbit Redux" is, like Mailer's "Armies of the Night," a major book about the sixties—the period when the struggles of the private self became political events and political events broke in on private lives.

Of the writers who are working in a professional way to help us come to some unsteady and evolving understanding of our human and cultural predicament as we slide into the seventies, two in recent years are complementary—Norman Mailer and John Updike. A metaphor might help us here. Mailer is a mountain-climber; Updike a miner. Mailer is heroically scaling the heights—of himself, of ideas, of urban life, of the future, of the sky, the outer spaces. He is aggressive, public, ostentatiously political, outrageously daring, unsparing of himself. Updike is an underground worker, chipping away at banal circumstances and minute feelings, trying to find jewels in a little space. Until this book he was nearly apolitical and even here he carefully grounds his characters' political opinions in their immediate social and psychological conditions. He is tender, not aggressive. His sexual descriptions are not boastful but reverent. His major characters include women as well as men—which is remarkable in American fiction. He is our finest writer about children. He treats his characters with respect; there are no villains.

In an interview in 1966 Updike said, "I like middles. It is in middles that extremes clash, where ambiguity restlessly rules." In an interview two years later he continued "Everything unambiguously expressed seems somehow crass to me . . . everything is infinitely fine and any opinion is somehow coarser than the texture of the real thing. . . . My work says 'yes, but.' Yes, in 'Rabbit, Run,' to our inner urgent whispers, but—the social fabric collapses murderously. Yes, in 'The Centaur,' to self-sacrifice and duty, but—what of a man's private agony and dwindling? No, in 'The Poorhouse Fair,' to social homogenization and loss of faith, but—listen to the voices, the joy of persistent existence. No, in 'Couples,' to a religious community founded on physical and psychical interpenetrations, but—what else shall we do, as God destroys our churches? . . . Domestic fierceness within the middle class, sex and death as riddles for the thinking animal, social existence as sacrifice, unexpected pleasures and rewards, corruption as a kind of evolution—these are some of [my] themes."

He has never treated them better than in his new novel. In "Rabbit Redux" all is ambiguous, dialectical and yet, finally, novelistically resolved. There are no "Updikean" curlicues of style or yawning gaps between symbol and event. All is dramatized. There are some structural faults, and moments when characters don't ring true. But I can think of no stronger vindication of the claims of essentially realistic fiction than this extraordinary synthesis of the disparate elements of contemporary experience. "Rabbit Redux" is a great achievement, by far the most audacious and successful book Updike has written.

MOCK INTERVIEW:

Henry Bech (John Updike), "Henry Bech Redux," *New York Times Book Review*, 14 November 1971, p. 3.

In this spoof-interview, Updike, posing as Henry Bech, interviews himself about the second novel in the Rabbit series.

The Book Review has been fortunate enough to persuade Henry Bech, the hero of John Updike's last book, to interview Mr. Updike on the subject of his newest work, "Rabbit Redux." Mr. Bech reports:

Updike's office is concealed in a kind of false-bottomed drawer in the heart of downtown Ipswich (Mass.), but the drowsy locals, for a mere 30 pieces of silver, can be conned into betraying its location. A stuck-looking door is pulled open; an endless flight of stairs, lit by a team of dusty fireflies, is climbed. Within the sanctum, squalor reigns unchallenged. A lugubrious army-green metal desk rests in the center of a threadbare Oriental rug reticulate with mousepaths; the walls are camouflaged in the kind of cardboard walnut paneling used in newly graduated lawyers' offices or in those Los Angeles motels favored by the hand-held cameramen and quick-tongued *directeurs* of blue movies. On these sad walls hand pictures, mostly souvenirs of his childhood, artistic or otherwise. On the bookshelves, evidently stained by a leopard in the process of shedding his spots, rest repellent books—garish schoolboy anthologies secreting some decaying Updikean morsel, seven feet of

John Updike with his wife, Mary, in 1972

James Buchanan's bound works adumbrating the next novel, some daffodil-yellow building-trade manual penumbrating "Couples"; and, most repellent of all, a jacketless row of the total *oeuvre*, spines naked as the chorus of "Hair," revealing what only the most morbid have hitherto suspected, that since 1959 ("The Poorhouse Fair," surely his masterpiece) Updike with Alfred A. Knopf's connivance has been perpetuating a uniform edition of himself. Beclouding all, the stink of nickel cigarillos, which the shifty, tremulous, asthmatic author puffs to sting the muse's eyes into watering ever since at the Surgeon-General's behest, he excised cigarettes from his armory of crutches.

Updike, at first sight, seems bigger than he is, perhaps because the dainty stitchwork of his prose style readies one for an apparition of elfin dimensions. An instant layer of cordial humorousness veneers a tough thickness of total opacity, which may in turn coat a center of heartfelt semi-liquid. Shamefacedly I confessed my errand—to fabricate an "interview" for one of those desperate publications that seek to make weekly "news" of remorselessly accumulating Gutenbergian silt. Shamefacedly, Updike submitted. Yet, throughout the interview that limped in the van of this consent, as the pumpkin-orange New England sun lowered above the chimney pots of a dry-cleaning establishment seen darkly through an unwashed window, Updike gave the impression of (and who wouldn't?) wanting to be elsewhere. He kept interjecting his desire to go "home" and "shingle" his "barn"; it occurred to this interviewer (the Interviewer, as Mailer would say), that the uniform books, varied in tint and size as subtly as cedar shakes, were themselves shingles, with the which this shivering poor fellow hopes to keep his own skin dry in the soaking downpour of mortality.

I observed, feinting for an opening, that he has stopped writing about Jews. He replied that the book about me had not so much been about a Jew as about a writer, who was a Jew with the same inevitability that a fictional rug-salesman would be an Armenian. I riposted that *he* was a writer, though a Wasp. With the languid shrug of the chronically pained, he bitterly inveighed against the term Wasp, which implies, he said, wealth where he had been poor, Calvinism where he had been Lutheran, and ethnic consciousness where he had had none. That his entire professional life had been spent among Jews and women, that his paternal grandmother had been partly Irish, that he had disliked James Gould Cozzens's last novel, that false loyalties were the plague of a divided Republic, that racism as an esthetic category was one thing but as an incitement to massacre another, etc.

With the chinks in his armor gaping before me like marigolds at the height of noon, I lunged deftly as a hummingbird. Didn't I detect, I asked, in his later work an almost blunt determination to, as it were, sing America? Would he describe himself, I asked, switching the tape recorder up to fortissimo, as (a) pro-American (b) a conservative? His turtleish green eyes blinked, recognizing that his shell was being tickled, and that there was no way out but forward. He said he was pro-American in the sense that he was married to America and did not wish a divorce. That the American style, and landscape was, by predetermination, his meat; though he had also keenly felt love of fatherland in England, in Russia, in Egypt. That nations were like people, lovable and wonderful in their simple existence. That, in answer to the second prong of my probe, there *were* some things he thought worth conserving, such as the electoral college and the Great Lakes; but that by registration he was a Democrat and by disposition an apologist for the spirit of anarchy—

our animal or divine margin of resistance to the social contract. That, given the need for a contract, he preferred the American Constitution, with its eighteenth-century bow to the pursuit of individual happiness, to any of the totalisms presently running around rabid. That the decisions of any establishment, though properly suspect and frightfully hedged by self-interest and the myopia power brings, must be understood as choices among imperfect alternatives; power participates in the weight and guilt of the world and shrill impotence never has to cash in its chips.

I inkled that this diatribe was meant to lead up to some discussion of his new novel, with its jacket of red, gray and blue stripes, but, having neglected to read more than the first pages, which concern a middle-aged ex-athlete enjoying a beer with his elderly father, I was compelled to cast my interrogation in rather general terms. Viz.:

Q.: Are you happy?

A.: Yes, this is a happy limbo for me, this time. I haven't got the first finished copies yet, and haven't spotted the first typo. I haven't had to read any reviews.

Q.: How do you find reviews?

A.: Humiliating. It isn't merely that the reviewers are so much cleverer than I, and could write such superior fictions if they deigned to; it's that even the on-cheering ones have read a different book than the one you wrote. All the little congruences and arabesques you prepared with such delicate anticipatory pleasure are gobbled up as if by pigs at a pastry cart. Still, the ideal reader must—by the ontological argument—exist, and his invisibility therefore be a demonic illusion sustained to tempt us to despair.

Q.: Do you envision novels as pills, broadcasts, tapestries, explosions of self, cantilevered constructs, or what?

Updike at work in his Ipswich office above the Dolphin Restaurant, 1972

A.: For me, they are crystallizations of visceral hopefulness extruded as a slow paste which in the glitter of print regains something of the original, absolute gaiety. I try to do my best and then walk away rapidly, so as not to be incriminated. Right now, I am going over old short stories, arranging them in little wreaths, trimming away a strikingly infelicitous sentence here, adding a paper ribbon there. Describing it like this makes me sound more Nabokovian than I feel. Chiefly, I feel fatigued by my previous vitality.

Q.: I'd like to talk about the new book, but the truth is I can't hold bound galley pages, my thumbs keep going to sleep, so I didn't get too far into this, what? "Rabbit Rerun."

A.: (*eagerly, pluggingly*): *Redux*. Latin for led back. You know Latin: *Apologia Pro Vita Sua*. The next installment, 10 years from now, I expect to call "Rural Rabbit"—you'll notice at the end of this book Janice talks about them getting a farm. The fourth and last, to come out in 1991 if we all live, is tentatively titled "Rabbit Is Rich." Nice, huh?

Q.: (*turning tape recorder down to pianissimo*): Not bad. *Pas mal*. Not bad.

A.: (*gratefully, his shingling hand itching*): Thanks. Thanks a lot.

Henry Bech's novels are "Travel Light," "Brother Pig," and "The Chosen." The working title for his fourth novel, in progress, is "Think Big."

> *The new generations, my impression is, want to abolish both war and love, not love as a physical act but love as a religion, a creed to help us suffer better. The sacred necessity of suffering no longer seems sacred or necessary, and Hemingway speaks across the Sixties as strangely as a medieval saint; I suspect few readers younger than myself could believe, from this sad broken testament, how we* did *love Hemingway and, pity feeling impudent, love him still.*

From Updike's "Older Americans," in his Picked-Up Pieces

BOOK REVIEW:

Arthur Schlesinger, Jr., "The Historical Mind and the Literary Imagination," *Atlantic Monthly*, 223 (June 1974): 54-59.

When asked why he did not like plays, Updike said, "The unreality of painted people standing on a platform saying things they've said to each other for months is more than I can overlook." Nonetheless, he wrote Buchanan Dying *(1974) in play form. Updike felt that his fellow-Pennsylvanian President James Buchanan has never received the recognition he deserved. Arthur Schlesinger, Jr., reviewed the work from a historian's point of view.*

. . . What possibly could have drawn John Updike to resurrect the nineteenth-century American politician regarded by many historians as the most tedious and unprofitable of all Presidents?

In a cocky and discursive Afterword, Mr. Updike strews a profusion of hints. With so premeditated a writer, one never knows whether his clues are designed to instruct or to mislead. But even misleading clues may be instructive. He began his research on Buchanan, he tells us, when he finished *Couples*. It is not unnatural that, after an elaborate study of the diversities of fornication in a place very much like Ipswich, Mass., an exhausted writer might begin to meditate about the only President to serve out his term as a bachelor. Still, this is a frivolous point, and I do not urge it. Mr. Updike goes on to urge on his own behalf that he, like Buchanan, is a Pennsylvanian, that Buchanan is the only Pennsylvanian to have become President and that the single Pennsylvania President remains to this day uncelebrated in the state of his birth—no monuments, Mr. Updike complains, no Buchanan Avenues, no picture books for the young. So local patriotism may have helped stimulate what Mr. Updike calls "my final volume of homage to my native state." But this seems a mildly superficial point too.

The first of Mr. Updike's parade of five epigraphs provides a stronger clue. He quotes a sentence from Kierkegaard's *Journals*: "I wanted to write a novel in which the chief character was to have been a man who had a pair of spectacles with one lens that reduced as powerfully as oxygas-microscope and the other that magnified equally powerfully; in his interpretation everything was very relative." Mr. Updike says that he decided to write such a novel himself. Then he learned that Pennsylvania's single President was nearsighted in one eye and farsighted in the other. "With one eye," as his niece Annie told his first biographer, George Ticknor Curtis (this should have been the sixth epigraph), "he could not distinguish the landscape at all, while with the other he could see very far." (It is perhaps typical of Buchanan that, according to his niece, he did not make this discovery about himself until middle age.) The coincidence of Kierkegaard's powerful image and Buchanan's ocular eccentricity evidently gave Mr. Updike his lead. For was not this the source of Buchanan's anguish, the ruin of his reputation—his compulsion to see the problems of the South through one eye and the problems of the North through another, his ineradicable relativity in an age of truculent absolutes? Mr. Updike's brave and singular ambition becomes clear. It is to make Buchanan nothing less than the tragic protagonist, if not the tragic hero, of the breakup of the American Union. . . .

His purpose is to display the Buchanan Administration as an ordeal of wisdom and sacrifice, in which Buchanan's selfless statesmanship prepared the way for Lincoln's canonization. But history, in "books written by Lincolnophiles and neo-abolitionists," has denied Buchanan's contribution, traduced his motives, and misrepresented his policy. Buchanan's equivocations, Mr. Updike suggests, far from being the expression of a feeble and evasive personality, were rather a noble response to an intolerable national dilemma. Buchanan's was not the tragedy of personal inadequacy. It was the distillation of the tragedy of the republic itself, a tragedy deeply rooted in the history which the "old public functionary," nearly sixty-seven when he ascended to the presidency, had seen from more places of civic responsibility than almost any other occupant of the White House. Instead of the historian's traditional *Rabbit, Run*, Mr. Updike, so to speak, offers Buchanan as *Rabbit Redux*.

He originally planned, as he tells us, to cast this interpretation in the form of a novel. Then he read Philip S. Klein's *President James Buchanan*, published in 1962, and found it so novelistic in its touches—not, it must be said, at the expense of its scholarly solidity—that "there seemed but little the fictionist could do but seek another form for the re-ordering of circumstances." The form he chose was a drama—an extended reverie, beginning and ending with Buchanan on his deathbed in 1868, in which the crucial scenes of his life recur amidst the fluid, wandering, dreamlike desolation of dying. Mr. Updike's stage directions, his asides to a potential director, his economy of set (one for the entire play) and of casting (the same players designated for a succession of roles)—all indicate that he hopes his drama may someday take the stage. I trust that he is right. *Buchanan Dying* is infinitely more interesting than most of the trash that finds its way to New York these days. Perhaps one of the regional repertory companies will undertake it; perhaps the Kennedy Center in Washington.

But the play undoubtedly presents practical difficulties. It is terribly long and filled, in addition, with *longueurs*, especially when Harriet Lane, Buchanan's vivacious niece—rather excessively vivacious as rendered by Mr. Updike—comes on the scene with her chatter of "Nunc." Nor has Mr. Updike, magician though he may be, quite solved the problem of language. He has, as he says, tried to blend actual utterance as recorded in letters, speeches, and memoirs with utterance imagined "in the rounded and scarcely idiomatic public language of the nineteenth century." Sometimes this results in speeches so stilted as to be unspeakable. Thus:

> Is it true, as all the tongues in Lancaster are wagging, that coming back from some days' absence you forthwith called upon Mrs. Jenkins and her sister Grace Hubley and made gay over tea, while Anne awaited your return at Colebrookdale?

Or Buchanan himself:

> Alas, our dusky brethren have been stirred to false hopes and vain aspirations by the delirious pamphlets of the abolitionists and by the freesoil rhetoric heard whenever Congress sits in session. Nothing grieves the President more, in these dark days, than that angelic Southern matrons must retire each night a-tremble for the safety of their children. Yet I would beg you, pity the black man in his impudent delusions, for the sudden suspension of the institution that enfolds and nurtures him would do no race greater harm than his own.

Yet it must be added that sometimes such speeches are deliberately satiric in intention—a point the author would have the director underline by starting up an applause machine at the back of the theater.

And very often Mr. Updike's fantastic talent for mimicry produces quite marvelous results. His reconstruction of the lost letter from Anne Coleman—the fiancée of Buchanan's youth, who, fancying herself ignored by the sedulous young politician, wrote Buchanan breaking the engagement and died shortly after—is a masterpiece. The talk Mr. Updike awards his romanticized Buchanan sometimes has immense style and felicity. Thus on his mother and the Bible:

> Ignoring my silent longing for her voice, she would dote upon that book as upon a black mirror. Ever

> since her death, I have carried it with me. Its substance is heaviness. Give me, instead, light, clear things: arithmetic and legal logic, whiskey and spring-water, Russian amber and British manners, the French language and Japanese procelain. Give me translucence and air . . . and a tingle on the tongue.

Or, in a Wilder mode,

> Dying, I discover, is rather like dancing, and not unlike diplomacy: legerity and tact are paramount. I was a fair country dancer in my time.

Buchanan is transformed from a sedate and rather ponderous old stager, weighty in words and legalistic in mind, into a worldly epigrammatist, emulating the La Rochefoucauld he constantly quotes. But, if Buchanan was not perhaps a pompous hypocrite out of a tirade by Charles Sumner, he was hardly a drawing-room dandy out of a comedy by Oscar Wilde. Henry S. Foote of Mississippi, who knew him well and acknowledged his facility in (here Foote quoted Dryden) "the horseplay of raillery," added, "I do not think he ever uttered a genuine witticism in his life." The Old Public Functionary frowned on dancing and card-playing in the White House as much as Mrs. Polk before him and Mrs. Rutherford B. Hayes after him. Still, Mr. Updike's myth of Buchanan serves a purpose. In this weary, somewhat cynical, fundamentally devoted old man he sees the emblem of the house divided against itself, the recapitulation of half a century of the American descent into chaos.

In a series of powerful flashes, the play illustrates this descent as refracted through Buchanan's own circumspect public career. Here the instinct of the professional novelist generally triumphs over the carelessness of the amateur historian. Thus Mr. Updike introduces a crucial encounter between Jackson and Buchanan in 1824 with a stage direction recalling that Jackson, as described by Albert Gallatin, was "a tall, lank, uncouth looking personage, with long locks of hair hanging over his face and a cue down his back tied in an eel skin." It is a marvelous description. The only trouble is that Gallatin wrote it in 1794. The Jackson of 1824 was a very different person, with manners "more presidential," as Daniel Webster, no fan, wrote that year, "than those of any of the candidates." Nor, so far as I know, did any friend of Jackson's ever refer to him as Andy, as Mr. Updike's Buchanan does in an earlier scene. Still, Mr. Updike's Jackson, when he appears, is splendidly realized, forceful and true. His Polk, whom Buchanan served as Secretary of State, is excellent also, without pretense or illusion, always speaking straight to the point: "In August of 1845, Mr. Buchanan, principally in order to keep a record of your remarkable variations of opinion, I commenced to keep a diary of my days as President"; and, later, "What is life, for any of us, but a busy dying?"

So history moved on, as Mr. Updike sees it, to its sullen necessity. The climax came when Buchanan and his Cabinet began to agonize over the decision of Sumter: what to do, as South Carolina headed toward secession, about Major Anderson and his federal troops in Charleston harbor? Buchanan, as usual, saw the problem as a relativist with disjunctive eyesight. On the one hand, he pronounced secession unconstitutional—a view that led his pro-slavery friends to accuse him bitterly of deserting the South. On the other hand, he said that neither the President nor Congress had any right to coerce into submission a state seeking to withdraw from the Union—a view that baffled and exasperated the North. And if he were wrong and Congress did have the power to authorize military action against seceding states, no President, Buchanan added, could exert such power on his own while Congress was in session; this would be usurpation and make the President "justly liable to impeachment." Nor, he pointed out, were there any federal civil officers—judges, district attorneys, marshals—left in South Carolina, all having resigned, to request and enforce federal intervention, as there had been when Jackson cracked down on nullification in the same state thirty years before.

Buchanan thus committed himself to a drastic doctrine of executive impotence. Even that most cautious of the cautious, his Secretary of State Lewis Cass, resigned when the President refused to reinforce the Charleston forts. Theories of presidential self-abnegation are particularly seductive this year, by which I do not, of course, imply that Mr. Updike's rehabilitation of Buchanan is an intellectual by-product of Watergate. But Buchanan was surely wrong in denying the federal government the power to put down secession; though he had a point in contending against presidential appropriation of congressional power while Congress was in Washington—which was why Lincoln delayed for ten weeks after the attack on Sumter before calling Congress back into session.

It was not just that Buchanan's reading of the Constitution might have made of it, in Arthur Goldberg's phrase, a suicide pact. It was even more the political consequences of his substantive judgments of the crisis. His annual message of December 3, 1860, made a number

Updike at his mother's farm near Morgantown, Pennsylvania in 1974, the year Buchanan Dying *was published*

of extraordinary points: not only the disclaimer of federal power to act but fervent expressions of sympathy for Southern grievances; exclusive blame for the crisis laid on the abolitionists who, Buchanan wrathfully said, had inspired the slaves with "vague notions of freedom"; a declaration that persistence by Northern legislatures in attempts to thwart the execution of the Fugitive Slave Act would justify the slave states "in revolutionary resistance to the Government of the Union"; all this leading up to the proposal of a constitutional amendment that would assure the security of slavery in the South and in territories not yet organized as states and assure as well the delivery by the free states of runaway slaves to their masters below the Mason-Dixon line. Such an array of attitudes on the part of a Northern President could only encourage the South to suppose it really would get away with its project of breaking up the nation.

Mr. Updike's interpretation of these events seems to me a bit muffled and confused. By dwelling on the rejection of the principle of secession, he glides over the substantive concessions Buchanan was prepared to make to slavery and thereby leaves him as a man in the precise middle between North and South: whereas on the issue that mattered most—the perpetuation of slavery—Buchanan stood firmly with the South. Mr. Updike, moreover, seems to endorse inconsistent, or at least diverging, theories of Buchanan's motives in choosing his course.

The obvious and familiar theory is that Buchanan decided not to play Andrew Jackson because he believed that, until the bombardment of Sumter, the Constitution forbade a Jacksonian response. This theory sufficiently explains Buchanan's inaction. He was a sterile legalist to the end and, though he had no personal use for slavery, did not understand it in 1860 as *the* fatal moral issue, any more, one cannot but feel, than Mr. Updike so understands it today. But Mr. Updike is not content to rest on the constitutional argument. He draws, in addition, on Professor Klein's defense of Buchanan—a defense, Mr. Updike revealingly admits, "more vigorous" than that made in 1866 by the former President himself (not, Mr. Updike, "the ex-President") in *Mr. Buchanan's Administration on the Eve of the Rebellion*. Conceivably Professor Klein's defense was more vigorous because he included arguments it did not occur to Buchanan to make. In any case Mr. Updike suggests that Buchanan was acting not only on constitutional principle but also, and perhaps even more, as a matter of tactics. He would not play Andrew Jackson because Jacksonianism would have been the inopportune response. Buchanan's restraint, Mr. Updike contends in his Afterword, expressed the "wise instinct" that in a democracy people will fight only for a cause that is made to appear righteous. "The North needed, perhaps, all these months of weakness and forbearingness in Washington to give a defensive coloring to the dubious cause of putting down secession with force." Once Sumter was shelled, "Lincoln could draw upon the moral capital Buchanan's conciliation had piled up."

One may be permitted to disagree with Mr. Updike's view that forcible opposition to slavery and secession was perceived in 1860-1861 as all that dubious a cause. Still, neither of us was there, and he may well be right. But historians well know the danger of reading back from result to intent. Whatever the result of Buchanan's policy, his intent was not to maneuver the Southerners into firing the first shot and thereby strengthen the moral case for suppressing the rebellion: nor was this an intent he ever claimed. Mr. Updike's Buchanan further argues: "For every day my administration staved off secession, another factory sprouted." If this implies that the Buchanan Administration deliberately bought time to rearm, it is not true. In any case it is rather like the English controversy over Munich: did Chamberlain's appeasement policy give Britain a year in which it made itself relatively stronger when war came? Maybe yes or maybe no, but, whether yes or no, this was not why Chamberlain was an appeaser. He was an appeaser because he thought Hitler could be successfully appeased. Buchanan's idea was not to gain time to rearm but to live by the Constitution as he saw it and hope against all reason that the nation would unite around a formula that would give slavery new constitutional guarantees.

There is a further ambiguity, if I read him correctly, in Mr. Updike's defense of Buchanan. If his theory that Buchanan acted tactically somewhat undermines the theory that Buchanan was acting according to constitutional principle, so a third theory—that Buchanan acted as he did because he could act no other way—somewhat undermines at least the second theory. By this third theory Buchanan would not play Andrew Jackson because it was psychologically impossible for him to play Andrew Jackson. Here we must return for a moment to Anne Coleman, the girl who died, who, some believed, killed herself, after she thought Buchanan had abandoned her. In the Updike play, Anne Coleman haunts Buchanan's dying hours. When his deathbed reverie flashes back to the secession winter, he asks Jacob Thompson to read aloud the response from the South Carolina Commissioners. Thompson reads but what Buchanan hears in his reverie is the last letter from Anne Coleman, the letter so brilliantly imagined by Mr. Updike, a letter rising to its awful climax: "My warmth greets in you a deceptive coolness as unalterable as the mask of death."

For Buchanan's incapacity to love, Mr. Updike appears to suggest, applies to the South as well as to Anne Coleman. In the play Buchanan is made to refer to the South as "her." "My tongue," he says, "tricks me into a telling gender; for so I imagine it to myself—the South is our wife." Later: "I loved the South . . . and she loved me, but I gulled her." Was Buchanan's desertion of the South, such as it was, no more then than a reenactment of the desertion of Anne Coleman? the response of a man endowed, in the phrase of the historian Roy Nichols, with an "inability to return affection adequately"? endowed, as Mr. Updike's Buchanan confesses to a pastor in August, 1860, with "a sense of impotent detachment and cool fatality," a witness who witnesses unmoved and is "enclosed within my destiny as within a crystal container"? "Break this man of crystal who encloses you," the minister exhorts the President. But Buchanan cannot. In his interpretation everything is very relative. With one eye he can see very far while with the other he cannot distinguish the landscape. So he stands passively by and watches the nation rush to war. All this is fascinating; but, if Buchanan was only doing what he could not but do, where does this leave Mr. Updike's argument about buying time?

Few historians, I imagine, will be convinced by Mr. Updike's glittering case for the Old Public Functionary as tragic hero. . . . The literary imagination is more closely allied to myth than to history. But this is far from saying that it is of no use at all to the historian. Though Mr. Updike himself calls *Buchanan Dying*, justly, a "strangely shaped, radically imperfect book," it is at the same time an abundant, even opulent, creative act. Such a book may well affect the historian not by virtue of its quasi-historical arguments but because of the intensity with which the artist reminds the historian that, if the past is another country, it is still a country populated by human beings.

. . . In breathing life into a historical figure, novelists and playwrights may well get things wrong and are not likely to alter professional verdicts. But the power of their imagination may force historians to look freshly at the frieze and to perceive historical figures not as abstractions but as human beings in all their idiosyncrasy and uniqueness, as human beings above all created by their own choices: "I am the man, I suffer'd, I was there." The artistic vision may thus reinvigorate that fundamental historical exercise, the imaginative leap into the past. For the passion to see things in the flickering light and shadow of the time itself and not with benefit of the knowledge of consequences remains the heart of the historical enterprise, at least in its narrative aspect. In this manner the literary imagination may fertilize the historical mind and serve to stretch and enrich historical understanding.

Why write? As soon ask, why rivet? Because a number of personal accidents drift us toward the occupation of riveter, which pre-exists, and, most importantly, the riveting-gun exists, and we love it.

From Updike's "Why Write?," in his Picked-Up Pieces

INTRODUCTION:

John Updike, introduction to "Leaves," *Writer's Choice*, ed. Rust Hills (New York: David McKay, 1974), pp. 391-392.

One of the least popular stories in The Music School *was "Leaves," a short prose-poem about a man's struggle to reorganize his life after divorce. When asked to select a story for* Writer's Choice, *a collection of writers' favorites among their own works, Updike chose "Leaves," defending it in his introductory note.*

An invitation to choose one's best makes an occasion to squirm. Contrary to popular impression, writers, unlike pole vaulters, do not know when they have done their best—there is no clatter of tipped bamboo to tell them they have failed, no statistic in tomorrow's paper to tell them they succeeded. We do our best with each piece; as with children no two look up at us with an identical face, and each demands separate treatment. Preferential treatment, indeed; and having satisfied ourselves that each pet has marched off past the mailbox with its hair as combed and its knickers as lint-free as caring can make them, we can only wave good-bye bravely and turn to the inspirations still waiting to be turned outdoors.

So a self-nominated anthology like this becomes an opportunity to rectify the slights of a harsh and hasty world and put forward a shy child. "Leaves" has never been, to my knowledge, included in any volume save my own collection *The Music School*. It is in a mode of mine, the abstract-personal, not a favorite with my critics. One of them, reviewing *The Music School*, expressed impatience with my lace-making, so-called. Well, if "Leaves" is lace, it is taut and symmetrical lace, with scarce a loose thread. It was written after long silence, swiftly, unerringly as a sleepwalker walks. No memory of any revision mars my backwards impression of it. The way the leaves become the pages, the way the bird becomes his description, the way the bright and multiform world of nature is felt rubbing against the dark world of the trapped ego—all strike me as beautiful, and of the order of artistic "happiness" that is given rather than attained. The last image, the final knot of lace, is an assertion of transcendental faith scaled, it seems to me, nicely to the mundane.

Enough of such. My clinching reason for selecting this story is its shortness, which I thought might offer, first to the editor and then to the readers of this anthology, a pleasant respite amid the no doubt extensive masterworks of my contemporaries.

BOOK REVIEW:

George Steiner, "Scarlet Letters," *New Yorker*, 51 (10 March 1975): 116-118.

A Month of Sundays *(1975) is a short novel dealing with Reverend Tom Marshfield, who is forced from his parish for sexual indiscretions and sent to a motel for fallen clergy in the desert.*

John Updike has been an enviable problem. Gifted at once with a supremely alert ear and eye for the pulse and sinew of contemporary American speech and with a passion for the rare word, for the jewelled and baroque precisions still vital beneath and around the current of common idiom, he has been able to write about literally *anything*. Whether it be the stubble in a Pennsylvania field, the swerve of a basketball under gymnasium lights, the rasp of a tire on gravel, the tightening at a man's temples under pressure of sexual fantasy, Mr. Updike has made these planes of experience brilliantly his own yet true to the evidence, penetrative into the fabric of American discourse and gesture to a degree that future historians and sociologists will exult in. He has written of rich and poor, of urban and rural, of science and political intrigue, of gregariousness and cold solitude with an unforgiving yet strangely solicitous, almost tender intelligence. The critic and the poet in him (a minor but sparkling poet of occasion and humor of a kind infrequent now) are at no odds with the novelist; the same sharpness of apprehension bears on the object in each of Updike's modes. But it is precisely this ubiquity, the sheer range of whatever elicits his luminous dispassions, that has made it difficult for him to find a mastering theme.

Not only in "The Centaur" but, indeed, in all of his novels Updike has tested elements of fable and allegory, ancient formal devices with which to knit into comely and probing shape the dazzling singularity, the vital ordinariness of his perceptions. "The Poorhouse Fair," still one of his finest achievements, aims at control, at a sharp and exemplary meaning, through compression. "Couples" is a panoramic mapping rescued from indiscrimination by recourse to deliberately symbolic, terminal devices (the raging fire at the close). "Bech" is a book held in place, mirrored within a book—again a fine solution to the problem of focus, of finding a structure both firm and supple enough to contain such wealth and scruple of style. Sexuality has over and over provided the key. Because it is simultaneously the most ordinary and the most individual of human rites, because sexual concourse in and out of marriage is not only general to all societies but highly distinctive of each, the erotic has provided Updike with an essential coherence. Our sexual lives are deep-rooted in the locale of our economic, regional, ethnic identity. They call on the masked as well as on the most public, brutal layers of contemporary language. They involve illusions of infinite particularity and recognitions, maturing no less than corrosive, of routine. And, inevitably, the erotic, even at its most vulgar and irresponsible—perhaps there more than elsewhere—touches on myth, on shadow-places and echoes, idyllic, cruel, scatological, as ancient as the human imagination itself. Through detailed accounts of sex, ranging from the physiological to the allegorical, Updike has found a center, a discipline for the prodigality of his art. At its best, the result is poignant and ironic: what is in lesser writers a dispensation is in Updike a severity. The more urgent, the more acrobatic the sexual moment, the tauter, the more contemptuous of facility is the writing. Eroticism is, in a serious artist, an ascetic pursuit.

To invoke the pathos, the enigmatic humanity of lust is, of course, to borrow the language of St. Augustine and of Kierkegaard. Where eros and sadness meet, theology begins. This realization has long been a part of Mr. Updike's work. Looking back, one comes to realize how deeply his sense of American experience is religious and religious in a vein related particularly to the history of New England Calvinism on the one hand and to the thought of Barth and Tillich on the other. It is a commonplace that recent American fiction and criticism have to a drastic extent been the product of a Jewish tone and explosion of talent. Updike is the counterpoise: his sensibility is, among practicing American novelists, the most distinctly Christian and Protestant. The eroticism of his fiction has been a long prelude to a radically theological view of American existence. In "A Month of Sundays" the sexual and the clerical, the scatological and the eschatological are intimately, almost violently meshed.

As a result of sensual indiscretions above and beyond the bounds of charity, the Reverend Tom Marshfield has been banished from his Midwestern parish. Under the veil of a nervous breakdown, scandal is avoided. Instead,

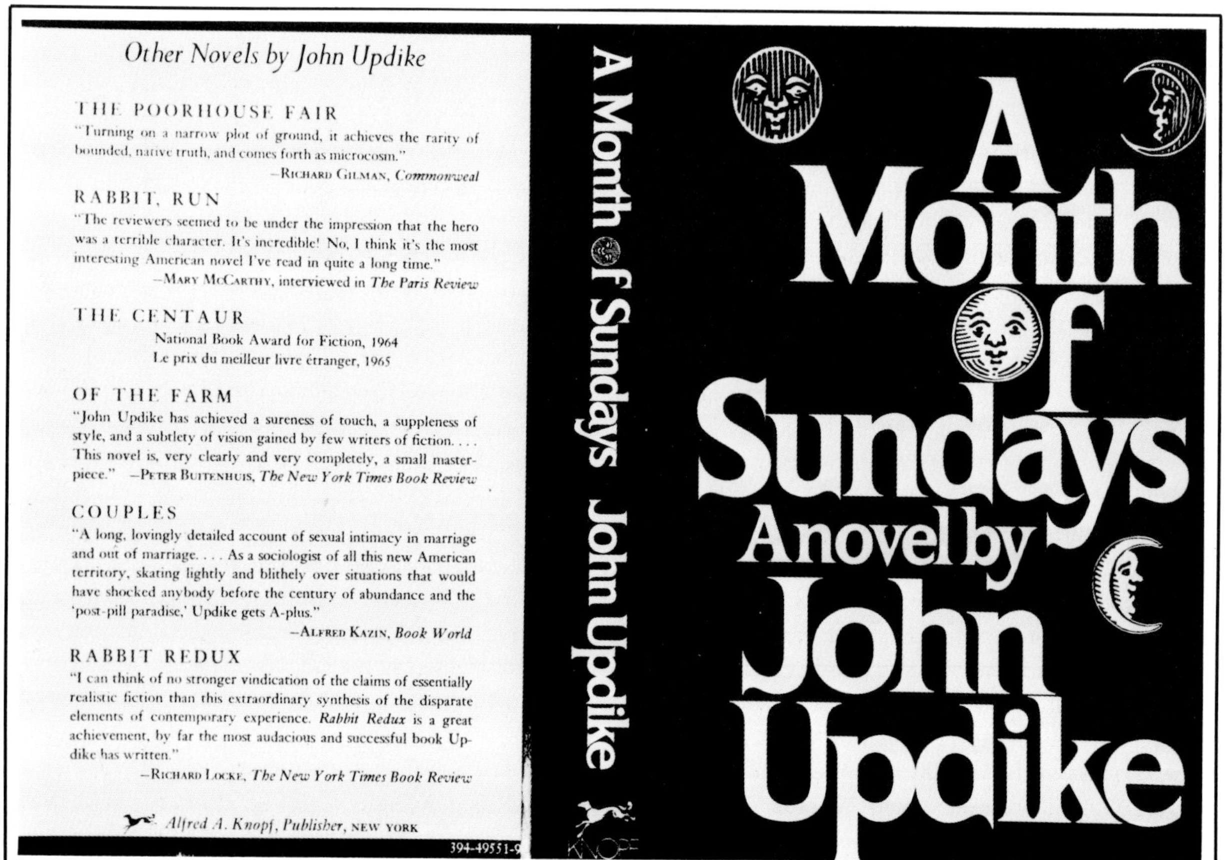

Dust jacket for Updike's novel about a clergyman enmeshed in adultery

the holy gentleman is to spend a month in a desert motel specifically intended for clergy in various modes of dishevelment (yielding to Updike's own obsession with puns, acrostics, and word games, one might describe his plot as nightshades of Tennessee Williams' "The Night of the Iguana"). The therapy for the Reverend Marshfield is a balanced diet of golf, masturbation, and written confession. He is to set down the chronicle of his fall from grace, together with his present thoughts, feelings, visitations of the spirit, holy or profane. What we have before us is this penitential journal—Marxist jailers call it self-criticism—together with a set of imaginary sermons. In the first place, however, these lucubrations (Mr. Updike's coruscated idiom becomes infectious) are meant not for the reader but for the guardian presence of the sanatorium. Her name is Ms. Prynne. The maiden name of Tom's wife, the name of her theologian father, is Chillingworth.

This, obviously, is the point. "A Month of Sundays" is a meditation on, a contradictory echo of that first classic of the American Protestant erotic imagination, Hawthorne's "The Scarlet Letter." Adultery was to Hawthorne the crucial, emblematic motif of the American condition, posing the full paradox of the inherited weakness of the flesh and of social institutions in a new Eden, in a world predestined to innocence and the renovation of man. Updike turns the tables on Hawthorne and on the legacy of Calvinist prohibition: "But who that has eyes to see cannot so lust? Was not the First Divine Commandment received by human ears, 'Be fruitful, and multiply'? Adultery is not a choice to be avoided; it is a circumstance to be embraced. Thus I construe these texts." The Reverend Marshfield's exegeses go further. Pondering the meaning of American experience, the location of this experience in God's scheme of things, he arrives at a new definition of American emancipation. It is marriage itself that has proved to be only a tentative sacrament in the crises and dispensations of what is, literally, the new world: "Separation arrives by whim (the last dessert dish broken, the final intolerable cigar-burn on the armchair) or marriages are extended by surrender. The race between freedom and exhaustion is decided. And then, in a religious sense, there is no more adultery, as there is none among schoolchildren, or slaves, or the beyond-all-reckoning rich." (It is in the placing of that word "reckoning" that Updike's parallel art, his conjunction of the colloquial with the liturgical, can be seen at its most exact.)

Given this doctrine and Marshfield's deepening doubts about the patriarchal deity of the Protestant tradition, his debauches seem at once inevitable and incidental. Alicia is something of a sexual athlete, Frankie's scapulae glint in the afternoon light of the motel—but these are the mere trappings of a subtler, sadder heresy. Ned, the curate, has taken to copulating with the beloved Alicia. Half-naked, the Reverend Tom has been peeping at their windows. Reviewing the desolate pain of the discovery, our confessor—observe the antique duplicity of the term—resorts to "Plotinian language." What is being violated is no less than "the body of my soul." Marshfield no longer accepts the bargain of transcendence. American spirituality is of the flesh, flesh-rooted and bound. Grace is of this world or it is of none. When John Updike launches on one of his inventories of the material scene:

> also visible through the window: houses with conical roofs, dormers, protrusions, scallop shingling, jigsawed brackets, ovals of stained glass tucked up under eave-peaks like single eyes under a massive gingerbread eyebrow; and hedges and shrubs, and a mailbox painted in patriotic tricolor, a birdfeeder hopping with feathered mendicants, a covetously onlooking squirrel, streetsigns, streetlamps, etc., etc. . . .

he is not primarily displaying his masterly eye and lexical virtuosity (that superbly apt "mendicants"). He is making an insistent point about the ephemeral substance of reality, about the possibility, profoundly heretical and grievous, that there is beyond the skin of things no firmer realm, no compensating deep. Poor Tom's gratifications have long been immanent: "Even the purgative sweep of windshield wipers gratifies me" (note "purgative"). Now, having by desultory license disrobed himself and been driven to the desert whence Christianity came in its dawn of promise, he finds himself "stripped." If there is a grace note at the close, it is, in the true sense, terminal. He who is down need fear no fall.

Working so near the innermost of his concerns, that congruence—at once farcical and tragic—of sexuality and religious feeling in post-Puritan America, Updike trusts himself almost blindly to his verbal skills. His use of puns, Freudian malapropisms, and portmanteau words—themselves symptomatic of Marshfield's nervous extremity—runs riot. Too often the level is that of a

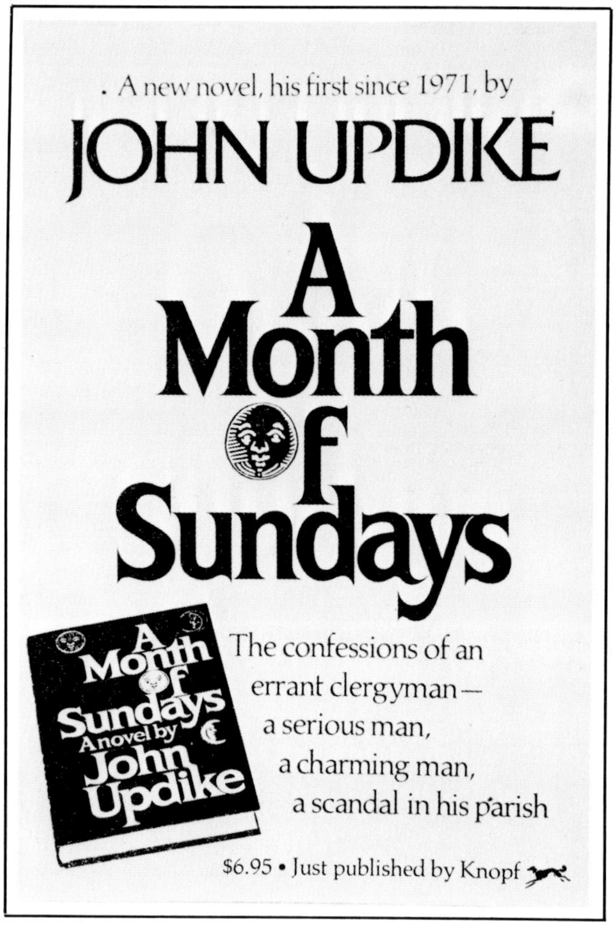

From New York Times Book Review, *2 March 1975*

Hasty Pudding script in an off year: "navish" for "knavery" in church; "Nixema, the noxious salve for liberal sores"; "Andman Willsin" for one of Mr. Updike's illustrious colleagues in American letters; "Near-Mrs.," no explanation needed. The prose is febrile in a manner expressive less of the Reverend Marshfield's troubles than of the writer's ungoverned cartwheels. An upper lip becomes "an arch of expectation, a gem of moisture"; passing car lights set Alicia's hair "on false fire"; a Dart is sea-changed into "a hydrofoil skimming above the asphalt waves of the highway of life"; golf-course sprinklers do "a dervish dance to keep the heartbeat of green alive." During a poker game, beer and tension induce dizziness. The result is "betting losers and folding winners in boustrophedonic alternation." Is there anything sadder than fireworks that last into the day?

However, as in Joyce, so in this latest Updike it is in the puns and acrostics, even at their most brutal, that the heart of meaning lies. When a wife's sexual organs (Updike's word is much shorter and simpler) are defined as "indentured," the triple connotation (pictorial, "pornographic," legal-economic) brilliantly, nauseatingly concentrates the intent of the book—its critique of those values and hypocrisies implicit in the Puritan ethic. When the Reverend Marshfield descants on "prick, pic, truthpic," he is not only mocking the mendacities of photographic realism or echoing back to "indenture" via "toothpick." He is proclaiming what he, and very probably John Updike, takes to be the locale and function of honesty, of authentic recognition. These are ugly devices toward an urgent vision.

Whether "A Month of Sundays" is substantial, controlled enough to make this vision emotionally plausible is less certain. It is an impatient text enforced by rather than enforcing its pyrotechnics. One would guess that it is a transitional novel in Updike's work, a rapid staking-out of territory that the next fictions will map at leisure. In the present instance the letter bullies the spirit. And is this not precisely the cause of Tom Marshfield's insurgence, of his peregrinations—randy, autistic, but fundamentally desperate—to the deserts of the heart?

BOOK REVIEW:

Lawrence Graver, "Even the Footnotes Sparkle," *New York Times Book Review*, 30 November 1975, p. 39.

Picked-Up Pieces *(1975), like* Assorted Prose *before it, collects Updike's nonfiction. It includes reviews, essays, introductions, speeches, and other writings from 1965-1975.*

With playful modesty Updike offers "Picked-Up Pieces" as consignments from an artist's workshop—miscellaneous prose made to order during the past ten years; but it looks more like a splendidly cluttered Italian museum where profane and sacred treasures, monuments and miniatures, make dizzying claims on our attention. Brilliant, sustained essays on Kierkegaard, Borges and Nabokov mix with travel sketches, accounts of golf, body cells, Indians, cemeteries, Satanism, and the ambiguous gratifications of the writing life. A garland celebrating our luck (and our children's) at having E. B. White's "The Trumpet of the Swan" is soon followed by thoughts on oral sex and buggery in the American novel. Across a table Voznesensky appears, "his pale face faintly bloated like a nun's squeezed in her wimple.". . .

Even the footnotes sparkle. Having said in 1968 that

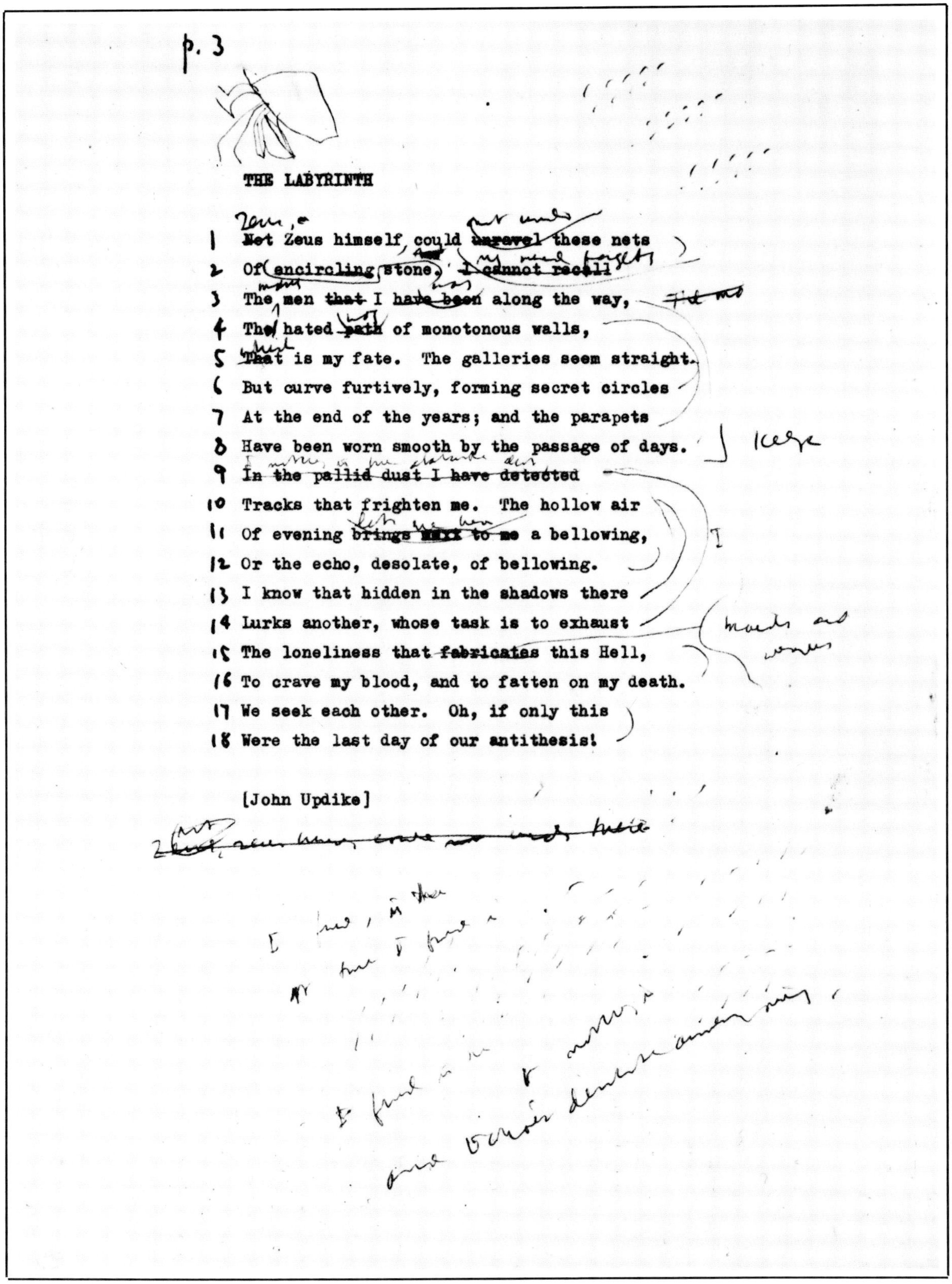

p. 3

THE LABYRINTH

Not Zeus himself could unravel these nets
Of encircling stone. I cannot recall
The men that I have been along the way,
The hated path of monotonous walls,
That is my fate. The galleries seem straight
But curve furtively, forming secret circles
At the end of the years; and the parapets
Have been worn smooth by the passage of days.
In the pallid dust I have detected
Tracks that frighten me. The hollow air
Of evening brings to me a bellowing,
Or the echo, desolate, of bellowing.
I know that hidden in the shadows there
Lurks another, whose task is to exhaust
The loneliness that fabricates this Hell,
To crave my blood, and to fatten on my death.
We seek each other. Oh, if only this
Were the last day of our antithesis!

[John Updike]

Working draft for Updike's translation of a Jorge Luis Borges poem, collected in Picked-Up Pieces *(Harvard University)* he must be one of the few Americans with a bachelor-of-arts degree never to have met either Robert Lowell or Norman Mailer, Updike now feels compelled to revise the record with an asterisk:

"*True in 1968 but no longer. Lowell who seemed to be leaning above me like a raked mast, later described me to a mutual friend as 'elusive and shy.' I think I was afraid he would fall on me from his height of eminence. Mailer, as much shorter than I had expected as Lowell was taller, danced about me on a darkened street corner (44th and Second Avenue, if memory serves), became not elfin but an entire circle of elves in himself, taunting me with my supposed handsomeness, with being the handsomest guy he had ever seen. I took it to be Maileresque hyperbole, absurd yet nevertheless with something profound in it—perhaps my secret wish to *be* handsome, which only he, and that by dim streetlight, at a drunken hour, has ever perceived."

Who else but Updike could offer in a footnote his talent in microcosm? Lowell as "raked mast"—the image is worth a thousand pictures of that looming, exposed, tormented poet; and metaphors as fresh animate much of "Picked-Up Pieces." The sentence that follows has that irresistible blend of vulnerability and pluck, self-effacement and self-regard that is often the quality of an Updike confession. With the appearance of Mailer, we get a bizarre, suggestive vignette: the prize-ring and the fairy tale, banter and illumination, plus a stubborn respect for mundane circumstance, the verifiable fact.

As one reads along in "Picked-Up Pieces" such dazzle becomes customary light, and a more confident feeling for the form of an Updike literary essay emerges. The initial impulse is usually celebratory: the reviewer wishes to share his enthusiasm for a book he admires. More often than not, the author is foreign, in some way exotic, in craft and vision unlike himself. Knut Hamsun—astringent, headstrong, irascible, defiant—manages to speak to Updike from a "human creatureliness that knows no accountability, no ideal systems"; and he can be vividly placed among "those tanned, clear-eyed truants (the Basque Unamuno, the Algerian Camus, the Egyptian Cavafy, the Russian Tolstoi) who jeer into the classroom of European civilization." At times, Updike's cosmopolitanism seems so imperial that no continent is alien to it. He speaks at Bristol on the future of the novel, in Adelaide on the creative impulse, in South Korea on why novels are funny. Narayan and Naipaul, Queneau, Grass and Gombrowicz, Sylvia Townsend Warner and Ivy Compton-Burnett—all present and more than satisfactorily accounted for.

Updike seems obsessed with finding out what the best people elsewhere are doing, partly from a desire to talk shop, partly from a need to peer through other masks, but also from an almost mystical passion for human connectedness in a clefted, precarious time. Bonds, ties, relationships, transactions, alliances—the urge to make them and the difficulty; how they are formed and dissolve; the joys they offer and the penalties they exact—this has been one of Updike's persistent subjects in fiction and in journalism. Rabbit runs and is lead back; "The Centaur" and "Couples" explore uncommon joinings; "Of the Farm" was originally "The Farm," but a preposition adds the vital note of linkage. The first item in "Picked-Up Pieces" is "On Meeting Writers" (better to connect in print than in person); the last is on Narayan, the writer as citizen (lucky the novelist who can "draw tales from a community of neighbors").

Updike's search for coexistence offers a clue to one of the most satisfying features of his best essays and reviews: the simultaneous expression of diverse, many-layered experience. Sometimes he does it through his remarkable gift for figurative speech. Describing the limits of Nabokov's "Glory," he isolates one of those "landlordly prefaces that slam shut the doors of unsightly closets, inveigh against the Freudian in the hall, and roughly nudge the prospective tenant toward the one window with a view." On a larger scale the effect works as a structural and thematic principle, as can be seen in the final tribute to Borges.

It begins quietly with facts about publication and translation history (in the clear, low-keyed style that can serve as cement for an Updike mosaic). A moment later comes personal reminiscence: "I myself had read only 'The Garden of the Forking Paths,' originally published in *Ellery Queen's Mystery Magazine* . . . [and] I was prompted to read Borges seriously by a remark made—internationally enough—in Rumania . . . by a young critic in a tone he had previously reserved for Kafka."

Funny yet unobtrusive, the juxtaposition does its work; our critic is equally relaxed with detective stories and the heady talk of a literary conference. The allusion to Kafka slides almost unnoticed into an analogy and a question. Will the appearance of Borges prove as important as the publication of Kafka in the 1930's? Unlikely; but might not his work "in its gravely considered oddity" provide a clue "to the way out of the dead-end narcissism and downright trashiness of present American fiction?" Three paragraphs into the essay and we have a compacted structure with four main elements: literary history, personal reminiscence, a promise of textual analysis, and generalized cultural commentary. From this point on, Updike's own delight in Borges's work, his skill at conveying its originality and felt life, its place in history, and its meaning for the present are elegantly woven together.

In the foreword to "Picked-Up Pieces," Updike laments that his flirtation with journalism has too often kept him away from fiction, his one true love; and he hopes that "for the sakes of artistic purity and paper conservation" the reviews to be gathered in 1985 will "make a smaller heap." Without wishing to hex his novels and stories, one might hope that for the sake of criticism he keeps his frustrating, fruitful balance.

BOOK REVIEW:

Peter S. Prescott, "To Have and to Hold," *Newsweek*, 88 (8 November 1976): 103.

Marry Me: A Romance *(1976) is the account of two couples' adulteries and the subsequent struggles to save their marriages. In the year it was published, Updike was divorced from his wife Mary after thirteen years of marriage.*

Let's hope the institution of marriage survives its detractors, for without it there would be no more adultery and without adultery two-thirds of our novelists would stand in line for unemployment checks. Adultery as a form of human anguish is the central theme of most of John Updike's novels; indeed, it has proven fiction's most trusty, least exhaustible resource since the days of medieval romances. "Romance" is the word that Updike applies to this story: clearly he is aware of the continuity. Like Chrétien de Troyes, he uses the narrow confines of an illicit affair to explore problems of choice, will and responsibility, the problem of a kind of love that is mostly pain, that precludes rational thought and, by becoming an obsession, threatens social order.

The time is spring and summer 1962, the place coastal Connecticut. Jerry is married to Ruth and Richard to Sally; they are all about 30 and have lots of young kids. Jerry and Sally are having an affair. They meet on beaches, fly separately to meet in Washington, tell a lot of lies. They want to get married. Sally feels she is already Jerry's wife and "this strange fact, unknown to the world but known to them, made whatever looked wrong right, whatever seemed foolish wise."

Jerry is more perceptive: "What we have, sweet Sally, is an ideal love. It's ideal because it can't be realized. As far as the world goes, we don't exist . . . any attempt to start existing, to move out of this pain, will kill us." In calm moments, Jerry knows that if they were to get married, they'd lose the kind of love they have; he also knows they'll lose it anyway. Love is not enough: it must become relaxed and right in the world's eyes or it will be lost.

Ruth discovers the affair before Richard does. In fact, she and Richard had had their own brief affair a few months earlier—an adventure that lacked the passion that breaks up families, that went unnoticed, that left Ruth feeling wiser and a better wife. Her discovery of Jerry and Sally's involvement strips it at once of its adolescent, idyllic character—not because of Ruth, who remains stoically sensible, but because of Jerry, who is a coward and smug in his grief and cannot decide what to do. He can't

Dust jacket for Updike's novel which offered the reader three alternative endings

bring himself to leave his family; he can't live without Sally; he wants Ruth to advise him, to tell him to go. "I'm not happy," Ruth tells him, "and I don't want a divorce." The summer dissolves in quarrels, discussions, confrontations, decisions made and then abandoned.

Updike shows us with appalling clarity the exact course of the disintegration of these two families. He manages to convey—for me, at least—a kind of spiritual fear, and he does it without resorting to violence or melodrama—no children die, there are no great drunken rows, not even much shouting. These are educated, civilized people and although Sally is greedy and Jerry spoiled, the four of them mean to behave sensibly, mean to do the least amount of damage. They worry about the children, about money, about destroying marriages that everyone admits are basically sound—about knowing what's right and doing what's wrong anyway.

This understatement, this unwavering vision fixed on only four characters, is a part of what makes the story so effective. Updike's best fiction has always been his most narrowly focused; in this novel the plot is direct—complex without becoming complicated by symbols thrashing obtrusively just behind the canvas—and refreshingly free from the portentousness that has marred several of his most ambitious novels. "Marry Me" is the best written and least self-conscious of Updike's longer fiction; it contains his most sophisticated and sympathetic portraits of women. It is, quite simply, Updike's best novel yet. I can't believe that anyone married or divorced could read it without being moved.

INTERVIEW:

Helen Vendler, "John Updike on Poetry," *New York Times Book Review*, 10 April 1977, pp. 3, 28.

Updike discussed his poetry in this interview a month before publication of Tossing and Turning.

Q.: You imply in a story, as I recall, that your mother wanted you to be a poet. Did her wish influence your writing, or did her taste guide yours?

A.: There was little, come to think of it, mention of poetry in my house while I was growing up. My mother remembered not remembering a poem she was reciting at about the age of 12. She felt permanently disgraced. The first poem I recall reciting in school was that passage from Sir Walter Scott that begins, "Breathes there the man with soul so dead. . . ." I got through it, and maybe that made the difference. The first poets I recall enjoying reading for myself were Phyllis McGinley, Arthur Guiterman, Robert Service and, somewhat later, Ogden Nash and Morris Bishop. I wonder how many 16-year-olds now have heard of any of these fine and funny writers.

Q.: Were these poets the chief models for your exquisite light verse?

A.: In the early fifties, when I did verse for the Harvard Lampoon, we looked toward Punch and toward the consoling notion, demonstrated in Punch week after week, that sheer metric neatness was halfway enough for a good light poem. That all seems long ago. Light verse died when it no longer seemed even the littlest bit wonderful to make two words rhyme. At about the same time, dancers in movies stopped going up and down stairs in white tie and tails. We had switched our allegiance from agility to energy. Auden was the last poet, I think, to make the one seem the other.

Q.: In your giddy self-interview, "Bech Meets Me," your gifted interviewer asks: "Do you envision novels as pills, broadcasts, tapestries, explosions of self, cantilevered constructs, or what?" The equally inventive interviewee answers that "they are crystallizations of visceral hopefulness extruded as a slow paste which in the glitter of print regains something of the original absolute gaiety." Would you like to say what you think lyrics are?

A.: I think you could say the same of lyrics except that the paste is faster, or the tube at least is smaller. Since I have never been taken very seriously as a poet and since I write less and less of what there seems no demand for, I am a poor one to theorize. As I recall, the poem comes with a perception—a breakthrough into nature, which encircles our numbness day and night. And married to the irruption of nature must be something live that surfaces out of language; the language even when rhyme and meter and syntax and punctuation are brushed aside, brings a formal element without which nothing happens, nothing is *made*. One of the charms of concrete poetry was that this element, after generations of *vers libre*, was reemphasized, from an unexpected direction. A lot of poetry I read now just washes through me, nothing has crystallized to ignite crystallization in me.

Q.: In "Why Write?" you say that as a child you used to

draw on a single sheet of paper "an assortment of objects—flowers, animals, stars, toasters, chairs, comic-strip creatures, ghosts, noses—" and then connect them with lines "so that they all became the fruit of a single impossible tree," and you added that the pleasure this gave you returns whenever you work "several disparate incidents or impressions into the shape of a single story." Does this apply to your poetry too?

A.: I have tried more than once to give this "collecting" impulse some place in esthetic theory. Rhyming words are in a sense a "set"—in a form like the ballade, a big set. Some of my light verse strings some similar things—French inventors, semi-extinct animals, new developments in particle physics—in a kind of necklace of stanzas, and steps back pleased. A kindred human urge, I suppose, is toward the exhaustive. We like a feeling of mopping up, of complete fullness. A jingle through the alphabet does this for us, and less obviously a Greek tragedy does also. We are *dismissed* by the work of art. I am talking as if art still pandered to our hopes or inklings of order. I'm not sure it does, except in this mysterious sense of fullness. In the days when I wrote poems habitually, I would know I had one, the idea of it, when my scalp crawled. When the skin on my head felt tight. My hand would shake and I couldn't write fast enough.

Q.: Recent lyric poetry (Ginsberg, Berryman, Lowell) has incorporated a lot of the detail hitherto reserved for fiction—family tales, social scenery, public affairs. Do you like this sort of thing, or is it better done in prose?

A.: Done better perhaps in the best prose. Prose, that is, can make tableaux move, cinematically, whereas in poetry the same material becomes a set of slides. Yes, I like some of Lowell's scenes and character sketches very much. In his poetry, human nature becomes quite tropical, stifling. I also like the late Ed Sissman's framed

On 30 September 1977 Updike married Martha Ruggles Bernhard. They are shown during a 1979 trip to Rome.

moments of his own history, and the palpable "others" in Anne Sexton, or Merrill, or Dickey. There is a limit, after all, to what can be done with daffodils and sunsets. Nor is this material novel; Chaucer, Shakespeare and Milton are all dramatic poets, and Romanticism unleashed a new passion for the psychological. Wordsworth turned it inward and Browning outward, but between them surely they covered all the anecdotal and confessional possibilities open to us now. Except perhaps that of sexual detail.

Q.: You've decided, in your new collection of verse, to prescind from "taste" altogether, in some of the poems about sex. Have you any sense that this has been done successfully by others? Is it possible to avoid the ridiculous in such enterprises?

A.: Well, why avoid the ridiculous? The poem in this collection you must have in mind, is meant to be among other things funny, and indeed is based like many of my light verse poems, on something that came in the mail. I think "taste" is a social concept and not an artistic one. I'm willing to show good taste, if I can, in somebody else's living room, but our reading life is too short for a writer to be in any way polite. Since his words enter into another's brain in silence and intimacy, he should be as honest and explicit as we are with ourselves. I find some of Donne's poems, and Whitman's, quite unridiculously sexual. Odd, that no modern celebrant comes to mind. Lawrence's poems seem to be mostly about animals.

Q.: Do you have any regrets that you turned out to be essentially a novelist rather than a poet?

A.: No. And yet I feel more at sea writing a novel than a poem, and often re-read my poetry and almost never look at my old novels. Also, poetry, especially since we have purged it of all that is comfortingly mechanical, is a sporadic activity. Lightning can't strike every day. It is always at the back of my mind to be a poet. Lately I had occasion to get out the collected poems of my fellow Pennsylvanian Wallace Stevens. He didn't publish his first collection until he was almost my present age and didn't publish another for 12 years more. Yet the total production, in the end, weighs like a Bible, a beautiful book as published by Knopf, with big print on big white pages, all this verbal fun and glory and serene love—what a good use of a life, to leave behind one beautiful book!

Q.: Would you like to do more reviewing of poetry?

A.: I try to deal with the poetry when it comes up in connection with a poet's biography, but no, I wouldn't presume to review it head on, and book upon book. I don't know how you do it, all these poets operating at what they think of as the height of intensity, exquisiteness, mystery. For me it would be like candling golden eggs. Did you notice, the Brancusi head on the jacket of "Tossing and Turning" is shaped like an egg? And my first book, a book of poems, was called "The Carpentered Hen." That was my first book, this is my 20th, and none in between has seemed more worth—how shall I say? crowing about.

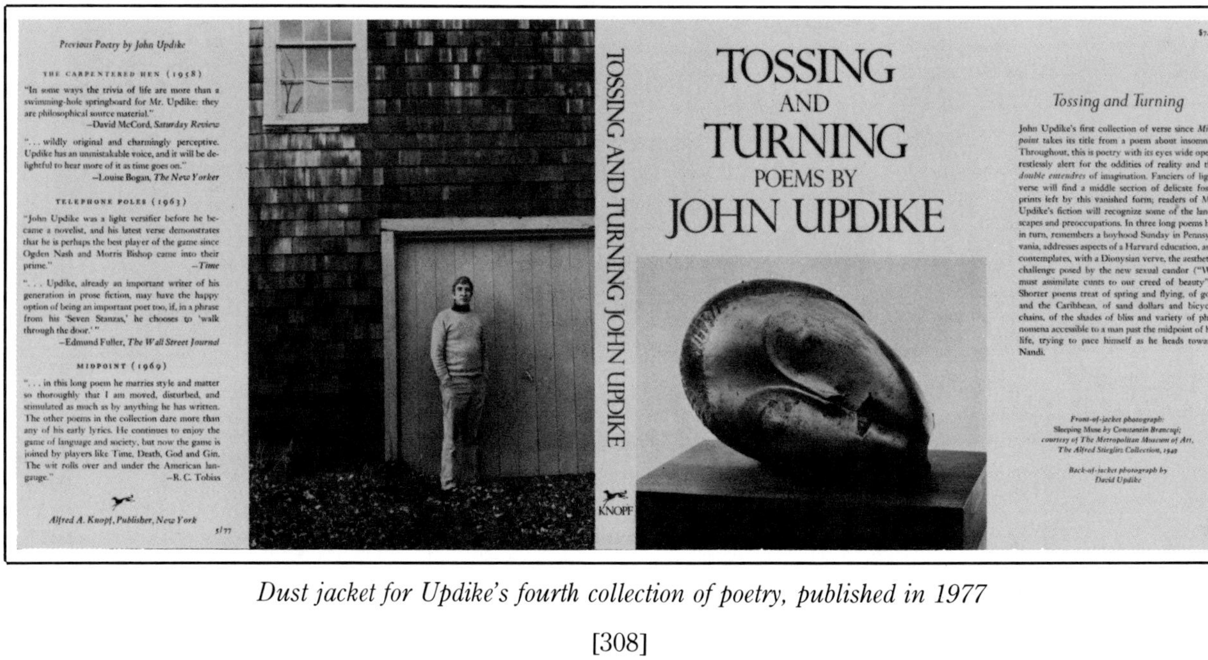

Dust jacket for Updike's fourth collection of poetry, published in 1977

BOOK REVIEW:

Joyce Carol Oates, "The Coup," *New Republic*, 180 (6 January 1979): 32-35.

Updike traveled to Africa, "the emptiest part of the world I could think of," as a Fulbright Lecturer in 1973. Five years later he used this setting in The Coup*—the fictitious memoirs of Ellelloû, recently deposed dictator of Kush. Novelist Joyce Carol Oates's admiring review is typical of the novel's critical reception.*

At a table in an open-air café in Nice there sits a small, prim, unprepossessing black man, the former president of the impoverished mythical state of Kush (formerly the mythical Noire), ex-Colonel Hakim "Happy" Felix Ellelloû. Having narrowly escaped death at the hands of Kush's new, pragmatic young president, Ellelloû (whose name means "freedom" in Berber) has been pensioned off, along with one of his four wives and a motley gang of children, so long as he remains "anonymous" and "silent." But Ellelloû sits at the café scribbling his memoirs, an account of his experience as dictator of Kush. What he has to say is mordant, outrageous, and bitterly self-mocking, a lengthy monologue that really *is* a coup of sorts, constituting Updike's most experimental novel to date. Kush is Ellelloû's fiction just as *The Coup* is Updike's fastidiously circumscribed fiction, a country set in an "Africa" of words. And what a virtuoso display Updike gives us! Not even *Pale Fire*, another inspired work by another displaced "ruler," is more darkly comic, more abrasively surreal, than Updike's Ellelloû's testimony.

Africa's most majestic feature, Ellelloû tells us, is the relative absence of Man. But where Man exists there is either pitiless suffering (northern Kush has suffered a five-year drought), or buffoonery (literally everyone Ellelloû encounters, from his four incompatible wives to his comic Russian "advisors" and the slangy, hearty, PR-minded Americans who call their exploitation of oil-rich Kush "philanthropy," are buffoons, locked into the most stereotyped of languages). Where Márquez's Faulknerian *The Autumn of the Patriarch* presented a bizarre dictator seen from without, filtered through the voices of a number of close observers, Updike's Nabokovian *The Coup* gives us the dictator in his own voice, as he sardonically and brokenly recounts the comic-opera events that led to his spiritual assassination. Nabokov's presence is felt throughout, but lightly and ingeniously, for Updike, unlike the self-indulgent Nabokov of *Ada*, that most relentlessly private of novels, has linked personal and authorial obsessions so gracefully with the outer chaos of Kush and the drama of the "superparanoids" America and Russia that Ellelloû's story works quite satisfactorily as a story, without self-referential props. Updike's homage to Nabokov is clear enough, and rather touching: it is Ellelloû's "opposite number," the Soviet Colonel Sirin, who saves his life at a characteristically absurd moment—and Sirin, as we know, was Nabokov's early pseudonym.

Ellelloû is, or was, a devout Muslim, and a jargon-ridden Marxist whose hatred for all things American—"America, that fountainhead of obscenity and glut"—is explained partly by the fact that he attended a small college in Franchise, Wisconsin where he received an unfair grade of B- in African history, from a trendy professor who was jealous of his relationship with a white girl named Candy, and partly by the fact that he married this girl and brought her back to his kingdom, where their marriage quickly deteriorated. (Candy, called "Pinktoes" by the blacks she compulsively pursues, is coarse-mouthed, nagging, stereotyped as any cartoon suburban wife; even her most ostensibly idealistic actions—like marrying a ragamuffin Negro who seemed so lonely at college—are motivated by clichéd notions of "liberalism." And of course she marries Ellelloû to enrage her bigoted father.)

Updike acknowledges numerous sources for his African information—books by contemporary historians and scholars, *National Geographic*, *Beau Geste*, children's books, *The Koran*—but his Africa, like his Kush, is a surrealist creation; and so, in part, is his increasingly debased and contemptible America. Ellelloû, composing his hallucinatory memoirs, pursues himself quixotically through a bewildering variety of masks. He views himself as a child, as a college boy in an alien country, as an ambitious though idealistic young soldier, as "dictator" of an ungovernable, indeed incomprehensible country, and finally as the hapless husband of four wives, chronically impotent, the passive butt of cruel jokes. Ellelloû experiences himself in stylish Cartesian terms, as two separate selves: "the one who acts, and the 'I' who experiences. This latter is passive even in a whirlwind of the former's making, passive and guiltless and astonished." He has sent many people to their deaths, and in person decapitates the former king, an elderly, blind, decadent fellow who was "like a father to him," but the reader hasn't the sense, any more than Ellelloû does, that he *is* a murderer: his elaborate syntax convinces us otherwise.

Difficult as Kush's mountainous terrain is to navigate, by camel or Mercedes (an air-conditioned Mercedes

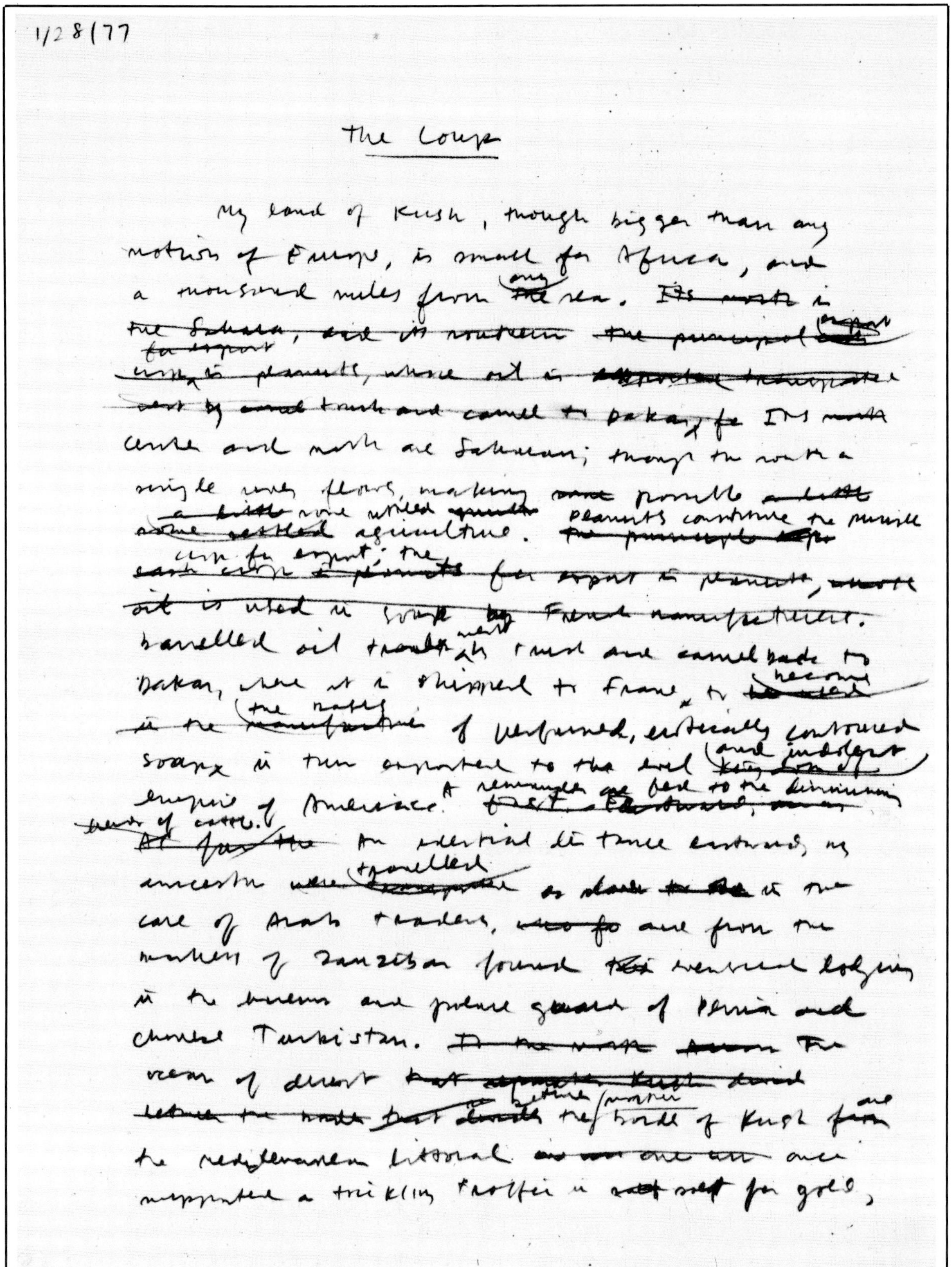

1/28/77

The Coup

My land of Kush, though bigger than any nation of Europe, is small for Africa, and a thousand miles from any sea. Its centre and north are Saharan; through the south a single river flows, making possible some settled agriculture. Peanuts constitute the single cash crop for export; the ... oil travels in trucks and camel back to Dakar, where it is shipped to France, to become the matter of perfumed, esthetically contoured soaps in turn exported to the ... and indulgent empire of America. ... In an identical ... our ancestors travelled as slaves in the care of Arab traders, and from the markets of Zanzibar found their eventual lodging in the harems and palace guards of Persia and Chinese Turkistan. The ocean of desert ... the trade of Kush from the Mediterranean littoral once supported a trickling traffic in salt for gold,

First page of the manuscript for The Coup *(Harvard University)*

follows the dictator as he travels disguised through his troubled country), the prose Updike has fashioned for him is even more difficult, and resembles nothing so much as an arabesque superimposed upon another arabesque. Motifs, phrases, "imagery," coarsely comic details from the "external world," Ellellоû's various and conflicting pasts, are rigorously interwoven into complex designs. The outer world, filling up slowly with American and Soviet junk, is a nightmare of vulgarity, and depressingly simple-minded; the inner world, the world of Ellellоû's ceaseless brooding, is correspondingly rich, elusive, teasing, ingenious. Updike has been accused in earlier, far more straightforward narratives like *Couples* and *The Centaur* (the novel that *The Coup* most resembles in its audacity and inspiration, if not in its tenderness) of writing self-indulgent, tortuous prose. That Updike has a painter's eye for detail, that he glories in what Joyce would call the suchness of a thing, and sees no reason, since it exists, *not* to describe it in detail, seems to me quite evident; but surely this is one of his strengths, one of the great virtues of his writing. By assigning the prose voice of *The Coup* to the defeated dictator Updike allows himself more freedom (or license) than he might ordinarily allow himself, and Ellellоû, plunging onward in his memoirs, as in his murky grotesque situation-comedy adventures, does the difficult work of characterizing himself. He remarks at one point that he knows his sentences are "maddeningly distended by seemingly imperative refinements and elaborations"; at another point—as he is about to execute the old king with a giant scimitar taken from its case in the People's Museum of Imperialist Atrocities—he thinks, "My mind in its exalted, distended condition had time to entertain many irrelevant images." Updike echoes or parodies earlier Updike, the earlier Updike (in the story "Wife-Wooing") paying homage to James Joyce of *The Sirens*: "Wide wadis remember ancient water, weird mesas have been shipped into shape by wicked, unwitnessed winds." When Ellellоû burns alive, on a pyramid of American gifts to the drought-stricken Kushians of the north, one Donald Gibbs, who assures him that his people really *want* this "manna" (*Kix Trix Chex Pops*, cream of celery coup, sorghum meant for cattle, and shipped in transparent sacks along with wood chips and dead mice) he thinks with characteristic scrupulousness:

> *I could smell on the victim, under the sweat of his long stale wait and the bland, oysterish odor of his earnestness, the house of his childhood, the musty halls, the cozy bathroom soaps, the glue of his adolescent hobbies, the aura of his alcoholic and sexually innocent parents, the ashtray scent of dissatisfaction. What dim wish to do right, hatched by the wavery blue light of the television set with its curious international shadows, had led him to the fatal edge of a safety that he had thought had no limits?*

This is Ellellоû's voice; and in sharp contrast to his indefatigable syntactical acrobatics the other voices of the novel are either flat and silly or a parody of US advertising rhythm and jargon. The wife who joins him in exile, the openly promiscuous Sittina, complains of lack of money "since you blew the dictatorship"; Candy greets his infrequent visits with "Holy Christ, look who it isn't," refuses to listen to his formal Islamic pronouncements which are, to her, "Kismet-crap," and says of his strategic execution of the old king: "Well, chief, how's top-level tricks? Chopping old Edumu's noggin off didn't seem to raise the humidity any." Updike does this all very skillfully, and one guesses that *The Coup* was immensely enjoyable to write, once the ankle-thongs of African "history" were disposed of. For instance, Ellellоû discovers that office supplies stolen from the capital city of Kush are being smuggled by camel caravan to Iran, and this embarrassment is explained cheerfully by the caravan's leader:

> *"The Shahansha has much wish to modernize. In his hurry he buys typewriters from West Germany and paper from Swedes and then discover only one type spool fit typewriter, only one type eraser not smudge paper. American know-how meanwhile achieve obsolescence such that only fitting spool stockpiled in Accra as aid-in-goods when cocoa market collapse. Formula of typewriter eraser held secret and cunning capitalists double, redouble price when Shah push up oil price to finance purchase of jet fighters, computer software, and moon rocks. French however operating through puppet corporations in Dahomey have secured formula as part of multi-billion-franc deferred-interest somatic-collateral package and erect eraser factory near gum arabic plantations. Much borax also in deal, smuggled by way of Quagadougou. Now Sadat has agreed to let goods across Nile if Shahanshah agrees to make anti-Israeli statement and buy ten thousand tickets to* son-et-lumière *show at Sphinx."*

Everything, every human act or gesture or vision, is explained away glibly in language taken from popular magazines or television shows: American women are "unbridled Amazons who drive our men outward from the home to perform those feats of engineering and merchandising that dumfound the world"; Ellellоû's mistress,

Dust jacket for Updike's ninth novel, which Joyce Carol Oates has called a coup of style

formerly a native wench whose grandmother was a leopard, soon acquires Western clothes, shoes, wristwatches, even contact lenses (which make her brown eyes blue), and assures Ellelloû that her response to his love-making is genuine: "Only my President can lead me so utterly to forget myself, I am led to the brink of another world, and grow terrified lest I fall in and be annihilated. It's neat."

Beneath, behind, informing every scene of this inspired novel, which a superficial reading might judge as almost *too* inspired (a *tour de force* against readers' expectations, like Updike's very first novel *The Poorhouse Fair*, which was anything but a "young man's novel"), is a passionate and despairing cynicism which I take to be, for all its wit, Updike's considered view of where we are and where we are going. No moral uplift here; no gestures, like Bellow's, toward the essential "health" of the commonplace. If American know-how is only another word for exploitation, if American statesmen (like the unctuous Klipspringer) and advisers are asinine jargon-filled fools, the Soviets are, if possible, even more ridiculous. "Islamic socialism" is "pure" of corrupting capitalistic investments, but it has the disadvantage of not working—so long as Ellelloû's anti-American policy holds, his people are doomed to die of thirst and starvation. Ellelloû is devoutly religious, and everyone who surrounds him is atheistic and materialistic, but what does faith in Allah matter when the sky is pitilessly blank, and all Ellelloû can think of in defense of his faith is the feeble observation, "The drought is a form of the Manifest Radiance, and our unhappiness within it is blasphemy. The book accuses: *Your hearts are taken up with worldly gain from the cradle to the grave*."

America, Updike hypothesizes, reached in the 1960s and early 1970s (and *The Coup* takes place during the Watergate hearings) "that dangerous condition when a religion, to contradict its own sensation that it is dying, lashes out against others. Thus the Victorians flung their Christianity against the heathen of the world after Voltaire and Darwin had made its tenets ridiculous; thus the impoverished sultan of Morocco in 1591 hurled troops across the Sahara. . . . a conquest that profited him nothing and destroyed the Songhai empire forever." And: "It may be . . . that in the attenuation, dessication, and death of religions the world over, a new religion is being formed in the indistinct hearts of men, a religion without a God, without prohibitions and compensatory assurances, a religion whose antipodes are motion and stasis, whose one rite is the exercise of energy, and in which exhausted forms like the quest, the vow, the expiation, and the attainment through suffering of wisdom are, emptied of content, put in the service of a pervasive expenditure whose ultimate purpose is entropy. . . . Millions now enact the trials of this religion, without giving it a name, or attributing to themselves any virtue."

("The Fifties were when all the fun was," Candy says bitterly, "though nobody knew it at the time.")

Judging from the stories in "another mode" in

Museums and Women, and the highly self-conscious voice of *A Month of Sundays*, it might have seemed that Updike's genius was for fiction and not metafiction. (For why parody art if you can create it, why devise clever paste pearls if you own genuine pearls?) But *The Coup*, which makes only the most perfunctory gestures toward old-fashioned realism, let alone naturalism, is an immensely inspired and energetic work, striking, on page after page, the comic brilliancy that leaps from Joyce's *Ulysses*, in such chapters as *The Cyclops*, for instance, in which ferocious exaggeration becomes an art that is self-consuming; in its possibly more immediate relationship to Nabokov and Márquez, the novel sets down the improbable beside the probable, creating a "fictional" nation that is altogether convincing, and yet populating it with fools and knaves and tough-talking nagging wives who have the depth, if not the distinctiveness, of playing cards. *The Coup*'s coup is style. If entropy is capitalism's goal, just as it is "socialism's" goal, if life in our time has become so sterile that even Ellellou's traitorous minister Ezana can say, casually, "Life is like an overlong drama through which we sit being nagged by vague memories of having read the reviews," there is all the more need for style, for art, for the unique, quirky, troubling visions that our finest artists force upon us.

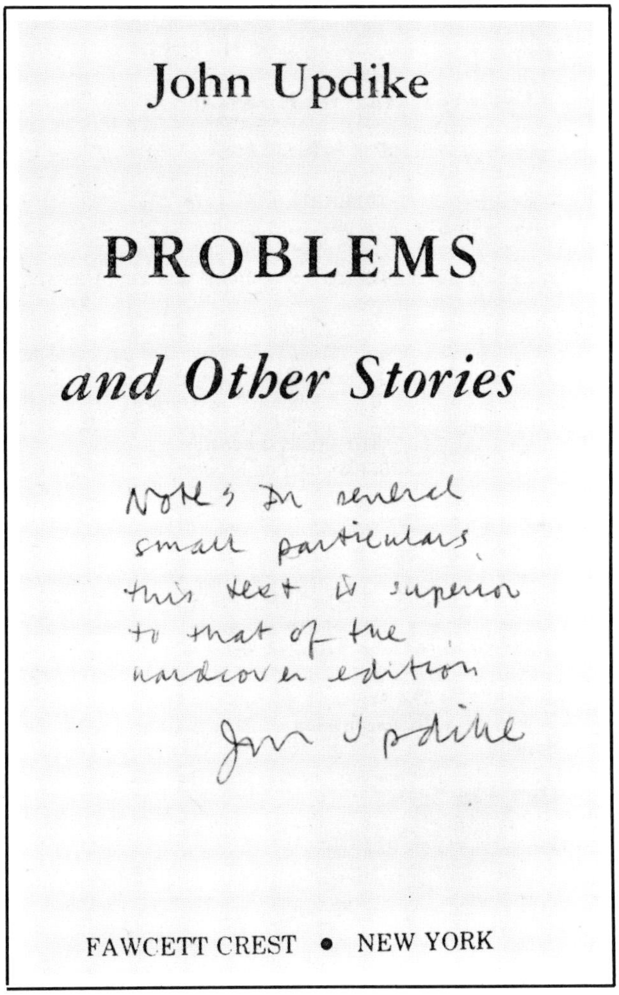
John Updike

PROBLEMS

and Other Stories

Note: In several small particulars this text is superior to that of the hardcover edition

John Updike

FAWCETT CREST • NEW YORK

Updike's textual note in the paperback edition of Problems and Other Stories *(Harvard University)*

Updike has grown amazingly cynical with the passage of time: how odd that the author of *Pigeon Feathers* should be evolving, before our eyes, into the Mark Twain of *The Mysterious Stranger*, or the Swift of Gulliver's final voyage, or the Samuel Beckett who says laconically that failure, not success, interests him! One would have not guessed the direction his novels might take, considering even the bitterly ironic ending of *Rabbit, Run* (which, if set beside *Rabbit Redux* of a decade later, is nevertheless characterized by an odd "Fifties" optimism despite the current of its remorseless plot—the sense of a world of promise, a world awaiting exploration, even exploitation, to which the dissatisfied Candy alludes in her banal fashion, calling it "fun"), and the understated, unheroic conclusion of *Couples*, in which the hero and heroine, about whose emotions we know so very much, in such exhaustive detail, become, merely, in the end, just "another couple" in suburban America. Admirers of Updike's sardonic Bech stories, however, have sensed quite clearly the drift of Updike's mind, which finds its sharpest, least muffled, and least sentimental expression through the *persona* of Henry Bech, Updike's daimonic opposite (bachelor, Jew, perpetually blocked novelist who, at the conclusion of a recent story, finds that he cannot even sign his own name); Bech's view of the universe and of man's striving within it is as droll as Céline's, and he would, adroitly, with an allegorical instinct as habitual as Updike's, sketch in quick analogues between the drying-up of creative powers and the drying-up of fertile lands.

The world in which "Kush" is located is, after all, a "global village" in which individuals no longer exist, and tribes are relocated in a matter of days, to make way for multi-level parking garages, shopping malls, and McDonald's hamburger restaurants. Ellellou's prophetic zeal is commendable, but who among his people cares?—if "You will be Xed out by Exxon, ungulfed by Gulf, crushed by the US, disenfranchised by France, not only you but your entire loving nation of succulent wives, loyal brothers, righteous fathers, and aged but still amusing mothers. All inked out, absolutely. . . . In the vocabulary of profit there is no word for 'pity.' "

Is such cynicism soluble in art? Indeed yes.

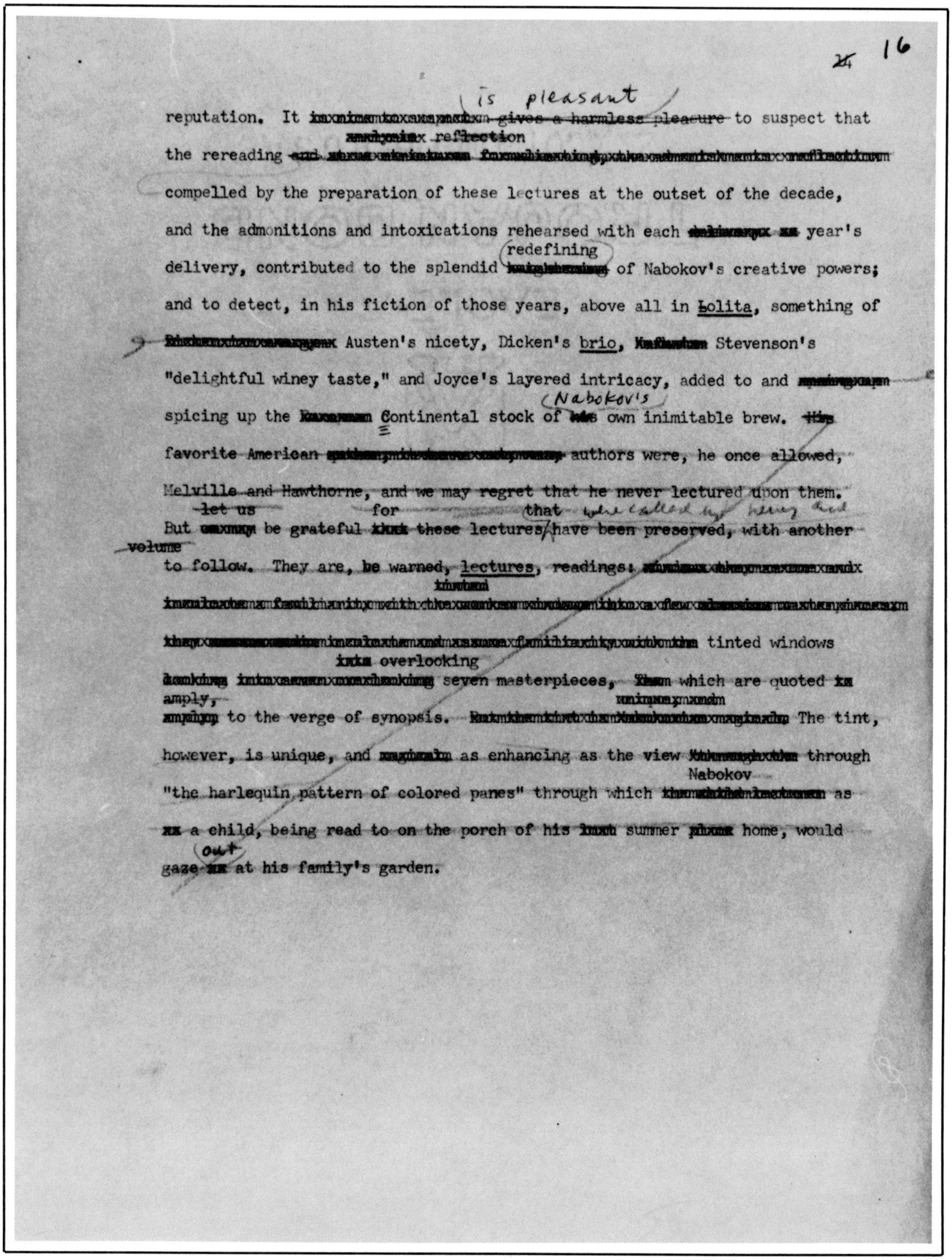
~~25~~ 16

reputation. It is pleasant to suspect that the rereading and reflection compelled by the preparation of these lectures at the outset of the decade, and the admonitions and intoxications rehearsed with each year's delivery, contributed to the splendid redefining of Nabokov's creative powers; and to detect, in his fiction of those years, above all in Lolita, something of Austen's nicety, Dicken's brio, Stevenson's "delightful winey taste," and Joyce's layered intricacy, added to and spicing up the Continental stock of Nabokov's own inimitable brew. ~~His favorite American authors were, he once allowed, Melville and Hawthorne, and we may regret that he never lectured upon them.~~ But let us be grateful for these lectures that have been preserved, with another volume to follow. They are, be warned, lectures, readings: tinted windows overlooking seven masterpieces, which are quoted amply, to the verge of synopsis. The tint, however, is unique, and as enhancing as the view through "the harlequin pattern of colored panes" through which Nabokov as a child, being read to on the porch of his summer home, would gaze out at his family's garden.

Final page of Updike's revised typescript for his introduction to Vladimir Nabokov's Lectures on Literature *(BC Research)*

Book Review:
Eliot Fremont-Smith, "Rabbit Ruts," *Village Voice*, 30 September-6 October 1981, pp. 35, 55.

Rabbit Is Rich, *the third novel featuring Harry "Rabbit" Angstrom, achieved the three top literary prizes for 1981: the Pulitzer Prize, the American Book Award, and the National Book Critics Circle Award.*

His hands lift of their own and he feels the wind on his ears even before, his heels hitting heavily on the pavement at first but with an effortless gathering out of a kind of sweet panic growing lighter and quicker and quieter, he runs. Ah: runs. Runs.

—Rabbit, Run (1960)

There is in Rabbit an engine murmuring. Undo, undo *. . . have it all unhappen.*

—Rabbit Redux (1971)

More timid than deer, customers.

—Rabbit Is Rich (1981)

These epigraphs tell the story; the title up top is a plug-in pun meant to convey affectionate resentment: my privilege. *Rabbit, Run*, that heart-stopping epiphany of 21 years ago, should never have had a sequel, and now it's got two. John Updike's privilege, I suppose; one must bend with the facts, if not forgive. *Rabbit Redux* still seems a rude trespass on what had become, after all, the property of my imagination; yet without it there could be no **RABBIT IS RICH**, no renewal of affection, no return of grace. The alter ego stuff aside, there's a juicy bravado to Updike's long loyalty to Harry "Rabbit" Angstrom that I can't help liking. The desperate, fleeing angel of *Rabbit, Run* is now, surprisingly, "family," and we're all growing older together. There's caring in this, and even some dignity—Rabbit still ruts as a rabbit will (his literally saving grace), but now he's most often called Harry, and jogs rather than runs. There's abrasiveness, too: Updike's mixed feelings, sense of challenge, volatile remnants of envy and anger, his flippancy. But in the main *Rabbit Is Rich* is an act of accommodation; it warms the rut we discover ourselves in together, and lubricates astonishment.

It's hard to imagine the effect on readers new to Rabbit. Of course, *Rabbit Is Rich* is technically discrete; in little bursts of efficiency it recapitulates what's gone before—e.g., Rabbit's desertion of his wife Janice and the pregnant Ruth, and the horrifying bathtub drowning of Rabbit and Janice's infant daughter in *Rabbit, Run*; Rabbit's guilt in his son Nelson's eyes for the death of the hippie Jill in the awful fire in *Rabbit Redux* ("undo, undo," pleads Rabbit's brain). And so on, the "essential" plot details. But the essence of Rabbit as he was cannot be synopsized: the degree of desperation (and release) at the end of *Rabbit, Run*, the *angst* in Angstrom, his love of basketball and yearning to remain a high school star ("the kids keep coming, they keep crowding you up," he thinks on the very first page of *Rabbit, Run*), his not knowing where to put his hand when Ruth fellates him (it flutters, then he rests it on his shoulder), the crucially intimate physics of his reconciliation with Janice at the end of *Rabbit Redux*—all this is, though acknowledged and told about or hinted at, missing.

"Relax," Janice says at the end of *Rabbit Redux*, "Not everything is your fault." And: "He lets her breasts go, lets them float away, radiant debris. The space they are in, the motel room long and secret as a burrow, becomes all interior space. He slides down an inch on the cool sheet and fits his microcosmic self limp into the curved crevice between the polleny offered nestly orbs of her ass; he would stiffen but his hand having let her breasts go comes upon the familiar dip of her waist, ribs to hip bone, where no bones are, soft as flight, fat's inward curve, slack, his babies from her belly. He. She. Sleeps. O.K.?"

Yes, O.K. But not for nothing has Updike's Rabbit saga been compared with Joyce's *Ulysses*, and the "O.K.?" is at once an apology to us, and maybe to Rabbit, for *Redux*, and a fist in the face (as most of *Redux* is). It's hard, too, to separate the books from other facts they generate, link onto, and diddle with—both "objective" facts and those of imagined history. Some important part of the Rabbit saga concerns how we negotiate facts born of manipulation, human and divine (and by writer's whim).

In the *Times Book Review* in 1971 Updike had himself interviewed on Rabbit by a very different and rival created character, Henry Bech of the funny *Bech: A Book*; and the trick is done again in the current *TBR* anent *Rabbit Is Rich*. "Let literature concern itself, as the Gospels do, with the inner lives of hidden men," Updike has Rabbit's creator spout to Bech. "The collective consciousness that once found itself in the noble must now rest content with the typical." Cute touch, the Gospels bit, and the device becomes part of our common surround. But it's not the way I think of Rabbit.

Indeed, the interview seems addressed to a more ancient history, the initial critical resistance to the moral and aesthetic character of Rabbit back in 1961, and Updike isn't espousing typicality so much as giving the finger again to an almost forgotten stuffiness. (Not dead, however. Peter Prescott in a *Newsweek* review has to quip that *Rabbit Is Rich* "is not . . . the kind of book you would want your parents to read." And James Wolcott in *Esquire* sullenly misreads the new novel as unabated rue, of which—making much of the opening line, "Running out of gas," and ignoring the denial, "So who says he's running out of gas?" 52 pages later—the critic sternly disapproves. You look too intently for bootstraps and none will float into view—even though down there, inside the book, in his and our middle life Rabbit is tugging away.)

Rabbit, Run is set in Brewer, Pa., in 1959; *Redux* in

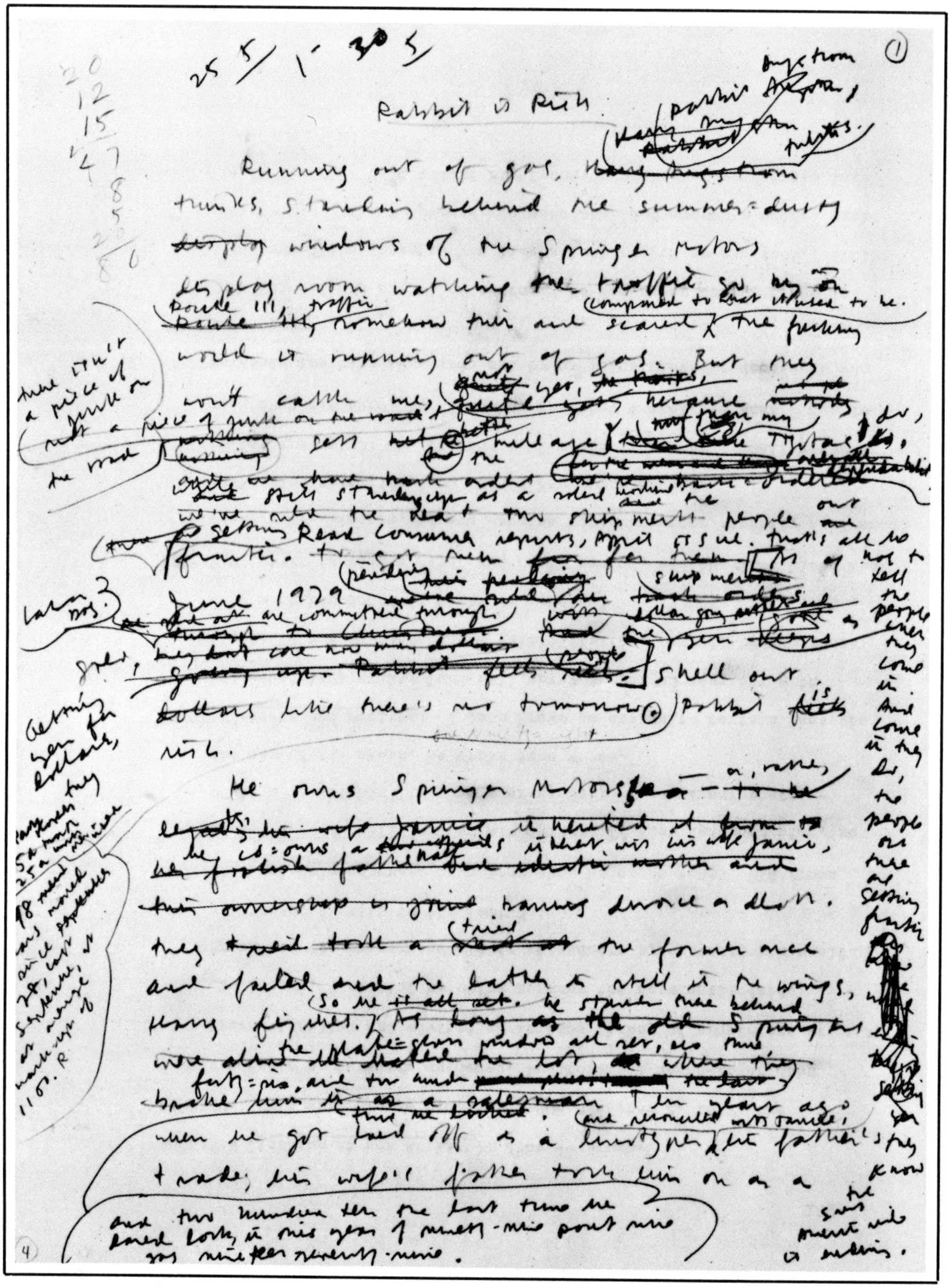

The first page of the working manuscript and revised typescript for Rabbit is Rich *(Harvard University)*

the same town in 1969; *Rich* ditto in 1979. The design-by-decade is slightly oppressive, yet as little time capsules of Americana, they do continuity duty; it's the background bustle and static and mood that's "typical," not Rabbit. In *Run*, it was the Eisenhower age (also the Existential age), blue collars into TV, upward mobility a new watchword but still a struggle (Rabbit seemed destined to follow his father in the printing trade). In *Redux*, we were exploring outer space and seething in local dissatisfaction; Rabbit is at once drawn to and an adversary of the counter-culture; his extended family blows up as his blood family begins to coalesce (an impossibility at the end of *Run*, Updike's fiat in *Redux*).

In *Rich*, Skylab is falling, Americans are held hos-

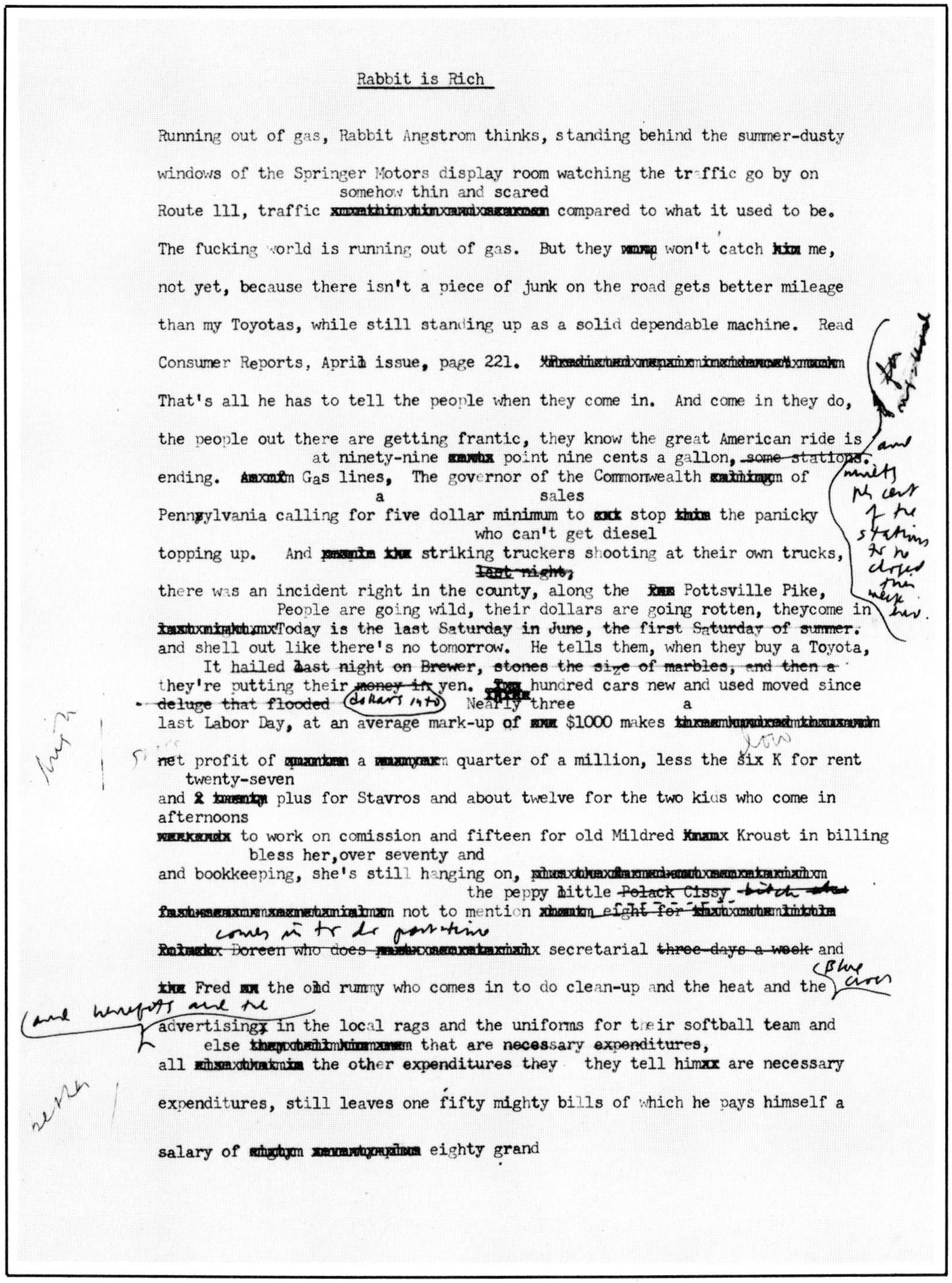

Rabbit is Rich

Running out of gas, Rabbit Angstrom thinks, standing behind the summer-dusty windows of the Springer Motors display room watching the traffic go by on Route 111, traffic somehow thin and scared compared to what it used to be. The fucking world is running out of gas. But they won't catch me, not yet, because there isn't a piece of junk on the road gets better mileage than my Toyotas, while still standing up as a solid dependable machine. Read Consumer Reports, April issue, page 221. That's all he has to tell the people when they come in. And come in they do, the people out there are getting frantic, they know the great American ride is ending. Gas lines, at ninety-nine point nine cents a gallon, ~~some stations~~. The governor of the Commonwealth of Pennsylvania calling for a five dollar minimum sales to stop the panicky topping up. And striking truckers who can't get diesel shooting at their own trucks, there was an incident right in the county, along the Pottsville Pike, ~~last night~~. People are going wild, their dollars are going rotten, they come in Today is the last Saturday in June, the first Saturday of summer. and shell out like there's no tomorrow. He tells them, when they buy a Toyota, they're putting their ~~money in~~ (dollars into) yen. It hailed last night on Brewer, stones the size of marbles, and then a deluge that flooded Nearly three hundred cars new and used moved since last Labor Day, at an average mark-up of $1000 makes a net profit of a quarter of a million, less the six K for rent and twenty-seven plus for Stavros and about twelve for the two kids who come in afternoons to work on comission and fifteen for old Mildred Kroust in billing and bookkeeping, bless her, over seventy and she's still hanging on, not to mention the peppy little ~~Polack Cissy~~ ~~bitch~~ Doreen who does secretarial ~~three days a week~~ and (comes in to do part-time) Fred the old rummy who comes in to do clean-up and the heat and the (Blue Cross) (and benefits and the) advertising in the local rags and the uniforms for their softball team and all the other expenditures they tell him are necessary else that are necessary expenditures, expenditures, still leaves one fifty mighty bills of which he pays himself a salary of eighty grand tage in Iran, Ipana toothpaste has disappeared, and life is pretty good. (Time-capsules aren't just nostalgia, they contain surprise.) Rabbit, now Harry, isn't really rich, but he's pulling about $42,000 as nominal boss of Brewer's Toyota dealership, owned by his wife Janice and her whiney, hard-beaked mother. He plays golf at the local country club, mouths complaints about Arab oil (though nothing could be better than OPEC for the Toyota biz), and reads *Consumer Reports*. He invests in Krugerrands and silver (he makes a profit on both), a Caribbean vacation (and terrific wife-swap), and a new house (to which he and Janice move at the end of the book). And he battles once more with his son Nelson, who is as accident-prone as Rabbit ever was—actually, Rabbit doesn't suffer accidents so much as bring them with him; accidents seem to slide off him onto others very close by—but utterly lacks Rabbit's special grace.

Ah, yes, the grace. It's convenient, as Thomas R. Edwards suggests in *The Atlantic*, to compartmentalize the books. Thus *Run* is religious in atmosphere, and *Redux* political (Rabbit too much distorted into Updike's mouthpiece), and *Rich* economic. But convenience elucidates only the nearest distance. Updike's great subject, in all his books but especially in the *Rabbits*, is grace—what it is, where and how it abides, how it manifests itself. It's Rabbit's grace—God's grace on him, which he perceives fleetingly but piercingly when the chips are down—that sustains Rabbit and our (and Updike's) interest in him. It's his grace that makes him acceptable now as "family"—why we are touched by him (and scared) and also want to touch, as if some of *it* might rub off. Disaster may follow Rabbit's every step and skittish feint; when it doesn't, we are surprised and laugh in relief (and *Rabbit Is Rich* has a lot of laughs). Yet he is a magnet. When people go away from him, it's with regret, and like Janice they return when they can. At the end of *Rich*, Rabbit comes face to face with Ruth—his hunt for Ruth and their illegitimate daughter is a running subplot—and she repells him with every vehemence at her command. The intensity of her rejection isn't because Rabbit's interest is merely narcissistic and sentimental (though it is that, with an overlay of "responsibility"), but because the magnetism of grace is so powerful. (If Rabbit is Bloom, he's also Prince Mishkin; also Joe Bffsstk.)

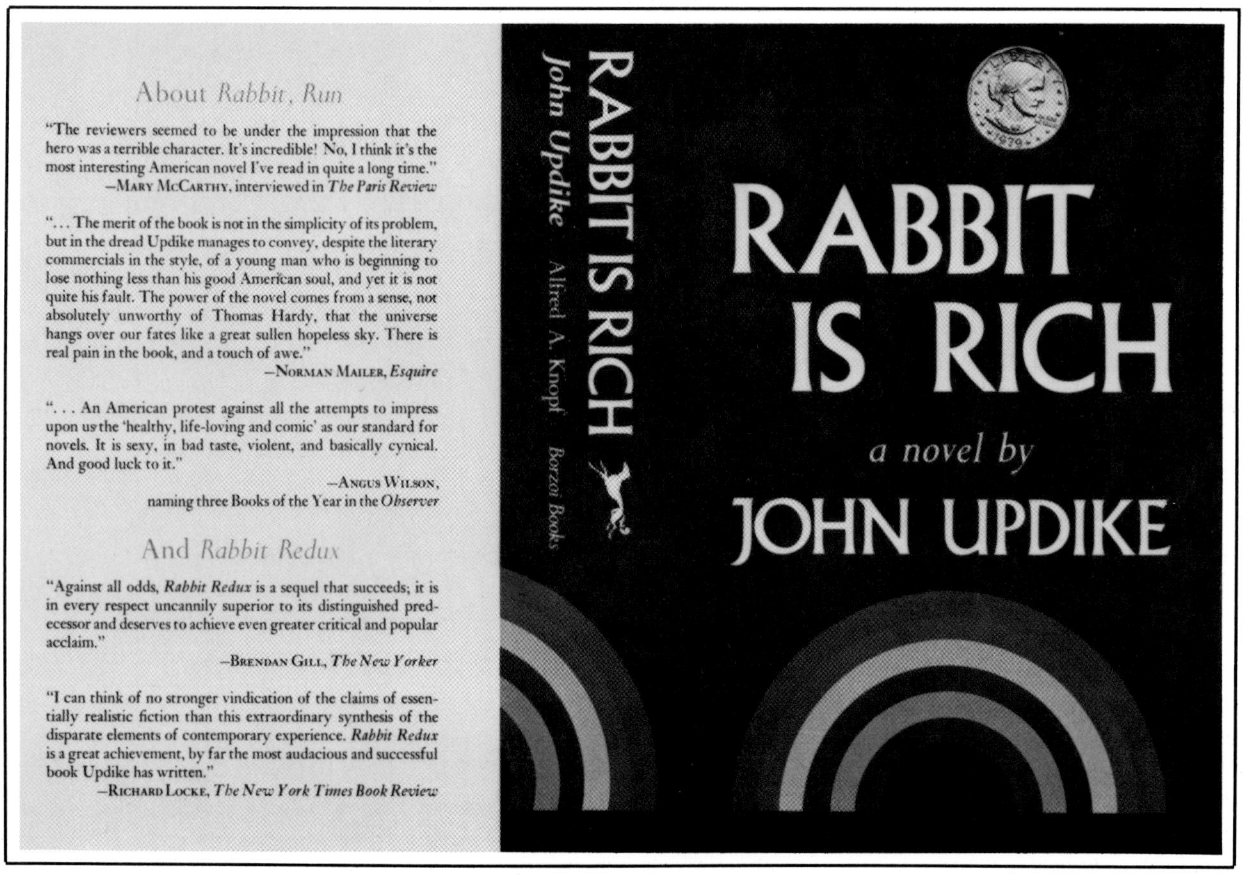

Dust jacket designed by Updike for the third novel of his projected tetralogy

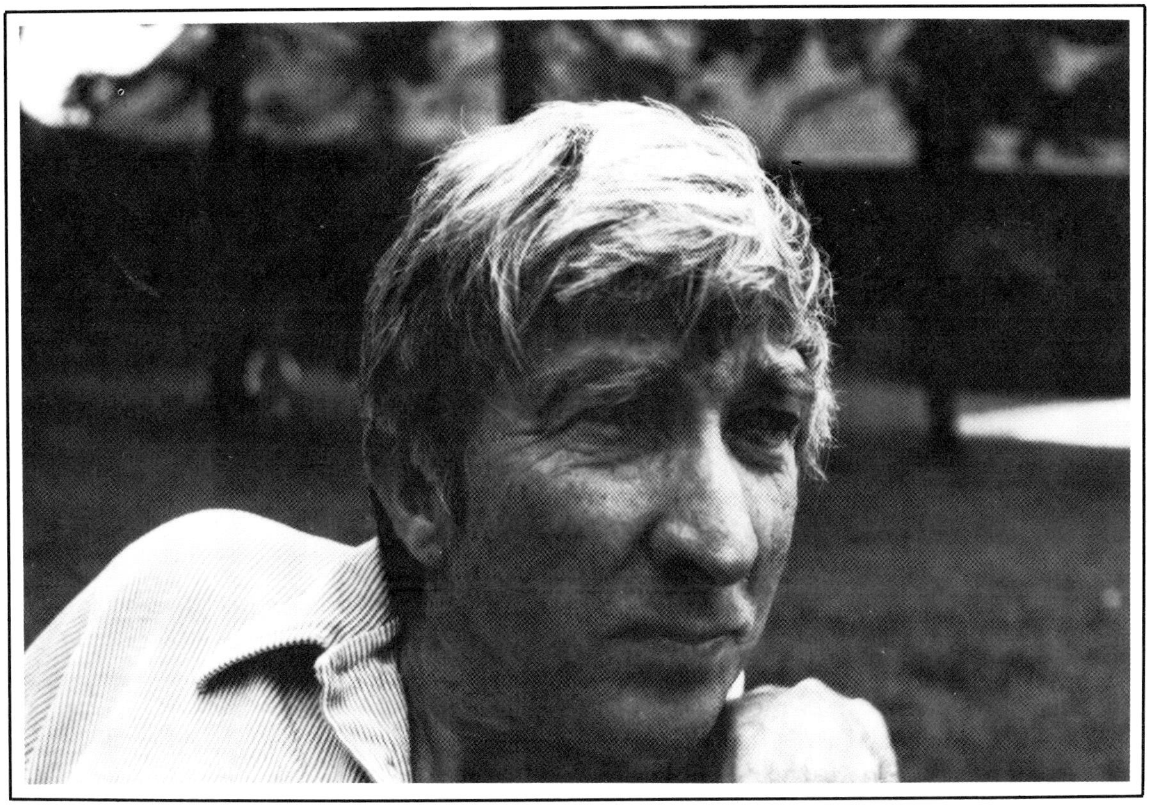

John Updike, summer 1981 (photo by Martha Updike)

The manifestation of grace in Rabbit comes in several ways—most weakly, perhaps, in his sense of "mission," most blatantly in his pervasive sexuality. The mission is vague (though explored in theological terms in *Rabbit, Run*), but has to do with his role in the ongoingness of life and particular lives, and with his amazement and awe that he is what and who he is, not something else or some other consciousness; and with the constant and sometimes appalling haul-and-tug between these phenomena.

This sense of mission connects to, is intimate with and inseparable from, his sexuality. Rabbit ruts all the time, if not in bed, then in his mind. But this isn't mere horniness, much less mere ability: the compulsion has basically to do with resolving the conflict of separateness, giving and receiving solace, experiencing grace. It contains many sentimentalities, but, arrestingly, no power trip, no cruelty. In fact, Rabbit's *lack* of a sense of cruelty may be one way of defining his grace; his vulnerability is him, and whatever surface assurance he has springs from that. Rabbit erect is the stunning delicacy of life, and of a piece with Rabbit sleeping in a curve of motherly flesh and dreams.

Looking back, it must have been the sexuality that so upset the respectable critics of *Rabbit, Run* in 1960. Their consternation had to do with what seemed a great divide between John Updike's exquisite command of prose—his lyrical beauty, emotional and metaphorical acuity, the wit and intelligence and *smoothness*—and the apparent no-good vulgar nothing he expended it on. Rabbit was simply unworthy of such talented refinement. He couldn't be tragic because his fall was, in classical terms, from such a low place. He couldn't be "existential" because his self-knowledge was too sensually determined. (Existentialism, in high culture as administered by middlebrows, was all the rage; it had also been turned on its head to give off vibes of optimism.) In short, Rabbit was a pathetic fallacy, and Updike—this was his second novel, and he was much regarded for his *New Yorker* stories—seemed to be slumming, and thereby dragging us down.

The respectables were wrong, of course; they simply couldn't recognize one of the great questing novels of our time. Yet the hangover—the idea that Rabbit is ignoble—persists. It's one of the great tensions in all the Rabbit books, especially *Run* and most clearly in *Rich*, that Rabbit is decent. His "innocence" irritates and quite often frightens, but within his sexuality a kind of goodness keens.

Rabbit Is Rich is in a sense Harry Angstrom's payoff. He has grown, is more melded now; the golf-club grass beneath his feet may sing of death (and his spirit, his inner voice, records the lament), but he is more morally alive than ever. It's a strange alertness (something else that bothered the hierarchal arbiters of moral taste), seemingly flat in its inability to distinguish the mundane from what is supposed to matter more. Thus in *Rich*, Rabbit fights to preserve a colleague's (Janice's old lover's) job at the Toyota dealership, and scrabbles around in a friend's bedside table for dirty Polaroids (and finds them, and is generously intrigued), and makes love with Janice in an orgy of gold coins, with the same intensity—and what is one to say? I think: that's life; in depression, inspiration; in guilt, surcease; in sensuous contentment, bravery. Rabbit's colleague's job rests on happenstance, but this doesn't alloy the commitment Rabbit—I should say Harry—makes, dredges up, deserves glory for.

There are flaws in *Rabbit Is Rich*. The early critics of Updike weren't entirely insensitive, and the jewellike prose at times promises a perfection that can be. The book is too long, and the time-capsule stuff, though not in the way, is less a tick than a tic. Rabbit's son Nelson is too much a nerd; he seems more programmed by Updike's loyalty to Rabbit than by Rabbit's genes or will.

But I almost love this book. Harry Rabbit Angstrom should never have returned. In *Rabbit, Run* he sighed for me; now he almost breathes for me. I am surprised, and a part of me will not forgive, but there is no choice but to wish Harry well. That there is no choice is Updike's triumph, and in 10 years' time he will no doubt pull off another, and tell us how Rabbit is to die. The prospect is grubby, scary, and appealing.

> To remain interested—*of American novelists, only Henry James continued in old age to advance his art; most, indeed, wrote their best novels first, or virtually first. Energy ebbs as we live; success breeds disillusion as surely as failure; the power of hope to generate action and vision lessens. Almost alone the writer can reap profit from this loss. An opportunity to sing louder from within the slackening ego is his. For his song has never been all his own: he has been its excuse as much as its source. . . . To become less and transmit more, to replenish energy with wisdom—some such hope, at this more than mid-point of my life, is the reason why I write.*

From Updike's "Why Write?," in his Picked-Up Pieces

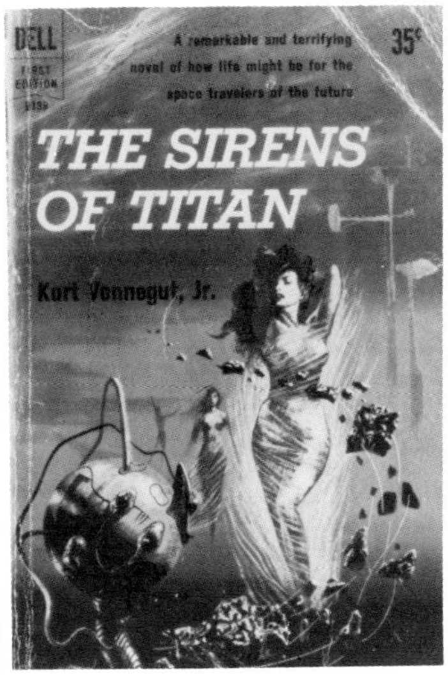

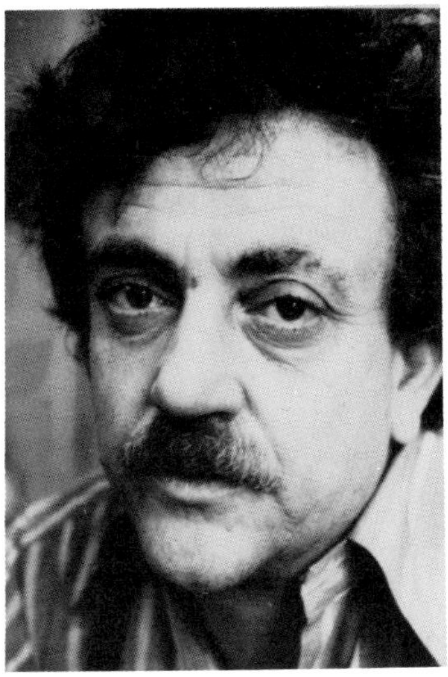

KURT VONNEGUT

(11 November 1922-)

See the Kurt Vonnegut entries in the Dictionary of Literary Biography, *volume 2,* American Novelists Since World War II; *volume 8,* Twentieth-Century American Science-Fiction Writers; *and* Yearbook: 1980.

MAJOR BOOKS:

Player Piano (New York: Scribners, 1952; London: Macmillan, 1953);

The Sirens of Titan (New York: Dell, 1959; London: Gollancz, 1962);

Canary in a Cat House (Greenwich, Conn.: Fawcett Gold Medal, 1961);

Mother Night (Greenwich, Conn.: Fawcett Gold Medal, 1962; London: Cape, 1968);

Cat's Cradle (New York, Chicago & San Francisco: Holt, Rinehart & Winston, 1963; London: Gollancz, 1963);

God Bless You, Mr. Rosewater, or Pearls Before Swine (New York, Chicago & San Francisco: Holt, Rinehart & Winston, 1965; London: Cape, 1965);

Welcome to the Monkey House (New York: Seymour Lawrence/Delacorte, 1968; London: Cape, 1969);

Slaughterhouse-Five, or The Children's Crusade (New York: Seymour Lawrence/Delacorte, 1969; London: Cape, 1970);

Happy Birthday, Wanda June (New York: Seymour Lawrence/Delacorte, 1971; London: Cape, 1973);

Between Time and Timbuktu (New York: Seymour Lawrence/Delacorte, 1972; St. Albans, U.K.: Panther, 1975);

Breakfast of Champions (New York: Seymour Lawrence/Delacorte, 1973; London: Cape, 1973);

Wampeters, Foma & Granfalloons (Opinions) (New York: Seymour Lawrence/Delacorte, 1974; London: Cape, 1975);

Slapstick, or Lonesome No More (New York: Seymour Lawrence/Delacorte, 1976; London: Cape, 1977);

Jailbird (New York: Seymour Lawrence/Delacorte, 1979; London: Cape, 1979);

Sun Moon Star, by Vonnegut and Ivan Chermayeff (New York: Harper & Row, 1980);

Palm Sunday (New York: Seymour Lawrence/Delacorte, 1981);

Deadeye Dick (New York: Seymour Lawrence/Delacorte, 1982).

BIBLIOGRAPHIES:

Betty L. Hudgens, *Kurt Vonnegut, Jr.: A Checklist* (Detroit: Bruccoli Clark/Gale Research, 1972);

Jerome Klinkowitz, "The Vonnegut Bibliography," in *Vonnegut in America*, ed. Klinkowitz and Donald L. Lawler (New York: Delacorte, 1977): pp. 217-252.

Kurt Vonnegut, Jr., was born in Indianapolis, 11 November 1922, the third child of Edith Lieber and Kurt Vonnegut. He attended P.S. 43 and then Northridge High School, where he wrote for the daily school paper, The Echo.

Kurt with his older brother and sister, Bernard and Alice, in 1923

Vonnegut in 1926

Vonnegut at age eighteen

After graduating from high school Vonnegut studied biology and chemistry at Cornell. In his junior year he joined the army and was trained as a mechanical engineer at the Carnegie Institute of Technology and then at the University of Tennessee. His mother committed suicide while he was in the army.

COLUMNS:

Vonnegut, "Well All Right," *Cornell Daily Sun*, 11 November 1941, p. 4; 4 March 1942, p. 4.

Vonnegut was an editor of the Cornell Daily Sun *during 1941-1942 and contributed to three of its columns—"Innocents Abroad," "Speaking of Sports," and "Well All Right."*

A Challenge to Superman! ! ! !

Wee kiddies are naturally mean, hate policemen, and love stories of Dillinger, Kelly, Luciano, and the Cleveland Butcher. Why are these natural instincts consistently thwarted by funny papers? We should like to introduce a new character, a cop hater, owing his superhuman powers to apple-jack, illiterate as hell, and fighting for the cause of crime all the way. Is it a bird? Is it a plane? Hell no—it's PEACHY-FELLOW! ! ! ! ! ! ! !

Chapter 1

Kent Trent coldly eyes the Sunday Mirror Magazine Section, shrugged his emaciated shoulders, blinked his watery blue eyes, and opened another pack of Twenty-Grands. Something had to be done! The boys at the sixth precinct police station had broken up Murder Incorporated, and there was only one man equal to the task of cleaning things up (go on, guess). Stripping off his blue twill sports jacket and gray flannels, drinking liberally from a bottle of seething amber fluid, Kent revealed

Vonnegut's mother was a member of a prosperous brewery family, and his father was an architect. Prohibition and the Depression put an end to their affluence, and the family was forced to give up their home at 4365 North Illinois Street, which his father had built.

himself in orchid shorts, polo helmet, and hip boots—PEACHY-FELLOW! ! ! ! ! !

Stepping to the window, a cool forty-six stories up, he easily cleared the sill and sailed into the street below. Impossible? Superhuman? In two graceful leaps and a bound, pausing for short beers, PEACHY-FELLOW was before the hated police station. Asphyxiating two detectives and a sergeant with his breath, he gained entrance to the offices of the crime hating Inspector Cobalt Cringe, an Eagle Scout if there ever was one. He bludgeoned the little man from behind, subduing his pitiful screams (this is the stuff, eh kids) with regular applications of a fifteen pound axe which we neglected to mention as an essential part of the uniform. PEACHY-FELLOW smiled wryly between luxurious burps—he had yet to fail on a mission.

The next step was simple. He took the keys from the bleeding corpse and opened the jail doors. Happy as little children, murderers, swindlers, burglars and other nifty people poured into the streets, no longer to be cruelly cooped up and treated like animals.

PEACHY-FELLOW would have none of their thanks; rather, he modestly passed out in an unobtrusive opium den, once more simply Kent Trent.

Don't miss next week's issue of OH SO NIFTY COMICS! ! ! ! PEACHY-FELLOW will challenge SUPERMAN! ! ! ! ! ! !

* * * * *

In Defense of the Golden West

In yesterday's column, Mr. Ted Eddy cut loose on the West with vicious generalities and the wit of a blotter.

A writer of merit.

With the brains of a parrot.

This, above all, is no time for a civil war, but if the steady flow of heckling from New York State doesn't stop, a breach is inevitable between the East and the West (the far West: Indiana, Illinois, and Ohio).

We of the Corn Belt are proud of our rolling fields of corn and wheat, our red barns, our stockyards, our factories. We make planes, tanks, shells, bombs, and guns—the best in the world. Our men were the healthiest and strongest in the Army of World War I.

More presidents have grown from our rich, black earth than from the gray sand and gravel that this state, New York, calls soil. The men who built up the Mid-West were the hardy men of their time, the strong men that could fight, clear forests, put in roads and fences, blast stumps and build forts and bridges. The weak stayed home. We hope the provincial Mr. Eddy is again safe and cozy.

Our country grew up out there, not in New York

Vonnegut left the University of Chicago after his M.A. thesis, "Fluctuations Between Good and Evil in Simple Tales," was unanimously rejected by the anthropology department. In 1947 he went to work as a public relations writer for General Electric in Schenectady, New York. When he began selling short stories to leading magazines, he quit his job and moved to Cape Cod. This photo was taken about the time his first story, "Report on the Barnhouse Effect," appeared in Collier's, *11 February 1950.*

City, the home of filth, corruption and unhappy people; nor did it grow up in Ithaca, the home of Mr. Eddy and Morse Chain.

Little men with glasses and thin, trembling lips, stick close to your fireside, and take care what poison you so glibly spread.

You see, we, Booth Tarkington, Hoagy Carmichael, Cole Porter, Wendell Willkie, Wilbur Shaw, Don Lash, James Whitcomb Riley, and myself are very proud people.

BOOK REVIEW:

David Goldknopf, "The Mechanistic Blues," *New Republic*, 127 (18 August 1952): 19.

Player Piano *did not attract much attention when it was published. This reviewer failed to detect any promise in the novel or the novelist.*

Player Piano is a preview of American life after the third World War and the fulfillment of the second, or electronic, Industrial Revolution, the one that is now getting under way. America has become a quasi police state in which vast numbers of willing workers, including some of the most skilled, are unemployed and indeed unemployable because electronically operated machinery has permanently displaced them. It is a country in which a man's station and future are totally controlled by a configuration of punched holes in a personnel card and men's minds have been ground down to a conformity as fine as our dust. That dust is occasionally stirred by ancient dreams and inchoate resentments, and such a stirring is taking place as the novel begins. But mostly America is a country in which life is intolerably dull.

That seems to be a quality shared by most versions of the future and it poses a very difficult problem for their creators: namely, how to write interestingly about a dull subject. *Player Piano*'s stereotyped or amorphous characters, inept construction, blunderbuss satire, and pedestrian prose help matters not at all.

And yet these defects, however serious, might be pardoned in a novel of ideas if the ideas themselves were profound or at least provocative. Mr. Vonnegut's are not; they are, in fact, demonstrably erroneous. Consider first the mildewed notion that machines create unemploy-

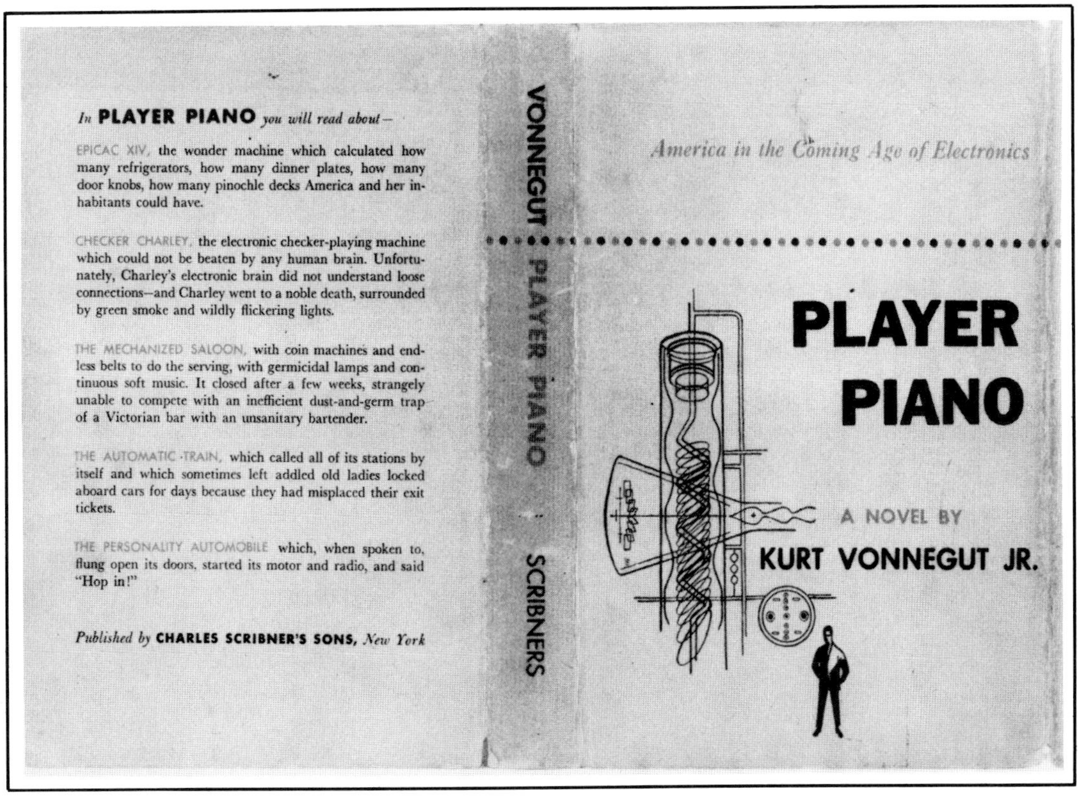

Player Piano, *an anti-utopian novel about an electronic world, was published in 1952. Vonnegut's first novel announced the theme that he would explore in all of his work: the dehumanization of modern man.*

ment. The fact is that machines create wealth and wealth creates jobs. More important still, it is in the nature of the machine to replace *unskilled* labor with *skilled* labor. We are still beguiled by the myth of craftsmanship, the absurd fancy, for example that the Middle Ages was an era of sword and chalice makers. Actually a far greater proportion of the population is engaged in skilled work in a truly mechanized society than in any other kind of society. In fact, many, if not most, of the jobs created by machines are not industrial; they provide new services of the sort that only a mechanized civilization can afford. Of course the author is talking about the future; but the future in his eyes is obviously an extrapolation of the present—that's what makes the novel "significant"—and there is, in the history of technological development, no support whatsoever for the situation which Mr. Vonnegut envisions.

More disappointing than the author's misconceptions, however, is his evasiveness. Having created a false issue, he lacks the courage to face up to it. The scientist-hero of *Player Piano*, after an abortive return-to-nature, lends himself to a Saturnalian uprising against the machine. As the novel ends he is seen sardonically yielding himself up to his executioners while the machine like the phoenix rises from the reeking ashes of its predecessor. Well now what does the author recommend? It may be objected that it is for the novel to propose problems not to answer them, but a work as doctrinaire and ill-natured as this one may reasonably be expected to offer some alternative to the evils it so grimly prophesies. Shall we return to brutalizing drudgery, to caste, to superstition? Shall we surrender our ease of movement, the spaciousness of our lives, in general—half our life-span for that matter. I'm sure the author would not seriously suggest that. Nor need he. Mechanization, blind and irresistible, can be directed if not resisted. We know now that the problems created by the machine are essentially political, not economic. We know too that they are susceptible of solution and that those solutions are not incompatible with freedom. Mechanization is as evil and beneficent as fire. It has vastly aggravated the horrors of war. The machine is, in the most literal sense, what we make it. It does what we make it do. It can be governed.

This novel, it seems to me, stems not so much from an intelligent apprehension as from the intellectual's sense of inferiority in the presence of the garage mechanic, at least while the mechanic is fixing the intellectual's car, or when he is presenting his bill. Why this feeling, which in its generalized state is one of non-participation in and non-contribution to society? Behind it may lie a sense of guilt. The intellectual despises the machine, but accepts its benefits—must accept them, willy-nilly. No Walden for him! That's only a suggestion of course, but it's one the writer of the next anti-machine novel might consider before he throws his sabots into the gears.

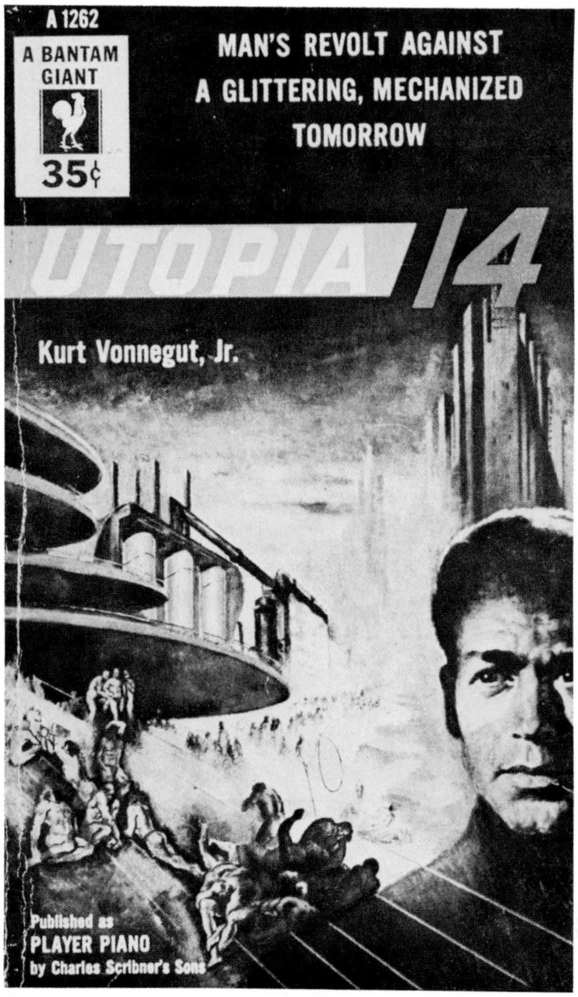

Player Piano *was republished by Bantam in 1954 as* Utopia 14.

As for literary criticism in general: I have long felt that any reviewer who expresses rage and loathing for a novel or a play or a poem is preposterous. He or she is like a person who has put on full armor and attacked a hot fudge sundae or a banana split.

From Vonnegut's "The People One Knows," in his Palm Sunday

ARTICLE:

Doris Lessing, "Vonnegut's Responsibility," *New York Times Book Review*, 4 February 1973, p. 35.

Lessing, a distinguished British novelist, re-appraised Mother Night *eleven years after its first publication.*

"Mother Night" is the Vonnegut book that has not been reviewed anywhere, ever, because it was sold first into paperback for a handy sum: he needed the money for his large family. And paperbacks don't get reviewed; so it has been ordained. Authors always feel that readers should know and care more about this kind of literary imperative than they do; there is more to what makes reputations than is taught in classes on literature.

"Mother Night" is odd-man-out in another way, being a straight novel. You needn't realize this at once or, indeed, at all; for it is a tale as monstrous as we read in the newspapers. As early as page 4 we find an 18-year-old Jew who guards our criminal hero in a Jerusalem jail; he does not know the name of Joseph Goebbels, but insists that Tiglath-pileser the Third, an Assyrian who burned down Hazar (a small town in Israel) in 732, was a man remarkable enough to be remembered by educated humanity. This sort of homely detail, instantly recognizable as the stuff of our zaniness, transports us further than any space-time warp and does not really need the addition of Vonnegut's elegant fantasy to make chimera land.

The criminal here is an American, Howard W. Campbell, Jr., an ordinary pleasant fellow, like us all. He was comfortably acclimatized, not being political by temperament, in Nazi Germany, but was recruited to be a spy for Us by an agent who recognized in him a fatal sense of the dramatic: he would never be able to resist seeing life as a battle between Good and Evil. During the war he invented and broadcast propaganda for the Nazis, while working reliably for Us. Fifteen years after the war, while living quietly with his memories in Greenwich Village, he was caught, mostly because of his own feelings of guilt or puzzlement about who really had done what—a specifically Vonnegut identification with the ambiguities of complicity.

Irrational, of course; because, judged by what he had done, he had been a very clever fellow and, indeed, a hero; and besides, he had survived, no mean achievement these days. His thoughts—well, they were another matter; and besides, he was no Eichmann or Calley to take orders and not know what it was he did: "My case is different. I know when I tell a lie, am capable of imagining the cruel consequences of anybody's believing my lies, know cruelty is wrong. I could no more lie without noticing it than I could unknowingly pass a kidney stone."

The force of Vonnegut's questioning is such that one has to sit down to think, to define degrees: Vonnegut simply cannot bear what we are, of course—like a lot of writers. The growl, the wince, the scream, that come off so many pages is due to this. But no other writer's sorrow, no other writer's refusal to play the child's game of Goodies and Baddies, is strong enough to make me remember, for instance, that before 1939 a great many people were shouting we should stop Hitler, that Nazism could be stopped if America and Britain wanted to. He makes me remember—he rubs our noses in the results of our missed chances—that when Nazism was not stopped, but flowered (to succumb to the associations of the word) into the expected and forecast war, how soon our judgments became warped by the horribleness of what was going on. The horribleness of the Nazis, of course: for almost at once Good and Evil became polarized into Us and Them and quite forgotten was the knowlege that the war could have been prevented if our governments had wanted. What Vonnegut deals with, always, is responsibility: Whose fault was it all—the gas chambers, the camps, the degradations and the debasements of all our standards? Whose? Well, *ours* as much as *theirs*.

This is so, that is, if you can believe in responsibility at all—it is here that Vonnegut is moral in an old-fashioned way. He does take the full weight of responsibility, while more and more people are shrugging off the *we should have* and *we ought to have* and *we can if we want* and coming to see history as a puppet show and our—humanity's—slide into chaos as beyond our prevention, our will, our choice. The strength of Kurt Vonnegut Jr., this deliberate and self-conscious heir, derives from his refusal to succumb to this new and general feeling of helplessness.

There is another way he is an original: for most of his career he has been in the category "space fiction" or "science fiction" where, for the most part, the chilliness of space derives from the writers' insistence that we do without the comforts of our own patterns of ethic, where we can see whole galaxies crumble with less emotion than we feel pouring boiling water into an ant's nest. Usually, in the center of Jex 132 (male) or Janni X56 (female) there is an emptiness which some claim is the proper imaginative response to the possibilities of all-space, but which in Vonnegut's people is filled with the emotions you and I would feel if we knew a molecule was

Vonnegut's third novel, Mother Night, *was published as a paperback original in 1962. It developed the strain of "black humor" with which he would become identified. The central figure is an American spy in Germany who became a Nazi propagandist and lost his true identity while performing as a double agent. Vonnegut wrote in the introduction for the 1966 edition: "We are what we pretend to be, so we must be careful what we pretend to be."*

loose that will freeze our world solid in a breath.

Precisely because in all his work he has made nonsense of the little categories, the unnatural divisions into "real" literature and the rest, because he is comic and sad at once, because his painful seriousness is never solemn, Vonnegut is unique among us; and these same qualities account for the way a few academics still try to patronize him: they cling to the categories. Of course they do: they invented them. But so it has ever gone.

Ordinary people, with whole imaginations, reading the newspapers, the comic strips and Jane Austen or watching the world reel by on television, keep an eye out for Ice 9 while hoping that we are indeed recognizing the members of our *karasses* when they come near, try to make sure that we don't pay more than what is due to the false *karasses*, and dare to believe that while there is life, there is still life—such readers know that Vonnegut is one of the writers who map our landscapes for us, who give names to the places we know best.

BOOK REVIEW:

Conrad Knickerbocker, "How To Love People Who Have No Use," *Life*, 58 (9 April 1965): 6-7.

Eliot Rosewater, the millionaire philanthropist of God Bless You, Mr. Rosewater or Pearls Before Swine *(1965) insists, "Goddamn it, you've got to be kind." This novel introduced the character Kilgore Trout, a destitute science-fiction writer, who reappears in Vonnegut's later work.*

It seems unjust that in this age of the super limelight, a writer as gifted and amusing as Kurt Vonnegut Jr. should be neglected. A black humorist, fantasist and satirist, a man disposed to deep and comic reflection on the human dilemma, he thus far has attracted a hard-core band of followers rather than a wide public. His supporters indicate his caliber: Graham Greene, Jules Feiffer, Conrad Aiken, Marc Connelly. *God Bless You, Mr. Rosewater* hopefully will earn the larger audience Vonnegut deserves.

His previous novels tackled religion, space, technology, doomsday, the nature of guilt, and the thousand ways science has amplified folly. *God Bless You, Mr. Rosewater* contemplates the screwy ways in which Americans regard money and never strays far from the essentials. Vonnegut's despair is the withering of true brotherly concern and the substitution of automated charity for love. His joy is all the non sequiturs that make up life. He conveys his feelings in an exuberant, crackling style—and with a frightening sense of the ridiculous in people and events.

Like the works of Jonathan Swift, his satires do not recount experience so much as they present parables that in turn demonstrate conditions. What redeems him from

Swiftian pessimism is his incapacity to take anything, even himself, seriously in the final analysis. Even so, he is one of the few writers not afraid to face up to the enormous social changes for which our times are a watershed—the technocratic revolution that will make the future so astonishingly different. Much of today's fiction has fled from this confrontation. Too many writers have hoped to find the truth in fragments of personal lives, when truth occurs less and less in individual arenas and more and more in the basement computer rooms of the Pentagon or in the boardrooms of huge and powerful organizations.

Such a power complex is the Rosewater Foundation, based on a fortune of $87,472,033.61 founded four generations ago by a "constipated Christian farm boy" turned speculator and briber in Indiana during the Civil War. At the helm of the foundation stands Eliot Rosewater, who went to Harvard, was a war hero, had a beautiful wife and seemed safe enough—until he actually gives some thought to the meaning of his money. From that point on, he becomes known in eleemosynary circles as variously "The Nut," "The Saint," "The Holy Roller" and "John the Baptist." His subsequent adventures as a self-confessed drunkard, utopian dreamer, tinhorn saint, volunteer fire department buff and all-around fool nearly cost him control of the fortune, but in the end his wily goodness bedazzles the shysters and crooks who try to dip into the moneypot.

During his pilgrim's progress, he crashes a convention of science-fiction writers to tell them they are the only ones who talk about the terrific changes going on and the only ones crazy enough to know that life is a space voyage. He frequently holes up with volunteer fire departments in places such as Clover Lick, West Virginia. Finally he runs to ground at the family homestead in Rosewater, Indiana, a fictional small town almost as terrible as a real one. There, in a flyblown office over a lunchroom, he directs the affairs of the Rosewater Foundation and lavishes his love on the worthless, unwanted inhabitants of the surrounding countryside. He makes a present of Nazi Berlin's main air raid siren to the Rosewater fire department and gives Rosewater Fellowships to suicidal machinists. He is a most enchanting millionaire, and we need more like him.

A fine set of rogues nearly tramples Eliot in its stampede toward what he calls the Money River. Vonnegut needs a chorus of hundreds to sound the true, rich scale of the national battiness, from Norman Mushari, the five-foot-three lawyer with the luminous posterior, to Diana Moon Glampers, the 68-year-old virgin who is afraid lightning endangers her kidneys. Groggy from booze and lunacy, Eliot still emerges as the sanest of the lot from his one-man battle in behalf of ordinary human beings.

In an earlier novel, *The Sirens of Titan*, which is generally misread as a work of science fiction, Vonnegut wondered if the entire human drama has not actually been the result of the planet Tralfamadore's quest for a spare rocket part. In *Player Piano* and *Cat's Cradle* he expounded basic doubts concerning technology. *God Bless You, Mr. Rosewater* ponders the problem of how to love people who have no use. It does so with humor and pity, and even if Vonnegut has no answers, he is sure asking the right questions.

Vonnegut's fifth novel, published in 1965 when he was forty-three, was the first to attract prominent review exposure. Playwright Marc Connelly called it "even better than Cat's Cradle *and the most truthful picture of a saint since El Greco's Sebastian."*

BOOK REVIEW:

C. D. B. Bryan, "Kurt Vonnegut on Target," *New Republic*, 155 (8 October 1966): 21-22, 24-26.

The breakthrough year for Vonnegut was 1966. Four of his novels were republished in cloth, and he went from a cult figure to a respected mainstream writer.

Kurt Vonnegut, Jr., is 44 years old and lives with his wife and six children in West Barnstable on Cape Cod. During the 1955-56 term he taught at the Writers' Workshop of the University of Iowa, and now teaches English in a private school on the Cape. He once worked for General Electric, his biography tells us, but Vonnegut "is a scientist only in as much as he is interested in the science of living reasonably and kindly." He was also volunteer fireman in Alpaus, New York—Badge 155. He has written six books and over a hundred short stories, articles, and reviews. Among his fans are Conrad Aiken, Nelson Algren, Marc Connelly, Jules Feiffer, Graham Greene, Granville Hicks, Terry Southern. Still Vonnegut has not received the acceptance due him from the reading public. Four of his books are available: *Mother Night*, published a few months ago; *God Bless You, Mr. Rosewater, or Pearls Before Swine*, 1965; *Cat's Cradle*, 1963, and *Player Piano*, 1952 reissued this year. Out of print are his two other novels, *Canary in a Cathouse* [*sic*] and the science fiction paperback, *Sirens of Titan*. What prevents Vonnegut from being a major satirist on the order, say, of John Barth is that Vonnegut takes very little seriously, and although he excels at that more gentle barb Irony, he lacks the anger and impatience which great satire demands. Nevertheless, he is the most readable and amusing of the new humorists.

Mother Night is narrated by Howard W. Campbell, Jr., an American citizen who broadcast anti-Semitic propaganda for the Nazis during the Second World War. Campbell had been recruited by a US counterintelligence agent in 1938, and Campbell's broadcasts carried coded information out of Germany. Campbell never knew what the information was. (Once the information was that Campbell's wife was captured and presumed dead.) Towards the end of the war Campbell is captured by Lt. Bernard B. O'Hare of the American Third Army, and taken to a nearby German concentration camp so that the American "traitor" would see the lime pits, the stacks of emaciated dead and the gallows capable of hanging six at a time. From the end of each rope hangs a camp guard. Campbell expects also to be hanged:

Vonnegut's second novel, The Sirens of Titan*, appeared seven years after* Player Piano *and was published as a paperback original in 1959. The book was not reviewed but eventually sold a half million copies and launched the Vonnegut cult.*

> "I took an interest in the peace of the six guards at the ends of their ropes.
>
> They had died fast.
>
> My photograph was taken while I looked up at the gallows. Lieutenant O'Hare was standing behind me, lean as a young wolf, as full of hatred as a rattlesnake.
>
> The picture was on the cover of *Life*, and came close to winning a Pulitzer Prize."

So that the Americans will not have to admit that he had been a counterspy, Campbell is freed on nonexistent technicalities. He returns to New York, moves into an attic in Greenwich Village and tries to start a new life. One of his neighbors is an alcoholic with the alias George Kraft, actually Colonel Iona Potapov, resident Soviet agent in the United States since 1935. Another character is the Reverend Doctor Lionel Jason David Jones, DDS, DD, who believes the teeth of Jews, Negroes, Catholics, and quite possibly Unitarians prove beyond question that these groups are degenerate, a theory he advances in his publication, *The White Christian Minuteman*. Jones is also founder of the Western Hemisphere of the Bible, a university which "held no classes, taught nothing, did all its business by mail. It awarded doctorates in the field of divinity, framed and under glass, for eighty dollars a throw." Campbell's wartime activities had made him a hero to Jones and his followers, one of whom is Jones' chauffeur, a 73-year-old Negro, Robert Sterling Wilson, the "Black Fuehrer of Harlem," who had been imprisoned as a Japanese agent during the war. The first time Campbell meets him, Wilson says:

> "The colored people are gonna rise up in righteous wrath, and they're gonna take over the world; White folks gonna finally lose!"
> "All right, Robert," Jones said patiently.
> "The colored people gonna have hydrogen bombs all their own," he said. "They working on it right now. Pretty soon gonna be Japan's turn to drop one. The rest of the colored folks gonna give them the honor of dropping the first one."
> "Where are they going to drop it?" I said.
> "China, most likely," he said.
> "On other colored people?" I said. He looked at me pityingly. "Whoever told you a Chinaman was a colored man?" he said.

Because of the publicity given Campbell by Jones' White Christian Minutemen, Campbell again comes to the attention of ex-lieutenant O'Hare, now the Americanism Chairman of the Francis X Donovan Post of the American Legion, who writes, "I was very surprised and disappointed to hear you weren't dead yet." Both O'Hare and the reverend dentist Jones had been informed of Campbell's whereabouts by the Soviet spy, George Kraft. Kraft wants to pressure Campbell into going to Mexico where he would then be kidnapped and flown to Moscow to be put on display "as a prime example of the sort of Fascist war criminal this country shelters."

What lifts *Mother Night* out of the realm of easy entertainment is Campbell's awareness of his guilt. His desire for punishment compels him to give himself up; and another neighbor, a Jewish doctor who had survived Auschwitz reluctantly arranges Campbell's capture by "Israeli agents"—a tailor, watchmaker and a pediatrician who, with Campbell's consent, turn him in the next morning to Israeli officials. While in Israel Campbell meets Eichmann who asks, "Do you think a literary agent is absolutely necessary?" Campbell replies, "For book clubs and movie sales in the United States of America, absolutely." Campbell knows that if the Israeli government will not punish him, he must. In the end he executes himself.

In his introduction to *Mother Night*, Vonnegut offers the following: "This is the only story of mine whose moral I know. I don't think it's a marvelous moral; I simply happen to know what it is: We are what we pretend to be, so we must be careful what we pretend to be." Howard W. Campbell, Jr., pretended to be a vicious, anti-Semitic

Vonnegut was a regular contributor to Collier's, Redbook, Cosmopolitan *and the* Saturday Evening Post *in the fifties. His early short stories were collected in the paperback* Canary in a Cat House *(1961) and have been included in* Welcome to the Monkey House *(1968).*

Nazi. His guilt lay in his knowledge that he had been far more successful at it than he needed to be.

Cat's Cradle is the account of a writer who wanted to record what important Americans had done on the day the first atomic bomb was dropped on Hiroshima. The book, to be called *The Day The World Ended*, "was to be a Christian book. I was a Christian then," explains the author narrator. "I am a Bokonist now." Bokonism is a religion invented by Vonnegut. The first sentence in the Books of Bokonon is: "All of the true things I am about to tell you are shameless lies." Another is, "Pay no attention to Caesar. Caesar has no idea what's *really* going on." Most of Bokonon's teachings are found in calypso "psalms" but the gist of it is captured in its "Genesis":

> "In the beginning, God created the earth, and he looked upon it in His cosmic loneliness.
>
> And God said, 'Let Us make living creatures out of mud, so the mud can see what We have done.' And God created every living creature that now moveth, and one was man. Mud as man alone could speak. God leaned close as mud as man sat up, looked around, and spoke. Man blinked. 'What is the *purpose* of all this?' he asked politely.
>
> 'Everything must have a purpose?' asked God.
>
> 'Certainly,' said man.
>
> 'Then I leave it to you to think of one for all this,' said God. And He went away."

Vonnegut's theology is also voiced in his science fiction novel, *Sirens of Titan*, in which religion is celebrated in the Church of God the Utterly Indifferent. Vonnegut is a proponent of the God is Dead theory and is convinced that all the evil in this world is perpetrated by man upon man. He is appalled by scientists and engineers. In *Cat's Cradle*, the author narrator interviews Dr. Breed, head of the Research Laboratory of the General Forge and Foundry Company—the laboratory in which Dr. Felix Hoenikker developed the atomic bomb. Dr. Breed is dismayed because "every question I asked implied that the creators of the atomic bomb had been criminal accessories to a murder most foul."

> "Dr. Breed was astonished and then he got very sore. He drew back from me and grumbled, 'I gather you don't like scientists very much.'
>
> 'I wouldn't say that, sir.'
>
> 'All your questions seem aimed at getting me to admit that scientists are heartless, conscienceless, narrow boobies, indifferent to the fate of the human race, or maybe not really members of the human race at all.'
>
> 'That's putting it pretty strong.' "

Vonnegut's hero in *Player Piano*, the novel which preceded *Cat's Cradle* by nine years, is again a man against science. But this time he is an insider, Dr. Paul Proteus, manager of the Ilium Works, a fully automated factory which produces just about everything. The time is the Electronics Age, perhaps 100 years in the future. But whereas in *Cat's Cradle* the rebellion is against that segment of science which produces better methods by which man can annihilate himself, in *Player Piano* Vonnegut attacks the science of automation through which man produces machines which replace man's pride, his usefulness, his meaning.

Vonnegut's best-known book is *God Bless You, Mr. Rosewater, or Pearls Before Swine*. Eliot Rosewater, whom Marc Connelly describes as "the most truthful picture of a saint since El Greco's Sebastian," is heir to the Rosewater fortune which provides an income of $3.5 million a year. The antagonists are everywhere, but the best articulated is Norman Mushari, a Lebanese hired by the Washington, D.C. law firm of McAllister, Robjent, Reed and McGee, designers of the Rosewater Foundation and Rosewater Corporation. The author points out that Mushari "would never have been hired if the other partners hadn't felt that McAllister's operations could do with just a touch more viciousness." Mushari's guiding principle in law had been stated by one of his former law school professors:

> "In every big transaction there is a magic moment during which a man has surrendered a treasure, and during which the man who is due to receive it has not yet done so. An alert lawyer will make that moment his own, possessing the treasure for a magic microsecond, taking a little of it, passing it on. If the man who is to receive the treasure is unused to wealth, has an inferiority complex and shapeless feelings of guilt, as most people do, the lawyer can often take as much as half the bundle, and still receive the recipient's blubbering thanks."

God Bless You, Mr. Rosewater hinges upon Mushari's knowledge that all he need do is prove Eliot Rosewater insane, and the fortune is transferred to the lesser branch of Rosewaters living in Rhode Island. Mushari has a good case. In every telephone booth in Rosewater, Indiana,

Vonnegut's fourth novel, Cat's Cradle *(1963), deals with the end of the world caused by the release of* ice-nine, *a form of ice stable at room temperature. This work introduced the terms* foma *("harmless untruths"),* karass *("teams that do God's will without ever discovering what they are doing"),* wampeter *("the pivot of a karass"), and* granfalloon *("a false karass").*

where Eliot lives, there is a sticker: "Don't kill yourself. Call the Rosewater Foundation." The stickers had been placed there by Eliot. If a person called, he was usually given some money, often with the suggestion that the caller take two aspirin with a glass of wine. Eliot had been under psychoanalysis; but the night after the psychiatrist resigned from the case, Eliot Rosewater and his wife, Sylvia, attend a new staging of *Aida* at the Met, for which the Rosewater Foundation had provided the costumes. "Everything was fine until the last scene of the opera, during which the hero and the heroine were placed in an airtight chamber to suffocate. As the doomed pair filled their lungs, Eliot called out to them, 'You will last a lot longer if you don't try to sing.' Eliot stood, leaned far out of his box, told the singers, 'Maybe you don't know anything about oxygen, but I do. Believe me, you must not sing.' " Eliot's wife led him away "like a toy balloon."

The only people with whom Eliot Rosewater feels complete identification are volunteer firemen. "We few, we happy few, we band of brothers," he tells them, "joined in the serious business of keeping our food, shelter, clothing, and loved ones from combining with oxygen." The one other group he admires are science fiction writers. On one of his alcoholic binges, Eliot crashes a science fiction writers' convention held in a motel in Milford, Pennsylvania. He interrupts their meeting to say, "I love you sons of bitches. You're all I read any more. You're the only ones who'll talk about the *really* terrific changes going on, the only ones crazy enough to know that life is a space voyage, and not a short one either, but one that will last for billions of years. You're the only ones with guts enough to *really* care about the future, who *really* know what machines do to us, what cities do to us, what big, simple ideas do to us, what tremendous mistakes, accidents, and catastrophes do to us. You're the only ones zany enough to agonize over time and distances without limit, over mysteries that will never die, over the fact that we are right now determining whether the space voyage for the next billion years or so is going to be Heaven or Hell."

Vonnegut was born in Indianapolis in 1922. During the Second World War he was a battalion scout in the US Army and was captured by the Germans. He became part of a prisoner work group employed by a Dresden factory which made a vitamin-enriched malt syrup for pregnant women. Dresden contained no troop concentrations or war industries. It was an "open city"—not to be attacked—and yet on the night of February 13, 1945, British and American bombers attempted to obliterate Dresden through the meticulous and scientific creation of a fire storm. They were about 75 percent successful. In his introduction to *Mother Night*, Vonnegut writes:

> "There were no particular targets for the bombs. The hope was that they would create a lot of kindling and drive the firemen underground.
>
> And then hundreds of thousands of tiny incendiaries were scattered over the kindling, like seeds on freshly turned loam. More bombs were dropped to keep the firemen in their holes, and all the little fires grew, joined one another, became one apocalyptic flame. Hey presto: fire storm. It was the largest massacre in European history, by the way. . . .
>
> We didn't get to see the fire storm. We were in a cool meat-locker under a slaughterhouse with our six guards and ranks and ranks of dressed cadavers of cattle, pigs, horses and sheep. We heard the bombs walking around up there. Now and then there would be a gentle shower of calcimine. If we had gone above to take a look we would have been turned into artifacts characteristic of fire storms: seeming pieces of charred firewood two or three feet long—ridiculously small human beings, or jumbo fried grasshoppers, if you will.
>
> The malt syrup factory was gone. Everything was gone but the cellars where 135,000 Hansels and Gretels had been baked like gingerbread men. So we were put to work as corpse miners, breaking into shelters, bringing bodies out. And I got to see many German types of all ages as death had found them, usually with valuables in their laps. Sometimes relatives would come to watch us dig. They were interesting, too.
>
> So much for Nazis and me.
>
> If I'd been born in Germany, I suppose I would have *been* a Nazi, bopping Jews and gypsies and Poles around, leaving boots sticking out of snowbanks, warming myself with my secretly virtuous insides. So it goes."

And so goes Vonnegut's most powerful writing. All the anger, the shame, the shock, the guilt, the compassion, the irony, the control to produce great satire are *there*. For sheer barbarity the fire storms of Dresden and Hamburg surpass the atomic bombing of Hiroshima and Nagasaki. Why, then, does Vonnegut settle for such lovely, literate amusing attacks upon such simple targets as scientists, engineers, computer technicians, religion, the American Legion, artists, company picnics?

ARTICLE:
"46—and Trusted," *Newsweek*, 73 (3 March 1969): 79.

Vonnegut's campus popularity grew enormously in the late sixties. This article appeared shortly before the publication of Slaughterhouse-Five.

If today's activist youth doesn't trust anyone over 30, then Herbert Marcuse is not 70 and Kurt Vonnegut Jr. is not 46. Marcuse is the house theoretician for New Leftists; and for many just plain college students, Vonnegut is a specialist George Orwell, a science-fiction writer who does more than write science fiction: he is a prophet, if not quite of doom then at least of some considerable unpleasantness, who manages to retain a wicked, pungent wit.

The mustached, strapping Vonnegut is an unlikely visionary, a married man who writes his novels and short stories in his rambling farmhouse in Barnstable, Mass., on Cape Cod, where he lives with his family and sheepdog. His reputation as both a science-fiction writer and a voice that communicates with many of the nation's youth has launched him on the lecture circuit; last month in New York he addressed the annual convention of the American Association of Physics Teachers on the "Virtuous Physicist"—the man "who declines to work on weapons." Indeed, he added pointedly, "some physicists are so virtuous that they're not going into physics."

Such wry moralizing obviously appeals to college

readers. "What J. D. Salinger was to me in high school," says Pat Gentry, 20, a junior English major at UCLA, "Kurt Vonnegut is to me in college." Courses at such schools as Harvard, Wisconsin and the University of Washington require students to read Vonnegut. One Vonnegut theme is the vulgarity that accompanies excessive wealth. In "The Sirens of Titan" (1959), a rich man uses the Mona Lisa in an advertising campaign for suppositories. "The whole idea is funny because we know it could happen," wrote a Harvard student in a full-page feature story on Vonnegut in a recent special supplement of the Crimson.

Vonnegut's works often feature modern Dr. Jekylls whose genius lies in creating a technology which eventually chops up man's humanity into little Shredded Wheat chunks of people. In one short story contained in the collection "Welcome to the Monkey House," he writes of the scientist who invents the "ethical" birth-control pill which, while it does not prevent conception, at least eliminates the copulatory desire by taking the fun out of sex.

But Vonnegut scoffs at the notion that his novels contain any so-called truths. He remarks dryly that if he were to look into what he has written a little more carefully, "there might be something there. I'm not about to investigate, unless, of course, my doing so would somehow save the life of a child." But, in fact, the "lessons" implicit in his novels often seem based on aspects of his own life. A combat infantry scout in the American Army during the second world war, Vonnegut, a fourth generation German-American, was captured by the Germans and held a prisoner of war in Dresden. There he managed to survive the immense Allied fire-bombing of Dresden only by keeping cool in a meat locker under a slaughterhouse, a nightmarish experience that forms the basis of his latest novel, "Slaughterhouse-Five," to be published this month. In the novel the protagonist says: "I have told my sons that they are not under any circumstances to take part in massacres, and that the news of massacres of enemies is not to fill them with satisfaction or glee." Vonnegut himself told *Newsweek*'s Thomas C. Plate: "I've got three kids Mark Rudd's age,

Vonnegut went overseas as a combat scout and was captured in the Battle of the Bulge. As a POW he survived the bombing of Dresden. In 1945 Vonnegut married Jane Marie Cox, whom he met in kindergarten. They are shown here in 1969.

and I share with them the sense that the system promotes to the top those who don't care about the planet."

Still, despite the patently prophetic nature of his fiction, Vonnegut is more than a little concerned that readers will take his glimpse into the future too seriously. "People are constantly demanding moralizing," he says. "There's going to be a lot of that this year—that's certainly what people want to hear when they ask me to lecture. Things like war crimes—that's what the kids are thinking about these days." But Vonnegut feels that a writer who takes his pronouncements as holy writ is about as mad as the scientist who blithely engages in research designed to make weapons that kill people better. After all, he says with a smile peeping out from under his mustache—and with a happy glimmer of the put-on in his eyes—"a writer is just a person who makes his living with his mental disease."

ARTICLE:

Leslie A. Fiedler, "The Divine Stupidity of Kurt Vonnegut," *Esquire*, 74 (September 1970): 195-197, 199-200, 202-204.

An assessment of Vonnegut's position in American letters after Slaughterhouse-Five.

I first read Kurt Vonnegut Jr., as I now know was proper, in paper, and at the urging of a fourteen-year-old son. He came to me, that is to say, not off the shelves of a library, but from the same world of disreputable entertainment to which comic books and beloved bad movies belong: the world of the pleasure rather than the reality principle, the world of the young rather than the old.

I grew up, for better or worse, in a generation and a class for which literature seemed more a duty than a self-indulgence. And I was a father before I was prepared to admit that books, even the very best of them, can, maybe should be used to subvert the world of duty and work and success. I don't mean that I did not in fact make such uses of some of them when I was myself still a son and an adolescent, merely that I insisted they be kosher, which is to say, checked out as classics and/or avant-garde masterpieces by accepted critics.

At any rate, I began, at the behest of my son, with Vonnegut's *Player Piano* (then called, as I remember, *Utopia 14*), which moved me oddly, though I still managed to avoid having to come to terms with it by tucking it away in the category of "Science Fiction." And I continued to read his books as science fiction whenever they came to hand on supermarket bookstalls. I am, like everyone else I know, an inveterate impulse buyer and commodity consumer.

Then, just three or four years ago, I was reminded that for some almost as young at this moment as my son was when he first introduced me to Vonnegut, his books seemed more scriptures than commodities. I had been asked for the first time to a university not under the auspices of the English Department, but on the invitation of the students themselves; and at the end of my three-week stay was given two books which, to my hosts, represented the kind of writing that compelled their deepest assent: Claude Levi-Strauss' *La Pensee Sauvage* and Vonnegut's *The Sirens of Titan*. It was still the point before student aspiration had been fully politicalized; and I suspect that now such secret scriptures are more likely to be Maoist or Trotskyist than structuralist and fantastic. Still, in this area one nail does not necessarily drive out another; and only last year a group of English students (who would supply me, before the official release date, with the lyrics of new Bob Dylan songs) were asking that two books be added to a reading list of post-World War II novels: Ken Kesey's *One Flew Over the Cuckoo's Nest* and Kurt Vonnegut's *Cat's Cradle*.

But Vonnegut seems an odd choice really, being not only immune to Left politics, but neither a pothead like Allen Ginsberg, or an acidhead like, say, Ken Kesey—or even a reformed heroin addict, like William Burroughs. He is—or so he claims in autobiographical asides—only an old-fashioned juicehead, a moderate boozer, now a couple of years past forty-five; and given—when liquored up—to remembering *his* war, which is to say, World War II, rather than World War III which didn't happen, or those smaller ones which did, in Korea or Vietnam. But it is those other wars which possess the imaginations of the young, especially the last, which may, indeed, be the first ever fought by Americans on marijuana rather than whiskey. What, then, has made Kurt Vonnegut an underground favorite of the young?

It is partly, I suppose, the fact that structurally, archetypally speaking, the space-odyssey is the same thing as the "trip"; and that having chosen the mode of science fiction, Vonnegut has subscribed to a mythology otherwise sustained by smoking grass or dropping LSD, or, for that matter, simply sitting half-stunned before the late, late show on TV. In a certain sense, it can be said that the taking of drugs is a technological substitute for a special kind of literature, for fantasy—an attempt to substitute chemistry for words; and it can thus be understood as a kind of midterm between science fiction and actual manned flights into outer space, those trips to the moon or Mars, which can be read as the final expression of technology imitating art. And, of course, becoming art once more as television records them.

Not Proust-Mann-and-Joyce, those "thick" books dense with realistic detail, symbol and psychological analysis, but the Western, Science Fiction and Porn, "thin" books all fantasy and plot and characters in two dimensions, possess our imaginations now; or at least so certain writers whom young readers prefer have come recently to believe. Novelists nurtured on the tradition of High Art and avant-garde, and therefore initially committed to a dream of surviving on library shelves and in classroom analyses, learn now that only the ephemeral lives the real life of literature these days, in living hearts and heads; and they begin, therefore, to emulate the Pop forms, which means begin to aspire to making it in paperback.

The long-predicted death of the Novel turns out to be the death of the Art Novel, the "poetic" novel read by an elite audience to whom high literature represents chiefly the opportunity of verifying their own special status in a world of slobs committed to the consumption of "mass culture." Quite "serious" writers, writers who kid neither themselves nor their readers, register their awareness of this in ways many of their most ardent readers seem not yet quite to understand. But only in this context is it possible to see clearly what John Barth was up to either in *The Sot-Weed Factor*, where in re-creating Pocahontas he created the Dirty Western, or in *Giles Goat-Boy*, where he married Rabelais to Science Fiction. So, too, the more recent work of William Burroughs, *The Ticket That Exploded*, for instance, only makes real sense to one who realizes how much in it comes from releasing the standard images of run-of-the-mill science fiction in a haze of junk. And he, too, begins now to move toward the classical form of the Western, first and most authentic variety of American Pop—that tale of the male companions, red and white, in flight from women and in quest of the absolute wilderness, which has recently been reborn in books as various as Ken Kesey's *One Flew Over the Cuckoo's Nest*, Truman Capote's *In Cold Blood* and Norman Mailer's *Why Are We In Vietnam?* It was all there in James Fenimore Cooper to begin with, has remained there in the Pop underground ever since, and rises to the surface whenever an American writer wants to indulge not his own exclusive fantasies of alienation and chosenness, but the dreams he shares with everyone else.

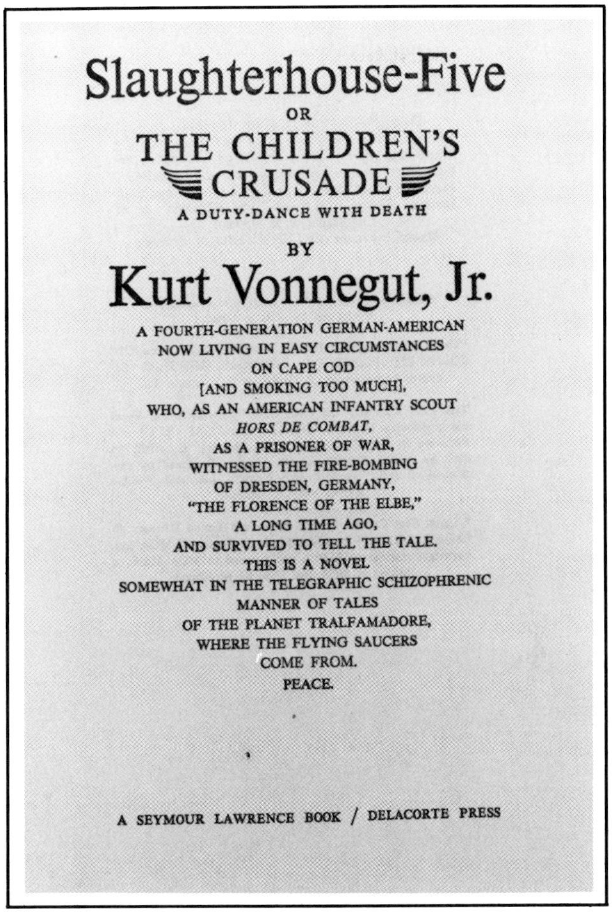
Slaughterhouse-Five
OR
THE CHILDREN'S
CRUSADE
A DUTY-DANCE WITH DEATH
BY
Kurt Vonnegut, Jr.
A FOURTH-GENERATION GERMAN-AMERICAN
NOW LIVING IN EASY CIRCUMSTANCES
ON CAPE COD
[AND SMOKING TOO MUCH],
WHO, AS AN AMERICAN INFANTRY SCOUT
HORS DE COMBAT,
AS A PRISONER OF WAR,
WITNESSED THE FIRE-BOMBING
OF DRESDEN, GERMANY,
"THE FLORENCE OF THE ELBE,"
A LONG TIME AGO,
AND SURVIVED TO TELL THE TALE.
THIS IS A NOVEL
SOMEWHAT IN THE TELEGRAPHIC SCHIZOPHRENIC
MANNER OF TALES
OF THE PLANET TRALFAMADORE,
WHERE THE FLYING SAUCERS
COME FROM.
PEACE.

A SEYMOUR LAWRENCE BOOK / DELACORTE PRESS

Title page for Vonnegut's most influential novel, which is about a man who becomes unstuck in time: "I would hate to tell you what this lousy little book cost me in money and anxiety and time."

Some American writers, John Updike, for instance, and Philip Roth, have been too inhibited by their own parochial commitments to the provinces of High Art as defined by *The New Yorker* or *Partisan Review* to make it back into the world of the Western or up and out into the world of Science Fiction. They, too, have felt the pressure to move toward the world of Pop and have responded by creating—in *Couples* and *Portnoy's Complaint*—fantasies of sex rather than of the Virgin Forest or Outer Space, turning to what Alberto Moravia once described as the last place where urban men (and who more urban than Roth, more suburban than Updike) live in nature. "I am not a Jewish sage," Roth has said recently, talking of his newest book, "I am a Jew Freak like Tiny Tim!" It is his instinct for survival which is speaking; and how splendidly he has survived the death of the Jewish Art Novel the record of sales for *Portnoy's Complaint* sufficiently indicates. But woe to writers, Jew and Gentile alike, who do not respond as he does, since the novel must cease taking itself seriously or perish.

Vonnegut has had what we now realize to be an advantage in this regard, since he *began* as a Pop writer, the author of "slick" fiction, written to earn money, which is to say, to fit formulas which are often genuine myths, frozen and waiting to be released. Fortunately, though he has sometimes written to suit the tastes of the middle-aged ladies who constitute the readership of the *Ladies' Home Journal*, he has tended more to exploit the mythology of the future. But he has, in any case—as writers of, rather than *about*, mythology must—written books that are thin and wide, rather than deep and narrow, books which open out into fantasy and magic by means of linear narration rather than deep analysis; and so happen on wisdom, fall into it through grace, rather than pursue it doggedly or seek to earn it by hard work. Moreover, like all literature which tries to close the gap between the elite and the popular audiences rather than to confirm it, Vonnegut's books tend to temper irony with sentimentality and to dissolve both in wonder.

Inevitably, however, critical approval has overtaken him; and he appears now elegantly produced between boards—misrepresented, as it were. And who could wish it otherwise, for criticism's sake at least, since he is a test case for the critics. When I was young, literary critics thought they knew for sure that it was their function to educate taste: to rescue a mass audience, largely middle-aged, from an addiction to outworn sentimentality and escapism, to prepare them to read what was newest and most difficult. Suddenly, however, it is the mass audience which leads the critics, educating them, for now it is the critics who are middle-aged, the big audience that is young; rescuing them from an addiction to outworn irony, and teaching them to read for the sake of a joy deeper than that of mere culture-climbing. Understandably enough, many survivors of the old critical regime find it difficult to persuade themselves that if, recently, they have come to esteem Vonnegut, it is not because they have been converted to the side of Pop, but because—though they did not at first realize it—he has all along belonged to the other side of High Art.

Confusion in this regard extends even to Vonnegut's publishers, or at least to the writers of his jacket copy, who assure us that "Once mistakenly typed as a science-fiction writer, he is now recognized as a mainstream storyteller. . . ." But all is presumably set straight; for we are also informed he has taught at the University of Iowa Writers Workshop. It is true, of course—however belatedly the universities and copywriters have come to acknowledge it—that Vonnegut *does* belong to what we know again to be the mainstream of fiction; it is not the mainstream of High Art, however, but of myth and entertainment: a stream which was forced to flow underground over the past several decades, but has now surfaced once more.

> *There is no shortage of wonderful writers. What we lack is a dependable mass of readers. . . . I propose that every person out of work be required to submit a book report before he or she gets his or her welfare check.*

From "Kurt Vonnegut: The Art of Fiction LXIV," Paris Review *(Spring 1977)*

To be, for a while, thus invisible is, in any case, not necessarily bad; art renews itself precisely in the dialectical process of disappearing, reappearing, disappearing. And just as the invisibility of the avant-garde, its unavailability to contemporary criticism at the beginning of the twentieth century, was a source of health and strength for an elitist, neoclassic tradition; so the invisibility of Pop, its immunity to fasionable judgment, seems in mid-twentieth century to have been a source of health and strength to what we now recognize as the New Romanticism: an art which prefers sentimentality to irony, passion to reason, vulgarity to subtlety. But sentimentality and passion and vulgarity had long been consigned to the outer darkness by such reigning critics as T. S. Eliot and Cleanth Brooks. And, as always when seeking renewal, art had to descend into that darkness which exists on the blind side of the critics' heads.

Moreover, for young readers the invisibility of Pop in general, science fiction in particular, has seemed a warrant of its relevance, a sign that by virtue of being unavailable to their elders, it belonged especially to them, to *their* "underground." And yet they could not forebear bringing the buried treasure they had discovered to the surface, bugging their presumed betters, urging their parents and teachers to share the pleasures of

Pop—in Vonnegut, or, for that matter, Andy Warhol and Lichtenstein, or vintage comic books or movies starring John Wayne. To do so, however, is to make the invisible visible, the hidden manifest, to translate certain artists from the paperback shelves or pornographic bookstores to the classroom and the required reading list, which creates confusion for all concerned.

And yet finally who can regret the whole ironic process; since to writers like Vonnegut, on the border between New Pop and Old High Art, their initial invisibility is a torment which leaves scars, if not disabling traumas. To check through the *Book Review Index*, for instance, and discover that from 1952 to 1963 no book of Vonnegut's is recorded as having appeared or been reviewed is to understand the persistent defensiveness which underlies his playful-bitter references to his status as "a writer of science fiction." Even in his latest collection of short stories and articles, which appeared in 1968 under the title of *Welcome to the Monkey House*, he is still fighting it out, saying ironically, "Here one finds the fruits of Free Enterprise"; then going on to explain, "I used to be a public-relations man for General Electric, and then I became a free-lance writer of so-called slick fiction. . . . Whether I improved myself morally by making the change I am not prepared to say. That is one of the questions I mean to ask God on Judgment Day. . . . I have already put the question to a college professor, who . . . assured me that public-relations men and slick writers were equally vile, in that they both buggered truth for money. . . ." The self-doubt in this latest comment is undercut by the irony. But Vonnegut was not always even this secure about what he was doing; since a writer, however much a pro, lives only days by what his stories earn him, must get through his nights on remembering what the critics say.

Perhaps Vonnegut's initial difficulty on this score, which turns out to be a final advantage, is that he is a transitional figure in a time of transition, a period in which we are rapidly leaving behind the values of Modernism: the notion propagated by such Modernist high priests as T. S. Eliot that "Culture" belongs to an elite, a tiny remnant saved by being able to appreciate an abstruse, hermetic, highly allusive and symbolic form of art. To the Modernist, Pop is a vice of the weak-minded majority, or alternatively, a sop thrown to the exploited by the Madison Avenue lackeys of their exploiters; to the Post-Modernist it is the storehouse of fantasy in which the present Future we now live was prefigured, the twenty-first century pre-invented.

Vonnegut is of two minds on the subject, alternatively, simultaneously. On the one hand, he has lived from the beginning by appealing to the great Pop audience on its own grounds, and yet something in him has always yearned to be a "serious writer," to win the respect of those professors whom he affects to despise, but whose colleague he has recently become all the same. And that something is betrayed in his habit—untypical in Pop fiction—of putting writers and artists at the center of his books. But this habit belongs essentially to the kind of Modernist book whose subject is art, whose hero the artist; and whose classic instance is Joyce's *Portrait of the Artist as a Young Man*.

Vonnegut has never, consequently, seemed to the first generation of hard-core science fiction fans a major figure in the genre, even Kingsley Amis in *New Maps of Hell*, the one broadly inclusive survey of the genre, dismissing him with a single friendly sentence. The older aficionados—weary scientists and hardworking technicians, for instance, to whom science fiction seemed a device for escaping rather than expanding their own sense of reality—have always preferred figures like Robert Heinlein, in whose earlier books the familiar conventions of the thriller and the detective story were transferred without fundamental change to interplanetary regions. But Heinlein ever since *Stranger in a Strange Land* has been remaking his own work on the model of Vonnegut's—using images of pursuit and discovery in Outer Space to indicate the possibilities of creating in Inner Space new values, a new language, in short, just such a New World as the New Romantics dream.

Meanwhile, Vonnegut himself, however, has been moving uneasily away from his science-fiction beginnings; in books like *God Bless You, Mr. Rosewater* and *Slaughterhouse-Five*, ironically playing with the form he once quite simply practiced. But disengaging from science fiction, Vonnegut seems on the point of disengaging entirely from words, and perhaps it is a weariness with the craft of fiction itself, with, at any rate, telling stories, i.e., making plots or myths, that impels him; as if he suspects the Pop Novel may be as dead as the Art Novel. More and more, he is impelled toward abstraction, the making of constellations or patterns, which may explain his recent statement that "I would enjoy becoming a painter for a while."

To understand how Vonnegut has moved, however, it is necessary to look more closely at his work to date, in particular at the six novels he has written since 1952. His short stories, collected in two volumes, *Canary in a Cat House* (1961) and *Welcome to the Monkey House* (1968), I shall refer to only in passing, since they seem to have been written with his left hand (he himself described them as "samples of work I sold in order to finance the writing of the novels") and he has no special talent for short fiction in any case.

Vonnegut's first novel, *Player Piano*, appeared in 1952, when he had just turned thirty, and was widely (if not always favorably) reviewed as a "serious" book; since, despite its projection into the future and its science-fiction gimmicks, it represented quite obviously the kind of earnest social criticism which suggests comparisons with quite respectable writers like Aldous Huxley and George Orwell. In its earlier pages especially, it seems now, in fact, *too* bent on suggesting such comparisons, more committed to morality than play, more concerned with editorial than invention; grimly intent on proving (once more!) that machines deball and dehumanize men—and that the huge corporation, called the Ilium Works but evidently modeled on the General Electric plant in Schenectady, for which Vonnegut once did P.R., corrupts those it nominates as an elite even as it strips of all dignity those it finds unworthy to program its computers. But before *Player Piano* is through, Vonnegut's sense of humor has mitigated his indignation, and he is pursuing (quite like those younger contemporaries, Jules Feiffer or Joseph Heller, for instance) any possibility of a joke, no matter how poor or in the midst of no matter what horror: anticipating, in fact, the mode later called, ineptly enough, "Black Humor."

What *Player Piano* conspicuously lacks, however, is a writer-spokesman at the center. Its point-of-view protagonist is a skeptical technocrat, an engineer who has lost faith in a world fashioned exclusively by those who share his skills; and among his enemies are included the kind of Pop writers who, in a world controlled by machines, provide ready-made dreams of man in a state of nature, whether bare-chested bargemen on the Erie Canal or Tarzan swinging homeward toward Jane in the treetops. Yet Vonnegut is at his best in the book when he himself indulges in Pop fantasy—anticipating what he can do best, as he invents the Ghost Shirt Society: that association of rebels against the white man's technology, who assume the bulletproof magic garb of those desperate Indians who fought vainly to stem the tide of European immigration in the late nineteenth century, and who, like their Indian counterparts, go down to defeat, destroyed by the technology of men too stupid to know the truth of magic.

Yet he seems not to have known how to deal with what he had begun to guess; for *Player Piano* is followed by seven years of silence—seven years in which he published no novels at all, only stories for the slicks. But he emerges from that silence with a pair of books which between them constitute his main achievement: *The Sirens of Titan*, which appeared in 1959, and *Cat's Cradle*, which was published in 1963. In these two fictions, at any rate, he seems at ease—in a way he was not earlier and would not be later—with science fiction; finding in its conventions not a kind of restriction, but a way of releasing his own sentimental-ironic view of a meaningless universe redeemed by love; his own unrecognized need to write a New Gospel or at least to rewrite the Old; his distrusted longing to indulge his fantasy without providing the unimaginative one more occasion for idle masturbation; his unconfessed desire to escape both the stifling inwardness of the traditional art-novel and the empty virtuosity of avant-garde experiment.

The Sirens of Titan appeared as a paperback original, perhaps because hard-cover publishers would have nothing to do with him. And yet, in a sense they did not intend, the publishers are right; what he begins in *Sirens of Titan*, confirms in *Cat's Cradle*, does not belong in hardcovers at all—being admirably suited to the not-quite-book snatched on the run in airports or picked up to allay boredom in bus terminals. Acquiring them so we are not tempted to hoard them, but lose them as good things should cheerfully be lost (sitting down to write this article, I discovered that *all* of my Vonnegut books had been mislaid or borrowed and not returned); and reading them, we are not tempted to believe ourselves set apart by the rareness of our pleasure or the subtlety of our understanding. Like all Pop art, they confirm our solidarity with everyone who can read at all, or merely dream over pages devoted to evoking the mystery of space and time, or to prophesying the end of man.

Mother Night, however, which appeared two years after *Sirens*, in 1961, temporarily interrupts Vonnegut's continuing exploration of the potentialities of science fiction—representing perhaps a desire to be more immediately topical, more directly political, more "serious" in short. It is not unsuccessful in its own terms, but finally irrelevant to Vonnegut's special vocation, though deeply concerned with Germany and World War II, which is Vonnegut's other obsessive subject matter: the past he remembers, rather than the future he extrapolates or invents. *Mother Night* does not quite manage to deal with the American fire-bombing of Dresden, through which Vonnegut actually lived as a prisoner of war—but it flirts with it throughout. This past year, he has come closer in *Slaughterhouse-Five*; but even that novel is less about Dresden than about Vonnegut's failure to come to terms with it—one of those beautifully frustrating works about their own impossibility, like Fellini's *Eight and a half*. And it is inevitable, perhaps, that Howard W. Campbell Jr., the protagonist of *Mother Night*, appears in the later book as well, quoted one more (final?) time in the tale Vonnegut could not make him tell first time around.

Eschewing science fiction in *Mother Night*, however, Vonnegut turns to another, more established Pop form, the spy novel. It is, in fact, dedicated to Mata Hari, the evocation of whose name introduces a disturbing note of irony; since she has become not merely a byword, but a comic one. The story itself is, however, serious enough; the tale of a double agent, unable to prove for a long time that he was really in the pay of the U.S. Government and unwilling, finally, to save himself from hanging when that proof is unexpectedly offered. Self-condemned and self-executed, Howard W. Campbell leaves behind a book intended to testify that one is always—hopelessly, irrecoverably—what he pretends to be, pretends to himself he is *only* pretending to be.

Campbell is, in fact, the first major author-protagonist in Vonnegut; and, like his own author, a Pop artist before history makes him an autobiographer. He has become for the large German public a successful playwright; and for the smaller public of two, constituted by himself and his wife, a private pornographer. Once the war is over, however, and he has fled back to his native America, his works fall into the hands of a Soviet writer who achieves a second round of best-sellerdom, claiming the translated versions as his own. And why not, since such fables are anonymous, international—pass not only from hand to hand, but from country to country as well. This Campbell does not really understand—but it does not deeply trouble him. What really does is the fact that his Russian counterpart has published (with illustrations) a large edition of his own private porn—titillating the great public with what was intended for the tiniest of elites.

And if Campbell responds so extravagantly to having become, inadvertently, a pornographer, this is surely because his author is especially hung up on the subject of porn, the sole Pop form which, in fact, evades him—despite a theoretical dedication to freeing men to lead full sexual lives. Vonnegut cannot ever quite manage to talk dirty enough to be explicit about sex: though (because?) he is haunted throughout his work by a vision of his own books ending up in the display windows of pornographic bookshops, confused by owners and customers alike with hard-core pornography. He is aware really that the confusion is, on the deepest level, somehow valid; that the best of science fiction has in common with the shabbiest sort of erotica, not sex but "fantasies of an impossibly hospitable world."

But he is not really at ease with the fact; and throughout his work, especially as it grows more and more unguardedly confessional, there appears over and over the image of that first of all pornographic photos, in which a girl is vainly trying to screw a Shetland pony: produced, he tells us, by the favorite student of Daguerre, and therefore an apt symbol of revolutionary art becoming (quickly, quickly) a Pop commodity, to be peddled to the unwary on street corners. Yet what bugs Vonnegut even more is the awareness that in his own time pornography is practiced, and accepted, as revolutionary art itself, a special way of telling the truth about the society we live in; and he parodies mercilessly, in *God Bless You, Mr. Rosewater*, a novelist presumably dedicated to absolute candor who ends up writing: "I twisted her arm until she opened her legs, and she gave a little scream, half joy, half pain (how do you figure a woman?) as I rammed the old avenger home"—which one suspects is intended as a put-down of Norman Mailer.

In the end, however, the spy novel proved for Vonnegut almost as unsympathetic as pornography itself—more unsympathetic, in fact, since the story of espionage posits a world of total alienation rather than one of impossible hospitality. He could not find room in it, moreover, for magic and wonder, the religious dimension so necessary to his view of man. Campbell is a writer, a popular artist, but he is not a guru, and Vonnegut could scarcely imagine him writing a new bible. What religious leaders appear in *Mother Night* are presented as comic nuts gathered together in a tiny American neo-Nazi Party: a defrocked priest and a dentist-minister, convinced that a man's teeth are the key to his character, and founder of the Western Hemisphere University of the Bible, by which, it turns out later, the witch doctor in *Cat's Cradle* has been ordained.

That shadowy figure of Dr. Vox Humana represents, in fact, the sole link between *Mother Night* and the book which follows it, in which Vonnegut returns again to the kind of science fiction he had already so successfully exploited in *The Sirens of Titan*, his best book, I think—most totally achieved, most nearly dreamed rather than contrived. In it, he evokes all the themes, along with their sustaining images, for which we remember him with special affection and amusement: the unreality of time and the consequent possibility of traveling therein, the illusory nature of free will and the consequent possibility of heroism and sacrifice; the impossibility of really choosing one's mate and the consequent necessity to love whomever, whatever happens to come to hand. It is, moreover, his most *chutzpahdik*, his most outrageously and attractively arrogant book; for in it he dares not only to ask the ultimate question about the meaning of human life, but to *answer* it.

But what sets *The Sirens of Titan* apart is that, inventing it, Vonnegut has escaped from the limitations of an imagination narrower and more provincial than it is ever possible quite to remember. Despite his dedication to a form predicated on space-travel, Vonnegut is oddly earthbound, American-bound really; there are, in fact, only three localities in which his invention is at home: Ilium, New York, the country around Indianapolis, and Cape Cod—not, one notices uneasily, any of those mythological metropolises so congenial to the minds of most writers of science fiction. In *The Sirens of Titan*, however, he imagined for the first time Tralfamadore, the transgalactic world he is to evoke again and again, but to which none of his space-travelers even actually go; until, perhaps, the Billy Pilgrim of his last book, and which we are free, therefore, to understand for the absolute Elsewhere, more easily reached by art or madness than by mere technology. And he has also described in its pages Mars and a Moon of Saturn called Titan, to and from which his protagonist, Malachi Constant, shuttles, returning at last to Indianapolis, where he dies waiting for a bus.

More central, though, to Vonnegut's own development is the antagonist, who is whirled at the book's close quite out of our solar system and our ken; that Winston Niles Rumfoord, who is both author and guru, as articulate and omnipotent as Prospero on his Island, and who seeming to want to rule the world turns out only to have longed to create a religion. He manages in fact to launch from Mars a doomed expedition of brainwashed mercenaries, whose intended defeat causes all men on Earth to recoil from conflict and self-delusion, and to live together in peace, worshipping according to the tenets of the Church of God the Utterly Indifferent, whose messiah-scapegoat is Malachi Constant himself. But in the end Rumfoord proves as little in charge of his own destiny as Constant; since not only his two books, but all of his complex maneuvering of men—and, indeed, the whole course of human history which made his actions possible—are revealed as having been plotted, by almost immortal Tralfamadorians, intent only on getting a spare part to one of their messengers, stranded on Titan with a trivial communication to another planet far across the universe. This is not, however, the work's final word, Vonnegut's final position; for that very messenger, it turns out, though an intricate machine, has learned somehow to love in the aeons he has spent as a castaway; and he provides—like a kindly Pop artist—a vision of Paradise to sustain Malachi's dying moments; a false vision sustained by posthypnotic suggestion, but sufficient to make dying more palatable than living. It is as much of a Happy Ending as Kurt Vonnegut could imagine at this point in his career, as much of a Happy Ending—he tries to persuade us—as we need or can use.

But in *Cat's Cradle*, his next work of science fiction, he does not even offer us this token Happy Ending, for that book begins and ends with a vision of the total destruction of mankind, to which only an eternal gesture of contempt is an adequate response. It is a book which has nothing to do with Heaven except insofar as it is not there ("No cat! No cradle!"), though it takes place largely on an island paradise in the Caribbean, which stirs in us once more memories of that Master of Illusion, Prospero. This time, however, the Prospero who regulates the actions of everyone else is dead before the fiction begins; a certain Dr. Felix Hoenikker, referred to throughout as "the father of the Atomic Bomb." He is a more equivocal figure even than Rumfoord, the hero-villain of *The Sirens of Titan*.

The name Rumfoord appears over and over in Vonnegut's stories and novels, always signifying the kind of Groton-Harvard-educated W.A.S.P., before whom—as a Midwestern German American—he feels that fascinated repulsion all of us Americans experience confronted by some absolute alien who happens to have got here before us. The Hoenikkers, father and children, like Vonnegut bear a name which memorializes their connection with a European people who made soap of dead Jews and were themselves roasted, boiled, turned to tinder by bombs from American planes. And before those Germans he feels the fascinated repulsion all of us Americans experience confronting the particular people abroad from whose midst our ancestors fled, but who persist still in our flesh, our dreams; and with whom therefore we die a little, when we come to bomb them.

Cat's Cradle is presented as if told by an almost anonymous narrator (we learn his first name John-Jonah, are left to guess his last—Vonnegut, perhaps?), who begins by trying to write the history of total destruction (called in his case, *The Day the World Ended*), with which Vonnegut himself was still wrestling in vain. For John-Jonah, however, it was to be a book about Hiroshima rather than Dresden, and in the end he does not even manage that—his imagination (and Vonnegut's) preempted not by the Atomic Bomb, which did not quite end the world, but by Hoenikker's next, posthumous invention, which did: not by the final fire, but the final ice—a kind of super-ice, called Ice-9, which melts at 114 degrees Fahrenheit, and with which Hoenikker was playing like a child at the moment of his death.

John-Jonah moves among the heirs who share the invention—old Hoenikker's children, along with their lovers and friends—learning slowly, painfully how to become yet one more Vonnegut sacrificial victim: the patsy and reluctant messiah of yet one more true, i.e., false, religion. At the book's close, he lies frozen for all eternity, his thumb to his nose and a history of the world clasped to his side. He has learned this sacred gesture of contempt for the God or not-God behind the universe from Bokonon, a Black Prophet who is Vonnegut's most impressive rebel-guru; and who, just before his own suicide, composed the final sentence of his Scriptures, as if for John-Jonah's special benefit:

"If I were a younger man, I would write a history of human stupidity; and I would climb to the top of Mount McCabe . . . and I would make a statue of myself, lying on my back, and thumbing my nose at You Know Who."

Indeed, the not-quite nihilism of the book's close is a product of the tension between the religion of Bokononism, which advocates formulating and believing sacred lies, and the vision granted to the dwarfed son of the Father of the Bomb of the emptiness behind all lies, however sacred. The voice of the White Dwarf and the Black Prophet are both Vonnegut's, and they answer each other inconclusively throughout; creating an ambiguity quite like that produced by the opposite claims of High Art (the Dwarf, an avant-garde painter, renders his view in monochrome abstraction) and Pop Art (Bokonon, an entertainer, sings his creed in calypso form).

But, as ever in Vonnegut, something more is presented than the unresolvable conflict of mutually exclusive theories: namely, the possibility of actual joy. John, at any rate, is revealed as having experienced two great joys before his tale is told: one slow and long-continued, as he learns who are the other members of his *karass*, the

Slaughterhouse-Five *is a novel that deals with four levels of time and two worlds. The principal subject is the 1945 destruction of Dresden. Vonnegut has denied that the experience of surviving the bombing was crucial to his work: "The importance of Dresden in my life has been considerably exaggerated because my book about it became a best seller. If the book hadn't been a best seller, it would seem like a very minor experience in my life. And I don't think people's lives are changed by short-term events like that. Dresden was astonishing, but experiences can be astonishing without changing you."*

handful of others in the world with whom, willy-nilly, he must work out the pattern of his destiny: one intense and momentary, as he plays footsie with the blonde Negress, Mona, whom he, and everyone else, loves: their naked soles touching in the ecstatic union called by Bokononists *"Boko-maru." Cat's Cradle* is then a book about loving; but it is even more, as my own language has been teaching me, the words that suggest themselves to me as I describe it, a book about learning, which means, inevitably, about learning a new language. It is Vonnegut's great good fortune to know this, and to be able to invent such new languages: to create terms like *karass* and *Boko-maru*, which seem to survive, in the heads of his readers, his plots and even his jokes.

Since *Cat's Cradle*, Vonnegut has written a pair of books, *God Bless You, Mr. Rosewater* (1965) and *Slaughterhouse-Five* (1969), which constitute, in fact, a single work, with common characters, common themes, common obsessions and a common whimsy—and which together rifle his earlier books for other characters, themes, obsessions and whimsical asides; as if he is being driven to make his total work seem in retrospect a latter-day Human Comedy or Yoknapatawpha series. But the last novels are quite different in their tone and effect, being essentially autobiographical rather than mythic: quasi-novels really, in which the author returns to his early material reflectively rather than obsessively—and so ends writing *about* it, rather than simply writing it; and thus falls, for better or worse, quite out of the world of Pop art. It is, perhaps, because of this fall that Vonnegut has become more available to established literary critics; or maybe his acceptance is only the inevitable triumph of time. Any writer who has lived so long (and he *has*) tends to seem at last respectable, even admirable—particularly if he is the sort of writer on whose behalf children tirelessly propagandize their parents.

Yet it is wrong finally to learn to love the late Vonnegut first, and to come to his earlier books backwards through the ones which followed. Ideally, a reader should learn his territory as he revealed it: be introduced to Ilium, New York, in *Player Piano*; to Indianapolis and Cape Cod and Tralfamadore in *The Sirens of Titan*. Vonnegut has, to be sure, returned in his last two novels to his three favorite American provinces and the single trans-galactic dream world in which he feels at home; but those worlds are oddly transmogrified. Tralfamadore, especially, has been distanced and ironized into the place "where the flying saucers come from," and serves no longer to release Vonnegut into the world of science fiction, but only as an occasion to make rueful jokes about it.

God Bless You, Mr. Rosewater is not science fiction at all—not even like *Mother Night* a spy story—but a work of "mainstream literature," in which Vonnegut has transposed from the Future and Elsewhere to the Present and Right Here the themes which he once mythologized in popular, fantastic modes: the compelling need to love the unlovable, whose ranks industrialization has disconcertingly swelled; the magical power of money and the holy folly of renouncing it; the uses and abuses of fantasy itself. But the profoundest and most central concern of *Rosewater* is new for Vonnegut; seems in fact more closely related to Norman O. Brown or Michel Foucault or R. D. Laing than what he himself had dealt with earlier. We remember the novel chiefly as a book about madness, or more particularly, as one about the relationship between madness and holiness; since Eliot Rosewater—a millionaire who becomes a Volunteer Fireman and one-man Counseling Service—is the first of Vonnegut's gurus who lives *in* madness rather than *by* lies. He does not, that is to say, choose deliberately to deceive for the sake of the salvation of mankind, but is hopelessly self-deceived: insane enough to accept as truth what Rumfoord was forced to justify as useful fictions, or Bokonon to preach as *foma*, "harmless untruths."

But if *God Bless You, Mr. Rosewater* is not science fiction, it is compulsively *about* science fiction; and this time the writer nearest to its center (Eliot Rosewater himself has only the unfinished scraps of a fantasy novel in his desk) is Kilgore Trout, the author of scores of neglected and despised science fiction novels. As the name itself betrays, however (it contains precisely the same number of letters as "Kurt Vonnegut," and, indeed, the four letters of "Kurt" insist on detaching themselves from the rest), Trout is a comic, self-depreciatory portrait of his author—or rather of what his author might have been, in some sense *was*, up to the moment he wrote the book in which Trout appears. As inappropriate to one on the verge of ambiguous success, Vonnegut portrays his alter ego as an absurd failure, driven to earn his living by supervising paper boys or redeeming Green Stamps, and obsessed by the fact that his books are only available in shops that peddle porn.

Yet it is given to Trout to play an equivocal St. Paul to Eliot Rosewater's absurd Christ: to rationalize Eliot's madness in terms acceptable even to his tycoon father; and yet to prepare Eliot himself for lapsing back into insanity, alcoholism and obesity, after he has been cured of all three by a regime of tennis and tranquilizers in a madhouse. And in *Slaughterhouse-Five*, Trout returns to play a similar role for a similar sub-messiah, this time an optometrist called Billy Pilgrim, who had, as a matter of fact, been introduced to the work of Trout by Eliot himself in the psycho-ward of a military hospital during World War II.

But Billy, unlike Eliot, travels in space and time, actually reaching Tralfamadore itself (invented first by Vonnegut in *The Sirens of Titan*, then reinvented by Trout in *God Bless You, Mr. Rosewater*), where he is displayed naked in a zoo, at work, at play, on the john, and in the arms of Montana Wildhack, a Hollywood starlet imported for mating purposes. Oddly enough, however—as Vonnegut pointedly informs us—Trout had already imagined the zoo episode in fiction, and Billy had read it before living it, or dreaming it, or falling through time and space into it. Vonnegut will not, to be sure, let us side with the cynics and realists who would, by psychiatric means, cure Billy of his belief that he has been and is forever on Tralfamadore; but he leaves suspended, not quite asked, much less answered, the question of whether he travels there through Outer Space or Inner, via madness or flying saucer—or merely by means of Pop fiction, in which each of these is revealed as the metaphor of the other.

Perhaps Vonnegut does not know at all what he is really doing in his last book. Perhaps he even believes what he so stoutly maintains in those sections of it which are more reminiscence and editorial than invention and fantasy; believes that he is at last writing the book he ascribed to John-Jonah in *Cat's Cradle*: the book which he precisely cannot, should not write, which is called archetypally *The Day the World Ended*, and which comes to him not out of his writer's imagination, but out of the duty he feels imposed on him by the fact that he himself lived through the fire-bombing of Dresden.

But though, like his author, Billy Pilgrim lives through that event—and returns to it eternally in contempt of time—he, like his author once more, can only return to it the way of Tralfamadore, which is to say, a world more comic and terrible and real than that of apocalyptic history. And if at last Vonnegut does not understand, all the better for him and for us. What he does not understand is precisely what saves him for readers like me who are disconcerted and dismayed as he grows more and more conscious of more and more in himself, turns more and more from fantasy to analysis.

Perhaps the process has begun to reverse itself, however, in *Slaughterhouse-Five*, or at least in those pages of it in which Billy takes his author back with him into the world of science fiction. I at least find occasion for hope in such passages, as I do in some remarks Vonnegut has included in a recent statement about his future plans and prospects. "I expect," he writes, "to become more and more stupid as time goes by." God bless him.

I was pleased to study anthropology, a science that was mostly poetry, that involved almost no math at all.

From "Kurt Vonnegut: The Art of Fiction LXIV," Paris Review *(Spring 1977)*

INTERVIEW:
60 Minutes, CBS Television (15 September 1970).

Harry Reasoner discusses with Vonnegut his status as a guru for young readers.

REASONER: As America begins, somewhat nervously, a new school year, we have an improbability. The current idol of the country's sensitive and intelligent young people is 47 years old. Young people snap up his books as fast as they are reissued. A reviewer says the books should be read aloud to children, cadets and basic trainees. He is suddenly a star, a luminary, a guru to youth. His gentle fantasies of peace and his dark humor are as current among the young as was J. D. Salinger's work in the 1950's and Tolkien's in the '60's.

Kurt Vonnegut, Jr. is a man who came out of my time of the century and my part of the country. He saw a good deal more of World War II than most of us did who talk about it, and when it was over he began a life-long, reserved brooding about it. He was a prisoner in Dresden, Germany, when the U.S. Air Force came over and fire-bombed it. He brooded about that for twenty years before he finally wrote "Slaughterhouse-Five"—Slaughterhouse Five was the name of the building where he was a prisoner—which is sort of a novel and sort of a cry out of his brooding: the world he has seen since he has left Indianapolis is insane.

Vonnegut spends most of his time in the tranquility of Cape Cod, where he lives, but now he can be found in New York, in a theater in Greenwich Village, agonizing over his new play, "Happy Birthday, Wanda June," a plea for pacifism, he says, which opens next month. He is reluctant to be interviewed for television, but he did agree to chat at the end of a day's rehearsal.

What do you think it is about what you've done that does make you so highly respected by young people who don't go around idolizing a lot of men your age?

VONNEGUT: Well, I'm screamingly funny, you know, I really am in the books. I think so. And that helps because I'm funnier than a lot of people, I think, and that's appreciated by young people. And I talk about stuff Billy Graham won't talk about for instance, you know, is it wrong to kill? And what's God like? And stuff like that. And they like to hear talk like that because they can't get it from the minister, and I show what heaven is like, you know, which you can't get a minister to talk about; that's part of the play. That is a good part of the play is in heaven. And so they want to know. They want to know what happens after you die. And I talk about it. That's a very popular subject.

REASONER: Does it please you to be liked by the young?

VONNEGUT: Older people read me too, you know. I've been writing for—hell, twenty years, so some people who read me when they were twenty, well, they're forty now and so I presume that they're still with me because I hear from people in fairly responsible positions. I heard from Sarge Shriver.

REASONER: (Indistinct)

VONNEGUT: Well, he's a grown-up. Former Ambassador to France.

REASONER: Your last book, "Slaughterhouse-Five," was—well, I wouldn't attempt to characterize it but it's been characterized as a very powerful anti-war book, and full of concern about things that have happened in the last fifty years, and yet in the last few months, you've been quoted a good many times talking to young people and saying don't get involved, take it easy and go out and look at the sunset. Is there a paradox there?

VONNEGUT: There's no paradox there. It's intolerable to me that they should be shot and I think they are in great danger of being injured. I know after the Kent State disaster, I spoke at Lehigh, just coincidentally spoke at Lehigh, and a lot of the students really wanted a call to battle. And my feeling as a grown-up was that they should be told what battle is like and so I have been delivering lectures on how to fight a tank and how to fight a machine gun and it's very hard to do and a very easy way to get killed.

REASONER: Are you talking—when you said to, I think it was a small girl's graduating class somewhere, when you said in effect, relax, there are a lot of beautiful things in life before you have to take on the burdens of the older generation.

VONNEGUT: I told the girls at Sea Pine, these little girls, please don't go out and save the world and don't let your parents tell you that it's your turn to save the world because it isn't yet. And there was a great cheer that went up from the student body as they were most relieved. I was telling, at a slightly more severe lecture for the Bennington girls, it's because they can do more. They're in a position to do more. But actually to be an effective person politically in this country, I think you have to be thirty or over, and also you have to be rich, well-placed, you have to be close to power. And I don't think that young people, because they look young, can do much, as I think they are counterproductive.

REASONER: Well, some of us journalists have been saying, since 1968, that it was a couple of thousand kids who went up into New Hampshire that to some extent did do a lot and turned the country around and drove an incumbent President out of office.

VONNEGUT: Yeah, that was exciting and I'm no political scientist, I simply sense that it won't happen again, if another children's crusade is launched. For one thing, the opposition has been firmed up as no one expected this successful attack in Vermont or New Hampshire. But it is expected now, and those who are opposed to college kids are waiting for them now to—to campaign against them. This was a surprise attack.

REASONER: You come out of all this, I would guess, calling yourself a pessimist. Would you accept that label?

VONNEGUT: Well, things do seem to get worse.

REASONER: Would it be fair to say you see no hope for the world and mankind?

Front page 'New York Times Book Review':

"An extraordinary success... A book we need to read, and to reread."

"Splendid art and simplicity . . . Kurt Vonnegut was present as a prisoner of war (so it goes, as he would say) at the Dresden fire-bomb raid in 1945—possibly the greatest atrocity ever committed by Americans and certainly the quietest . . . Vonnegut says it took him more than 20 years to write a novel about it, and in a sense he hasn't written one yet. As though blinded by the glare of the fire bombs, he has turned his back on the raid and written a parable instead . . . SLAUGHTERHOUSE-FIVE is written with nerve-racking control: a funny book at which you are not permitted to laugh, a sad book without tears, a book of carefully strangled emotions. A tale told in a slaughterhouse."
—*Wilfrid Sheed, Life Magazine*

"Very tough and very funny; it is sad and it is delightful; and it works... Kurt Vonnegut knows all the tricks of the writing game. So he has not even tried to describe the bombing. Instead he has written around it in a highly imaginative, often funny, nearly psychedelic story."
—*Christopher Lehmann-Haupt, New York Times*

"A work of keen literary artistry . . . by one of our most gifted and incisive novelists . . . On the basis of one brief meeting and a few short novels, the suspicion grew on me that Kurt Vonnegut, Jr. was perhaps the best person of all in this nation of ours that now numbers more than two hundred million citizens. His new novel, SLAUGHTERHOUSE-FIVE, strengthens that strange notion considerably."
—*Joseph Heller, author of 'Catch-22'*

"Uniquely fascinating on a level attained by only our best novelists."
—*Barbara Bannon, Publishers' Weekly*

"Vivid reading . . . [It is] in a class above war books that tell it straight—this is a deliberately staged hunt for the poetry there's supposed to be in the pity, but which isn't there at all. Vonnegut's patient but loaded account of Billy Pilgrim's misadventures in the abattoir called history is his way of specifying the meaninglessness of war . . . A work of sensitive acerbity, in which imagination triumphs in the presence of so much human ash, SLAUGHTERHOUSE-FIVE is also an object-lesson in the mind's agility and fecundity. It shows what the mind can manage to do with itself when confronted with horrors it cannot dismiss and cannot change."
—*Paul West, Chicago Sun-Times Book Week*

"Terrifying implications . . . Vonnegut really is a sardonic humorist and satirist in the vein of Mark Twain and Jonathan Swift . . . His satire sweeps widely, touching on education, religion, advertising, and many other subjects. There is a passage about free will that Mark Twain might have written in his late and bitter years . . . There is some amusing business about pornography . . . But the central target is the institution of war . . .

"As I read it, I could hear Vonnegut's mild voice, see his dead pan as he told a ludicrous story, and gasp as I grasped the terrifying implications of some calm remark . . . Vonnegut lives and breathes in the book, and that is one reason why it is the best he has written."
—*Granville Hicks, Saturday Review*

"Funny, compassionate and wise . . . Serious critics have shown some reluctance to acknowledge that Vonnegut is among the best writers of his generation. He is, I suspect, both too funny and too intelligent for many, who confuse muddled earnestness with profundity. Vonnegut is not confused. He sees all too clearly . . . He is a true artist."
—*Robert Scholes, front page New York Times Book Review*

1st, 2nd and 3rd printings sold out! 4th printing just off press—$5.95 at all bookstores now.

a seymour lawrence book

delacorte press

DELL PUBLISHING CO., INC.

From New York Times, *14 April 1969*

VONNEGUT: Yeah, I see some, as I can see maybe forty years' more hope. And I can see help for people like myself and kids like mine, as we can retreat. I don't have to stay anywhere in order to hold a job. I can go run away, as my son has gone to British Columbia now. He's straight with the draft, he's not there as a resister, although he would have resisted. But he went up there and he's bought himself eighty-two acres on salt water. He's got a salt-waterfront there and he can continue to retreat up into British Columbia as things get tougher. And I'm thinking of getting off of Cape Cod now and moving somewhere out, but there are a hell of a lot of people who are cornered. And when they finally get me it's going to be like getting Marie Antoinette, you know, the very last one.

REASONER: Does your ability to run away, or the ability of the people you know, your children and my children, to run away, in effect give you any kind of guilt feeling? Do you think we ought to be in helping or pitching in?

VONNEGUT: I feel guilty about my children running away because I think I must have told them something wrong. I'd like them to stay. I would like them to become professionals because they are intelligent and college isn't tough for them. And if they would do what their father told them to do, they'd become lawyers and they'd become doctors, that sort of thing. People with really useful skills. And so far they've declined to do this. I'm embarrassed about that.

REASONER: If you were seventeen or eighteen now, would you not run away to write novels in a room? Would you become an activist?

VONNEGUT: If I were seventeen or eighteen and had decided to be a political activist, there's a very good chance I would become a bomb-maker, because at seventeen or eighteen, that isn't very old you know, and I might decide that that was the thing to do.

REASONER: But at forty some you deplore it?

VONNEGUT: Oh, yes. Yeah, if it would work, you see, if the bombs would work then you'd have something else, but they're not going to do any good.

REASONER: You say that you would advise seventeen or eighteen-year-olds to be uninvolved for a while, and yet you say if you were seventeen or eighteen you would probably be making bombs. Can you clarify that?

VONNEGUT: Well, I remember what it was to be seventeen or eighteen, what it was like to be me and I was a follower of fashion and I did want a big rep, and I also wanted to be socially effective and I think I would probably decide that bombing was useful and I'd probably do it. It would be wrong but I would do it. It would be wrong because it wouldn't work.

REASONER: Does it worry you talking to the young, in other words, you're speaking to them about heaven and God and the nature of life.

VONNEGUT: No, it doesn't worry me. I don't think I've corrupted anybody.

REASONER: Are you giving them the information that they need, a philosophy that will be good for them?

VONNEGUT: Well, I'm giving them information that will make them kinder. You know, you can give them certain kinds of information that would make them extremely tough, you know, about what God wants and all that, so you just make up something that would tend to make people gentle. It's all made up anyway, you know, we really don't know anything about that stuff.

REASONER: It may be that Kurt Vonnegut speaks so clearly to youth because he doesn't think of them as any different from the rest of us: just people who are younger but growing older as he speaks to them, which is something most of them sense. In any event it is reassuring that a man of my age can be an idol of the young. He reminds me of a man I knew who was asked if he didn't sometimes feel overwhelmed when he thought of all the young people crowding on from below as he got older. No, he said, I don't think of myself as getting older: I think of them as rapidly becoming contemporaries.

While looking as much like a bloodhound as possible, announce that you are working twelve hours a day on a masterpiece. Warning: All is lost if you crack a smile.

From Vonnegut's "Funnier on Paper than Most People," in his Palm Sunday

REVIEW:

Jack Kroll, "No More Heroes," *Newsweek*, 76 (19 October 1970): 123.

When Vonnegut read The Odyssey *for a "great books" course in 1955, "Odysseus the war hero coming home from the wars really got to me," and he wrote a play, "Penelope." Rewritten as* Happy Birthday, Wanda June, *it had a run of 142 Off-Broadway performances.*

Almost every time an American novelist writes a play he shows up most of our thumb-tongued playwrights, who lack the melody of mind, the wit, dash and accuracy of Saul Bellow and Bruce Jay Friedman. And the same thing must be said of the writing in *Happy Birthday, Wanda June*, the first play by novelist Kurt Vonnegut, Jr., to be produced. Vonnegut's dialogue is not only fast and funny, with a palpable taste and crackle, but it also means something. And his comic sense is a superior one; "Wanda June" has as many laughs as anything by Neil Simon.

But of course there is more to plays than writing, and here, just as with Bellow and Friedman, Vonnegut has far to go. "Wanda June" means to be a play of ideas, with characters who embody social vectors and moral assumptions. Vonnegut wants to attack those dreadful fake heroes whose crushing handshakes imply moral impotence, who believe in violence and the false rituals of machismo. But Vonnegut is no Shaw; there is a lot of uncarbonated Saroyan in his punch, a lot of good old American media-vaudeville willing to settle for the kind of message-entertainment that ultimately befogs the moral atmosphere with an aerosol cloud of speciously sweet righteousness.

Vonnegut has cleverly built his play on the Odyssey, when Ulysses returns home after the wars. Vonnegut's Ulysses is Harold Ryan (Kevin McCarthy), a rich hunter, who returns after having been lost in the South American jungle for eight years with a buddy, Looseleaf Harper (who had dropped the atom bomb on Nagasaki), to find his wife (named Penelope, of course) besieged by two suitors—a loudmouth vacuum-cleaner salesman who brings his XKE experimental vacuum cleaner on dates so it won't fall into competitors' hands, and a peace-loving, violin-playing physician.

Ryan is a silly brute and male chauvinist who has spent his life killing animals—and men—in jungles and on battlefields with everything from guns and knives to piano wire, cyanide capsules and his bare hands. The poles of his life have been the killing ground and the bedroom, but we learn that his lovemaking is as quick as his trigger finger.

The wife had been a mindless carhop whom Ryan had scooped up one day along with his hamburger. In the years her dazzling husband (a blend of Hemingway and Howard Hughes) has been missing she has grown from the "springbok" he remembers to a creature with a mind and moral sensitivity. She has just about decided to marry the gentle physician (who tests his masculinity by going into the park at midnight, to make sure his pacifism is not a front for cowardice), when Harold returns.

The confrontations among all of the characters occur in a series of scenes which also include, amusingly, interludes in Heaven involving among others a Nazi officer who delivers a hilarious monologue in which he admiringly recounts his own wartime death at the hands of the intrepid Ryan. In the end, the brutal hunter is outfaced and spiritually broken by the doctor and the wife, who tell him he is a ludicrous fossil and that "new heroes are trying to save the planet. They have no time for useless killing." (One of the ways in which the play is fatally soft for serious purposes is the begging of the question of violence as part of the new social sensibility.)

Under Michael J. Kane's somewhat soft direction the actors produce a kind of middle charm just this side of style. Closest to it are Marsha Mason, who has the grown-up gamin quality of Barbara Harris and Brenda Vaccaro,

Marsha Mason and Kevin McCarthy in Happy Birthday, Wanda June

After a run of 142 performances, Happy Birthday, Wanda June *was made into a movie starring Susannah York and Rod Steiger. Calling the 1971 Columbia Pictures release "one of the most embarrassing movies ever made," Vonnegut said he was quite pleased when "it sank like a rock." He is shown above with producer/director Mark Robson.*

and veteran Method-man William Hickey, who turns Looseleaf into a creature festooned with discomfitures. "The world is teeming with women—ours to enjoy," booms McCarthy. "You know, every time I think like that," replies Hickey, "I get the clap."

BOOK REVIEW:

J. G. Keogh and Edward Kislaitis, "*Slaughterhouse-Five* & The Future of Science Fiction," *Media & Methods* (January 1971): 38-39, 48.

This review analyzes Vonnegut's method, characterizing his use of science fiction as a means to convey a surrealistic view of existence.

Kurt Vonnegut's latest novel *Slaughterhouse-Five* is a minor masterpiece which ticks away as smoothly as the barometer clock powered by the alterations in atmospheric pressure described in it. Its hero Billy Pilgrim is an unwilling time-traveller whose science-fictionlike predicament increasingly reminds us of the plight of modern man, not sure whether he's living in the past or the future, and sometimes having the baffled conviction that he is living in all times at once. Billy Pilgrim is a victim of future shock. And if clocks can be run by atmospheric pressure—itself conditioned by the attraction of gravity—then perhaps time itself, which we like to consider an absolute, is subject to the whims of unknown forces.

Billy's problem is that he keeps coming "unstuck in time," bounced back and forth between his experiences as a German prisoner of war (like Vonnegut, he survives the firebombing of Dresden) and his post-war career as a successful optometrist in Ilium, N.Y. What Billy calls time-travelling some people may call memory, to be sure, and the ultimate effect of the novel's technique may simply be to give us a glimpse of that timeless thing that most people call "personality." The novel's many space-warps and time-jumps are simply a conventional science-fiction plot used as metaphoric frame for a bit of genuinely popular surrealism (much as Graham Greene uses the dream-vision).

The surreal experience is of course nothing new, having been around in France these past hundred years, but for a book like Vonnegut's—a best-seller list staple for a long time—it comes as a bit of a shock. Human death, for example, is mentioned quite casually as only one more instant in anyone's full lifetime. Death is mentioned as a matter of course, always followed by the fatalistic phrase, "So it goes," and eventually propelling us into a sort of stoic mysticism. Vonnegut has always been a cynic, and while people in this novel may die as a result of something, they never die *for* something. It's all much the same, whether it's Jesus Christ (who was "well-connected") or a glass of water:

> There was a still life on Billy's bedside table—two pills, an ashtray with three lipstick-stained cigarettes in it, one cigarette still burning, and a glass of water. The water was dead. So it goes. Air was trying to get out of that dead water. Bubbles were clinging to the walls of the glass, too weak to climb out.

This spot of description is from the section showing Billy in the Veteran's Hospital after the war, being visited by his mother, and follows the twin laws of surrealism as revealed by James Thurber and Nathanael West. (1) Treat the wild things with nonchalance, and the tame things wildly. (2) Take violence as a matter of course, but describe the most innocent things (like glasses of water) with violent intensity. It is a prescription for symbolist poetry which can perhaps only be understood in an age of urban technology, where violence is taken for granted, and the most innocent things can hurt and kill.

There are of course less tame moments in Billy's prison camp and they are ruthlessly domesticated, if not thoroughly broken, by the rigorous reins of scientific law. Billy hangs "self-crucified" from the ventilator of a cattle-car, en route to the camp, as a sort of subhuman

The 1972 movie of Slaughterhouse-Five, *written by Stephen Geller and directed by George Roy Hill, was highly successful. Michael Saks (Billy Pilgrim) and Valerie Perrine (Montana Wildhack) are shown in this still.*

mediator of all feces. (When he isn't passing down food, he passes out waste.)

> Billy coughed when the door was opened, and when he coughed he shit thin gruel. This was in accordance with the Third Law of Motion according to Sir Isaac Newton. This law tells us that for every action there is a reaction which is equal and opposite in direction:

If Vonnegut is rather late arriving on the surrealist bandwagon (which the Beatles have driven for the last half-decade), and if he is an almost too patient explicator of his own mode (every flashback and flashforth has its key transitional phrase), perhaps the best excuse that can be offered for his hard, gemlike prose is its unqualified success. *Slaughterhouse-Five* (the satiric analogue to *Catch 22*) burns with a hard, phosphoruslike flame, and drops on its readers like a stick of firebombs.

Billy Pilgrim, fat, fiftyish and optometrist, leads a triple existence in Ilium, N.Y. as a staid businessman, young prisoner of war, and zoo specimen for the curious inhabitants of the musical planet Tralfamadore four billion light years away, who look at all things *sub specie æternitatis* through eyes in the palms of their hands. Billy's mind jumps back and forth quite unpredictably from the Children's Crusade (the book's code subtitle for World War II) to the over-solemn carnival of grown-up suburbia. All this furious mental activity gyrates around one horrible still point, the fire-bombing of Dresden and the resultant incineration of nearly 200,000 civilians. Billy weeps after the event—not so much out of shame for being an American, but because he is rebuked by an old refugee couple for maltreating a horse. Vonnegut does not say much about the fact that Dresden had been full of Eastern refugees, but one can only look on with awe at the Allies' final solution to the displaced persons problem. Thanks to the ingenuity of modern technology, an entire city was turned into a mass-grave overnight, and Billy almost alone comes out of it alive to tell the story, as Vonnegut did to write the novel. Dresden was indeed an apocalyptic event quite out of time (though the novel was published only after the twenty-five-year limit covering the documentation of such massacres), and one that for Billy must be viewed eternally, from all possible dimensions of time, if only to preserve one's sanity. The shock has to be spread out over a lifetime, and it is this multiplicity of dimensions which gives Vonnegut's book (as it gave Eliot's *Waste Land*) its guts of compassion.

Slaughterhouse-Five builds on several of the themes from Vonnegut's earlier work (philanthropist Rosewater, fascist Campbell, Tralfamadore) which intersect each other in an intriguing polyphony that can only mean that perhaps at last Vonnegut has produced his masterwork. It is an astute parody of several of his earlier books—and while good writers often steal from others, and bad writers always imitate themselves, perhaps only the master writers are ever able successfully to parody themselves.

Traditionally, science-fiction has worked like the most conventional medieval allegory, with the content adjusted to the twentieth century. Spaceships and modern technology are the hardware which symbolizes the myth of eternal progress. Once reality catches up with such predictions (even Christ was a prophet of doom) the images are sure to lose their symbolic value. Vonnegut once said that most science-fiction is a popularization of technology invented fully thirty years before it (perhaps in order to assist its marketing by Madison Ave.). Once the myth is dead, and in the interim before the generation of an entirely new set of symbols, the *rictus mortis* known as black humor begins to set in—if only to fill the vacuum. Vonnegut's new book, together with his earlier departure from the clique of professional science-fiction writers, is as plain an indication of the death of science-fiction old-style, as is the new writing of J. G. Ballard and Brian Aldiss. Even Kubrick's *2001* seems to be composed more of religious than of scientific mysticism. HAL is not only a cryptogram for the initials IBM, but is also an exact transcription of one of the seven oldest of the nine billion names of God, the Semitic name 'AL (perhaps more familiar to us as 'ALLAH).

Slaughterhouse-Five crosses the border-line from science-fiction into black humor when it becomes obvious that the s-f plot is there to provide dramatic contrast with the only too real (super-real) technology of mass civilian bombing practiced during the twentieth century, when conscripted civilian soldiers bombed the defense-counterparts. The fire-bombing of Dresden was more dramatic because it was done to Europeans (always more human than Orientals, although perhaps less so to speakers of English). For some strange reason the carnage resulting from mass bombing-raids has always proved more acceptable to the general public than the assembly-line slaughter of civilian conscriptees during the WWI. Perhaps it was merely more acceptable to the soldiers themselves. It was certainly more efficient in the extinction of excess, unwanted population. And modern war is perhaps only the most obvious example of the extent to which the latest technology brings regress to barbarism, which may be the only "progress" ever worshipped by the primitives of a new civilization. Unlike the satirist or the apologist, the black humorist adopts a more conservative stance which is disliked by both sides. Unlike the movies *Catch 22* or *MASH*, the surrealist simply provides us with an artfully juxtaposed version of the facts, a "documentary" account of the cultural impact of any new technology, as did Heller's original novel.

Both Jacques Ellul and Marshall McLuhan pointed out years ago that the barbarism in which most new technology results is a direct consequence of the establishment of technocracies run for the sake of machines, whether mechanical or political, as opposed to societies run for people—all done according to the only esthetic principle which a machine understands, efficiency. Mass man, the end-product of such assembly lines, has been the subject of many satires from Kafka through Orwell, but it is only recently that the subject of these predictions (both encaustic and encomniac) has become enough of a reality to be dealt with realistically. The result is surreal (super-real): intelligent computers competing with mechanical men for a decent livelihood, and it is a result predicted by both H. G. Wells and Wyndham Lewis. But whereas they could only prophesy, we live with the results, and our reactions are neither wholly hostile nor implacably optimistic. We look at our reflections in the polished chrome as if laughing through a gas, darkly.

The future arrives when man makes the discovery that human technology is neither all good nor all bad, but like Adam's legendary "knowledge," a mixture of good and evil, with both good and bad consequences inextricably mixed together. After a technical revolution, about the only thing it is possible to be sure of is that the previous culture has irrevocably changed, and a new one has taken its place. Surrealism is thus a matter of tradition and the individual technology. The conflict between generations, in which for one generation at least the surreality which is the meaning of black humor is the interface between the faces that we meet and the masks we make, too many of them unfortunately tragic. Black humor takes the tragic experience, and treats it comically, leaving the purer forms as the vehicles of survival emotion for later and less affected generations. The result is either melodrama (as in the case of the Victorians) or, in the case of Vonnegut and Ballard, dark satyr plays.

What does all this mean? Among other things, that we are headed for the end of literature and science-fiction as we know it, hardly surprising perhaps but nonetheless surreal. In a transitional age the simpler and more "sublime" forms (tragedy, ode, romance) are quite impossible, and men opt instead for the grotesques of satire and the burlesques of the comically absurd, or the tragically comic. To do anything else is both academic and irrelevant, a procedure no more sensible than that of those writers of Senecan tragedy in the age of Shakespeare. The products of course are monsters, hardly likely to be cherished as "classics" by later generations, and certainly not written for them. A secular apocalypse, surrealism remains a vision of an afterlife that most of us are unlikely ever to live to witness—bejeweled and multifaceted—an after-life gleams dully in the remote present as though it were a semi-precious stone.

Book Review:

Benjamin DeMott, "Vonnegut's Otherworldly Laughter," *Saturday Review*, 54 (1 May 1971): 29-32, 38.

This omnibus review of Vonnegut's first six novels attempts to account for his "youthcult" appeal and to assess the strengths and weaknesses of his work.

Bulletin: Kurt Vonnegut, Jr., has broken out of the pack in the Youthcult Hero Stakes, leaving Norman Mailer, Herbert Marcuse, R. D. Laing, A. S. Neill, *et al.* behind at the top of the stretch. Can this upset-in-the-making be explained? Will a Vonnegut victory hurt letters? Hurt the kids? Hurt anybody?

Answers are easier to come by now than they once were, for the earlier novels by the author of *Slaughterhouse-Five, or The Children's Crusade, a Duty-Dance with Death* (1969) are back in print, permitting sober inquiry into literary and other lines of development. As it happens, the literary lines are pretty simple. The novelist's first try—*Player Piano* (1952)—is tentatively deferential to conventions of plot, characterization, and social detail. Its setting is a factory town resembling Schenectady, where Vonnegut once worked as a PR man for General Electric. Its hero, Paul Proteus, conducts a rebellion against tyrannies of automation and abstraction, and the story is told in orthodox, cause-and-effect narrative rhythms. The tyrannies themselves, moreover—competition, enforced company loyalty, country club parties, ambitious wives, and other matters that were examined in William Whyte's *Organization Man* are familiar stuff.

Yet, while the surface is in the main traditional, several large cracks do appear in the form of visionary elements. The factory world is, for one thing, futuristic—not today's GE but tomorrow's, fully automated. For another, the portrait of the lives of the townies—people whose test scores exclude them from meaningful work—borrows heavily from Orwell (the proles in *1984*). And the secondary story, detailing a visit to America by a Naïve Stranger, repeatedly touches the fabulous. Symptoms of impatience with "reality" are, in other words, visible from the beginning, hints that for Vonnegut the fabulous could easily become the norm.

And so it does. In the works that follow *Player Piano* fact occasionally asserts itself, usually in historical bits. *Mother Night* (1961) draws on the wartime activities of Lord Haw Haw and Ezra Pound, and on earlier types like Gerald L. K. Smith and Father Coughlin, in telling the tale of an American double agent named Howard W. Campbell hired by Nazis to vilify Jews on the radio. And, as everybody knows, *Slaughterhouse-Five* takes as its crisis the Allied bombing of Dresden and the subsequent firestorm that wiped out hundreds of thousands of lives. But neither book is anything like a chronicle. *Mother Night* is satirical-confessional throughout, and the reportage in *Slaughterhouse-Five* gives way in the end to sci-fi fantasy that flies up from the local disaster to a fanciful, cosmological redefinition of death.

And so it also goes with Vonnegut's major pop hits of the Sixties: *God Bless You, Mr. Rosewater* (1965), *Cat's Cradle* (1963), and *The Sirens of Titan* (1959). Each story floats free of attachment fo dailiness. *Rosewater* introduces a rich, bibulous eccentric addicted to kindness (ROSEWATER FOUNDATION/HOW CAN WE HELP YOU?) and determined to outwit the gaggle of sharpies who seek to strip him of his power to do good. *The Sirens of Titan* tells of another quixotic moneybags, Malachi Constant, a man lured by sirens from another planet into magical space wanderings—again few touchdowns on any recognizably human base. And *Cat's Cradle* is still another imaginary voyage, a "novel" that begins as a probe of the behavior of the fathers of the atomic bomb on the day of Hiroshima, but quickly shapes up as a journey to the end of the world. These three books attempt in their opening pages to create momentary plausibilities of setting—Newport, R.I., "Ilium," N.Y., a law office in Washington, D.C.—and they also venture a word or two of explanation about the origins of the inheritance or the conscience or the interest in space exploration that's the initial focus of the narrative. But the explanations are only teasers: the writer's evident intention is to slip the nets of ordinary life—to fight off the documentary sensibility of the age. And, partly because of the increasing familiarity of the sci-fi mode and partly because of Vonnegut's relaxed good humor, the escape from everyday is usually brought off with grace and ease.

Is this the key to Vonnegut's charm for the young? Certainly escape is attractive, and so too is the *Yellow-Submarine*, Brechtian world of mixed tones that his withdrawal enables Vonnegut to construct. A free-form universe of discourse—fantasy-sermon-satire—can function as a kind of alternative community, a refuge from the oppressive rule of things as they are. But that free-form world, the promise of a truly fresh deal, is obviously only one element of the success. (A comparable promise is made, after all, by Terry Southern, Donald Barthelme, and a number of other writers unconstrained by commonplace social fact; yet none of them has achieved, or seems likely to achieve, Vonnegut's authority among the young.) The case is that Vonnegut is loved not alone for his breakout from boring norms of realism, but for a congeries of opinions, prejudices, and assumptions perfectly tuned to the mind of the emergent generation. Consider the record:

- Youthcult holds that everyone in power is hung up on procedures and forms, blind to the great issues, scared of looking the facts of the age in the eye. Vonnegut says the same. Nobody "will talk about the *really* terrific changes going on," says Mr. Rosewater furiously. Nobody except maybe a sci-fi writer here and there has "guts enough to *really* care about the future . . . *really* notice what machines do to us, what wars do to us, what cities do to us, what big, simple ideas do to us, what tremendous misunderstandings, mistakes, accidents and catastrophes do to us."

- Youthcult holds that we are living in a world about to be trashed, a hair or two away from cataclysm. Vonnegut says the same.

"Daddy," cries the narrator of *Cat's Cradle* (a person who's written a work called *The Day the World Ended*), "Daddy, why are all the birds dead? Daddy, what makes the sky so sick and wormy? Daddy, what makes the sea so hard and still?"

- Youthcult holds that the work ethos at once begets and is begotten by cruelty and hatred. Vonnegut says the same. "Americans have been taught to hate all people who will not or cannot work, to hate even themselves for that," says Kilgore Trout, the sage of *Rosewater*. "We can thank the vanished frontier for that piece of commonsense cruelty. The time is coming, if it isn't here now, when it will no longer be common sense. It will simply be cruel."

• Youthcult holds that the attempt of the elders to hide the prevalence of brutality from the young (and from themselves) is both criminally evasive and doomed to failure. Vonnegut says the same. At the end of *Mother Night* Howard Campbell, on trial for genocide, receives some junk mail from Creative Playthings pitching for toys that prepare kids for life and help them to "work off aggression." Campbell answers:

> I doubt that any playthings could prepare a child for one millionth of what is going to hit him in the teeth, ready or not. My own feeling is . . . [against] bland, pleasing, smooth, easily manipulated playthings like those in your brochure, friends! Let there be nothing harmonious about our children's playthings, lest they grow up expecting peace and order, and be eaten alive. As for children's working off aggressions, I'm against it. They are going to need all the aggressions they can contain for ultimate release in the adult world. . . . Let me tell you that the children in my charge. . . . are spying on real grownups all the time, learning what they fight about, what they're greedy for, how they satisfy their greed, why and how they lie, what makes them go crazy, the different ways they go crazy and so on. . . .

• Youthcult holds that openness is the highest virtue, and that moral and intellectual rigidity—the belief that absolute right or wrong can be known by men—is the root of our sickness. Vonnegut says the same. In *Slaughterhouse-Five* the writer notes that he "never wrote a story with a villain in it," attributing this to the University of Chicago's Anthropology Department ("they taught . . . that nobody was ridiculous or bad or disgusting"). Howard Campbell preaches solemnly against self-righteousness in *Mother Night*: "There are . . . no good reasons ever to hate without reservation, to imagine that God Almighty Himself hates with you, too. Where's evil? It's that large part of every man that wants to hate without limit, that wants to hate with God on its side." And Vonnegut is forever imagining loony battlefields in the void wherein the collected Mr. Cocksures of the universe can blow themselves to nothingness—"remotes" like the "Chrono-Synclastic Infundibula" described, in children's encyclopedia jargon, in *The Sirens of Titan*:

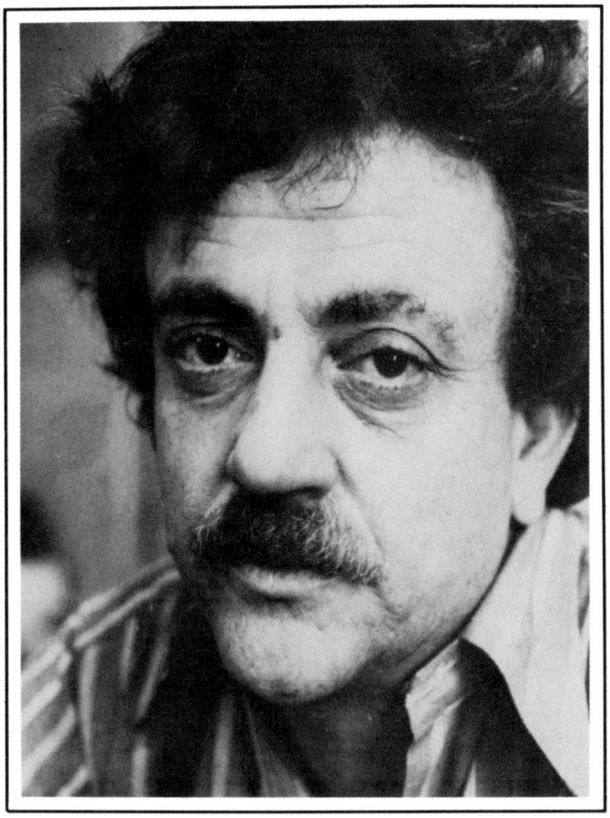

Vonnegut in 1971

> Just imagine that your Daddy is the smartest man who ever lived on Earth, and he knows everything there is to find out, and he is exactly right about everything, and he can prove he is right about everything. Now imagine another little child on some nice world a million light years away, and that little child's Daddy is the smartest man who ever lived on that nice world so far away. And he is just as smart and just as right as your Daddy is. Both Daddies are smart, and both Daddies are right. Only if they ever met each other they would get into a terrible argument, because they wouldn't agree on anything. Now, you can say that your Daddy is right and the other little child's Daddy is wrong, but the Universe is an awfully big place. There is room enough for an awful lot of people to be right about things and still not agree. The reason both Daddies can be right and still get into terrible fights is because there are so many different ways of being right. There are places in the Universe, though, where each Daddy could finally catch on to what the other Daddy was talking about. . . . We call these places chrono-synclastic infundibula. . . . You might think it would be nice to go to a chrono-synclastic infundibula and see all

the different ways to be asbolutely right, but it is a very dangerous thing to do.

• Youthcult holds that Possibility is all, that men must trip out to the borders of self and experience, penetrate the countries wherein ordinary sequences of time break down and past and future coexist, wherein ego and isolation vanish—wherein, like, thought and feeling, man, like, they just flow. Vonnegut says the same. Time and time over he imagines those countries and populates them with instructive (if not model) creatures—the inhabitants of Mercury, for example, as described in *The Sirens of Titan*:

> There is only one sex.
> Every creature simply sheds flakes of his own kind, and his own kind is like everybody else's kind.
> There is no childhood as such. Flakes begin flaking three Earthling hours after they themselves have been shed.
> They do not reach maturity, then deteriorate and die. They reach maturity and stay in full bloom, so to speak, for as long as Mercury cares to sing.
> There is no way in which one creature can harm another, and no motive for one's harming another.
> Hunger, envy, ambition, fear, indignation, religion, and sexual lust are irrelevent and unknown.
> The creatures have only one sense, touch.
> . . . They have only two possible messages. . . . The first is, "Here I am, here I am, here I am." The second is, "So glad you are, so glad you are, so glad you are.". . .
> Because of their love for music and their willingness to deploy themselves in the service of beauty, the creatures are given a lovely name by Earthlings. They are called *harmoniums*.

As should be said at once, the dogmas just summarized aren't highly supportive to careerists, lads on the way up, pushers, drivers, scrappers. Instead of toughening wills, they foster softness, acquiescence, an indisposition to stamp your mark on life. And the general thrust, furthermore, like that of hundreds of writers from Blake to Hesse, is "anti-intellectual": don't burn the books, but don't crack them, either. "You can safely ignore the arts and sciences," says Eliot Rosewater. "They never helped anybody." See my Pop, the Nobel Laureate physicist, father of the atom bomb, says Newton Hoenikker in *Cat's Cradle*. The morning Dr. Hoenikker left for Sweden "Mother cooked a big breakfast. And then, when she cleared off the table, she found a quarter and a dime and three pennies by Father's coffee cup. He'd tipped her." Where would true brilliance wind up, asks Vonnegut, if it ever materialized in our midst? Not at the top, is his answer, but in some Green Stamp redemption center, clerking—witness the case of Kilgore Trout.

It also needs to be said that Vonnegut's best literary self is neither dogmatic nor sermonical, nor as simplistic as most of the foregoing themes. It seldom appears, this best self, in comic-strip send-ups of greed like *God Bless You, Mr. Rosewater*. Neither do you meet it in the sci-fi, futuristic, or cataclysmic corridors of *Slaughterhouse-Five* or *The Sirens of Titan* or *Cat's Cradle*. The strongest writing in this *oeuvre* is found in the least fanciful, most tightly made tales—*Player Piano* and *Mother Night*. And again and again in both books the comedy cuts cleanest when the subject in view is that of classical satire—namely, self-delusion. *Player Piano* is a rich survey of ways in which inflexibility and self-simplification exact respect as "integrity," and a mocking indictment of the conception of civilization "as a vast and faulty dike, with thousands of men . . . in a rank stretching to the horizon, each man grimly [and self-congratulatingly] stopping a leak with his finger." The memorable set piece, a brilliantly worked conceit, matches a machine-mesmerized manager against Checker Charley, a sick computer, and dramatizes swiftly, precisely, fiercely a dozen brands of contemporary superstition. The computer plays poorly, is obviously shot—yet the human opponent can't believe in his own success:

> To Paul's surprise, he took one of [Charley's] pieces without, as far as he could see, laying himself open to any sort of disaster. And then he took another piece, and another. He shook his head in puzzlement and respect. The machine apparently took a long-range view of the game with a grand strategy not yet evident. Checker Charley, as though confirming his thoughts, made an ominous hissing noise, which grew in volume as the game progressed.

And when the explosion comes, human hearts—self-conned into faith that men are machines and vice versa—are torn and "good men" weep:

> "Fire!". . .
> A waiter came running with a fire extinguisher and sent a jet of fluid into Checker Charley's entrails. Steam billowed up as the jet fizzed and sputtered on the glowing parts. The lights on Charley's steel bosom were skittering about the board wildly now, playing a demoniacal and swift game according to rules only the machine could

> understand. All the lights went on at once, a hum swelled louder and louder, until it sounded like a thunderous organ note, and suddenly died. One by one, the little lamps winked out, like a village going to sleep.
>
> "Oh my, my, oh my". . . .
>
> The engineers crowded around Checker Charley, and those in the front rank probed through the ashes, melted tubes, and blackened wires. Tragedy was in every face. Something beautiful had died.

(The feigned grief, raspingly tender, of the sleeping-village metaphor is vintage Vonnegut.)

And in *Mother Night* a precisely analogous kind of comedy is achieved in a dramatization of the mind of a Jew-baiter that simultaneously illuminates the capacity of the meanest of men to see himself as virtuous, and the incapacity of the best men to name their virtues in terms that don't trivialize them. (Fascists engaged in organizing a bully-boy, storm-trooping Iron Guard describe themselves—earnestly—as "working with youngsters . . . just ordinary kids from all walks of life . . . kids who would ordinarily be at loose ends and getting into trouble. . . .") At his best, powered by the pressure of his own astonishment at the spectacle of the moral gymnastics of contemporary compartmentalized man, the creature who invariably "serves evil too openly and good too secretly," Vonnegut is a potent satirist, with a fine eye for the self-deceit built into mod vocabularies of altruism.

But at certain moments in the history of letters the nature of a writer's best or worst self in literary terms matters less than the function the man performs for his primary audience. The present is one of those times—and the function performed by Vonnegut isn't negligible. It is, as indicated, that of articulating the blackest suspicions of a skeptical, cynical generation without running on into orgies of hate or ironical partisanship of evil. Vonnegut's fictional world is often formally incoherent, a mix of jokebook turns, fantasies, cartoon and sermonical bits, Luddite posturings, outcries against cruelty and greed. Lax, rambling, muzzy, sad-eyed, Beatle-toned, sticky at intervals, the writer can be damned as soft at his center, self-advertising in his proclaimed vulnerability to pain and suffering, deeply *un*fascinated by anything difficult.

But viciousness has no dominion over him, and this makes the considerable difference. The author of *Mother Night* may dream of black comedy, but kindness keeps breaking in—there and everywhere else. The man of despair hums on about the profound wretchedness of men and things, but always he's challenged by the inventor inside him, a fabulist in love with images of goodness, generosity, hope, and forever on the verge of declaiming, flat out, with no embarrassment whatever, that, dammit, men and things ought to be—*could be*—infinitely better than they are. The results, viewed "esthetically," aren't uniformly exhilarating: both art and intellect vanish periodically; bull-session simplisms often mound up and drift.

But, to repeat, the work as a whole does serve a function. Its unbrutal laughter is a surcease from high-fashion meanness and knowingness, a patch of dry land on which, by pumping a little more breath into "silly," "innocent" faith in love, moral aspiration can avoid killing itself off prematurely. Say it out straight: on balance, the kids' lighting on Kurt Vonnegut is an undeservedly good break for the age.

ARTICLE:

" 'Slaughterhouse' Burned in N.D.," U.P.I., 15 November 1973.

After his books were taught in high school, Vonnegut became the target of censorship, as in this North Dakota event. In 1976, a Long Island schoolboard, citing twelve examples of vulgar language in Slaughterhouse Five, *removed it, along with eight other books, from the library at Island Trees High School. A group of students and parents sued to have the books reinstated. After a summary judgment in favor of the school board and a reversal by the District Court of Appeals, the Supreme Court voted 5 to 4 in June 1982 to affirm the Court of Appeals decision remanding the case for trial on its merits.*

Author Kurt Vonnegut Jr., whose "Slaughterhouse Five" novel was confiscated and burned by school officials in Drake, N.D., said Wednesday, "those children will have a ridiculous memory of adults. It's a rotten education for the kids to see."

Drake School superintendent Dale Fuhrman and the town school board ordered three dozen copies of the anti-war novel burned last Thursday after a high school sophomore girl complained about profanity in it.

"I'm glad of the freedom to make soldiers talk the way they do talk," Vonnegut said.

"The normal way to get rid of trash is to burn it," Fuhrman said in explaining the book burning.

Vonnegut said in his New York apartment, "The only effect of 'Slaughterhouse' is to make the reader a pacifist. Nothing in the book urges people to take any sexual action at all."

The novel, a strong antiwar statement, describes

the Allied firebombing of Dresden, Germany, in World War II, through the eyes of five characters who survived the ordeal by taking shelter in a slaughterhouse meat locker. Vonnegut was among the five.

The school board of Drake, population 600, also ordered confiscated "Deliverance" by James Dickey and "Short Story Masterpieces," which includes tales by Hemingway, Faulkner, Steinbeck, Joyce and others.

The other titles were included in the ban because "the board wanted to make a clean sweep," Fuhrman explained.

Vonnegut, asked for his reaction, said, "It's grotesque and ridiculous. It's like asking how do I feel about man-eating sharks."

Did he ever think his novel would be burned? "I didn't think anybody's books would be burned," he replied.

Opposing the School Board are English teacher Bruce Severy, many of his students and the Minot, N.D., chapter of the American Civil Liberties Union.

"The issue here is denying students access to those books," Severy said. He said "Slaughterhouse Five" is a "moral" book—one that "addressed itself to current problems in an honest and straightforward manner."

An advertisement for Vonnegut's seventh novel in Publishers Weekly, *12 February 1973*

INTERVIEW:

Nan Robertson, "Vonneguts, Father and Son, Discuss Insanity Interlude," *New York Times*, 23 October 1975, p. 45.

Kurt Vonnegut has six children: Mark, born 1947; Edith, born 1949; and Nanette, born 1954; and three sons he adopted when his sister and her husband died in 1958. In 1975 Mark Vonnegut wrote an account of his schizophrenic breakdown in The Eden Express.

"When Mark went crazy," Kurt Vonnegut Jr. said, "he didn't go away from me. He always had a core of wisdom to which I could speak." The author of "Slaughterhouse-Five"—and other celebrated novels urging the abandonment of rationality as the only way to survive a cruel and insane planet—was in his New York City brownstone, musing about his son. The next day, in an apartment in Boston, Mark Vonnegut said, "I could relate to him as I had known him. I could not relate to him as a physical presence. I wasn't sure it was really him." But while insane, he added with a grin, "I had some great chats with my father when he wasn't there."

Mark Vonnegut wrote "The Eden Express," a just-published Frank E. Taylor/Praeger book on his descent into schizophrenic madness in a counter-culture wilderness commune in British Columbia, Canada.

He is now 28 years old, a first-year student in the Harvard Medical School, married since May to Pat O'Shea—and recovered.

Reviewers whose interest in Mark was aroused because he is his famous father's son have called him, among other things, "a brilliant natural storyteller" (The Village Voice), "an immensely likable young man with no distinct capacity to write" but with "a believable sincerity" (Newsweek), and a person who has produced "a searchingly vivid, if sometimes voluble account of the inside of a schizophrenic breakdown, the struggle to recover, to understand" (The New York Times Book Review).

What emerge in interviews with the two Vonneguts and in "The Eden Express" are tenderness, a faith in family despite the parents' breakup, confidence on the part of each about the other's writing judgment that made comment unnecessary and ambivalence about great success.

Physically the two men are unlike: Mark with cornsilk-fine brown hair and bespectacled dark eyes, slender, 5 feet 10. His father is 6 feet 4, with a wild tumble of curls on his head and a bushy moustache. "I was the only male in the family that didn't crack 6 feet, and that really hurt," said Mark.

"The Eden Express," written while Mark was in a hospital near Vancouver, is dedicated to one of the young Vonnegut's best friends, who held his hand during the "time warps" Mark was ricocheting through like his father's anti-hero, Billy Pilgrim, in "Slaughterhouse." It is also dedicated to the doctor who brought him out of madness and "To my father. Without you I wouldn't have known how to fight."

Kurt Vonnegut said: "Any book that has anything on its mind is an important book. Mark had something terribly on his mind. He had the special experience of going insane and recovering, so he's worth listening to. I had a feeling about the book that it would probably be worthwhile. Nobody expected that it would be a perfectly wonderful book, which this is."

Mark Vonnegut: "The fact is, my memories of being crazy give me an almost sensual glee. I feel very privileged and lucky to have gone through what I went through. I felt it (the book) would be affecting a lot of people's lives and would cut a lot of pain. Everybody knows a couple of people who are going under, really wigging out."

The father gave Mark no advice on writing the book. "I made no suggestions," he said. "He didn't ask for any. Mark worked on his own."

Mark believes he learned a lot about writing "by osmosis." The father concurred, saying that male writers, working at home, are "more domesticated than other males" and may even unconsciously pass on some insights even if they do not discuss their solitary labors.

Both spoke in a dialogue, separated by more than 200 miles, of what it is like to be the son of a prominent man:

"I'm Kurt Vonnegut Jr.," said the writer. "Kurt Vonnegut Sr. was a very well known man in Indianapolis," an architect and painter, an important figure in the community, a source of pride.

"But it was a connection of manageable dimensions; it meant nothing outside Indianapolis," Kurt Vonnegut said. Nonetheless he confessed it felt convenient to get "treated right in department stores and by cops."

For his own son, being the offspring of an international counterculture hero was a bitter brew to swallow.

"When it first started, I liked it," Mark said. "You always like to see your father make good. After a while it did seem twisted and evil. There seemed to be too much money around, dinners at Sardi's, people who had never read a Vonnegut book.

"It still doesn't look good to me but it doesn't make me sick to my stomach. I saw him as a victim—exploited and used. I see pretty clearly now that he wanted to be a successful writer. If I'd known it at the time, it would have bugged the hell out of me."

Mark is the oldest of Kurt Vonnegut Jr.'s three biological children, the others being Edith, 26, an artist who is married to the television newsman Geraldo Rivera; and Nanette, who has just turned 21. When Mark was 11, a double tragedy added three more boys to the Vonnegut family—the sons of Kurt Vonnegut's sister, Mrs. James C. Adams. The sister died of cancer the day after her husband was killed in a train crash. The three Adams orphans were adopted forthwith by the Vonneguts.

When his son went mad, Kurt Vonnegut experienced helplessness and guilt. "I thought perhaps he would never recover." Now, as a "vested interest I'm deeply relieved that I'm not to blame for his insanity. You can make other persons insane by treating them badly. Still I always thought schizophrenia was a real disease and not something society induced."

Mark responds now: "There's no shame, there's no blame, there's hope. That's what the book is all about."

His friends clung to a hippie precept that schizophrenia is a sane response to an insane society. Finally, on Valentine's Day, 1971, Mark was committed to Hollywood Psychiatric Hospital near Vancouver.

For a man who writes about the randomness of life, with no individual control over his fate, Kurt Vonnegut nonetheless spoke of his son's will to recover.

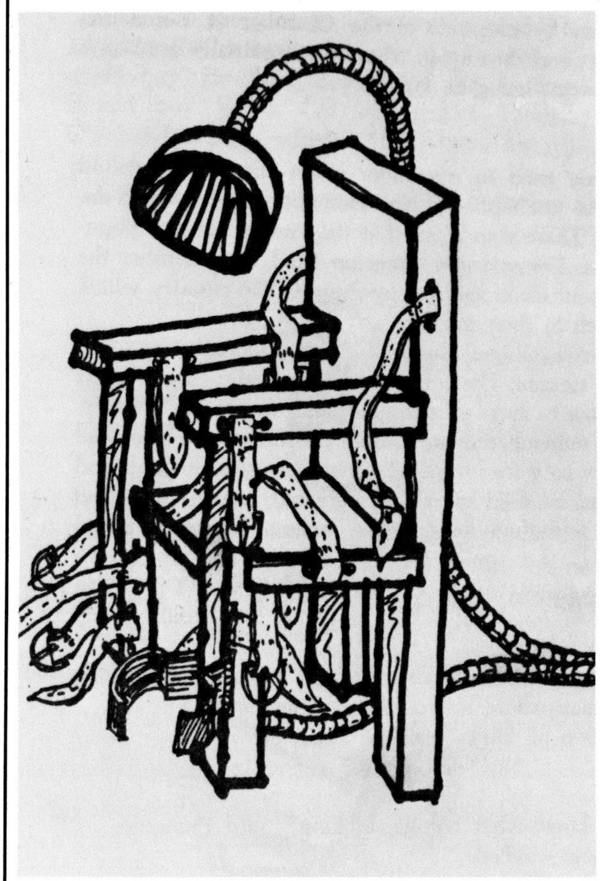

Vonnegut wrote himself out of a period of malaise in Breakfast of Champions or Goodbye Blue Monday!, *which he described as "my fiftieth birthday present to myself." The novel, which brought back Kilgore Trout, was illustrated with the author's drawings.*

"It's called grit—the determination to get out of trouble and a hole," he said. "Mark had this core. He has a tremendous wisdom about life. He has pursued happiness very intelligently. A lot of people don't have anything to come back to. He's got lots of supportive relatives and friends."

Mark also told his father that medical school "was like a candy store, with so many wonderful things to learn."

In his preface, the son writes that "colds, ulcers, flu and cancer are things we get. Schizophrenic is something we are."

"If I had had a well-defined role in a stable culture, it

might have been far simpler to sort things out," he said. "For a hippie, son of a counter-culture hero, B.A. in religion, genetic bio-chemical disposition of schizophrenia, setting up a commune in the wilds of British Columbia, things tended to run together."

ARTICLE:

John Irving, "Kurt Vonnegut and His Critics," *New Republic*, 181 (22 September 1979): 41-49.

In this article subtitled "The Aesthetics of Accessibility," novelist Irving defended Slapstick *and* Jailbird *against charges that Vonnegut had sacrificed content to readability.*

More than 10 years ago, John Casey—the author of the novel *An American Romance* and the recent collection of stories, *Testimony and Demeanor*—interviewed Kurt Vonnegut for a magazine then published in West Branch, Iowa, and now defunct. In that interview Vonnegut said:

> *We must acknowledge that the reader is doing something quite difficult for him and the reason you don't change point of view too often is so he won't get lost and the reason you paragraph often is so that his eyes won't get tired, is so you get him without him knowing it by making his job easy for him. He has to restage your show in his head, costume and light it. His job is not easy.*

Neither is Vonnegut's. Making a reader's job easy is difficult work, although there's always been a great misunderstanding of Vonnegut on this point. In the *New York Review of Books*, for example, Jack Richardson called Vonnegut an "easy writer," and—among other charges—accused Vonnegut of not being Voltaire. And in the interview with Casey, Vonnegut tells the story of meeting Jason Epstein, the Random House editor—whom Vonnegut calls "a terribly powerful cultural commissar"—at a cocktail party. When they were introduced, Epstein thought a minute, then said, "Science fiction," turned and walked off. "He just had to place me, that's all," Vonnegut said. Other "cultural commissars" have been trying to "place" Vonnegut for years; more often, like Richardson, they tell us what Vonnegut is *not*. If he's not Voltaire, for example, it's possible he's not Swift, either. At least in part, I think, it is the childlike availability of his prose, its fast and easy-to-read surfaces, that seems to be so troublesome to Vonnegut's critics.

The assumption that what is easy to read has been easy to write is a forgivable lapse among non-writers, but it is self-incriminating how many critics, who also (in a fashion) write themselves, have called Vonnegut "easy." In one of the worst broadsides ever published on Vonnegut (in the *New York Times Book Review*, in the disguise of a review of *Slapstick*), Roger Sale seemed especially upset with Vonnegut's audience—the "minimally intelligent young," he called them. "I think I would be less bothered by Vonnegut were it not that one of my major tasks is to try to pose hard questions for the semi-literate young," says the long-suffering Mr. Sale, slaving in the trenches of ignorance. There is something self-serving in this criticism; these are the remarks of a critic who wants a work to need him—to explain it to us, perhaps. "Nothing could be easier," Sale assures us about Vonnegut's writing. On the other hand, Sale tells us, "it takes stamina, determination and crazy intelligence" to read Thomas Pynchon. More self-congratulation—Sale is not an easy reader, we have to give him that. And despite Sale's invitation to comparison, it is not my desire to knock Thomas Pynchon, a writer as serious about his work as Mr. Vonnegut is about his; I would say, however, that there are many "serious people who take fiction seriously" (as Sale calls us) who think that Pynchon's kind of writing is the easiest to write. And the hardest to read: a struggle with ideas and language where we, the readers, provide much of the struggle; where the writer, perhaps, has not struggled hard enough to make himself more readable.

Why is "readable" such a bad thing to be these days? Some "serious people" I know are gratified by the struggle to make sense of what they read; as Vonnegut says, "So it goes." Let them be gratified. As someone who, like Roger Sale, has struggled many hard hours with the "semi-literate young," I am more often gratified by a writer who has accepted the enormous effort necessary to make writing clear. Vonnegut's lucidity is hard and brave work in a literary world where pure messiness is frequently thought to be a sign of some essential wrestling with the "hard questions." Good writers have always shown that hard questions must also be posed and answered cleanly and well. It is as if Roger Sale—and he's hardly alone; I use him as an example of many—is championing a literature for second-year graduate students, a literature dependent on interpretation; and, of course, in our shameful semi-literacy, perhaps we will need to call upon the "crazy intelligence" of someone like Mr. Sale to interpret it for us.

Mr. Sale tells us he'd be surprised if Robert Scholes, "who once expressed fondness for Vonnegut," likes Vonnegut now as much as he once did. I would be astonished if Mr. Scholes didn't feel all the more convinced of his earlier appraisal. Writing about *Slaughterhouse-Five* in the *New York Times* Mr. Scholes offered gentle chiding to those, like Roger Sale, who find Vonnegut difficult to accept as serious. Scholes pointed out that Vonnegut's critics too often confuse muddled earnestness with profundity—that is, if you *sound* serious, you must be. Indeed, Sale seems to be telling us that if the work is tortured and a ghastly effort to read, it must be serious; or, as Sale tells us in the case of Joseph Heller's *Something Happened*, another valuable way to judge a book's seriousness is to note how many years it took to write. (Mr. Heller is a serious and good writer, but not for the years between his books.) Roger Sale's logic leads to this: if the work is lucid and sharp and the narrative flows like water, we should suspect the work of being simplistic, and as light and as lacking in seriousness as fluff. This is simplistic criticism, of course; it is easy criticism, too.

There is no shortage of this kind of criticism around; Vonnegut is a frequent victim of it. No fewer than five graduate students I have taught over the past 11 years have delighted in showing me this polemic of John Middleton Murry's (as if they'd made a rare discovery): "Criticism should be less timid; it should openly accept the fact that its final judgments are moral." No kidding; but all the more reason, then, that those judgments should be careful. We should judge writers for what they've done, and what they mean—not for their audience or their press (or for their lack of either). Another popular person to quote—in the environs of no fewer than four English departments I've been associated with—is Cyril Connolly. "Never praise. Praise dates you." Maybe; but not as much as remarks like Epstein's "science fiction" and Richardson's "easy writer" date *them*.

"It is the duty of critics," Alvin Rosenfeld writes in the *Southern Review*,

> *to make a good poet's work harder for him to perform, for it is only in the overcoming of genuine difficulties that strong poetry emerges. A corollary of this view . . . is that a critic should do his work in such a way as to make a* reader's *work also more difficult for him to perform, and for much the same reasons, namely, to achieve interpretations strenuous enough to be adequate to the age.*

It may seem inexact to respond to that as I do, but what a lot of crap that is! For *whom* is this difficulty satisfying? Good writers have always been more than "adequate to the age"; in fact, they have always had to fight against how boring, and limiting, the mere adequacies of their age are to them. . . .

In his introduction to the work of Celine, Vonnegut writes:

> *He was in the worst possible taste, by which I mean that he had many educational advantages, becoming a physician, and he was widely traveled in Europe and Africa and North America—and yet he wrote not a single phrase that hinted to similarly advantaged persons that he was something of a gentleman.*
>
> *He did not seem to understand that aristocratic restraints and sensibilities, whether inherited or learned, accounted for much of the splendor of literature. In my opinion, he discovered a higher and more awful order of literary truth by ignoring the crippled vocabularies of ladies and gentlemen and by using, instead, the more comprehensive language of shrewd and tormented guttersnipes.*
>
> *Every writer is in his debt, and so is anyone else interested in discussing lives in their entirety. By being so impolite, he demonstrated that perhaps half of all experience, the animal half, had been concealed by good manners. No honest writer or speaker will ever want to be polite again.*

Of course "the more comprehensive language of shrewd and tormented guttersnipes" is the language Vonnegut also loves and uses so well. "My motives are political," he admits in [a 1973] *Playboy* interview.

> *I agree with Stalin and Hitler and Mussolini that the writer should serve his society. I differ with dictators as to* how *writers should serve. Mainly, I think they should be—and biologically* have *to be—agents of change. For the better, we hope. Writers are specialized cells in the social organism. They are evolutionary cells. Mankind is trying to become something else; it's experimenting with new ideas all the time. And writers are the means of introducing new ideas into the society, and also a means of responding symbolically to life.*

Vonnegut admits that he couldn't survive his own pessimism if he didn't have "some kind of sunny little dream." His work is full of those dreams—"harmless untruths," he has called them (in *Cat's Cradle*). Religions, charitable organizations, world planners, utopian schemers, absent-minded inventors bent on change, do-gooders atoning for terrible crimes (or accidents), lovable and not-so-lovable men of power and men of money; they all fail, they all bungle the job of improving the species in usually funny and well-meaning ways. "The biggest laughs," Vonnegut has said, "are based on the biggest disappointments and the biggest fears." It's nothing that new; Freud, as Vonnegut likes to point out, has already written about gallows humor. "It's people laughing in the middle of political helplessness," Vonnegut says. "I have customarily written about powerless people who felt there wasn't much they could do about their situations."

"It goes against the American storytelling grain," Vonnegut says,

> *to have someone in a situation he can't get out of, but I think this is very usual in life. There are people, particularly dumb people, who are in terrible trouble and never get out of it, because they're not intelligent enough. And it strikes me as gruesome and comical that in our culture we have an expectation that a man can always solve his problems. There is that implication that if you just have a little more energy, a little more fight, the problem can always be solved. This is so untrue that it makes me want to cry—or laugh.*

He points out that the science-fiction passages in *Slaughterhouse-Five* are

> *just like the clowns in Shakespeare. When Shakespeare figured the audience had had enough of the heavy stuff, he'd let up a little, bring on a clown or a foolish innkeeper or something like that, before he'd become serious again. And trips to other planets, science fiction of an obviously kidding sort, is equivalent to bringing on the clowns every so often to lighten things up.*

In fact, Vonnegut even *speaks* lucidly about his own work—a subject even lucid writers can be clumsy about. It's remarkable, considering how clear he's been, to consider how badly understood he is. But listen to this: "A good critic," according to Jacob Glatstein, "is armed for war. And criticism is a war, against a work of art—either the critic defeats the work or the work defeats the critic." Well, with that kind of demand put on the critic, I guess it's always possible to misunderstand *anything*.

Vonnegut is not Shakespeare, either, of course, but in that fun field—of trying to prove who Vonnegut is *not*—Shakespeare comes closer than some others. They both feel that art and entertainment are not uncomfortably married; indeed, they feel that art ought to be entertaining. But this idea is not in literary vogue. William Gass—the eloquent philosopher whose good language and clear thinking are marvels to me—noted recently what he thinks happens to "almost any writer who has gained some popularity. That popularity," according to Gass, "is almost invariably based on what is weakest in the writer's work, and then the tendency is for the writer to lean in the direction of that quality which encourages the weakness rather than counteracting it." A puzzling notion: would a lack of popularity assure a writer that he has no weaknesses? And knowing that most serious writers have always seen themselves as speaking to a deaf world (Vonnegut included), isn't it odd to assume that a writer—once popular—would indulge his so-called weakness by writing to an audience? A writer always mistrusts his audience, whether he is conning them or seducing them or ignoring them (and indulging himself); I think a writer especially mistrusts his audience when he discovers that he has one. Gass's theory is intellectually interesting, but it makes him sound like a poor judge of human nature—

Vonnegut stated in the "Prologue" to Slapstick, or Lonesome No More *(1976): "This is the closest I will ever come to writing an autobiography. I have called it 'Slapstick' because it is grotesque, situation poetry—like the slapstick film comedies, especially those of Laurel and Hardy, of long ago." It is about Dr. Wilbur Daffodil-11 Swain, a seven-foot tall, 100-year-old man, a former President of the United States who lives in the lobby of the Empire State Building amid the ruins of Manhattan.*

more particularly, writers' natures—which I'm sure he isn't. His idea, though, is connected to his misgivings about entertainment and art. "Even people of considerable intelligence are not interested in literature per se," Gass has said. "They want things that are fundamentally not upsetting. They want entertainment." A bad word, for Gass—"entertainment." (Perhaps it's like "readable.") And yes, and no—people do want entertainment, certainly; but I think they also want things that are fundamentally upsetting, which—easy or hard to read—good literature usually is. Catharsis—perhaps it is also an unpopular word today, or at least an old-fashioned one—relies on upsetting readers. You purge fear through evoking it, you purify pain by rendering it, you bathe the heart with tears. Vonnegut can hurt you, and he does; he means to, too. When the sunny dreams and the harmless untruths evaporate—and they always do—a ruined planet is what we look upon; his books make us wish we were better. That's a moral harshness Conrad and Dickens surely share with him; Dickens, by the way, was also an entertainer. Vonnegut may not make us weep for little Nell; there are no little Nells, or other characters of her kind, in his spare books. In his books we weep, instead, for *us*. Which reminds me of what Vonnegut said more than 10 years ago, about what you do to a reader . . . "you get him without him knowing it by making his job easy for him." Like the pharmacist who really knows what's good for you: he understands the sugar coating on some very bitter pills. So many of Vonnegut's critics have noticed only the coating—or the pills: his bleak impoliteness (as he would say of Céline). It is in the combination of such dreaming and such reality, in his work, where his ambition is both large and realized.

One of Vonnegut's critics has at least tried harder than some others, and this is John Gardner—although Vonnegut, and nearly everyone else, is mowed down by Gardner's religious crusade to make literature optimistic again. "He's making a shrill pitch to the literary right wing that wants to repudiate all of modernism and jump back in the arms of their 19-century literary grandfathers," John Barth accuses Gardner; that's fair to say. But Gardner's "morality," *his* political motives for writing—for improving the world—are not unlike Vonnegut's own aims, and Gardner sees some of what Vonnegut is doing more clearly than most. Vonnegut's "problem," as Gardner sees it, is that "he's overcritical of himself, endlessly censoring, endlessly reconsidering his moral affirmations." That's a "problem" more writers should have, I think. Gardner goes on to say that this "would explain the seeming cold-heartedness and trivial-mindedness of his famous comment on the American fire-bombing of Dresden, 'So it goes,' a desperate, perhaps overcensored attitude mindlessly echoed by the turned-off and cynical." And here Gardner falls into the old sin of accusing a writer for the audience he keeps. Even so, Gardner is wise to point out that "Vonnegut's cynical disciples read him wrong." He adds: "It is Vonnegut himself who points out the vast and systematic modern evils that he then appears to shrug off or, for some reason, blame on God. But the misreading is natural. Vonnegut's moral energy," Gardner calls it, "is forever flagging, his fight forever turning slapstick." Yes, but slapstick is Vonnegut's response to despair; Gardner doesn't approve of despair. John Updike (who has been especially wise about Vonnegut) has said of Gardner: "Morality in fiction is accuracy and truth. The world has changed, and in a sense we are all heirs to despair. Better to face this and tell the truth, however dismal, than to do whatever life-enhancing thing [Gardner is] proposing." Gardner, speaking morally, says that Vonnegut "sighs, grins, and sidles away. He's most himself when . . . he's most openly warm-hearted and comic," Gardner complains. "His lack of commitment—ultimately a lack of concern about his characters—makes his writing slight." But what Gardner calls "slight"—or worse, "a lack of concern"—is really the haunted soul of Vonnegut's vision itself: Vonnegut sees little light at the end of the tunnel, though he keeps looking; Gardner wants him to come up with more light. It is Gardner's aesthetic, not necessarily Vonnegut's, that "art is essentially and primarily moral—that is, life-giving—moral in its process of creation and moral in what it says." Well, Vonnegut *is* a do-gooder, but none of us, according to Gardner, is do-gooding enough.

It surprises me only because—for other, wiser things Gardner has written—I would expect him to like Vonnegut more than he likes anybody else. "Dullness is the chief enemy of art," Gardner writes, "each generation of artists must find new ways of slicing the fat off reality." And Vonnegut does that so well—his novels are *skeletons* of people and events, lit up in such a bare, hard light that we can't fail to recognize all our evils and hopes—lovingly carried to human extremes. "By its nature," Gardner also writes,

> *criticism makes art sound more intellectual than it is—more calculated and systematic. . . . The best critical intelligence, capable of making connections the artist himself may be blind to, is a noble thing in its place; but applied to the making of art, cool intellect is likely to produce superficial work, either art*

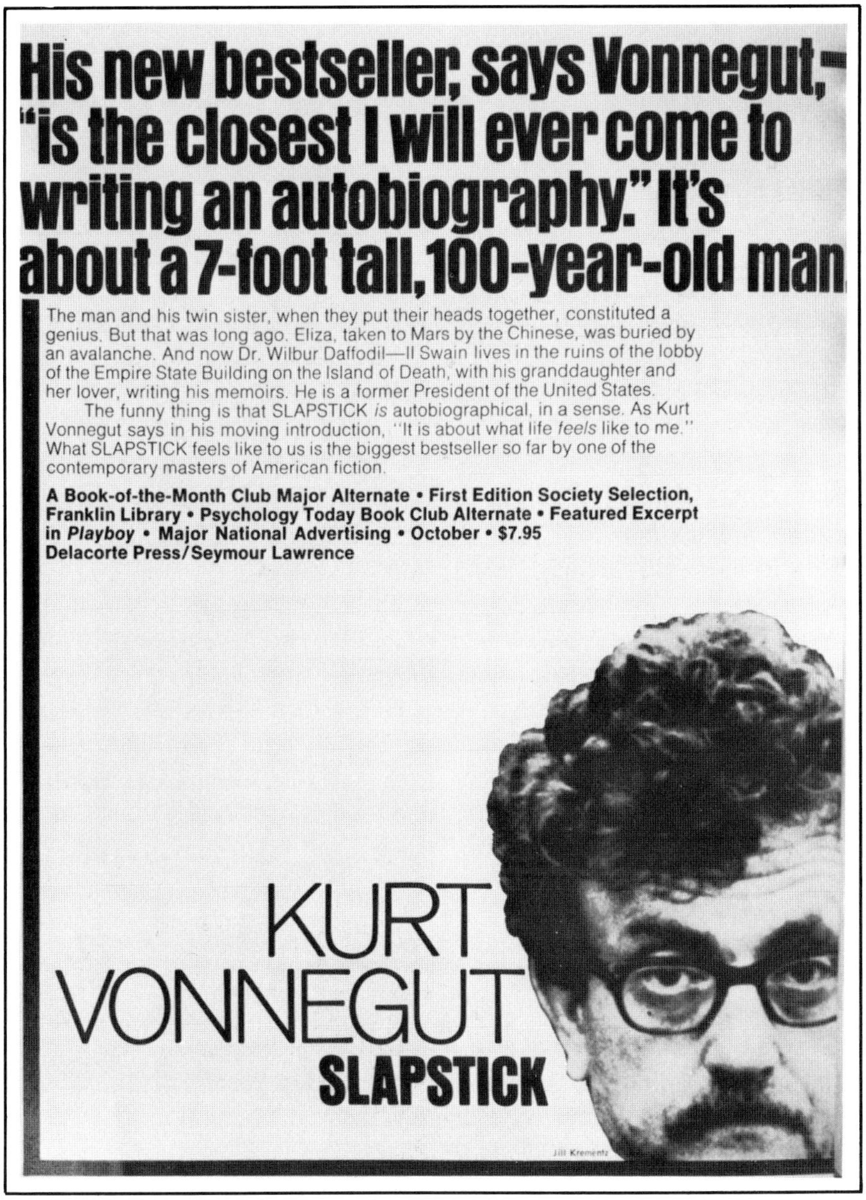

His new bestseller, says Vonnegut,– "is the closest I will ever come to writing an autobiography." It's about a 7-foot tall, 100-year-old man
The man and his twin sister, when they put their heads together, constituted a genius. But that was long ago. Eliza, taken to Mars by the Chinese, was buried by an avalanche. And now Dr. Wilbur Daffodil—11 Swain lives in the ruins of the lobby of the Empire State Building on the Island of Death, with his granddaughter and her lover, writing his memoirs. He is a former President of the United States.
The funny thing is that SLAPSTICK *is* autobiographical, in a sense. As Kurt Vonnegut says in his moving introduction, "It is about what life *feels* like to me." What SLAPSTICK feels like to us is the biggest bestseller so far by one of the contemporary masters of American fiction.
A Book-of-the-Month Club Major Alternate • First Edition Society Selection, Franklin Library • Psychology Today Book Club Alternate • Featured Excerpt in *Playboy* • Major National Advertising • October • $7.95
Delacorte Press/Seymour Lawrence
KURT VONNEGUT
SLAPSTICK
Jill Krementz

Publishers Weekly, *209 (21 June 1976)*

> *which is all sensation or art which is all thought. We see this whenever we find art too obviously constructed to fit a theory, as in the music of John Cage or in the recent fiction of William Gass.*

I think it is fair to make such a generalization, but there can be no accusing Vonnegut of that kind of playing around. He can't be accused of another kind of playing around that Gardner wonderfully describes, either. "The trivial has its place," Gardner writes. He adds,

> *I can think of no good reason that some people should not specialize in the behavior of the left-side hairs on an elephant's trunk. Even at its best, its most deadly serious, criticism, like art, is partly a game, as all good critics know. My objection is not to the game but to the fact that contemporary critics have for the most part lost track of the point of their game, just as artists, by and large, have lost track of the point of theirs. Fiddling with the hairs on an elephant's nose is indecent when the elephant happens to be standing on the baby.*

But Vonnegut is always concerned for the baby, he is no fiddler with the hairs—or even with the elephant. I would think Gardner would like him for that. Vonnegut's novels have been about—roughly—the destruction of human individuality by the team-sports mentality of corporations and the technological age; the origins of our universe, and the proof that there is no life after death; the viciousness of political propaganda and the definition of "war criminal"; the end of the world, through technological playfulness and crack-pot morality; the problems of the rich having so much money, and getting richer, and the poor growing poorer and also more stupid; more war crimes; the problems of making it, whatever "it" is, when you're too old to enjoy it—whatever "it" is; and another end of the world. In fact, it's the end of the world, again and again, with him. That's a pretty big baby; that's not fiddling with the hairs on an elephant's nose. Vonnegut would surely find that "indecent."

I intend (obviously) to praise him; he is among living writers—together with John Hawkes and Günter Grass—the most stubbornly imaginative. He is not anybody else, or even a version of anybody else, and he is a writer with a cause. He likes to refer to our potential to belong to "artificial extended families," and he intends to keep trying to make us belong—in spite of ourselves. He is unique and wise, graceful and kind, and he can fool you by how "easy" he is to read—if you don't *think* carefully. In the prologue to *Slapstick* he wrote—of his brother Bernard, a scientist, and himself—

> *Because of the sorts of minds we were given at birth, and in spite of their disorderliness, Bernard and I belong to artificial extended families which allow us to claim relatives all over the world.*
>
> *He is a brother to scientists everywhere. I am a brother to writers everywhere.*
>
> *This is amusing and comforting to both of us. It is nice.*
>
> *It is lucky, too, for human beings need all the relatives they can get—as possible donors or receivers not necessarily of love, but of common decency.*

As a cause—not to mention a literary theme—"common decency" is worth praising. I do not fear being "dated" for it. As John Middleton Murry also wrote, "The critic should not be cheap," and I would add that there are times when praise is more difficult and worthy to articulate than scorn. As Thomas Mann said:

> *We all bear wounds; praise is a soothing if not necessarily healing balm for them. Nevertheless, if I may judge by my own experience, our receptivity for praise stands in no relationship to our vulnerability to mean disdain and spiteful abuse. No matter how stupid such abuse is, no matter how plainly impelled by private rancors, as an expression of hostility it occupies us far more deeply and lastingly than the opposite. Which is very foolish, since enemies are, of course, the necessary concomitant of any robust life, the very proof of its strength.*

Kurt Vonnegut certainly has enemies. Not only because of them, but because of the constancy of his light-dark work, he is our strongest writer. Now he gives us *Jailbird*, his ninth novel.

Kilgore Trout, the science-fiction genius, is back. "He could not make it on the outside," Vonnegut writes. "It is no disgrace. A lot of good people can't make it on the outside. I think it's a wonder that I have." Kilgore Trout is in jail, it turns out. In *Jailbird* we learn that Trout has all along been just one of the pseudonyms of Dr. Robert Fender, "a veterinarian and the only American to have been convicted of treason during the Korean War." He fell in love with a North Korean and tried to hide her, and now

Vonnegut with photographer Jill Krementz (whom he married in November 1979) and novelist William Price Fox at the University of South Carolina in February 1979

he is the supply clerk and a lifer in a Federal Minimum Security Adult Correctional Facility in Georgia; in the supply room, he plays Edith Piaf records all day long—he is especially fond of her song, "Non, Je ne Regrette Rien." Or: "No, I am not sorry about anything."

Fender, or Trout as he often does in Vonnegut books, tells us stories about beings from other planets. Under the pseudonym of Frank X. Barlow, he tells us about the planet Vicuna. An escaped judge explains that the "people" on his planet had the same word for "hello" and "goodbye" and "please" and "thank you." The word was "ting-a-ling." The judge tells us that "back on Vicuna the people could don and doff their bodies as easily as Earthlings could change their clothing. When they were outside their bodies, they were weightless, transparent, silent awarenesses and sensibilities." The judge, in fact, has come to earth looking for a body to occupy; he makes an awful mistake concerning the body of his choice; he chooses a wasted old man, a fellow prisoner of Kilgore Trout's—and the hero of *Jailbird*—Walter F. Starbuck, a Watergate criminal and formerly President Richard M. Nixon's special adviser on youth affairs (a position so little valued by Nixon that Starbuck works in a basement office without windows and never has a secretary). But before the judge makes the mistake of occupying Walter F. Starbuck's body, we hear about what happened on the planet Vicuna.

"They ran out of time," the judge says.

> The tragedy of the planet was that its scientists found ways to extract time from topsoil and the oceans and the atmosphere—to heat their homes and power their speedboats and fertilize their crops with it; to eat it; to make clothes out of it; and so on. They served time at every meal, fed it to household pets, just to demonstrate how rich and clever they were. They allowed great gobbets of it to putrefy to oblivion in their overflowing garbage cans.
>
> 'On Vicuna,' says the judge, 'we lived as though there were no tomorrow.'
>
> The patriotic bonfires of time were the worst, he says. When he was an infant, his parents held him up to coo and gurgle with delight as a million years of future were put to the torch in honor of the birthday of the queen. But by the time he was fifty, only a few weeks of future remained. Great rips in reality were everywhere. People could walk through walls. His own speedboat became nothing more than a steering wheel. Holes appeared in vacant lots where children were playing, and the children fell in.
>
> So all the Vicunians had to get out of their bodies and sail into space without further ado.
>
> 'Ting-a-ling,' they said to Vicuna.

"Ting-a-ling" is one of nearly a dozen jangling refrains in this novel. When Walter F. Starbuck has served his Watergate term, and has had another run for the money "on the outside," he is found to be a criminal again— "and on and on," as Vonnegut says. "I am a recidivist," Starbuck says at the end, defining the word as describing a person who habitually relapses into crime or antisocial behavior. He receives a telegram from good old Kilgore Trout, the lifer—sent as a kind of welcome home card before Starbuck returns to the slammer. "Ting-a-ling," the telegram says.

Other refrains in *Jailbird* are: "Nobody home," "Live and learn," "Small world," "Imagine that," "Peace," "Times change" and "Time flies." My favorite is "Strong stuff," because the book *is* such strong stuff, and Vonnegut's ability to freshen the clichés in our language by using them when we're most vulnerable to the truth in them has never been sharper.

Another, larger "cliché" he employs in a startlingly vulnerable way is the Sermon on the Mount. That's the one about the poor in spirit receiving the Kingdom of Heaven, about the meek inheriting the earth; those hungering for righteousness actually find it, and the merciful are treated mercifully; the pure in heart get to see God, and the peacemakers are called the sons of God; "and on and on." Walter F. Starbuck is an idealist; he suffers from a disease described by Vonnegut as long ago as *God Bless You, Mr. Rosewater* (1965), for Eliot Rosewater also suffers it—"it attacks those exceedingly rare individuals who reach biological maturity still loving and wanting to help their fellow men." Starbuck's idealism does not even die in the Nixon White House, it does not die in prison, or even when he becomes—before his final arrest—a vice president of the Down Home Records Division of The RAMJAC Corporation. RAMJAC, at the time of Starbuck's employment there, owns quite a lot of things, McDonald's and the *New York Times* among them. In fact, Walter F. Starbuck's son, who hates him—and who is a most unpleasant person—is a book reviewer for the *Times*; "imagine that." Yet Walter F. Starbuck says that he *still* believes "that peace and plenty and happiness can be worked out some way." He also admits, "I am a fool." Of his years in the Nixon White House, as the president's special adviser on youth affairs, even Starbuck is forced to conclude that he might have sent the same telegram each week "to limbo," instead of compiling his countless memos to the president. Here is the telegram: "YOUNG PEOPLE STILL REFUSE TO SEE THE OBVIOUS IMPOSSIBILITY OF WORLD DISARMAMENT AND ECONOMIC EQUALITY. COULD BE FAULT OF NEW TESTAMENT."

There seems to be little, on the surface, that Vonnegut refuses to see; at least he tries to see the possibilities for human improvement. But he misleads us, as we *are* misled—by our own optimism, our own idealism, our own good intentions, all along.

In the opening of *Slaughterhouse-Five* he admits that writing an antiwar book is like writing an anti-glacier book; then he tries to write one anyway. The war happens just the same. He calls *Slaughterhouse-Five* a failure—"and had to be," he writes "since it was written by a pillar of salt." He says he loves Lot's wife for looking back at the fire and brimstone, when God told her not to look back, "because it was so human." He concludes: "People aren't supposed to look back." *Jailbird*, and almost every Vonnegut novel, has its pillar-of-salt person.

Walter F. Starbuck is the son of immigrant hired help, but his benefactor—Alexander Hamilton McCone, the man who sends young Starbuck to Harvard and advises him on how to conduct himself—is a multimillionaire pillar of salt. McCone witnesses his family's bridge and iron company of Cleveland under the siege of a pre-union strike; Vonnegut's invention, called the Cuyahoga Massacre, takes place in the 1890s, and the young McCone is so traumatized by the shooting of several striking workers, their women and children, by Pinkerton marksmen, that he develops a crippling stammer, drops out of factory life and becomes a reclusive donor to the arts. There is often a crippled rich man in a Vonnegut book, and Vonnegut always has recognized the safety of the arts. *Jailbird* is his most socially demonstrative novel.

Sacco and Vanzetti, whose story is retold in Vonnegut's voice, are the real-life heroes of the book. Walter F. Starbuck has his ideals in the right place, but his heart, as an ex-girlfriend points out to him, just isn't in the workers' revolution. "It's all right," she tries to reassure him (her dying words). "You couldn't help it that you were born without a heart. At least you tried to believe what the people with hearts believed—so you were a good man just the same." Strong stuff, but the common man and economic equality—forms of a humane socialism—have long been a part of Vonnegut's overall plea for human dignity and common decency. In the end, though, even these are usually stripped away. "You know what is finally going to kill this planet?" Starbuck tries to tell his friends at his farewell party before returning to jail. "A total lack of seriousness," he says. "Nobody gives a damn anymore about what's really going on, what's going to happen next, or how we ever got into such a mess in the first place." But his friends are all "full adults" and can only, of course, find this hysterically funny; they crack up with laughter over it. They all tell each other jokes. In fact, the most touching relationship in the novel—that Starbuck has with a girl he loved but never made love to, a girl who jilts him and marries his best friend—is a relationship based on telling jokes, sometimes long-distance (over the phone). She works in a hospital and is especially eager to tell jokes on the days when she loses the most patients.

"I gave up on saying anything serious," Starbuck tells us at the end and sits back to listen to a tape of his last remarks to Congressman Nixon, when Nixon asks him why, "as the son of immigrants who had been treated so well by Americans, as a man who had been treated like a son and been sent to Harvard by an American capitalist," *why* had he been "so ungrateful to the American economic system"? He was a Communist, in his younger days—that's all Nixon means; Starbuck's answer, as he admits, is not very original. His answer to Nixon is: "Why? The Sermon on the Mount, sir."

It's a weak answer, but Vonnegut's wisdom is such that he won't insult our intelligence with anything pretentious or—frankly—unlikely; he won't make a grander claim. His heroes slump at the endings, they drag their heels—and they all start out running so hard, meaning so well. Finally, at their best, all they can do is try to be kind; they forgive whomever is around to be forgiven, but their pessimism is extreme.

Starbuck's dog is experiencing a false pregnancy. She believes that a rubber ice-cream cone with a squeaker in it is her puppy. "She carries it up and down the stairs of my duplex," Starbuck tells us.

> She is even secreting milk for it. She is getting shots to make her stop doing that.
>
> I observe how profoundly serious Nature has made her about a rubber ice-cream cone—brown rubber cone, pink rubber ice cream. I have to wonder what equally ridiculous commitments to bits of trash I myself have made. Not that it matters at all. We are here for no purpose, unless we can invent one. Of that I am sure. The human condition in an exploding universe would not have been altered one iota if, rather than live as I have, I had done nothing but carry a rubber ice-cream cone from closet to closet for sixty years.

Dr. Robert Fender, alias Kilgore Trout, in prison

for life, writes "a story about a planet where the worst crime was ingratitude. People were executed all the time for being ungrateful." The immigrants Sacco and Vanzetti were guilty of ingratitude, too, of course. Who seems more ungrateful to us than anarchists? Especially "foreign" anarchists. Kilgore Trout was writing, as he is always writing, about *our* planet. May he live—even in prison—in peace!

The committeemen named by the state (of Massachusetts) to advise us what to do with Sacco and Vanzetti were two college presidents (from Harvard and MIT) and a retired probate judge. Despite the advice of Albert Einstein, George Bernard Shaw, Sinclair Lewis, and H. G. Wells, among others, this triumvirate declared that in the electrocution of Sacco and Vanzetti justice would be served. "So much for the wisdom of even the wisest human beings," Walter F. Starbuck says. "And I am now compelled to wonder if wisdom has ever existed or can ever exist. Might wisdom be as impossible in this particular universe as a perpetual-motion machine?"

Earlier, Starbuck cries out in warning: "What a book this is for tears!" Oh yes; and he admits to still further embarrassment. "The most embarrassing thing to me about this autobiography, surely, is its unbroken chain of

In 1976 Vonnegut replied to complaints that his plots had become too loose: "There'll be more and more to complain about in my fiction. People will say it's not fiction any more, it's editorializing." Jailbird *(1979) blends history, fiction, autobiography, and preaching. In this novel Vonnegut, who describes himself as "a Christ-worshipping agnostic," advocates the Sermon on the Mount as a corrective for the economic power system.*

proofs that I was never a serious man. I have been in a lot of trouble over the years, but that was all accidental. Never have I risked my life, or even my comfort, in the service of mankind. Shame on me." And so Vonnegut shames us all.

Of course, not many of us will feel compelled to action. Some of us might merely wish we were better. Neither response is a typical response to nihilism, which has been the easiest criticism of Vonnegut of all. If something is more pessimistic than you think it should be, call it nihilism. If I had to call what Vonnegut does any one thing, I would opt for something like "responsible soap opera"—"soap opera" being a good thing to write, in my opinion; it is only bad art that has given soap opera a bad name. Good soap opera simply means writing about people as if the people were important; "responsible" soap opera means representing people as people really are. "Nowhere in the world was this sort of theater being done anymore," Walter Starbuck writes of the soap opera of his own life. "For what it may be worth to modern impresarios: I can testify from personal experience that great crowds can still be gathered by melodrama."

Starbuck's real crime—not his Watergate crime, which is an accident, and not the crime that ends the book, for which he is again imprisoned (it being a crime of mild heroism)—is that he "told a fragmentary truth which has

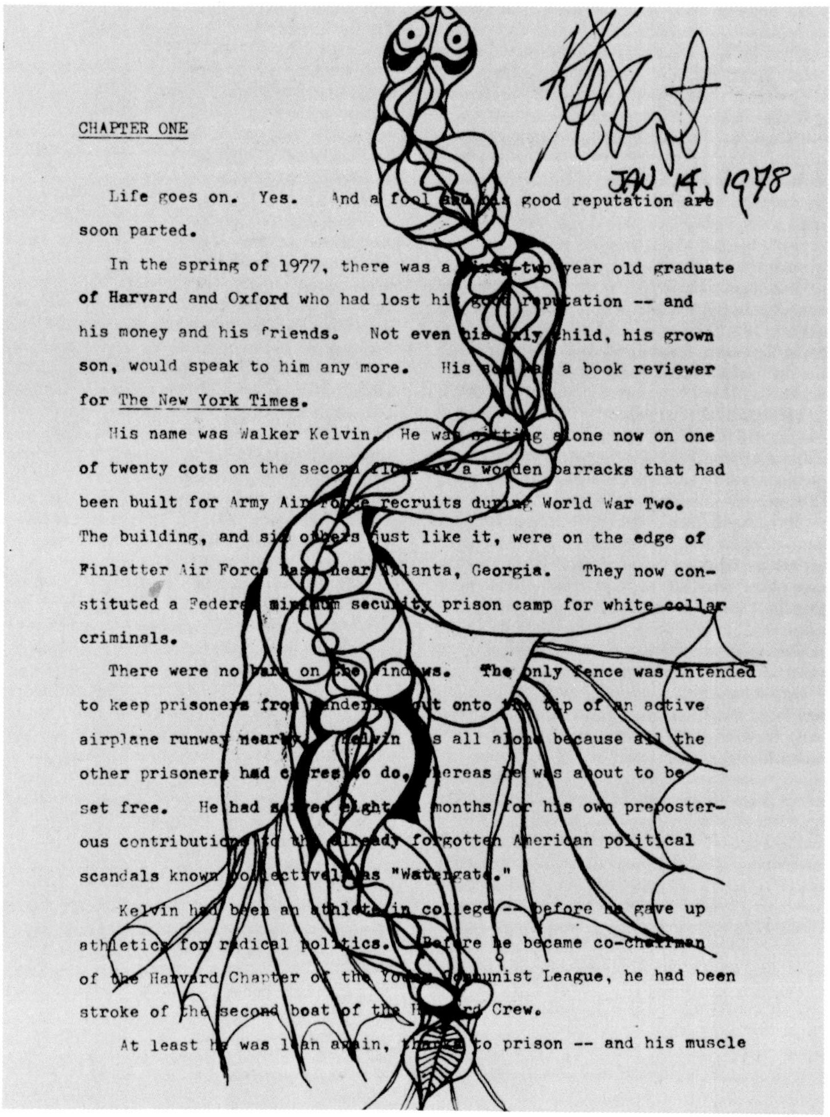

CHAPTER ONE

Life goes on. Yes. And a fool and his good reputation are soon parted.

In the spring of 1977, there was a sixty-two year old graduate of Harvard and Oxford who had lost his good reputation -- and his money and his friends. Not even his only child, his grown son, would speak to him any more. His son was a book reviewer for The New York Times.

His name was Walker Kelvin. He was sitting alone now on one of twenty cots on the second floor of a wooden barracks that had been built for Army Air Force recruits during World War Two. The building, and six others just like it, were on the edge of Finletter Air Force Base near Atlanta, Georgia. They now constituted a Federal minimum security prison camp for white collar criminals.

There were no bars on the windows. The only fence was intended to keep prisoners from wandering out onto the tip of an active airplane runway nearby. Kelvin was all alone because all the other prisoners had chores to do, whereas he was about to be set free. He had served eighteen months for his own preposterous contributions to the already forgotten American political scandals known collectively as "Watergate."

Kelvin had been an athlete in college -- before he gave up athletics for radical politics. Before he became co-chairman of the Harvard Chapter of the Young Communist League, he had been stroke of the second boat of the Harvard Crew.

At least he was lean again, thanks to prison -- and his muscle

It is Vonnegut's custom to doodle on his rejected drafts, as shown in these two versions of the opening for Jailbird.

now been allowed to represent the whole." He is "yet another nincompoop, who, by being at the wrong place at the wrong time was able to set humanitarianism back a full century." A harsh charge, but a usual one—in the best of Vonnegut's work. In Starbuck's words: "Much talk about human suffering and what could be done about it—and then infantile silliness for relief." Strong stuff.

I am reminded of Eliot Rosewater's heroizing of Kilgore Trout, long ago. "The Hell with the talented sparrow-farts who write delicately of one small piece of one mere lifetime," Eliot boozily crows, "when the issues are galaxies, eons, and trillions of souls yet to be born." Vonnegut does have a way of making me feel that the accomplishments of his contemporaries are somehow less—though this, I know, he would be the first to deny. As Vonnegut says, of old Senator Rosewater's view of Kilgore Trout: "The Senator admired Trout as a rascal who could rationalize anything, not understanding that Trout had never tried to tell anything but the truth." And the truth, as we say, can hurt.

If someone hurts us more than we think is fair, perhaps we feel better if we dismiss that person by calling him a "nihilist." To say so to Vonnegut is to be tone-deaf, for in his tone of voice is always a plea for human kindness, for common decency. He has always been more than a satirist.

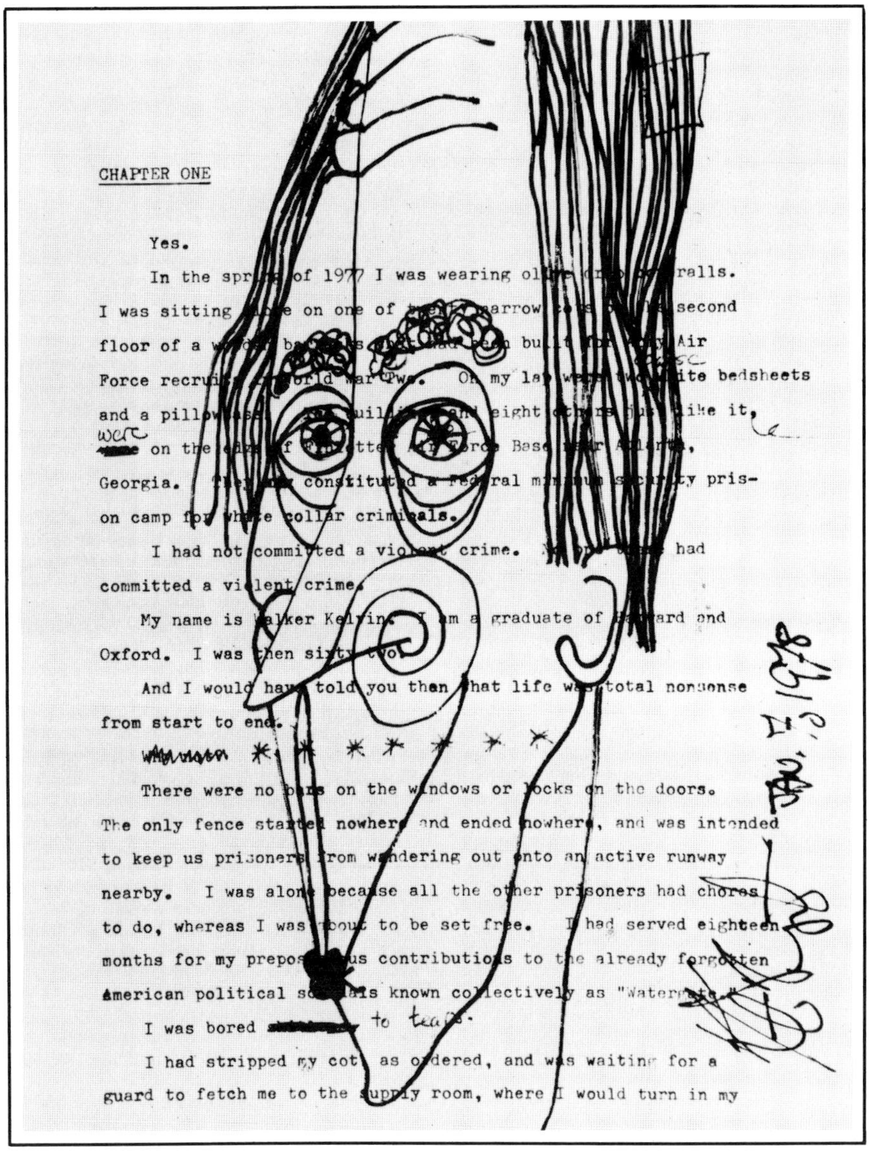

CHAPTER ONE

Yes.

In the spr[illegible] of 1977 I was wearing ol[illegible]ralls. I was sitting [illegible] on one of [illegible] narrow [illegible] second floor of a [illegible] bu[illegible] Air Force recru[illegible] World War Two. On my lap [illegible]ite bedsheets and a pill[illegible] [illegible]ike it, were on th[illegible] of [illegible] Base [illegible], Georgia. [illegible] constituted a Federal m[illegible]y prison camp f[illegible]e collar criminals.

I had not committed a vi[illegible] crime. [illegible] had committed a violent crime.

My name is [illegible]lker Kelvin. [illegible] a graduate of [illegible]ard and Oxford. I was then sixty-two.

And I would have told you then that life was total nonsense from start to end.

* * * * * *

There were no b[illegible] on the windows or locks on the doors. The only fence started nowhere and ended nowhere, and was intended to keep us prisoners from wandering out onto an active runway nearby. I was alone because all the other prisoners had chores to do, whereas I was about to be set free. I had served eighteen months for my prepos[illegible]us contributions to the already forgotten American political s[illegible]s known collectively as "Watergate."

I was bored to tears.

I had stripped my cot as ordered, and was waiting for a guard to fetch me to the supply room, where I would turn in my

He is also such an artist at the structure of a novel, we could satisfy ourselves by praising him for that alone. His plots—especially in *Jailbird*—would have made Dickens glow; it takes away from his surprises to reveal the story of *Jailbird* in that way. It is wonderfully Dickensian, intricate and risky, with a beginning, a middle, and an end. There is even an epilogue. There is always a kind of epilogue in Vonnegut because he sees things, as many writers can't, in their entirety. The epilogue in *Jailbird* begins: "There was more. There is always more." And we are prepared for it throughout because of his deliberate foreshadowing: every character is introduced with a minor history, and of many we are told, from the first meeting, what *would* become of them. There is also a prologue, where Vonnegut neatly fuses the most trivial autobiography with the most daring inventions, and shows us how they belong together. In this he includes an assessment of his own work, sent him by a high school student from Indiana. The student states that a single idea lies at the core of Vonnegut's work so far. "Love may fail, but courtesy will prevail." Vonnegut says that this sounds true and complete to him, but he has always been modest. "Our language is much larger than it needs to be," he writes: a hard truth many writers are pained to discover. And I have to admire that the Indiana high school student is certainly closer to understanding Vonnegut than are several of his most outspoken critics.

Jailbird is Vonnegut's best book since *Slaughterhouse-Five*; it is the equal of that book, and the equal of *Sirens of Titan*, *Rosewater*, *Mother Night*, and *Cat's Cradle*, too. It is vintage Vonnegut. "What a book this is for tears!" Indeed. Its last word—with a proper chill, and a proper sadness—is "Good-bye."

Remember Salinger's Glass family? In the heart of *Seymour: An Introduction*, Seymour, a writer, is arguing with his brother Buddy, also a writer, about why it's necessary to believe in a kind of aesthetics of accessibility; Seymour always thinks of the old librarian of his childhood, a Miss Overman, whenever he judges his own work. "He said he felt he owed Miss Overman a painstaking, sustained search for a form of poetry that was in accord with his own peculiar standards and yet not wholly incompatible, even at first sight, with Miss Overman's tastes." Buddy argues; he points out to Seymour Miss Overman's "shortcomings as a judge, or even a reader, of poetry." But Seymour persists. Says Buddy:

> He then reminded me that on his first day in the public library (alone, aged six) Miss Overman, wanting or not as a judge of poetry, had opened a book to a plate of Leonardo's catapult and placed it brightly before him, and that it was no joy to him to finish writing a poem and know that Miss Overman would have trouble turning to it with pleasure or involvement.

And so Buddy backs down; he admits that

> *you can't argue with someone who believes or just passionately suspects, that the poet's function is not to write what he must write but, rather, to write what he would write if his life depended on his taking responsibility for writing what he must in a style designed to shut out as few of his old librarians as humanly possible.*

That strikes me as admirable. It is not an aesthetic of condescension, or of writing down to one's reader. It is an aesthetic of the most demanding order. Kurt Vonnegut's "old librarians," and the rest of us, should be proud of him.

Player Piano	B
The Sirens of Titan	A
Mother Night	A
Cat's Cradle	A-plus
God Bless You, Mr. Rosewater	A
Slaughterhouse-Five	A-plus
Welcome to the Monkey House	B-minus
Happy Birthday, Wanda June	D
Breakfast of Champions	C
Wampeters, Foma & Granfalloons	C
Slapstick	D
Jailbird	A
Palm Sunday	C

Vonnegut graded his work in this report card. From "The Sexual Revolution," in his Palm Sunday.

In 1980 Vonnegut had a one-man show of his "felt-tip calligraphs." He explained: "The human face is the most interesting of all forms. So I've just made abstracts of all these forms. Because that's how we go through life, reading faces very quickly."

How to write with style

By Kurt Vonnegut

International Paper asked Kurt Vonnegut, author of such novels as "Slaughterhouse-Five," "Jailbird" and "Cat's Cradle," to tell you how to put your style and personality into everything you write.

Newspaper reporters and technical writers are trained to reveal almost nothing about themselves in their writings. This makes them freaks in the world of writers, since almost all of the other ink-stained wretches in that world reveal a lot about themselves to readers. We call these revelations, accidental and intentional, elements of style.

These revelations tell us as readers what sort of person it is with whom we are spending time. Does the writer sound ignorant or informed, stupid or bright, crooked or honest, humorless or playful – ? And on and on.

Why should you examine your writing style with the idea of improving it? Do so as a mark of respect for your readers, whatever you're writing. If you scribble your thoughts any which way, your readers will surely feel that you care nothing about them. They will mark you down as an egomaniac or a chowderhead – or, worse, they will stop reading you.

The most damning revelation you can make about yourself is that you do not know what is interesting and what is not. Don't you yourself like or dislike writers mainly for what they choose to show you or make you think about? Did you ever admire an empty-headed writer for his or her mastery of the language? No.

So your own winning style must begin with ideas in your head.

1. Find a subject you care about

Find a subject you care about and which you in your heart feel others should care about. It is this genuine caring, and not your games with language, which will be the most compelling and seductive element in your style.

I am not urging you to write a novel, by the way – although I would not be sorry if you wrote one, provided you genuinely cared about something. A petition to the mayor about a pothole in front of your house or a love letter to the girl next door will do.

2. Do not ramble, though

I won't ramble on about that.

3. Keep it simple

As for your use of language: Remember that two great masters of language, William Shakespeare and James Joyce, wrote sentences which were almost childlike when their subjects were most profound. "To be or not to be?" asks Shakespeare's Hamlet. The longest word is three letters long. Joyce, when he was frisky, could put together a sentence as intricate and as glittering as a necklace for Cleopatra, but my favorite sentence in his short story "Eveline" is this one: "She was tired." At that point in the story, no other words could break the heart of a reader as those three words do.

Simplicity of language is not only reputable, but perhaps even sacred. The *Bible* opens with a sentence well within the writing skills of a lively fourteen-year-old: "In the beginning God created the heaven and the earth."

4. Have the guts to cut

It may be that you, too, are capable of making necklaces for Cleopatra, so to speak. But your eloquence should be the servant of the ideas in your head. Your rule might be this: If a sentence, no matter how excellent, does not illuminate your subject in some new and useful way, scratch it out.

5. Sound like yourself

The writing style which is most natural for you is bound to echo the speech you heard when a child. English was the novelist Joseph Conrad's third language, and much that seems piquant in his use of English was no doubt colored by his first language, which was Polish. And lucky indeed is the writer who has grown up in Ireland, for the English spoken there is so amusing and musical. I myself grew up in Indianapolis, where common speech sounds like a band saw cutting galvanized tin,

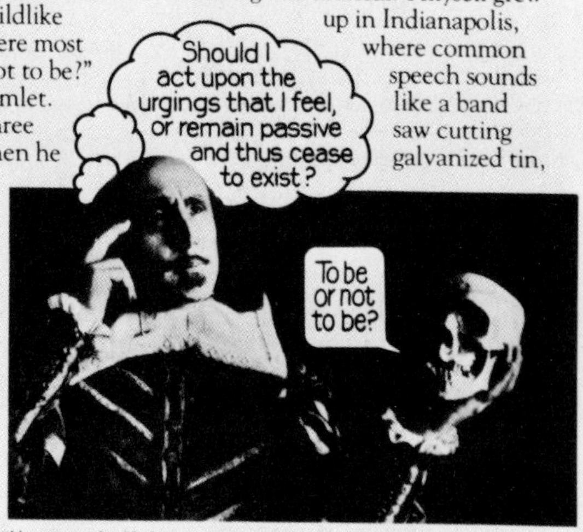

Should I act upon the urgings that I feel, or remain passive and thus cease to exist?
To be or not to be?

"Keep it simple. Shakespeare did, with Hamlet's famous soliloquy."

Vonnegut wrote this 1982 article for the International Paper Company's "Power of the Printed Word" series.

"Be merciless on yourself. If a sentence does not illuminate your subject in some new and useful way, scratch it out."

and employs a vocabulary as unornamental as a monkey wrench.

In some of the more remote hollows of Appalachia, children still grow up hearing songs and locutions of Elizabethan times. Yes, and many Americans grow up hearing a language other than English, or an English dialect a majority of Americans cannot understand.

All these varieties of speech are beautiful, just as the varieties of butterflies are beautiful. No matter what your first language, you should treasure it all your life. If it happens not to be standard English, and if it shows itself when you write standard English, the result is usually delightful, like a very pretty girl with one eye that is green and one that is blue.

I myself find that I trust my own writing most, and others seem to trust it most, too, when I sound most like a person from Indianapolis, which is what I am. What alternatives do I have? The one most vehemently recommended by teachers has no doubt been pressed on you, as well: to write like cultivated Englishmen of a century or more ago.

6. Say what you mean to say

I used to be exasperated by such teachers, but am no more. I understand now that all those antique essays and stories with which I was to compare my own work were not magnificent for their datedness or foreignness, but for saying precisely what their authors meant them to say. My teachers wished me to write accurately, always selecting the most effective words, and relating the words to one another unambiguously, rigidly, like parts of a machine. The teachers did not want to turn me into an Englishman after all. They hoped that I would become understandable – and therefore understood. And there went my dream of doing with words what Pablo Picasso did with paint or what any number of jazz idols did with music. If I broke all the rules of punctuation, had words mean whatever I wanted them to mean, and strung them together higgledy-piggledy, I would simply not be understood. So you, too, had better avoid Picasso-style or jazz-style writing, if you have something worth saying and wish to be understood.

Readers want our pages to look very much like pages they have seen before. Why? This is because they themselves have a tough job to do, and they need all the help they can get from us.

7. Pity the readers

They have to identify thousands of little marks on paper, and make sense of them immediately. They have to *read*, an art so difficult that most people don't really master it even after having studied it all through grade school and high school – twelve long years.

"Pick a subject you care so deeply about that you'd speak on a soapbox about it."

So this discussion must finally acknowledge that our stylistic options as writers are neither numerous nor glamorous, since our readers are bound to be such imperfect artists. Our audience requires us to be sympathetic and patient teachers, ever willing to simplify and clarify – whereas we would rather soar high above the crowd, singing like nightingales.

That is the bad news. The good news is that we Americans are governed under a unique Constitution, which allows us to write whatever we please without fear of punishment. So the most meaningful aspect of our styles, which is what we choose to write about, is utterly unlimited.

8. For really detailed advice

For a discussion of literary style in a narrower sense, in a more technical sense, I commend to your attention *The Elements of Style*, by William Strunk, Jr., and E.B. White (Macmillan, 1979). E.B. White is, of course, one of the most admirable literary stylists this country has so far produced.

You should realize, too, that no one would care how well or badly Mr. White expressed himself, if he did not have perfectly enchanting things to say.

Years ago, International Paper sponsored a series of advertisements, "Send me a man who reads," to help make Americans more aware of the value of reading.

Today, the printed word is more vital than ever. Now there is more need than ever before for all of us to *read* better, *write* better, and *communicate* better. International Paper offers this *new* series in the hope that, even in a small way, we can help.

For reprints of this advertisement, write: "Power of the Printed Word," International Paper Co., Dept. 5- , P.O. Box 954, Madison Square Station, New York, NY 10010. ©1980 INTERNATIONAL PAPER COMPANY

INTERNATIONAL PAPER COMPANY

We believe in the power of the printed word.

Printed in U.S. on International Paper Company's Springhill® Offset, basis 60 lb.

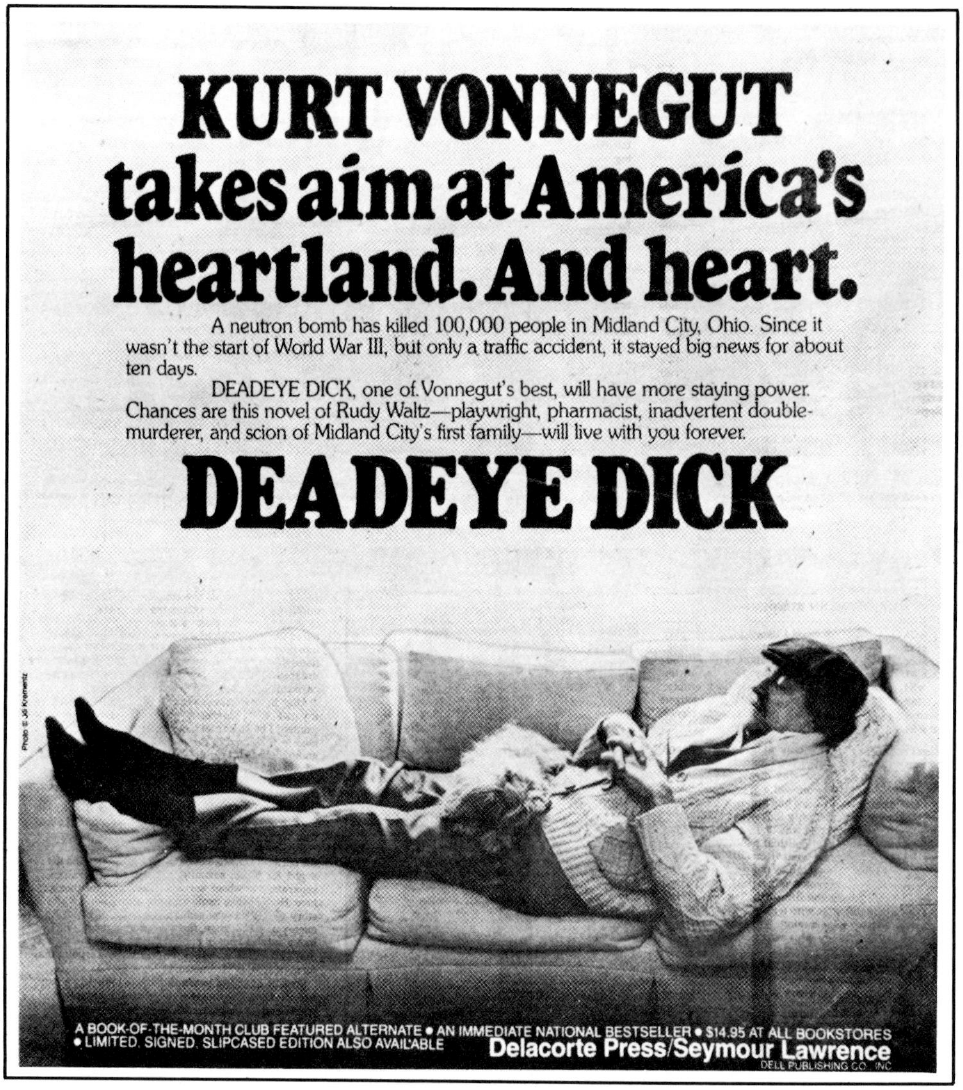

From New York Times Book Review, *24 October 1982*

It was dishonorable enough that I perverted art for money. I then topped that felony by becoming, as I say, fabulously well-to-do. Well, that's just too damn bad for me and for everybody. I'm completely in print, so we're all stuck with me and stuck with my books.

From "Kurt Vonnegut: The Art of Fiction LXIV,"
Paris Review *(Spring 1977)*

Cumulative Index

Dictionary of Literary Biography, Volumes 1-13
Dictionary of Literary Biography Yearbook, 1980, 1981
Dictionary of Literary Biography Documentary Series, Volumes 1-3

Cumulative Index

DLB before number: *Dictionary of Literary Biography*, Volumes 1-13
Y before number: *Dictionary of Literary Biography Yearbook*, 1980, 1981
DS before number: *Dictionary of Literary Biography Documentary Series*, Volumes 1-3

A

B

C

D

E

F

G

H

I

J

K

L

M

Q

R

Cumulative Index

T

U

V

W

Y

Z

VISIONS OF CODY
VISIONS OF CODY
JACK KEROUAC
Introduction by Allen Ginsberg
McGRAW-HILL
JACK KEROUAC
HERZOG
SAUL BELLOW